W9-CKJ-648

WORD, MEANING, POEM

All poetry is difficult to read.

ROBERT BROWNING, *The Ring and the Book*

I learnt that Poetry, even that of the loftiest and, seemingly, that of the wildest odes, had a logic of its own, as severe as that of science; and more difficult, because more subtle, more complex, and dependent on more, and more fugitive causes.

SAMUEL TAYLOR COLERIDGE, *Biographia Literaria*

The prime obstacle in general education is a feeling of helplessness before the unintelligible. Every problem is new to the mind which first meets it and it is baffling until he can recognize in it something which he has met and dealt with already. The all important difference between the mind which can clear itself by thought and the mind which remains bewildered and can proceed only by burying the difficulty in a formula—retained, at best, by mere rote memory—is in this power to recognize the new problem as, in part, an old conquest. Language with its inexhaustible duplications (which here are duplicities), ceaselessly presents to us the old as though it were new, familiar ideas in novel disguises, understood distinctions as fresh opportunities for confusion, already assimilated combinations as unforeseeable conjunctions. The teacher meets with all this whenever he reads anything which stretches his intelligence; the pupil meets with it all the time, and if he is being well taught he should be expecting it and enjoying the sense of increasing power that his progressive mastery of it can afford. For this growth in power is, fundamentally, the vitalizing incentive with which education builds.

I. A. RICHARDS, *Interpretation in Teaching*

WORD, MEANING, POEM

MORSE PECKHAM

SEYMOUR CHATMAN

University of Pennsylvania

Thomas Y. Crowell Company New York

Established 1834

Library of Congress Catalog Card Number: 61-6172

Designed by Edwin H. Kaplin
Manufactured in the United States of America
by Vail-Ballou Press, Inc., Binghamton, N.Y.

ACKNOWLEDGMENTS

Acknowledgment is gratefully made as follows on pages iv–vii for permission to reprint copyrighted material:

W. H. Auden: "Petition," "May with its light behaving," "Casino" copyright 1934, 1937, and 1937 respectively by The Modern Library, Inc., W. H. Auden, and Random House, Inc. Reprinted from *The Collected Poetry of W. H. Auden* by permission of Random House, Inc. and Faber and Faber Ltd.

Robert Bridges: "The sea keeps not the Sabbath day" from *The Poetical Works of Robert Bridges,* 1914, reprinted by permission of The Clarendon Press, Oxford.

Thomas Campion: "Song" reprinted from *English Madrigal Verse,* edited by E. H. Fellowes, 1925, by permission of the The Clarendon Press, Oxford.

John Clare: "Secret Love" from *Poems Chiefly from Manuscript,* edited by E. Blunden and A. Porter, published by Richard Cobden-Sanderson, 1920.

Arthur Hugh Clough: "Italy" ("O land of Empire, art and love") from *The Poems of Arthur Hugh Clough,* edited by H. F. Lowry, A. L. P. Norrington, and F. L. Mulhauser, reprinted by permission of The Clarendon Press, Oxford.

William Collins: "Dirge in Cymbeline," "Ode to Evening," and "Ode Occasion'd by the Death of Mr. Thomson" from *Poems of Gray and Collins,* edited by Paget

Toynbee, Leonard Whibley, and Frederick Page, third revised edition, 1937. Reprinted by permission of Oxford University Press.

Alec Comfort: "A Rider Turned to Stone" from *And All but He Departed,* 1951, reprinted by permission of Routledge & Kegan Paul Ltd., London.

Hart Crane: "To Brooklyn Bridge" from *The Collected Poems of Hart Crane.* By permission of Liveright, Publishers, N.Y. Copyright (R) 1961, Liveright Publishing Corp.

E. E. Cummings: "anyone lived in a pretty how town," copyright, 1940, by E. E. Cummings. Reprinted from *Poems 1923–1924* by E. E. Cummings by permission of Harcourt, Brace and Company, Inc.

Walter de la Mare: "Forests" from *Fleeting,* reprinted by permission of the Literary Trustees of Walter de la Mare and The Society of Authors as their representative.

Emily Dickinson: "The Soul has Bandaged moments," "After great pain, a formal feeling comes," "A narrow Fellow in the Grass." "After great pain, a formal feeling comes" copyright 1929 by Martha Dickinson Bianchi; copyright, ©, 1957 by Mary L. Hampson. All three poems reprinted by permission of the publishers from Thomas H. Johnson, editor, *The Poems of Emily Dickinson.* Cambridge, Mass., The Belknap Press of the Harvard University Press. Copyright, 1951, 1955 by The President and Fellows of Harvard College.

Richard Eberhart: "If I Could Only Live at the Pitch That Is Near Madness" from *Poems New and Selected, 1944,* copyright 1945 by New Directions. Reprinted by permission of New Directions.

T. S. Eliot: "A Cooking Egg," "Gerontion," "Animula" from *Collected Poems 1909–1935* by T. S. Eliot, copyright, 1936, by Harcourt, Brace and Company and reprinted with their permission and that of Faber and Faber Ltd.

Kenneth Fearing: "Art Review" from *New and Selected Poems* by Kenneth Fearing, published by Indiana University Press.

Robert Frost: "Birches," "In Time of Cloudburst," and "A Lone Striker" from *Complete Poems of Robert Frost.* Copyright, 1930, 1949, by Henry Holt and Company, Inc. Copyright, 1936, by Robert Frost. By permission of Holt, Rinehart and Winston, Inc.

Robert Graves: "The Cool Web" from *Collected Poems* published by Doubleday & Co., Inc., and Cassell & Co. Ltd., by permission of Robert Graves. © 1955 by Robert Graves.

Donald Hall: "The Body Politic" from *Exiles and Marriages* by Donald Hall. Copyright 1955 by Donald Hall. Reprinted by permission of The Viking Press, Inc.

Thomas Hardy: "A Commonplace Day," "A Night of Questionings," and "He Abjures Love" from Thomas Hardy, *Collected Poems,* copyright 1925 by The Macmillan Company and used with their permission. Reprinted from *Collected Poems of Thomas Hardy* by permission of the Trustees of the Hardy Estate, Macmillan & Co. Ltd., and The Macmillan Company of Canada Limited.

Gerard Manley Hopkins: "Hurrahing in Harvest," "The Windhover," and "Pied Beauty" from *Poems of Gerard Manley Hopkins,* edited by R. Bridges and W. H. Gardner, 1952, reprinted by permission of Oxford University Press, Amen House.

A. E. Housman: "From far, from eve and morning" from *A Shropshire Lad* by A. E. Housman. By permission of Holt, Rinehart and Winston, Inc., The Society of Authors as the literary representative of the Trustees of the Estate of the late A. E. Housman, and Messrs. Jonathan Cape, Ltd., publishers of A. E. Housman's *Collected Poems*.

Sidney Keyes: "The Promised Landscape" from *The Cruel Solstice*, 1944, reprinted by permission of Routledge & Kegan Paul Ltd., London.

Rudyard Kipling: "An American" by Rudyard Kipling from the book *Rudyard Kipling's Verse*. Reprinted by permission of Doubleday and Company, Inc. Reprinted from the book *The Seven Seas* by permission of the Macmillan Company of Canada Ltd., and Mrs. Bambridge.

D. H. Lawrence: "Dolour of Autumn" from *Collected Poems* by D. H. Lawrence. Copyright 1929 by Jonathan Cape and Harrison Smith, Inc., 1957 by Frieda Lawrence Ravagli. Reprinted by permission of The Viking Press, Inc.

Robert Lowell: "Mr. Edwards and the Spider" from *Lord Weary's Castle*, copyright, 1944, 1946, by Robert Lowell. Reprinted by permission of Harcourt, Brace and Company, Inc.

Archibald MacLeish: "Immortal Autumn" from *Collected Poems, 1917–1952*, reprinted by permission of Houghton Mifflin Company.

Louis MacNeice: "Picture Galleries" from *Poems, 1925–1940*, by Louis MacNeice, reprinted by permission of Faber and Faber Ltd.

John Masefield: Sonnet "Here in the self" from John Masefield, *Collected Poems*, copyright 1916 by John Masefield, copyright renewed 1944, and used with permission of The Macmillan Company.

Wilfred Owen: "Dulce et Decorum Est" from *The Poems of Wilfred Owen*, all rights reserved. Reprinted by permission of New Directions.

Robert Pack: "The Way We Wonder" reprinted with the permission of Charles Scribner's Sons from *Poets of Today II, The Irony of Joy: Poems*, copyright 1955 Robert Pack.

Ezra Pound: Canto XVII from *The Cantos of Ezra Pound*, copyright 1934 by Ezra Pound. Reprinted by permission of New Directions.

Lizette Woodworth Reese: "Wild Geese" from *The Selected Poems of Lizette Woodworth Reese*, copyright, 1926, by Rinehart & Company. Renewed 1954 by C. Reese Dietrich. Reprinted by permission of Holt, Rinehart and Winston, Inc.

I. A. Richards: From *Interpretation in Teaching*, reprinted by permission of Routledge & Kegan Paul Ltd., London.

Edwin Arlington Robinson: "Old Trails" From Edwin Arlington Robinson, *Collected Poems*. Copyright 1916 by The Macmillan Company, copyright renewed 1944, and used with their permission.

Carl Sandburg: "Interior" from *Cornhuskers* by Carl Sandburg. Copyright, 1918, by Henry Holt and Company, Inc. Copyright, 1946, by Carl Sandburg. By permission of Holt, Rinehart and Winston, Inc.

Delmore Schwartz: "I am to my own heart merely a serf" from *In Dreams Begin Responsibilities*, copyright 1938 by New Directions. Reprinted by permission of New Directions.

Karl Shapiro: "Elegy for a Dead Soldier" copyright 1944 by Karl Shapiro. Reprinted from *Poems 1940–1953* by Karl Shapiro, by permission of Random House, Inc., and Faber and Faber Ltd.

Edith Sitwell: "The Higher Sensualism" reprinted by permission of the publishers, The Vanguard Press and Gerald Duckworth & Company, Ltd., from *The Collected Poems of Edith Sitwell.* Copyright, 1954, by Edith Sitwell.

Stephen Spender: "Polar Exploration" copyright 1942 by Stephen Spender. Reprinted from *Collected Poems, 1928–1953,* by Stephen Spender, by permission of Random House, Inc. and Faber and Faber Ltd.

Wallace Stevens: "Peter Quince at the Clavier," "Anecdote of the Jar," and "Not Ideas about the Thing but the Thing Itself" reprinted from *The Collected Poems of Wallace Stevens,* by permission of Alfred A. Knopf, Inc. Copyright 1923, 1931. 1952, 1954 by Wallace Stevens.

Dylan Thomas: "Do Not Go Gentle into That Good Night" from *The Collected Poems of Dylan Thomas,* copyright 1952, 1953 by Dylan Thomas. Reprinted by permission of New Directions and J. M. Dent & Sons Ltd.

Thomas Traherne: "The Vision" from *Centuries, Poems and Thanksgivings, by Thomas Traherne,* edited by H. M. Margouliouth, 1958, reprinted by permission of The Clarendon Press, Oxford.

Henry Treece: "In the dark caverns of the night" reprinted from *Collected Poems* by Henry Treece, by permission of Alfred A. Knopf, Inc. Copyright 1946 by Henry Treece.

Henry Vaughan: "Corruption" from *The Works of Henry Vaughan,* edited by L. C. Martin (Oxford English Texts), 1957, by permission of The Clarendon Press, Oxford.

Robert Penn Warren: "Crime" from *Eleven Poems on the Same Theme,* copyright 1942 by New Directions. Reprinted by permission of New Directions.

Richard Wilbur: "Love Calls Us to the Things of This World" from *Things of This World,* © 1956, by Richard Wilbur. Reprinted by permission of Harcourt, Brace and Company, Inc.

W. B. Yeats: "Sailing to Byzantium" and "Vacillation" from W. B. Yeats, *Collected Poems, Variorum Edition,* copyright 1928, 1933 respectively by The Macmillan Company; "When You Are Old" from W. B. Yeats, *Collected Poems,* copyright 1906, renewed 1934 by The Macmillan Company and used with their permission. By permission also of Mrs. W. B. Yeats and The Macmillan Company of Canada Ltd.

Dedicated to

JUDITH STALBERG FRIEDMAN

Contents

APPENDICES

To the Instructor

This book is focused upon one problem: the comprehension of the semantic aspect of a poem. Although our theoretical commitments are as limited as we can make them, it appears to us that the semantic aspect can be considered apart from the formal aspect. This is neither to deny nor to assert that the formal aspect has some kind of sign function; but it is our belief that the response to the formal aspect must necessarily be inadequate if the semantic aspect is not comprehended. If "understanding poetry" means to have an adequate response to both aspects, then by "comprehending poetry" we mean "identifying the segment of the environment to which the words of the poem, as words, refer and the orientation toward that segment which the words of the poem imply." Hence the second theoretical position which we occupy: A poem, like any work of literature, has as primary function the dramatization of an orientation toward some segment of the environment, including the self as other, i.e. as part of the environment.

We do not maintain that to "comprehend" a poem is the only thing one can do with it, or the only thing one ought to do with it—merely that it is the first thing one must do with it. Thus we have no particular opinions about whether a poem is or is not autotelic, or autonomous, or a "world in itself"; at least we have no opinions on this matter which are at work here or which are related to what we propose. We conceive the problem of "comprehension" as primarily a pedagogical problem, and this book is designed to help a college student (as well as superior secondary students, graduate students, and the general reader) to remedy his linguistic and semantic inadequacies and failures when he attempts to read a poem. These our experience has shown to be of several orders and kinds.

There is first the problem of common student attitudes: Either that a poem has no specific meaning and can mean anything that the reader wishes it to mean; "This is what it means to me and my opinion is as good as yours because the meaning of a poem is no more than an opinion." Or that a poem is far too difficult for the ordinary mind to comprehend; "Poetry is for longhairs, for eggheads, for highbrows." Or that a poem which is not immediately comprehensible is not communicating, and since a body of language that does not communicate is a failure, poetry that resists immediate comprehension can be ignored as no good anyway. Or that poetry is for women and the effeminate and offers no discipline or intellectual challenge for the tough and masculine mind. It seems to us that the only way to show that poetry has determinable meaning, that the average college student can be trained to grasp that meaning, that it does communicate to those willing to raise themselves to its level—like the language of philosophy and physics—and that much of it was written by mature tough-minded men for mature tough-minded men—is to *demonstrate* these truths, not merely assert them. Either poetry can sustain and repel such attacks, or it cannot, and the only way to show that it can repel them is to show how it does so.

These attitudes can be rooted out only by openly acknowledging them in the classroom, by being continuously aware of their presence, and by showing how the student himself may and does destroy them. The principal means is to engage his mind precisely at the point where he encounters those difficulties which set up his resistance and rouse his defenses. These difficulties may be classified: First, the lexical problem: does he understand all the words? More important, does he know whether he understands them or not? Second, the syntactic problem: has he observed the syntactic disturbance and has he resolved it? Is he aware that there is a syntactic disturbance? Third, the problem of metaphor: can he analyze a metaphor, presenting a complete scheme of the corresponding terms of vehicle and tenor and identifying the connection? Can he recognize a metaphor when he sees one? Can he determine whether or not a term implied by the metaphor is or is not relevant to the meaning of the poem? Fourth, the interpretational problem: can he construct a consistent interpretation based upon as much of the information in the poem as he can manage to observe? Or does he proceed by selecting from the poem bits of information he can comprehend and constructing some kind of interpretation from that essentially random selection? This book is designed to separate the first two of these problems from each other and from the third and fourth.

Part I consists of twenty-five poems together with a full analytic apparatus. These poems are by poets most of whom would find a place in almost any informed list of the best twenty-five poets of the language, from the middle of the sixteenth century to the present. Many of the poems are familiar, but we have also included less well-known works. They are arranged, not in chronological order, but in order of difficulty, an order determined by the ratio of the length of the poem to the length of the Interpretational Hypothesis—a term to be explained below. Facing each poem is a diagram of the sentence structure of each poem; the special signs used are explained in "Notes to the Student." Whether he feels he understands the sentence or not, the student should be required and trained to compare this "Syntactic Gloss" with the poem itself. The most difficult problem in reading is not knowing when one is not comprehending. The object of the constant employment of the Syntactic Gloss is to teach the student to make a similar gloss of the poems he studies in the second and third parts of the book, and to give him a method by which he may extricate himself when he has progressed to the point of being aware that he is confused. Below each poem is to be found a "Lexical Gloss." We have attempted to include every word which might conceivably cause anybody any trouble. For some students this glossing will be too heavy; for others, perhaps, inadequate, though we suspect that anyone for whom it is inadequate had better not be in college. This gloss, which is to be used constantly and consulted in its entirety, has three functions. First, it is there to train the students to be sensitive to words, the variety of their meanings, and particularly their historical shifts in meaning—in short, to train the student to use a dictionary. Second, it is to save him time and interruptions in the process of interpretation. Third, it is to make him sensitive to his failures in lexical comprehension, which arise from a confusion of one word with another, from a confusion of one meaning with another meaning of the same word, from not knowing that a word has undergone a subtle semantic change since the poem was written. Hence the student must always consult the entire list, whether or not he thinks he understands a word. The object is not to give him meanings which he needs but to make him aware that he needs a meaning other than that in his accessible repertoire of meanings. As far as possible, he should be trained to refer frequently to the *Shorter Oxford English Dictionary* and, if it is at all convenient, to the complete work.

Each of these twenty-five poems is followed by what we call an "Interpretational Hypothesis." We use this term instead of such a term as "interpretation" or "critical analysis" or "close reading" because we wish to suggest several notions. To begin with, there is the fact that, paradoxically, though a poem does have an ascertainable meaning, that meaning can never be stated with finality. With poetry we must assume the attitude we must assume toward all statements: they have consistent and determinable meaning until analysis or experience proves otherwise. In practice, complete agreement is rarely reached about the meaning of a poem or of any other statement; in theory, it can never be reached. And this for several reasons. In interpreting a poem we do two things: we reduce a multi-level semantic structure to a one-level structure (for example, we identify the tenor of each metaphor), and we locate the segment of environment referred to and the attitude implied, by using a different set of words, or linguistic conventions, from that found in the poem. But the sets of words will vary from individual to individual; only a rough kind of agreement can be reached. Furthermore, an interpretation relatively adequate in one generation will be, or at least can be, relatively inadequate in another. In addition, an interpretation should be based upon consideration of all the semantic information the poem presents. Again, in practice it is virtually impossible to do so. Finally, we use the term "Interpretational Hypothesis" to bring out a parallel, which we think to be just, to the theoretic constructs of scientists. Such a construct is not "right" or "wrong" or "true" or "false"; and the aim of the scientist is to demonstrate the inadequacies of his construct. For if he considers his construct finally "right" or "true," he ceases to be a scientist and enters the realm of metaphysics, whither many literary critics have preceded him.

These "IH's," as we call them, are presented to serve several functions. First, they are models of how to go about creating an interpretation. But this does not mean that they are final or perfect models. They are, second, there to be criticized. Like the syntactic and lexical glosses, they are to be used in conjunction with the poem. Have we omitted any data? And if we have, does the inclusion of such data change our interpretation? And if it does, is the change one of a minor shading of meaning, or does it involve a radical change in the direction of the interpretation? We have played fair. These are as adequate interpretations as we can present, and at the time of going to press we believe them to be "true," that is, relatively reliable and adequate. But we are not in a position of claiming, "This is what the poem *really* means." Third, they are not to be regarded as ends in themselves. This book is designed to teach students to comprehend poetry, not to train them to write interpretational hypotheses. The most delicate step of the whole process of creating an Interpretational Hypothesis and its whole purpose is the rereading of the poem, preferably by the instructor, and aloud, so that the attitude discovered by the IH may be signified and reinforced by the instructor's tone of voice—dry, witty, richly emotional, disturbed, subdued, passionate, or ecstatic, as the case may be. At this point "the butterfly broken upon the wheel of analysis" is miraculously reborn; comprehension is substituted for interpretation; the word is reincarnated. In short, the goal of studying, writing, and constructing IH's is to give the student a repertoire of analytical devices to fall back upon when he is in difficulties, but principally to comprehend poems without recourse to the mechanics of constructing an interpretational hypothesis. Since the possibilities of poetic difficulty are in theory infinite and in practice inexhaustible, no book could hope to present an example of each. Finally, we have pointed out nearly all instances of metaphor and have identified tenor, connection, and vehicle. (In a few instances we have not felt it necessary to do so, since the metaphor involved is very simple or so much a part of the normal language spoken today as to be an inoperant or dead metaphor.)

In using Part I we recommend that the instructor begin by assigning one of the first four poems. These are relatively easy, and it is best to begin by spending one or two classroom hours on one of them. It is at this point that the most difficult problem in interpreting a poem will, or should, appear. In poetry what happens between the statements is the crucial matter. The attitude toward the area of experience referred to by the poem is implied both by statements and, more frequently, by the implied connection between statements. Hence the IH's contain a good many questions in order to give examples of appropriate questions. The task of the instructor at this stage is to train the students to consult the complete apparatus and to learn the primary function of the IH. That is, if a student disagrees with the interpretation offered, he must (a) point out neglected data, (b) point out a non sequitur or some kind of logical failure, (c) demonstrate the superior consistency of the interpretation he proposes. In short, he must *prove* by semantic consistency a failure in our IH and the superiority of a differing interpretation. The function of the IH is to make the meaning of a poem public as well as to correct idiosyncratic and inadequate interpretation.

The next twelve poems (Hardy to Swinburne) form a group of graded difficulty, but as a group are more difficult than the first four. The third group (Yeats to Shakespeare), the fourth (Dickinson to Keats), and the fifth (Wordsworth) offer similar increases in difficulty. The teacher may advance from group to group or may skip a group, or may start at a higher level than that of the first four, as his experience and his estimate of the quality of his group of students may determine. We recommend that at least three other poems in Part I be assigned and subsequently worked out in class. We think it unwise to assign the students any other preparation at first. The difficulty inherent in interpretation is one that arises from treating your own language as a foreign tongue, and the creation of an IH is, in many ways, comparable to a translation that includes within it the justifications for the decisions that the translator makes.

In *Part II* the real difficulty begins. Here the students must apply what they have learned about the syntactic problem and the lexical problem from Part I, but the Lexical Gloss is different. It provides only dictionary information, and is presented to save the teacher and the student both class and preparation time and to minimize the necessary suspension of interpretation while a dictionary or encylopedia or annotated edition is consulted. The poems in Part II are presented in chronological order, not in order of difficulty. Since we have not made IH's of these fifty poems (one of which by each author is ordinarily well known, the other, less famous and less frequently anthologized), we do not know that order. However, it is our empirical observation that each poet has a certain style or degree of difficulty as well as, more or less continuously through his poetry, or at least his mature poetry, of kinds of difficulty. Thus we have chosen fifty poems by the twenty-five poets of Part I, so that the teacher may have some notion of where to take his class next. A class that in the first three weeks has not progressed beyond the second group had better be limited to the same poets in Part II.

We recommend the following method for Part II. The student should be asked to prepare a Syntactic Gloss and an IH for each class; it is of no importance how much of the poem he covers. The more experienced he becomes, the less of the poem will he be able to cover in the allotted preparation time, because he will see so much to discuss. And we suggest that he be required to spend not more than an hour on the preparation. If it is desired to assign him two hours of preparation, he can do nothing better than to read, at such depth as he wishes, in Part III. The teacher is not advised to use these papers in the class. He can learn something by reading them; but we do not even advise correcting them and returning them—for this reason. The whole function of these assignments is to get the students to engage themselves with the preliminary problems. If the poem is not finished in one class meeting, the student may be assigned the task of rewriting his hypothesis from the point at which the class discussion broke off. Repetition will do him no harm and an infinite amount of good.

The class time should be devoted to the oral construction of an IH. We have found it useful not to prepare the poem before the meeting of each class. As much of the interpretation must be drawn from the students as possible; the fewer ideas the teacher already has the better. He should approach each poem as freshly as he can. Hence we have designed the book so that the teacher may use it for some years without repeating any material; he need not repeat a poem until his memory has faded. If he has two sections of the same course, he should use different poems in each. His job is to approach the poem as freshly as the students do, if he possibly can. And he must not only point out difficulties; he must also admit to perceiving difficulties which he himself cannot yet solve. In this kind of instruction the omniscient teacher is the greatest hindrance to the development in the students' minds of the realization that a poem is a public statement and that anyone may have something pertinent to say on the subject, that anyone's special linguistic or nonlinguistic experience may enable him to see something vital which no one else has observed. Students need not be told of difficulties; they need to experience them. Thus the teacher's classroom formula is not, "Such and such is the problem here," but, "Does anyone see a problem here?" The first half of the course will be and should be filled with long silences.

In developing an oral IH, the following rules, practiced for nearly a decade, we have found to be invaluable, and indeed are the basis of our method of teaching the comprehension of poetry and of writing the IH's.

1. *Use no material outside of the poem except dictionary and encyclopedia material.* Who wrote the poem is important only in giving a way to find out what meanings were in circulation during the poet's lifetime. To make this information as exact as possible, when it needs to be so, we have provided a bibliographical appendix which gives the date and place of first publication in book form, that is, in the text as we now have it. (There are of course certain exceptions, such as Donne and Traherne and Dickinson; and in one modern instance we have not been able to determine the date of first publication.) The teacher must be, to some extent, an encyclopedia, but all such information must be kept at a minimum. The only safety is in wielding Occam's razor. The less use is made of special knowledge, the easier it is to interpret the poem, the more reliable is the interpretation, and the more the students become aware that a poem is a public document, accessible to a reader who is willing to think. The IH's give numerous examples of how such special knowledge is either to be incorporated or excluded.

2. *Interpret the poem in the order in which the semantic data is presented.* Proceed by major syntactic units, as they are numbered in the syntactic glosses. After the obviously unknown words have been identified and meanings or a range of meanings tentatively accepted, the next step is to untangle the syntax. It is often a good idea, when the occasion arises, to let a student begin at the second or third line in order to show how the question asked or the interpretation proposed is vitiated by the failure to begin at the beginning. The more time spent on the early part of the poem, the more satisfactory the IH. In a disorienting situation our tendency is to grab onto the most recognizable feature and insist that it is the major clue to the situation. The student must be constantly disabused of the reliability of this device. Further, a poem is a dramatization. Just as it is an error to interpret something in Act I of a play by referring to Act III, so it is a mistake to explain something in the first stanza of a poem by skipping to the last without working one's way through the earlier portion. Even at the most sophisticated levels of interpretation or "criticism" there is a plaguey tendency to select from the poem, almost at random, recognizable statements, images, phrases, and so on, and interpret the poem from those. It is, of course, an obvious error, but it is almost irresistible in literary in-

terpretation because of the complexity of the material and the disorienting effect produced by an odd syntactic and semantic structure. The problem is to resist it. And the only way is to go through the poem, as demonstrated in the IH's, unit by unit, proceeding by as small a unit as seems appropriate, whether it be a sentence or a phrase. Further, in the final and most important step, reading the poem as a unit, comprehension and not interpretation is the goal. To comprehend something we must comprehend it as it is presented and in the order in which it is presented. All modern criticism has moved in one direction: to observe what the poem says; and to do so, one must examine each bit of information as it comes along.

3. *Do not proceed until the entire group is in virtual agreement.* Nothing is better calculated to demonstrate that a poem is a public statement, designed to be understood. Further, nothing is better designed to get rid of the idiosyncratic interpretation, including the teacher's. Whatever is proposed must be accepted not because it is appealing, but because it functions in the consistent structure of meaning which is being unfolded. But even more important—and of this the teacher must be constantly aware—a student may stubbornly hold out for his position because he is right and everybody else, including the teacher, is wrong. Consequently, every suggestion must be given serious attention—subject of course to the general classroom discipline of squashing the bumptious and controlling the psychopathic. Classes can be become extremely heated and noisy in such situations. But passions rarely rise; tempers rarely flare; and a general spirit of responsibility toward interpretation begins to emerge as the students perceive that their views and consents are being seriously considered. It is astonishing how students become both at once suspicious of their judgments and aware of unknown powers. A warning and a suggestion may be appropriate. The technique of orally constructing an Interpretational Hypothesis can be very exhausting to both teacher and class, and usually is. It is as demanding as logic and mathematics. On the other hand, one two-hour class is probably better than three one-hour classes, while one three-hour class or seminar is ideal, if there is an intermission and if the teacher remembers to break the tension from time to time with a joke or an absurdity.

4. *Avoid all value questions during the construction of an IH.* We recommend the consistent omission of value questions and statements—for several reasons. Since the inescapable human tendency is to negate the value of a disorienting stimulus, value sentences are constantly used to erect barriers, to defend ourselves, to rationalize our failures to respond, to give ourselves a good reason for not continuing the effort to comprehend. To omit valuations in the interpretational process is to strip our-

selves of those defenses which serve so excellently to conserve the energy which must be spent if we are to comprehend complex linguistic structures. In the most disorienting kind of linguistic situation in which it is possible to find ourselves, poetry, the more value impedimenta we get rid of, the better we can expose ourselves to the onslaught of the enemy's forces, and the better we can engage in the battle. Further, the value of what is said in any situation is totally irrelevant to the comprehension of what is said. Valuing comes after comprehension, and the profounder the comprehension, the more significant to the personality is the act of valuation. We agree with Matthew Arnold; evaluation should be postponed as long as possible, until it is irresistible and inevitable. When it comes to poetry which is widely accepted as part of the canon, it makes little difference whether I like it or not. The important question is: Does the poem like me?

Further, it is our conviction that values are best imparted indirectly, not verbally taught. They are to be learned in the classroom, not from the textbook, at least for the beginner in poetry. Only the highly sophisticated reader of poetry, one who is deeply involved in the process of including and excluding poems from the constantly shifting canon, which proceeds through history like a sand dune drifting across a beach, or in creating his own individual canon, should trouble himself too much with reading evaluational criticism. For the young, values are best learned indirectly and by personal transmission. From a thousand clues in the teacher's behavior, the student develops a sensitivity to poetic values; for a teacher is a role-model when he is not a drillmaster. In this process of teaching how one interprets poetry and comprehends it, he is both. When interpreting poetry he is indirectly a model for the role of valuing poetry. The more the student incorporates poetic valuations unconsciously, the better; for only values thus absorbed are lasting—and truly convincing. To be sure, there are always students for whom everything about a particular teacher is offensive, but we can do nothing about that; at least we can try to train them to read.

Part III consists of one hundred poems by a hundred authors not represented in Parts I and II. The poems are arranged in chronological order and have been selected according to the following scheme: After Wyatt and Surrey, one poet born per decade from 1540 to 1570, two poets born per decade from 1570 to 1790, three poets (two English, one American) born per decade from 1790 to 1870, and five poets (two English, three American) from 1870 to 1930. (There is one exception: the 1740's suffered a critical shortage in the births of poets, and we have used three from the 1730's.) For this scheme there are several reasons. It is not difficult to make an anthology of a hundred poems worth studying; considering the enormous wealth of material in the English language, nothing is easier. The problem is to create a representative selection, not primarily on the basis of merit but rather on the basis of style and for the purpose of including the greatest possible variety of interpretational problems.

Some of these poems are magnificent; all of them are worth reading. Each, however, presents a syntactic, lexical, or interpretational problem which makes it worth paying attention to. Furthermore, an anthology based on merit is necessarily limited by the evaluative limitations of the anthologizer and of the generation of which he is a part. Thus, our examination of certain recent anthologies has revealed what is, to at least one of us, a scandalous neglect of eighteenth-century poetry, as well as, oddly enough, of Elizabethan poetry. To be sure, even with the scheme used here personal taste plays a part, but, we think, a less significant part, simply because the selection of poets and thus of styles has a built-in randomness. In addition, an anthology without such planned randomness tends, because of the interests of the anthologizer, to present problems of interpretation for which the anthologizer has a special taste. If he is particularly interested in the sustained metaphor, or conceit, or if—a common case in a now aging generation—he is convinced that a "good" poem must be so organized, that is what he will look for, often quite unconsciously. If, however, a random scheme involves styles he has no great personal commitment to, he will be able to discern a greater variety of problems. Finally, this scheme necessarily includes a considerable amount of fresh and infrequently or never anthologized material. It will, we hope, not only offer the jaded teacher a lift, but it will particularly help him to get out of the omniscient role, which is harmful in this kind of instruction.

From the historical point of view, the scheme has further advantages. By increasing the number of poets born per decade at 1570, 1790, and 1870, we have presented a rough approximation of the growth of the volume of English and American poetry from the early sixteenth century to the present. From 1870 to 1930 there are more American poets than English because we feel that the poetic accomplishment in America since 1910 has been perhaps even more impressive in America as compared with England than our proportions indicate. Further, the reader has before him a kind of historical museum of poetic styles, with, we think, no major and few minor styles omitted, especially if taken in conjunction with Parts I and II. For this reason the names, together with titles of the poems, of the poets in Parts I and II have been inserted in Part III at the chronologically appropriate place.

We recommend that Part III be used in two ways. From the beginning, the student should be required—and perhaps checked by brief quizzes —to spend a certain amount of time reading and rereading, consecutively, the entire section. In any literature course intensive and extensive reading, even if it amounts to mere scanning, should be combined. Only thus can the student escape the necessary intellectual and aesthetic parochialism consequent upon attention given to a very limited number of texts. He needs not only to be trained in minute examination; he needs also to expand the range of his responses and power of comprehension. After all, one of the best ways, when all is said and done, though not the only best way, to learn to read is to read a lot.

But of course the most important function of Part III is to provide a wide range of texts to be used after three or four texts in Part II have been thoroughly explored and comprehended. In Part III, the student is entirely on his own, and as many of these poems should be done as time permits and the class level allows. But this is not to imply that a course in poetry using this volume will be successful if twenty or thirty poems are covered. If our basic rules are put into practice, forty-five hours devoted to six poems may very well be far more valuable than forty-five hours devoted to thirty.

Testing. We have found that very satisfactory results are obtained from examinations which follow closely classroom practice. The examination should be a written example of what the student has been doing at home and what the teacher and students have been doing in class, interpretation and explication. In an adequate examination the student is asked to explicate a short poem from Part III of this book (or a self-contained portion of a longer one) which he has worked over at home. Notes and books should be allowed on examinations to confirm to the student that he is being asked to read more closely, not to exercise his memory. It is important to keep these examinations from being vague summaries. They should show at least three things very precisely: (1) the recognition and glossing of all words whose precise sense in the context is important to the meaning of the poem as a whole; (2) the working out of syntactic difficulties, the filling in of ellipses and identification of the referents of all pronouns; and (3) the recognition and explication of all metaphors in terms of tenor, vehicle, and their connection (see "Notes to the Student").

A good way to assure uniformity for grading purposes is to ask that the class keep the words of the poem intact (although not in the inverted poetic order) and to insert all explanations and glosses in parentheses; thus, the first lines of *The Rape of the Lock:*

What dire offense from am'rous causes springs,
What mighty contests rise from trivial things,
I sing—

could be written "I sing (sing about or celebrate) what (sort of) dire (horrible, dreadful) offense springs from am'rous causes (matters of the heart), (and I sing about) what mighty contests (struggles, fights) rise from trivial (unimportant, extremely minor) things." Some students will have difficulty with the first requirement above because they will tend to put in too few glosses. Their attitude may be that since they "know" the word they do not think it necessary to do anything with it. Therefore it might be helpful for the instructor to tell the class at the outset approximately how many words he thinks need to be glossed.

Prosody. Since our aim is concentrated on the semantic dimension of the poem, we have separated it from the formal dimension; but that is not to say that the formal dimension need be neglected, although poetry can be taught this way with a high degree of effectiveness, i.e. without mentioning prosodic matters at all. Or prosody can be introduced at the beginning and used constantly. However, we have included little material on the subject, and for a particular reason. At the present time, the problem of prosody is in the greatest confusion. There is no firm agreement on anything, and a state of warfare obtains throughout the academic world. We feel that it is best that each instructor teach what he thinks proper. However, we have included in Appendix I what we consider the most probable basic prosodic patterns for the first twenty-five poems. The teacher may find this useful, or he may find it so offensive that he prefers to ignore it, or better yet, have the students tear these pages out of the book.

Texts. We have made an effort to get a good text for each poem. The source of the text is to be found, together with the date, when known, of its first publication, in Appendix II. Each poem has either been photographed from the text we have used or a photograph has been collated against a copy of that text. Many of them have also been checked against modern editions of high repute, and a few poems have been taken directly from such editions, particularly when an early edition was not available. We have used editions either known to have been seen through the press by the author or by someone directly connected with him, or editions for which there is a considerable presumption that either the author or a friend was responsible. We have made every effort to reproduce the punctuation and capitalization of the originals, and only very rarely have we been eclectic, preferring to depend on the judgment and taste of someone contemporary with the author, even if it were not the author himself. For instance, no one is sure of the meaning of the rise and fall of internal capitalization from the sixteenth to the nineteenth centuries; yet there it is, and it certainly is not an orthographic device, nor a purely decorative one. It seems to have added a delicate emphasis, like a subdued italicization, until eventually it came to be so overused that it no longer served its function. Then it was gradually abandoned. But this theory is perhaps not much more than a guess. Only very rarely, and then only in instances of obvious textual corruption or typographical error, have we changed the punctuation. We find the punctuation of the original, whether it be the author's or one of his contemporaries', far more expressive and informative than attempts to punctuate in a modern style, which, furthermore, often distorts or changes the meaning. After all, the punctuation is just as much a part of the semantic dimension of a written piece of language as the words themselves, and it forms an inseparable part of the total body of linguistic information which the text presents. Because this fact has been so often ignored, in many modern editions punctuation has even more textual uncertainty than words.

After long and anxious discussions, we decided to modernize the orthography. It does not seem to us to belong to the same level of information as punctuation and words. That is, it serves to identify the word, but it has nothing to do with the semantic aspect, or significance of the word. To preserve it would put still another barrier before the student's comprehension. Our principles have been simple and not always absolutely consistent, though as consistent as we have been able to make them. We modernize a word if we can do so without changing its phonetic character. Thus "thankt" is printed "thank'd," since in modern English the final "d" is pronounced "t." But "thank'd" in an original is never printed as "thanked," because, well into the nineteenth century, almost all poets made a careful distinction between syllabic and unsyllabic endings. Again in Shakespeare's Sonnet 116, the original "highth" is printed "heighth," rather than "height," although the form is now dialectic or uneducated. Since Shakespeare texts present a special and notorious case, and since we wish to provide the teacher an opportunity to make the students aware of the textual problem, we have printed both the Second Quarto and the First Folio texts for the passage from *Hamlet*, unchanged except for orthography. There is no reason for students to imagine that we know precisely what our poets wrote, when, in fact, we do not.

To conclude, so that the instructor will know whom to swear at, we append a note on responsibility. Chatman wrote the paragraphs on testing above, Note III in "Notes to the Student," and the syntactic and lexical glosses in Parts I and II. Peckham is responsible for "To the Instructor," Notes I and II in "Notes to the Student," the interpretational hypotheses, and the selecting and editing of all the poems. Except for the anthology, the final text has been determined by consultation and approximate agreement. The idea of doing some such book was the former's; the plan and the preparation for the press, the latter's. It is a pleasure to acknowledge the aid of Miss Estelle Cohen, who arranged the photographing of the texts; of Mrs. Ruth Perlmutter, who assisted in the preparation of the lexical glosses; of the Photography Staff of the University of Pennsylvania Library, and of the rare-book room staffs of the Pennsylvania and Princeton University Libraries.

Notes to the Student

The student will find in this book a few words used in a special or technical sense with which he may not be familiar, as well as, for each poem in Part I, a diagram of the poem which makes use of certain special signs. These notes are designed to explain these terms and signs.

I. *Metaphor, Vehicle, Tenor, Connection.* Poetry, like all language, employs metaphors, but tends to use them with greater care, expressiveness, and complexity. These terms are used to discuss the different parts of a metaphor. To use a metaphor is to substitute one word for another, or to assert that such a substitution is possible, in such a way that some of the attributes of the thing to which the substituting word refers (the referent) are transferred to the referent of the substituted word. For example: "A mighty fortress is our God," implies that, for certain purposes of meaning, "fortress" can be substituted for "God." The substitution is possible because God and a fortress have certain attributes in common: both have strength, security, reliability; both offer circumstances for restoring one's strength and issuing forth to fight one's enemies; both offer refuge in a time of crisis. In this metaphor "fortress" is the *vehicle,* that is, that word which "carries" the special meanings to be ascribed to the substituted word, or *tenor,* "God." The latter is called "tenor" because it "holds" the meaning of the passage or discourse in which the metaphor occurs (Latin *tenere* means "to hold"). The attributes in common to the referents of the two words are called the *connection.* The connection is the important element, since we use metaphors for the purpose of selecting the attributes in the connection. Thus, the author of this metaphor wished to select out of all the infinite attributes of God certain particular attributes. It is these attributes, he informs us in the metaphor, that he wishes to talk about, to the exclusion of others. Dante, wishing to talk about other attributes of God, used the vehicle "rose," thus selecting a different set of divine attributes, beauty, preciousness, order, inclusiveness (a rose has a myriad petals). In "A mighty fortress is our God," the speaker asserts that because certain attributes are common to the referents of the words "God" and "fortress," the word "fortress" may be substituted for the word "God." In the following sentence the substitution has actually been carried out. "I worship our mighty fortress." The original sentence contained an explicit metaphor: both tenor and vehicle were identified.

This is an implicit metaphor; only the vehicle is named. All by itself such an expression might not be comprehensible, but if placed in a proper context, it would be. For example, "I worship our mighty fortress, the Creator and Sustainer of Man and the Universe." Fully to understand a metaphor, it is necessary, first, to recognize it as a metaphor, and then to identify the vehicle, the tenor, and the connection, and finally to fit it into the structure of meanings in the poem. In the Interpretational Hypotheses of Part I are numerous metaphors; in most instances all three elements of each metaphor have been pointed out. The student will find it a useful exercise to examine some of these metaphors; they may be located by the appearance of the analytic terms in the text.

II. *Orientation, Dramatization.* The student will perhaps find it helpful to think of a poem in the following way: At every moment of his waking life each human being is face-to-face with some thing, some person, some area of his environment. In the experience of this encounter, there are two ingredients: (1) The object or person or group of objects and persons in his environment, and (2) his attitude toward that segment of his world. If it is his beloved, does he feel overcome by her beauty, or does he hate her for her indifference, or is he, as happens to us, in one of those states of mind in which he himself is indifferent to the woman whom at other times he loves? If the object is a landscape, is he awed by it, is he entranced by it, or does it bore him? The poet is concerned with presenting such attitudes, or states of mind, or, to use the most inclusive term, such *orientations.* However, we must not imagine that the poet is offering for our consideration something which actually exists within his environment. He invents, he imagines something environmental that will reveal as precisely as possible an orientation. Nor, on the other hand, are we to believe that he is presenting, as a psychologist might, an actual or real orientation. His task is to create, as far as imagination will carry him, a new orientation, something perhaps which no one has ever experienced but the creation and contemplation of which adds to the range of human experience. Thus we are to read a poem as if it were spoken by an imaginary human being in an imaginary situation. Just as the author of plays dramatizes the relations among human beings, so the poet dramatizes a relation between a human being and some thing, some force, some object, some stimulus, which is not that human being, something other than that human being himself. Consequently, at the conclusion of nearly every Interpretational Hypothesis which follows in Part I, there is a statement which sums up the orientation which the poem is dramatizing. In real situations, when a man speaks, his attitude or orientation is revealed by the tone of voice, by gesture, by bodily movement, by a thousand sources of information to which we respond, for the most part unconsciously. But poetry is language stripped of these aids which reveal, to the acute observer, the orientation which governs what a man is saying and what, in his environment, he is interested in and paying attention to. Hence the ultimate question in comprehending a poem is, "In what tone of voice should it be spoken?" Whether reading the poem aloud or silently, we are like a radio actor studying his part, who must say to himself, constantly, "How shall I say this line so that I may reveal the orientation of the speaker toward the person he is addressing?" So the poet wishes us to say to ourselves, "How shall I say this poem so that my tone of voice may reveal the orientation of the speaker of the poem to his beloved—or to the landscape—or even, and most subtly, to himself?"

III. *Syntactic Gloss.* Opposite each of the first twenty-five poems the student will find a diagram which displays in a very simple way the sentence structure of the poem. Many beginning readers have difficulty understanding poetry because, despite the fact that they may know the meanings of all the words in a sentence, they do not understand how the sentence fits together. The diagrams or "syntactic glosses" are designed to help the student when he has difficulty of this sort. They can be used in the same way as the lexical glosses at the right side of the selections. It is always wise to consult it whether the student thinks he understands the syntax of the sentence or not; he may be mistaken; and in poetry, at the first reading, he probably is.

Although the diagrams look a little complicated, they are actually very easy to use, and one can learn how to use them in a few minutes. What we have done is simply to rewrite the poem so that the principal structure (usually the main clause) is farthest to the left, and then to place the modifiers above and beneath and to the right. These modifiers are placed under the expressions which they modify. For example, the first sentence of Ben Jonson's "To the Immortal Memory and Friendship . . ." (the sixth poem in Part I), which reads:

Brave Infant of *Saguntum,* clear
Thy coming forth in that great year,
When the Prodigious *Hannibal* did crown
His rage with razing your immortal Town.

is written as follows:

<Brave Infant of *Saguntum,*>
Thy coming forth [was] clear
↑
in that great year,
↑
When the Prodigious *Hannibal* did crown His rage
↑
with razing your immortal Town.

Notice that the arrow drawn from "in that great year" to "coming," the one drawn from "When the Prodigious Hannibal did crown His rage" to "year," and the one drawn from "with razing your immortal Town" to "did crown" indicate at a glance what goes with what. Wherever a single word is modified in this way, an arrow is drawn; wherever a phrase or clause is modified, no arrow is drawn, since it is understood that the modificational relationship is sufficiently shown by the indentation.

Note in the example above that the main clause "Thy coming forth [was] clear" is written between asterisks (**). These asterisks are used to indicate that the words which occur between them have been rearranged into an order which would be more usual in modern American English. Poets frequently utilize inversions of words for metrical and other reasons, and students sometimes have trouble rearranging them in their own minds so that they can understand the sense of the poem. This device should raise to a conscious level a process which all readers of poetry use to understand what they read. The student will appreciate how complex poetic inversions may be by considering the Syntactic Gloss to the selection from Milton's *Paradise Lost* (the eighth poem in Part I).

A few other symbols are used to show structural relationships; these can simply be listed, since they are so easy to learn:

<> show apostrophe, or direct address to some person, being, or thing:

<Brave Infant of *Saguntum,*>

{} show parallel structures, at any level:

Thou <Wise child> { did'st hastily return,
And mad'st thy Mother's womb thine urn

[] show interpolations introduced by the editors to make the structure of the sentence clearer:

How summ'd a circle *of deepest lore thou didst leave mankind*
[if] *we could find the Center*!

↕ (double-headed arrow) shows apposition:

For here's a tun of Midnight-work to come,
↕
Og *rolling home from a Treason Tavern*.

Finally, note that the punctuation and capitalization of the poem have been kept intact in the syntactic glosses, but that the lines have been rearranged and numbered by sentences. Some students are confused by poetry because it is arranged in metrical lines or stanzas; they think that the metrical arrangement has something to do with the structure of the sentence of the poem. This, of course, is untrue; the meter of a poem is one thing, and the syntax is something else. The same principles of syntax are used in poetry as in prose. The arrangement in the syntactic glosses by sentences is designed to show at a glance what the sentences of the poem are, so that one never need make the mistake of beginning to read a sentence in the middle merely because that is where a line of poetry starts, or the mistake of thinking a sentence ends merely because the line of poetry comes to an end.

PART I

TWENTY-FIVE POEMS WITH SYNTACTIC AND LEXICAL GLOSSES AND INTERPRETATIONAL HYPOTHESES, ARRANGED IN ORDER OF DIFFICULTY

1\. Farewell {
<thou Thing,
↑
{so known, / so dear To me,} as blood to life and spirit:
↑
[in] *pass'd time*
[thou] Near,
Nay, thou more near than {
kindred,
friend,
man, wife,
Male to the female,
soul to body:
Life To {quick action, / or the warm soft side Of the {resigning, / yet resisting Bride.>

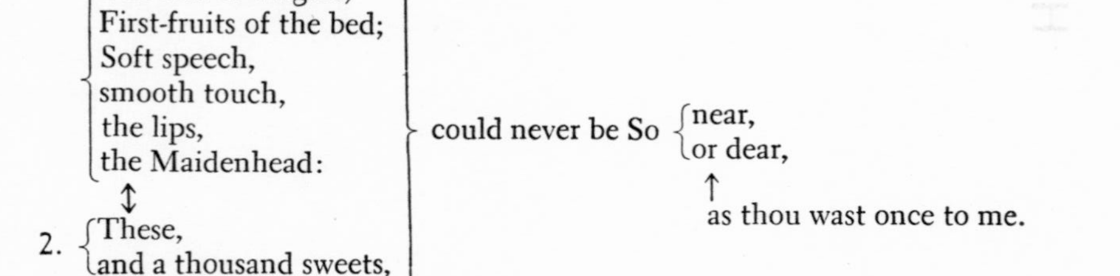

{The kiss of Virgins;
First-fruits of the bed;
Soft speech,
smooth touch,
the lips,
the Maidenhead:}
↕
2\. {These,
and a thousand sweets,} could never be So {near, / or dear,
↑
as thou wast once to me.

1.

ROBERT HERRICK (1591–1674)

His Farewell to Sack

Farewell thou Thing, time-pass'd so known, so dear
To me, as blood to life and spirit: Near,
Nay, thou more near than kindred, friend, man, wife,
Male to the female, soul to body: Life
To quick action, or the warm soft side
Of the resigning, yet resisting Bride.
The kiss of Virgins; First-fruits of the bed;
Soft speech, smooth touch, the lips, the Maidenhead:
These, and a thousand sweets, could never be
So near, or dear, as thou wast once to me.

Title. Sack: a white wine of Spain.

1. *time-pass'd:* (in) time passed.

1. *so . . . so:* as . . . as.

2. *spirit:* a vital and highly refined substance or fluid thought in the older physiology to permeate the blood and the vital organs.

3. *kindred:* family relations.

6. *resigning:* surrendering.

7. *First-fruits:* the pleasures of deflowering a virgin.

8. *Maidenhead:* virginity.

3. <O thou the drink of {Gods, / and Angels!
↕
Wine
↑
That scatter'st Spirit and Lust;
*whose purest shine shows
↑
More radiant than the Summer's Sun-beams*;

[that is] {*illustrious, / brave;
↑
[in] Each way*

and like to {
those Comets we see by night;
↑
whose shagg'd portents Foretell the coming
↑
of some dire events:

Or some full flame,
↑
which *aspires with a pride*,
↑
Throwing about his {wild, / and active fires.>
}

O thou the drink of Gods, and Angels! Wine
That scatter'st Spirit and Lust; whose purest shine,
More radiant than the Summer's Sun-beams shows;
Each way illustrious, brave; and like to those
Comets we see by night; whose shagg'd portents
Foretell the coming of some dire events:
Or some full flame, which with a pride aspires,
Throwing about his wild, and active fires.

12. *scatter'st Spirit and Lust:* distribute and endow drinkers with vigor and desire.

13. *shows* (used here intransitively): appears.

14. *illustrious:* bright, luminous, shining.

14. *brave:* beautiful.

15. *shagg'd:* hairy (a reference to the tail of the comet).

15. *portents:* omens (comets were thought to be bad omens).

17. *aspires:* mounts up.

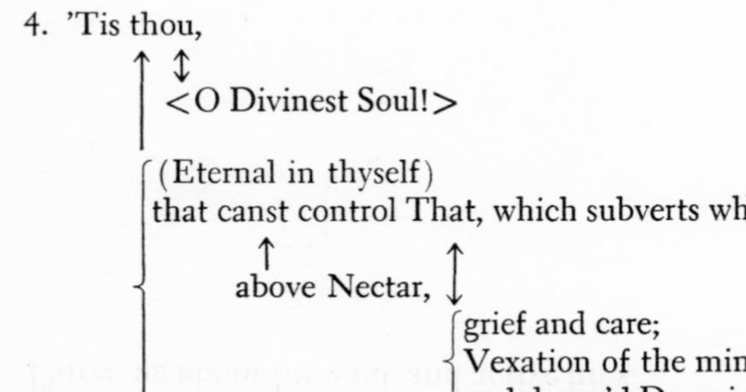

4. 'Tis thou,
<O Divinest Soul!>
(Eternal in thyself)
that canst control That, which subverts whole nature,
above Nectar,
grief and care;
Vexation of the mind,
and damn'd Despair.

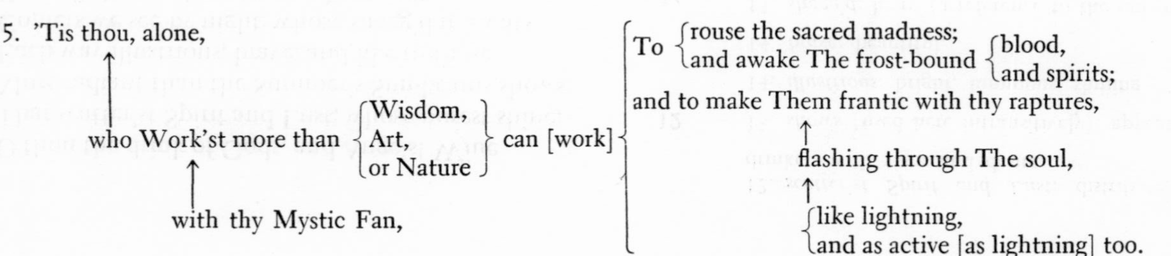

5. 'Tis thou, alone,
who Work'st more than {Wisdom, Art, or Nature} can [work]
with thy Mystic Fan,
To {rouse the sacred madness; and awake The frost-bound {blood, and spirits;}}
and to make Them frantic with thy raptures,
flashing through The soul,
{like lightning, and as active [as lightning] too.}

6. 'Tis not [i.e. Not even] {*Apollo or those thrice three *Castalian* Sisters,} can sing*,
if [they are] wanting thee.

'Tis thou, above Nectar, O Divinest soul!
(Eternal in thyself) that canst control
That, which subverts whole nature, grief and care;
Vexation of the mind, and damn'd Despair.
'Tis thou, alone, who with thy Mystic Fan,
Work'st more than Wisdom, Art, or Nature can,
To rouse the sacred madness; and awake
The frost-bound blood, and spirits; and to make
Them frantic with thy raptures, flashing through
The soul, like lightning, and as active too.
'Tis not *Apollo* can, or those thrice three
Castalian Sisters, sing, if wanting thee.

19. *above:* more than.

19. *Nectar:* the drink of the gods.

20. *control:* to exercise restraint upon.

21. *That:* those (things) which . . . , i.e. grief, care, vexation of the mind and damn'd Despair.

23. *Mystic Fan:* one of the objects associated with Bacchus, the Greek god of wine, was a magical fan used for winnowing grain (i.e. blowing the chaff and refuse away).

24. *Work'st more:* hast a greater effect.

25. *sacred madness:* of poetic inspiration.

26. *spirits:* see line 2.

27. *frantic:* out of control, delirious.

27. *raptures:* act of seizing and carrying off as prey. Wine carries off the blood and spirits of the drinker.

29. *'Tis not:* It is not that; i.e. not even.

29. *Apollo:* god of poetry.

30. *Castalian:* Castalia was a fountain on Mount Parnassus near Delphi, Greece, sacred to the nine ("thrice-three") Muses. Its waters were said to be a source of inspiration.

30. *wanting:* lacking.

7. {*Horace*, / *Anacreon*} both had lost their fame,
[if] thou Had'st not fill'd them with thy fire and flame.

8. {*Phœbean* splendor! / and thou *Thespian* spring!
↑
Of which, sweet Swans must drink,
before they sing {Their true-pac'd-Numbers, / and their Holy-Lays,
Which makes them worthy {*Cedar*, / and the *Bays*.>

9. But {why? / why *do I gaze longer upon Thee*
↑
with the eye of admiration?
Since I {must leave thee; / and [being] enforc'd, must say To all thy witching beauties, {"Go, / Away."

Horace, *Anacreon* both had lost their fame,
Had'st thou not fill'd them with thy fire and flame.
Phœbean splendor! and thou *Thespian* spring!
Of which, sweet Swans must drink, before they sing
Their true-pac'd-Numbers, and their Holy-Lays,
Which makes them worthy *Cedar*, and the *Bays*.
But why? why longer do I gaze upon
Thee with the eye of admiration?
Since I must leave thee; and enforc'd, must say
To all thy witching beauties, Go, Away.

31. *Horace:* Latin lyric poet (65 BC–8 BC).

31. *Anacreon:* Greek lyric poet (around 550 BC–465 BC).

31. *had:* would have.

33. *Phœbean:* pertaining to Phoebus Apollo, the sun god in Greek mythology, god of the Muses. The splendor of the wine is as pure and bright as the sun and inspires one to write great poetry.

33. *Thespian:* Thespiae was a city near Thebes, Greece, whose population worshipped the Muses in a sacred grove on nearby Helicon. Hence, one of the fountains on Helicon, Hippocrene or Aganippe, which were sacred to the Muses.

34. *Swans:* it was once believed that swans sang immediately before they died; as a result "swan" was figuratively used for "poet."

35. *true-pac'd:* measured truly, i.e. written with correct metrical scansion.

35. *Numbers:* lines of verse, particularly as metrical constructions.

35. *Lay:* a short poem.

36. *Cedar:* cedar oil was used to preserve papyrus; hence, it symbolizes poetry worth preserving.

36. *Bays:* leaves of the bay tree were used as a wreath for poets.

39. *enforc'd:* constrained or compelled by circumstances.

40. *witching:* bewitching.

But if thy whimp'ring looks do ask me why?

10. Then know, that {Nature bids thee go,
not I.

11. 'Tis her erroneous self
↑
[which] has made a brain
↑
Uncapable of such a Sovereign,
↑
As is thy powerful self.

12. Prithee {*smile not*;
Or smile more inly;
lest thy looks beguile My vows
↑
{denounc'd in zeal,
which *show thee thus much*,
↕
That I have sworn, to know thee
↑
but by thy looks.

But if thy whimp'ring looks do ask me why?
Then know, that Nature bids thee go, not I.
'Tis her erroneous self has made a brain
Uncapable of such a Sovereign,
As is thy powerful self. Prithee not smile;
Or smile more inly; lest thy looks beguile
My vows denounc'd in zeal, which thus much show thee,
That I have sworn, but by thy looks to know thee.

41. *whimp'ring:* appealing.

41. *looks:* glances.

43. *erroneous:* human nature is capable of error.

46. *more inly:* less observably.

46–47. *beguile My vows:* to charm or divert my attentions so that I give up my vows.

47. *denounc'd:* proclaimed, announced, published.

47. *zeal:* great moral enthusiasm, often religious or puritanical enthusiasm.

48. *but:* only.

13. Let others { drink thee freely;
and desire Thee and their lips [to be] espous'd; }
while I { admire,
And love thee;
but [do] not taste thee. }

14. Let my Muse { Fail of thy former helps;
and only use Her inadult'rate strength: }

15. what's done by me Hereafter, shall smell { of the Lamp,
not thee. }

Let others drink thee freely; and desire
Thee and their lips espous'd; while I admire,
And love thee; but not taste thee. Let my Muse
Fail of thy former helps; and only use 52
Her inadult'rate strength: what's done by me
Hereafter, shall smell of the Lamp, not thee.

50. *espous'd:* married, united.

52. *Fail of:* do without.

52. *helps:* assistance.

53. *inadult'rate:* unadulterated, unmixed.

Interpretational Hypothesis

The title tells us the occasion of the poem: the poet is going to stop drinking sack, a white wine from Spain and the Canary Islands, very popular in England in the sixteenth and seventeenth centuries. He begins, then, with a direct address to the wine, as if it were a person, although he calls it a "Thing," a peculiar expression, but it serves to individualize what is after all only an infinitely extensive liquid. It has not only been known to the poet; it has been "dear," which one would take to mean simply "desirable" or "important," were it not for the simile. It is as dear to the speaker as blood is to life and spirit. Since blood is dear to life and spirit because it is essential for their maintenance, it follows that sack has been in the same way essential for the life of the poet. Next, in order to explain the special meaning he gives to "near," he introduces a whole series of comparisons of increasing length, complexity, and importance. The nearness to him of wine is greater than any feelings of nearness provided by one relation to another, or friend to friend, or husband to wife, or wife to husband. The last two words lead by association to the next comparison: the nearness of male and female, or man and woman as sexual partners. Now he introduces an even closer relationship, that of soul to body, which is associated with the previous two by the fact that man and wife, or male and female, are traditionally compared to body and soul. But since soul and body are separated after death, he finds an even closer relationship: quick action is always the sign of life, and the two are virtually inseparable. This leads to the last comparison. Syntactically we have little choice, though at first it seems odd, but to read, "As near as life is to the warm soft side of the bride." Since the comparisons have proceeded by a kind of association, a subtle and indelicate connection appears to exist between quick action and the bridal bed, where life as quick action certainly is inseparable from and is aroused by the presence of the bride, with her charmingly ambiguous response. And this last nearness, since the passage has proceeded by steps of increasing nearness, is the nearest of all. "Near," then, means "close to, a natural concomitant, essential, inseparable, not to be thought of without, irresistible." Sack has been all this to him.

By a natural association with the last of the series, he goes on in the next statement to say that all the delights of love could never be so essential to him and inseparable from him as sack once was. Having said this much, he bursts forth in an apostrophe to wine, hailing it as divine, and thus continuing a very ancient tradition: to the Greeks, Bacchus, the bringer of wine to man, was a god. Wine has a divine origin, the speaker insists, referring not only to its power to arouse vigor and potency, but also comparing its brilliancy to summer sun-beams. Like them, it is in every way shining and noble ("illustrious") and beautiful ("brave"). It also has the character of comets, which with their strange tails, are signs ("shagg'd portents") that something terrible is going to happen: it arouses our expectancies. Again, wine is like a flame, mounting up proudly from the fuel which produces it and tossing its branches ("fires") wildly and vigorously. In the same way wine enhances our sense of vitality and vigor. He continues with wine's divine nature, which, almost irreverently, he claims to have the character of the godhead, in that it sustains itself eternally and is not sustained by another force. The proof of its divinity is that it can control grief and care, mental torments and despair, the most damnable kind of emotional depression. These things subvert nature, by which is meant here human nature. They turn it upside down. Anything which keeps human nature in its proper emotional course is surely divine and is worth more than nectar, the gods' drink. Further, it works like a fan which can make a fire burn better. It has a mysterious or divine power to arouse the sacred madness, the traditional term for poetic inspiration, which is far less responsive to the power of wisdom, the traditions of human skill, or the unaided strength of human nature. It stirs up the blood and the emotions ("spirits") and drives them to a divine madness. Both in its speed and its ability to cause an effect ("active") it is like lightning. In fact neither Apollo himself, the god of poetry, nor the Castalian sisters can sing, or perform their proper duties, without the aid of wine. The Castalian sisters are the nine Muses. They take their name from the Castalian spring, which flows on Mt. Parnassus, their home and that of Apollo, symbol of poetic inspiration. Thus wine is the greatest source of poetic inspiration. And the two great lyric poets of the ancient world, the Roman Horace and the Greek Anacreon, were both dependent on wine for their power.

Again he apostrophizes wine. It has the splendor of Apollo ("Phoebus" was his first name) and it is itself the spring from which all true poets must drink. Poets are here referred to as swans, partly because of the beauty of these birds and partly because, though they sing only when they are dying, legend has it that then they sing with extraordinary beauty. Poets, then, need wine to inspire them before they can compose their poems in the right rhythms, and before they can write their truly divine poems ("holy-lays"), which give them the right to wreaths of cedar (a symbol of immortality because it is always green and yields a preserving oil) and of bays (by ancient tradition the plant from whose leaves wreaths for poets were woven when they had won in poetic contests).

But to hail wine as necessary for true poetry puts the speaker in an unhappy position, for he too is a poet; and if he says farewell to sack he must forego his proper source of inspiration. This explains the sudden break in continuity which occurs in line 37. The speaker checks himself, remembering that he is saying farewell to sack, and that praising its virtues is no way to make the parting easier. And now we learn that he is *forced* to leave wine and its enchanting and inspiring beauties; and he orders sack, now personified, to go away. But sack is presented as whimpering at the prospect of departure and wondering why it must leave. Now comes what has been put off so long, the reason for the farewell. "Nature," here used in the sense of "bodily constitution," is responsible, not the poet himself, i.e. his spirit or soul. His bodily constitution has endowed him with too weak a brain to endure the masterful powers of wine. But merely looking at wine, thinking of it, or writing a poem about it tempts him, and he begs wine not to look at him so attractively and invitingly, or at least somehow to conceal its beckoning charms. Otherwise he may be persuaded to forget what he has sworn with such earnestness, to know wine only by its appearance and not by experiencing it or drinking it. "Know" seems to be used here almost in the Biblical or sexual sense, for the lips of drinkers and wine are often said to be married. It may be all right for others to drink wine, but he can only admire and love it from a distance, not by drinking it.

And now as a poet he has to face what this farewell to wine must cost him. His Muse, his poetic inspiration, must get along without the help of wine, which it once had. His inspiration must depend only on its native ("inadult'rate") strength. Thus from now on the speaker will be able to write only poetry that "smells of the lamp"—the symbol of the scholar, for in it he burns the midnight oil. And poetry written by the lamp will have the oily smell of poetry written from knowledge, craftsmanship, and unaided, uninspired talent ("Wisdom, Art, Nature," l. 24). It will not have the smell of the grape, or of divine inspiration. Thus half humorously, half sadly, the poet looks forward to a far less interesting life and poetic career.

The poem, then, is a dramatization of how a disagreeable necessity is made acceptable by humor and good nature.

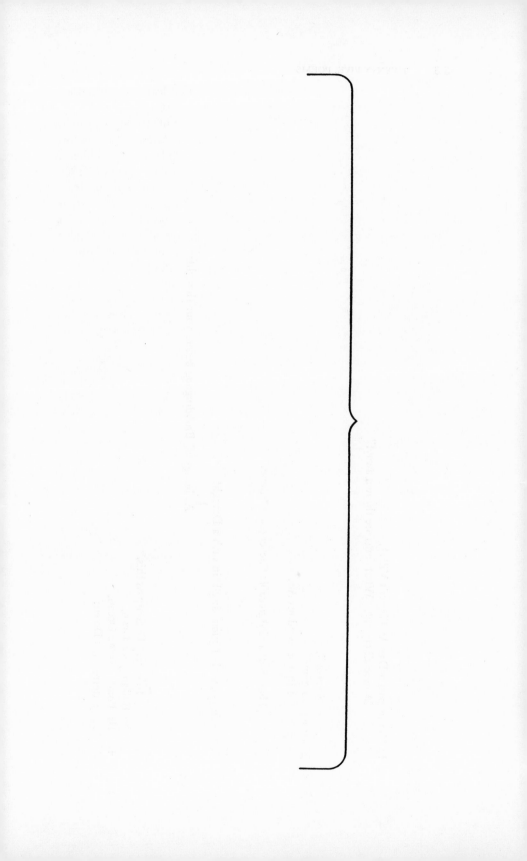

1. *let us pass a Day At _Timon's Villa_*,
   Where all cry out, "What sums are thrown away!"

2. [It is] { So proud,
   so grand,
   of that stupendous Air,
   ↑
   [That] _Soft_ and _Agreeable_ *never come* there.

3. Greatness, with _Timon_, dwells in such a Draught
   ↑
   As brings all _Brobdingnag_ before your thought:

4. [In order] To compass this,
   { his Building is a Town,
   His Pond [is] an Ocean,
   his parterre [is] a Down:

ALEXANDER POPE (1688–1744)

Timon's Villa

From Of False Taste, An Epistle to the Right Honourable Richard Earl of Burlington

At *Timon's Villa* let us pass a Day,
Where all cry out, "What sums are thrown away!"
So proud, so grand, of that stupendous Air,
Soft and *Agreeable* come never there.
Greatness, with *Timon*, dwells in such a Draught
As brings all *Brobdingnag* before your thought:
To compass this, his Building is a Town,
His Pond an Ocean, his parterre a Down:

1. *Timon's*: a classical name (cf. Shakespeare's *Timon of Athens*) used as a pseudonym for the great English lord whose architectural tastes Pope is satirizing. It was customary in eighteenth-century satiric poetry to refer to one's enemies in this way, and much ingenuity has been used by later editors in discovering who the originals were.

1. *Villa:* a country estate.

3. *of that:* of so; of such a.

3. *Air:* style, scale.

4. *Soft and Agreeable:* soft and agreeable things, pleasant aspects of architecture.

5. *Greatness:* hugeness, great size.

5. *with:* in Timon's view, as far as Timon is concerned.

5. *Draught:* draft, excessive air-current. Timon's villa was built on a site which was very breezy.

6. *Brobdingnag:* a country visited by Swift's Gulliver in his travels in which everything (including the inhabitants) was of gigantic size, so that Gulliver appeared extremely small in comparison.

7. *compass:* encompass, stretch around and contain.

7. *this:* this scale or expanse, this "stupendous" air.

8. *parterre:* level space in a garden occupied by flower-beds ornamentally arranged.

8. *Down:* a large expanse of open, elevated land.

5. Who but must laugh,
        when he sees the Master?
                    ↕
                    A puny Insect, shiv'ring at a Breeze!

6. Lo! what huge Heaps of Littleness [are] around!

7. The Whole, [is] a labor'd Quarry above ground.

8. Two *Cupids* squirt before:
a Lake behind Improves the keenness of the Northern Wind.

9. His *Gardens* next *call [forth] your admiration*,
behold the Wall On ev'ry side you look!

10. No pleasing Intricacies intervene,
No artful Wildness [intervenes] to perplex the Scene:

11. Grove nods at grove,
each Alley has a Brother,
And half the Platform just reflects the other.

Who but must laugh, the Master when he sees?
A puny Insect, shiv'ring at a Breeze!
Lo! what huge Heaps of Littleness around!
The Whole, a labor'd Quarry above ground.
Two *Cupids* squirt before: a Lake behind
Improves the keenness of the Northern Wind.
His *Gardens* next your admiration call,
On ev'ry side you look, behold the Wall!
No pleasing Intricacies intervene,
No artful Wildness to perplex the Scene:
Grove nods at grove, each Alley has a Brother,
And half the Platform just reflects the other.

9. *Who but must laugh, the Master when he sees:* anyone, when he sees the master, can only laugh; or, no one can help laughing when he sees the master.

11. *huge Heaps of Littleness:* "little" in the sense of being intrinsically of little worth, no matter how great in size.

12. *labor'd:* worked over.

12. *Quarry:* a large mass of rock in natural state.

13. *Cupids:* statues of Cupid as fountains.

13. *before:* in front.

13. *behind:* in back.

14. *Improves:* (notice the sarcasm implicit in this word).

14. *keenness:* unpleasant sharpness.

15. *call:* call forth, attract.

17. *Intricacies:* interesting complexities.

18. *perplex:* to make something complex or intricate.

19. *Grove:* a plot of trees.

19. *Alley:* a walk or passage in a garden, usually bordered with trees or bushes.

20. *Platform:* terrace on the garden façade.

12. The suff'ring Eye *sees Nature inverted*,
↑
Trees cut to Statues,
Statues thick as Trees,
With here a Fountain, never to be play'd,
And there a Summer-house, that knows no shade;

13. Here *Amphitrite* sails thro' Myrtle bow'rs;
There Gladiators fight, or die, in flow'rs;

14. see { the drooping Sea-horse mourn,
↑
Un-water'd
And Swallows roost in *Nilus*' dusty Urn.

15. My Lord advances with majestic mien,
↑
Smit with the mighty pleasure,
↕
to be seen:

The suff'ring Eye inverted Nature sees,
Trees cut to Statues, Statues thick as Trees,
With here a Fountain, never to be play'd,
And there a Summer-house, that knows no shade;
Here *Amphitrite* sails thro' Myrtle bow'rs;
There Gladiators fight, or die, in flow'rs;
Un-water'd see the drooping Sea-horse mourn,
And Swallows roost in *Nilus*' dusty Urn.
  My Lord advances with majestic mien,
Smit with the mighty pleasure, to be seen:

21. *inverted:* upside down.

23. *play'd:* turned on, allowed to work.

25. *Amphitrite:* Greek goddess of the sea, daughter of Nereus and wife of Poseidon. The reference is explained by a line in *The Guardian*, No. 173: "There ships of myrtle sail in seas of box." The poet is satirizing the practice of trimming bushes and trees into odd shapes like "giants, animals, monsters, coats of arms, and mottoes" (Horace Walpole).

25. *Myrtle:* a shrub having shiny evergreen leaves and scented white flowers.

26. *Gladiators:* Pope remarks in a footnote that he refers specifically to the two famous Roman statues of the Fighting Gladiator and the Dying Gladiator.

29. *mien:* appearance, manner.

30. *Smit:* smitten, struck.

16. But soft—by regular approach—not yet—
First [you must] *sweat thro' the length of yon hot Terrace*,

And when *you've dragg'd your thighs up ten steep Slopes,
17. he'll bless your Eyes Just at his Study-door*.

18. His *Study!* with what Authors is it stor'd?

19. *my Lord is curious { In Books,
not Authors*; }
*he turns you round To all their *dated Backs**,
**Aldus* printed These*,
**Du Süeil* has *bound* those*.

20. Lo { some are V*ellum*,
and the rest [are just] as good For all his Lordship knows,
↑
but they are W*ood*. }

21. *'tis in vain to look For *Locke* or *Milton**,
These Shelves admit not any Modern book.

But soft—by regular approach—not yet—
First thro' the length of yon hot Terrace sweat,
And when up ten steep Slopes you've dragg'd your thighs,
Just at his Study-door he'll bless your Eyes.
 His *Study!* with what Authors is it stor'd?
In Books, not Authors, curious is my Lord;
To all their *dated Backs* he turns you round,
These *Aldus* printed, those *Du Süeil* has *bound*.
Lo some are *Vellum*, and the rest as good
For all his Lordship knows, but they are *Wood*.
For *Locke* or *Milton* 'tis in vain to look,
These Shelves admit not any Modern book.

31. *soft:* "Easy!" "Just a minute."

31. *regular approach:* i.e. taking no short-cuts, going via the architecturally prescribed routes. "Approach" in the architectural usage means "access, entranceway."

32. *Terrace:* large open porch or patio, often with balustrade.

33. *thighs:* synecdoche (i.e. part for whole) in which thighs stand for legs in general.

36. *curious:* inquisitive, skilled as a connoisseur.

37. *Backs:* the spines of the books.

37. *he turns you round To:* he shows or calls your attention to.

38. *Aldus:* Aldo Manutio (1449–1515), Venetian printer, founder of the Aldine press and publisher of the first printed editions of Greek authors.

38. *Du Süeil:* Abbé du Süeil, noted Parisian binder of the period.

39. *Vellum:* fine parchment made from calfskin.

40. *Wood:* a reference to the practice, still common, of painting wood panels in studies to give the impression of filled bookshelves.

41. *Locke:* John Locke (1632–1704), English philosopher.

22. And now *you hear the Chapel's silver bell*,
↑
That summons you to all the Pride of Pray'r:

23. Light Quirks of Music, Make the Soul dance upon a Jig to Heaven.
↑
broken and uneven,

24. *you devoutly stare On painted Ceilings*,
↑
Where *the Saints of *Verrio* or *Laguerre* { sprawl*, / *lie On gilded Clouds in fair expansion*, / And bring all Paradise before your Eye. }

25. *the { Cushion / and soft *Dean* } invite [you] To Rest*,
↑
Who never mentions Hell to *polite Ears*.

26. But hark! the chiming Clocks *call to Dinner*;
A hundred Footsteps scrape the marble Hall:

And now the Chapel's silver bell you hear,
That summons you to all the Pride of Pray'r:
Light Quirks of Music, broken and uneven,
Make the Soul dance upon a Jig to Heaven.
On painted Ceilings you devoutly stare,
Where sprawl the Saints of *Verrio* or *Laguerre*,
On gilded Clouds in fair expansion lie,
And bring all Paradise before your Eye.
To Rest, the Cushion and soft *Dean* invite,
Who never mentions Hell to Ears polite.
But hark! the chiming Clocks to Dinner call;
A hundred Footsteps scrape the marble Hall:

43. *Chapel's:* many large mansions in England have private chapels.

44. *Pride:* pomp, splendor, magnificent display. The irony of "proud worship" should be obvious, since the greatest of all Christian sins is pride.

45. *Quirks:* sudden turns, fantastic phrases.

46. *dance upon a Jig:* dance under the influence of the music of a jig, a lively old dance rhythm, apparently identified by Pope with *gigu*, a French word for a sophisticated dance rhythm.

48. *sprawl:* an 18th-century editor writes: "this single verb has marked with felicity and force the distorted attitudes, the indecent subjects, the want of nature and grace so visible in the pieces of these two artists, employed to adorn our royal palaces and chapels."

48. *Verrio:* Antonio Verrio (1639–1707), who decorated Windsor Castle.

48. *Laguerre:* Louis Laguerre (1663–1721) decorated Blenheim, Burleigh, and other famous houses.

49. *fair expansion:* beautiful extent or space.

51. *Dean:* a church official lower in rank than a bishop or archdeacon; in this case, the clergyman presiding over the lord's chapel.

52. *Ears polite:* Pope writes in a footnote: "This is a fact; a reverend Dean preaching at court threatened the sinner with punishment in 'a place which he thought it not decent to name in so polite an assembly.' "

27. *well-color'd *Serpents* grace The rich Buffet*,
And gaping *Tritons* spew to wash your face.

28. Is this a Dinner?
[Is] this a Genial Room?

29. No, 'tis {a Temple,
{and a Hecatomb;

[The dinner being] A solemn Sacrifice,
↑
perform'd in State,

30. You {drink by Measure,
{and *eat to Minutes*.

The rich Buffet well-color'd *Serpents* grace,
And gaping *Tritons* spew to wash your face.
Is this a Dinner? this a Genial Room?
No, 'tis a Temple, and a Hecatomb;
A solemn Sacrifice, perform'd in State,
You drink by Measure, and to Minutes eat.

55. *Buffet:* a side-board upon which refreshments were spread.

55. *well-color'd Serpents:* serpents with open mouths ejecting liquids were frequently used in the eighteenth century as decorative fountains or tap heads.

55. *grace:* adorn.

56. *Tritons:* images of imaginary sea deities, depicted as bearded men with tails for legs and holding tridents and shell-trumpets.

56. *spew:* spit, eject water.

57. *Genial:* festive, pleasantly cheerful.

58. *Hecatomb:* a great public sacrifice at which large numbers of animals are slaughtered.

59. *in State:* ceremonially; while participating in a ceremony of wealth, splendor, and magnificence.

60. *by Measure, and to Minutes:* according to a prescribed and carefully timed schedule.

31. *each flying Course retires So quick*

↑ [that] you'd swear [that] { *Sancho's* dread Doctor / and his Wand } were there.

32. *the trembling salvers ring Between each Act*,

↑ From soup to { sweet-wine, / and *God bless the King*. }

So quick retires each flying Course, you'd swear
Sancho's dread Doctor and his Wand were there.
Between each Act the trembling salvers ring,
From soup to sweet-wine, and *God bless the King*. 64

61. *retires:* is removed by the waiters.

61. *Course:* course of the meal, as soup, fish, dessert, etc.

62. *Sancho's dread Doctor and his Wand:* a reference to *Don Quixote*, Book II, Chapter 47. Sancho Panza, Don Quixote's wily servant, has taken possession of the island of Barataria and has been made perpetual governor. He is carried to a palace and seated at a great table. At his side stands a physician who holds a wand made of whalebone. The waiters remove a cloth from the dishes, grace is said, and a lace bib tied around Sancho's neck. Sancho takes a bite, but the physician touches the dish with his wand and it disappears. A waiter brings another dish, but this one is also touched and disappears before Sancho can even taste its contents. The doctor then explains his reason for making the food disappear. As a personal physician to the governor, he is so solicitous of his health that he finds fault with literally every dish prepared for him. Sancho, in a rage, orders him to be imprisoned.

63. *Act:* transaction, hence course of the meal.

63. *salvers:* trays.

64. *soup to sweet-wine, and God bless the King:* from the beginning to the very end when the toast to the king was given. The British national anthem "God Save the King" is not supposed to have been sung until 1745; since this poem is dated 1731, it is to be supposed that this refers to a toast to the King's health.

{*starving In Plenty*,
tantaliz'd in State,
And complaisantly help'd to all I hate,
Treated, caress'd and tir'd,

33. I take my leave,
Sick of his civil Pride from Morn to Eve;

34. I { curse { such lavish Cost, / and [such] little Skill,
And swear no Day was ever pass'd so ill.

35. Yet hence { the *Poor* are cloth'd,
the *Hungry* [are] fed;
*The Lab'rer bears { *Health* to himself, / and *Bread* to his Infants*:

36. *His charitable Vanity supplies What his hard Heart denies*.

37. Another age shall see { the golden Ear { Embrown the Slope, / and nod on the Parterre,
Deep Harvests bury all [that] his Pride has plann'd,
And laughing *Ceres* reassume the Land.

In Plenty starving, tantaliz'd in State,
And complaisantly help'd to all I hate,
Treated, caress'd, and tir'd, I take my leave,
Sick of his civil Pride from Morn to Eve;
I curse such lavish Cost, and little Skill,
And swear no Day was ever pass'd so ill.
  Yet hence the *Poor* are cloth'd, the *Hungry* fed;
Health to himself, and to his Infants *Bread*
The Lab'rer bears: What his hard Heart denies,
His charitable Vanity supplies.
  Another age shall see the golden Ear
Embrown the Slope, and nod on the Parterre,
Deep Harvests bury all his Pride has plann'd,
And laughing *Ceres* reassume the Land.

65. *In:* amid.
66. *complaisantly:* obligingly, courteously.
68. *civil:* refined.
69. *Cost:* expense.
71. *hence:* from this.
73. *his:* the lord's.
75. *Ear:* of corn, i.e. wheat.
76. *Embrown:* make brown.
78. *Ceres:* Greek goddess of corn-bearing earth.
78. *reassume:* take over once again.

Interpretational Hypothesis

The subject of Pope's satirical attack is probably named Timon after Shakespeare's Timon of Athens, who, so long as he was rich, lived a life of splendor, surrounded by hosts of friends, but who became a misanthrope after he lost his fortune, having discovered that his friends cared for his wealth but not for him. Since this Timon still has his villa, it is a Timon still wealthy and still throwing his money away on stupid grandeur. Hence all who visit him are impressed only with what his villa cost, and we are immediately told why. It is so proud and so grand, built in so imposing a style ("air") that there is nothing pleasing about the place, nothing beautiful. Consequently, Timon has not created a true greatness of style and beauty and taste. He has simply created something so big that you are quite unprotected from the wind (in England a serious consideration), and all you can think of is that you are like Swift's Lemuel Gulliver in Brobdingnag, the land of the giants, lost in something utterly inappropriate to real human beings. In line 7 "this" is used ironically. "To compass *this*," means "to achieve this pointless and useless size," hence, "this absurdity"; the house is as big as a whole town, the pond is as big as an ocean, and the parterre, the great open and level space in front of the main façade, is as big as a plain. Timon has confused great size with excellence, and hence anyone must laugh at him to see his puniness against this vast background. He seems by contrast as tiny as an insect which has no resistance against a light breeze. Here the speaker picks up the "draught" in line 5 and again suggests that the whole place is windy and barren.

Now he turns to the details of the place, having established a general impression and having made a fundamental contrast between greatness of excellence and greatness of size. He begins by repeating that idea in contrasting the size ("huge") of the various edifices in the grounds with their aesthetic triviality. The place has no more shape or meaning than a quarry, the natural mass of stone from which were hewn the materials of which the villa was built. The mansion represents a lot of work ("labour'd") but that is all. The implicit connection to the next couplet is "for example." In front of the building there are two fountains with cupids, holding, in the fashion of the time, some decorative ornament from which water flows out. The speaker is suggesting that a place so big should have enormous fountains. Instead, the fountains are piddling in size; the water "squirts" from them in a thin stream instead of grandly flowing. The place lacks the consistency of grandeur and thus has yet another aesthetic fault. On the other hand, behind the building is a whole lake, but all that it does is to make the north wind keener by presenting to it a total absence of any protective barrier. So even where there is a consistent grandeur, common sense is lacking. "Improves" is ironic; one usually applies the word to things which make a building better, but here the word is used in connection with one of the elements which make the building worse. So foolish was Timon that he has managed to help the wind make the house uncomfortable, rather than controlling its effects. In the eighteenth century, in fact, "improve" was almost a technical term used to refer to building a new house and creating splendid gardens on an old estate. These floods of water behind the house should have been in the fountains in front of it.

Next you are invited to admire Timon's gardens. But there is nothing to see except the wall around them. At a glance you see it all, because you see nothing. It totally lacks any surprises: between you and the wall of the garden there are no complex arrangements which please because you cannot quite understand them and are tempted to go and look. Further, everything is rigidly formal: there are no areas of the garden planted to look as if they had grown that way naturally. There are no pleasing "accidents." On the contrary, the garden is laid out with absolute symmetry, on either side of an axis. Wherever there is a stand of trees, there is another one exactly like it in the corresponding place on the other side of the axis. In the same way, every "alley" (a drive or walk between two rows or groups of trees) has *its* exactly symmetrical counterpart. Likewise, one half of the platform, or terrace on the garden façade of the house, is precisely like the other half. On the other hand, nature is inverted or turned upside down. Trees are trimmed into the shape of statues, but the stone statues are so thick that they seem like trees, that is, seem all alike. In one part of the garden is a fountain, but it has no water piped to it. Elsewhere there is a summer house, but it has no roof (or perhaps is shaded by no trees). This meaninglessness is compounded by the way the flowers and bushes are arranged. Bowers or trellises of myrtle, a thick vine, are trimmed to look like waves through which sails a statue of the sea-goddess Amphitrite, usually presented at the time as gliding over the waves in a sea-shell. With equal absurdity, beds of flowers inappropriately surround statues of fighting and dying gladiators, who actually fought and died on bloody sand. Elsewhere are other fountains, without water, one of a sea horse, and one of the god of the river Nile, with an urn or vase from which water should flow but does not.

And now we meet the owner and builder of this fantastic pile of absurdity. He comes toward you swollen with his own importance, and his pleasure is not to see you but to let you see him. "But soft" means "But wait, not in such a hurry." You are not to see him yet. You must go to him by "regular approach"; you must go to him according to the rules, for, as we have seen, everything here is done by senseless, inconvenient rules; this lordship tortures his guests as he has tortured stones, trees, and flowers—by rule. These ideas add another dimension to Timon. He is a man quite without human feelings; hence his life of display. Thus he makes you walk in the hot sun across the terrace and drag yourself up ten steep flights of stairs. Only *then* will he receive you at his study door; he would not under any circumstances go to meet you. That the sight of him will be a "blessing" to your eyes is bitterly ironic: Timon imagines that the sight of him will be a blessing to you, but in fact it is an exasperation. It is a "blessing" only in the sense that your weary walking and climbing is done.

And now you look around his study. What kind of books does a man like this read? Well, he is interested in books, not in authors; in the appearance and value of books, not what is written in them. He makes you look at the dates stamped on the spines, to show you how old and valuable they are. You have to observe that a famous printer printed these and a famous binder bound those. How astonishing! some are actually printed on vellum, and the rest might as well be, for all his lordship knows about it. The fact is that many are dummy books, beautifully bound slabs of wood, but Timon, having never looked inside them, does not know it. There is no point in looking for the books of the great philosopher (Locke) and the great poet (Milton) of modern times. His lordship pretends to have no interest in anything but the ancient classics. However, the fact is that he is really as ignorant of these classics as he is of his great modern contemporaries. He is a man without taste, feeling, or learning.

The next thing on the agenda is to attend chapel, where everything is devoted to the display of religious feeling ("Pride or pray'r") and, by implication, nothing to religious experience and genuine worship. This implication is immediately borne out. You hear light quirks of music, trivial and unmeaning trills and runs. The music has no even and solemn flow. Rather, it is like dance music, utterly inappropriate to a religious service. The ceilings are decorated by the fashionable painters of the day, whose comprehension of religious emotion may be measured by the fact that their saints, instead of showing dignity or religious fervor in the worship of God, lie around on golden clouds to show how beautiful they are; the painting claims to be an image of Paradise. The inappropriateness of their attitudes indicates the falseness of this picture of Heaven. But in a way such a picture is suitable, for in this chapel the cushioned seat invites you to comfort, as does the pleasing Dean, the preacher (Timon would never have a mere rector as his chaplain), who never speaks of the terrors of religious faith. To Timon's other failings may now be added religious hypocrisy.

Now the expensive clock-chimes summon you to dinner. Line 54 may mean either that you have to walk a hundred paces to get across the enormous marble hall to the dining room, or that a hundred people are coming to dinner. In either case, overwhelming size is emphasized. The first thing that strikes your eye is a great side-board ("buffet") covered with silver and gold plate (a custom still observed in great English houses and American imitations of such houses). But, another absurdity, it is decorated with repulsively realistic snakes. Likewise from the mouths ("gaping" and "spew") pour torrents of water, enough to wash your face, instead of a small stream of water, or basin of water, to rinse your fingers. You are astonished at the amount of food prepared. Is this enormous display a dinner? Is this huge room a place that invites you to relax your spirits ("genial")? On the contrary, its size makes you think it is a temple and the enormous display of food reminds you of a sacrifice to the gods. The kind of sacrifice called a hecatomb involved the slaughter of dozens of animals. The speaker repeats that it is a sacrifice, with the ironic implication that it is a sacrifice to the pride of Timon, and like a religious or civil ceremony or a play it is "perform'd in state," with no thought of individual comfort or pleasure. Everything is planned ahead of time. You have exactly so much time to eat a course and so much time to drink a glass of wine. Furthermore, the whole thing is so rapidly timed that you almost think it done by magic. The salvers or serving dishes are taken up and set down so rapidly that they are constantly ringing, since of course they are made of solid silver, as they touch the table and each other. And this goes on from the first course, soup, to the last course, sweet wine and the toast to the king, with which a proper English dinner concludes. The poet starves, surrounded by food; he is like Tantalus, who was tortured in Hell by never being permitted to get a drink of water or to grasp fruit, both of which were always just beyond his reach. And all this is done in high style and ceremony. When the speaker does get anything, it is because he is helped to something he does not like, and his host does this disservice with complete self-satisfaction. Timon is, in fact, utterly indifferent and insensitive to other people's desires and needs. Although he "treats" the poet, i.e. constantly gives him things, and though he makes much of him ("caresses"), he is in fact indifferent to him and does it only from "civil Pride." Here the "Pride" cancels out the "civil," since self-importance and real courtesy are incompatible. The poet, sick of the whole thing, which has gone on in the same stupid way all day long, departs. He curses Timon's expenditure which, because of stupidity and ignorance, benefits no one.

In line 71 he seems to relent, to admit that there is something good about Timon. After all, all this cost means employment for many; the poor are clothed, the hungry are fed, and the laborer gets health for himself and bread for his children. But this admission is a satirical trap. The source is not concern for the welfare of men but the vanity of appearing charitable. Timon's heart is hard; his intention is to please and glorify himself, not to help others.

In a later age, an age different in time and character, ripe wheat will cover the slope on which the villa is built, and its heavy heads will bend where the parterre once was. Timon's vast and stupid villa and gardens will have disappeared, and the place will be used for its proper purpose, agriculture: Ceres, the goddess of the harvest, will rule. A stupid, ignorant, tasteless man, devoid of common sense, fellow-feeling, religion, and interest in the comfort of his guests, filled with pride and hypocrisy, has misused his riches by building a vast and ugly villa and garden. But since it is the product of vanity, it will disappear.

1. Yes! { *enisled in the sea of life*,
With echoing straits *thrown between us*,
Dotting the shoreless watery wild, }
We mortal millions live *alone*.

2. The islands feel the enclasping flow,
And then *they know their [the islands'] endless bounds*.

3. But when { the moon *lights their hollows*,
And they are swept by balms of spring,
And *The nightingales sing divinely in their glens*,
↑
on starry nights,
And lovely notes *pour, from shore to shore, Across the sounds and channels*— }

4. Oh! then a longing like despair Is *sent to their farthest caverns*;

5. For, *they feel, [“] surely once we were Parts of a single continent*!

MATTHEW ARNOLD

(1822–1888)

Switzerland

5: To Marguerite—Continued

Yes! in the sea of life enisled,
With echoing straits between us thrown,
Dotting the shoreless watery wild,
We mortal millions live *alone*.
The islands feel the enclasping flow,
And then their endless bounds they know.

But when the moon their hollows lights,
And they are swept by balms of spring,
And in their glens, on starry nights,
The nightingales divinely sing;
And lovely notes, from shore to shore,
Across the sounds and channels pour—

Oh! then a longing like despair
Is to their farthest caverns sent;
For surely once, they feel, we were
Parts of a single continent!

1. *enisled:* made into isles.
2. *straits:* narrow bodies of water between land.
3. *wild:* wilderness.
6. *their:* the islands.
6. *bounds:* limits, boundaries.
7. *hollows:* valleys.
8. *balms:* balmy breezes.
9. *glens:* narrow, secluded valleys.
12. *sounds:* bodies of water.

6. Now *the watery plain spreads round us*—

7. Oh might our marges meet again! ["]

8. Who order'd, that their longing's fire Should be cool'd?
↑
as soon as kindled,

9. Who renders their *deep desire vain*?—

10. A God,
a God { *ruled their severance*!
And bade *The unplumb'd, salt, estranging sea to be betwixt their shores*.

Now round us spreads the watery plain—
Oh might our marges meet again!

Who order'd, that their longing's fire
Should be, as soon as kindled, cool'd?
Who renders vain their deep desire?—
A God, a God their severance ruled!
And bade betwixt their shores to be
The unplumb'd, salt, estranging sea.

18. *marges:* margins, boundaries.

22. *severance:* separation.

22. *ruled:* decreed, required.

23. *bade:* commanded.

24. *unplumb'd:* unfathomed, not measured for depth.

24. *estranging:* causing to be strangers.

Interpretational Hypothesis

Arnold published this poem under various titles: "To Marguerite, in Returning a Volume of the Letters of Ortis" (1852), next as number V in the sequence of poems called "Switzerland" with the title as simply "To Marguerite" (1853), next as number VI in that series and with the same title (1854), then as number VII but with the new title "Isolation" (1857), again as number 7 of "Switzerland" with the title as given above (1869), and finally as number 5 (1888). Since these titles were used at various times for other poems in the same series, this poem is best identified and remembered by its first line.

Of these various titles only that of 1857, "Isolation," is the kind of title that gives some information about the poem itself. "Insula" in Latin and "isola" in Italian, "îsle" in French, and "isle" or "island" in English all have the same meaning. The land of an island is separated by the surrounding sea from other land. Hence an "isolated" person is separated from other persons. What physically isolates a prisoner from society is concrete: stone walls and bars. What emotionally isolates an individual from society is a sense of separation from others because he does not share with them feelings which emotional communication makes possible. All these uses are metaphorical developments of "to be an island." In the first line the poem states that it is true, emphatically true ("Yes!"), that we are islands in the sea of life. The separating medium, then, is life itself, or the conditions of existence in which we find ourselves. Between us are echoing straits. Two questions arise here. Why "echoing" and why "thrown"? An echo is the return of one's voice to oneself by other than a human agency. The word brings out the failure of communication between the islands, or individuals. Although isolated individuals may attempt to establish emotional communication with others, they "hear only their own voices," i.e. they experience no answering emotional response. "Thrown" implies that some power external to the conditions of life is responsible for the existence of the straits. But that power is not identified. It raises the expectation that it will be. Whether that expectation will be fulfilled or disappointed remains to be seen. The "wild" or wilderness of the water is appropriate because it is consistent that there is no communication, as we have seen, between the islands; and thus the wild is shoreless. But this word raises a question. Do not islands have shores? Yes, but so do continents. The sea of life, then, is different from the actual seas of the earth which are bordered by the shores of continents. In the sea of life, the conditions of existence in which we find ourselves, there are no continents, continuous bodies of lands; there is no such thing as human solidarity. Thus "we mortal millions live alone," each separate on his own little island. The italicization of *alone* is a typographical device to indicate emphasis.

At first glance, lines 5–6 seem to add nothing to what has been said, until we consider "feel" and "know." The metaphor is now extended. Not only are human beings isolated; they are also aware of being isolated. They are clasped or firmly caught in the "flow" or continuously changing medium of isolation. When the individual feels that he is inescapably separated from other human beings by the continuously shifting conditions of experiences, then he is aware, consciously, of his "endless bounds." This last phrase is a paradox, since a "bound" or frontier *is* an "end" or limit. Thus the phrase means "boundless bounds," or "no bounds at all." The phrase is a way of saying, "There are no bounds, no frontiers, to the personality; that is, one personality never genuinely impinges on, confronts, meets, and contacts another personality." The two lines, then, are concerned with the raising of an emotional response to the level of an intellectual conception.

This explains the force of the "But" in the first line of the next stanza (l. 7): "In spite of their knowledge, in spite of their intellectual certainty that this isolation is the condition of life and always will be—." The implication is that a longing for communication and a sense of solidarity and communication with other human beings will appear and will be felt. The rest of this stanza, then, is concerned with the conditions under which such a longing will occur. Having established that the metaphor of "island" equals "individual human personality" and "sea" equals "conditions of existence," the poet now speaks for a time entirely in terms derived from the vehicle. When the moonlight shines into the dark and hidden places of the islands, when the sweet winds of spring blow across them, when the nightingales, the birds of spring and love, sing on perfect nights, and their notes are heard across the straits, the sounds, and the channels, then the islands feel in their deepest caverns a desire which is like despair, that is, a desire which involves an awareness that the desire cannot be gratified. With "feel" the language of the tenor is reintroduced. If the whole preceding passage is expressed in the language of the tenor, we have something like this: When the individual finds himself experiencing a great sensuous gratification (the moonlit spring nights) and a great emotional gratification (the song of the nightingales from island to island), that is, considering the traditional significance of the nightingale, when he is in love (the poem, after all, is addressed to a woman) and finds himself experiencing the feeling of communication, then, to the very depths of his personality (the farthest caverns), he experiences a longing which he knows cannot be gratified. The "for" in line 15 connects the ensuing statement with the preceding one. It implies, "We are justified in feeling this longing. Surely, all men at one time were part of a single, continuous human solidarity ('single continent'). Although the conditions of life separate us from each other, we have a terrible longing to experience that continuity" (that is, in the language of the vehicle, that the islands' edges or marges ["bounds," l. 6] meet and the islands join together to form a single continent).

In the next stanza the voice of the islands has ceased and the poet speaks. In "order'd" is picked up and developed the implication of "thrown" in line 2. The conditions of life do not merely exist; they were made that way. A new metaphor is now introduced. The vehicle is the kindling and then cooling or extinguishing of a fire. The tenor is the arousing and then suppression of emotional desire, or longing, among human beings. The longing is suppressed as soon as felt, because it is futile ("vain"); and it is futile because he has already raised the feeling of isolation to intellectual certainty (ll. 5–6), and because he has further concluded that longing is hopeless. Again the question is asked (l. 21): "What force makes it impossible that the deep desire of the islands for communion be satisfied?" The poet again shifts into the language of the basic vehicle of the poem. "A God decreed that islands should be separate and that between their shores should always exist the unfathomable, salty, and separating sea." In the language of the tenor: "Some force which we cannot control or understand" (i.e. it is "a God," not the Christian God or some particular non-Christian God; the God involved is not identified) "is responsible for the fact that some barrier always prevents the emotional communication of human beings with one another and that that barrier is at once incomprehensible ('unplumb'd'), sterile or destructive of emotional gratification ('salty'), and capable of making us feel like strangers to one another, people with nothing in common ('estranging')."

The poem, then, is concerned with the emotional isolation of human beings from each other, with the desire that that isolation should be transcended or destroyed, and with the knowledge that that desire can never be gratified, even in love under the most sensuously and aesthetically perfect conditions.

1. <Great V*enus*,>
↕
Queen {of beauty / and of grace,
The joy of {Gods / and men,
that {Dost *shine fairest*, / and [dost] most adorn thy place,
↑
under sky
That {*dost pacify The raging seas with thy smiling look*, / and mak'st the storms to fly:

2. *the winds, / the clouds } do fear {Thee <goddess,> / thee*

And when thou spread'st thy mantle forth on high,
3. {The waters play
and pleasant lands appear [or, *lands appear [to be] pleasant*],
And heavens laugh,
and all the world shows joyous cheer.

EDMUND SPENSER (1552?–1599)

A Hymn to Venus

From *The Faerie Queene*
(Book IV, Canto X, stanzas xliv–xlvii)

Great *Venus*, Queen of beauty and of grace,
 The joy of Gods and men, that under sky
 Dost fairest shine, and most adorn thy place,
 That with thy smiling look dost pacify
 The raging seas, and mak'st the storms to fly:
 Thee goddess, thee the winds, the clouds do fear,
 And when thou spread'st thy mantle forth on high,
 The waters play and pleasant lands appear,
And heavens laugh, and all the world shows joyous cheer.

2. *under sky:* anywhere.
3. *fairest:* most beautifully.
3. *place:* situation, function in life.
4. *look:* glance.
4. *pacify:* make peaceful.
7. *mantle:* cloak.
9. *cheer:* appearance.

4. Then *the dædale earth doth throw forth abundant flowers to thee*:
↑
Out of her fruitful lap

5. And then all living wights,
↕
They all do learn to play the Paramours;
[as] soon as they see The spring break forth out of his lusty bowers,

6. First *the merry birds
↑
thy pretty pages
↕
Privily pricked with thy lustful powers,
do Chirp loud to thee out of their leavy cages*,
And *call thee to cool their kindly rages*.
↕
their mother,

7. Then *the salvage beasts do* begin to play Their pleasant frisks,
and loathe their wonted food:

Then doth the dædale earth throw forth to thee
  Out of her fruitful lap abundant flowers:
  And then all living wights, soon as they see
  The spring break forth out of his lusty bowers,
  They all do learn to play the Paramours;
  First do the merry birds, thy pretty pages
  Privily pricked with thy lustful powers,
  Chirp loud to thee out of their leavy cages,
And thee, their mother, call to cool their kindly rages.

Then do the salvage beasts begin to play
  Their pleasant frisks, and loathe their wonted food:

10. *dædale:* variously adorned.

12. *wights:* beings, anything alive.

13. *his:* spring's.

13. *lusty:* joyful.

13. *bowers:* a sleeping place.

14. *Paramours:* lovers.

15. *pages:* young male attendants on persons of importance.

16. *Privily:* secretly.

16. *pricked:* spurred on, incited.

16. *lustful:* provocative of desire, inciting to desire.

16. *powers:* ability to act upon a person or thing; influence.

17. *leavy:* leafy.

18. *kindly:* natural; also pertaining to the power to reproduce one's kind, i.e. sexually desirous.

18. *rages:* passions.

19. *salvage:* savage.

19–20. *play . . . frisks:* frisk, caper, cavort about.

20. *loathe:* to feel an aversion for.

20. *wonted:* accustomed, usual.

8. The Lions roar,
the Tigers loudly bray,
The raging Bulls { rebellow through the wood,
And dare [to] tempt the deepest flood,
↑ breaking forth,
↑ To come where thou dost draw them
↑ with desire:

9. So all things else *seek to quench their inward fire In generation*.
↑ that nourish vital blood,
[As] Soon as *thou dost inspire them with fury*,

10. So all the world *was made at first by thee*,

11. And daily yet thou dost *repair the same*:

The Lions roar, the Tigers loudly bray,
The raging Bulls rebellow through the wood,
And breaking forth, dare tempt the deepest flood,
To come where thou dost draw them with desire:
So all things else, that nourish vital blood,
Soon as with fury thou dost them inspire,
In generation seek to quench their inward fire.

So all the world by thee at first was made,
And daily yet thou dost the same repair:

21. *bray:* in the earlier meaning, this was applicable to all large animals.

22. *rebellow:* to bellow in reply to urgings of Venus.

23. *tempt:* to try, to attempt to cross.

23. *flood:* body of water, in this context a pond, lake, or river.

24. *To come:* in order to go.

25. *all things else:* all other things.

25. *nourish:* to maintain, strengthen within one's body (i.e. with food, oxygen, etc.).

25. *vital:* life-giving.

26. *Soon as:* as soon as.

26. *fury:* sexual appetite.

27. *generation:* reproductive activity.

28. *So:* in that way.

29. *repair:* renew, renovate, revive.

12. ⎧ Ne [is there] ought on earth
↑
that *is merry and glad*,
Ne [is there] ought on earth
↑
⎩ that *is lovely and fair*,
But thou *didst prepare the same for pleasure*.
[i.e. there is nothing on earth except that which you prepared for pleasure.]

13. Thou art the root of all that *is joyous*,

14. <Great God of men and women,
↕
⎧ queen of th'air,
⎨ Mother of laughter,
⎩ and wellspring of bliss,>
O grant that *I may not miss of my love at last*.

Ne ought on earth that merry is and glad,
Ne ought on earth that lovely is and fair,
But thou the same for pleasure didst prepare. 32
Thou art the root of all that joyous is,
Great God of men and women, queen of th'air,
Mother of laughter, and wellspring of bliss,
O grant that of my love at last I may not miss. 36

30–31. *Ne ought:* nor [is there] anything.
32. *But thou . . . didst:* which you did not.
34. *God:* goddess.
35. *wellspring:* source, fountainhead.
36. *at last:* eventually.
36. *may not:* should not, not be allowed to.

Interpretational Hypothesis

It is sufficient to know that these four self-contained stanzas from *The Faerie Queene* are addressed to a statue of Venus, but that could almost be deduced from the hymn itself. Our current notion of Venus as the equivalent of the Greek goddess, Aphrodite, is that she is the goddess of simple sexual love, or of erotic love, that is, sexual love combined with emotional intoxication. It is to be seen whether or not this poem conforms with such a notion.

The poem, as is proper with a hymn, begins with a direct address to the goddess, indicating her basic character. She is presented as a queen; she has power and control of power. The "of" can relate "beauty" and "grace" to her in several ways: she can be herself characterized by beauty and grace; she can control the assignment of beauty and grace, dispensing them to human beings as she wills; or she can control the beauty and grace which man finds in the world about him. Possibly all three meanings are at work. Since she is presented as queen, however, the most likely notion is that she controls these qualities wherever they may be found, and is thus to be considered as the ultimate source of them. Thus, wherever these qualities exist, her influence is at work. The distinction between beauty and grace seems at first unnecessary, but if we remember that "grace" is beauty in motion, then "beauty" implies beauty at rest. Her next attribute is that she is both an object of joy and a source of joy, as is demonstrated in the next two clauses. Men and gods find joy in her because she shines fairest under the heavens. Since "of what objects" she is the fairest is not specified, she is the fairest of all objects, a notion that is confirmed by "most adorn thy place." She is better suited to her place in the world than anything else is, and she is more beautiful in it than anything else is in its place. The next clause demonstrates her power as the source of joy: she quiets the seas and chases away storms with a glance.

We come to the first independent clause, observing that "great Venus" is in apposition with "thee" and "goddess." (In grammatical punctuation today we would put a comma after the first "Thee.") The fear she inspires in the winds and the clouds repeats the notion of the fleeing storms in the preceding lines, not merely for greater detail, but to emphasize that when Venus dispenses her influence, winds and clouds, the accompaniment of raging seas and storms, depart, leaving windless air and clear blue sky.

"Mantle" is a metaphor for "blue sky," the connection being that both the sky and a cloak have the power of covering, protecting, and sheltering. All the world is now joyful. It will be noticed that the organization of the stanza leads us from the sphere of heaven, Venus's dwelling-place, down through the skies, the place of storms and winds, to the appearance of pleasant lands, made possible by the spreading forth of the sheltering mantle. The goddess thus descends to the earth to spread forth her power.

And in the next stanza the earth responds to the influence which Venus has sent forth. The variously adorned goddess of the earth greets her arrival with flowers thrown from her lap, used here also in the sense of "womb." Venus, then, is the goddess of spring, or at least the goddess who releases the power of spring, for spring in line 13 is presented as a young god or spirit breaking out of where he had been sleeping, the earth itself, which is now joyful ("lusty," a word which implies sexually potent) with the leaves and flowers of the spring. On his appearance all living things learn how to become lovers, combining his joy with earth's fruitfulness and Venus's love, as is proper, for she is the ultimate source of all of these qualities. The first to appear in this joyful scene are the birds, who are said to be pages to Venus, youthful attendants or cupids who are secretly aroused by the sexual powers of Venus. The cages from which they sing are leafy; they are trees, and thus the birds are free, bound only by their kindly rages, their natural passions. But there is probably another meaning in "kindly"—"desirous of reproducing one's own kind." The use of "mother" carries on the comparison of the birds to Venus's pages, since a feudal or chivalric page was of noble birth and was a surrogate (substitute) son for the lord or lady whom he served.

The scene now becomes more furious as the savage beasts are aroused. First they play, as their spirits are aroused by the spring; then, as the power of Venus begins more intensely to assert itself, their passions make them spurn eating. Lions and tigers and wild bulls roar and bellow in the woods, and the bulls break out of the woods and dare to plunge into the deepest river in order to go where Venus's power of desire calls them, to their cows. Thus all things that carry within themselves the blood of life (in the sense of good heredity, as in "He is of noble blood," i.e. a true source of vital energy and power) try in sexual activity to rid themselves of the fury with which Venus has incited them. This fury is compared to a fire in the blood which they seek to put out ("quench").

This is the climax of the poem, and now we are given a kind of generalized conclusion, which rises to its own climax. In this way ("so"), by descending to earth, by bringing warmth and spring and sexual desire, Venus made the earth originally and (l. 29) by her continuous activity maintains it, making up for what dies by creating new life. Thus everything on earth that is glad and beautiful was prepared by Venus for the gratification of its own sexual desire. Hence she is the source or root of all joy, and hence the Great Divinity, the supreme divinity of men and women. She is queen of the air, because the air surrounds the earth. From her laughter is born, and from her flows bliss, probably meant here as the gratification of sexual desire. She creates the drive and she creates its satisfaction. In the next line we see the reason for the shift from flowers, birds, and animals in stanzas two and three to men and women in stanza four; the speaker begs that Venus grant him also the gratification of his love, which is thus clearly presented as having a sexual origin. And it is right that his prayer be granted, he maintains, because if it is, he too will enter into the great process by which Venus creates and sustains the life of the earth.

Thus the conception of Venus presented is far greater than our ordinary notion of that goddess. But it is to be noted that the conception is personalized. That is, the hymn is not a religious or philosophical statement to be "believed" or "taken seriously." Rather, it represents the attitude of a lover. To him Venus—not Jupiter or Zeus or any other god—is the supreme deity. The poem is a dramatization of the rationalizing psychology of the lover, to whom all values are as nothing except the gratification of his desire, and who justifies his attitude by claiming that desire and its gratification create and sustain the life of earth.

1. At last I put off love,
↕
The daysman of my {thought, And hope, and doing;
↑
For twice ten years
Being {ashamed thereof, And faint of {fears And desolations,} wrought In his pursuing,
Since first ↑ in youthtime {those Disquietings Became my housefellows,
↑
That heart-enslavement brings To {hale and hoary,
And, I turned from {kith and kind
↕
{fool and blind,
To give him [i.e. love] glory.

2.

THOMAS HARDY
(1840–1928)

He Abjures Love

At last I put off love,
  For twice ten years
The daysman of my thought,
  And hope, and doing;
Being ashamed thereof,
  And faint of fears
And desolations, wrought
  In his pursuing,

Since first in youthtime those
  Disquietings
That heart-enslavement brings
  To hale and hoary,
Became my housefellows,
  And, fool and blind,
I turned from kith and kind
  To give him glory.

Title. *Abjures:* swears off.

3. *daysman:* arbitrator, in the older meaning of one who has a matter under his sole control; hence, a kind of foreman or task-master.

4. *doing:* action.

5. *thereof:* of that, namely of love.

6. *faint of:* faint from.

7. *wrought:* worked upon himself (by the speaker).

8. *his pursuing:* the pursuit of him (i.e. love).

12. *hale:* the healthy.

12. *hoary:* the old.

15. *kith and kind:* acquaintances and relatives.

2. I was as children be
↕
Who have no care;

3. I did not shrink or sigh,

4. I did not sicken;

5. But lo, Love beckoned me,

6. And I was { bare,
And poor,
and starved,
and dry,
And fever-stricken.

7. *I Did Return the anxious smiles Of friendly faces.

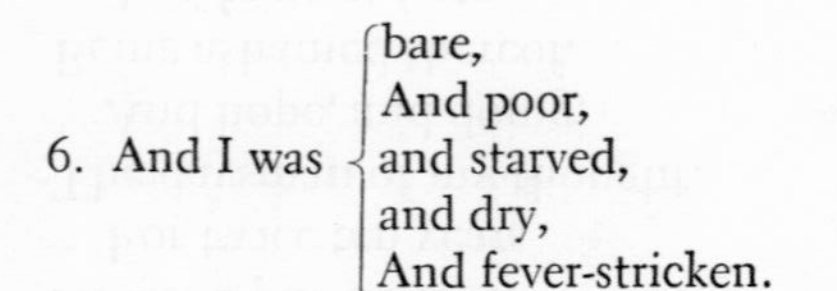

by { wilful ways
And baseless ires,
Too many times
ablaze With fatuous fires,
↑
Enkindled by his [i.e. love's] wiles To new embraces*,

I was as children be
  Who have no care;
I did not shrink or sigh,
  I did not sicken;
But lo, Love beckoned me,
  And I was bare,
And poor, and starved, and dry,
  And fever-stricken.

Too many times ablaze
  With fatuous fires,
Enkindled by his wiles
  To new embraces,
Did I, by wilful ways
  And baseless ires,
Return the anxious smiles
  Of friendly faces.

26. *fatuous:* foolish, stupid.

27. *Enkindled:* lighted, ignited.

27. *wiles:* tricks, deceits.

29. *wilful:* obstinate.

29. *ways:* behavior.

30. *baseless:* for no apparent cause.

30. *ires:* shows of anger.

8. *I will now No more rate* {
The common [to be] rare,
The midnight drizzle [to be] dew,
The gray hour [to be] golden,
The wind [to be] a yearning cry,
The faulty [to be] fair,
dreamt Things [to be] of comelier hue,
↑
Than *beholden things*! . . .

9. —I speak as {
one who plumbs Life's dim profound,
One who at length can sound {Clear / and certain} views.

10. But—*what comes after love*?

11. {
A scene that lours,
A few sad vacant hours,
And then, the Curtain.

No more will now rate I
  The common rare,
The midnight drizzle dew,
  The gray hour golden,
The wind a yearning cry,
  The faulty fair,
Things dreamt, of comelier hue
  Than things beholden! . . .

—I speak as one who plumbs
  Life's dim profound,
One who at length can sound
  Clear views and certain.
But—after love what comes?
  A scene that lours,
A few sad vacant hours,
  And then, the Curtain.

33. *rate:* consider, i.e. see the common thing as being the rare thing.

39. *comelier hue:* more attractive appearance.

40. *beholden:* actually seen, not imagined.

41. *plumbs:* ascertains the depth of.

42. *profound:* vast depth.

43. *can sound:* can plumb, can ascertain the depth of.

46. *lours:* frowns, looks threateningly.

48. *Curtain:* of death.

Interpretational Hypothesis

The title of the poem informs us at once what the theme of the poem is going to be. But it raises questions as to why, how, and with what consequences. These, presumably, will be answered in the poem.

The first line informs us that the process of abjuring or swearing off love either has already taken place at the time the poem is spoken or else is taking place. The decision as to which time "put" refers to must be suspended. (That is, what is the sense of "put"?) Lines 2–4 indicate love's importance in the speaker's life for the twenty years preceding its rejection. "Daysman" metaphorically implies that love was a kind of foreman and taskmaster who directed and controlled the speaker's conception of a project, his ability to sustain hope for its success, and the putting it into effect. Lines 5–16 consist of a single syntactical unit modifying "put off." The connection is causal. The speaker swore off love, gave it up as a bad practice, because he was ashamed of this emotion (l. 5); because he was weary of all the fears and desolations, or completely destructive activities, which he has been responsible for ("wrought") in the pursuit of love (wrought either upon himself or others, and thus probably both). These fears and desolations have been a part of his life ever since the first time, when he was young, that the emotional disturbances ("disquietings") of love came to live with him (l. 13), became, that is, his constant companions, a permanent part of his emotional life. Nor does he imagine that this experience was unique to himself. "Heart-enslavement," the subjection of one's emotional life to the domination of love, comes to everyone, whether he becomes a healthy or a feeble old man. That is, whatever the ultimate effect of life's experiences on an individual, whatever kind of human being he is, if he subjects himself to love, his life will be disturbed. When those disquietings became part of the speaker's life, he turned away from his friends and relatives (foolishly and ignorantly, not knowing what he was letting himself in for) in order to give the maximum value in his life to love (ll. 14–17).

The connection between this and the next stanza is one of repetition with elaboration. Before he had turned to love, when he was as a child, still devoted to kith and kind, he had had no cares, no sources in his life for emotional disturbance or disquietings. "Shrink" means to turn timidly away from something; "sigh" and "sicken" are clear enough. Thus, before love came to him, nothing could frighten or upset him. "Love" is here capitalized to indicate that it is now referred to as a god, a being with complete control over its worshipper. The consequence of Love's beckoning and the speaker's obeying was that he was left bare, poor, starved, dry, and fever-stricken, all of which are physiological metaphors for corresponding emotional states: feelings of being unprotected, without emotional resources, conscious of need for the gratifications of love and also desiring them, and finally emotionally over-stimulated to the point of illness. These are reasons for his swearing off love. And in the next stanza he gives a further reason. Love made him deceitful. When, far too often, he was violently ("ablaze") and stupidly and foolishly ("fatuous") in love, aroused again and again to new erotic desires by the tricks and schemes ("wiles") of his own emotions, and when his friends were worried about his state, he responded to their anxiety by "wilful ways and baseless ires." Wilful habits ("ways") of action are those in which the individual acts quite without regard to the feelings or interests of others. "Baseless ires" are fits of temper quite unjustified by the stimulus which causes them. His friends were worried, though considerate, about his emotional state; he responded with unjustified inconsiderateness and anger.

There are further reasons for abjuring love. He will no longer be a victim of those illusions which are the consequences of love: of thinking that common things are rare things, that a feeble midnight rain is the dew of the morning, that a dismal sky is beautiful, that the wind is a cry which echoes his own yearning, that women with ordinary faults are lovely, and that things of the imagination are more attractive than what one sees with one's own eyes.

The dots at the end of line 40 and the dash at the beginning of line 41 indicate a break in thought or continuity of attitude. The implied connection is "however." The present tense of "speak" informs us that he has been speaking in lines 1–40 about the past. Thus "put" in line 1 must be in the past tense. It informs us that at the time of speaking the poem he has already abjured love.

All these illusions, then, he has given up, and in the last stanza, he tells us the consequences. He has become a man who really understands the mysterious depths of life and has come to the foundations of things. In consequence, his ideas about life are straightforward and to be relied on. In the metaphor "plumbs—profound—sound" the vehicle refers to casting a weighted line over the side of a ship in order to ascertain the depth of the water. The tenor, then, is, as indicated above, comprehending the truth about life and its conditions, including the falsehood and unreliability of love. But now, after the self-satisfaction and self-possession of line 44, comes an entirely new and disturbing idea. He asks himself, "Now that I have rid myself of the greatest source of the illusions of life, what is life going to be like?" The new metaphor is taken from the theater. In the vehicle, the stage-setting is gloomy; the performance gives no pleasure or distraction; and when it is over, the curtain will come down—and that is all. The connection between the tenor (his life) and the vehicle (the spectator at the theater) is that without the illusions of love he is a mere spectator of life who is not emotionally involved with it, just as a member of a theater audience is bored if he cannot become emotionally involved in the performance on the stage and cannot believe in the theater's illusion. Thus, without love and its illusions, life is ugly, meaningless, a stupid way of passing the time until we die.

The poem is concerned with a conflict of values. If our lives are governed by the emotions of love, we become dissatisfied, frustrated, angry, cruel, and filled with illusions. But if we live without love, life is without value. Love makes life bitter and illusory, but perhaps bitterness and illusions are better than no values at all. To this conflict between truth and value there is no solution; but this failure to find a solution is not stated—it is only implied. The poem, then, is a dramatization of the successive emotional states which have led the speaker to the discovery of what he perceives as a basic conflict in human experience.

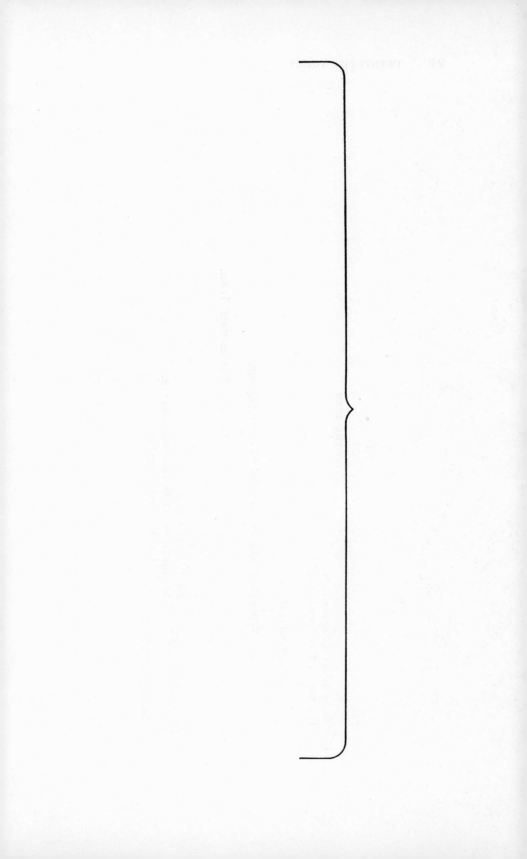

THE TURN

1. <Brave Infant of *Saguntum*,>
Thy coming forth [was] clear
↑
in that great year,
↑
When the Prodigious *Hannibal* did crown His rage,
↑
with razing your immortal Town.

2. Thou, <Wise child,> {did'st hastily return,
{And mad'st thy Mother's womb thine urn.
↑
looking then about,
Ere thou wert half got out,

BEN JONSON (1572–1637)

To the Immortal Memory, and Friendship of That Noble Pair, Sir Lucius Cary, and Sir H. Morison

THE TURN

Brave Infant of *Saguntum*, clear
Thy coming forth in that great year,
When the Prodigious *Hannibal* did crown
His rage, with razing your immortal Town.
Thou, looking then about,
Ere thou wert half got out,
Wise child, did'st hastily return,
And mad'st thy Mother's womb thine urn.

Title. Sir Lucius Cary (1610–1643) and Sir Henry Morison (?–1629) were close friends. In 1631 Cary wrote an "Anniversary" of Morison's death in which he addressed Jonson as their "father."

Turn, Counter-turn, Stand: Usually called Strophe, Anti-strophe and Epode, these are the three different kinds of stanza that form the ode. The strophe and the anti-strophe are usually identical in structure, while the epode is different. In this poem, the strophe and anti-strophe are in couplets, while the epode has a more complicated structure: *ababccdeedff* with the second and fourth lines short.

1. *Saguntum*: a town in ancient Spain conquered by Hannibal in 219 BC, an event which caused the Second Punic War. The prodigious birth of the child is described in Pliny L, vii, 3.

1. *clear:* understandable.

2. *coming forth:* birth.

3. *Prodigious:* unnatural, amazing.

3–4. *crown His rage*: fully satisfy his anger. Hannibal had conquered all the country south of the Iberus river in northeastern Spain (now the Ebro), and only the town of Saguntum prevented him from controlling all of southern Spain. By this means he cleared the way for a direct attack on Rome.

6. *wert half got out:* were half born.

8. *urn:* funeral urn.

3. How summ'd a circle *Of deepest lore thou didst leave mankind*,
[if] *we could find the Center*!

THE COUNTER-TURN

4. Did wiser Nature draw thee back,
↑
From out the horror of that sack?
↑

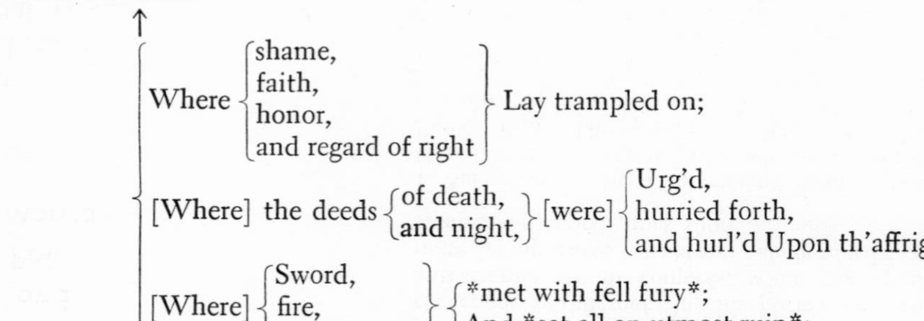

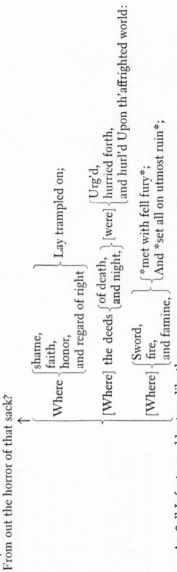

Where {shame, faith, honor, and regard of right} Lay trampled on;
[Where] the deeds {of death, and night,} [were] {Urg'd, hurried forth, and hurl'd Upon th'affrighted world:}
[Where] {Sword, fire, and famine,} {*met with fell fury*; And *set all on utmost ruin*;}

As, *all Infants would return like thee.
↑
No doubt
[if] they could but foresee life's miseries*,

How summ'd a circle didst thou leave mankind
Of deepest lore, could we the Center find!

THE COUNTER-TURN

Did wiser Nature draw thee back,
From out the horror of that sack?
Where shame, faith, honor, and regard of right
Lay trampled on; the deeds of death, and night,
Urg'd, hurried forth, and hurl'd
Upon th'affrighted world:
Sword, fire, and famine, with fell fury met;
And all on utmost ruin set;
As, could they but life's miseries foresee,
No doubt all Infants would return like thee.

9. *summ'd a circle:* one "sums" or computes a circle's area by finding its center and measuring its diameter.

9. *didst thou leave:* you would have left.

9–10. *circle of lore:* great and perfect piece of knowledge as represented by the prodigious birth.

10. *could we:* if we could only.

11. *wiser:* i.e. wiser than the child, line 7, whose natural urge was to be born.

11. *draw thee back:* pull you back into the womb.

12. *From out:* out of.

12. *that sack:* the plundering of Saguntum by the Carthaginians.

13. *regard of right:* concern for law.

17. *fell:* savage.

18. *on:* in.

19. *As:* did you return, as any infant would return if he . . . etc.

19. *could they:* if they could.

19. *but:* only.

THE STAND

5. For, what is { life, if measur'd by { the space, / Not by the act? }
Or masked man, if valu'd by his face, Above his fact? }

6. Here's one
↑
[who] { out-liv'd his Peers,
And told forth fourscore years; }

7. He { vexed time,
and busied the whole State;
Troubled both { foes,
and friends; } } ←But ever to no ends:

8. What did this Stirrer [do], but die late?

9. How well [it would have been if] at twenty *he had* { fall'n,
or stood! }

For three of his fourscore,
↓
10. he did no good.

THE STAND

For, what is life, if measur'd by the space,
Not by the act?
Or masked man, if valu'd by his face,
Above his fact?
Here's one out-liv'd his Peers,
And told forth fourscore years;
He vexed time, and busied the whole State;
Troubled both foes, and friends;
But ever to no ends:
What did this Stirrer, but die late?
How well at twenty had he fall'n, or stood!
For three of his fourscore, he did no good.

21. *space:* mere duration or length.

22. *Not by:* instead of by.

22. *the act:* one's deeds.

24. *Above:* instead of, assuming his appearance is more important.

24. *fact:* his deeds.

25. *Here's one out-liv'd:* here's one who out-lived.

25. *Peers:* contemporaries.

26. *told forth:* counted out.

26. *fourscore:* a score is twenty.

29. *ever to no ends:* always to no real purpose.

30. *did this Stirrer?:* did this Stirrer do?

30. *but:* except.

30. *die late:* live too long.

31. *How well . . . had:* how much better it would have been if he had . . .

31. *stood:* stood firm against an enemy.

THE TURN

11. He { enter'd well,
↑
by virtuous parts,
Got up and thriv'd with honest arts: }

12. He { purchas'd { friends,
and fame,
and honors then, }
And had his noble name advanc'd with men: }

13. But He { stoop'd To { sordid flatteries,
acts of strife, }
↑
in all men's sight
And sunk *So deep in that dead sea of life*,
↑
as [that] he did *sup [i.e. would have supped] death's waters then*;
But that the Cork of Title buoy'd him up. }
↑
weary of that flight,

THE TURN

He enter'd well, by virtuous parts,
Got up and thriv'd with honest arts:
He purchas'd friends, and fame, and honors then,
And had his noble name advanc'd with men:
But weary of that flight,
He stoop'd in all men's sight
To sordid flatteries, acts of strife,
And sunk in that dead sea of life
So deep, as he did then death's waters sup;
But that the Cork of Title buoy'd him up.

33. *enter'd well:* entered life's scene.

33. *by virtuous parts:* with honest and manly talents.

34. *Got up:* rose to prominence.

34. *arts:* endeavors.

35. *purchas'd:* not "bought" but "won."

36. *with:* among.

37. *that flight:* his original honest, if (perhaps) slow climb to prominence.

38. *stoop'd:* 1. lowered himself in dignity; 2. plunged down, like a hawk.

40. *sunk:* sank.

40. *dead sea of life:* see IH.

41. *as he did . . . sup:* that he would have drunk . . .

42. *But that:* except for the fact that.

42. *Cork of Title:* his rank and power served as a life-preserver.

THE COUNTER-TURN

14. Alas, but *Morison* fell young:

15. He never fell, thou fall'st,
↕
<my tongue.>

16. He stood,
↕
a Soldier to the last right end,
A perfect Patriot,
and a noble friend,
But most, a virtuous Son.

17. All Offices were done By him,

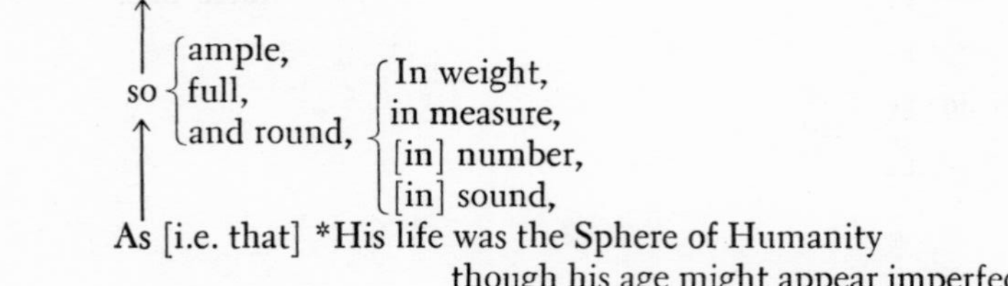

↑
so ampl,
full,
and round,
In weight,
in measure,
[in] number,
[in] sound,
↑
As [i.e. that] *His life was the Sphere of Humanity
though his age might appear imperfect*.

THE COUNTER-TURN

Alas, but *Morison* fell young:
He never fell, thou fall'st, my tongue.
He stood, a Soldier to the last right end,
A perfect Patriot, and a noble friend,
But most, a virtuous Son.
All Offices were done
By him, so ample, full, and round,
In weight, in measure, number, sound,
As though his age imperfect might appear,
His life was of Humanity the Sphere.

45. *last right end:* very end, dying a virtuous death.

47. *most:* mostly.

48. *Offices:* tasks.

49. *ample:* amply.

49. *full:* fully.

49. *round:* "roundly" in the sense of "thoroughly."

50. *In weight, in measure, number, sound:* that is, in every respect. See IH for further implications of these terms.

51. *his age:* the era in which he lived.

52. *the Sphere:* the sphere is often taken as symbolic of the perfect whole. See IH.

THE STAND

18. Go now,
and tell out days
↑
summ'd up with fears,
And make them years;

19. Produce thy mass of miseries on the Stage,
↑
To swell thine age;

20. Repeat *a throng of things*,
↑
To show thou hast been long,
Not liv'd;

21. for Life doth *spell her great actions*,
↑
By what was done
and wrought In season,
and so brought To light:

22. her measures are, how well Each syllab'e answer'd,
and *how fair [each syllable] was form'd*;

THE STAND

Go now, and tell out days summ'd up with fears,
And make them years;
Produce thy mass of miseries on the Stage,
To swell thine age;
Repeat of things a throng,
To show thou hast been long,
Not liv'd; for Life doth her great actions spell,
By what was done and wrought
In season, and so brought
To light: her measures are, how well
Each syllab'e answer'd, and was form'd, how fair;

53. *tell out:* count up (see l. 26).

54. *make them years:* exaggerate them as if they were years.

56. *age:* life.

58. *hast been:* you have merely existed, not *lived.*

59. *spell:* set the standards for. See IH.

60. *wrought:* achieved, created.

61. *In season:* at the appropriate moment.

61. *so:* in that fashion.

62. *measures:* 1. standards; 2. vertical lines in musical scores indicating musical rhythm.

63. *answer'd:* suited the occasion.

63. *fair:* beautifully.

23. {These [syllables as separate entities] make the lines of life,
{and that [a succession of syllables, taken as an entity]'s her air.

THE TURN

24. It is {not growing like a tree In bulk,
{Or standing long [like] an Oak,
↑ ↑
three hundred year,
To fall [like] a log at last, } [which] *doth make man be better*;
↑
{dry,
{bald,
{and sere:

25. A Lily of a Day, Is *far fairer*, in May,
Although it {fall,
{and die that night;

26. It was the {Plant,
{and flow'r of light.

27. {*we see just beauty In small proportions*:
{*And life may be perfect in short measures*.

These make the lines of life, and that's her air.

THE TURN

It is not growing like a tree
In bulk, doth make man better be;
Or standing long an Oak, three hundred year,
To fall a log at last, dry, bald, and sere:
A Lily of a Day,
Is fairer far, in May,
Although it fall, and die that night;
It was the Plant, and flow'r of light.
In small proportions, we just beauty see:
And in short measures, life may perfect be.

64. *These . . . air:* see IH.

64. *her:* Life's.

66. *doth make:* which doth make.

68. *sere:* withered.

69. *of a Day:* living only a day.

72. *flow'r:* blossom, considered independently of the plant itself.

73. *just:* perfect.

74. *measures:* meaning 2 of line 62, musical measures.

THE COUNTER-TURN

28. Call, <noble *Lucius,*> then for Wine,
And let thy looks *shine with gladness*:

29. Accept this garland,
plant it on thy head,
And think, nay know, thy *Morison's* not dead.

30. He leap'd the present age,
↑ ↑
To see that bright eternal Day:
Possess'd with holy rage, ↑
Of which we *Priests,* and *Poëts* say Such truths,
↑
as we expect for happy men,

THE COUNTER-TURN

Call, noble *Lucius*, then for Wine,
And let thy looks with gladness shine:
Accept this garland, plant it on thy head,
And think, nay know, thy *Morison*'s not dead.
He leap'd the present age,
Possess'd with holy rage,
To see that bright eternal Day:
Of which we *Priests*, and *Poëts* say
Such truths, as we expect for happy men,

76. *looks*: features.

77. *garland*: a head-wreath of flowers worn at a feast in antiquity, symbolizing good spirits.

79. *leap'd*: jumped out of.

79. *age*: era.

80. *with*: by.

80. *rage*: eagerness, desire.

81. *bright eternal Day*: heaven.

83. *Such truths, as*: the sort of truths which.

THE STAND

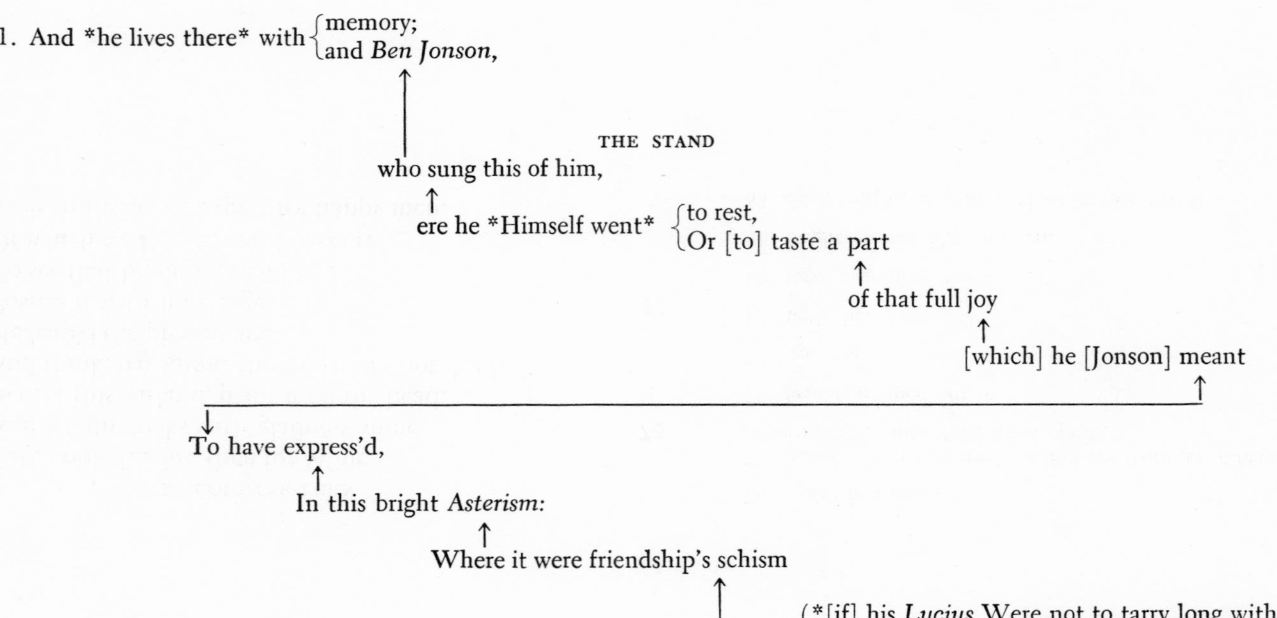
31. And *he lives there* with memory; and *Ben Jonson*,
who sung this of him,
ere he *Himself went* to rest, Or [to] taste a part
of that full joy
[which] he [Jonson] meant
To have express'd,
In this bright *Asterism:*
Where it were friendship's schism
(*[if] his *Lucius* Were not to tarry long with us*)
To separate these twi-Lights, the *Dioscuri:*
And [to] keep the one half from his *Harry*.

And there he lives with memory; and *Ben*

THE STAND

Jonson, who sung this of him, ere he went
Himself to rest,
Or taste a part of that full joy he meant
To have express'd,
In this bright *Asterism:*
Where it were friendship's schism,
(Were not his *Lucius* long with us to tarry)
To separate these twi-
Lights, the *Dioscuri;*
And keep the one half from his *Harry*.

84. *lives with memory:* in a condition of immortality.

84–85. *with . . . Jonson:* see IH.

85. *sung:* sang.

85. *him:* Morison.

85. *he:* Jonson.

87. *taste:* to taste.

89. *Asterism:* constellation, hence the poem itself, since it yokes the "stars," Cary and Morison, together.

90. *Where:* in which.

90. *were:* would be.

90. *schism:* rupture, splitting.

91. *Were . . . tarry:* if it were not for the fact that Cary would stay alive for many years yet.

92–93. *twi-Lights:* twin lights (or stars).

93. *Dioscuri:* in classical mythology, the Constellation Gemini, "the twins," made up of Castor and Pollux, sons of Zeus. The affection of these two was so great that they are often held up as a paragon of brotherly love.

94. *Harry:* Morison.

32. But fate doth so alternate the design,
↑
[that] Whilst {that [light] [must shine] in heav'n,
this light *must shine on earth*.

THE TURN

33. And [you must] shine
as you are exalted;
↕
{Two names of friendship,
but one Star:
the union Of hearts.
↑
And those [hearts] not {*Made by chance*,
or indentured,
or leas'd out t'advance The profits for a time.

But fate doth so alternate the design,
Whilst that in heav'n, this light on earth must shine.

THE TURN

And shine as you exalted are;
Two names of friendship, but one Star:
Of hearts the union. And those not by chance
Made, or indentured, or leas'd out t'advance
The profits for a time.

95. *alternate the design:* make the plan, arrangement, or disposition of the stars such that . . .

96. *Whilst:* while.

96. *that:* that light, i.e. Morison.

96. *this light:* Cary.

97. *And shine:* and you must shine.

97. *as:* since, because.

99. *hearts:* affections.

99. *those:* the hearts.

100. *indentured:* linked together by legal agreement.

100. *leas'd out:* rented.

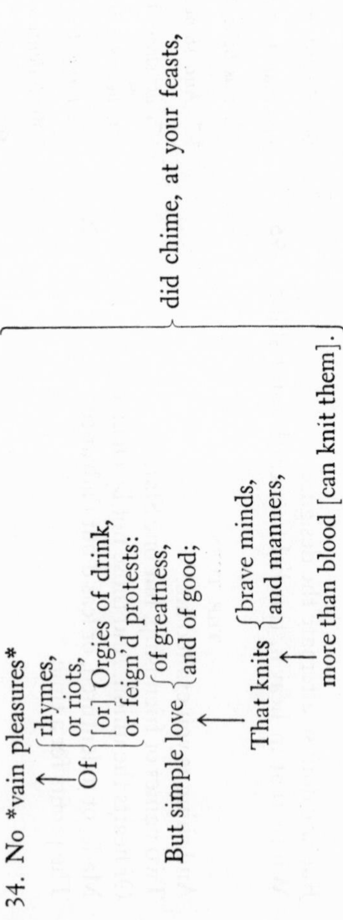
34. No *vain pleasures*
Of
rhymes,
or riots,
[or] Orgies of drink,
or feign'd protests:
did chime, at your feasts,
But simple love
of greatness,
and of good;
That knits
brave minds,
and manners,
more than blood [can knit them].

No pleasures vain did chime,
Of rhymes, or riots, at your feasts,
Orgies of drink, or feign'd protests:
But simple love of greatness, and of good;
That knits brave minds, and manners, more than blood.

102. *vain:* stupid, worthless.

102. *chime:* to be joined, because they are in harmony.

103. *riots:* disruptions, noisy revels.

103. *feasts:* parties.

104. *feign'd protests:* expressions of pretended or counterfeited affection.

105. *good:* whatever is good; moral excellence.

106. *blood:* blood or family relationships.

THE COUNTER-TURN

35. This made you {
first to know the Why You lik'd,
then after, to apply That liking;
and approach so one the t'other,
Till either grew a portion of the other:
↕
Each styled, The Copy of his friend.
↑
by his end,
}

36. You liv'd to be {the great surnames,
And titles,}
↑
by which all made claims Unto the Virtue.

37. Nothing perfect [could be] done,
↑
But as a CARY, or a MORISON.

THE COUNTER-TURN

This made you first to know the Why
You lik'd, then after, to apply
That liking; and approach so one the t'other,
Till either grew a portion of the other:
Each styled, by his end,
The Copy of his friend.
You liv'd to be the great surnames,
And titles, by which all made claims
Unto the Virtue. Nothing perfect done,
But as a CARY, or a MORISON.

107. *This:* the mutual recognition of excellence.

108. *lik'd:* liked each other.

108. *apply:* make proper use of.

109. *approach:* to become so close as to adjust exquisitely to each other's personality.

109. *so:* in that way.

109. *t'other:* other.

110. *either:* each.

111. *styled:* engraved.

111. *end:* purpose.

113. *You:* both Cary and Morison.

113–114. *surnames, And titles:* by-words or synonyms for excellence.

114. *all:* everybody.

115. *the Virtue:* the quality of excellence.

115–116. *Nothing . . . Morison:* nothing was done perfectly by anyone unless he was acting like a Cary or a Morison.

THE STAND

38. And *the fair example had such a force*,
As [i.e. that] they were glad That such a Law Was left yet to Mankind;
that {saw The good,
and durst not practise it,
Where they might {read,
and find
[that] *Friendship*, *was written, {in deed,*
not in words:
And with {the heart,
not [the] pen,
Of two so early men,
{Whose lines *were {her rolls*,
and records.
Who, Had {sow'd these fruits,
and got the harvest in.
ere the first down bloomed on the chin,

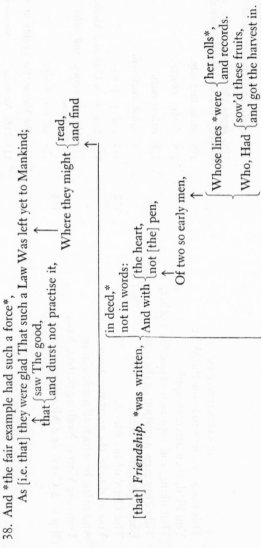

THE STAND

And such a force the fair example had,
As they that saw
The good, and durst not practise it, were glad
That such a Law
Was left yet to Mankind;
Where they might read, and find
Friendship, in deed, was written, not in words:
And with the heart, not pen,
Of two so early men,
Whose lines her rolls were, and records.
Who, ere the first down bloomed on the chin,
Had sow'd these fruits, and got the harvest in.

118. *As:* that.

119. *durst not:* did not dare.

120. *Law:* the Virtue, i.e. excellence.

122. *they:* mankind.

123. *in deed:* in deeds.

125. *early:* young.

126. *lines:* lineaments, appearances, and features of personality.

126. *rolls:* scrolls, parchments upon which a record is written, then rolled for storage.

127. *down:* fuzz, face hair.

128. *harvest:* virtue, the product of friendship.

Interpretational Hypothesis

The form of the poem, with its translations of the Greek terms "strophe," "anti-strophe," and "epode" into the English "turn," "counter-turn," and "stand," tells us that it is an ode. In Jonson's time the ode was considered the highest and most dignified lyric form, to be used for several purposes. If, as here, it is addressed to human beings, it is used to praise them and the human values they embody. Nevertheless, the poem begins by addressing an infant of Saguntum instead of Cary and Morison. Why?

The first turn is concerned with the confrontation of two prodigies, events out of the normal course of human affairs, thought of as either monstrous (abnormal), or else as superhuman, things brought into existence by a divine power, or at least of human power beyond its normal range of strength and achievement. The first prodigy is that of the infant of Saguntum who began to be born as Hannibal was sacking the town; it returned or was withdrawn into its mother's womb, and there of course died. In the poem, the event is prodigious because the child is represented as wise enough, even before its birth was completed, to perceive the horror of the circumstances around it, to decide that life was not worth living, and to withdraw to the womb whence it came and where it died.

The second prodigy is Hannibal himself, the great Carthaginian. Enraged by the eight months' siege of the town which barred his way to Rome, he sacked and destroyed it, and marched on to his prodigious crossing of the Alps. The prodigious nature of the child's birth, then, is clear, or easy to understand: it went against the natural process of birth because it judged life and withdrew. But (ll. 9–10) how it could make such a judgment and be so correct remains a mystery. It made a perfect judgment, or circle, but since we do not know the center or basis or method of its judgment, we cannot compute the area of the circle; that is, we cannot judge its value by applying it to other situations of life. We can only admire it, not use it. We are left with the question: How are we, who are not prodigies, to make adequate judgments on the value of life?

Now we can answer our question as to why the poet begins by addressing the infant instead of Morison or Cary, or some figure to symbolize friendship. Morison died young—considering his excellence as a human being, a tragic loss. Or was it? Indeed, how shall we measure the value of a life unless we have a measure for the value of life itself? And so the poet begins by meditating on this second problem, the measure for the value of life itself. And he dramatizes this meditation by directing his attention to an infant who, mysteriously, measured life adequately and left it, but whose basis for judgment we cannot know. We must look elsewhere.

And this the poet proceeds to do in the first counter-turn. Was Nature responsible for the child's returning to its mother's womb (l. 11)? The capitalization of Nature indicates that we are to conceive of it as a divine or at least superhuman force, so that the prodigy is a natural prodigy, unexpected, unusual, but not monstrous. Was Nature, he asks, wiser than the infant? Did natural forces, rather than human judgment, decide that the infant should not be fully born? In that sack of Saguntum all things that decent human beings value were dishonored and trampled on. There was a hurling forth of deeds of death and night; and with sword, fire, and famine were combined the savage fury of a frustrated conqueror. Indeed, all the men of the conquering army were set on total destruction, in the sense that we "set our hearts on something." But we must note that the question is strange. In statement form it is: "Wiser Nature drew thee back, just as all infants would return, if they could foresee the miseries of life." It appears inconsistent to say that Nature is responsible for drawing the child back, and in the same sentence to say that the child made the decision, or that all children would make the decision. The "would" indicates that the will of the infants is involved, or would be involved if they could foresee what life would be like. But this apparent inconsistency can be reconciled. If infants had foreknowledge, their will would correspond with the will of Nature. Their judgments on life's value would be Nature's judgment. The apparent inconsistency, then, is a way of dramatizing this statement: "If we knew life's *real* value, if, when infants, we could predict its horrors, it would be natural to refuse to be born." And in question form: "Is it not natural to refuse to be born? Is it not understandable, clear, acceptable?" But the poet does not answer his own question. Why not? Just as at the end of the first turn we are left in ignorance as to the basis for the infant's decision, so here we are left wondering whether or not Nature provides a basis for that decision.

The first stand begins with further questions. But why does the first line begin with "For" (l. 21)? We must inquire further what the stand says before we can arrive at the answer to this question. "Space" and "act" are presented as opposites. Duration of time is thus opposed to a deed done in that time; yet the two terms have in common the implication that both can be used as measurements of life. It is meaningless to ask, "What is the quantity of life if measured by the quantity of time it takes to live it?" But it is meaningful to ask, "What is the *quality* of life if measured by the quantity of time, or duration, that it takes to live it?" The poet, then, is organizing his questions around the fact that measurement can refer to either quantitative measurement or qualitative measurement, that is, either How much? or How good? And this continues the poet's question of how we can know the value of life, or its quality. To measure according to the quantity of an act, how big the act is, or how long it takes, would also be meaningless, since the quality of something cannot be measured in quantitative terms. The question then is, "What is the value of life if it is measured by its duration instead of the quality of the deeds which are performed during it, as life should be judged?" The answer, since it has been established that quality cannot be measured by quantity, is: "Life has no value if measured by its mere duration." Thus one possible way of judging the value of life has been disposed of.

Now we can turn to the question with which we began. Why "For"? The answer is that the word implies a causal relation between this stand and what precedes, either the counter-turn or the turn and counter-turn taken together. Thus, "If it is true that the value of life cannot be judged by its duration, then . . ." Now, since we cannot know whether or not Nature drew the child back, we must continue to judge his act as a great and prodigious one, in spite of the brief duration or almost non-duration of his life. Hence we can finish our sentence: ". . . then we are justified in judging the action of the infant of Saguntum by its prodigious decision and not by the brevity of its life. Since we did make such a judgment, we are right in eliminating length as a criterion for the value of a life."

The next question (ll. 23–24) immediately forces us to ask, Why the parallel construction? The construction requires us to supply the missing parts from the first sentence. Thus: What is the quality or value of a man who is masked, if we judge him by his face, rather than by what he really is as demonstrated by his deeds? And again, we are required by the parallelism to answer, "Nothing." But there is a further parallelism. Why does the positioning and rhyme of the words force us to equate "space" with "face" and "act" with "fact"? The face of a masked man is, of course, his mask, or what we see, as opposed to what lies underneath, his fact or reality, that is, what he actually does. We have then an opposition between appearance and reality, parallel with the opposition between quantity and quality. Reality, the poet tells us, lies in quality or value, not in quantity or duration, which are merely aspects of appearance. This is, to begin with, a way of reinforcing the statement we worked out in the preceding stanza, namely, ". . . it is true that . . ." and is thus clear enough. But we are, nevertheless, forced by the parallelism to ask, Does the "For" govern the second question as well as the first? If it does, we should be able to say: "If it is true that the value of a man cannot be judged by his appearance, then we are justified in judging the infant as genuinely great in spite of the fact that in appearance it was only an infant. That is, a man can live a short life, but by doing great deeds be a great man."

We turn now (l. 25) from questions to statements. The poet points some "one" out to us. Who is "one"? Since it is one who lived a long life, it cannot be Cary, who died young (see Lexical Gloss). "One" is, then, a real person or an imagined person used as an example. Let us assume that we should read it as follows, until we are given contrary information: "Here, for example, is one who outlived his contemporaries (or perhaps social equals). He counted out eighty years of life. He annoyed and irritated the times in which he lived and occupied the whole central government, or governing aristocracy and monarchy, with himself; not content with disturbing his foes, a natural way of acting, he also disturbed his friends in the same way. But all of his activity was pointless (l. 29). He accomplished nothing except to live a long time." With lines 31–32, however, we must slow down. The poet states that if this man had fallen in battle when he was twenty, or successfully stood his ground against the enemy, he would have lived well. The conditional ("had" equals "would have been, if he had") tells us that he did neither, and the last line of the turn states that for the remainder of his life, the next sixty years, he did nothing of value. We are then faced with the question: Why does the poet state that this man's first twenty years were of value? The next turn should provide an answer.

The stanza is organized around a contrast between the first four lines (ll. 33–36) and the last six (ll. 37–42) beginning with "But." He was, as line 36 tells us, a nobleman who made a good entrance on the great stage of public life, because he had the talents suitable to a man among men, to the masculine role as conceived in the seventeenth century. (He had "virtuous parts.") He rose to prominence and improved his position or reputation by honest methods ("arts"). He won ("purchas'd") friends, fame, and honors, and his already noble name acquired new luster. However (l. 37) . . . Why "flight," which is not parallel with the "entered, got up, thrived," and so on? It is a metaphorical term, and the metaphor is continued by "stoop'd." The two words together identify the vehicle as that of a hawk which stoops to, or plunges down on, a lure or bait; the man is tempted to plunge from his noble high course by sordid flatteries. The connection between "hawk" and "nobleman" is that both are noble fighters, that both fly high in their respective spheres, and that both swoop down from above on their prey. But why are "acts of strife" bracketed with flatteries as a lure? Because, as we saw in the previous stand (ll. 27–28), this man was especially characterized by his creation of unnecessary disturbances. In line 40 the problem is whether there is a reference to the

Dead Sea of the Bible or whether "dead" modifies "sea of life." The question may be resolved by examining the significance of "death" or "death's waters" in line 41. The simplest meaning of "supping death's waters" would be to die, but as we know, he lived. The waters found in the dead sea of life, then, would appear to be the waters of oblivion, of which indeed the Dead Sea of the Bible may be regarded as a symbol. Thus, the poem says that the man would have been forgotten had not the fact that he was a nobleman supported him and kept him before people's attention.

In the counter-turn the "but" (l. 47) raises the first question. It carries us back to line 31, contrasting Morison's short life with the long life of the unnamed Disturber. The repetition of "fall" and the apparent reversal of the statement of line 43 suggests a double meaning for "fall," i.e. he fell physically but not morally. Indeed (l. 45) the poet states that on the contrary it is the poet's own powers (l. 44) that fail before Morison's virtues. The contrast with the Disturber is now continued. Morison, instead of causing trouble, was the source of social order, perfect in every respect, whether we think in terms of space, of weight, of length, or mathematically or aurally. The syntax of lines 51–52 is difficult only because, in the sixteenth and seventeenth centuries, "so . . . as" was commonly used where we should say "so . . . that." The sense then is, "He acted so perfectly that his life was the perfection ('sphere') of humanity, although the shortness of his life makes his life seem imperfect." (Since a sphere is the most perfect shape, it is a metaphor for the idea of perfection.) But has not a somewhat similar idea appeared before, also connected with a short life? If we look back to the opening turn, we will see that the infant's judgment was also perfect, that is, a circle. Morison is thus linked with the infant as a model of perfection, but his value is even greater, for a sphere is more perfect, being three-dimensional, than a flat circle. The implication is that although to withdraw from life may be prodigious, since we cannot know the basis for such a judgment, it is better to stand up to life and its evils, to live, though briefly, as Morison did, and assume one's duties. The example of the infant, as we have seen, is impressive but useless. Morison's example is more impressive—and useful.

In the second stand (l. 53), whom is the poet addressing? Whoever it is, he is told, defiantly (as we today say, "O.K., go ahead and do it, since you think you're so superior"), to do the following things: first, to exaggerate the scale of his life by treating fearful days as if they were years; second, to display them publicly, like a playwright drowning a stage in tears in order to impress people with the enormous importance of his life; third, to say over and over everything he can think of to show that a long time has elapsed since his birth. This individual, not identified, is to be taken as another kind of bad example.

Although this complainer has existed ("been"), he has not really "lived," i.e. lived meaningfully, or lived a valuable life, however noisy a life it may have been. After "for" the mood changes from the imperative to the indicative, suggesting that an ellipsis must be filled out, thus: "Go ahead and make a big fuss; it will do you little good; for Life 'spells out her great actions' not by the sort of thing you're doing, but by whether or not a deed is done and done beautifully ('wrought,' as a work of art is 'worked') at a time and place appropriate to it and in that way brought to light," that is, in that way only. The important thing about a deed is its suitability to the circumstances under which it was performed and the thoroughgoing excellence and beauty with which it was carried out. That is, it must solve well a genuine problem. "Spell" is a metaphor. When we write down a spoken word, we must have certain standards of orthography which determine how we shall set down the sounds. The tenor of this vehicle is "to employ standards to determine whether or not a deed is to be remembered." This idea of determining value is continued in the metaphor of lines 62–64. "Measures" first means "standards by which the quantity or quality of something is determined"; here, since quality is under discussion, the word means "standards by which the quality or excellence of a life is determined." Second, it means the vertical lines which indicate the rhythmic structure of a piece of music. Life, in her capacity of writing down, or recording, a meaningful or valuable life, regards a life as a song, consisting of words and music. Each syllable must be appropriate to its place in the song and must be well formed or sung. The succession of the syllables makes the lines; the succession of the musical notes in which the syllables are sung forms the air, or melody. It is thus apparent that "measures" in its second meaning is not at work within the metaphor, since a measure has to do with rhythm, not syllables and notes, or lines and melodies. Although "measures" is a musical metaphor, it is separate from what follows "how." In reading music, these vertical lines tell us how to organize the words and notes rhythmically. They tell us, then, how to make musical sense out of the work. Hence, in the second meaning of "measures" the tenor is "that which makes sense out of." The first and second meanings taken together, therefore, mean "that which gives standards of value or makes sense out of." Hence, Life's measures are what makes sense out of life by giving it value, or, to make sense out of life is to give it value. Turning again to what is now to be understood as a second musical metaphor, beginning with "how," we may now determine the tenor: If an act is appropriate, a succession of such acts ("the lines of life") makes a life meaningful, just as a succession of individual words properly put together makes a meaningful sentence; again, if an act is beautiful in itself, a succession of such acts (an air) makes a whole life beautiful, i.e. using the metaphor in "measures," valuable. Hence "done" (l. 60) is equivalent to syllables and lines, and "wrought" is equivalent to fair notes and melodies. To sum up, the standards by which we determine whether or not a life is a great act and worth recording are its meaningful relations to its time, its intrinsic beauty, and its continuousness in both qualities. Morison's was such a life, and the titled Disturber's was not. This new certainty, after the bafflement of the beginning of the poem, and after the rejection of a quantitative measure for value, accounts for the tone of confident statement we encounter in the third turn.

This next turn is a summing-up of the main ideas so far presented. It contrasts a quantitative measure of the value of a man's life (the tree, the oak) with the qualitative measure (the lily). Although the oak may live three hundred years, when it falls, it is sapless, with few leaves, and those leaves are withered. The lily may live only a day, but it was in its whiteness, the product of light. ("Flower" is used here in the sense of "blossom considered independently of the plant itself.") The light is the light of purity, the light from the sun that makes things grow, the light that gives beauty to the world, intellectual and spiritual light, since the sun's light is ultimately from God. And so the poet draws the moral which, as we have seen, is already implicit in the poem. Just (perfect and appropriate) beauty can be seen, as in the lily, in small things; in the same way, the perfection of life may be seen even though the span of life may be short, just as perfect music may be found in a composition which consists of only a few measures. But why, we may properly ask, does the poet present in the form of a statement what has already been worked out in the poem? The answer lies in the complexity with which the first half of the poem developed the idea. The poem dramatizes the encounter with the problem (Is life worth living?), the conditions for a solution (What is the proper basis upon which to judge a life?), and the solution (The proper measure is not length but excellence, which is to be judged by appropriateness and originality). Having arrived at a solution, the poet celebrates coming to a conclusion with a statement of that conclusion in clear and confident tones. Here the poet dramatizes not merely the truth of the statement but the certainty with which it may be now uttered. (It is thus worth noting that this stanza of the poem is often published separately as a complete poem. But notice how much it loses by the omission of the intellectual struggle which leads up to it.)

In the counter-turn (l. 75) the first problem is the force of "then." The poet urges Lucius, the surviving friend, to celebrate the death of

Morison, not lament it, to let his features glow with happiness, for he may be confident that, short though Morison's life was, it was a perfect life. Consequently, Cary may be sure that Morison is in heaven. He was so fired with the love of excellence that he could not endure the conditions of our ordinary life and rose to eternal light; thus the poem resumes the idea of the lily as the flower of light. But why is there now introduced the notion that poets, as well as priests, say what heaven will be like for happy men? First, priests tell us of the character of heaven, but it is the function of poets to maintain great men in our memories. Thus we are reminded that the poem is titled "To the immortal memory" and that the formal ode, in ancient times, was used to preserve the memory of noble men. Therefore, second, it gives the poet the opportunity to bring himself into the poem by linking himself with memory, and his dramatic emergence into the poem is brought out by the way his name is split between the counter-turn and the ensuing stand. This device adds to the drama of the poem by justifying the direct address to Cary (l. 75) and increases the nobility of the two friends by presenting the admiration of a poet-priest in his own person; for a priest sanctifies and makes divine and immortal whatever he considers in his role as priest, that is, whatever he blesses. Finally it permits him to state the purpose of the poem, to celebrate, to be joyful, in spite of the perplexity and disgust with many men's lives in the first half of the work.

However, the use of the past "sung" in line 85 is strange. At once it makes us imagine Jonson as having had already sung the song which, in fact, he is now addressing to the reader and in which he has just addressed the still living Lucius. The explanation of this oddity is that the poet now imagines himself as having finished the poem and indeed as having finished with life. For Morison is in heaven and Ben Jonson is with him. He now thinks of himself there, projecting himself into the future, and he tells us that he sang this poem about Morison before he, Jonson, died and before he tasted, in heaven, a part of that heavenly immortality which he meant to be expressed "in this bright Asterism," i.e. set forth in this bright constellation. (The function of "asterism" must be postponed for a moment.) The implication is that by celebrating the immortality of the two friends he has added to his own. It is a graceful way of saying that just as he, as prophet-priest, conferred sanctity and immortality on Morison, so the nobility of the subject of his poem confers immortality on the poet-priest.

An asterism is a constellation or yoking together in the imagination of two stars. By celebrating the two friends in the same poem, Jonson has created a constellation, or asterism. It would be the breaking up of a friendship to separate Morison and Cary, were it not for the fact that

Lucius is going to continue to live. The two friends are properly inseparable, like the heavenly twins of the Romans, the Dioscuri, who were symbolized by the morning and the evening stars. The myth also stated that one was divine and one mortal. After death, one went to heaven, the other to Hades, but daily they met in the heavens, and daily were separated. Fate, then, as in the case of the Dioscuri, has decreed that Morison must be in heaven, while Cary must remain on earth; but both are stars, nevertheless. The implication is that the friends are equally noble and must be considered together as a unity, an inseparable oneness.

In the final turn, "and shine" seems to involve a switch to the imperative mood, but it most simply is thought of as an ellipsis: "and you, Harry and Lucius, must shine (together, as we have seen) as is proper for beings so raised up by friendship, or ennobled." In fact, the two names are simply different ways of referring to one friendship, one star, which is the symbol of the union of two hearts. Nor are they ordinary hearts, that is, common or vulgar capacities for affection. Such capacities did not come into existence by mere luck or circumstances, nor were they linked together by a legal agreement, nor were they "rented" to each other for the sake of mutual profit. At the feasts, or formal dinners, which the two friends gave, there was no joining together ("chime") of stupid amusements ("pleasures vain"), which reinforced each other by making the guests act more stupidly than they would have if they had participated in only one such amusement. Such amusements would be silly rhyming games, or indulgence in general turmoil, shouting and singing: other such amusements would be getting excessively drunk, or pretending to affection which people do not really feel but which, it is implied, comes from too much drinking. Rather, at their dinners the simple love of greatness chimed with the simple love of whatever is good. Such a simple love unites in a single endless web (like the interlocking chains of knitted work) brave minds and good manners, even more powerfully than a blood relationship can.

The counter-turn continues this line of reasoning with the consequences. The mutual recognition of excellence explained to the two friends why they were brought together and how to make proper use of that affection. They were now so close to each other that to the imagination they were no longer separable. The metaphor in lines 111–112 comes from engraving. The purpose of each, to achieve nobility and excellence, was like an engraving tool which copies a picture. Thus each was a model to the other. Furthermore, they became models to others besides themselves. The first step in this process (ll. 113–116) was to call superior people a Cary or a Morison in recognition of the superiority of such people. The second step appears in the final stand. By this process Cary and Morison became not merely verbal equivalents of excellence but models of excellence. Even those who did not dare to be good at least were glad that in these degenerate days the two men were the proof of the law of excellence, a law which might be read, and where one could find that true friendship is revealed not in words but in deeds.

This is explained and developed in an elaborate metaphor. The vehicle: The law of such men is written in words with the pen; thus the law has rules, and records, statements which guide us and which preserve the memory of that which is right. The tenor: The Friendship of two such men is written in deeds with their capacity for affection; thus Friendship has rolls or records, which guide us and which preserve the memory of that which is right. The metaphor works because noble men, as previously shown, are remembered just as laws and records are remembered. And this model or law is made all the more remarkable by the fact that it was formed by the lineaments ("lines") of two young men in the first spring of their life, before they had beards, which are compared with the blossoms of spring. They had planted virtue (had determined to love greatness and excellence) and brought in the harvest (done noble deeds). Thus the last quarter of the poem is the praise of the highest achievement of mankind, to become an ideal. The memory and friendship of the truly noble pair is immortal because they have provided us with a standard by which to measure the value of a life, and have also given us a standard, or model, by following which we ourselves may learn to live nobly. They have provided a better answer to the problem of life than the infant of Saguntum, who refused to be born.

The poem is dramatization of the movement of the mind from the question, "Is life worth living?" to the answer, "Yes, because my two noble friends have shown me and other men how to live."

1\.
For Godsake
hold your tongue,
and let me love,
Or chide {my palsy, / or my gout,}
flout {My five gray hairs, / or ruin'd fortune,}
improve {your state With wealth, / your mind with Arts,}
Take you a course,
get you a place,
*Observe {his honor, / or his grace,}
Contemplate Or [i.e. either] the King's {real, / or his stamped} face,
approve, what you will,
So [i.e. as long as] you will let me love.

JOHN DONNE (1573–1631)

The Canonization

For Godsake hold your tongue, and let me love,
  Or chide my palsy, or my gout,
My five gray hairs, or ruin'd fortune flout,
  With wealth your state, your mind with Arts improve,
    Take you a course, get you a place,
    Observe his honor, or his grace,
Or the King's real, or his stamped face
  Contemplate, what you will, approve,
  So you will let me love.

Title. Canonization: the ceremony by which one is recognized a saint after one dies. (See IH.)

1. *Godsake:* God's sake.

2. *chide:* scold, expose, and correct.

2. *palsy:* a nervous disease.

2. *gout:* a form of rheumatism.

3. *fortune:* inheritance, and/or prospects in life.

3. *flout:* deride, make fun of.

4. *state:* personal circumstances, estate.

4. *Arts:* learning.

5. *Take you a course:* enter into competition for some position.

5. *place:* position at Court, i.e. in the government.

6. *Observe his honor, or his grace:* Watch, and thereby determine (for the purpose of personal advantage) the disposition of some great man ("his honor") or duke, archbishop, or other socially lofty personage ("his grace") toward you.

7. *Or . . . or:* either . . . or.

7. *stamped:* impressed on coins.

8. *Contemplate:* fill one's mind with his real face (see l. 6 *observe*) or his face on coins (i.e. become a miser).

8. *what you will:* whatever you want.

9. *So:* as long as.

2. Alas, alas, who's injur'd by my love?

3. What merchant's ships have my sighs drown'd?

4. Who says my tears have overflow'd his ground?

5. When did my colds *remove a forward spring*?

6. When did the heats which *fill my veins* Add one more [name] to the plaguy Bill?

7. {Soldiers [still] find wars,
{and Lawyers *still find out* Litigious men,
↑
which [i.e. who] *move quarrels*,
Though she and I do love.

Alas, alas, who's injur'd by my love?
What merchant's ships have my sighs drown'd?
Who says my tears have overflow'd his ground?
When did my colds a forward spring remove?
When did the heats which my veins fill
Add one more to the plaguy Bill?
Soldiers find wars, and Lawyers find out still
Litigious men, which quarrels move,
Though she and I do love.

12. *ground.* fields, land.

13. *colds:* low spirits.

13. *a forward spring remove:* delay an early spring.

15. *plaguy Bill:* official report of deaths caused by the Plague.

16. *find out still:* continue to find.

17. *Litigious:* fond of going to law.

17. *which:* who.

17. *move:* start (in order to go to law).

8. Call us what you will,

9. we are made such [what you call us] by love;

10. Call {her one,
me another} fly,

11. We' {are Tapers too,
and *die at our own cost*,

12. And we *find in us [i.e. ourselves]* th' Eagle and the Dove.

13. {The Phœnix riddle hath more wit By us,
we two are it.
↑
being one,

14. So *both sexes fit to one neutral thing*.

15. We {die and rise the same,
and prove Mysterious by this love.

Call us what you will, we are made such by love;
  Call her one, me another fly,
We'are Tapers too, and at our own cost die,
  And we in us find th' Eagle and the Dove.
    The Phœnix riddle hath more wit
    By us, we two being one, are it.
So to one neutral thing both sexes fit.
  We die and rise the same, and prove
  Mysterious by this love.

19. *will:* want to.

19. *such:* whatever you want to call us (or whatever condition you say you find us in).

21. *Tapers:* candles.

21. *at our own cost:* to our own expense, i.e. we consume ourselves.

21. *die:* a pun: (1) cease to live; (2) achieve sexual consummation.

22. *us:* ourselves.

22. *Eagle:* represents strength. See IH.

22. *Dove:* represents mildness. See IH.

23. *Phœnix:* the Phœnix was a fabulous bird which was believed regularly to be consumed by fire and thereafter to arise reborn from its own ashes.

23. *hath more wit:* makes more sense.

24. *By us:* because of what we are.

25. *to . . . fit:* become.

26. *the same:* unchanged.

16. We can die by it [love],
    if not live by love,

And if *Our legend be unfit for tombs and hearse*,
17. it will be fit for verse;

And if *we prove no piece of Chronicle*,
18. We'll build *pretty rooms in sonnets*;

19. *a well wrought urn becomes The greatest ashes,
↑
As well as half-acre tombs*,

20. And all {shall approve Us *Canoniz'd* for Love.
↑
by these hymns,
And [shall] thus invoke us;

We can die by it, if not live by love,
And if unfit for tombs and hearse
Our legend be, it will be fit for verse;
And if no piece of Chronicle we prove,
We'll build in sonnets pretty rooms;
As well a well wrought urn becomes
The greatest ashes, as half-acre tombs,
And by these hymns, all shall approve
Us *Canoniz'd* for Love.

30. *legend:* anything that may be read, a written account: and more especially (1) a saint's biography; or (2) an inscription, motto, or epitaph, something written on the outside of something.

31. *if:* although.

31. *prove no piece of Chronicle:* prove to be not worth recording in historical treatises.

33. *well wrought:* well, even beautifully, constructed.

33. *becomes:* suits becomingly, is appropriate to.

34. *The greatest ashes:* ashes of the greatest people.

34. *half-acre tombs:* tombs so huge that they cover half an acre.

35. *by these hymns:* by means of these songs of praise (i.e. the love sonnets).

35. *approve:* confirm authoritatively, recognize, and find to be true by experience.

36. *Canoniz'd:* see note on title.

21. [“]You whom reverend love Made one another’s hermitage;
You, to whom love was peace,
↑
that now is rage,
[You] Who {did *contract the whole world’s soul*,
and drove *Countries, Towns, Courts Into the glasses of your eyes
↑
So made {such mirrors,
and such spies,
That they [eyes] did *epitomize all to you*,*:

Beg [for us] from above A pattern of your love![”]

And thus invoke us; You whom reverend love
  Made one another's hermitage;
You, to whom love was peace, that now is rage,
  Who did the whole world's soul contract, and drove
    Into the glasses of your eyes
    So made such mirrors, and such spies,
That they did all to you epitomize,
  Countries, Towns, Courts: Beg from above
  A pattern of your love!

37. *And . . . us:* for SG see page 132.

37. *invoke:* pray to a saint so that he will exercise his power of intercession with God in one's behalf.

37. *reverend:* worthy of deep respect.

38. *hermitage:* the retreat or sanctuary of a religious recluse or hermit.

39. *rage:* sexual appetite.

40. *contract:* make small, squeeze together.

40. *drove:* the object is "Countries, Towns, Courts."

41. *glasses:* mirrors.

42. *spies:* spy-glass, telescopic lenses. The eyes of each lover at once reflected and observed the whole world in the eyes of the other.

43. *all:* everything that exists.

43. *to you:* as far as you are concerned.

43. *epitomize:* to comprise in brief.

44. *Countries:* the countryside or rural regions.

44. *Courts:* places where sovereigns hold their state.

44. *Beg from above:* beg from God for us (the "saints," the poet and his mistress, are to intercede with God for their suppliants).

45. *pattern:* an example or model deserving imitation; a model of a particular excellence.

Interpretational Hypothesis

A saint is a human being of such extraordinary religious merit that after his death the Church formally states its belief that he is among the saved and that even the Last Judgment will not change his status. He is in heaven, in the presence of God; he is a privileged spirit who can be persuaded by the prayers of the still living (if they are worthy) to intercede with God that He might grant them favor and mercy and help. The ceremony at which it is announced that the Church believes that a dead man has achieved the status of sainthood is called a canonization.

The poem begins with a cry of annoyance. Apparently a friend or acquaintance of the speaker has been upbraiding the speaker for being in love and for giving it too great importance. The speaker replies, to use the language of today, "For Heaven's sake, be quiet; let me alone, don't bother me, don't interfere; it's none of your business." He attempts to divert his accuser's attention by admitting that he has weaknesses; he has the palsy (an inability to control minor bodily movements), thus implying that he has led a life of sexual debauchery; he has the gout (a painful inflammation of toes and joints), thought to be the result of drinking too much wine; he admits he is growing old, probably before his time. He even admits that his accuser would be justified in deriding him for having run through his inheritance. Having attempted to divert the accuser by focusing attention on the speaker's real faults, he tries to persuade him to think of his own problems, suggesting that he try various things to solve them: to build up his own fortune, or to acquire learning, or to enter on some course of competition for a valuable position in the Royal Court or in the government, or actually to get such a place; or attentively to watch the behavior of some notable person or duke to determine the chances of getting their favorable notice; or either to fill his mind with the King's greatness or to devote himself to money coined by the King and stamped with his image, that is, become a miser. The speaker urges his accuser to do anything he wants to, so long as he doesn't interfere with the speaker's love. The rush of suggestions dramatizes the speaker's impulse to defend himself against attack, implying perhaps that he is in a rather weak position and that he feels its weakness. At any rate, in the next stanza he tries a different line of defense.

"After all," he says, "I'm not hurting anybody." None of his sighs have been so stormy that they have capsized merchant ships. His tears haven't flooded anyone's land. His shivers of emotion have not delayed the spring. The heat of lust in his blood has not so raised the temperature of the air that the death rate from the plague has gone up. (Plague was thought to be caused by overheated and therefore corrupt air.) These overstatements ironically imply that the accuser's suggestions about the undesirability of the speaker's love are equally exaggerations. ("You are making too much of the whole thing, anyway.") Moreover, to speak of more normal things, soldiers still can find wars to fight and lawyers can still find men who like to go to law so much that they deliberately stir up quarrels in order to get the chance to take the quarrels to a court of law. (I.e. "who move quarrels." A second possibility is "whom quarrels move." The first interpretation has the advantage of greater syntactical simplicity, which must always be the guiding factor in decisions of this sort. It also appears to be more consistent: Soldiers look for wars, lawyers look for men who are always looking for chances to go to law.) "What we do has no effect upon anyone else; things pursue their ordinary course, though she and I do love." Again we have the rush of suggestions, indicating that all of the speaker's wits are aroused in self-defense, but there is a difference in tone between this stanza and the first. Not only is it wittier, in the implication by his own exaggeration that the accuser has been exaggerating, but the choice of things which his love does not affect is limited to natural disasters and the aggressive passions. By implication, his love is disconnected from such things. It is to be seen whether or not this limitation has any relation to what follows.

The speaker's next line of defense begins with a statement that love has made the speaker and his beloved whatever they are, good, bad, or indifferent. Thus he testifies to love's power. If the accuser wants to, he can call the lovers flies, the very symbol of a base and nasty lust, for flies copulate indiscriminately in public. But, he goes on, it would be just as fair to call them candles; they may be destroying themselves, but they are not destroying anyone else and, the implication is, like candles, they shed light. Here we begin to see more clearly the nature of the accusation that has been made; the accuser has said that the lovers are guilty of an excessive preoccupation with their love; it has become an obsession to them. But the speaker is recovering rapidly from the attack by turning it to his own credit, by justifying the obsession. Thus from flies he goes on to candles, and thence to the eagle and the dove. Each metaphorical step increases the value of the tenor (the lovers) by increasing the value of the vehicle. The eagle is a traditional symbol of strength and power, and the dove of peace and innocence. Further, in England the eagle and the dove are part of the royal insignia used in coronations, symbolizing the duty of the king to combine both of these principles in his rule. And this, the speaker says, he and his love do. Their love has made them the very symbols of power and innocence. He further raises their value by comparing them to the phoenix, the mysterious bird which, just before its death, builds for itself a nest of spices, with which it then burns itself up; and from the ashes it rises new-born to live for another thousand years. It is a symbol of resurrection. "By us" can best be interpreted thus: "Our behavior makes more sense out of the riddle of the phoenix. It may be a myth, but we are a real instance of what it symbolizes. The reason is that we two lovers form a single entity." This raises a question: How can the lovers be one? The next sentence explains: The phoenix breed does not need two sexes to reproduce its kind. In the same way (l. 25) male and female united together become one thing without sexual differentiation, the perfect hermaphroditical being, a self-enclosed and self-sustaining entity which does not have to turn outside itself for gratification. At the time of the poem, "die" meant, in an erotic environment, as this poem is, to have a sexual experience. Thus, he claims, after each such experience, his love and he are resurrected, come again to life, unchanged and immortal like the phoenix. They have discovered a mysterious and transcendent (or superhuman) secret. He implies that his friend has accused him of being in the grips not merely of an emotional obsession but in fact of a physical, a sexual one. The accuser, it is implied, has said to the speaker, "If you go on this way, you'll kill yourself."

And indeed, in stanza four the speaker admits the justification for the accusation. The "die-live" antithesis, replacing the "die-rise" antithesis, suggests that "die" is now used in a different sense, its normal sense. The rest of the stanza confirms this hypothesis. Using the word "die," then, in its ordinary sense, he admits that he cannot live in such a way. But once again he defends himself. Even though the story of their love might not be suitable for a pompous funeral procession ("hearse") or to be written in detail on their tombs, still it is at least something worth recording in poetry. Moreover, even if it may not be worth putting down in the history of the times ("Chronicle"), nonetheless the lovers will at least have "pretty rooms" in sonnets, brief, charming, and intense love poems. But what is the tenor in the metaphor "rooms"? The speaker explains his meaning by a new metaphor. The vehicle is: A beautifully carved urn or vase is as suitable for the ashes of great men as pompous tombs that cover half an acre. And the tenor: A brief but perfect poem will ensure our memory as well as a big book of history. "A pretty room," then, is a small, charming tomb, or place of memory. Furthermore, these poems will be hymns, versified prayers to something divine, and by repeating them, everyone shall admit that the lovers are properly canonized by reason of their love. Just as a saint is canonized to heaven for religious merit, so they shall be canonized to heaven by reason of erotic merit. And, it is implied, everyone shall pray to them (l. 36).

The rapidity with which all this develops, the ease with which a complex idea is sustained, as opposed to the brief and hurried suggestions of the first two stanzas, indicates that the speaker feels that he has arrived at a successful line of defense. But it is not the one that he began with. The emotional release, it is to be noted, comes after the admission that the accusation of sexual obsession is justified. And now we see why the exaggerations of stanza two employed images of turmoil and brutality: ordinary life is so ugly that the lovers felt themselves justified in turning away from it. The lovers *are* living a life apart from ordinary life, but ordinary life is filled with natural and human ugliness. They have turned in upon themselves to create a world of perfection. That perfection may be unlivable, but even if it is and leads more rapidly to death, it is at least an inspiration to all who come after them. And such lovers of a later time, as we have seen, will pray to them as if they were saints, as indeed they are, for they have created perfection. And the prayer will be of this nature (ll. 37–45):

First the lovers (now in heaven) will be addressed as individuals who, by the permission and power of sacred love, the god of love himself, made each other into a holy refuge from the brutality of the world.

Then they will be addressed as individuals to whom love was a source of peace, not as it has become since their death, a source of frustration and fury.

Then they will be addressed as lovers who saw in each other's eyes the entire world; each became to the other everything that exists, whether separate countries, or cities, or royal courts; for each pair of eyes functioned both as a lens through which to see the world (since each lover contained the world) and as a mirror to reflect the beloved's own image of the world back into his or her own eyes. The result was an infinite series of reflections and perceptions that summed up, in a single mutual perception, all existence.

But is there a reason for the order in which these three qualities are presented? Love was a refuge; therefore it was a place of peace; therefore it was a more than adequate substitute for the rage and fury of the world. For this reason men and women of the future will pray to the two lovers, now saints, to request the God of Love to grant to the lovers still on earth a pattern by which to understand love—a pattern which would make it possible for others to love as did the canonized lovers.

The drama of the poem lies in the sequence of defenses put up by a man who is accused and feels the accusation is justified. First he tries distraction, then he tries ridicule of the accusation, then he insists on the value of what he is doing, then he grants fully the accusation and admits that he is guilty, but insists that his crime is nobler than the world against which it is committed.

1. Descend from Heav'n <*Urania,*>
If thou art call'd rightly by that name,
↑
Following whose divine Voice, *I soar, { above th' *Olympian* Hill*,
Above the flight of *Pegasean* wing.

JOHN MILTON (1608–1674)

Paradise Lost

From *Book VII*

Descend from Heav'n *Urania*, by that name
If rightly thou art call'd, whose Voice divine
Following, above th' *Olympian* Hill I soar,
Above the flight of *Pegasean* wing. 4

1. *Urania:* the word means "heavenly" in Greek. Urania was the name given to at least two classical figures: (1) the Muse of astronomy; (2) Aphrodite (Venus), who in one of her cults was the queen of the heavens and who from her seat in heaven ruled earth, sea, and air. Her father was Uranus. She was carefully distinguished from the "common" Aphrodite, daughter of Zeus and Dione, surnamed Pandemos. But for Milton, Urania is the "heavenly Muse" of Book I, a Christian spirit of divine inspiration to the poets of the Scriptures and a daughter of God.

3. *Olympian Hill:* Mount Olympus, residence of the Greek gods.

4. *Pegasean wing:* a wing like the wings of Pegasus, the flying horse of Greek mythology who, striking the ground with his foot, produced the Hippocrene fountain on Mt. Helicon, a stream sacred to the Muses and the source of all classical artistic inspiration. But, as was pointed out above, to a Christian poet, the inspiration of the "Heavenly Muse," Urania, is both more sanctified and also aesthetically more powerful. Thus, one inspired by her could fly above the pagan poets who had only *Pegasean* wings, that is, the inspiration of less powerful deities.

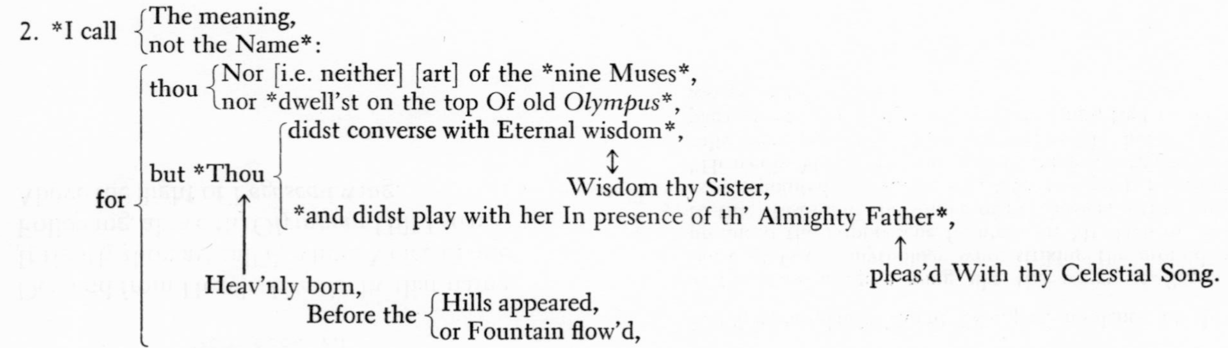
2. *I call
The meaning,
not the Name*:
for
thou
Nor [i.e. neither] [art] of the *nine Muses*,
nor *dwell'st on the top Of old Olympus*,
but *Thou
didst converse with Eternal wisdom*,
Wisdom thy Sister,
and didst play with her In presence of th' Almighty Father,
pleas'd With thy Celestial Song.
Heav'nly born,
Before the
Hills appeared,
or Fountain flow'd,

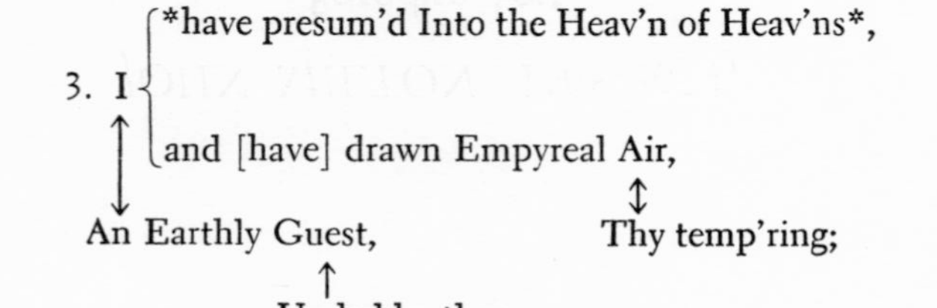
3. I
have presum'd Into the Heav'n of Heav'ns,
and [have] drawn Empyreal Air,
Thy temp'ring;
An Earthly Guest,
Up led by thee

The meaning, not the Name I call: for thou
Nor of the Muses nine, nor on the top
Of old *Olympus* dwell'st, but Heav'nly born,
Before the Hills appear'd, or Fountain flow'd,
Thou with Eternal wisdom didst converse,
Wisdom thy Sister, and with her didst play
In presence of th' Almighty Father, pleas'd
With thy Celestial Song. Up led by thee
Into the Heav'n of Heav'ns I have presum'd,
An Earthly Guest, and drawn Empyreal Air,
Thy temp'ring; with like safety guided down

5. *The meaning, not the Name:* see IH.

6. *Nor . . . nor:* neither . . . nor.

6. *Nor of the Muses nine:* neither [art] thou of the nine Muses.

7. *born:* originating in heaven.

8. *Hills, Fountain:* the Olympian hills and the Hippocrene fountain (see above).

12. *Celestial:* heavenly.

13. *I have presum'd:* I have taken it upon myself to go (in the preceding portions of *Paradise Lost*).

14. *drawn:* breathed.

14. *Empyreal:* heavenly.

15. *temp'ring:* "to temper" means to mix something with something else so as to reduce it to a suitable condition; hence, the empyreal air, which would be too rare for humans to breathe, has been adjusted by Urania for human consumption so that the poet could survive.

15. *with . . . down:* for SG see p. 144.

15. *like safety:* safety like the safety which you provided when you allowed me to soar.

guided down with like safety
↓
4. Return me to my Native Element:
Lest *I fall on th' *Aleian* Field*
↑
{*unrein'd from this flying Steed*,} ←(as once *Bellerophon*, though from a lower Clime)
{Dismounted,}
to wander there Erroneous and forlorn.

5. {Half yet remains unsung,
{*but [it is a half which is] bound narrower Within the visible Diurnal Sphere*;

Return me to my Native Element:
Lest from this flying Steed unrein'd, (as once
Bellerophon, though from a lower Clime)
Dismounted, on th' *Aleian* Field I fall
Erroneous there to wander and forlorn.
Half yet remains unsung, but narrower bound
Within the visible Diurnal Sphere;

16. *Native Element:* the denser air of the earth which is "native" or usual to humans.

17. *Lest:* for fear that.

17. *flying Steed:* Milton's Pegasus, which is a Christian horse.

17. *unrein'd:* thrown.

18. *Bellerophon:* while drinking at a fountain, the winged horse Pegasus was caught by the Greek hero, Bellerophon, with a golden bridle given to him by Athena. With the aid of Pegasus, Bellerophon conquered the Chimaera, a fire-breathing monster, part dragon, part goat and part lion. Bellerophon tried to fly to heaven on Pegasus, but fell off; Pegasus continued flying until he reached the sky and dwelt ever after among the stars.

18. *Clime:* climate, meaning here area of the atmosphere.

19. *Aleian Field:* the Aleian plain is the place in Asia Minor upon which Bellerophon landed when he fell off Pegasus. The name means "field of error" and it was Bellerophon's fate to spend the rest of his life wandering through this desolate region.

20. *Erroneous:* roving aimlessly.

20. *forlorn:* utterly lost, without hope of being found.

21. *Half:* half the poem.

21–22. *narrower bound Within:* more narrowly confined to.

22. *visible Diurnal Sphere:* the astronomical universe of man, which appeared to revolve around the Earth daily in twenty-four hours.

{Standing on Earth,
{not rapt above the Pole,
↓
6. *I Sing More safe* with mortal voice,
↑ ↑
| unchang'd To hoarse or mute,
| {though fall'n on evil days,
| {*though fall'n On {evil days*,
| { {and evil tongues;
| {[though] {In darkness,
| { {and *compass'd round with {dangers*,
| { {And solitude;
| {yet not alone,
| { while thou Visit'st my slumbers
| { ↑
| { {Nightly,
| { {or when Morn Purples the East:

7. still {govern thou my Song, <*Urania,*>
{and *find {fit audience*,
{though few.

Standing on Earth, not rapt above the Pole,
More safe I Sing with mortal voice, unchang'd
To hoarse or mute, though fall'n on evil days,
On evil days though fall'n, and evil tongues;
In darkness, and with dangers compass'd round,
And solitude; yet not alone, while thou
Visit'st my slumbers Nightly, or when Morn
Purples the East: still govern thou my Song,
Urania, and fit audience find, though few.

23. *rapt:* carried away by force.

23. *above the Pole:* the topmost point of the astronomical universe.

24–25. *unchang'd To hoarse or mute:* the poet's voice has not become hoarse or mute.

25. *fall'n on evil days:* a reference to the poet's personal difficulties—he was blind, old and out of political favor.

27. *compass'd round:* encompassed, surrounded by.

30. *Purples:* makes red.

30. *govern:* to direct and guide.

8. But drive far off the barbarous dissonance
↑
Of *Bacchus* and his Revellers,
↕
the Race Of that wild Rout
↑
that tore the *Thracian* Bard
↑
in *Rhodope*,
↑
where {Woods / and Rocks} had Ears To rapture,
↑
{till the savage clamor drown'd Both {Harp / and Voice;
{nor could the Muse defend Her Son.

9. So fail not thou, [him] who *implores thee*:
For {thou art Heav'nly,
{she [is only] an empty dream.

But drive far off the barbarous dissonance
Of *Bacchus* and his Revellers, the Race
Of that wild Rout that tore the *Thracian* Bard
In *Rhodope*, where Woods and Rocks had Ears
To rapture, till the savage clamor drown'd
Both Harp and Voice; nor could the Muse defend
Her Son. So fail not thou, who thee implores:
For thou art Heav'nly, she an empty dream.

32. *dissonance:* harsh noise.

33. *Bacchus:* the god of wine; his "revellers" would be the participants in orgies enjoyed in his honor.

33. *Race:* a group of persons having some common feature, in this case, their rowdiness.

34. *Rout:* a disorderly crowd.

34. *Thracian Bard:* Orpheus, the fabled singer of classical mythology, whose musical powers were so great that he was able to charm the woods and rocks and all living things, and even temporarily to deliver his wife Eurydice from Hades.

34–35. *wild Rout . . . In Rhodope:* Orpheus was killed on the banks of the river Hebrus, in Thrace, by Bacchanalian women because he spied on their rites or treated them with contempt.

37. *Muse:* Calliope, the Muse of epic poetry.

39. *she:* Calliope, the classical Muse, who, in comparison to Christian inspiration, is an empty dream of paganism.

Interpretational Hypothesis

These are the first thirty-nine lines, or first verse paragraph, of Book VII of *Paradise Lost,* which tells the story of the fall of man and his expulsion from Paradise. Book VII is concerned with the creation of the world and its creatures, and the rest of the poem (Books VIII–XII) with the fall of Adam and Eve and with Old Testament history up to the coming and crucifixion of Christ, that is, to the promised redemption of man from the penalties of Adam's sin. Thus it differs from the first half of the poem, which is principally concerned with events outside of the world, in heaven and hell.

The poet begins by addressing Urania, a figure, as is indicated in the Lexical Gloss, taken from classical mythology. He asks her to descend from heaven. Presumably this passage is an instance of a poet's appeal to his Muse, and we will proceed on that hypothesis, though it may be mistaken. The next question is raised by the phrase, "by that name/If rightly thou art called." Why should the poet express doubt about her name? For one thing, "Urania" means merely "Heavenly," a word which could refer only to an attribute of the spirit he is addressing, rather than to the spirit itself. A further explanation may be forthcoming. The poet proceeds now to explain why he is addressing Urania. Following her divine voice he has soared above the hill of Olympus. Olympus was the residence of the gods of Greece. She has led him, then, to a higher realm of reality than those gods attained; this is emphasized by referring to Olympus as a hill instead of by its more customary term, Mount. By implication, then, she has raised him above the spiritual level to which Greek poets could attain, since they could sing of nothing higher than their own gods. This implication is verified in line 4: she has led him above the level to which Pegasus, the winged horse, symbol of pagan poetic inspiration, could ever attain. Thus she is not a Greek muse, even though her name is taken from Greek mythology: she is called Urania only because Greek mythology had names for Muses. Hence he is ignorant of her true name and he uses instead a word for her attribute as a dweller in the Christian heaven.

The next statement (l. 5) by raising a question answers a previous one. The difference between a word and its meaning is the difference between any sign or symbol and what it refers to. Why this careful distinction? As we have seen, he is not sure if he is calling her by her right name, since her name only means "heavenly" or "divine." Here he returns, then, to the problem, and he resolves it by calling upon the distinction between a sign and what it refers to. Since he knows what the name refers to, the spirit that has so far guided him in his poem, it is a matter of indifference if he uses the right name or not. He is being very modern here, or what seems to us to be very modern; for he is saying that the word we use to refer to something is only a convention and there is no necessary or real connection between a word and its referent.

Why "for" at the beginning of the next clause? We must interpret that statement before this question can be answered. Certainly an interpretation that reads, "I address the meaning of the word because she was born in heaven, etc." seems rather odd. The whole clause provides a considerable amount of information: (1) Urania was not one of the nine Muses; that is, though an inspirer of poets she is not of those who inspired Greek and Roman poets; she is, then, a Christian muse. (2) She did not dwell on Olympus; therefore, since she is divine, she dwelt in the Christian heaven, infinitely higher, as we have already seen. (3) Consequently she was born in the Christian heaven. (4) Her existence was prior to the creation of the world, another fact that differentiates her from the pagan Muses. (5) She communicated with the eternal wisdom, the wisdom that existed before the creation of the world, infinitely, and will continue to exist infinitely after its destruction. We might think at first that this means God himself, but (6) eternal wisdom is the sister of Urania; presumably both are the offspring of God, a point (7) which seems to be emphasized by referring to God as the Almighty Father in the presence of whom Urania and Wisdom played, as children, for to God all creatures are children. This sisterhood, by putting Urania on a level with Wisdom, brings out her divine splendor. (8) God was pleased with the divine song of Urania. Thus the poet claims to know a great deal about Urania, and now we can answer the question about "for." The poet is saying: "I call upon the meaning, that is, I have the meaning in my mind, rather than just the name, because, although I am uncertain of the name, I am certain of the meaning." This further explains the connection between the first sentence (ll. 1–4) and the second (ll. 5–13). He knows a great deal about Urania because he has already had, in writing the first half of the poem, a great deal of experience with her, i.e. with the poetic inspiration which is on a level with divine wisdom. He now repeats this idea, in order to make a transition to his next point. Led by her, he, a guest from earth, has dared to penetrate to the Heaven of Heavens, the abode of God. There he has breathed the air of the highest heavens, because it was "tempered" by her, because her presence and aid made it possible for him, a mere mortal, to breathe it. Now he is requesting her to guide him back to earth, to his own air. If she does not help him he may not be able to stay on the horse he has been riding (the Christian equivalent of Pegasus, for as we have seen, he has been flown above the range of the Greek Pegasus), just as Bellerophon was thrown from Pegasus and spent the rest of his life wandering on the field of error. From this we learn two important things. First, the hypothesis that this is a poet's address to the Muse to descend to him is incorrect. It is a prayer that she descend *with* him. It is not a prayer for new inspiration but a prayer for continued inspiration under new and different circumstances. And second we learn why he has made this request. Twice he has said that only with her aid has he penetrated the Heaven of Heavens, and thus he emphasizes his fear that when he writes about earthly events he may lose his inspiration and make a mess of the rest of his poem. Thus he emphasizes the sense of the greatness of his accomplishment so far, and his sense of its difficulty, as if he had been walking a kind of poetic tightrope. We must ask, however, if the difficulty is his only fear. One other source of fear may properly be deduced from the nature of the whole poem. Although the place of the events in the rest of the poem will be earth, those events will still have a divine significance, and thus he will continue to need divine aid. However, both of these reasons are so far based on implication only. We may hypothesize, therefore, that he will state more clearly his reasons for his fear and his conviction that Urania's help will continue to be essential to him.

He begins by admitting that, although half of the poem remains to be written, that half will take place on earth—within the sphere that is illuminated by the ordinary light of the sun and the moon, not by the divine light of the Heaven of Heavens. And he further admits that he is safer there within the realm of ordinary mortal knowledge. Moreover, he admits that his voice has not become hoarse (that his power to write poetry has not declined), that he has not become mute (that he has not been forced to stop writing poetry), even though times have changed, and that his poetic gift exists in a world that is evil. At this point the syntax becomes tricky and surprising. "Unchang'd" depends on "voice," and the parallelism of "fall'n" (l. 25) with "unchang'd" at first seems to indicate a similar dependency. However, though we may imagine a *voice* falling on evil ears, it is more normal to think of a *person* falling on evil days. It is, in fact, a common expression. "Fall'n on evil days" and what follows depend, therefore, on "I." Thus the poet is saying, "I continue to sing even though I have fallen on evil days, and though I am being accused or slandered by the tongues of evil people; even though I am surrounded by darkness, dangers, and solitude, yet I am not alone so long as you, Urania, visit me in my dreams or when I awake at dawn." (Probably the last refers to the fact that many people experience an unusual clarity of mind and vigor of imagination when they first wake up in the morning.) This gives us the answer as to why he is afraid that his poetic powers might be suspended if Urania no longer guides him; he is helpless and alone in dangerous circumstances. He is writing under two difficulties, the difficulty of theme and the difficulty of environment. But now we wonder why these days are evil.

Now he makes Urania three requests (l. 30): (1) to continue to help him write his poem; (2) to find him the proper audience for his poem, even though that audience might be very small, the implication being that only readers who themselves have something of divine inspiration will be able to understand his poem (but why will they be so few?); (3) to "drive far off the barbarous dissonance of Bacchus and his Revellers." When Bacchus, the god of wine, rouses men to drunken frenzy, they present a danger to the poet: (1) they make an uncivilized and dissonant music through which such poetry as his own divinely inspired harmonies cannot be heard; (2) they are particularly dangerous to divinely inspired poets. Here the reference is to Orpheus, at whose voice and harp the very woods and rocks were emotionally stirred and even, the legend is, moved closer to him to hear better and to be nearer the source of such beauty. But once a group of women, driven insane by Bacchus, caught Orpheus when he was spying on their monstrous rites and tore him to pieces. Even his Muse could not save him. This is the specific danger, then, of the evil days on which the poet has fallen. Not only are there people who cannot hear such poetry as his, because the social environment is too uncivilized and maddened, but also it is an environment actively inimical to the divinely inspired poet. Thus he begs Urania not to fail him, as Orpheus's Muse failed, for, since Urania is heavenly, she can save him, inspire him, and protect him, since she really exists, while the Muse of Orpheus was only the unreal product of the pagan imagination.

Thus the poet resolves a problem felt from the beginning: how can he compare Christian inspiration to pagan inspiration, since one is true and the other false? He can do so, not because he is comparing two things on the same plane of reality, but because Christian inspiration is a divine reality, while pagan inspiration was only the product of the unredeemed imagination; it was false. Thus he indicates that his task is not only greater than the task of pagan poets but that it is radically different: they wrote of pagan lies; he writes of Christian truth. A further implication follows. Since his environment is riotous, uncivil (inspired by Bacchus), it is not truly Christian. The only Christians are himself and the small audience he hopes to discover and appeal to.

Complex as the passage is, it resolves itself into a simple emotion: May I continue to experience the same poetic inspiration that has made me successful so far in my great undertaking; I am afraid that I will lose it, especially since I am living in a society which is not only indifferent but actually hostile to poets and to Christians like myself.

FIRST SPIRIT

1. <Palace-roof of cloudless nights!

2. Paradise of golden lights!
↑
Deep, immeasurable, vast,
Which art now,
and which wert then!

3. *Presence-chamber,
temple,
home,
Ever-canopying dome, ⟵ Of the present and the past,
Of the eternal where and when,
Of acts and ages yet to come*!>

PERCY BYSSHE SHELLEY
(1792–1822)

Ode to Heaven

Chorus of Spirits

FIRST SPIRIT

Palace-roof of cloudless nights!
Paradise of golden lights!
  Deep, immeasurable, vast,
Which art now, and which wert then!
  Of the present and the past,
Of the eternal where and when,
  Presence-chamber, temple, home,
  Ever-canopying dome,
  Of acts and ages yet to come!

Spirit: bodiless being or existence.

4. *then:* any moment in the past, no matter how remote.

6. *where:* place.

6. *when:* time.

7. *Presence-chamber:* chamber in which a sovereign or other great personage makes his appearance.

8. *canopying:* covering like a canopy or tent.

4. Glorious shapes have life in thee,
↕
Earth,
and all earth's company;
↕
Living globes
↑
which ever throng Thy deep chasms
and wildernesses;
And green worlds that glide along;
And swift stars with flashing tresses;
And icy moons most cold and bright,
And mighty suns beyond the night,
↕
Atoms of intensest light.

Glorious shapes have life in thee,
Earth, and all earth's company;
   Living globes which ever throng
Thy deep chasms and wildernesses;
   And green worlds that glide along;
And swift stars with flashing tresses;
   And icy moons most cold and bright,
   And mighty suns beyond the night,
   Atoms of intensest light.

11. *company:* other astronomical bodies in space, seen as companions.

15. *tresses:* hair; the reference is to the tails of comets whose very name in Greek means "long-haired star."

18. *Atoms:* minute particles.

5. Even thy name is as a god, <Heaven!>
for thou art the abode Of that power
↑
which is the glass
↑
Wherein man *sees his nature*.

6. Generations Worship thee with bended knees.
↑
as they pass

7. Their unremaining gods and they roll away:
↑
Like a river

8. Thou remainest such alway.

Even thy name is as a god,
Heaven! for thou art the abode
  Of that power which is the glass
Wherein man his nature sees.
  Generations as they pass
Worship thee with bended knees.
  Their unremaining gods and they
  Like a river roll away:
  Thou remainest such alway.

20. *abode:* home.

21. *glass:* mirror.

22. *nature:* the inherent dominating power of man by which action or character is determined and directed.

23. *Generations:* the whole body of individuals born about the same period.

27. *such:* as you are, the same.

27. *alway:* always.

SECOND SPIRIT

9. Thou art {but the mind's first chamber,
        ↑
        Round which its young fancies clamber,
                ↑
                Like weak insects in a cave,
                        ↑
                        Lighted up by stalactites;
    But the portal of the grave,
        ↑
        Where a world of new delights Will make thy best glories seem But a {dim / and noonday} gleam
                                                                                        ↑
                                                                From the shadow of a dream!

THIRD SPIRIT

10. Peace! the abyss is wreathed with scorn At your presumption,
    <atom-born!>

11. What is heaven?

12. and what are ye
        ↑
        Who *inherit its brief expanse*?

SECOND SPIRIT

Thou art but the mind's first chamber,
Round which its young fancies clamber,
Like weak insects in a cave,
Lighted up by stalactites;
But the portal of the grave,
Where a world of new delights
Will make thy best glories seem
But a dim and noonday gleam
From the shadow of a dream!

THIRD SPIRIT

Peace! the abyss is wreathed with scorn
At your presumption, atom-born!
What is heaven? and what are ye
Who its brief expanse inherit?

29. *clamber*: climb with difficulty.

31. *stalactites:* icicle-like mineral deposits hanging from the roofs of caves, sometimes containing luminescent materials.

32. *But:* only.

32. *portal:* gateway.

37. *abyss:* the vast regions of the visible heaven.

37. *wreathed:* twisted, contorted into an expression (of scorn).

38. *presumption:* impertinence.

38. *atom-born:* produced by atoms.

13. What are {suns
and spheres

↑
which flee With the instinct of that spirit

↑
Of which ye are but a part?

14. [They are only] Drops

↑
which Nature's mighty heart Drives through thinnest veins.

15. Depart!

16. What is heaven?

17. [It is] a globe of dew,

↑
Filling *Some eyed flower in the new morning*

↑
whose young leaves waken On an unimagined world:

What are suns and spheres which flee
With the instinct of that spirit
Of which ye are but a part?
Drops which Nature's mighty heart
Drives through thinnest veins. Depart!

What is heaven? a globe of dew,
Filling in the morning new
Some eyed flower whose young leaves waken
On an unimagined world:

42. *spirit:* see IH.

48. *eyed:* marked as with eyes, spotted.

49. *unimagined world:* a world beyond the imagination.

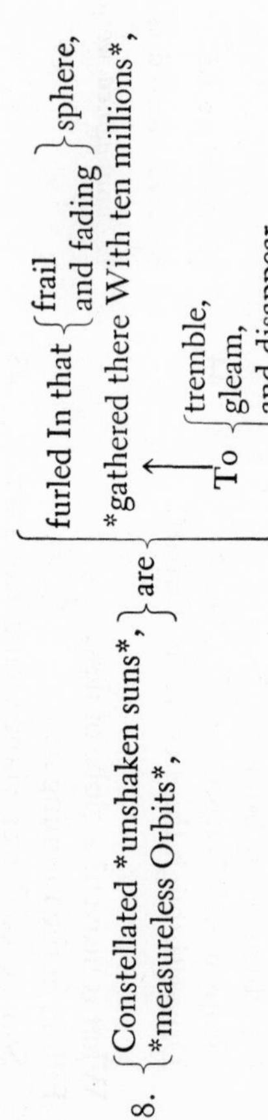
18.
Constellated *unshaken suns*,
measureless Orbits,
are
furled In that
frail
and fading
sphere,
gathered there With ten millions,
To
tremble,
gleam,
and disappear.

 Constellated suns unshaken,
Orbits measureless, are furled
 In that frail and fading sphere,
 With ten millions gathered there,
 To tremble, gleam, and disappear.

50. *Constellated:* clustered together as stars.

50. *unshaken:* not yet "shaken out" of what "furls" them, the dew-drop.

51. *Orbits:* a confusion with orb, "a heavenly body."

51. *furled:* rolled up into small compass.

52. *sphere:* the dew drop.

53. *ten millions:* ten million other orbs.

Interpretational Hypothesis

A glance at the poem indicates that this is a novel kind of ode, a poem which is usually spoken by a single speaker to some higher power; an ode is ordinarily a kind of prayer. However, this ode is spoken by a chorus of three spirits, each of whom speaks separately.

The first spirit hails heaven (thus following the ordinary formula of an ode) as a palace roof which can be seen on cloudless nights. A palace is the residence of greatness and power, and heaven is thus thought of as a roof or dome which governs the visible universe. Yet this picture of heaven as a roof is immediately changed in the next line to a picture of heaven as a place. It is a paradise, a place of supreme and divine worth; it is paradise where, traditionally, all contradictions are resolved, where there is no disorder. Within that paradise dwell the golden lights of the stars. In line 3 this image of a place of limited extent is replaced by a conception of something that has great depth, cannot be measured, and is vast; just as it is immeasurable in space, so it is (l. 4) immeasurable in time. It exists now, and it existed "then," that is, at any time in the past. In lines 5–9 the concepts of place and time and of roof and palace are combined. Reading in normal syntactical order, and beginning with line 7, as a "presence-chamber," it is a place where a monarch makes his appearance; as a "temple," it is a place where a god makes his appearance; and as a "home," it is a place where man feels comfortable and adjusted. The term "ever-canopying dome" combines time and space; and "dome" (referring to the apparent roundness of heaven as the Spirit sees it) means here both the roof over a semi-spherical hollow space and the space itself, a dual meaning emphasized by the fact that "dome" is in apposition with the three space-names of line 7. Thus the poet is simultaneously employing the three normal meanings of heaven as a visible and experienced fact: It seems to be a dome or covering; scientifically, it is not, but rather a three-dimensional space of indefinite size; it is everything beyond the surface of the earth, including earth in its space. It is at once the abode of the divine, of all power, and of the human spirit. Thus it is the place of the present and the past, of eternal time and space, and of the future (ll. 5, 6, and 9).

The next stanza lists those things whose existence in heaven makes it an abode of such splendor. These things are "glorious shapes" which in heaven have life, i.e. the planet earth and all the other planets and the stars. They are presented as living beings rather than as inanimate parts of a universal machine. The first category of these shapes consists of earth and earth's company, i.e. those shapes which are like earth. In lines 12 and 13 the nature of their similarity is explained: "earth and her company are living globes." Heaven is compared to an unexplored area of earth, a place with canyons and unknown areas. But these heavenly areas are thronged with the company of earth. But what does "living" mean? The answer comes in line 14, with the mention of green worlds; presumably they are green because they are covered with vegetation, though with no life of a higher order. This contrast with "living" suggests that the "living globes" are so called because they sustain conscious life, or at least life more conscious than the life of vegetation. Further, there are rapidly moving stars with shining hair—comets. There are cold, brilliant moons of ice, like our moon. Line 17 refers to the astronomical idea that what we call night is only apparent night. Half the time we are on a side of the earth away from the sun and too far from other stars to get an illumination equivalent to that of the sun. Thus beyond our apparent night are other suns as great as ours but too distant to appear to us as great. Even so, in the vast spaces of heaven these suns are only pinpoints of light, brilliant though that light may be.

The first spirit is now raised to a high pitch of rapture and exaltation by this picture of the immense life of the universe. He cries that even the name of heaven has the characteristics of a god; even the name of heaven is to be worshipped. The "for" explains why. Heaven is not only the abode of past and future, space and time, the stars and suns and planets; it is also the abode of "that power" which is a mirror in which man sees what he really is. Consequently the generations of man worship heaven as they come into existence and die. Both they and their transient gods, presumably created by themselves, pass away steadily and inevitably, but the power in the universe is always the same, unchanging in past, present, or future.

The first spirit sees a universe which is composed simultaneously of the material objects in the universe and the power which controls those material objects. This is borne out by the statements that both the objects and the power have the same relation to the universe: the heavens are the abode or dwelling-place of both. Since the objects are presented as alive, and all as having the same life, it seems reasonable to hypothesize that the ultimate power of the universe, which is also presented as alive though it is unknown (we worship the name, not the power itself, presumably because we cannot understand the power)—that ultimate power is identifiable with the objects themselves, or with some aspect of the objects.

The second spirit disagrees with this point of view. The heavens, or the universe, he says, are only, or nothing but, the first dwelling chamber of the mind. That is, the heavens are only the nursery or cradle of the mind. The metaphor is continued in the next three lines. The vehicle is that young insects, still unable to fly, climb around the walls of a cave, lighted only by the weak reflected glimmers of stalactites. Since insects are alive, but rock is, by contrast, dead, the tenor is that the ideas projected by the mind onto the universe are the only genuine life in the dead universe, where there is in fact no real life at all. This spirit denies the tremendous value given to the visible universe by the first spirit, maintaining that the real life of reality is in the mind, and that by contrast the visible world has no life. Consequently it has no reality. It is only the gateway to death. In human existence, mind is aided but limited by matter. The insects clamber on the walls of the cave, but they are limited by the fact that it is a cave and is weakly lighted. When they become mature and can fly, they can fly out of the portal of the cave into the unlimited world outside. Thus, the universe exists only to bring the mind into life, to protect it in its infancy, to provide it something to exercise itself on, and to guard it from the intense light of the day, which lies outside the cave of the universe and which the mind reaches after it no longer needs the body (which the mind rids itself of in death); that light is real reality. Thus after the body has died, the mind enters into a world of such pleasure that the most brilliant stars and suns will seem to have no more light or reality than the faint light ("gleam") which is to be seen in the darkness of a dream, in which even when we dream of noon the light is as nothing compared to the real light of the day.

The first spirit has said that the power in the universe is identifiable with or inherent in the visible objects of the universe. The second spirit has said that the visible objects of the universe have, on the contrary, no life or even reality at all, that the real life of the universe is the life of the mind, which will find its true home or paradise after death and after escaping from the physical universe.

The third spirit tells them both (as indicated by the "ye" or plural of "you" in line 39) to be quiet ("Peace!"). The abyss, the vast depths of the visible universe, is filled with scorn at the presumption or unjustified boldness of the two spirits who attempt to define its nature. It is "wreathed" with scorn, as we say of a face which is all good humor that it is wreathed with smiles. In comparison with what they are attempting to talk about, the spirits are creatures produced by atoms, the smallest entities in the universe (according to early nineteenth-century physics). Then comes a series of questions, all of which have the same answer, given in lines 44–45. The spirits ask what heaven is, but they who ask are nothing. They only inherit from preceding generations a heaven which, great as it is, has but a brief life. The first spirit was wrong in thinking that it has comprehended the universe; the second wrong in thinking that it can get out of the world of time and space which is the universe. Even the suns and the spheres do not have their own life but fly through the universe impelled by the same Spirit of which the two spirits are only a part. How can they hope to understand something from which they cannot separate themselves? Thus is attacked the first spirit's idea that the power in the universe is a mirror for man (l. 21), and the second that it is but a training ground for the mind in which it learns to understand itself, and by this understanding separate itself from the universe. Heaven, and the spirits, and the suns and spheres, are, using the vehicle of the metaphor, like drops of blood driven through the smallest veins in the human body by the mighty heart of Nature. They are the tiniest of all things in the enormous natural universe. Even the power which activates them, the heart, is but a part, though the life-giving part, of a nature which is utterly beyond comprehension. Having exposed contemptuously both the materialism and the idealism of the first two spirits, the third spirit dismisses them. (Materialism is the doctrine that matter is the only reality and that everything in the world, including thought, will, and feeling, can be explained only in terms of matter. Idealism, here, is the doctrine that the objects of perception are actually ideas of the perceiving mind and have no reality.)

Alone now (the first two spirits presumably having obeyed the order to depart) the third spirit asks the question: What is heaven? What is the visible universe? The answer is expressed in a metaphor. The vehicle is: In the morning a dewdrop fills the cup of a tiny flower which opens up for the first time. To comprehend the full impact of this metaphor, it is necessary to place it against the scale of things presented in the poem. Within the visible universe there is an immeasurable number of stars and planets. On one small planet, earth, there is a flower so small that its cup is filled with a single dewdrop. The *visible* universe, then, bears the same relation to the *total* universe, as a dewdrop bears to the *visible* universe. But space is not all that is involved. The tiny flower, with its little eye which looks forth on a world which it could not have imagined as existing, wakes in the morning and perceives this world. How long will it live? Certainly far longer than the dewdrop which fills its cup. "Dewdrop" is the vehicle for "heaven," that is, the minute heaven or tiny visible universe which we can see. In that "frail and fading sphere," the dewdrop, or visible universe, are suns or stars arranged in constellations which seem eternal ("unshaken"). The suns follow paths ("orbits") so vast as to seem measureless. Besides those we can see, there are "ten millions" more, but even all these together are infinitesimal compared with what lies beyond. The whole vast visible and conceivable universe is not more than a dewdrop, with just as short a life, when it is compared with the inconceivable size and unimaginable time span of the total universe. And as a dewdrop trembles when the sun strikes it, gleams momentarily in the sunlight, and then disappears, or evaporates, so this vast visible and conceivable universe (as yet "unshaken") will have the briefest of lives, compared with the immense and unimaginable time span of the life and the unknown and unknowable universe.

Finally, who are the spirits? Each represents a certain philosophical attitude. The first two, as we have seen, materialism and idealism, the third, skepticism. The poem is thus a dramatic allegory, a work in which a dramatic or fictional character stands for and is equivalent to an abstract conception. By having the third spirit dismiss and expose the inadequacy of the first two, the poet indicates his preference for the third position. The poem is a dramatization of an intellectual experience which considers materialism and then idealism as alternate but, in their own terms, at least, adequate theories of the nature of the physical universe; and then he rejects them both in favor of a kind of scientific skepticism which recognizes the existence of the physical universe but denies that the human mind, with its limitations of its own nature and of space and time, can comprehend it.

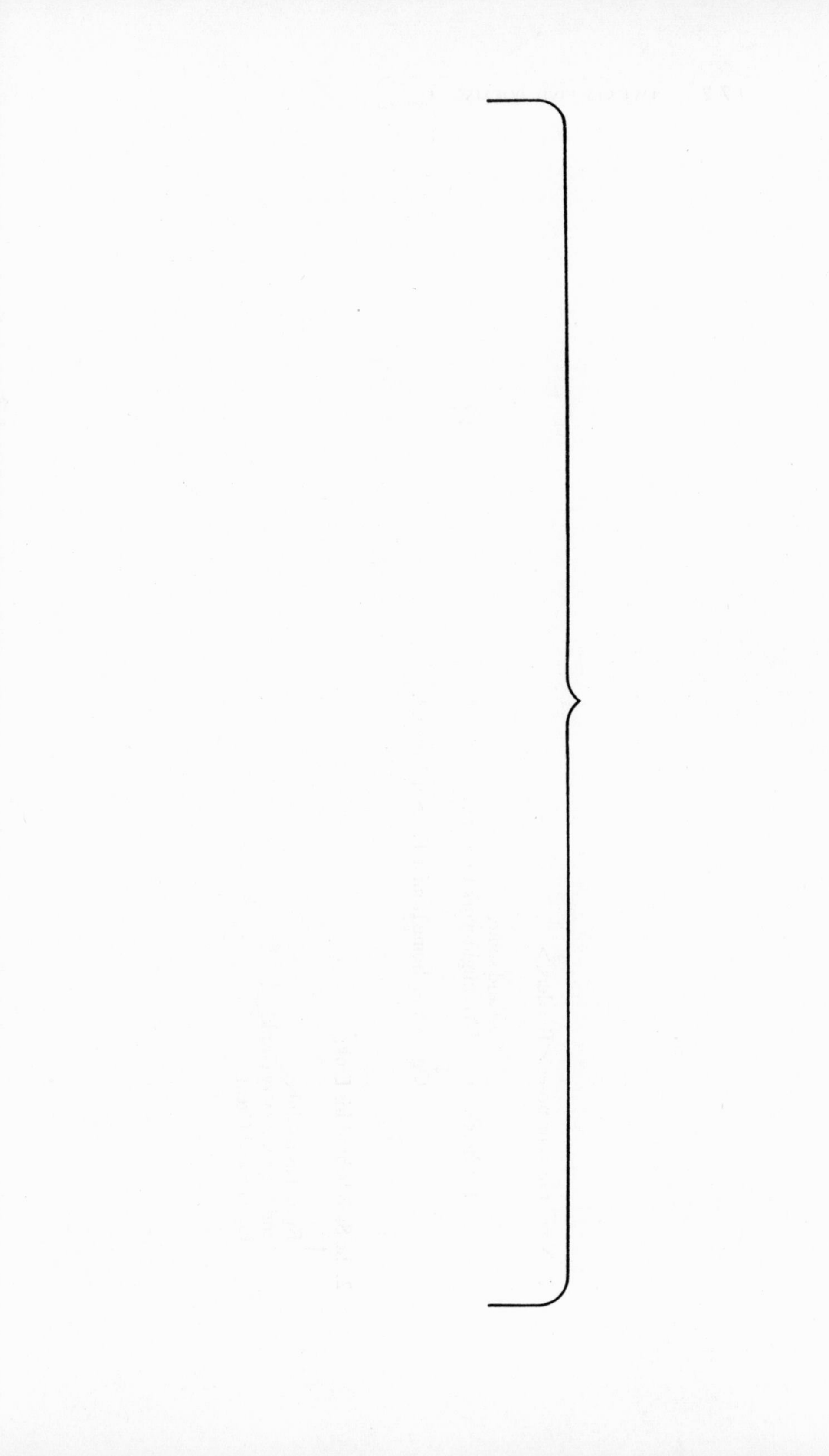

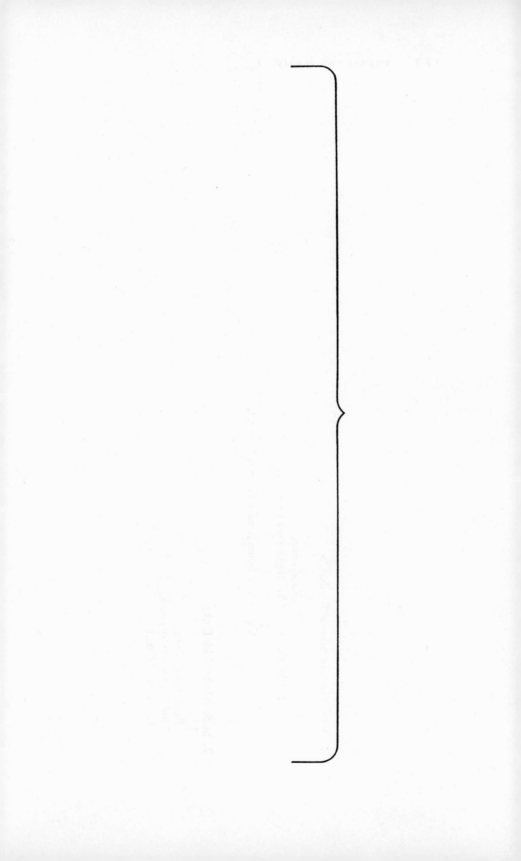

1. Now stop your noses <Readers,>
↑
all and some,
For here's a tun of Midnight-work to come,
↕
Og *rolling home from a Treason Tavern*.

2. he Sails behind his Link;
↑
{Round as a Globe,
{and Liquor'd ev'ry chink,
{Goodly and Great

JOHN DRYDEN (1631–1700)

A Character of Og

From *The Second Part of Absalom and Achitophel*

Now stop your noses Readers, all and some,
For here's a tun of Midnight-work to come,
Og from a Treason Tavern rolling home.
Round as a Globe, and Liquor'd ev'ry chink,
Goodly and Great he Sails behind his Link;

Title. A "Character" is a brief descriptive sketch of a personage who typifies some special quality or trait.

1. *all and some:* the sum total, everybody.

2. *tun:* a large barrel or cask.

2. *Midnight-work:* night-soil, human excrement collected and used as fertilizer.

3. *Og:* the powerfully built King of Bashan, who was defeated by Israel at Edrei, the Bashan capital (Num. 21:33). But in this allegorical poem, Og represents Thomas Shadwell (1642?–92), a Whig poet, poet laureate after the Revolution, whom Dryden had also satirized in *Mac Flecknoe*. As Sir Walter Scott wrote, "Shadwell's corpulence, his coarse and brutal debauchery, his harsh and clumsy style of poetry" all come under Dryden's lash here.

3. *Treason Tavern:* a tavern where treason is being plotted. (Here, presumably, the hangout of Whigs.)

4. *chink:* open spaces between the barrel staves. He is so full of liquor that it seems almost to be leaking out of the cracks in his skin.

5. *Goodly:* both large in size and well suited to its function.

5. *Link:* a torch made of tow and pitch for lighting people along the streets. Thus also the boy who carries the torch.

3. there's nothing lost in *Og*
↑
With all this Bulk
For ev'ry inch that is not Fool is Rogue:

4. [he is] A Monstrous mass of foul corrupted matter,
As [if] all the Devils had spew'd to make the batter.

When wine has given him courage to Blaspheme,
5. He Curses God,
But God before Curs'd him;

And if man could have reason
6. none has more [reason to curse God],
↑
That made his Paunch so rich and him so poor.

7. *he was not trusted With wealth*,
for Heav'n knew What 'twas of Old to pamper up a *Jew*;

8. To what [size] would he *swell on Quail and Pheasant*,
↑
That ev'n *could rebel on Tripe and Carrion*?

With all this Bulk there's nothing lost in *Og*
For ev'ry inch that is not Fool is Rogue:
A Monstrous mass of foul corrupted matter,
As all the Devils had spew'd to make the batter.
When wine has given him courage to Blaspheme,
He Curses God, but God before Curs'd him;
And if man could have reason none has more,
That made his Paunch so rich and him so poor.
With wealth he was not trusted, for Heav'n knew
What 'twas of Old to pamper up a *Jew*;
To what would he on Quail and Pheasant swell,
That ev'n on Tripe and Carrion could rebel?

6. *With:* despite.

7. *Rogue:* rascal.

8. *matter:* pus, discharge.

9. *As:* as if.

9. *spew'd:* spit.

9. *batter:* mixture; i.e. the composition of his body.

12. *none:* no one.

13. *Paunch:* belly, and hence, appetite.

13. *rich:* desirous of rich foods.

15. *pamper up:* to feed up, make prosperous.

15. *Jew:* see IH.

16. *what:* what size.

17. *Tripe:* cattle stomachs prepared as food.

17. *Carrion:* putrefying or putrefied flesh.

17. *rebel:* rebel against God.

But though Heav'n made him poor,
(*speaking with rev'rence*,)
9. He never was a Poet of God's making;

10. The Midwife laid her hand on his Thick Skull, With this Prophetic blessing—

11. ["]*Be thou Dull;*
Drink, Swear and Roar,
forbear no lewd delight
↑
Fit for thy Bulk,
do any thing but write:

12. Thou art {of lasting Make like thoughtless men,
{A strong Nativity—
↑
but for the Pen;

13. Eat Opium,
mingle Arsenic in thy Drink,
Still thou may'st live
↑
avoiding [i.e. as long as you avoid] Pen and Ink.["]

But though Heav'n made him poor, (with rev'rence speaking,)
He never was a Poet of God's making;
The Midwife laid her hand on his Thick Skull,
With this Prophetic blessing—*Be thou Dull*;
Drink, Swear and Roar, forbear no lewd delight
Fit for thy Bulk, do any thing but write:
Thou art of lasting Make like thoughtless men,
A strong Nativity—but for the Pen;
Eat Opium, mingle Arsenic in thy Drink,
Still thou may'st live avoiding Pen and Ink.

20. *Midwife:* a woman trained to deliver babies.

22. *Roar:* be a wild man-about-town.

22. *forbear no lewd delight:* do not abstain from any vulgar or unchaste pleasure.

24. *Make:* fabric, constitution.

25. *Nativity:* birth; here more specifically, bodily fabric or constitution; also in an astrological sense, see IH.

25. *but:* except.

27. *Still thou may'st live:* you can continue to live.

27. *avoiding:* providing that you avoid.

14. I see, I see 'tis Counsel given in vain,
        For Treason botch'd in Rhyme will be thy bane;

15. Rhyme is the Rock on which thou art to wreck,
    ↕
    'Tis fatal to thy Fame and to thy Neck:

16. Why should thy Metre *blast good King *David**?
    A Psalm of his will Surely be thy last.

17. Dar'st thou presume *to meet thy foes in verse*,
        ↑
        Thou whom the Penny Pamphlet foil'd in prose?

18. *Doeg* O'er-tops thy talent in thy very Trade;
    ↑
    whom God *has made for Mankind's mirth*,

I see, I see 'tis Counsel given in vain,
For Treason botch'd in Rhyme will be thy bane;
Rhyme is the Rock on which thou art to wreck,
'Tis fatal to thy Fame and to thy Neck:
Why should thy Metre good King *David* blast?
A Psalm of his will Surely be thy last.
Dar'st thou presume in verse to meet thy foes,
Thou whom the Penny Pamphlet foil'd in prose?
Doeg, whom God for Mankind's mirth has made,
O'er-tops thy talent in thy very Trade;

28. *Counsel:* advice.

29. *botch'd:* messed up.

29. *bane:* that which causes ruin or woe.

30. *Rhyme:* verse as a whole.

31. *'Tis:* rhyme is.

32. *Metre:* his verse as a whole.

32. *King David:* the Biblical king (Book of Samuel) standing for King Charles II (reigned 1660 to 1685) whose sympathies were against the Whigs.

33. *Psalm:* David is supposed to have written some of the psalms in the *Book of Psalms*. Here the psalm stands for the royal command of execution.

35. *Penny Pamphlet:* a cheap pamphlet distributed in the streets.

35. *foil:* to defeat, to frustrate or baffle.

36. *Doeg:* a man from Edom whom Saul placed in charge of his herds or runners (I Sam. 21:7) and who also spied on David's activities. Doeg represents Elkanah Settle (1648–1724), a Whig writer who later replied to Dryden's attack in a poem entitled "Absalom Senior or Achitophel Transposed." Dryden writes in preceding lines that Doeg's poetry was harmless although noisy: "Free from all meaning, whether good or bad, And, in one word, heroically mad."

37. *very:* very same.

[since] thy paintings are so Coarse,
19. *Doeg* [in comparison] to thee *is A Poet*,
though he's the Poet's Horse.

20. *thou dost pull A Double Noose on thy Neck*,
↑
{For Writing Treason,
{and for Writing dull;

21. To die for Faction is a Common evil,
But to be hang'd for Nonsense is the Devil:

Had'st thou [if thou had'st] *express'd the Glories of thy King*,
22. Thy praises had [i.e.would have] been Satire at the best;

23. But thou Hast Shamefully defied the Lord's Anointed:
↑
in Clumsy verse,
↑
{unlick'd,
{unpointed,

Doeg to thee, thy paintings are so Coarse,
A Poet is, though he's the Poet's Horse.
A Double Noose thou on thy Neck dost pull, 40
For Writing Treason, and for Writing dull;
To die for Faction is a Common evil,
But to be hang'd for Nonsense is the Devil:
Had'st thou the Glories of thy King express'd, 44
Thy praises had been Satire at the best;
But thou in Clumsy verse, unlick'd, unpointed,
Hast Shamefully defied the Lord's Anointed:

38. *to thee:* in comparison to thee.

39. *Poet's Horse:* see IH.

42. *Faction:* political party strife.

45. *had been:* would have been.

45. *at the best:* at best.

46. *unlick'd:* new-born bears were reputed to come into the world unformed and to be licked into proper shape by their parents; hence, not presentable, not well-formed.

46. *unpointed:* the verse has not been given "point," force, piquancy, prominence, or distinction; or, more probably, not properly punctuated.

47. *Anointed:* to smear with oil and hence to consecrate or make sacred, a reference to the King, who rules by divine right.

24. I will not rake the Dunghill of thy Crimes,
For who would read thy Life
↑
that reads thy rhymes?

25. But *[let] this be the Doom of King *David's* Foes*,
↕
May all be like the Young-man *Absalom;*

26. And [as] for my Foes *may this be their Blessing*,
↕
{To talk like *Doeg,*
{and to Write like Thee.

I will not rake the Dunghill of thy Crimes,
For who would read thy Life that reads thy rhymes?
But of King *David's* Foes be this the Doom,
May all be like the Young-man *Absalom;*
And for my Foes may this their Blessing be,
To talk like *Doeg*, and to Write like Thee.

49. *would:* wants to.

50. *Doom:* judgment, sentence passed.

51. *Absalom:* third son of David by Maacah (II Sam. 3:3), noted for his beauty. He plotted to seize the throne but was defeated in the woods of Ephraim and killed by three dart shots while his long beautiful hair held him entangled in a tree. Absalom represents James Scott, Duke of Monmouth (1649–1685), son of Charles II and Lucy Waters. Although at first preferred by his father and the people to his brother, the Duke of York (later James II), he became embroiled in the plots of Shaftesbury (Achitophel in this poem, the evil counselor). Vexed by this association with his political opponent, Charles called York back from exile and banished Monmouth in turn to Holland. He came back at Shaftesbury's instigation without his father's permission (in 1679) and proceeded, treasonably, to make a royal march through the west of England seeking the people's favor. He was arrested in 1682, banished again to Holland, and finally beheaded in 1685 after an unsuccessful rebellion against Charles's successor, James II.

Interpretational Hypothesis

Dryden wrote all of the first part of *Absalom and Achitophel,* but the second part was written principally by Nahum Tate; Dryden contributed certain sections, of which this is the most notable. It is not necessary to be familiar with the complicated politics of the time to understand this section, or indeed the whole poem. It is enough to know that it is an allegorical political satire; that Dryden is writing on the side of the King, Charles II, whom he calls here King David, and against the King's enemies, including his illegitimate son, the Duke of Monmouth, here called Absalom; and that Achitophel and Doeg are all Whigs, while the King's party is known as the Tories. Even this much is scarcely necessary if we are familiar with the Biblical story of how King David's beautiful and beloved son, Absalom, rebelled against him. The story has become a symbol of the rebellion, abetted by unscrupulous friends and politicians, of any gifted but wild son against a loving but imperious father. In the hundreds of satirical pamphlets and poems written about the conflict, innumerable minor figures were involved: one of them was Og, or Thomas Shadwell, who was on the side of the King's enemies and therefore one of Dryden's antagonists.

The opening lines inform us that this is the kind of poem in which the author directly addresses the reader. The author assumes the role played by a master of ceremonies in a nightclub or on a television show. He has a direct relation with his readers, and his purpose, as the next few lines tell us, is not to present evidence from which the readers may judge Og, but rather to direct and determine their attitude toward him. It is just the opposite of saying in a loud and enthusiastic voice, "Let's all give the lovely lady a great big hand." Here the poet warns the readers to hold their noses, because the next character is so unsavory that he is properly compared to an enormous barrel of night soil; in London at that time, as in the cities of the Orient today, human excrement was collected at night from slop pails set in front of the doors of the city houses and taken to the farms to be used as fertilizer. The character, Og, is next presented to the readers as rolling from a tavern where treason is hatched. "Treason" was often used then as "Communist" often is today; anybody who was not of the King's party and whom one wished to disparage, one called a traitor. Og rolls for two reasons, first, because a tun of night soil was carried on wheels, and second, because then, as today, when you wanted to indicate the movements of a dissipated drunkard, you spoke of him as "rolling," e.g. "He rolled home at three o'clock in the morning." Dryden then continues this second meaning of "roll" by comparing Og to a sphere, thus referring to his gross fatness. In the next phrase he refers to something else that can be rolled, a barrel of beer or wine. "Liquored" is used in precisely the same way that we say today, "He surely was liquored up." Og then is as full of liquor as a barrel in which the liquor has penetrated into the tiny crevices between the staves and is leaking out. It would be impossible for anybody to have more liquor in him than Og. In line 5 Dryden compares him with a ship (he "sails"). "Goodly" means "fulfilling a function in the most thorough-going fashion possible," and also "considerable in size, quantity, or number." Both meanings are at work. Since Og's function is to be full of liquor, he is "great" because he does a vile thing superbly; he is also physically huge. But why the comparison to a ship? Several explanations seem appropriate. A prime function of a ship is to carry goods; so, Og's primary function is to carry liquor, an interpretation reinforced by "goodly." Another reason is that he has been already represented as in motion, and "sails" continues this image very appropriately, because the steady motion of a rolling barrel is similar to the steady motion of a ship. And both are motions, which, because of the law of inertia, once set going are difficult to control and stop. They have the character of inevitability. The "link" is the final touch to the stage setting, for a link was a boy who at night went ahead of the foot-passenger with a torch to light his way through the dark, filthy, and dangerous streets of seventeenth-century London.

The next line prepares an ironical trap. Line 6 by itself means that there is, after all, something good about the man, "good" used in a minimal meaning of "acceptable." The connection between this line and the preceding statement is "despite" ("with all"). The "for" continues the preparation of the trap. The poet is going to tell us what there is that is good about him. And it turns out that Og is good because whatever in him is not foolish is irresponsibly antisocial. He is "good" because he is so *thoroughly* bad. Today we use the same device when we say of someone we wish to disparage utterly, "At least he's consistent" in whatever stupid or vicious thing he may be guilty of. To emphasize that consistency, the poet introduces a particularly repellent comparison in the next couplet (ll. 8–9). "Matter" is used in the now obsolescent sense, still to be found in country districts, of "pus," the discharge from a festering sore or wound. Hence it is both foul and corrupted, for "corrupted" is here used as in the phrase the "corruption of the flesh," the breakdown and decay of organic material, referring back to the first picture of Og as a tun of night soil.

He is in fact so loathsome that it seems as if the very devils in hell had vomited to furnish batter (material) which when baked (created) became Og. Og, then, is not even like the rest of the descendants of Adam, made from clean clay.

Once we realize this we understand the at first somewhat unclear transition to the next sentence. Since he has been made of something inhuman but has been given the qualities of a human, he curses God for having created him, at least when wine gives him the courage to do so. But such cursing and blasphemy will not bring down the wrath of heaven on his head, because God has already cursed him, that is, damned him. He is unredeemable; nothing can save his soul. Indeed, the poet says, if anybody was ever justified in cursing God (as Job, for example, felt he was) Og is justified. Here again an ironic trap is being prepared. We seem to feel that the speaker has a bit of sympathy for Og. But at once the trap is sprung. The reason for Og's justification in cursing God is that he has a champagne stomach but a beer pocketbook. His paunch is "rich," not only because it is so big but also because it desires rich and expensive food. Thus the apparent justification for Og's blasphemy is overwhelmed by the trivial source of his complaints. Further, Heaven was justified in not giving him the money to satisfy the rich and gross demands of his stomach. Heaven had already experienced what happens when a Jew is made prosperous: he cries out and rebels against his God; he is never satisfied. (All the characters, it must be remembered, are Jews; that is, allegorically, Englishmen.) The prophets of the Old Testament allude thousands of times to this characteristic of the people they are denouncing and warning for their neglect of their religion. The point is made clearer in the next couplet (ll. 16–17): "What would he swell to if he could eat quail and pheasant, since he would rebel against God and King even on a diet of tripe and carrion?" Quail and pheasant are game birds, protected by the English aristocracy for their own pleasure in hunting and eating. Only the rich, therefore, could eat them legally and in abundance. "Swell" is used in two senses. His stomach would swell and his pride and his rebelliousness would swell. Tripe, the lining of the cow's stomach, is a cheap food, as is carrion, rotten meat, in the late seventeenth century often the only meat the poor could get. He was not made rich, then, because God knew he would be rebellious and treasonable even on the worst food. On good food, he would have been absolutely uncontrollable.

The connection between this couplet and the next is obvious, but the connection between the two lines of the couplet (ll. 18–19) is not. What has poverty to do with his not being a poet? If we remember that poets are traditionally and notoriously poor, particularly, as in the seventeenth century, when they were dependent upon the aristocracy, the connection is clear. "Since God made Og poor, it might be expected that He made him a poet, but such is not the case." ("With rev'rence speaking" implies that the speaker does not wish to be thought as presumptuously claiming a knowledge of God's will.) Therefore, although apparently God did not make him a poet, he insists upon trying to be one anyway. The speaker now imagines that even the midwife who officiated at Og's birth warned him against trying to write (l. 23). Her blessing was prophetic, for she was aware of what his chief danger would be. Like a fairy godmother she gave him the negative virtue of being "dull," which at this time meant not merely stupid but actively hating intelligence (l. 21). Dullness was thought to be a kind of intellectual viciousness. She warns him that he will get along well enough and will even be able to indulge safely in all the vices ("roar" means to be a wild-man-about-town), so long as he does not write. She tells him that like most men without brains he has a vigorous constitution ("lasting Make") and was born under physically auspicious stars and other astrological signs ("a strong Nativity"), but that his one danger is writing. He can even eat opium and drink diluted arsenic and live, so long as he doesn't write.

Here a problem arises. Where does the midwife's speech end? Does the "I" in line 28 refer to the midwife or the speaker? It is not easy to decide, and in a sense the midwife's speech can be considered as continuing until the end of the passage. However, whoever speaks from line 28 on has a knowledge not merely of what will constitute his danger—writing—but also that Og has written and continues to write. He even knows the political and literary details of Og's writings, and in the last couplet "my" could hardly refer to "midwife." Presumably the midwife would know only what the danger would be. The most satisfactory hypothesis, then, seems to assume that the midwife's speech ends at line 27, and that what follows serves to confirm her prophecy.

Thus the speaker, resuming his own role, perceives that the midwife's advice was of no use; and he prophesies on his own account that treason, or political opposition to the King, wretchedly set forth in verse, will be the undoing of Og. Perhaps picking up the comparison to a ship in line 5, he tells Og (of course he continues to be heard by the readers and is really speaking to them) that he will be destroyed by poetry, as a ship is destroyed by a rock which it cannot avoid. And he states that not only will poetry destroy his reputation but that it will also hang him. The question in line 32 implies that it is dangerous for Og to attack King David (Charles II) in poetry. Why? "A psalm of his will surely be thy last." The Biblical David wrote the Psalms, at least according to a tradition accepted at that time. The psalm was his normal form of utterance. It is true that Charles did not write poetry, but as King he too had a normal form of literary utterance, the royal command. Such a command, which would be the "last" for Og, would of course be an order to hang him.

Continuing the subject of Og's attacking his enemies in verse, the speaker now warns him against attacking those of less importance than the King. Even the ordinary pamphleteer who writes in prose and sells his wares for a penny (anywhere from five to fifteen cents in our currency) can defeat Og in the pamphlet war and show up his stupidity. The connection between this couplet and the preceding is "even." "It's dangerous for you to attack the King; it's even dangerous for you to attack a political literary hack." The same connection works for the next series of couplets. "Even Doeg is better than you are." This places Doeg, of course, at an even lower level than the penny pamphleteer. And no wonder, for God *made* Doeg to be laughed at. Even Doeg, then, is more talented than Og in everything that Og tries to do. Compared to Og, Doeg is a poet, since Og's "paintings" (i.e. the poetic equivalent of paintings: description and character portrayal) are so badly done. Even so, Doeg is not a real poet; he's only the poet's horse. What is a poet's horse? Could it be Pegasus, the winged horse who carried poets to the heaven of poetic inspiration? But this notion seems odd here; there is nothing to indicate that the speaker wishes us to think of Doeg as in any way inspired. Such a notion would be inconsistent with Doeg's status, which is even below that of the penny-pamphleteer. It seems best, then, to reject the possibility of a reference to Pegasus. It is necessary, therefore, to break the question into two questions: (1) Why is Doeg a horse? (2) Why is he a *poet's* horse? As for (1), since Doeg is given the credit for having at least more brains than Og, and since the speaker wishes to denigrate Doeg because he also is an enemy of the King, and since the more he denigrates Doeg, the worse Og seems, by calling Doeg a horse, the poet implies that even a horse is better than Og. As for (2), a poet's horse is something a poet rides, exploits, makes use of. The suggestion seems to be, then, that Doeg is a kind of ghost writer.

The speaker now goes back to the suggestion in line 32 and line 34. Og will end by hanging, not just for treason but also for writing so abominably. The first (writing treason causes death for reasons of faction or adherence to a political party) is common enough, but what could be worse than being hanged for sheer silliness? Dullness bad enough to be hanged for is really the abyss of dullness, the hell of dullness. The return in the next two couplets (ll. 44–47) to Og's disloyal writing against the King raises a question of connection. The link seems to be: "Yet, in spite of all this, you wrote against the King." If Og had written on the King's side, it would not have helped him much, for he writes so badly that it would have seemed like an attack against the King. (The suggestion is that it would have been impossible to believe that anyone so stupid, gross, and talentless would be on the King's side and that therefore praise from such a person would have been misunderstood and taken for satire.) But Og did even worse than writing so badly that his work as an author was misunderstood; he wrote against the King, and everybody, since it came from such a person, knew what he meant. His verse was so incorrect, so unrevised, unedited, unpolished (all these are involved in "unlickt," which refers to the old legend that when a bear is born it is shapeless and has to be licked into shape by its mother) and even so badly punctuated ("pointed") that the defiance of the King was shockingly offensive. The King is called the "Lord's anointed" because at David's coronation he was anointed with holy oil by Samuel, thus indicating that it was God's will that he be King. (The practice was revived by the kings of western Europe and is part of the coronation ritual of the English monarchs to this day.) The implication is that a king is holy because he has been selected for his position by God. To attack him, therefore, is to attack and defy God; as we were told in line 11, Og is a man who curses God.

Suddenly the speaker breaks off from his description of Og's misdeeds, which he compares to a dunghill. After all, to read his poetry is sickening enough. Who, having done that, would want to read the whole story of his life? The connection with the two final couplets (ll. 50–54) is: "I won't say anything more, but let this be my warning to you." May all the King's foes suffer the fate of Absalom, who was defeated in his rebellion against the King when he was caught in a tree by his own hair and killed. That is, may the King's foes be destroyed by their own wicked characteristics. As for my foes (implying that whoever is the enemy of the King is my enemy too), I will give them a blessing, but of course the blessing one gives one's foes is a curse. "May this be the *best* thing that happens to you." May their conversation be as silly as Doeg's (whose ideas, we have seen, insofar as he had any, have been obtained from somebody else) and may their writing be as bad as Og's.

Poor Og! Poor Shadwell! By combining abuse with a wit that makes the abuse palatable and justifies it, Dryden blackened his appearance, his habits, his intelligence, his ability, his patriotism, and even, cruellest of all, his ability to be politically dangerous. And Dryden was successful, for Shadwell became a kind of symbol or ideal of Dullness in the ensuing centuries. Only recently has modern scholarship shown that the real Shadwell was far more gifted as a writer than anyone, judging by Dryden's "Character of Og," would ever have guessed.

1. I wonder do you feel to-day
↑
As I have felt
↑
since, We sat down on the grass, [in order] to stray In spirit better through the land,
↑ ↑
hand in hand, This morn of {Rome / and May?

[As] For me,
2. I touched a thought, I know,
↑
[which] Has tantalized me many times, for rhymes
↑ ↑
(Like turns of thread To catch at and let go.
↑
[that] the spiders throw Mocking across our path)

ROBERT BROWNING
(1812–1889)

Two in the Campagna

I

I wonder do you feel to-day
  As I have felt since, hand in hand,
We sat down on the grass, to stray
  In spirit better through the land,
This morn of Rome and May?

II

For me, I touched a thought, I know,
  Has tantalized me many times,
(Like turns of thread the spiders throw
  Mocking across our path) for rhymes
To catch at and let go.

3. *to:* in order to.

8. *turns:* single rounds, as of a coiled twine or tape.

3. Help me to hold it!

4. First it left The yellowing fennel,
↑
{run to seed There,
{branching from the brickwork's cleft,
↕
Some old tomb's ruin:

5. yonder weed Took up the floating weft,
↑
Where one small orange cup amassed Five beetles,—
↕
they grope Among the honey-meal:
↑
blind and green

6. and last, *I traced it Everywhere on the grassy slope*.

III

Help me to hold it! First it left
  The yellowing fennel, run to seed
There, branching from the brickwork's cleft,
  Some old tomb's ruin: yonder weed
Took up the floating weft,

IV

Where one small orange cup amassed
  Five beetles,—blind and green they grope
Among the honey-meal: and last,
  Everywhere on the grassy slope
I traced it. Hold it fast!

11. *it:* the thought.

12. *fennel:* a very common field plant.

12. *run:* gone.

13. *brickwork's cleft:* break in a bricked wall.

15. *weft:* the woof or filling yarn on a loom, but more generally a tangled, floating thread.

16. *amassed:* collected.

18. *honey-meal:* the pollen.

20. *it:* the thought.

7. Hold it fast!

↑

The champaign with its endless fleece Of feathery grasses everywhere!
Silence and passion,
joy and peace,
An everlasting wash of air—

↕

Rome's ghost since her [Rome's] decease.
Such life here, through such lengths of hours,
Such miracles

↑

performed in play,
Such primal naked forms of flowers,
Such letting nature have her way

↑

While heaven looks from its towers!

8. How say you?

9. Let us, <O my dove,>
Let us be unashamed of soul,

↑

As earth lies bare to heaven above!

V

The champaign with its endless fleece
  Of feathery grasses everywhere!
Silence and passion, joy and peace,
  An everlasting wash of air—
Rome's ghost since her decease.

VI

Such life here, through such lengths of hours,
  Such miracles performed in play,
Such primal naked forms of flowers,
  Such letting nature have her way
While heaven looks from its towers!

VII

How say you? Let us, O my dove,
  Let us be unashamed of soul,
As earth lies bare to heaven above!

21. *champaign:* countryside.

24. *wash:* flow, air thought of as a liquid washing the countryside.

25. *her:* Rome's.

25. *decease:* death.

28. *primal:* original, primeval.

10. How is it under our control To love or not to love?

11. I would that you were all to me,
↕
You that are {just so much, no more.
Nor yours nor mine,
nor slave nor free!

12. Where does the fault lie?

13. What [is] the core O' the wound, since wound [it] must be?

14. I would I could {adopt your will,
See with your eyes,
and set my heart Beating by yours,
and drink my fill At your soul's springs,—
↑
your part [being] my part In life, for good and ill.

How is it under our control
To love or not to love?

VIII

I would that you were all to me,
You that are just so much, no more.
Nor yours nor mine, nor slave nor free!
Where does the fault lie? What the core
O' the wound, since wound must be?

IX

I would I could adopt your will,
See with your eyes, and set my heart
Beating by yours, and drink my fill
At your soul's springs,—your part my part
In life, for good and ill.

44. *part:* role.

15. No. I { yearn upward,
touch you close,
Then stand away.

16. I { kiss your cheek,
Catch your soul's warmth,—

17. I { pluck the rose
And love it more than tongue can speak—

18. Then the good minute goes.

19. Already how am I so far Out of that minute?

20. Must I *Still go Onward*,
↑
{ like the thistle-ball,
[with] no bar,
Fixed by no friendly star?
whenever light winds blow,

x

No. I yearn upward, touch you close,
  Then stand away. I kiss your cheek,
Catch your soul's warmth,—I pluck the rose 48
  And love it more than tongue can speak—
Then the good minute goes.

xi

Already how am I so far
  Out of that minute? Must I go 52
Still like the thistle-ball, no bar,
  Onward, whenever light winds blow,
Fixed by no friendly star?

53. *Still:* always.

53. *like the thistle-ball:* i.e. floating on the wind.

53. *bar:* obstruction.

21. Just when I seemed about to learn!

22. Where is the thread now? Off again!

23. The old trick!

24. Only I discern— { Infinite passion,
and the pain Of finite hearts that yearn.

XII

Just when I seemed about to learn!
  Where is the thread now? Off again!
The old trick! Only I discern—
  Infinite passion, and the pain
Of finite hearts that yearn.

57. *thread:* the thought of line 6.

58. *discern:* perceive, distinguish.

Interpretational Hypothesis

The title gives us the setting and the number of people involved. The Campagna is the great and, in the mid-nineteenth century, empty plain around Rome, notable for its beauty and its wildness. The title tells us that the "I" in the first line indicates that one person is speaking to the other, "you." Shortly before the speaker begins, the two lovers ("hand in hand") have sat down on the grass. Their purpose in thus halting in their walk or wandering has been to satisfy their feeling that to wander in imagination ("in spirit") would be more rewarding than physical movement through the Campagna on this Roman May morning. This seems an odd idea, until we remember that bodily activity is to a certain extent an impediment to intellectual-emotional activity, the minimum meaning that may be given to "spirit" at this point in the poem. For example, the better-run art museums place chairs and benches in front of their greatest works of art, so that visitors may concentrate exclusively on the paintings and be free from the subtle half-conscious strain of standing. Thus the speaker introduces into the poem a conflict between body and spirit. If this hypothesis is correct, that conflict will be one of the main themes of the poem. The effect on the speaker has been to start in him a special strain of feeling, and he wonders if the girl or woman with him shares that feeling. ("Hand in hand" suggests the probability of two sexes. Since the speaker appears to be originating the action, the traditional behavior proper to the masculine role, it seems best to hypothesize that the speaker is a man, until evidence to the contrary is forthcoming.) Hence, it follows that he does not know if the girl shares his feeling. Again, from this it seems reasonable to hypothesize that one of the themes of the poem will be the inescapable barriers to perfect emotional communication between two people.

In stanza II the speaker goes on to explain what this feeling was ("For me" means "As for me"). A thought has come to his mind which has often tantalized him. Here he introduces a parenthetical explanation of what he means by "tantalize." Anyone who has walked in the countryside knows that he is continually encountering single strands of thread spun by spiders from bush to bush, or tree to tree, across the path he is following. But why are spiders "mocking" the passer-by? The thread is a barrier and yet is not a barrier, it is so weak. You feel it across your face or an arm, but it is so slight that you are not absolutely sure that you have encountered it. Above all, it cannot be easily anticipated or grasped and detached when you have struck it. The tenor to this vehicle is the "thought." It has tantalized the speaker because the "thought" and the spider thread are connected by the fact that both are encountered by accident, without prediction or anticipation or willing, and that when either is felt it cannot be seized upon and held, or remembered. The effect of this "thought" on the speaker, who is now revealed as a poet, is that rhymes (metaphorically compared with hands or instruments, or his power of rhyming or composing poetry) want to catch hold of the idea, examine it, and then let it go, just as his hands want to catch hold of the ungraspable spider web, examine it, and then let it go. He wants to grasp the thought, examine it, and then forget about it. The full form of the sentence is: "As for me, I touched a thought, which I am familiar with and which has tantalized me many times, and which would be just the thing to be grasped and then let go in rhymes." "For" (l. 9) is purposive, as in "apples for eating."

In stanza III "Help me to hold it!" is more than a simple request for aid. First, he wants now to keep the "thought" long enough to understand it. Second, if the girl can help him to hold the idea, then she can share it. So the request is really a wish that full communication of thought and feeling be established between them, since, as stanza I told us, the poet is not sure that such a sharing does exist. In stanzas III and IV the speaker describes the "thought" as if it were a spider thread, and at the same time shows its development in his mind. It first came to him as he was looking at the fennel, already turning yellow from the heat of a Roman May. The fennel has already stopped flowering, and is dying, its seed pods having been formed. It is rooted in a cleft or crevice of a brick wall or half-ruined structure, the remains of an old tomb, of which the Campagna has thousands. Next, the thought continued growing in his mind as his eye moved to a weed which has a small orange flower crowded with five beetles. Blind, or, probably, thoughtlessly, the beetles are pushing about in the flower's pollen. Pollen is here compared to ground wheat, or meal, a coarser form of flour, and to the beetles this pollen is a food as sweet and desirable as honey. Finally, the "thought" is to be found everywhere on the grassy slope. "Hold it fast!" implies that he has now made the thought clear to himself and that communication between the two can be established. But what has he made clear? The "thought" is not immediately explained. We must wait. First, however, the thought this time has not eluded him. He sees it everywhere. He realizes what inspired it: as it moves from the dying but fruitful fennel, growing out of the tomb, to the weed flower filled with greedy beetles, he sees everywhere the vitality of nature springing out of the ruins of man's activities. Thus a homogeneity, a unity is given to the landscape.

In stanzas V and VI the syntactical material is not organized into sentences. The speaker gives us a series of short phrases, each, for the most part, consisting of a noun or substantive with modifying dependents. Thus is represented an excitement so intense that the normal structure of speaking is abandoned. These phrases consist of indications of what he sees and of how his thought gives meaning to these sights. Thus his "thought" begins to come clear. The plain is unified by its covering of feathery grasses, like the wool of a fleece. Everywhere there is both silence and in the vitality of nature, passion, or life. There is joy in the landscape but also peace, the vitality of growth and life and complete satisfaction. There is a steady current or wave of air. This further contributes to the unity of the landscape. But why is that "wash" of air called the ghost of Rome? A ghost is one name for the haunting memory of something that no longer exists. Since the air is "everlasting" it is eternal like Rome itself. Thus the landscape is unified by the memory of Rome. This picks up, of course, the "old tomb's ruin" of line 14.

In stanza VI the implications of V are spelled out. What impresses him, what his "thought" consists of, is the sense of the continuity of life over vast lengths of time; the sense of the absolute ease with which the miracles of nature, such as a plant growing out of brick, are performed, but performed in play, without purpose or moral significance; the sense that the flowers have the "primal" forms they had when they were created and that they are "naked" forms, innocently shameless. Nothing interferes with the energy and vitality and continuity and renewal of nature (all these qualities have been implied in the previous lines). Even Heaven doesn't interfere. This seems odd, and is half-humorous in its statement. But Heaven (or God) interferes when something is going wrong or bad. Its interference is moral. Hence this world of the Campagna is a kind of Paradise where the problems of good and evil do not arise, as well as a place where the past (the tombs and the ghost of Rome) is of no consequence. Thus in the Campagna on this May morning, the poet has found a symbol for his "thought": this is a world of absolute spontaneity, homogeneity, and freedom, and his "thought" is that these qualities are valuable as a guide to conducting one's life.

Thus, in stanza VII, he at once asks his beloved what she thinks of such an attitude, and to make his attitude unequivocal, he applies it to their situation. Calling her his dove, a creature of the natural world and a symbol of innocence, he insists ("Let us" is repeated) that they too should be absolutely innocent, unshamed, and spontaneous, that these values should rule their souls. Soul is, as usual, a vague word, but here it is consistent with the poem to define it as that aspect of personality which determines what values we should live by. We should have, he says, the same relation to Heaven that the Campagna does. Should we live this way, innocent, free, ignorant of the past, and spontaneous like nature, Heaven will no more interfere with us than it does with the world of the Campagna. The connection between this and the next statement can best be thought of as "after all." That is, this is why we should act this way, since, after all, love is not an emotion which is really under our control. We should follow the way of life symbolized by the Campagna, and thus create the right emotional condition in which love might flourish.

The statement in line 36 implies, however, that the girl is *not* everything to the speaker, as she would have to be were they to organize their lives entirely around love by imitating the Campagna, i.e. there are limits to the importance she has for him. Thus the complete communication which he was attempting to achieve, and which seemed to be on the point of arriving in stanza VII, not only does not occur but is rejected as impossible. She does not belong completely to herself or to him. She is neither under the complete control of some power not within herself, nor is she wholly free from the influence of such a power. She cannot give herself completely, nor withhold herself entirely. Thus she may give the impression that she can surrender herself to perfect communication, but she is, in fact, unable to do so. To perfect communication there is, then, some impediment. This idea makes more explicit the suggestion in the first stanza that there are impediments to the free activity of the spirit. "Fault" may be thought of as equivalent to "guilt," as in "Whose fault is it?" but since the next metaphor, which refers to the failure of communication as a wound, is physical, "fault" may here have the sense of a geological fault, an internal weakness rather than a guilt. This seems to be more probable, since the failure of perfect communication is thought of as a wound upon the personality, something, then, for which the individual is not responsible, something, perhaps, necessarily in the nature of things. This problem should be resolved in the course of the poem.

"To adopt your will" means in the context of the poem, to enter into a state of perfect communication with another, thus achieving the homogeneity or unity and spontaneity of the Campagna. He wishes that he might become part of her in a kind of fusing of two personalities through the process of identification of himself with her, not only morally ("will") and physically ("eyes" and "heart") but spiritually. He wishes to do what he has perceived that she cannot (stanza VIII). The sense of "soul" seems consistent with that suggested for the word in line 32. Thus, whether for good or bad, her part in life would be his. This interpretation is consistent with the moral innocence or indifference of the Campagna, indicated by the noninterference by Heaven (l. 30) and applied to the lovers (l. 33).

But (stanza X) it is impossible. The fault (l. 39) is in him as well as in her. The speaker may long for this higher state; he may even achieve it momentarily by embracing her; but then he stands away. A barrier is perceived, the fault is experienced, the wound is felt. Though he may kiss her and thus catch for a moment what he wants, the sense of complete communication with her, the life of her soul, it is like picking a rose. His love of the flower is so intense that it is beyond speech. But that feeling lasts only a minute and is gone.

In fact, in stanza XI, he is already a long way from that "good minute" which arrived when he realized that his "thought" was symbolized in the Campagna and that it might be applied to themselves (stanzas VI and VII). He compares himself to a bit of thistledown, to which there is no barrier (i.e. nothing to hold it back from wandering), without any will of its own, blown onward whenever there is a light wind. The winds are the environment of the thistle-ball. So the circumstances of life are the environment of the feelings of the speaker. He is the will-less victim of them, without the capacity to control them. The metaphor now shifts, pivoting on "winds," which propel ships as well as thistledown. In navigation, to be fixed by a star is to ascertain one's position by determining the star's place in the heavens. But "star" is also a metaphor for something of supreme value which guides us through life. Thus the tenor is that he will never be able to relate himself to life and find something that will always guide him. He is saying, "Must I never be able to find an answer to all my questionings—an answer which will give my life final meaning and purpose?" He had thought that the grasping of the "thought" and its application to themselves would be such a "star."

Just as he seemed to be about to learn that final purpose and meaning in emotional communication with his beloved, the thread disappeared. That thread, as we have seen, was the idea of a completely satisfactory life lived in innocence, spontaneity, and homogeneous fusion with another person. But now the "thought" is off again. He no longer can remember what it was, so far is he now out of that minute. Circumstances have played the same old trick on him. That is, the failure to hang onto the thought does not come from any weakness of his own but from the circumstances of his environment. (A trick is played upon an individual by somebody else.) All that he has left of the experience is the realization that "finite hearts," that is, the emotions of human beings frustrated by the limitations of the human environment, are capable of yearning for an emotional life with no such limitations, a life of infinite exaltation and passion. The pain of human life comes from the contrast between, on the one hand, our capacity to have the idea of perfect, innocent, spontaneous, and limitless emotional gratification, absolute harmonization with the environment, and complete identification with the beloved, and even to experience it for a moment; and, on the other hand, our inability to fix and stabilize such an ideal in our lives.

The poem, in short, dramatizes how our failure to achieve perfect communication with another, even a beloved, is caused by our general inability to achieve any state of complete and perfect fulfillment, except in lucky, accidental, and evanescent moments which are gone as soon as they come.

1. <My God,>
I heard this day, That none doth build a stately habitation,
↑
But he that means to dwell therein.

2. What house* {hath there been, / Or can [there] be,} more stately*,
↑
than *Man is*?
↑
[in comparison] to whose creation All things are in decay.

3. For Man is {ev'ry thing, / And more:

4. He is {a tree, yet bears more fruit; / A beast, yet is, or should be more [than a beast]:

5. *we only bring Reason and speech*.

6. Parrots may thank us,
if they are not mute,

GEORGE HERBERT (1593–1633)

Man

My God, I heard this day,
That none doth build a stately habitation,
But he that means to dwell therein.
What house more stately hath there been,
Or can be, than is Man? to whose creation
All things are in decay.

For Man is ev'ry thing,
And more: He is a tree, yet bears more fruit;
A beast, yet is, or should be more:
Reason and speech we only bring.
Parrots may thank us, if they are not mute,

2. *none:* nobody.
3. *But he that:* except the one who.
3. *therein:* in that.
5. *to whose creation:* in comparison to whose creation.
6. *All things:* all non-human things.
9. *more:* better than a beast.

7. They go upon the score.

8. Man is { all symmetry,
Full of proportions,
↑
{ one limb to another,
And all [parts] to all the world besides:

9. Each part may call the furthest [part], brother:
For { head *hath private amity with foot*,
And both [have private amity] with moons and tides.

10. Nothing hath got so far,
But Man hath { caught
and kept it, } as his prey.

11. His eyes dismount the highest star:

12. He is *all the sphere in little*.

13. Herbs gladly cure our flesh;
because that they Find their acquaintance there.

They go upon the score.

Man is all symmetry,
Full of proportions, one limb to another,
And all to all the world besides:
Each part may call the furthest, brother:
For head with foot hath private amity,
And both with moons and tides.

Nothing hath got so far,
But Man hath caught and kept it, as his prey.
His eyes dismount the highest star:
He is in little all the sphere.
Herbs gladly cure our flesh; because that they
Find their acquaintance there.

14. *proportions:* satisfying harmonic relationships.

17. *private amity:* significant and special, therefore friendly and mutually agreeable relations.

18. *moons:* phases of the moon.

19. *got:* traveled away from man.

20. *But Man hath caught it:* which man has not caught.

21. *dismount:* to take out of their setting; see IH.

22. *in little:* in miniature.

22. *sphere:* universe.

23. *because that:* because.

24. *their acquaintance:* correspondence, resemblance.

14. *the winds do blow For us*,
The earth doth rest [for us],
heav'n [doth] move [for us],
and fountains flow [for us].

15. *we see Nothing*, but [that which] means our good,
↑
[either] As our *delight*,
or as our *treasure:*

16. The whole [universe] is, either our cupboard of food,
Or [our] cabinet of *pleasure*.

17. The stars have us to bed;
Night draws the curtain,
↑
which the sun withdraws;
Music and light attend our head.

18. *All things are kind
unto our *flesh**
↑
In their *descent* and *being;*
to our *mind*
↑
In their *ascent* and *cause*.

For us the winds do blow,
The earth doth rest, heav'n move, and fountains flow.
Nothing we see, but means our good,
As our *delight*, or as our *treasure:*
The whole is, either our cupboard of food,
Or cabinet of *pleasure*.

The stars have us to bed;
Night draws the curtain, which the sun withdraws;
Music and light attend our head.
All things unto our *flesh* are kind
In their *descent* and *being*; to our *mind*
In their *ascent* and *cause*.

27. *Nothing . . . good:* we see nothing which does not intend to help us.

29–30. *cupboard . . . pleasure:* things which are either useful or ornamental.

31. *have:* to conduct; see IH.

33. *attend:* to wait upon.

34. *kind:* (1) friendly; (2) similar, related, akin to.

35. *descent and being:* see IH.

36. *ascent and cause:* see IH.

19. Each thing is full of duty.[:]
↑
Waters { united are [for] our navigation;
Distinguished, [are for] our habitation;
Below, [are for] our drink;
above, [are for] our meat; }
Both [i.e. waters from both places] [are for] our cleanliness.

20. Hath one such beauty?
Then how are all things neat?

21. More servants wait on Man,
↑
Then he'll take notice of:

22. in ev'ry path He treads down that
↑
which doth befriend him,
↑
When sickness makes him pale and wan.

23. <Oh mighty love!>
Man { is one world,
and hath Another to attend him. }

Each thing is full of duty.
Waters united are our navigation;
Distinguished, our habitation;
Below, our drink; above, our meat;
Both are our cleanliness. Hath one such beauty?
Then how are all things neat?

More servants wait on Man,
Then he'll take notice of: in ev'ry path
He treads down that which doth befriend him,
When sickness makes him pale and wan.
Oh mighty love! Man is one world, and hath
Another to attend him.

38. *Waters united:* in oceans and other large bodies.

38. *are our navigation:* are for our navigation.

39. *Distinguished:* bodies of water are separated from each other by land upon which we dwell.

40. [*waters*] *Below:* in wells.

40. [*waters*] *above:* rain.

40. *meat:* food, i.e. they water the fields.

41. *Both:* waters from both places, heaven and earth.

41. *one:* one thing, i.e. water.

43. *wait on:* serve.

44. *Then:* than.

45. *that which:* i.e. herbs and medicines.

47. *mighty love:* God.

Since then, <my God,> thou hast *built So brave a Palace*;
24. O dwell in it,
[so] That it [Palace, i.e. man] may dwell with thee at last!

25. Till then, afford us so much wit,
↑ ⎧ we may serve thee,
That, ⎨ ↑
⎪ as the world serves us,
⎩ And both [we and the world may] *be thy servants*.

Since then, my God, thou hast
So brave a Palace built; O dwell in it,
That it may dwell with thee at last!
Till then, afford us so much wit, **52**
That, as the world serves us, we may serve thee,
And both thy servants be.

50. *brave:* beautiful.
50. *Palace, it:* man.
52. *afford:* give us, provide us with.
52. *wit:* intelligence, understanding.
53. *as:* in the same way, just as.
54. *both:* both the natural world and man.

Interpretational Hypothesis

The poem opens with an address to Deity. It seems to be in the form of a prayer; but the casualness of the next phrase, "I heard this day," and the generalization in the following clause, "No one builds a magnificent residence unless he intends to live in it," indicates that this is neither a public prayer (Common Prayer) nor a private prayer, but a Meditation. A Meditation is "The continuous application of the mind to the contemplation of some religious truth, mystery, or object of reverence, as a devotional exercise," and thus, "A discourse, written or spoken, of a meditative character." But the generalization is presented as hearsay, not as absolute truth. We may expect an informal meditation, one without a conventional pattern. Anything may be said, but if it is some kind of meditation, we may hypothesize that a religious truth will be arrived at.

The question asked in the next sentence, implying that the stateliest possible house is man himself, establishes "house" as the vehicle of a metaphor, the tenor being "man," and the connection being "something to live in." But who has created man and who is to live in the house that is man? To this question we must await an answer. The stanza concludes by asserting that in comparison with man everything else is decaying, or moving toward death. But why is not man also moving toward decay and death? We are thus faced with another question: How can man be so superior to the rest of nature that he does not decay?

"For" (l. 7) implies that the sentence which it introduces is the answer to this last question, presented in the form of an abstract proposition supported by data. Man is everything; that is, he is a tree and a beast, representative examples of the non-human organic worlds, the kingdoms of plants and of animals. Each kingdom is introduced in the order of its distance from man, beginning with the most distant. Thus, by implication, man has the qualities of each created thing plus additional qualities unique to himself. Like a tree, he bears fruit (his ability to bring things into the world which otherwise would not be there). "More" may be interpreted not only quantitatively (in the sense that man has a longer creative life than a tree; i.e. he produces all the year round and perhaps lives longer), but also qualitatively (man bears more varied kinds of fruit than does a single tree). In the same way he is more than a beast, having a beast's qualities and yet something unique to himself. But why the doubt expressed in "or should be more" (l. 9)? The implication is that man can sink to the level of a beast. Only man has reason and speech, something which differentiates him always from the beast, though there are men who behave irrationally and misuse or even forget speech. Why "bring"? To carry out the idea of "bears" (l. 8), or "carries into," of bringing something to the created world which otherwise would not be there. The poem now descends to the next level of evidence, a specific case to prove the difference between man and beast. Parrots can talk only because of men's speech. Thus "they go upon the score." "Score" means tally-sheet or stick on which an innkeeper kept his customer's account or reckoning. When presented to him, the customer must pay according to what the "score" states. That is, the "score" controls his behavior. Thus parrots may speak only according to the directions or control we present to them. In speaking, they have no power of independent action. They can no more speak as they will than a customer can pay according to his whim.

The next stanza begins, like the second, with another general statement asserting man's excellence or stateliness. If the pattern of the poem continues, supporting evidence will continue to be produced. Our use of "symmetry" is more limited than the seventeenth century's; to us it generally means that one half of an object, such as a building, is a mirror reflection of the other half. But the word was once more general, referring to a "mutual relation of parts in respect of magnitude and position; relative measurement and arrangement of parts; proportion" (OED). In man, then, every limb of his body is related in mathematically expressible terms to every other limb. Furthermore, the body as a whole has symmetrical and proportional relationships to the entire created universe (l. 15). This statement is based on the old idea that the microcosm or little world of man repeats in organization and activity the macrocosm or great world of the universe which God has created. In the next three lines the idea of lines 13–15 is repeated in new terms. A metaphor of human relationships is employed, first on the private or familial level, then on the level of the relationship of the family to the total human society. Every part of the body may call even that part most distant from itself, "Brother." The reason is that even the two extremes of the body, the head and the foot, have a "*private* amity" with each other, that is, brotherhood, since both are part of the same organism and microcosm. Furthermore, since both are related in the same way with moons and tides, that is, have a *public* amity or natural alliance and relationship with elements of the macrocosm, they are therefore related to each other.

Stanza 4 (ll. 19–20) continues the pattern with another general statement or reason for man's excellence, followed by supporting evidence. The statement is presented in metaphorical form. Man as a hunter has so successfully pursued and captured the things of the macrocosm that nothing is too remote to be his proper prey. "Hunter" is the vehicle, and the tenor is man's reason and intellectual control. The tenor of "prey" is the structure and significance of the macrocosm. Thus man can abstract intellectually ("dismount") the highest star, that is, figuratively, take it out of the sky, turn it around in his mind, and comprehend the laws of its movements. And he can do this because (l. 22) of the microcosm-macrocosm relation. He is a miniature version of the universe. Thus, to be more specific, naturally growing plants, or herbs, are happy to cure our illnesses, the reason being that they find their physico-chemical correspondences ("their acquaintance") in our bodies.

But this introduces a new idea. So far (ll. 1–22) man has been likened to the rest of nature, from which he may be distinguished only by his superior creativity. This line of thought is concluded by the generalization, "He is in little all the sphere." But the "gladly" suggests a willing subservience of the non-human world to the human. Stanza 5 continues and develops this new idea. Winds blow, the earth stands still at the center of the created universe, the heavens rotate around the earth, and springs flow with water. Everything exists for man's sake, either for his pleasure or for his use. The whole universe is like a piece of furniture ("cupboard" or "cabinet") used for storing either useful things, as food, or beautiful things for pleasure.

Stanza 6 continues the idea that the things in the universe have the relationship to us of servant to master. Thus the stars are like chamberlains or personal body-servants who light us to our beds with their candlelike flames. Night, another chamberlain, draws the curtains around the bed, and the sun, still another, draws them back again in the morning. The metaphor is continued in line 33, music and light also being servants. They attend our heads, for music comforts us and light makes the world visible for our pleasure and profit. The next lines (ll. 34–36) present problems. The speaker makes two statements: (1) When we consider all things in terms of their descent and being, we perceive that they are kind to our bodies; and (2) When we consider all things in terms of their ascent and cause, we perceive that they are kind to our minds. There are two possible senses of "kind": "related to by belonging to the same category" and "generous and gentle." The two statements are built around three antitheses and one identity (ascent-descent, being-cause, bodies-minds; kind-kind). The double possibility of "kind" creates two possible propositions for the whole sentence. It would seem, then, that the speaker is making the following statements. (1) All things are in the same category as our bodies because both things and our bodies have been created by God. However, since these other things are generous and gentle to us and wait upon us gladly, they are (in their actual state of being) in a category different from our bodies'. (2) All things are in a category different from that of our minds because in terms of their distance from God ("ascent") they are less than our minds and thus ought to serve us. However, in terms of their ultimate cause, God (the Creator of everything), they are in the same category as that of our minds. The real antithesis lies within each half of the statement. We may, then, supply "and" or "moreover." The implications of these statements then, are: Since all things in terms of their creation and ultimate cause are in the same category as our bodies and minds, they feel an affinity with us. Hence they serve us gladly. On the other hand, in terms of their place in nature and their distance from God, they are in a different category from ours and a less valuable one. Hence they ought to be our subordinates and servants. They are willingly subservient because of their affinity to us, but they also ought to be subservient because of their difference from us.

Consequently, in the next stanza, the first line (l. 37) states that it is the duty of all things to serve us, in whatever condition they may be found. Thus where two bodies of water flow together, water serves as a means whereby we can sail from one place to another. Where two bodies of water are separated, the absence of water serves as a means to provide us a place to live. We drink the water which is found in streams and pools; and the water from above, the rain, by aiding the growth of the edible products of nature, provides our food. ("Meat" is here used in the old sense of all food.) If only one thing (water) has such beauty, is it not wondrous that all things are "neat" (that is, put or kept in good order, perfectly adapted for their function)? Thus the notions of use and beauty introduced in the previous stanzas are here combined. (If the idea had been fully presented the sentence might read, "If one thing has such beauty, isn't it amazing that all things are beautiful." By substituting "neat" for "beauty," the speaker says, "If one thing is so beautiful [and neat], then all things are [beautiful and] neat.")

The superiority of man has now been amply demonstrated; but he is even greater than we have yet been informed. Man has so many servants that he does not even bother to notice them all. Indeed he is even destructive of his natural friends and servants, such as herbs which aid him when he is sick. (In modern punctuation the comma after "him" would indicate that the following clause is nonrestrictive and therefore modifies "treads," but this usage has been established, and not universally, only in the past seventy-five years.) Hence the love which has created man is "mighty." Great as is God's love for all created things, his love for man is so much greater that man is permitted to destroy even what God has created. Hence the progressive sundering between man and nature, begun with "man is everything, and more," now reaches its climax. In the created universe there are two worlds. It is not a simple case of correspondence between them. Although that correspondence exists, it is more than that. The two worlds are different in kind. First, the human world is more creative; second, the natural world provides a beautiful setting and is in continuous service to the human; third, man can even be destructive to the natural world because of its superabundance of attendants. Hence the force of the last line and a half of this stanza is that the natural world is not merely coexistent with man; it exists to attend him. It exists only because man exists. Man is the prior and necessary condition for the existence of nature. Man is not merely God's prime concern but his only one.

Hence the speaker can with confidence appeal to God to dwell in the palace, man himself, the stately habitation (of l. 2) that He has, the speaker now comprehends, created. This answers our first question, "Who has created man and who is to live in the house that is man?" And our next question ("How can man be so superior to the rest of nature?") is also answered, both implicitly and explicitly. Man is superior to nature because nature does not exist in its own right, but only to serve man, whose ultimate destiny is to dwell with God, if only God will dwell within him. That is, "The builder dwells in the house that he built" is the vehicle for "God's Grace descends upon the Human Soul." Thus may man be immortal and free from nature's decay, and the final problem of the second question is resolved. But having thus sundered man from nature, the speaker now restores the relationship. Until we enter the immortal world, we must live in the natural world. To live in it with wit (i.e. with intelligence), we must recognize that we are to God as the world is to us. Thus although nature was created to serve us, we are created to serve God. In that sense, both nature and man are equally servants to God. Great as the distance is between man and nature, the distance between man and God is so great that, from the Divine perspective, both man and nature are at one level. Thus the speaker, having given the most splendid possible conception of man's place in nature, saves logically himself from pride by returning from logical argument and demonstration to prayer and humility. The structure of the poem is argument inside of informal meditation, not a continuous application of the mind to the contemplation of some religious truth, but rather the discovery of a religious truth by the analysis of a truism. By an intellectual process, the speaker humbles the intellect and thus dramatizes how an individual may use all his intellectual resources to arrive at a profound but willing and joyous abasement before the Deity.

1. Lo! where the rosy-bosom'd Hours, { appear,
Disclose the long-expecting flowers,
And wake the purple year!
↕
Fair Venus' train

2. The Attic warbler pours her throat,
↑
Responsive to the cuckoo's note, } ⟷ The untaught harmony of spring:

3. Cool Zephyrs *fling Their gather'd fragrance thro' the clear blue sky*.
↑
While whisp'ring pleasure as they fly,

THOMAS GRAY (1716–1771)

Ode on the Spring

Lo! where the rosy-bosom'd Hours,
Fair VENUS' train appear,
Disclose the long-expecting flowers,
And wake the purple year!
The Attic warbler pours her throat,
Responsive to the cuckoo's note,
The untaught harmony of spring:
While whisp'ring pleasure as they fly,
Cool Zephyrs thro' the clear blue sky
Their gather'd fragrance fling.

1. *Lo!:* look! see!

1. *Hours:* the companions of the Greek goddess Venus who ushered in the seasons. They guarded the doors of Olympus and promoted the fertility of the earth. They are depicted in paintings as blooming maidens or youths.

2. *Venus':* of the goddess of Love.

2. *train:* a retinue, a number of persons attendant on a person of rank.

3. *Disclose:* open up.

3. *long-expecting:* long-expected.

4. *purple:* bright-hued, brilliant (of any color).

5. *Attic:* pertaining to Attica, a division of Greece whose capital is Athens.

5. *warbler:* song-bird; but the *Attic warbler,* in particular, is the nightingale, in Greek mythology, Philomela, the metamorphosed daughter of the king of Athens.

7. *untaught:* instinctive.

8. *they:* Zephyrs.

9. *Zephyrs:* the pleasant west winds of spring.

10. *Their:* the flowers'.

10. *gather'd:* from the flowers.

{Where'er the oak's thick branches stretch A broader browner shade;
{Where'er the rude and moss-grown beech O'er-canopies the glade

4. *the Muse shall {sit With me Beside some water's rushy brink*,
and think {How vain the ardour of the Crowd [is],
{How low, how little} *the Proud are*,
How indigent the Great [are]!

↑ (At ease reclin'd in rustic state)

Where'er the oak's thick branches stretch
A broader browner shade;
Where'er the rude and moss-grown beech
O'er-canopies the glade
Beside some water's rushy brink
With me the Muse shall sit, and think
(At ease reclin'd in rustic state)
How vain the ardour of the Crowd,
How low, how little are the Proud,
How indigent the Great!

11. *Where'er:* wherever.

13. *rude:* rugged, rough, uncultivated.

14. *O'er-canopies:* covers over like a canopy.

14. *glade:* clear open space in the woods.

15. *water's:* body of water's, i.e. pond's or stream's.

15. *rushy brink:* bank covered with rushes and water weeds.

16. *Muse:* an inspiring goddess of song.

17. *reclin'd:* reclining.

17. *rustic state:* in rural pomp, like a king holding his court.

18. *ardour:* heated passion or desire.

20. *indigent:* poverty-stricken.

5. *the toiling hand of Care is Still*:

6. The panting herds repose:

7. Yet hark, how *The busy murmur glows thro' the peopled air*!

8. The insect youth are on the wing,
↑
Eager to {taste the honied spring,
And float amid the liquid noon:

9. Some *skim lightly o'er the current*,

10. Some show their gaily-gilded trim
↑
Quick-glancing to the sun.

Still is the toiling hand of Care:
The panting herds repose:
Yet hark, how thro' the peopled air
The busy murmur glows!
The insect youth are on the wing,
Eager to taste the honied spring,
And float amid the liquid noon:
Some lightly o'er the current skim,
Some show their gaily-gilded trim
Quick-glancing to the sun.

22. *repose:* rest.

23. *peopled:* filled with animal life.

24. *glows:* puts forth a steady emanation.

26. *honied spring:* flowers, which are the source or fountainhead of honey.

27. *liquid noon:* see IH.

28. *current:* the current of a stream.

29. *trim:* dress, adornment.

30. *Quick-glancing:* causing flashes of (reflected) light by rapid movements.

11. *Such is the race of Man To Contemplation's sober eye*:

12. { And they that creep, / and they that fly, } Shall end where they began.

13. * { the Busy / and the Gay } Alike* But flutter thro' life's little day,
↑
dress'd In fortune's varying colors:

14. *They leave their airy dance, to rest in dust*.
↑
{ Brush'd by the hand of rough Mischance,
Or chill'd by age,

To Contemplation's sober eye
Such is the race of Man:
And they that creep, and they that fly,
Shall end where they began.
Alike the Busy and the Gay
But flutter thro' life's little day,
In fortune's varying colors dress'd:
Brush'd by the hand of rough Mischance,
Or chill'd by age, their airy dance
They leave, in dust to rest.

31. *sober:* serious, reflective.

32. *race of Man:* mankind in general.

33. *they:* insects, and thus, men, who resemble them in their mortality.

34. *end where they began:* "dust to dust."

35. *the Busy and the Gay:* busy people and gay people.

36. *But:* only.

37. *fortune's:* blind chance's.

15. Methinks I hear The sportive kind reply:
↑
in *low accents*

16. <Poor moralist!> and what art thou?
A solitary fly!

17. *no glittering female meets Thy Joys*,

18. *thou hast { No hive of hoarded sweets*,
No painted plumage to display:

19. *thy youth is flown On Hasty wings*;

20. Thy sun is set,

21. thy spring is gone—

22. We frolic,
↑
while 'tis May.

Methinks I hear in accents low
The sportive kind reply:
Poor moralist! and what art thou?
A solitary fly!
Thy Joys no glittering female meets,
No hive hast thou of hoarded sweets,
No painted plumage to display:
On hasty wings thy youth is flown;
Thy sun is set, thy spring is gone—
We frolic, while 'tis May.

41. *accents:* speech.

41. *low:* quiet.

42. *sportive kind:* the insects.

47. *plumage:* feathers, adornments.

Interpretational Hypothesis

According to the title, the poem is an ode. But it is an "ode on" rather than an "ode to." It is not, therefore, a hymn, but what was known as an Horatian ode, modeled on the *Odes* of the Latin poet Horace. "Ode" here has little more significance than such a simple term as "a poem." We may think of the title as meaning "A poem about the spring."

The poem opens with the poet urging himself, or a companion, or the reader to observe the coming of the spring. It is not clear to whom the poem is addressed. Since the reader is not in the same place as the speaker, he can probably be excluded. The first possibility seems the most attractive, since nothing as yet seems to indicate the presence of anyone else. The Hours, here used as goddesses or symbols of time, are in the train of Venus; they are her attendants. In mythology and poetry Venus is usually the goddess of love; but here, since her attendants open up the flowers, which have long been awaiting her coming, and awake the many-colored year, she is the goddess of love in the whole natural world: i.e. she is the goddess not of constant fertility, but of annually recurring fertility, as her attendance by the Hours, the time-symbols, indicates. In what sense do these Hours "wake . . . the year"? Until shortly before this poem was written, the year legally began March 21, rather than on January 1. The coming of the spring, in the attitudes and feelings of the people of the time, coincided with and meant the coming of the new year.

The implied connective to the next sentence appears to be "consequently" or "as a result." The Attic warbler is the nightingale; she is represented as pouring forth her song, an allusion to the very long phrases of the nightingale's song. The term "Attic" may be only a bit of decoration, but it is to be remembered that to the eighteenth-century mind, civilization began in Greece and especially in Attica, the capital of which was Athens. Such an interpretation would be consistent with the subject of the poem, spring; i.e. Attic culture was the springtime of civilization, and had spring's grace and purity. The nightingale is presented as having a kind of duet with the cuckoo. That the harmony is untaught indicates that their music is unsophisticated, natural, and spontaneous. The phrase adds to the idea of a bursting forth of life under the influence of Venus and the Hours and is consistent with the note of freshness suggested by "Attic." The line presents another problem. On what is it grammatically dependent?

By contiguity, the principle that any modifier must be interpreted as modifying the nearest word or phrase susceptible of modification (unless the context forbids such an assignment), the "cuckoo's note" is the "untaught harmony." However, the commas after "throat" and "note" suggest the possibility that "harmony" refers to the idea of line 5 by ellipsis. Thus, "The warbler pours her throat," that is, produces harmony. Yet both the cuckoo and the nightingale each produce only a melody of separate notes, while harmony is the consequence of the coincidental sounding of two or more notes. Hence, the "untaught harmony" seems to be best thought of as the consequence of the duet of the two birds. "In responding to the cuckoo, the nightingale produces a melody which harmonizes with that of the cuckoo." Although they are untaught, the birds produce melodies which relate harmoniously one to the other. This interpretation reinforces the naturalness of the music and the scene.

The next three lines (ll. 8–10) also present a bit of a syntactical problem. First, is "they" "the birds" or "the zephyrs"? Since "they" are whispering, they can hardly be the singing birds. Second, should we read, "While they are whispering pleasure, the zephyrs fling fragrance" or "While the zephyrs, whispering pleasure, fling their fragrance"? In the first reading the three lines form an independent clause, indicated by the colon (l. 7). In the second, the clause is dependent upon "the warbler pours her throat," and the colon is equivalent to a comma which separates a subordinate from its main clause. It is not easy to decide between these two readings, but there are several clues. First of all, there is no comma between "while" and "whisp'ring." Secondly, the first reading, taking the clause as independent, would carry out the pattern of independent statements established in lines 1–4 and 5–7. Finally, the wiser tendency in understanding English sentences is to understand something in terms of what has preceded it, unless we get further information which may make us change our minds. The first reading, then, seems to be the more desirable. The Zephyrs or breezes, presented as deities like the Hours, whisper pleasure as they move along because they are (1) making only a faint sound as they move through the leaves and branches of the trees, and (2) they are subtly hinting that pleasure should now be the thing we ought to desire. "Hint" or "suggest" or "insinuate" are old and common meanings for "whisper," used when the notion thus communicated is something we do not quite dare or quite wish to say aloud. Since, in the orthodox Christian tradition of values, pleasure is not to be sought for itself, the zephyrs are hinting at the value of something not to be publicly approved but to be privately enjoyed—sensuous pleasure. The zephyrs fling their gathered fragrance, because they are spreading abroad the scents of the flowers which they have collected from the fresh countryside.

The next stanza, by contrast, consists of only one sentence. The connection between the two stanzas must be postponed until we have an interpretation of the second. The poet states that wherever he can find under an oak tree a shade thicker than other trees provide, or wherever he can find an old beech tree hanging like a canopy over a grassy spot next to the edge of a pool or brook overgrown with rushes, he will be with his muse, that is, he will think, or write poetry. There he will lie as comfortably as a king holding his court in the countryside ("in rustic state"). The subjects of his meditation will be how pointless is the passionate desiring (for gain?) of the mass of men, how really insignificant are those who think themselves important, and how poor in truly valuable experiences are the world's powerful people. The connection with what has preceded is not immediately obvious, until we remember that the Zephyrs whispered pleasure. The poet is saying that in his present attitude, induced by the charm of the spring, he possesses everything (hence the comparison of himself to a king), and he realizes that what men think to be important is in fact worthless. He has listened to the Zephyrs and has accepted their suggestion that simple, naïve, spontaneous, sensuous pleasure is the best thing in the world.

In the next stanza the time of day has subtly changed. In the opening stanza the emphasis upon waking and rousing and the song of the birds suggested morning. Now it is noon. The peasants have stopped working in the fields; the cattle panting from the heat are not grazing but resting. There is, now, a new sound. The air is filled with life, the life of insects and their hum. However, the expression that their "murmur glows," referring to a "visible sound," is an odd one. It is a metaphor. The vehicle is "glows" and the tenor is "is audible." The connection is, as always, that characteristic of the vehicle which can be meaningfully applied to the tenor. "Shedding light" is certainly not such a characteristic; but a "putting forth of a steady and continuous emanation" is. Now, in line 25, comes the explanation for this hum that has the steadiness and continuity of light. It comes from the newborn insects, who are presented as eager to enjoy the nectar in the spring flowers. The next line (l. 27) presents a problem somewhat similar to the glowing murmur. "Noon" confirms the deduction about the time of day made from lines 21 and 22; and the insects float in it because it is pictured as a liquid. But how can the noon be thought of as liquid? "A watery noon" would mean, if anything, that it is raining, but clearly it is not. However, water is only one kind of liquid, which is a general term. To be liquid is to have the qualities of density, unlimited dispersal, absence of form, and homogeneity. The poet, then, is referring to the fact that as far as the eye can see, the landscape is absolutely homogeneous, with no clouds to cast shadows and nothing to interrupt the impression of the heat and quasi-palpability of a spring noontime.

Line 28 informs us that there was some significance in talking about the oak before the beech. He has chosen not the oak but the beech beside water, and "current" indicates that it is a brook or stream, rather than a pool or pond. Some of the insects fly down close to the water, while others display their wings. "Trim" is used in the sense of a ship's trim, or sails and ropes. The insects' wings, which are brightly colored, are visible as they flutter rapidly and catch the light of the sun. All these details add up to a sense of the spontaneous joy of the insects in being alive.

Hence we feel the quick contrasting movement to the next stanza: the poet thinks not of their beauty but continues to follow the train of thought which he started in stanza 2. He has been thinking of the purposelessness and meaninglessness of man's existence, and he sees the insects in the same way. Whether they crawl on the ground or fly in the air, they shall end up where they began, in the earth, dead. Among men, those who work hard and those who enjoy themselves are like the insects who have only a day to live. Like the insects, who are dressed in different colors, men are dressed in the different colors which fortune gives them, whether drab or brilliant. Like insects, men must leave their activities, which have no more importance than dancing in air, and they must die and be buried. This can happen either because they have bad luck and are struck down by ill fate, just as an insect can be killed by the blow of a man, or because both insects and men can simply die of the cold of age. But this attitude raises a problem. In stanza 2 the poet mocked the self-importance of people who live a life of activity as opposed to pleasure; but here he sees that pleasure, which he had decided was the great good, is also ephemeral and illusory. Sensuous enjoyment and ambitious activity are equally unsatisfactory.

To resolve this problem, the speaker imagines the insects replying to his conclusions. They call him a "poor moralist," not because he moralizes badly but because to moralize at all is the really vain thing. He need not imagine he is more important than they are (or, by implication, other men are) just because he can moralize. He, too, is only a fly, destined to all the mischance and brevity of life of his kind. Furthermore he is a solitary fly; he is alone; he lacks the pleasures of company. No charming woman waits to welcome the pleasures he brings. He has none of the good things of life which he has gained through his efforts. He is not even very attractive. The reasons are given in the next two lines. With his melancholy attitude about the vanity of activity and pleasure, his youth has gone with nothing to show for it; it is over before he knows it. Consequently, the time for real life for him is over ("thy sun is set") and the best time for activity and pleasure has also passed. The insects, on the other hand, enjoy themselves, but, as we have seen, their enjoyment includes both pleasure and purposeful activity.

The argument of the poem is as follows, when it is stripped of its sensuous charm: "Pleasure is better than activity, which is vain because life is short. But then pleasure is also vain. It follows that far better than thinking about life is finding our satisfaction in uniting pleasure and purposeful activity. The moralizing separation of the two is the mistake."

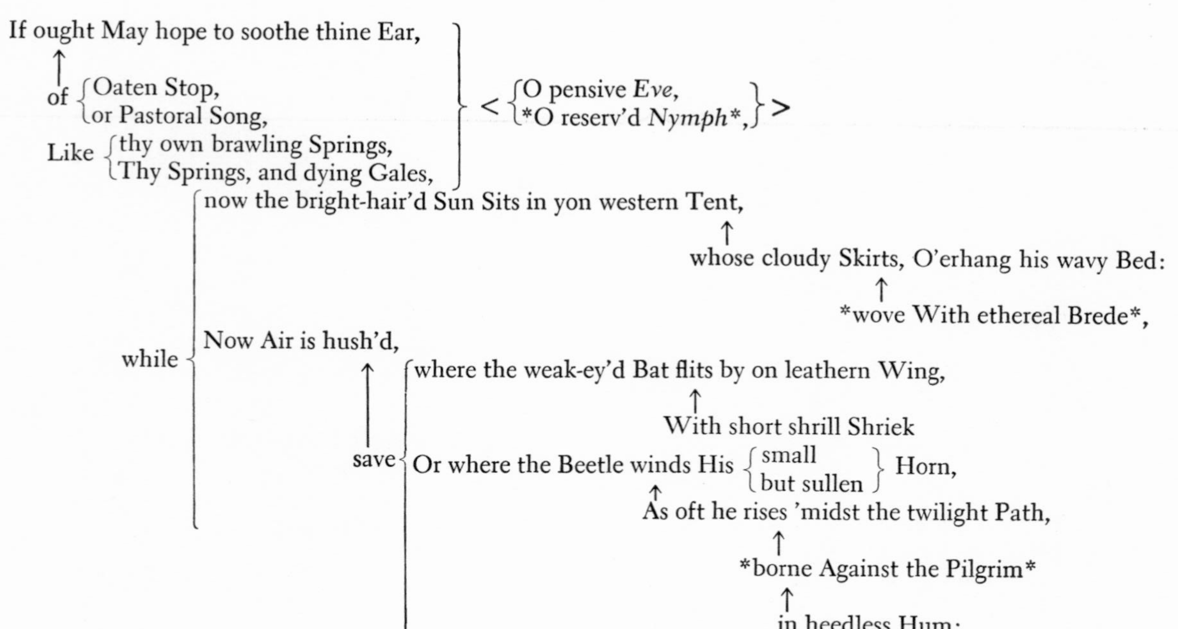
1. If ought May hope to soothe thine Ear,
of Oaten Stop,
or Pastoral Song,
Like thy own brawling Springs,
Thy Springs, and dying Gales,
< O pensive *Eve*,
*O reserv'd *Nymph**, >
now the bright-hair'd Sun Sits in yon western Tent,
whose cloudy Skirts, O'erhang his wavy Bed:
wove With ethereal Brede,
while
Now Air is hush'd,
where the weak-ey'd Bat flits by on leathern Wing,
With short shrill Shriek
save
Or where the Beetle winds His small but sullen Horn,
As oft he rises 'midst the twilight Path,
borne Against the Pilgrim
in heedless Hum:

WILLIAM COLLINS (1721–1759)

Ode to Evening

If ought of Oaten Stop, or Pastoral Song,
May hope, O pensive *Eve*, to soothe thine Ear,
    Like thy own brawling Springs,
    Thy Springs, and dying Gales,
O *Nymph* reserv'd, while now the bright-hair'd Sun
Sits in yon western Tent, whose cloudy Skirts,
    With Brede ethereal wove,
    O'erhang his wavy Bed:
Now Air is hush'd, save where the weak-ey'd Bat,
With short shrill Shriek flits by on leathern Wing,
    Or where the Beetle winds
    His small but sullen Horn,
As oft he rises 'midst the twilight Path,
Against the Pilgrim borne in heedless Hum:

1. *ought:* anything.

1. *of Oaten Stop:* played on a reed pipe used by shepherds; a "stop" is a hole in a reed instrument.

2. *pensive:* thoughtful.

3. *Like:* in the same way as.

3. *brawling:* making a loud confused noise, as water running over stones.

4. *Gales:* gentle breezes.

5. *Nymph:* in classical mythology, a semi-divine female creature inhabiting natural places, hence, a beautiful woman.

5. *reserv'd:* sedate, restrained, dignified.

7. *Brede:* embroidery.

7. *ethereal:* airy.

7. *wove:* woven.

8. *his:* the sun's.

9. *save:* except.

10. *leathern:* leatherlike.

11. *winds:* blows.

12. *sullen:* melancholy; dull or deep.

13. *'midst:* in the middle of.

14. *Pilgrim:* one who travels to a shrine or sacred place.

14. *borne:* carried.

1. *cont.*

Now teach me, <*compos'd *Maid**,> To breathe some soften'd Strain,
↑
Whose Numbers May *suit not unseemly with its Stillness*,
↑
stealing thro' thy dark'ning Vale,

As I hail Thy genial lov'd Return!
↑
musing slow,

For when thy folding Star shows His paly Circlet,
↑
arising

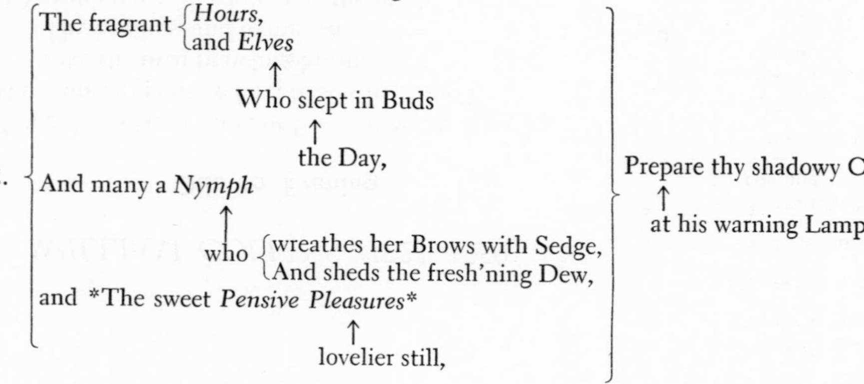

2. The fragrant {*Hours*, and *Elves*}
↑
Who slept in Buds
↑
the Day,
And many a *Nymph*
↑
who {wreathes her Brows with Sedge, And sheds the fresh'ning Dew,}
and *The sweet *Pensive Pleasures**
↑
lovelier still,
} Prepare thy shadowy Car.
↑
at his warning Lamp

Now teach me, *Maid* compos'd,
To breathe some soften'd Strain,
Whose Numbers stealing thro' thy dark'ning Vale,
May not unseemly with its Stillness suit,
As musing slow, I hail
Thy genial lov'd Return!
For when thy folding Star arising shows
His paly Circlet, at his warning Lamp
The fragrant *Hours*, and *Elves*
Who slept in Buds the Day,
And many a *Nymph* who wreathes her Brows with Sedge,
And sheds the fresh'ning Dew, and lovelier still,
The *Pensive Pleasures* sweet
Prepare thy shadowy Car.

15. *compos'd:* quiet, collected.

16. *Strain:* song, music, poem.

17. *Numbers:* the meter of the poem.

17. *Vale:* valley.

18. *unseemly:* inappropriately, unbefittingly.

18. *its:* the Vale's.

18. *suit . . . with:* agree with, be in harmony with.

19. *slow:* slowly.

20. *genial:* comforting, sympathetic.

21. *folding:* the star which signals that it is time for shepherds to put their sheep into folds.

22. *His:* the star's.

22. *paly:* pale.

22. *Circlet:* ring, nimbus.

22. *at:* at the moment that the lamp shines.

23. *Hours:* the classical goddesses of the seasons and weather who send down dews and rain. Hence, they are further associated with the youthful bloom and grace of the springtime and are often confused with the three Graces.

25. *Sedge:* any of a group of tall marsh grasses (Carex), like the sweet flag, the yellow iris, growing in dense tufts and traditionally supposed to have been used by river nymphs to adorn their heads.

27. *Pleasures:* see IH.

28. *Car:* chariot.

3. Then let me { rove some { wild / and heathy } Scene,
Or find some Ruin 'midst its dreary Dells,
↑
Whose Walls *nod more awful*
↑
By thy religious Gleams. }

Or if { chill blust'ring Winds, / or driving Rain, } Prevent my willing Feet,

4. *[Let] the Hut be mine*,
↑
That { Views { Wilds,
and swelling Floods,
And *brown Hamlets*,
and dim-discover'd Spires, }
↑
from the Mountain's Side,
And hears their simple Bell,
and marks Thy Dewy Fingers draw The gradual dusky Veil. }
↑
o'er all

Then let me rove some wild and heathy Scene,
Or find some Ruin 'midst its dreary Dells,
    Whose Walls more awful nod
    By thy religious Gleams.
Or if chill blust'ring Winds, or driving Rain,
Prevent my willing Feet, be mine the Hut,
    That from the Mountain's Side,
    Views Wilds, and swelling Floods,
And Hamlets brown, and dim-discover'd Spires,
And hears their simple Bell, and marks o'er all
    Thy Dewy Fingers draw
    The gradual dusky Veil.

29. *heathy:* like a heath or desolate open wasteland.

30. *its:* the scene's.

30. *Dells:* ravines, small secluded valleys.

31. *nod:* seem to sway or waver in the uncertain light.

32. *By:* in response to, or in the light of.

34. *Prevent:* presumably from roving and finding.

36. *Wilds:* wild scenes.

36. *swelling:* from the rain.

36. *Floods:* rivers.

37. *Hamlets:* small villages.

37. *dim-discover'd:* the church steeples are hard to perceive or make out.

38. *their:* the spires'.

38. *marks:* perceives.

While *Spring* shall {pour his Show'rs,
And bathe thy breathing Tresses,} as oft he wont, <meekest *Eve!*>
While *Summer* loves to sport,
↑
Beneath thy ling'ring Light:
While sallow *Autumn* fills thy Lap with Leaves,
Or [while] *Winter* {Affrights thy shrinking Train,
And rudely rends thy Robes,
↑
yelling thro' the troublous Air,

5. So long Shall {*Fancy*,
Friendship,
Science,
smiling *Peace*,} {*own Thy gentlest Influence*,
And love thy fav'rite Name!
↑
regardful of thy quiet Rule,

While *Spring* shall pour his Show'rs, as oft he wont,
And bathe thy breathing Tresses, meekest *Eve!*
    While *Summer* loves to sport,
    Beneath thy ling'ring Light:
While sallow *Autumn* fills thy Lap with Leaves,
Or *Winter* yelling thro' the troublous Air,
    Affrights thy shrinking Train,
    And rudely rends thy Robes,
So long regardful of thy quiet Rule,
Shall *Fancy*, *Friendship*, *Science*, smiling *Peace*,
    Thy gentlest Influence own,
    And love thy fav'rite Name!

41. *his:* Spring's.

41. *as oft he wont:* as was often his custom.

42. *Tresses:* hair.

43. *to sport:* to frolic, frisk.

45. *sallow:* of a sickly yellowish or brownish color.

45. *Lap:* the earth is seen as Eve's lap.

46. *troublous:* not "troublesome," but "troubled, disturbed."

47. *Affrights:* frightens.

47. *shrinking:* cowering for fear.

48. *rends:* tears.

49. *regardful:* heedful, attentive to.

50. *Fancy:* creative imagination, perhaps here even artistic endeavor.

50. *Science:* learning in general.

51. *gentlest:* gentler than any other deity's, very gentle.

51. *own:* admit, acknowledge.

Interpretational Hypothesis

The poem begins with a long introductory clause, from "If ought" (l. 1) to "heedless hum" (l. 14); and the main statement of the opening sentence is "Teach me" (l. 15). The first problem is the relation between these two parts of the sentence. The title has told us that the poem is an ode, an address to something or somebody. The information in lines 3 and 4 that Eve governs springs and gales suggests that this ode is to a goddess who controls certain aspects of nature, and her name tells us that she is the goddess of evening, or, in the poem, "Eve," that period when day has ended but night has not begun. An ode to a deity has the same function as a hymn. It praises the power of the deity, refers to his attributes and achievements, and frequently makes a request. The request may be that the deity grant the suppliant a special favor or that the deity bestow on the speaker some of the deity's own qualities or attributes. We shall hypothesize, therefore, that this poem will have one or some combination of these characteristics.

The opening statement of lines 1 and 2 amounts to a hope that the goddess may be propitious and listen to the speaker: "If music played on a pipe made of hollow oat stems, or if a song like that which shepherds sing is pleasing to you (then teach me . . . [l. 15])." The speaker hopes that the goddess may be best propitiated and prayed to by naïve, simple music and poetry such as shepherds create to pass away the lone time of guarding sheep. Since Eve is pensive, musingly thoughtful, such music seems right to the speaker; for it will have the character of brooks running over stones ("brawling" did not have the meaning of loud confusion it now has) or of breezes which are dying away (gales did not then mean violent winds but gentle ones), such things being under Eve's power and therefore pleasing to her. She is a reserved nymph, one who does not mingle with other deities. The time is also propitious for his prayer. The sun has descended to the west and only its rays ("bright hair") are visible, for the sun itself is behind the clouds ("sits in yon western tent"). Since a tent is made of woven material, the edges of the clouds colored by the rays of the concealed sun are described as being interwoven or decorated with embroidery. It is ethereal embroidery, because the colors are made of light and air.

At first glance this description seems inappropriate, for evening, the period when Eve rules, comes after sunset. It also seems pointless. Why this elaborate description of the sun behind the clouds? But these questions are resolved when we realize that evening has not yet come. The time of the poem is late afternoon. The speaker is thinking of evening before its arrival. Hence "reserv'd" means also "held back." Eve is withholding herself. The poet is begging her to come. Why this plea is made should become clear later on. Further, the fact that the late afternoon sun is behind a cloud means that a darker period (of Eve's reign) is foreshadowed. Hence the lavishness of the description. The speaker is moved by the beauty of the clouds covering the later afternoon sun because they foreshadow the coming of evening.

The time to address Eve ("nymph" confirms Eve as a nature goddess) is further propitious because of its quietness. Only the little cry of the bat, whose eyes are too sensitive to light to be useful by day, may be heard, or the drone of the beetle. The sound of the latter is compared with the sound produced by a horn when it is blown or "winded." A sullen person is dull, melancholy, and insistent on maintaining his emotional state. The last trait, the most striking thing about a sullen emotional state, is probably the most useful meaning here. "Sullen," then, refers to the monotonous or tuneless buzzing of the beetle. Another human being is now introduced, a pilgrim whom the beetle flies heedlessly into. What is the pilgrim doing here? A pilgrim is one who has vowed to visit a religious shrine to gain the favor of a saint or of God. He is often thought of as traveling alone. Although it cannot be certainly stated, it seems possible that the pilgrim is the speaker himself, since he is making a visit to the shrine, the evening landscape of a saint or goddess, Eve, with the purpose of making a devotional act and a request or prayer.

It is now appropriate to ask why these details are here introduced. Do they have a purpose? Do they have anything to do with Eve and her characteristics and attributes? They should, since they are all grammatically dependent upon a statement that refers directly and by implication to Eve's nature. Listing them in order of appearance, we have simple and naïve rusticity, musing thoughtfulness, solitude so quiet that even the gentlest and most easily ignored sounds are audible, beauty, half darkness, and fading light. It is characterized, then, by separateness from the rest of humanity and by trembling sensitivity. The only human figures appropriate are a poet and a pilgrim, or quite likely, a poet-pilgrim, one who has turned his back on ordinary life and is seeking a special kind of experience, the blessing of a god or saint. The speaker has established thus indirectly the attributes of the goddess.

Now begins his plea. "Teach me to write your kind of poetry," "strain" referring originally to a bit of music and by metaphor, common in the early eighteenth century, to a bit of poetry. It is poetry not to be spoken, but only breathed, barely whispered. It is the kind of poetry appropriate to the goddess, and therefore the capacity of the speaker to create such poetry would mean that he had taken on the attributes of the goddess. The further implication is that since he has to be taught to write Eve's kind of poetry, he does not know. It implies that he desires such attributes as quietness, solitariness, thoughtfulness, and peace because at the time of speaking or of making his prayer he has just the opposite attributes; he is disturbed and unhappy, in a state of emotional wretchedness. This kind of poetry ("numbers," which usually refers to the metrical organization of a poem, was commonly used in the eighteenth century to refer to poetry in general) will fit most appropriately the stillness of the darkening valley. And he will breathe this poetry while he is musing, having become pensive like the goddess. He hails her return, a return which is "genial" or suitable to his "genius," or, as we would say today, personality. "Musing" may mean meditating, or more literally, being subject to the Muse, slowly composing poetry or composing poetry with a slow movement. This further resolves the question raised in the preceding section of the poem, the apparent inconsistency between the evening setting and the fact that the sun is still in the sky, though behind clouds. The poet is waiting for the goddess to return to her proper place, the landscape of evening. The prayer is addressed to an absent deity, and it is a request that the speaker be attuned emotionally to her arrival.

The next sentence (ll. 21–28) requires first that we ask, What is the proper interpretation of "for"? But the answer must be postponed until the entire sentence has been interpreted. The folding star is the star that warns shepherds that it is time to put the sheep in the folds. It has a "paly Circlet" because the mist of the evening makes it appear to have a faint halo of light around it. Next we have a whole series of mythological beings. First are those Hours which are fragrant because as evening hours they release the scents of the countryside. Then, the elves who slept in buds all day are no doubt the perfumes of the flowers released into the dampened air of the evening. Next come nymphs who are water spirits, since they wear crowns of sedge, water plants that grow at the edges of streams and ponds. They shed, or cause to descend on the scene, the freshening dew; i.e. from the streams and pools rises the freshly moistened air that seems to put a halo around the star and releases the scents of the flowers and of the countryside. Finally come the "pensive pleasures," mythological creatures like hours, nymphs, and elves. They are still lovelier because Eve herself is pensive and thus they are her particular handmaidens. This repetition of "pensive" requires that we consider the word a little more carefully. It is usually used (as when we ask of someone, "Why are you so pensive?") to refer to the state of a person who is turned in upon himself. He forgets the rest of the world in pursuing some hidden chain of thought; but the word would not be used if it were suspected that the person so addressed were thinking over some difficult logical argument. Rather it implies an emotional state half sad, half pleased, and a current of consciousness not directed but drifting. It seems to imply not so much thinking as observing one's own stream of ideas, images, and impressions. These "pensive" deities, then, prepare the car of Eve. Traditionally, each deity of a period of day has a chariot, which he drives across the sky during the hours when he rules. The chariot has the attributes of those hours. The chariot of the sun is fiery gold, blindingly bright; and the chariot of Eve is of course "shadowy."

We can now answer the question about "for." "I love to see evening return, because of its frequent freshness and especially because it is a time when I can be pensive," with all that the word implies.

"Then," at the time when Eve is governing the hours, will be the time, Eve instructing and permitting, to wander about a countryside which is wild, or uninhabited, and covered with heath, or uncultivated. Or to find some ruin whose high walls are made even higher and more threatening by the religious light of evening. It is a religious light because it is the light that old churches and cathedrals always have, dim and mysterious. Or if it is cold and windy, or if it is raining, and unpleasant for wandering abroad, it will be best to stay in some hut on a mountainside, from which can be seen uncultivated heaths and forests, rivers swelling from the rain, and a brown little village with church spires which can barely be made out through the rain and the darkening evening. From such a hut can be heard the simple bell ("simple" as opposed to the complicated chimes of great cathedrals, and hence the bell of a village church) and can be seen misty darkness gradually concealing everything.

This is the simplest part of the poem so far, and again it is proper to ask the question asked about the first section: Do all these details have any function? It is possible to discern a pattern, running from the loneliness and least humanized scene at the beginning, through ruins, once inhabited, to a hut more recently inhabited, since it is built of lighter construction than stone ruins, to, in the distance, not only a village but also a church and its bell, the symbols of human community. There is movement therefore from a desire for absolute loneliness to an approach, even if it is only a momentary one, to ordinary humanity. It is a curious pattern, for at the beginning Eve was presented as absolutely alone. On the other hand, in the second sentence she was presented as accompanied by other mythological beings. The two patterns seem to coincide, the second being a repetition of the first. Clearly there seems to be a movement from a complete turning away from the rest of humanity to a tentative turning toward it.

It remains to be seen if the rest of the poem carries this movement further.

The first clause of the last sentence can be reduced to "All year long." In the spring it often rains, but the rain serves the goddess. "Breathing tresses" are hair flowing with the quality of life, hair, perhaps, that appears to float of its own power in the wind. In the summer, the god of summer plays in the evening, but in autumn the pale yellow god strips the leaves from the trees. In winter the winds howl. They make her daily visit unpleasant for the goddess. They tear her robes and frighten her attendants. "So long regardful . . ." indicates that the first clause had better be put: "Whatever the season of the year, such and such things shall happen." The "shall" (rather than the simple third singular "will") indicates that the speaker wants these things to happen. It is first to be noticed that there is an increasing activity and unpleasantness in the description of the seasons. Hence it would be better yet to put the first clause thus: "No matter what the season and its comforts or discomforts—if Fancy (imagination), Friendship, Science (learning), and Peace submit themselves to the power of evening, they shall admit ('own') the advantages of Eve's gentle influence and will love her name, which shall be the name of their favorite goddess." Fancy and Science, or imagination and learning, may be regarded as deities or personifications of purely subjective experiences; but Friendship and Peace involve other people. The repetition of "shall" emphasizes the willingness, the desire, of the speaker that these things shall occur. Now he has said: "If I please Eve, then she will teach me those of her qualities which I need, for they bring me the pensive pleasures. With these I can wander freely in solitudes and, from a distance, even observe humanity. Having come under her influence, I shall be able, no matter how disturbing the world may be, to enjoy the things I like: the exercise of poetic imagination and learning, friendship and freedom from jarring relations with other people. I shall be able to accept, even to welcome, the disturbances of life, just as Eve survives under all conditions of the year, for I shall have the compensations of Eve." Or, "If I had a real inner tranquillity I could enjoy the world, approach a little closer to general humanity and society, and I should have defenses against disturbing influences so that I could observe and make the most of my gifts and my friends."

The poem is the dramatization of the feelings of a man who wishes to be other than he is. Disturbed, he desires tranquillity. Alone, he desires friends, and, timidly enough, some contact with the rest of men. Unable to use and enjoy his gifts, he deeply desires to do both.

1. Let the downpour roil and toil!

2. The worst it can do to me Is [to] carry some garden soil A little nearer the sea.

3. 'Tis the world-old way of the rain
   ↑
   To exact *A little of future harm for a present gain*.
   When it comes to a mountain farm

4. And the harm is none too sure,
   For {
   {when all that was rotted rich Shall be scoured poor,
   ↑
   in the end
   When my garden has gone down ditch,}
   Some force has but to apply,
   And {summits shall be immersed,
   The bottom of seas [shall be] raised dry—
   The slope of the earth [shall be] reversed.}
   }

ROBERT FROST (1875–   )

In Time of Cloudburst

Let the downpour roil and toil!
The worst it can do to me
Is carry some garden soil
A little nearer the sea.

'Tis the world-old way of the rain
When it comes to a mountain farm
To exact for a present gain
A little of future harm.

And the harm is none too sure,
For when all that was rotted rich
Shall be in the end scoured poor,
When my garden has gone down ditch,

Some force has but to apply,
And summits shall be immersed,
The bottom of seas raised dry—
The slope of the earth reversed.

1. *to roil:* to rend water turbid or muddy by stirring up sediment.

7. *to exact:* to levy, to take away in payment of.

10. *all that was rotted rich:* all the soil that was made fertile by the decay of matter.

11. *scoured:* effaced, rubbed away by erosion.

13. *apply:* to apply itself, to put itself into effect.

14. *summits:* mountaintops.

14. *immersed:* submerged.

16. *slope of the earth:* not the globe, but rather the geological structure, e.g. the slope of a mountain. The idea is that the point where the bottom once was shall now be the point where the top is.

5. Then all I need do is {run To the other end of the slope,
{And Begin all over to hope.
↑
on tracts laid new to the sun,

6. Some worn old tool of my own Will be turned up by the plow,
↑
{The wood of it changed to stone,
{But as ready to wield as now.

7. May my application To so endless a repetition Not make me {tired
{and morose
{And resentful of man's condition.
↑
so close

Then all I need do is run
To the other end of the slope,
And on tracts laid new to the sun,
Begin all over to hope.

Some worn old tool of my own
Will be turned up by the plow,
The wood of it changed to stone,
But as ready to wield as now.

May my application so close
To so endless a repetition
Not make me tired and morose
And resentful of man's condition.

19. *tracts:* stretches of land for farming.

25. *application:* close inspection and consideration of or concentration on (geological process).

26. *repetition:* the repetition of natural processes of creation and destruction.

27. *morose:* sullen, gloomy.

Interpretational Hypothesis

The title tells us that the poem is to be imagined as being spoken during a cloudburst. In the first line "roil" and "toil" indicate that the speaker is thinking not of the rain when it is coming down but after it has penetrated the earth and has become muddy and is working into and across the ground. The implied connection between the first line and the second is "after all." "I don't care if we are having a torrential downpour of rain; after all the worst it can do as far as I am concerned . . ." But his consolation for the loss of his garden soil, however, is not that, after all, he is only losing some soil which is merely going a little farther on its way to the sea. Rather, in adjusting to the loss of valuable ground through runoff, his mental device is to recognize it as a natural process. ". . . and after all, it's only natural." This theme is developed in the next stanza. This is what the rain always does to mountain farms. For the benefit of life-giving moisture in the present, the farm must pay in the future by having lost some of its soil. Not only is it a natural process, therefore, but there is even a better reason to accept it. We see here, the speaker says, the balance of nature.

So far the drama of the poem, then, is adjustment to an undesirable situation by a reorientation. But the process of reorientation having begun, it continues, apparently irresistibly. Why it should continue is not immediately apparent, and is a problem that must be postponed. At any rate, the speaker continues. What's more, he says, the good that the rain is doing may very well outweigh the bad. The reason for arriving at this attitude is that when all of the good soil, which has become rich through the natural processes of organic decay ("rotted rich"), has been washed away, and when all the garden has disappeared as if it had been drained down a ditch, the new problem of how to find a place to grow food will be easily solved. That solution is presented in the next stanza.

"Some force has but to apply" itself, and mountains will be covered by the sea and the bottom of the sea will be raised to dry out and be ready to be used for new gardens. The force, then, is a geological force, and the consequences of its application is that "the slope of the earth" will be "reversed." That is, what was downhill will now be uphill, and vice versa.

Then all the speaker will have to do is to run to the other end of the slope. That is, when this reversal happens, his mountain farm will be under the sea, and all he has to do is to run up to the sea-bottoms which are now high above him and laid freshly to the sun, covered with the soil which was once on his mountain farm. Then he can begin all over again to hope. And his hope for a good garden and crops, he goes on to say in the next stanza (ll. 21–24), will be justified; plowing once more, in the soil which drained off his farm, found its way to the sea bottom, and was raised once again into dry land, he will find a garden tool of his own. It was washed away with soil, its wooden handle was petrified, but even so it will be as ready to be used as it is now. The simple future tense permits no doubt about this event. It is an expression of complete confidence. In spite of temporary losses, man's future is assured.

Yet the final stanza begins with a wish that this concentration of his on the endless alternation of dry land and sea bottom may not make him weary and dispirited and unable to adjust to the fact that man cannot control the natural forces inimical to him. At once several questions arise. First, since "may not" indicates the possibility that his application "may indeed" make him "tired and morose and resentful," we have a sudden shift from the confidence of lines 21–24 to a foreboding and anxiety. His confidence makes him afraid. A curious state of affairs. Why should it occur? Is the thought of the endlessness of this repetition the stimulus that introduces the emotional shift from confidence to anxiety? That is, has his mood darkened at the thought that this shifting of the life-giving soil between sea bottom and mountaintop is without termination and therefore without purpose, and that consequently, since man is inescapably bound to the soil, man's life is purposeless? Such an explanation would seem adequate were it not for the fact that the anxiety appears before this reason for it is offered. That is, he doesn't say, "I hope that this endless repetition won't depress me." He says, "I hope that my *application* to this endless repetition won't depress me." The causative factor, the stimulus for the shift from confidence to anxiety, is his concentration on man's condition, not his fear that man's suffering is pointless. It is apparent that something in the process of application has shifted his mood from confidence to anxiety. It follows, therefore, that his concern over the pointlessness of man's suffering helplessness is the product or reflection or expression of his anxiety, not the cause of it. What, then, is that "something" in his application which caused the anxiety?

Looking back to the preceding stanza, where the process of application culminates in a mood of confidence, we find that the confidence conceals an absurdity. As a human being with an ordinary life span he cannot possibly live long enough to enjoy the results of a geological process which will take aeons to occur. His confidence is based upon a nonreality, a fantasy, an illusion. What has happened? Looking back still farther, we can see that the "I" of line 17 is not the I implied by the "my" of line 12. In line 12 the speaker was an ordinary man watching the rain wash away his topsoil; in line 17 he is thinking of himself as Man, a personification of the whole human race. Only in the last stanza does the appearance of "my" in the same sentence as "man" indicate that the two roles have become separated. The cause of the separation is the absurdity of lines 21–24, which made it no longer possible to sustain the illusion that he was Man as well as a man. Instead of explaining that absurdity, the poet dramatizes its effect by shifting from confidence to anxiety. Lines 4–24 are revealed as a rationalization. Faced with an intolerable situation before which we feel helpless, we console ourselves by shifting to a way of looking at things that makes us comfortable. The process is called rationalization and is an illusion or lie or self-deception. The confidence of lines 21–24, then, is the product of a lie which the speaker of the poem has told to himself. We can now answer the question it was necessary to suspend at lines 8–9. Why does the speaker's reorientation continue? Because his impulsion is not rational but emotional. Thus the lie or rationalization is the source of the anxiety. Although the speaker is not aware that he has lied to himself, the fact that he has done so is dramatically revealed to the reader by the lack of a reason to continue after line 8, by the absurdity of the form the consolation or reorientation takes, by the use of "may not" to imply "may very possibly," and by the separation of the two roles in the use of "my" and "man."

The poem, then, is not an argument for making the best of things. It is a dramatic revelation that making the best of things, when it involves rationalization or self-delusion, is paid for by anxiety.

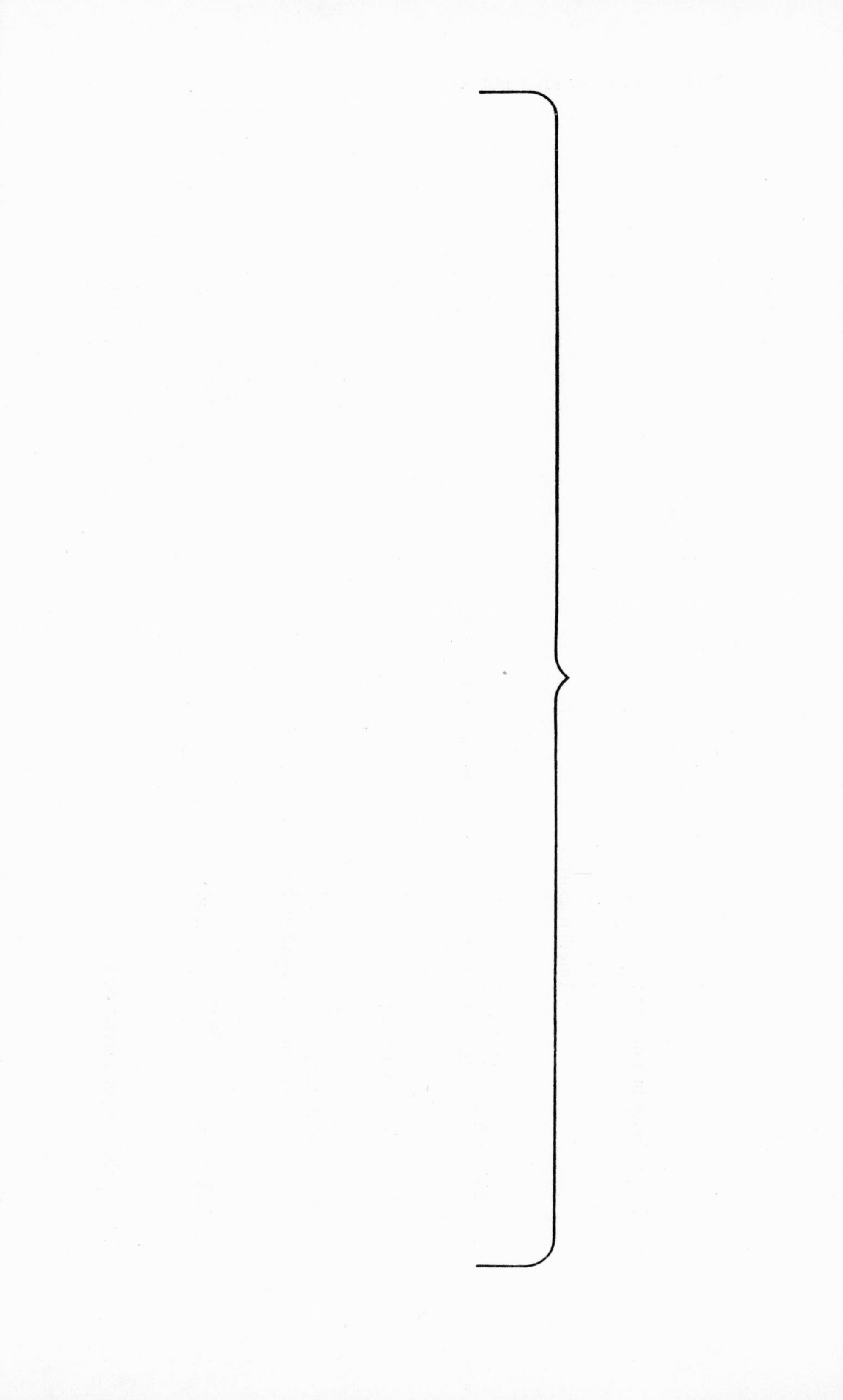

1. I hid my heart in a nest of roses,
↑
{Out of the sun's way,
{hidden apart;

2. *I hid my heart {Under the roses
{In a softer bed than the soft white snow's [bed] is*.

3. Why would it *not sleep*?

4. why should it start,
When never a leaf of the rose-tree stirred?

5. *What made sleep {flutter / and part} his wings*?

6. Only the song of a secret bird.

ALGERNON CHARLES SWINBURNE (1837–1909)

A Ballad of Dreamland

I hid my heart in a nest of roses,
  Out of the sun's way, hidden apart;
In a softer bed than the soft white snow's is,
  Under the roses I hid my heart.
  Why would it sleep not? why should it start,
When never a leaf of the rose-tree stirred?
  What made sleep flutter his wings and part?
Only the song of a secret bird.

Title. "Ballad," in the sense in which Swinburne uses it, is usually spelled "ballade." A ballade is a French verse form consisting of a varying number of stanzas each of which ends in a refrain (here "Only the song of a secret bird"). The last stanza is called an "envoi," which is French for "a sending-forth" and is a "peroration," an emphatic recapitulation or summary of the whole poem. "Ballade" has nothing to do with "ballad," which is a narrative poem transmitted orally by the folk, or an imitation thereof.

3. *snow's:* snow's bed.

5. *start:* to spring up, to awaken.

7. *part:* spread.

7. [“]Lie still,[”] I said,
[“]for { the wind’s wing closes,
And mild leaves muffle the keen sun’s dart;

8. Lie still,
for { the wind *dozes on the warm sea*,
And the wind is unquieter yet than thou art.

9. Does a thought *still smart in thee as a thorn’s wound*?

10. Does the fang *of deferred hope still fret thee*?

11. What bids the lids of thy sleep dispart?[”]

12. Only the song of a secret bird.

13. The green land’s name that *encloses a charm*,
↕
It *was never writ* in the traveller’s chart,

Lie still, I said, for the wind's wing closes,
  And mild leaves muffle the keen sun's dart;
Lie still, for the wind on the warm sea dozes,
  And the wind is unquieter yet than thou art.
  Does a thought in thee still as a thorn's wound smart?
Does the fang still fret thee of hope deferred?
  What bids the lids of thy sleep dispart?
Only the song of a secret bird.

The green land's name that a charm encloses,
  It never was writ in the traveller's chart,

14. *fret:* to torment.
14. *deferred:* put off.
15. *dispart:* open, separate.
17. *charm:* magic spell.
18. *chart:* map.

And [as] sweet as the fruit *that grows on its tree is*,
14. It *was never* sold in the merchant's mart.

15. The swallows of dreams *dart through its dim fields*,
And sleep's [tunes] are the tunes *heard in its tree-tops*;

16. No hound's note } wakens the wildwood hart,
Only the song of a secret bird. }

17. *I have chosen my part In the world of dreams*,
↕
{ To sleep for a season
{ and hear { no word { Of true love's truth
{ or of light love's art,
{ Only the song of a secret bird.

And sweet as the fruit on its tree that grows is,
  It never was sold in the merchant's mart.
  The swallows of dreams through its dim fields dart,
And sleep's are the tunes in its tree-tops heard;
  No hound's note wakens the wildwood hart,
Only the song of a secret bird.

ENVOI.

In the world of dreams I have chosen my part,
  To sleep for a season and hear no word
Of true love's truth or of light love's art,
  Only the song of a secret bird.

21. *its:* green land's.
22. *sleep's:* sleep's tunes.
23. *hart:* deer.
25. *part.* role.

Interpretational Hypothesis

The first question comes from the title. What is meant by "dreamland"? A land which one dreams of? A land where dreams live? Is it a metaphor for daydreaming or reverie? "Dreamland" requires an explanation, which will presumably be forthcoming in the poem. At least, however, let us hypothesize that whatever happens in the poem happens in dreamland, unless we are otherwise informed.

In the first line "heart" requires explanation. Traditionally, it is a metaphor for the emotional life in general; in more limited senses it may mean a capacity to sympathize with the emotions of another person or to respond to them, or it may refer specifically to the capacity for erotic love. Until something in the poem restricts the meaning, it is best to use the most inclusive meaning: the individual's emotional life. The first line also sets up the basic metaphor of the poem. In dreamland there are roses. Their soft warm protectiveness makes a bunch of them like a nest. The tenor, then, is that the speaker has so managed his emotional life that it has been hidden from other people and that it has been warmly and deliciously protected. Since its place of concealment is a nest, a place where infant birds are protected, the implication is that he has so manipulated his emotions that they have returned to the conditions of infant immaturity. He has then turned away from and has determined to avoid the emotions of the mature adult. His heart was hidden out of the sun's way. Since the sun is responsible for life and growth, he has protected his emotional life so that it might neither develop nor be noticed by others, and thereby be subjected to emotional stimuli from other people ("hidden apart"). Its bed was even softer than snow. Why is this metaphor introduced? The obvious connection is whiteness and softness, but there appears to be a less obvious connection. Snow is inimical to life because an individual who goes to sleep in deep snow is numbed. This metaphor implies, then, that the desire of the speaker was not only to return his emotional life to the conditions of infancy and to protect it from growth, but even to anaesthetize it. The repetition in line 4 of "I hid my heart," with the substitution of "under" for "in a nest of," serves to indicate the intensity of the desire to protect himself from emotional stimuli. Nevertheless, as the questions in lines 5–7 imply, his heart did not sleep, his emotions did not cease to respond. The implied connection between line 4 and line

5 is "but." His heart "started," i.e. made some response to external stimulus, even in such perfectly tranquil conditions that not even a leaf stirred of the rose-tree in which it was concealed. When an individual starts he is in a state of some tension rather than in one of complete relaxation. The sleeping heart is compared to a bird, or more probably to an infant winged deity, like a sleeping cupid. (The second interpretation becomes more probable by the appearance of "the secret bird" in the next line. It is simpler to assume that the "sleep," i.e. the sleeper, of line 7 is not a bird; for then we would be required to distinguish between two different birds.) As protected as the infant deity, i.e. the heart, was in its warm nest, nevertheless it fluttered its wings and parted them, or opened and closed them a moment. That is, even when the speaker's emotional life was so suppressed, or asleep, that it seemed impossible that it could respond to anything, nevertheless it did. What was this stimulus? "The song of a secret bird."

Can we yet say what "dreamland" refers to? What is the tenor of this vehicle? To begin, it obviously refers to "the conditions proper for suppressing the emotional life." But are these conditions subjective or objective, inside the speaker or outside him in the environment? Since "dreams" have only subjective *existence* (although they may be described or symbolized in language objectively understandable), "dreamland" is inside the speaker; it is subjective. It is some portion or area of the personality. (Talking about a personality as if it were a landscape is a very old literary tradition. Indeed, it is almost impossible to discuss the personality without using spatial metaphors.) "Dreamland" is an area into which the speaker has willed to put his emotional life so that its activity might be suppressed. That is, he has placed his emotional life under a control which he has consciously willed. Of such a person we would say, "His attitude toward himself is such that he is suppressing (or attempting to suppress) his emotional life." A "land" in the personality, then, is an attitude or orientation toward oneself, i.e. a self-orientation. "Dreamland" is a metaphor for which the tenor is "a self-orientation which is designed to inactivate my (the speaker's) emotional life." But can we be more precise? Emotional life equals "heart" equals "sleeping winged little God," i.e. Cupid, the god of erotic love. We may hypothesize, then, that "heart" is specifically the capacity for erotic emotions. Finally, is it possible to identify the "secret bird," which keeps the heart from being perfectly at rest? "Secret" from whom? Cupid or the speaker? Presumably, since the speaker uses the word, the bird is secret or hidden from him. Within the personality area which "dreamland" symbolizes is some force working against the efforts to suppress his erotic emotions; but he does not understand what the force is. He now has a choice. Shall he attempt to understand that force, or shall he increase his efforts to achieve the anaesthesis of his erotic emotions? If the former, he will, we may hypothesize, direct his attention to the bird; if the latter, he will attempt to increase the charm and magical somnolence of dreamland.

The answer to this question appears at once, in the next stanza, where he describes his efforts to persuade his heart to sleep by telling it how wonderful dreamland is for emotional anaesthesis. Even, he tells us he said to his heart, the "wing" of the wind was closing, i.e. the wind's capacity to produce movements of the air was ceasing to be effective. But why "for"? "Lie still because the wind is ceasing to blow" implies that the circumstances were right for sleeping. "For" also governs the next statement, and for the same reason: the leaves of the rose-tree excluded the rays of the life-stimulating sun. In the same way, it was proper to sleep because the wind was half asleep on the warm sea, and even so was less quiet than the perfectly protected heart. That is, he urged the heart to lie still because it already was quieter than the half-asleep or dying wind. It should have been still, then, not only because the conditions for sleep were perfect, but also because, by having already exceeded the quietness of the wind, it had indicated that it wanted to sleep, that its desire was for sleep, or emotional suppression. The landscape of dreamland has now been broadened to include not only the rose-nest, the sun, and the rose-tree, but also the wind and the sea. The speaker said to himself, "I have created perfect conditions for the suppression of my erotic emotions. Why (l. 13) should they continue to be active?" The questioning indicates that something indeed is keeping the heart awake, and now the speaker tries to imagine what. Did it still suffer from a thought as painful and deep as a wound which a thorn from a rose or a hawthorn can cause in the flesh? Did some disappointed or frustrated hope disturb his emotional life with the relentless persistence of a dog gnawing on a bone? "What keeps waking you up, or keeps you from going completely to sleep?" What caused the eyelids of the little sleep-god to open? And he receives the same answer as to the questions of lines 5–7, "Only the song of a secret bird." It was not identifiable feelings that kept him from achieving the suppression of erotic emotions.

The next stanza shifts from the past to the present tense. It consists of general statements about dreamland; it explains why dreamland should be a perfect place to hide his heart. That is, the speaker insists that the conditions for emotional suppression can be achieved. Such conditions do not exist in the ordinary world of human relations. They are disconnected from ordinary experience by a "charm," that is, by magic, by some suspension of the normal character of human behavior and feeling. The disconnection is further emphasized in the next extensions of the basic metaphor, the landscape of dreamland. Dreamland has never been mapped. Further, although dreamland produces fruit, it is not fruit that can be sold in the marketplace. The tenor of this metaphor is satisfactions that cannot be used in relations with other people. The connection is bartering or interchanging or giving something in return for something else. Further, in the landscape of dreamland the only swallows are dreams. The only sights in motion are fantasies utterly useless in the ordinary life of human interrelations. And the sound of the wind in the tree-tops induces sleep; there is nothing in dreamland of that flow of stimulus from outside ourselves that normally keeps us awake. There are no hounds to waken and pursue the deer in the forests; there is no activity which has pursuit and gain as its object. The landscape of dreamland has now been even further extended. It is now a complete world divorced utterly from ordinary life and without any activity significant to other human beings. Yet the secret bird wakens the wildwood hart. In spite of its enclosed completeness and perfection, dreamland still contains a disturbing but unidentified and unlocated stimulus within itself.

The summary or concluding "envoi," through the use of the present perfect form "have chosen," informs us that the activity of the poem, the attempt at emotional suppression, having been begun in the past, continues into the present. The role ("part") the speaker chose was to disconnect himself from ordinary human life, to respond in no way to the values either of love that involves profound emotional commitment or of the most frivolous flirtation (love pursued for the purposes of amusing stimulation). This line confirms the hypothesis that "sleep," the sleeping god, is Cupid, and that "heart" means specifically erotic emotions. The last line contains a surprise. Throughout the poem the implication has been that the secret bird, or the element within the desire for total suppression of erotic emotions which prevents that suppression, was something to be regretted, since it was presented as a stimulus that frustrated the satisfaction of that desire. Yet "to sleep for a season" implies that the speaker had no desire that this emotional suppression should be permanent. Hence his "part," or the role in which he temporarily cast himself, has been to hear nothing of the emotions of serious or trivial love, yet to continue to respond to something, still unidentified and unlocated, that will prevent him from entering a state of complete nonexistence of erotic emotion. "I have chosen to hear no word, only the song of a secret bird," indicates that he has chosen to hear the song. Thus, even though he may regret the disturbance of the song, fundamentally he hears it because he wills to. The "secret bird" is now discovered. Beneath the speaker's desire to suppress his erotic emotions lay a deeper desire *not* to suppress them. "Bird" is a peculiarly appropriate metaphor. A bird is small and fragile; it easily blends with its surroundings. But it is capable of uttering sounds which are entrancing, disturbing, and inescapable.

The poem is about a conflict between two desires. The simultaneous satisfaction of both of them is impossible, and one of them is not even understood. Such a conflict is resolved through the realization that what one thinks one desires most profoundly, is not, in the long run, one's deepest desire, and that by postponing the gratification of the profounder desire so that the more superficial desire may be gratified at once, one may achieve emotional calm.

1. That is no country for old men.

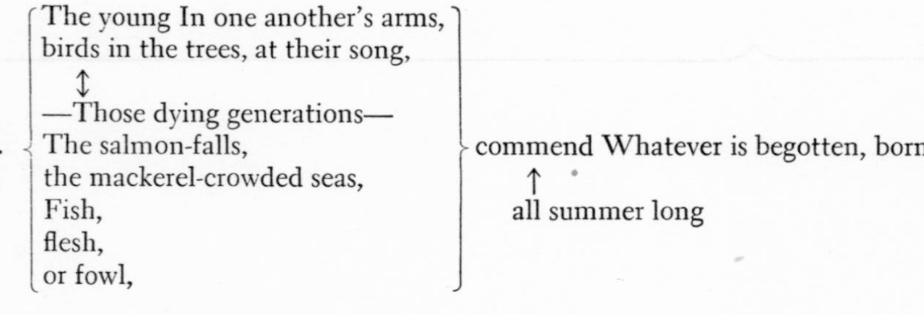

2. The young In one another's arms,
birds in the trees, at their song,
↕
—Those dying generations—
The salmon-falls,
the mackerel-crowded seas,
Fish,
flesh,
or fowl,
commend Whatever is begotten, born, and dies.
↑
all summer long

Caught in that sensual music
↓
3. all neglect Monuments of unageing intellect.

4. An aged man is but {a paltry thing, / A tattered coat upon a stick,
unless [his] Soul {clap its hands / and sing, / and *sing louder* For every tatter in its mortal dress,

3.

WILLIAM BUTLER YEATS

(1865–1939)

Sailing to Byzantium

I

That is no country for old men. The young
In one another's arms, birds in the trees,
—Those dying generations—at their song,
The salmon-falls, the mackerel-crowded seas,
Fish, flesh, or fowl, commend all summer long
Whatever is begotten, born, and dies.
Caught in that sensual music all neglect
Monuments of unageing intellect.

II

An aged man is but a paltry thing,
A tattered coat upon a stick, unless
Soul clap its hands and sing, and louder sing
For every tatter in its mortal dress,

1. *That:* that country.

3. *generations:* offspring, that which is generated or given birth to, hence living things.

4. *salmon-falls:* spawning salmon fight their way up waterfalls to get back to their birthplace; hence waterfalls which salmon climb.

5. *commend:* praise, treat as worthy of acceptance or regard.

6. *begotten:* sexually conceived and given birth to.

6. *Whatever . . . dies:* i.e. anything which is natural or organic.

7. *that sensual music:* the music of life, the music of the senses.

8. *Monuments:* not merely edifices but anything that survives by virtue of its excellence.

10–11. *unless Soul clap:* unless the soul claps.

12. *For:* the more tatters, the louder the song.

5. Nor is there [any] singing school but studying Monuments of its own magnificence;

6. And therefore I have { sailed the seas
and come To the holy city of Byzantium.

7. <O sages standing in God's holy fire
↑
As in the gold mosaic of a wall,>

8. Come from the holy fire,
perne in a gyre,
And be the singing-masters of my soul.

9. Consume my heart away;
↕
It knows not what it is;
↑
{ sick with desire
And fastened to a dying animal
and gather me Into the artifice of eternity.

Nor is there singing school but studying
Monuments of its own magnificence;
And therefore I have sailed the seas and come
To the holy city of Byzantium.

III

O sages standing in God's holy fire
As in the gold mosaic of a wall,
Come from the holy fire, perne in a gyre,
And be the singing-masters of my soul.
Consume my heart away; sick with desire
And fastened to a dying animal
It knows not what it is; and gather me
Into the artifice of eternity.

13. *Nor is there singing school but studying:* there is no singing school but studying.

14. *its:* the soul's.

16. *Byzantium:* the ancient name for Constantinople, capital of the Eastern division of the Roman Empire and for centuries one of the leading art centers of the world, particularly in painting and architecture and the two arts mentioned later in the poem: ceramics and metal enamelling.

17. *sages:* a sage is a wise man; the reference is to the great artists of history.

17. *God's holy fire:* the fire of the artificer, at once cleansing things of their organic impurities and molding them into artistic shapes of ideal beauty.

18. *gold mosaic of a wall:* perhaps the greatest achievements of Byzantium art are the representations of Christ, angels, saints, and kings in mosaic on the walls of its churches.

19. *perne in a gyre:* "perne" does not appear in the OED; it is an Irish word meaning bobbin or spool as a noun, and to spin like a bobbin or spool as a verb. A "gyre" is a spiral or vortex. See IH for further implications.

22. *dying animal:* the aged body of the poet.

23. *It:* the heart.

24. *artifice:* that which art produces.

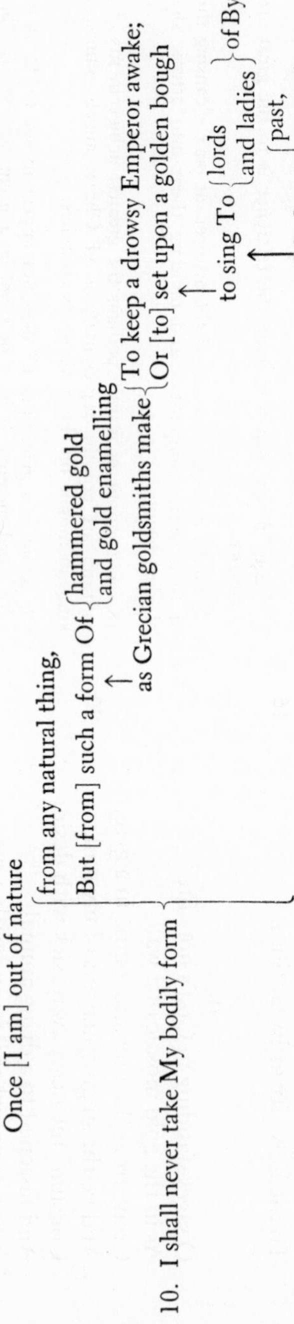
Once [I am] out of nature
10. I shall never take My bodily form
from any natural thing,
But [from] such a form Of
hammered gold
and gold enamelling
as Grecian goldsmiths make
To keep a drowsy Emperor awake;
Or [to] set upon a golden bough
to sing To
lords
and ladies
of Byzantium
Of what is
past,
or passing,
or to come.

IV

Once out of nature I shall never take
My bodily form from any natural thing,
But such a form as Grecian goldsmiths make
Of hammered gold and gold enamelling
To keep a drowsy Emperor awake;
Or set upon a golden bough to sing
To lords and ladies of Byzantium
Of what is past, or passing, or to come.

27. *form*: Yeats wrote: "I have read somewhere that in the Emperor's palace at Byzantium was a tree made of gold and silver, and artificial birds that sang."

28. *gold enamelling*: the gold can be covered with a colorful glossy coating which fuses with it under great heat and then hardens.

Interpretational Hypothesis

Byzantium, or Constantinople, now Istanbul, was the capital of the Greek or eastern half of the Roman empire, which survived long after the western half had fallen to the barbarians. In fact, it continued as a great center of Christian and medieval culture until its fall to the Turks in 1453. It is famous for its learning, its wealth, its beauty, its longevity, and particularly today for its style of non-naturalistic, severe, and glowing art. The title may indicate that the poem is a historically based account of sailing to Byzantium in the past, or it may indicate that the term "Byzantium" is to be used as a symbol of some concept or emotional attitude or orientation toward the world which the speaker is attempting to grasp or believe.

The speaker begins by referring to a country unsuitable for old men. Two questions at once arise. Is the speaker young or old? Is "that country" Byzantium or some other place? (1) If he is young, and if that country is Byzantium, then he is going to Byzantium because it is a proper place for him. (2) If he is young, and if that country is not Byzantium, then he is going to Byzantium because it is not the proper place for him and the country is the proper place (i.e. he is acting improperly and wilfully). (3) If he is old, and if that country is Byzantium, then he is going to Byzantium because it is not a proper place for him. (4) If he is old, and if that country is not Byzantium, then he is going to Byzantium because it is the proper place for him and that country is not the proper place. Although it may be of some value to hypothesize that the speaker is probably not going to a place he doesn't want to go to, there is so far nothing in the poem to justify even this reduction of the possibilities. The solution to the problem must be postponed until sufficient information has been presented to select a solution.

In that country young people make love, the birds sing in the trees. The comma after "trees" implies that "dying generations" refers to both the young and the birds. A generation is the product of an engendering, i.e. an initiation of the process of biological reproduction; or it is a group of organic beings born at about the same time; or it is a group of organic beings with a parent or parents in common. What all these meanings bring out is the notion of a repetitiveness and transiency of reproductive activity. However, in this country the falls up which salmon leap to reach their breeding grounds, the seas crowded as the result of the enormous reproductive capacity of mackerel, of fish, flesh, fowl—in short, all living things there spend the summer asserting the value ("commend") of biological creativity. Further, from the description of their activities, they commend biological creativity by participating in reproductive activity. And since they are not presented as doing anything else, since they are totally engaged in commendation by example, they are presented as thinking of nothing else but these activities, which are most appropriate to potent and vigorous youth. In the summer their thoughts do not dwell upon what the winter will bring. However, the speaker is aware of the transiency of each generation of biological life, that each generation exists, from his point of view, only to reproduce its kind and to die. Hence he interpolates "dying generations" and implies the coming of winter, the time of age and death, by referring to summer. Since youth thinks only of reproductive activity, it is unaware of transiency and death, and since the speaker is aware of these things and is thus unsuited to that country because he cannot be totally involved in reproductive acts, it follows that the speaker is old. Further, since by now "country" has been identified not merely as a place but also a "countryside" as opposed to a city, or the natural world, and since Byzantium is a city, it follows that Byzantium is not to be identified with that country. The speaker is, then, going to Byzantium because it is the proper place for him to be. This interpretation is confirmed in the next sentence. The creatures of that country, including, of course, the young, are completely involved in the entrancing actions of sensual pleasure and sexual reproduction, just as the whole personality can be entranced by music. Since the speaker observes this fact, he is outside the situation, and is therefore old. In consequence of their entrancement, the country's inhabitants all neglect to affirm the value of "monuments of unageing intellect." A monument is a memorial that testifies to the value of whatever it memorializes. It is designed to be permanent, or as permanent as possible. It is logical that all the creatures in that country should neglect monuments, since they are interested in the transient, not the permanent. Since they are sensually involved, it is equally logical that they should neglect "monuments" of intellect. Since they are unaware of ageing, it is consistent that they should ignore "monuments" of unageing intellect. However, the relation of "monuments" to intellect may mean either "monuments *dedicated to* intellect" or "monuments *created by* intellect." That is, they may be monuments which stand for or symbolize the values of intellect, or they may be monuments which embody those values. But since monuments which embody the values of the intellect necessarily symbolize those values, these are monuments *both* dedicated to and created by the intellect. However, if the speaker is sailing or planning to sail to Byzantium, at what point in the journey is he speaking the poem? This question must remain suspended.

In the second stanza, since we know that the speaker is an old man, it is at once obvious that in referring to the apparent worthlessness of aged men he is talking about himself: his usefulness in the country which he has left, the country where the prime value is the enjoyment of sexual reproduction, is obviously limited. In such a place he is only a scarecrow. His body has no more significance than a dead stick which holds up old clothes to frighten birds with. All this is true unless the old man's soul clap its hands, as for a dance, and sing, and compensate by the strength of its singing for every loss of physical vitality, for everything that damages and destroys its usefulness in the world of sensual music. "Mortal dress" is the physical or bodily clothing of the soul. As the flesh becomes wasted by time, the soul must rejoice the more. Only thus can it be something other than a "paltry thing," something almost totally without value, something that, at best, like a scarecrow, can only frighten away that which is dangerous to young life. But such a function is exceedingly paltry. In that country all organic life is equally valuable (l. 6). Whether the crows eat the seeds and seedlings in the scarecrow's field, or whether they are frightened away by the scarecrow, organic life is served. The scarecrow is superfluous to a society in which only organic life—life of no matter what kind—is important. But now (l. 13) the speaker tells us that if the value of the aged man is to be retained or re-created by singing, the soul must learn how to sing. The soul must go to a singing school, and there is no other singing school than the one in which monuments of the soul's own magnificence are studied. The soul's own magnificence is antithetical to the implicit magnificence of the flesh. This line (l. 14) offers a difficulty similar to that of line 8, the interpretation of "of." The parallelism of the two lines appears to imply the reading: "Monuments created by and dedicated to the soul's magnificence." The soul must find its value (learn to sing) by studying monuments characterized by the values of the soul, since it cannot celebrate the values of the flesh through action. This is not a poem, it follows, about the conflict between flesh and soul: the pleasure of the flesh has been given the value of entrancing music. Rather, the idea is that when the body no longer has the physical resources with which to celebrate the values of sensual and sexual pleasure, if the individual is to maintain a sense of his own value, he must discover a new source of value in the magnificence of his soul and he must learn to express that value adequately. Therefore, the speaker has sailed the seas and come to the place where the monuments of intellect are valued, where he will feel once again at home; he has come to Byzantium. "Sailing the seas," consequently, means making a transition from a psychological orientation which values the pleasure of sexuality and the flesh to one which values things of the mind and spirit and soul.

But why does the speaker call Byzantium "holy"? As we have seen, the poem is built upon an antithesis between "that country" and "Byzantium," the natural world versus a city. A city is a purely human place, created, ideally at least, as Byzantium was, by tradition, according to the human values of intellect, learning, and order. The speaker has presented the following antitheses: country-city; sexuality-intellectuality; dying-unageing; body-soul; flesh-spirit. "Unholy" is implied by "holy." By using the epithet "holy," the speaker informs us that he is giving a much higher value to the right-hand member of each antithesis than to the left. He is asserting that he regards sailing to Byzantium not as an unsatisfactory compensation for the pleasure of the country of sensual music, or as something of equal value, but rather a deliverance from the demands and conditions of that country which his age makes possible. He asserts that he is about to enter onto a higher level of experience.

It is now possible to answer the question raised at the end of the first stanza. At what point in the voyage is the poem spoken? The speaker says he has sailed to Byzantium and has arrived there, and in the next stanza he addresses the sages or spirits of the city. In explaining why he left the world of nature he has clarified the antithesis between the two worlds. Now understanding what he must do to achieve his new value, the only value open to an old man, he prepares to do so by uttering a prayer. We may imagine him, then, speaking at the point of arrival at the city, at that moment when the transition from the old orientation to the new is about to be completed by entering the city itself.

The "sages" are those who have created the monuments of unageing intellect. The whole poem is, in fact, addressed to them; it is his prayer. They stand in God's holy fire; that is, they are dead and are in heaven. They have become saints who protect and bless whatever in man transcends or rises above and out of the natural world and has rid itself of that world's demands. Even the fire of God, that extreme splendor in which no organic or natural thing can survive, does not harm them. The speaker describes the sages as resembling the non-naturalistic mosaic images of human beings, standing against a background of pure gold. (Byzantium was famous for its mosaics.) This comparison emphasizes the sages' non-natural or superhuman and divine qualities, and at the same time confirms the interpretation that they are sacred beings, saints and guardians of Byzantium. The speaker prays that they descend and teach him to sing (as in older poems the Muse was prayed to that she might descend to inspire the poet). The repetition of "holy fire" reinforces the idea that they have achieved a complete transcendence over the sensual and transient. They are requested to "perne in a gyre." "Perning" is what a spool or bobbin of thread does when it whirls rapidly as thread is drawn off it or whirled onto it. A "gyre" is the motion of a gyroscope in whirling about while maintaining its balance at any angle. It seems almost to defy gravity. To "perne in a gyre," when applied to the sages or wise men who have created monuments of unageing intellect, refers to their power to maintain an extraordinarily rapid motion while not losing their balance. But clearly, this is metaphor. The tenor, then, would be the power to maintain entirely self-sustained and self-involved intellectual activity independently of the natural world. Thus we see why the sages are to be the singing-masters of the speaker's soul. He wishes to assert the value of purely intellectual-spiritual activities and he wishes to be absolutely free of nature, to have no temptations to listen to that sensual music, to suffer no backward step from his new orientation. This interpretation is confirmed and developed in the next lines (ll. 21–24). He prays to the sages to consume his heart away, to destroy his capacity for emotional involvement with the world he has left, i.e. his capacity to love and thus the desire to achieve physical expression for that love. The reason for this prayer is that his heart no longer knows what it is; that is, there remains to it no activity by means of which it can recognize itself. Lines 21 and 22 explain why. It still desires the pleasures of "that world," the gratifications of unself-conscious sexuality; but his body is no longer capable of achieving those gratifications. He has come on his voyage not merely to achieve a new and better way of life but to solve a torturing problem; his emotional life continues, but without a function, or means of expression. Resuming his prayer, he begs the sages to gather him into "the artifice of eternity." The antithesis of such a phrase would be, "the naturalness of temporal life." The tenor of the metaphor is, "May my emotional-sensual life be destroyed. It prevents me from freeing myself from the values of the natural-temporal life. Only when it is destroyed will I be able to enter into a life devoted to the values of that which is free from nature and time, the life of the eternal and the intellectual." The vehicle is, "I have landed at Byzantium. May God's sages teach me to be a good Byzantine, and may they destroy my heart so that I may enter the city."

In stanza IV he imagines the consequences of the granting of such a prayer, and in so doing he explains to the sages that he is worth their granting his prayer. Once he is free from the temptation to think that he can still find sexual gratification, once he is free from the limits of a personality which exists to gratify the body, once, that is, he has been admitted to Byzantium, he will not think of himself as a natural product (ll. 25–26). He will think of himself as a work of art (l. 27). The goldsmiths of Byzantium were famous, so runs the legend, for their skill in making artificial birds which could flutter their wings and sing. As we have seen, "to sing" in this poem means to assert one's value by praising the soul and the intellect and their products. The significance of the idea that the purpose of these marvelous toys was only to keep awake a drowsy Emperor is this: the Emperor of Byzantium rules the city of the artifice of eternity. His gratification does not come from any sensual music which praises the world of nature, but only from a perfect art, unrelated to the demands of human flesh and personality, which will not rouse him to any activity in the real world. In the same way another function for this artificial bird is to sing to the members of the emperor's court. It sings of past, present, or future with equal indifference. It is outside of time. As an artificial bird, it is totally detached from nature, an indifferent spectator of human life. The bird of the emperor or the bird of the lords and ladies will be the model or pattern according to which the old man will think of himself, and to which he will mold his behavior, if he is admitted to Byzantium, if the sages grant his prayer and lead him into the city of which they are the patron saints, the spiritual lords. By showing that he understands Byzantium, he proves that he is worthy to enter it.

The poem dramatizes the efforts to achieve a new orientation by a man who has found gratification and his own value in the pleasure of participating in the sexually maintained continuity of organic life. Unable any longer, because of his ageing body, to achieve such gratification and value, he desires to live a life of absolute intellectual and aesthetic indifference to the natural world and the course of ordinary human life. And he asserts that such a life will be superior to his previous life.

```
                     ⎧are living;
1. Only the hands   ⎨              ⎧as deer trek desperately towards a creek
          ↑          ⎩Are moved    ⎨          ↑
          |                         |    Through the dust and scrub of the desert,
          |                         ⎩or gently As sunflowers turn to the light.
     *attracted to the wheel*,

                                ⎧               ⎧the cries of feverish children,
                                ⎪     takes up  ⎨The cravings of lions in dens,
             And, as the night  ⎨               ⎩the loves of dons,
                                ⎪                       ↕
                                ⎩Gathers them all and remains the night,
2. the Great room is full of their prayers.

3.     *They ⎧flock To the last feast of isolation*,
             ⎩and *are joined in the rite of disbelief*;
         ↑
     self-invited

4. *all their stars are recreated From numbers*,
         ↕
        ⎧The enchanted,
        ⎨the world,
        ⎩the sad.
```

WYSTAN HUGH AUDEN (1907–   )

Casino

Only the hands are living; to the wheel attracted,
Are moved as deer trek desperately towards a creek
  Through the dust and scrub of the desert, or gently
  As sunflowers turn to the light.

And, as the night takes up the cries of feverish children,
The cravings of lions in dens, the loves of dons,
  Gathers them all and remains the night, the
  Great room is full of their prayers.

To the last feast of isolation self-invited
They flock, and in the rite of disbelief are joined;
  From numbers all their stars are recreated,
  The enchanted, the world, the sad.

3. *scrub:* low shrubbery and bushes.

5. *as:* in the same way as.

5. *takes up:* merely absorbs.

6. *don:* a fellow, usually a teacher at an English university.

7. *them:* the cries of children, the cravings of lions, and the loves of dons.

7. *remains:* keeps on being, doesn't change from being.

8. *Great room:* the gambling hall.

8. *their:* the players.

10. *rite:* ceremony.

11. *numbers:* on the roulette wheel.

11. *recreated:* made new, put fresh life into, reconstructed.

5. Without,
the rivers flow among the wholly living,
↑
Quite near their trysts;
and the mountains part them;
↕
and the bird Sings towards their work.
↑
Deep in the greens and moistures of summer

6.
But here no nymph comes naked to the youngest shepherd;
The fountain is deserted;
the laurel will not grow;
The labyrinth is safe but endless,
and *Ariadne's thread Is broken*.
As *their fortune is grooved deeper in these hands*:
↕
"*few Were Lucky*,
and it is possible that none was loved;
And what was godlike in this generation Was never to be born."

Without, the rivers flow among the wholly living,
Quite near their trysts; and the mountains part them; and the bird
  Deep in the greens and moistures of summer
  Sings towards their work.

But here no nymph comes naked to the youngest shepherd;
The fountain is deserted; the laurel will not grow;
  The labyrinth is safe but endless, and broken
  Is Ariadne's thread.

As deeper in these hands is grooved their fortune: "Lucky
Were few, and it is possible that none was loved;
  And what was godlike in this generation
  Was never to be born."

13. *Without:* outside.

14. *their:* of the wholly living.

14. *trysts:* secret meeting places.

14. *part:* to separate.

14. *them:* the wholly living.

16. *Sings towards their work:* toward the work of the wholly living.

17. *here:* in the Casino.

17. *nymph:* a beautiful semi-divine creature inhabiting woods, streams, etc. in classical mythology.

18. *fountain . . . laurel:* the fountain of Helicon, and the plant from which wreaths are made; both are emblems of poetry.

19. *labyrinth:* maze of paths bordered by high hedges or walls.

20. *Ariadne's thread:* Ariadne, in Greek mythology daughter of Minos and Pasiphae, gave Theseus a thread which he let out as he went into the labyrinth, thereby saving his life.

21. *As:* at the same time.

21. *fortune:* fate.

23. *this generation:* the gamblers, conceived of as being all of the same sort of birth and conditioning.

Interpretational Hypothesis

A casino is any building built solely for pleasure and amusement. At the present time the word ordinarily refers to a gambling casino; and in the first line of the poem the reference to "the wheel" indicates that this is indeed a gambling casino: the wheel is a roulette wheel. The only living things are the hands of the gamblers. The rest of their bodies are dead, that is, without spirit, feeling, or purpose. The hands show movements in two ways. Either they behave like deer seeking water in a desert, or like sunflowers gently turning to the light. In the first metaphor the connection is that both thirsty deer and one type of gambler suffer from a desperate urge to satisfy a need. In the second, another type of gambler is distinguished, one who has the same need but whose need is immediately and easily satisfied, who can afford to be gentle rather than desperate. What is that need? Is it simply money, or is it something else? It may be hypothesized that the poem will answer this question it has raised.

The first line of the second stanza at once raises two problems. Why the "and"? What connection does it indicate? This question must be postponed until the whole stanza is understood. The second question is: Does "as" mean "while, the same time that" or "in the same way that"? To read, "While the night does various things and remains the night, the great room is full . . ." seems to make little sense because a connection between the statements seems to be nonexistent. However, "Just as (in the same way that) the night does various things and remains the night, so the great room is full of their prayers and remains the great room" seems more helpful. It implies that there is something in common between the cries, the cravings, and the loves outside in the night and the prayers inside the casino. Feverish children are miserable and unrestrainedly complaining; the cravings of lions, whether for food or love, are violent and brutal; the loves of dons—English university professors—are, at least in legend, notoriously timid, frustrated, and inhibited. To all of them the night is indifferent; it absorbs their feelings and cries and is unchanged; they have had no impact on the night. In the same way the great room of the casino where roulette is played is indifferent to the prayers of the players. It follows that the personalities of the players are like those of feverish children, lions, and dons. The equivalence takes on more force still if the dens of the lions are thought of as dens in zoos rather than natural dens. The dens, then, are prison cells and the gamblers are in a kind of prison. Thus extreme frustration is added to those other qualities which the gamblers share with lions, children, and dons. Now it becomes possible to interpret the "and" of line 5. The gamblers have a terrific drive to satisfy a need; and their need is not money but the necessity to satisfy the illness, craving, and inhibition of their personalities. And to all of this sick craving, the room, *their* environment, *their* night, is indifferent.

Hence they are here self-invited. No one cares if they come or not. Gambling is a feast of isolation because at a feast one can eat as much as he wants of what he most desires. What these people want is isolation; it follows that their great driving need, the sickness of their personalities, is for complete emotional separation from other human beings. In this they are alike as sheep are like each other ("they flock"). But why is this "feast" also a "rite," a religious celebration? One kind of feast is a communion feast in which individuals, by sharing food and drink, symbols of the necessities of life, assert their emotional relation to each other and their common belief in a divine source both of life's necessities and of that very emotional relation which they feel. Gamblers do just the opposite. The gambler has no interest in anything but whether he wins or loses on the next spin of the wheel. Hence gambling becomes the basic necessity of life, and gambling with other people is an assertion of emotional isolation and of a complete disbelief that there is any divine or other source which creates either gambling or isolation. They are joined merely because they are in the same place and doing the same thing and satisfying the same interest, not because there is any real emotional communication among them. Consequently, as the semicolon suggests, their stars are recreated from numbers. A star is traditionally a symbol of something valuable, as when we say "My lucky star." More narrowly it is a symbol of some personal value which guides one through life. But the expression "my lucky star" derives from astrology, according to which our lives are governed by the stars. Hence, the important things, the valuable things to these people are the numbers which identify the slots into which the roulette ball is whirled. Further, just as the believer in astrology, a pseudoscience, governs his life by the stars, so these people govern their lives by the numbers of the roulette wheel. But there is a further implication. The believer in astrology thinks that he can predict the course of events; the typical gambler has a "mathematical system," but he is deluded: gambling establishments take in more money than they pay out. Each of these gamblers, then, lives in an atmosphere of self-imposed delusion in which abstractions (nothing is more abstract than a number) are substituted for real human values. This idea is given additional force by "recreated." The implication is that their former "stars," their former symbols of value, have died, or have been destroyed; but that in gambling they have a new guide to life, a new system of values.

The last line in the stanza is at first puzzling, and on two accounts. First, what does this series of terms modify? And second, why are dissimilar parts of speech—an adjective, a noun, and a second adjective—put into parallel construction? Turning to the first problem, the most likely candidate for modification is "stars," but it seems more likely that at least "enchanted" and "sad"—and therefore, somehow, "world"—modify the "they" or "theirs." Since for some lines the poem has been talking about the gamblers as "they" and in fact has never given them a name but refers to them only as "they," this seems the best solution. They are enchanted; they are caught in their own self-imposed emotional magic. They are sad; they may satisfy their need for isolation, but they know nothing of the gratification that comes from emotional communion. But how about "world"? The syntactical problem is resolved if we observe that "the enchanted" is not an ellipsis for "the enchanted ones" but a conversion of an adjective into a noun by putting it into a syntactical position normally occupied by a noun. This syntactical shift is very common in the English language. The oddity of the line comes, then, from the fact that the first and third words are not normally used as nouns, while the second always is. The gamblers are the enchanted and the sad. But in what sense are they the "world"? They have enchanted themselves and made themselves sad from their self-imposed illusions; and by the same self-imposed illusion they think that they are the world; they do not recognize the reality of any human beings but themselves; or more precisely, each gambler recognizes the human reality only of himself. Each is an entirely self-enclosed world.

The opening "Without" in the next stanza (l. 13) at once indicates that they are indeed self-deluded. The implied connection between the two stanzas is "However." However, outside of the casino is the real world of people who are emotionally alive all the way through, not just in their hands (to go back to l. 1). Such people love each other ("trysts") and are close to the natural world ("rivers" and "mountains"). When the mountains part them, the implication is that they feel it, just as they are filled with feeling when they are close together. Even the birds among the damp and juicy leaves of the summer woods sing toward them and their work. Outside of the casino is a community of nature and man.

But inside the casino (l. 17) matters are different; there is nothing of the atmosphere of the idylls of the Greek poets, in which, in innocent and natural shamelessness, the deities of nature ("nymphs") made love to human beings. The juxtaposition of "fountain" and "laurel," the bush from which was made the crown for successful poets, suggest that the deserted fountain is Helicon, the fountain of the Muses from which poets drank to be inspired. In the next two lines we have a metaphor based on a famous Greek myth: Dedalus created on Crete a labyrinth which had the man-bull Minotaur at the heart of it. Ariadne gave Theseus a ball of thread to unwind so that he could find his way back again after killing the Minotaur. "Here" still governs "labyrinth is safe" because of the semicolons and the parallelism. Hence, in the casino is a labyrinth which has no Minotaur in it but on the other hand has no end. Furthermore, there is no way to find your way out of it again. What is the labyrinth of the casino? What is the tenor of this vehicle? It can scarcely be gambling itself, for gambling is by no means safe. It must, then, be "the world" of line 12, the self-inclosed emotional life of each gambler. It follows, then, that he feels safe in the casino; we have seen why; there he can be as isolated as he wishes. To be isolated, then, is to be in an emotional labyrinth, a dark place you cannot understand but which you feel is safe, although you cannot come to the end of it or go back to the entrance point. Labyrinth, then, is a vehicle for the complexities of the emotional life. The labyrinth of normal people has a Minotaur at the center; by discovering and slaying the Minotaur they uncover and resolve the source of their difficulties; they find an answer, a resolution to the tension. After encountering the Minotaur and slaying it, the normal person returns to normal life, resumes normal relations with other people. But the gambler's labyrinth has no Minotaur, no answer, no resolution, and no return.

The stanza now leaves us with one further question. Why is all the imagery taken from classical mythology? We have seen that the labyrinth is a metaphor. Since "labyrinth" is parallel with the other three statements in this stanza, it may be assumed that they also are metaphors. Then the tenor of the first (l. 17) is that here in the casino there is no experience of innocent and natural eroticism; the tenor of the second ("The fountain is deserted") is that here there is no free impulse of the imagination; the tenor of the third ("The laurel will not grow") is that here there are no rewards for achievement. And finally, the negative tenor of the last ("the labyrinth") is that here there is no challenge to which one can make an heroic response. The implication is that in the real world outside of the casino these are the real values.

The "As" of the first line of the last stanza implies that something is going on while their fortune is grooved into their hands. That something is, of course, the whole gambling situation and the life of the world outside of the casino presented in the preceding five stanzas. The colon after "fortune" indicates that what follows is a statement of that fortune. But why is it enclosed in quotation marks? The fact that their fortune is grooved in their hands implies that it may be read from their hands by a palmist, someone who purports to make predictions about an individual's future on the basis of lines in the palm of his hand. That is, in the quotation marks is a palmist's report or prediction. Palmistry is a pseudoscience, like astrology; the palmist purports to read a man's character and his future. People of a specific character, according to the palmist, will have a specific and unavoidable future. Literally, line 21 states that continuous gambling cuts more deeply into the gamblers' hands those lines ("grooves") from which the palmist determines character and predicts the future. For two reasons we may assume that this notion is metaphorical: (1) Palmistry, like astrology, is a pseudoscience; since astrology has been used metaphorically (l. 11), there is high probability that palmistry is also being used metaphorically; (2) even if astrology hadn't been alluded to earlier in the poem, the very fact that palmistry is a pseudoscience, and recognized as a pseudoscience in modern times by everyone of any intellectual sophistication, suggests that line 21 is metaphorical. (That is, we have to read Chaucer [14th century] with the assumption that he believed in astrology; we cannot so read Rossetti, who, in the 1860's and 1870's when he wrote *The House of Life*, used astrology metaphorically.) The tenor, then, of this vehicle is: Continuous gambling reinforces in the gamblers' characters those needs which originally drove them to gambling; consequently, the more they gamble the greater their need to gamble. This interpretation is consistent with the rest of the interpretational hypothesis, and specifically reaffirms the notion presented in the Minotaur metaphor. (Their labyrinth is endless and has no Minotaur.) Moreover, the repetition of "hands" (ll. 1 and 21) can hardly be accidental. Although palmists cannot read character and future from the lines in the hands, the speaker of the poem does read character and future from the continuous movement of the hands and now proposes to state both the cause of the gambling and the future of the personalities enmeshed in it. He returns to the problem of his initial observation. Why are only the hands living? And we now see the poem as an explanation of a fact which differentiates gamblers from normal people outside of the casino.

The speaker, then, continuing the metaphor of line 21, assumes the role of the palmist, with the difference that since he has had made a real observation ("Only the hands are living"), he can provide a reliable explanation and prediction about the future of the gamblers. His explanation is that, first, few of them were lucky; that is, life, as we would say, gave few of them a decent, or lucky, break. Victims of circumstance to a greater degree than other people, they felt their unusual fortune or fate and expressed that feeling in their sense of isolation. Second, it is possible that none was loved. The speaker is here less sure of his proposed causality, but he suggests that none of them had the experience of being loved, the primary experience that breaks through an individual's sense of isolation. The consequence, and the prognosis, is presented in the next statement, beginning, "And what was godlike . . ." A god creates the world and makes it valuable. In a human being a godlike quality is one that makes it possible for him to make the world meaningful and valuable for himself and others. A generation, all born approximately at the same time, is a group of people with something in common. These people have in common the fact that they are gamblers. Because they were unlucky and unloved, they have become isolated and can satisfy their isolation only in gambling. Consequently their ability to create and give value to the world was fated never to be expressed. It was fated because their sickness necessarily destroyed their creative powers.

The poem, then, is the meditation of someone in a gambling casino watching the gamblers and wondering what makes them act as they do. He perceives that they gamble from some inner necessity, that the world is indifferent to them, that they desire that indifference and isolation, that the world of healthy human beings is utterly alien, that these people have none of the achievements and rewards of the healthy world, that only in the gambling casino can they feel safe. They are failures as human beings, but, he suggests, they are victims of the chances of the world and of psychological deprivation.

1. Let me not *Admit impediments to the marriage of true minds*,

2. love is not love
   ↑
   Which alters *when it { finds alteration
   { Or bends to remove with the remover*.

3. O no, it is an ever fixed mark
   ↑
   That { looks on tempests
   { and is never shaken;

4. It is the star to every wand'ring bark,
   ↑
   Whose worth's unknown,
   ↑
   although his [the star's] heighth be taken.

WILLIAM SHAKESPEARE (1564–1616)

Sonnet 116

Let me not to the marriage of true minds
Admit impediments, love is not love
Which alters when it alteration finds,
Or bends with the remover to remove.
O no, it is an ever fixed mark
That looks on tempests and is never shaken;
It is the star to every wand'ring bark,
Whose worth's unknown, although his heighth be taken.

2. *Admit:* acknowledge the possibility of.

2. *impediments:* obstructions.

4. *bends:* turns away, departs.

4. *remover:* one who leaves, one who is inconstant.

4. *to remove:* to leave, to go away.

5. *mark:* a sea-mark, a conspicuous object distinguishable at sea which serves to guide or warn sailors in navigation.

7. *bark:* any ship.

8. *worth:* real significance or value.

8. *his:* its. (The possessive form "its" only became regular in the late 17th century. The normal possessive in the 16th century for "it" was "his." No personification is implied.)

8. *heighth:* the measure of the star taken with the cross-staff, for determining one's latitude at sea.

5. Love's not Time's fool,
↑
though rosy lips and cheeks *come Within his [Time's] bending sickle's compass*,

6. Love {alters not with his [Time's] brief hours and weeks,
But bears it out even to the edge of doom:

If this be {error
and *proved upon me*,

7. {I never writ,
nor no man ever loved.

Love's not Time's fool, though rosy lips and cheeks
Within his bending sickle's compass come,
Love alters not with his brief hours and weeks,
But bears it out even to the edge of doom:
   If this be error and upon me proved,
   I never writ, nor no man ever loved.

9. *fool:* court jester.

9–10. *though . . . come:* although young people grow old.

10. *bending:* bending down, lowering in order to encompass.

10. *sickle:* scythe, a curved knife for cutting crops.

10. *compass:* range, area of coverage.

11. *his:* Time's.

12. *bears it out:* lasts.

12. *doom:* Doomsday, the day of final judgment, i.e. the end of time. ("Doom" does not mean "tragic fate" or "impending death.")

13. *upon me proved:* proved against me.

14. *writ:* wrote.

Interpretational Hypothesis

The poem begins with an appeal. Do not permit me to admit the truth of the proposition that any obstacle can frustrate (or stand in the way of) the permanent devotion to each other of faithful minds. "Mind" is probably best thought of here as mental intention, as in "I have a mind to do so-and-so." But to whom is the request addressed? It has a peculiar urgency, coming as it does at the beginning of the poem without any prelude or explanation. It is as if the speaker were desperately crying out, "Don't let me do it! I don't want to!" The request implies a powerful impulse to do whatever the speaker is begging not to be permitted to do. It may be addressed to the beloved, or it may be addressed to the speaker himself. But if to the former, an insistence that there *are* no impediments would seem more likely. There is also the possibility that the speaker is addressing a third individual, a god or a friend. But since there is no information as to who such a person might be, it is best to adopt, until the poem requires us to do otherwise, the simplest hypothesis. We shall go on the assumption, therefore, that the speaker is addressing himself, and is, in some agony, attempting to quell his doubts about the permanence of love. "True" is used in the sense of "faithful in love," and is associated with "marriage," because to plight one's troth, to declare one's truth or faithfulness, precedes marriage. "Marriage of true minds," then, can be interpreted as the unchanging devotion to each other of personalities who have declared that they would maintain such devotion. The speaker is trying to resist considering the possibility that the declaration of love does not assure love's permanence, that "saying so does not make it so." If this hypothesis is correct, the doubts which the speaker is trying to suppress will make themselves apparent in the poem.

The first attempt to achieve conviction is by definition. An emotion which one has taken to be love is not really love which changes simply because its object (i.e. the beloved) has changed. Even if a partner in love (i.e. the beloved) exhibits a lessening or cessation of love, a true lover continues to love. Nor is an emotion really love if its direction is turned away from the beloved toward another love-object just because the beloved's emotion has shifted *its* direction toward another love-object (l. 4). It follows that the speaker is not so much anxious about a change in the love of his partner as he is about what would happen to his own feelings if his partner's love changed. If, the implication is, the speaker's love should change as a consequence of a change in the beloved's love, then the speaker's love was not really love to begin with. That is, if it should turn out that there are impediments to a love which appears to be a true love, then it was not true love in the first place. But this conclusion is not satisfactory, because the speaker doesn't want to find out if his love is true or not; he wants to believe that there is no possibility that it is not true love. Does his anxiety stem from a suspicion, hidden even from himself, that there is such a possibility? Else, why all the shouting?

It is not surprising, then, that the next statement begins with a cry of denial that his love could change, that it could not be true love. A metaphor follows: The vehicle is a sea-mark which guides sailors and can be relied on even in storms. The tenor is an emotion which remains unaffected even while the individual who feels that emotion is in the throes of emotional disturbance. The connection is fixity. Again he assures himself that his love cannot change even if he experiences emotional turmoil within himself, for, as we have seen in the interpretation of lines 1–4, his anxiety is really about his own emotions and their reliability, not his partner's.

The speaker now introduces another metaphor taken from life at sea. But why does he continue to use sea-metaphors? The reason is that the sea is an ancient and standard metaphor for changefulness and unreliability. In order to establish his position at sea a sailor determines how high above the horizon a star may be. By using an instrument (in the sixteenth century, a cross-staff) he measures the angle between the horizon and a star. Thus he determines his latitude or how far north he is. His judgment is all the more reliable if he can sight the North Star. But even then he cannot determine his longitude, for before the nineteenth century it was impossible to determine longitude. A wandering ship, then, one which has lost its way, may very well determine the height of a star above the horizon, but will be unable to chart its course from such meager information. Thus to the individual lost in the turmoil of his emotions love is something of enormous value (a standard tenor for a star-metaphor) but in a sense it is also quite useless to him because he cannot predict even while experiencing love what his future course will or should be. The contrast between the assurance of line 7 and the revelation in line 8 of the worthlessness of that assurance reveals that the speaker is *not* sure of the permanence and reliability of his love and therefore is not sure that it will last.

The speaker now shifts his metaphorical world from the sea to court life, another standard symbolization for changefulness and unreliability. Here the vehicle is the king and the king's jester, whose function is to be amusing. If he is not—off with his head! A jester was also a privileged character; he could say things to the king which other courtiers could not, so long as he was witty and amusing. Otherwise—! At best he suffered dismissal. A jester, then, is someone who is allowed to get away with something, who is allowed certain privileges, but those privileges are likely to be withdrawn at the whim of the jester's master. In the first half of line 8, therefore, the speaker asserts that love is not a jester at the mercy of Time (the king) or of its whims and unpredictability. And this independence from Time is true even though the original inspiration for love, personal beauty and youth ("rosy lips and cheeks"), must submit to the power of Time. Time is presented in the traditional way as a man with a scythe or sickle, and Time mows down men as a reaper mows down grass. In the same way Time mows down beauty. Love survives, then, what originally caused it, the beauty of the beloved. Consequently it does not change under the impact of the passing of the paltry hours and weeks of time, but survives even to the day of the Last Judgment, when all things shall end. The old term was "doomsday." We have a situation like that of lines 7 and 8. There is a contrast between the brief passage of hours and weeks and the vast reaches of time which separate us from the end of the world. The very exaggeration and desperation of the statement implies a doubt. That is, in the context of this interpretational hypothesis the hyperbole (exaggerated statement) seems to be a defense against an emotional pressure of uncertainty about the validity and permanence ("trueness") of the speaker's own feelings of love.

It is not surprising, then, that the poem ends with another exaggerated statement: if the speaker is wrong about the reliability of his love under the impact of time and change, then he never wrote this poem and no man was ever in love. But the assurance of the statement is undermined by the doubts that have intruded and by the fact that the statement may very well be untrue. That is, his attitude ("this," l. 13) is unquestionably an error if it is a fact that what people call "true love" does indeed change, weaken, and die. At the very least, there is no agreement on the matter: probably as many people think "true love" can die as think it cannot. The final statement, then, is questionable when judged by ordinary human experience, and probably untrue. Thus the poet has presented the speaker as reassuring himself and, simultaneously, revealing the hollowness of that assurance. The drama of the poem is concerned with the efforts of a man to keep from thinking what he suspects is very possibly true. Since the process of self-deception in order to make an unacceptable situation acceptable is called rationalization, it may be said that the poem simultaneously presents a rationalization and reveals, at least to the reader, if not, apparently, to the speaker, that it *is* a rationalization.

4.

EMILY DICKINSON (1830–1886)

Poem 512

The Soul has Bandaged moments—
When too appalled to stir—
She feels some ghastly Fright come up
And stop to look at her—

Salute her—with long fingers—
Caress her freezing hair—
Sip, Goblin, from the very lips
The Lover—hovered—o'er—
Unworthy, that a thought so mean
Accost a Theme—so—fair—

The soul has moments of Escape—
When bursting all the doors—
She dances like a Bomb, abroad,
And swings upon the Hours,

As do the Bee—delirious borne—
Long Dungeoned from his Rose—
Touch Liberty—then know no more,
But Noon, and Paradise—

The Soul's retaken moments—
When, Felon led along,
With shackles on the plumed feet,
And staples, in the Song,

The Horror welcomes her, again,
These, are not brayed of Tongue—

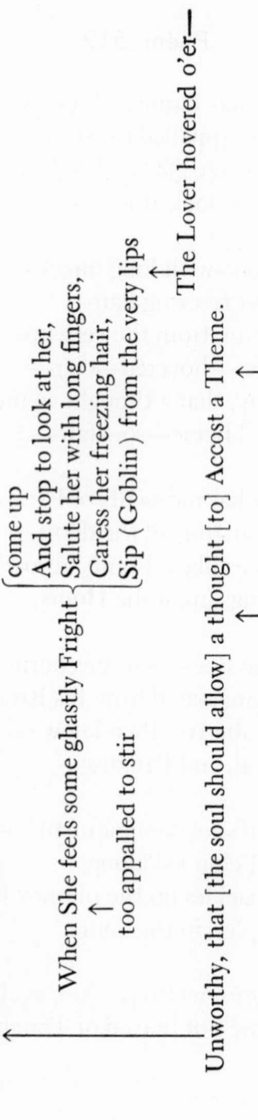
1. The Soul has Bandaged moments,
When She feels some ghastly Fright
too appalled to stir
come up
And stop to look at her,
Salute her with long fingers,
Caress her freezing hair,
Sip (Goblin) from the very lips
The Lover hovered o'er—
Unworthy, that [the soul should allow] a thought [to] Accost a Theme.
so mean
so fair

Punctuated Text

The Soul has Bandaged moments,
When too appalled to stir
She feels some ghastly Fright come up
And stop to look at her,

Salute her with long fingers,
Caress her freezing hair,
Sip (Goblin) from the very lips
The Lover hovered o'er—
Unworthy, that a thought so mean
Accost a Theme so fair.

1. *Bandaged moments:* moments when the soul is bandaged.
2. *appalled:* horrified, made pale with fear.
3. *ghastly:* fearful; like a ghost.
4. *her:* the soul.
5. *Salute:* greet.
7. *Goblin:* a devil.
9. *mean:* nasty, unpleasant.
10. *Accost:* make advances to.
10. *Theme:* subject, here the soul.
10. *fair:* lovely.

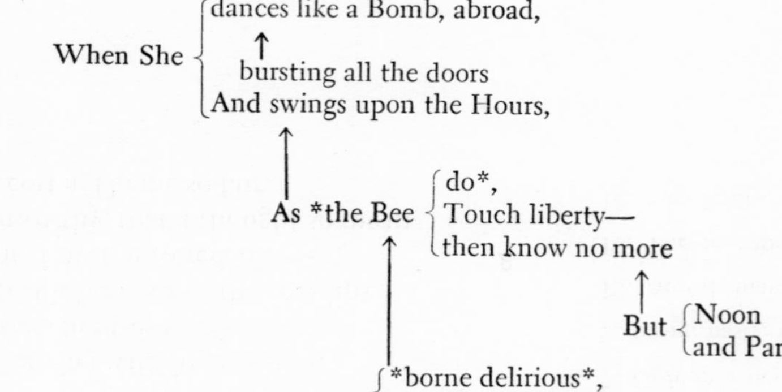

2. The soul has moments of Escape,
When She {dances like a Bomb, abroad,
↑
bursting all the doors
And swings upon the Hours,
↑
As *the Bee {do*,
Touch liberty—
then know no more
↑
But {Noon
and Paradise.
↑
{*borne delirious*,
Long Dungeoned from his Rose,

3. The soul's [has] retaken moments,
When, The Horror welcomes her again:
↕
Felon led along,
↑
With {shackles on the plumed feet
And staples in the Song,

4. These [moments] are not brayed of Tongue.

The soul has moments of Escape,
When bursting all the doors
She dances like a Bomb, abroad,
And swings upon the Hours,

As do the Bee, delirious borne,
Long Dungeoned from his Rose,
Touch Liberty—then know no more
But Noon and Paradise.

The soul's retaken moments,
When, Felon led along,
With shackles on the plumed feet
And staples in the Song,

The Horror welcomes her again:
These are not brayed of Tongue.

14. *Hours:* time.

15. *do:* subjunctive form for "does."

15. *borne:* carried aloft.

16. *Dungeoned from:* locked away from.

17. *Touch, know:* subjunctive forms for "touches" and "knows."

19. *soul's:* soul has.

20. *Felon:* criminal.

21. *shackles:* leg-irons.

22. *staples:* fastening nails.

24. *brayed:* to make a raucous noise.

24. *of:* by the.

Interpretational Hypothesis

In the first line it is not moments that are bandaged, but moments when the soul is bandaged. "Bandaged" has several possible interpretations. One is that the soul is thought of as a body so thoroughly wound in bandages that it cannot stir; the other is that the soul is blindfolded. Both seem to work equally well. The first would be consistent with the statement that the soul cannot stir because it is too horrified; in this interpretation the bandage would stand for the soul's horror-stricken immobility. The second is consistent with the statement that the soul feels, rather than sees, the approach of the ghastly Fright. Something has blinded the soul and rendered it motionless and helpless. What? The poem should provide the answer.

A ghastly fright is dreadful because it is like a ghost, a terrifying unreality which is the remembered image of a past experience. Since, as we have seen, the soul is appalled because it is blindfolded and cannot see normal reality, we may conclude that the Fright appears because the soul cannot see. Separated from normal reality as it is, the soul remembers something from the past which horrifies it; the speaker is identifying, then, what psychologists would call a compulsive memory or image. Helpless, the soul feels the approach of this memory and senses that instead of fading away it stops to look. Since "appalled" is dependent on "come up and stop," the latter also contributes to the sense of horror. The feeling of being examined adds to the soul's appallment. Such distress is felt when one has something to hide, i.e. when one feels guilty. "The something from the past," then, is something the soul has done, the memory of which involves guilt and shame.

In the next stanza we must ask why the approach of the frightful memory is presented as it is, in language appropriate to sexual advances. The Fright touches the soul's body, caresses the hair, which freezes under the touch, and, Goblin, creature of the night that the Fright is, it kisses the lips once hovered over (that is, not actually kissed) by a lover. It dares what even a lover did not dare. "Unworthy" presents a difficult problem. One would think that the Goblin-Fright was the unworthy one in this drama, but the word modifies "soul." In "A thought . . . accost a theme," the "thought" is the Goblin-Fright and the "theme" is the soul. The full form is, "The soul is unworthy that so mean a thought should accost so fair a theme as the soul"; or, more clearly, "A soul must be unworthy if so mean a thought may accost it." This unworthiness of the soul reinforces the interpretation that the soul is or feels itself guilty. The poet is making the usual distinction between soul and mind, or, roughly, between our feelings or emotional life on the one hand, and, on the other, our reason, our power to examine and judge all things, including our emotional life. A "theme" is a matter or a subject which the mind examines. To provide itself an instrument for examining that theme, the mind produces a thought. Here, the mind uses a thought to examine the soul in such a way as to reveal the soul's guilt. The remaining problem is "accost." Literally, the word means to go to the side of someone, to get next to someone. But it is almost always used in a shameful situation, as when a prostitute accosts and solicits a prospective client. This is entirely consistent with the sexual tone of the approach of the Goblin to the soul (ll. 5–8). However, the soul is presented here as feminine. Thus the situation is one in which an erotically interested man approaches a woman who pretends to be sexually unapproachable but actually is not; who pretends to be sexually pure, but is in fact quite the opposite; who pretends, then, to be guiltless but is guilty, as we have seen. It is the soul's fault that the horror should be able to approach her, that the mind can examine and judge her. We can now answer the question posed above: "What has so blinded the soul that it can be subject to this dreadful threat of violation?" The answer is that because its own unworthiness has made the accosting possible, the soul has blinded itself. In our lives come moments when we are blind and helpless. We feel our guilt, but, because we are blind, we cannot understand the nature of the accusation that we are making against ourselves. We feel guilty; we do not know why or what we are guilty of; and we are helpless if we attempt to understand the reasons for our self-accusation or to deny its truth and justification.

What is the connection with the next stanza? The contrast between lines 10 and 11 indicate that we may supply a "but," or "on the other hand." "But the soul has moments when it escapes from the Goblin." We can, then, assume that the "doors" are meant as confining doors or prison doors which at certain moments can be burst or broken through. The soul escapes from the prison and dances outside the prison "like a bomb." A bomb has the potential of enormous explosive energy. The closeness of "burst" and "bomb" implies that this very energy not only enables the soul to dance in freedom, outside of the prison, with a sense of great potential energy for further activity ("dancing"), but also that that very energy was responsible for its escape from prison. The connective "but" can now be made more precise. "Although the soul can be rendered helpless by guilt, it also has a tremendous reserve of energy with which it can free itself from guilt."

But what is meant by "Swings upon the hours"? In this metaphor there are several possibilities. One is that the soul swings upon a rope swing; thus each hour would be a support for the swing, or, perhaps, a tree from which the swing hangs. Another is that the soul swings as a trapeze artist swings, freely from one flying bar to the next. Each hour is a flying trapeze. Now, although it is virtually impossible to decide which is preferable, both vehicles have in common the notion of play, of easeful mastery, and of freedom from normal laws of physics and gravity. That is, under ordinary circumstances, we are subject to the hours, ruled by them. But here the soul is not subject to the hours; it plays with them, as a child plays with toys, or on them. In short, it is in control of time. In those moments when the soul is freed by its great potential of energy, it is not subject to time, but rather dominates time and does with time what it pleases. When in prison, or bandaged, it is subject to time in the sense that it is confined by the guilt of something done in the past. To swing upon the hours, then, means to be free of the past and to live solely in the present.

In the next stanza, the sentence continues and compares the soul in this state with the bee. Here "bee" is used in a very strange way. At first it looks as if a singular subject were being used with a plural verb. However, "touch" and "know" are also verbs for "bee" and are also singular. The form used is actually a subjunctive; thus, "As a bee would do, would touch Liberty, and would know no more." The use of the subjunctive brings out the hypothetical character of the vehicle, and suggests a similar hypothetical character for the tenor. The bee is presented as having been previously dungeoned, or kept in prison, locked away from his rose, to plunder and gather the nectar, an action which is his sole aim and function. He is now borne, or carried away—by what? Turning back to the tenor, we observe the parallel with the implied prison and by implication with "bursting" and hence with "bomb." He is borne by his own internal force, and the release of that potential into activity makes him delirious with joy, just as the soul danced. By achieving his delicious goal, the rose, he touches liberty, and in consequence loses all knowledge of his surroundings, except the knowledge that it is noon, the apex of the day, and that he is in Paradise. That is, turning to the vehicle, he is in the state the soul is in when it swings upon the hours, free of the binding sense of time and of the guilty past. Thus when the soul achieves *its* true object, *its* rose, it is in Paradise, the place which is the equivalent of the noontime, as the parallel construction tells us. Thus the true object of the soul is to be free from the compulsive memories which bind it to the past, that is, to time, and to live in the present moment of pure joy and fulfillment, which is infinite.

Now, suddenly, there is another break, like that after line 10. The parallel with lines 1 and 11 suggests that "Soul's" should be read as "soul has." This is common and even normal elision in spoken English, as in "Mike's had it." A further parallel with line 1 indicates that we should not read, "The soul has moments that are retaken," but, "The soul has moments when it is retaken." In these retaken moments the soul is compared to a criminal. On its plumed feet, those which once carried it out of its prison to dance abroad, are the shackles which will keep it from escaping again. Even its song is "stapled," fastened down, so that even the utterance of the soul at liberty is treated as if it were a criminal act. That is, the soul is prevented from any expression of itself and its internal potential. Its position is now worse than in the first section. There horror rendered it immobile. But in the second section it burst out of that horror, those bandages, and escaped. Now, however, it is chained, more firmly bound down. The Horror welcomes her as a jailer receives back an escaped prisoner, brought back in shame. Between the tenor, soul, and the vehicle, felon, then, the connection is guilt. "Welcomes" has a peculiar force here. We are welcomed to a place when it is right and proper that we should enter into it, whether or not we want to go there. If the soul is welcomed, it is right and proper that it should once again enter its prison. It is, then, guilty. This, of course, is entirely consistent with the interpretation of the first section that a sense of guilt in the soul permitted the Horror to accost it. These terrible moments of recapture are "not brayed of tongue." "Of" in this context means "by" and "to bray" is to make the big raucous grotesque noise by which a donkey or an ass calls attention to its foolish self. This sound suggests what happens when an unworthy creature makes a big noise, calls attention to itself, boasts. Nobody, the speaker says, boasts about such moments. You may boast of your suffering or your joy in escape from suffering. But who boasts of those moments when you re-enter into a condition of psychological suffering which you realize is entirely produced by your own weakness and guilt? These are the moments of shame which you keep quiet about because you cannot blame them on anyone else. Shame, and the realization of shame, is the subject of the poem. The soul's capacity for shame is what makes it susceptible to being accosted and imprisoned by the mind. It seems not unreasonable to translate the idea into modern terminology. Since "soul" can be identified in this poem with the emotional life (there is nothing to suggest that a theological or religious sense of "soul" is at work) the subject of the poem is the psychology of emotional inhibition through self-conscious shame.

```
                {At the earliest ending of winter,
                {In March,
                   ↓
1. a scrawny cry Seemed like a sound in his mind.
                ↑
                from outside

2. He knew that he heard it,
                      ↑    ↕
                      |    A bird's cry,
                     {at daylight or before,
                     {In the early March wind.

3. The sun was rising at six,
      ↑
    No longer a battered panache above snow . . .

4. It would have been outside.
```

WALLACE STEVENS *(1879–1955)*

Not Ideas about the Thing but the Thing Itself

At the earliest ending of winter,
In March, a scrawny cry from outside
Seemed like a sound in his mind.

He knew that he heard it,
A bird's cry, at daylight or before,
In the early March wind.

The sun was rising at six,
No longer a battered panache above snow . . .
It would have been outside.

2. *scrawny:* scraggy, lean, thin.

8. *panache:* ornamental plume or tuft of feathers, usually on a hat or helmet.

5. It was not from the vast ventriloquism Of sleep's faded papier-mâché . . .

6. The sun was coming from outside.

7. That scrawny cry—
↕
it was A chorister whose c preceded the choir.

8. It was part of the colossal sun,
↑
Surrounded by its choral rings,
↑
Still far away.

9. It was like A new knowledge of reality.

It was not from the vast ventriloquism
Of sleep's faded papier-mâché . . .
The sun was coming from outside.

That scrawny cry—it was
A chorister whose c preceded the choir.
It was part of the colossal sun,

Surrounded by its choral rings,
Still far away. It was like
A new knowledge of reality.

11. *papier-mâché:* a combination of shredded paper and glue, used for making furniture.

14. *chorister:* member of a choir.

14. *c:* the musical note "C."

16. *rings:* perhaps a pun: (1) encompassing circles, (2) reverberations of the music.

Interpretational Hypothesis

The title raises a number of perplexities. How should it be completed? "This poem is not about ideas about the thing but about the thing itself?" Or, "Not ideas about the thing but the thing itself is what I am interested in," or ". . . is what we ought to value," or ". . . is what we never can grasp or understand"? This last is a little odd, perhaps, but it seems possible. In other words, the poem should make it possible to complete the sentence implied by the title. From the title, however, we seem to be informed of at least one important point: the poem will be concerned with the distinction between the mind's ideas of the real world and the objects in the real world to which those ideas refer. It implies that the mind's ideas are related to things outside of the mind. But this implication also may be a trap.

The first line and part of the second, through "March," present the first problem. It is apparent that this line and a half sets the time of the poem. We can grasp that the events of the poem take place in March, but "the earliest ending of winter" is a peculiar phrase. Faced with such odd locutions, it is advisable to attempt to find an analogous phrase in ordinary language. If for "ending of winter" we substitute the more general "point of time," and if for that we substitute "moment," we have "at the earliest moment." Such a phrase usually is concluded by "possible," and hence, when "possible" is omitted, implies that word. The phrase now reads: "At the earliest ending of winter that is possible (and that moment comes in March)." But "earliest" implies that the word it modifies may also be modified by "less early" or "later." The implication is that winter may end at any one of a number of times during March. Since by the calendar it can end at only one time (on March 21), one of a series of other endings to winter must be referred to. In another mode of reckoning the end of winter, a common method is to determine it by the appearance of some sign of spring, the coming of warm weather, the appearance of certain flowers, or the coming back of the birds from the south. The last of these is perhaps the most commonly accepted sign of spring. We may hypothesize at this point (1) that the problem of what ends winter will be resolved, and (2) that the poem may very well be about some kind of transition.

At this point of time, then, the speaker thinks or says that a scrawny cry from outside seemed to be in "his" mind. But who is the "he" of "his"? This question must be suspended until additional information is forthcoming. "Scrawny" usually implies both thin and ugly. A "scrawny cry" would be a cry not easily heard, not far above the level of perception, and hoarse and scratchy. "Outside" in its ordinary sense means outside of some enclosure, ordinarily a house or a room. Here, the antithesis between "outside" and "in his mind," emphasized by the fact that both phrases end a line, suggests that "outside his mind" is meant. The speaker tells us that the cry was outside "his" mind. But "he" thinks that it is inside. Can we identify such an experience? Dreams in which a stimulus from outside the body finds its place in a dream and as part of a dream are not uncommon, particularly in the morning when we are gradually coming awake and are more responsive to exterior stimuli. This seems to be such a case, and virtually confirms the idea that it is the ending of night and that, since "he" is waking up, one of the themes of the poem is transition from one state to another.

"He" then is a dreamer, gradually awaking from sleep, who is incorporating exterior stimuli into his dreams. The next stanza takes the process one step further. Now the dreamer knew that he heard it, did not dream it, and he identified it. It was the cry of a bird. This resolves the problem of what ends winter. It is the moment of the return of the birds, which we are aware of when we first see a bird or, as here, when we first hear one. It is either at the first light of day or before (the dreamer does not know which), and he is aware of the wind, and aware of it as the wind of early March.

Now (l. 6) the speaker tells us first that the sun is rising at six, another indication that winter is ending as well as information that instructs us that time is passing, since it is now past the time of first light; and second, that the rising sun no longer has the paleness of the sun in midwinter. It no longer seems like a gorgeous plumed feather for a helmet, somewhat the worse for wear. It is no longer shedding its light on snow. Spring has come; the snow is gone. The three dots and the next line present a difficulty. The shift from past indicative to past conditional indicates that some shift in point of view has taken place. In the present tense line 9 would read "It will have been," an obsolete or at least obsolescent and noncolloquial way of saying, "It must have been outside." The dots, then, and line 9 indicate that the speaker is imagining what the half-awake dreamer was saying to himself. "Now that would be something going on outside my mind, not inside." But what is the antecedent of "it"? At first glance, either the bird's cry or the sun serves equally well, but the "sun" is the nearer to "it." Although it is always advisable to assume that the nearest possible antecedent for a pronoun is the word meant until some reason is discerned for not so assuming, the repetition of "outside" makes more plausible the interpretation that "it" refers to "cry." "Outside" serves to define the antecedent of "it."

The parallel in construction and punctuation between stanzas 3 and 4 suggests that in all probability the first two lines (ll. 10–11) are from the speaker, a notion fairly well confirmed by the shift back from the conditional mode to the indicative. The speaker is now interested in confirming the feeling of the sleeper. "It," like the preceding "It" (l. 9), refers to the cry, since between the two "its" is nothing which can serve as antecedent for a second "it." This is confirmed by "ventriloquism," the illusory projection of a sound to a point other than its actual point of origin. "Papier-mâché" is made by combining shredded paper with glue and then forming it to imitate elaborate woodcarving. The forming is done by pressing the still unsolidified "mash" of paper and glue into a mold. Hence "papier-mâché" is a cheap and, like ventriloquism, illusory imitation of the real thing; it is molded, not carved, and is therefore, though a reverse copy of its mold, an exact copy of the object from which the mold was made. Making papier-mâché objects is now an old-fashioned nineteenth-century technique, and things thus made are faded from age and their out-of-dateness. This is the vehicle. The tenor is dreams, since the images of sleep, the things that sleep makes, are dreams. The connection is that dreams are cheap imitations of real things and are out-of-date in the sense that they are formed from past experiences. But they delude us just as ventriloquism deludes us. In the next line, the dreamer (as the dots indicate) becomes aware of the sun. Or rather, the sun enters his dreams but he is a little more awake. Instead of thinking, "That cry must have come from outside," he thinks, "The sun is coming from outside." The past indicative is used here, just as the past subjunctive was used in line 9, because the speaker is not quoting the dreamer but constructing or imagining his thoughts.

The speaker now connects the cry and the sun in one concept. In a choir one singer sounds a note (here C, the basic note of the scale of the basic and most common scale, C major) and the other singers take their pitch from him. He gets a chorus under way. Thus the cry of the bird sounded a note which will be taken up later by other birds. But how can the cry be part of the sun? And why is the sun called colossal? The first question is answered in line 16. The choir of the birds form rings of sounds ("choral rings") around the sun, or *will* form rings of sounds when they come, for they are now still far away. The bird who utters the scrawny cry is but the first of the many birds who will come north as spring goes on and who will sing at dawn. This interpretation provides a further explanation for "preceded." The chorus has not yet arrived because it is so early in spring, at the earliest moment at which winter may be thought of as ending. When the birds' chorus does arrive, there will be one great vision, the rising sun surrounded by the choral rings of the birds, of whom the sounder of the scrawny cry will be one. Inseparable from the sun, it will be part of it, since it will be part of the vision that unites both the sun and the birds' songs. The sun is colossal because it is just above the horizon (l. 7), and at rising and setting the sun always appears surprisingly larger than it does when it is an hour in the sky.

The cry was like a new knowledge of reality to the dreamer. Why "new"? First, this word confirms the hypothesis that the poem is about some kind of transition, and this transition from "old knowledge," the source of dream images, to "new knowledge," images entering the mind from outside it, is the transition itself. The transitions involved are from winter to spring, from night to day, from dreaming to waking, and from imitation (ventriloquism and papier-mâché) to reality. The contrast between the inferior nature of the old, also indicated by the worn-out sun of winter, and the new—the choir of birds, the colossal sun, the glory of light and music united in the vision of the sun and the birds' song—indicates that the poet is affirming the superior value of the new knowledge over the old.

The poem is a dramatization of the perceptual, intellectual, emotional, and aesthetic discovery of reality as the foundation of human value. The problem posed by the title may be resolved: "The human experience to be valued is not to have ideas about reality but to confront reality itself; to do this is to be awake, really awake, and to encounter the prime source from which we derive the value of human existence."

1. Pipit sate upright in her chair
 ↑
 Some distance from where I was sitting;

2. *Views of the Oxford Colleges* Lay on the table, with the knitting.

3. {Daguerreotypes
 and silhouettes,}
 ↕
 Her {grandfather
 and great great aunts,} } Supported *An Invitation to the Dance.*
 ↑
 on the mantelpiece

THOMAS STEARNS ELIOT
(1888–   )

A Cooking Egg

En l'an trentiesme de mon aage
Que toutes mes hontes j'ay beues . . .

Pipit sate upright in her chair
  Some distance from where I was sitting;
Views of the Oxford Colleges
  Lay on the table, with the knitting.

Daguerreotypes and silhouettes,
  Her grandfather and great great aunts,
Supported on the mantelpiece
  An *Invitation to the Dance.*

. . . . .

Title. A *Cooking Egg*: an egg used when absolute freshness is not at issue.

Epigraph. The first lines of *The Great Testament* of François Villon (15th-century French poet), which has been translated, "In my thirtieth year, when I have drunk all my shame . . ." Villon was in prison at the time and this was his "last and only Testament." The poem is written in a spirit of melancholy resignation. Villon sees himself as "Not all fool nor yet all sage," but he feels keenly the passing of youth and merriment and looks forward with misgivings to the future and inevitable death. The general atmosphere in which he finds himself is as stale as the cooking egg.

1. *Pipit*: critics have taken Pipit as both an old nurse and a little girl, but the current view seems to be that she is "I" 's wife. A pipit is a small larklike bird; does this suggest a birdlike quality in her? See IH.

1. *sate*: old form of "sat."

3. *Views of the Oxford Colleges*: an old book.

5. *Daguerreotype*: an early kind of photograph.

5. *silhouettes*: old-fashioned portraits of the outline of the face cut out of black paper.

8. *Invitation to the Dance*: a dance program in which a girl's partners wrote their names.

4. I shall not want Honour in Heaven
For I shall { meet Sir Philip Sidney
And have talk with { Coriolanus
And other heroes of that kidney.

5. I shall not want Capital in Heaven
For I shall meet Sir Alfred Mond.

6. We two shall lie together,
↑
lapt In a five per cent. Exchequer Bond.

7. I shall not want Society in Heaven,
[for] Lucretia Borgia shall be my Bride;

8. Her anecdotes will be more amusing
↑
Than Pipit's experience could provide.

I shall not want Honour in Heaven
   For I shall meet Sir Philip Sidney
And have talk with Coriolanus
   And other heroes of that kidney.

I shall not want Capital in Heaven
   For I shall meet Sir Alfred Mond.
We two shall lie together, lapt
   In a five per cent. Exchequer Bond.

I shall not want Society in Heaven,
   Lucretia Borgia shall be my Bride;
Her anecdotes will be more amusing
   Than Pipit's experience could provide.

9. *want:* both senses of the word are implied: "to lack" and "to desire."

10. *Sir Philip Sidney:* English poet and statesman (1554–1586).

11. *Coriolanus:* Gaius Marcus, a Roman patrician, immortalized in Shakespeare's *Coriolanus.* He got his nickname from the great valor he displayed in the capture of Corioli, a town at war with Rome. Later he became a vindictive opponent of Rome after being banished for political reasons. Were it not for the pleas of his mother and wife, he would have conquered Rome with a Volscian army. He is reputed to have answered to his mother's entreaty for the city, "Oh, mother, thou hast saved Rome, but destroyed thy son."

12. *kidney:* class, stamp, nature, sort.

13. *Capital:* funds.

14. *Sir Alfred Mond:* (1868–1939) British politician and industrialist who had interests in gas and nickel. He became Minister of Health in 1921.

15. *lapt:* wrapped up in.

16. *Exchequer Bond:* an English government bond constituting part of the unfunded debt.

17. *Society:* companions; "high" society.

18. *Lucretia Borgia:* (1480–1519) Duchess of Ferrara, patroness of a brilliant court that included artists and intellectuals like Ariosto, Titian, Dosso Dossi, and Aldus Manutius.

9. I shall not want Pipit in Heaven:
Madame Blavatsky will instruct me In the Seven Sacred Trances;

10. Piccarda de Donati will conduct me.

11. But where is the penny world I bought To eat with Pipit
↑
behind the screen?

12. The red-eyed scavengers are creeping From Kentish Town and Golder's Green;

13. Where are the eagles and the trumpets?
Buried beneath some snow-deep Alps.

14. Weeping, weeping multitudes Droop in a hundred A.B.C.'s
↑
Over buttered {scones / and crumpets}

I shall not want Pipit in Heaven:
  Madame Blavatsky will instruct me
In the Seven Sacred Trances;
  Piccarda de Donati will conduct me.

. . . . .

But where is the penny world I bought
  To eat with Pipit behind the screen?
The red-eyed scavengers are creeping
  From Kentish Town and Golder's Green;

Where are the eagles and the trumpets?

  Buried beneath some snow-deep Alps.
Over buttered scones and crumpets
  Weeping, weeping multitudes
Droop in a hundred A.B.C.'s

22. *Madame Blavatsky:* Helena Petrovna Blavatsky (1831–1891) was an organizer of the Theosophist Society, an organization interested in mystical and occult experience.

23. *Seven Sacred Trances:* varying states of mystical elevation or removal from reality.

24. *Piccarda de Donati:* Dante's spiritual guide in the Paradiso (Canto III) of the *Divine Comedy.*

25. *penny world:* see IH.

28. *Kentish Town, Golder's Green:* slums of or near London.

29. *eagles:* standards of the Roman legions.

31. *scones and crumpets:* hot breads or muffins.

33. *A.B.C.'s:* Aereated Bread Company, a chain of English tea shops.

Interpretational Hypothesis

A cooking egg is good enough to be used in baking a cake but not fresh enough to be boiled and eaten from the shell, or to be fried or made into an omelet. It is usable only when it is mixed with other ingredients. The title implies that the poem is going to have something to do with the second-rate.

The epigraph gives further information about the attitude of the speaker. His emotional condition—one may hypothesize—will be one of consciousness of shame and failure. All his potentiality for shameful actions has been exploited at the early age of thirty.

At some unspecified time before the poem is spoken the speaker was sitting in a room with Pipit. Of Pipit we are given a suggestion in her name, but that suggestion is perhaps no more precise than simply that she is of no or very little importance. "Sate" instead of the ordinary "sat" is odd. It suggests something both old-fashioned, even archaic, and something ceremonious. It would be said that a queen "sate" on her throne. Pipit, then, is characterized by stiff, old-fashioned dignity. If, as the epigraph indicates, the speaker is about thirty, Pipit is considerably older. This is further reinforced by "upright in her chair." Her dignity and ceremoniousness suggest that she has the habits of a lady, that she has been trained in the manners of the upper classes. In the nineteenth century such ladies were taught that in the presence of others they must never permit their backs to come into contact with the back of the chair. Even today you never, in photographs or newsreels, see the Queen of England lounging in her throne or chair of state. Further, Pipit is some distance away. A polite distance must always be maintained, particularly between a lady and a gentleman. Moreover, she has on the table only an extremely proper book; nothing could be more correct and harmless and unexciting than *Views of the Oxford Colleges*. She occupies her mind with only the most proper books, and she occupies her hands in an equally proper manner; she knits. The room is decorated with the kinds of pictures which were popular two and three generations back. These pictures hold up an *Invitation to the Dance*. The italics and capitalizations indicate that it would be a mistake to think simply of a formal invitation to come to a dance. When Pipit was young, ladies at dances had silk-covered booklets in which prospective partners, with permission, wrote their names. On the cover was stamped the phrase

Invitation to the Dance in sentimental reference to a famous concert-waltz by Weber, the German composer, written in 1819. Pipit's world, then, is old-fashioned, restricted, without contact with the modern world, in effect, dead, useless, a world of memories.

There now comes a sudden break in the continuity of the poem, indicated not only by the dots across the page but also by the shift in tense. At the time of speaking, the present of the poem, the speaker first thinks of a visit, or some contact, he has had with Pipit. Now his mind turns in a different direction. He thinks of what he shall enjoy in Heaven. What is the connection, then, between the first two stanzas and the next four? Specifically, does "want" mean that Heaven will have the same qualities as Pipit's room or that it will have different qualities? (To be sure, the room where the speaker sits with Pipit is not clearly identified as Pipit's, but it is "her chair." The simplest assumption is that the room is Pipit's, and this hypothesis will be used unless it becomes necessary to abandon it. Indeed, unless we assume that it is her room, the subsequent details of the first two stanzas become no clues to her character. Almost insuperable problems would thus be raised.) And does "want" mean "lack" or "desire"? Before these questions can be answered, the next four stanzas, up to the second break indicated by a line of dots, must be interpreted. He begins by saying that in Heaven he shall not want Honour, that is respect for his own personal courage and ability. The reason is that there he will meet and talk with people like Sir Philip Sidney, the perfect example of Elizabethan chivalry, and Coriolanus, the noble, courageous, and embittered Roman hero, the subject of a play by Shakespeare, and "other heroes of that kidney." The last phrase indicates not only that the other heroes will be of the same quality, but that the speaker will even be able to speak of them and think of them in a casual manner. He will be able to use a kind of slang in referring to them. This reinforces the idea that he will mingle with such men on their own plane, as an equal. Such familiarity indicates further that his own great qualities will be admitted and respected.

Similarly, stanza four: in Heaven he will be so wealthy that he will be regarded as an equal by Sir Alfred Mond, one of the great capitalists of England. As snug as two bugs in a rug, they will be wrapped up together in a bond issued by the British Government, paying five per cent interest. At the time the poem was written, before the First World War, no better investment could be imagined.

Similarly, in Heaven he will be a member of such good society that he will marry Lucretia Borgia, one of the most beautiful, wicked (by legend), and cultivated women of the Italian Renaissance. By parallelism, the causal relation of lines 10 and 14 is continued. Lucretia was the daughter of Pope Alexander Borgia and the sister of Cesare Borgia, the very symbol of unscrupulous political adventurers. She was rumored to have had incestuous relations with both of them. Finally, after two brief marriages, productive of further scandal, she married Alfonso I, Duke of Este, Lord of Ferrara, one of the most sophisticated courts and cities in Italy, where she patronized artists and writers, lived a life of charity, and died honored and loved by her people and friends. What she can tell him about her life and the life of her times will certainly be more interesting than what Pipit can tell him about her experiences as a Victorian Lady. Thus, though now he is not a member of Society, in Heaven he will belong to the most elite of societies. The reference to Pipit settles the question of whether Heaven will be a continuation of Pipit's room or its opposite. It is clear now that Heaven will provide satisfactions he does not now enjoy. This is confirmed in the next stanza.

In Heaven he will neither need nor desire Pipit. This involves a sudden break in the pattern. Why the shift from Honour, Capital, and Society to Pipit? The pattern implies that Pipit belongs to the same category as the first three. In that case she must at this point in the poem symbolize some aspect of experience, as the first three have done. The colon after Heaven implies a causal relation. "I shall not want Pipit in Heaven, because Madame Blavatsky . . ." Whether Madame Blavatsky's claim to mystic insight into the religious character of the universe was justified or not, her religion was very exciting, a mixture of Eastern and Western ideas; she claimed that if one were properly instructed in certain psycho-physical practices, the seven sacred trances or mystical states, one could know God directly. Hence the name of her religion: theosophy, or god-knowing. Furthermore, Picarda de Donati, a pure and religious woman of medieval Italy whose spirit guided Dante through a part of Paradise in the third part of the *Divine Comedy*, will conduct the speaker of the poem. Thus the most exciting of modern religious experiences and the loftiest of medieval religious experiences will be his in Heaven. In line 21, then, Pipit stands for religion. The implication is that her religion and the religious experience she offers is most narrow, neither noble nor exciting. But though such religion is what the speaker has on earth, in Heaven it will be different. He will no longer want great religious experiences, for he will have them.

To sum up this section: the speaker imagines that if he were in Heaven, if all his wants were satisfied, he would have honor, money, society, and a satisfying religion. As it is, he lacks these things, or more specifically, he lacks honor and money, and the only society and religion he has are provided by Pipit. Since he lacks these things, he desires them; he dreams of having them in Heaven. It is thus apparent that he must also desire them now. That is, his statement that he lacks them and his precise vision of what having them would involve, dramatize his desire for them and thus his dissatisfaction with the way he is living his life. He desires a first-rate life, with all the richness that experience can offer, but he has, instead, Pipit's kind of life. That is, there is implied some kind of inescapable, unbreakable bond between the speaker and Pipit. Unable to get the gratifications he really desires, he has two choices: (1) the compensations of imaginary pleasures, or (2) the narrow, restricted, unimaginative, out-of-date, second-rate, and ultimately unsatisfying pleasures offered by an association with Pipit. The implication is that his real choice is between the world of Pipit and nothing at all: not only no honor or money, but not even the narrow range of Pipit's memories and her equally narrow and unimaginative religion.

This interpretation is consistent with and appears to be confirmed by the third section of the poem. Again the direction of his mind shifts, a shift indicated as before by dots and by a change of tense. Now instead of a past characterized by minimal delights or a future characterized by impossible pleasures, we are suddenly in a real present. The speaker here comes to grips with his actual situation. The connection from line 24 to line 25 is clear if we read it as follows: "These are the pleasures which I can imagine, but where is even the pleasure I have had with Pipit?" What *is* "the pleasure I have had with Pipit"? The answer is: "Eating a penny world." A "penny world" is a world worth only a penny. But because it is a world, a self-contained and self-existent unity, it is better than nothing. But this is a penny world one *eats*. It is some kind of cheap treat, a cake or some sweet such as children or the poor can buy and enjoy. And "world" also refers to the very character of Pipit's room and what happens there, since her room has already been presented as a self-centered universe. (This sense of "world" is employed in such expressions as "the world of the novel" and "the world of baseball.") Thus the "world" is at once comfortable and secure, but cheap, i.e. easily procured and worth very little. The speaker and Pipit eat behind a screen, because Pipit has to use one room both for sitting and for eating, and a screen is necessary to separate the two areas. But screen presents another possibility. Besides being a piece of furniture, "screen" is also a metaphor. One hides behind a screen. But what is the speaker hiding from? The other "world" in which he has neither honor nor money. What is really being said is: "I have traded my empty life and imagined pleasures for the real though cheap, restricted, and out-of-date experiences which I can have with Pipit."

All this is presented as question; and the question is, "What is the reality of even that little pleasure?" And the implied answer is: "The penny world does not exist; even that little pleasure is an illusion." Where is the penny world? Nowhere. We wonder why this unhappy state of affairs should exist, and we are immediately told. That is, since the next statement immediately follows a question it is presumably the answer to that question. The lowest classes of society, their eyes red with drink or anger or both, are spreading out from the slums of London in which hitherto they have been confined. "Creeping" implies that they are moving slowly and cautiously, and the "red-eyed" and "creeping" together suggest a stealthy and sinister or threatening activity. This interpretation is supported by "scavengers," people from the bottom level of society who live on the discards of the economic classes above them. The penny world is nowhere; the illusion of a little happiness cannot be sustained because of the speaker's awareness of the new movement outward of the scavengers. It is a new movement because the scavengers have hitherto been confined to the slums, Kentish Town and Golder's Green. But why this change in the activity of the scavengers? Presumably, it may be hypothesized, because there is now more to scavenge. The classes superior to the scavengers are using less and less of what they have. This interpretation appears to be sustained by the rest of the sentence, a question. Because it is not a new sentence and is separated from the first part of the sentence by a semicolon, the question is a consequence of something apprehended in the statement about the scavengers.

Eagles, the standard or pole topped with a metal eagle, gold or gilded, functioned as the flag for a Roman regiment. They symbolized the fact that the regiment was an organized social body; they were a symbol of the pride and self-respect of that body; and they served as guides and rallying points on the march and in battle. Likewise, the trumpets served to control the army in march and battle, and to synchronize its action. Where are these symbols of power and grandeur and heroism and social order? The parallel with the preceding question indicates that the answer is, Nowhere. And this interpretation is confirmed by line 30. The regiments have been crushed and buried, perhaps by avalanches, as they were crossing the Alps. But why is this power presented in Roman symbols? When the Romans crossed the Alps, they brought to the barbaric tribes north of the Alps not only military and political power, but also, eventually, peace, order, prosperity, and civilization. Since the statement about the scavengers gives rise to the question about the eagles and trumpets, and since the Roman empire has long since ceased to exist at the time the speaker is uttering the poem, the eagles and trumpets are to be taken as the vehicle of a metaphor in which the tenor is peace, social order, prosperity, civilization, power, grandeur, authority, and heroism. The meaning of the passage from lines 25–30 is: "I cannot enjoy even the minimal pleasures offered by my association with Pipit, because I am all too conscious that even that little area of peace and civilization is threatened by the uncivilized and barbaric proletarian hordes of the great cities, and that there is no power on earth that can control them, subdue them, and civilize them. Civilizing power and authority have gone out of life. No Roman empire will rescue us."

It is no wonder, then, that the multitudes weep and despair. A.B.C.'s are the tea shops of the Aereated Bread Company, at that time a large chain of stores in which bread and cakes and so on were sold, and which served afternoon tea. They were patronized by members of the middle classes who could afford to enter clean and well-kept tea shops and order and consume the rich hot breads of various kinds (scones and crumpets), spread with butter. At this time, as for a long time after, the lower classes in England used not butter but oleomargarine. The use of butter, as well as the patronage of the A.B.C.'s and the consumption of rich scones and crumpets, indicates the class. But what is the connection between the loss of authority and order and the fact that middle-class people are weeping and eating in A.B.C.'s? The breakup of the normal stanzaic structure and the juxtaposition of lines 30 and 31 in the same stanza indicate that there is a close connection. They weep, of course, because they are helpless in the face of the loss of power, order, and authority. But if we interpolate "They *merely* weep," or "They *do nothing but* weep and eat," we have a further explanation for the scavengers. Faced with a disastrous loss, the middle classes turn to minor gratifications and fail to use the resources of their society to meet the danger. Since these resources are not used, they are the proper prey of the scavengers, who are thus seen, as suggested above, as a metaphor for all the deprived classes who have not shared in the possessions of the classes superior to them in the past but who are now inheriting or threatening to inherit the possessions which the middle classes can no longer use.

There is further implication to be derived from the multitudes of the middle classes eating in despair in tea shops. The parallel between the inexpensive food eaten by the speaker and Pipit in her quarters, and the speaker's despair and Pipit's out-of-dateness and uselessness in contemporary society, on the one hand, and on the other hand, the scones and crumpets and the drooping behavior of the multitudes, identifies the class of the speaker with the class of the multitudes. They despair and are deprived of all energy (they "droop"). The speaker also, then, is deprived of energy, and for the same reason. The middle classes, settling for a second-class world, are threatened by the invasion into their areas of the lower classes: yet they lack the energy and do not know where to find the power to defend themselves and civilize these half-brutalized human beings from the deprived classes.

The poem, then, dramatizes the perplexity of a man of the middle classes whose life is empty, without any experience of life's potentiality of richness, but who still finds a minimum kind of pleasure when his imagination fails him. Trying to locate the sources of this failure of his life, he realizes that his fellow members of the middle classes are in the same position. Though their world is threatened by the lower classes, the real trouble lies not in himself or the middle classes, or even in the lower classes, but instead arises from the fact that in the modern world there are no strong forces of power, splendor, and civilization, qualities he thinks necessary for the richness of life which he can now only imagine.

The "cooking egg" is the second-best world which he has to put up with but which is not really satisfactory and which cannot really be depended upon to continue. His shame ("*mes hontes*") is the shame he feels for the failure of himself, his class, and his age. And this despair is reinforced by the disappearance of the orderly rhyme-scheme and stanzaic structure in the last five lines of the poem. That disappearance symbolizes the collapse of order which is the subject of the poem.

(*Note:* A number of theories have been advanced by various critics as to who Pipit is: an old nurse, a little girl, the speaker's wife, a childhood sweetheart, and so on. The only things these various theories have in common is their irrelevancy and the fact that there is no basis in the poem for preferring one to the other. Although, for example, she appears to be old, for the reasons given in the Interpretational Hypothesis above, she may very well be a young woman living in the rooms of her dead great-aunt. Who knows? The important thing is her function in the poem, and the function of her environment. The speaker has a particular relation to her and to her rooms, and that relation is carefully presented.)

1. Summer ends now;

2. now, the stooks arise Around;
↑
barbarous in beauty,

3. up above, { what wind-walks!
what lovely behaviour Of silk-sack clouds! }

4. has wilder, wilful-wavier Meal-drift *ever { moulded*
and melted across skies? }

5. { I walk,
I lift up,
I lift up { heart,
eyes, } Down all that glory in the heavens }
↑
to glean our Saviour;

6. And, <éyes, heárt,> { what looks,
what lips } yet gave you a Rapturous love's greeting { of realer,
of rounder replies? }

GERARD MANLEY HOPKINS (1844–1889)

Hurrahing in Harvest

Summer ends now; now, barbarous in beauty, the stooks arise
  Around; up above, what wind-walks! what lovely behaviour
  Of silk-sack clouds! has wilder, wilful-wavier
Meal-drift moulded ever and melted across skies?

I walk, I lift up, I lift up heart, eyes,
  Down all that glory in the heavens to glean our Saviour;
  And, éyes, heárt, what looks, what lips yet gave you a
Rapturous love's greeting of realer, of rounder replies?

1. *stooks:* shocks or haystacks.

1. *arise:* grow (into a pile).

2. *wind-walks:* see IH.

3. *silk-sack:* see IH.

3. *wilful-wavier:* more wilfully wavy.

4. *Meal-drift:* a drifting of meal bit by bit, as in "piecemeal"; spreading out in a flow as flour spreads out from a granary.

4. *moulded:* formed into a mould.

5. *lift up:* see IH.

6. *Down:* along the sky toward the horizon.

6. *glean:* to gather from the field what has been left by the reapers.

7. *looks:* glances.

7. *yet:* ever.

8. *Rapturous:* ecstatic, transporting.

8. *rounder:* more complete, and thus more satisfying.

7. And the azurous hung hills are { his world-wielding shoulder
{ Majestic—
↑
as a *stalwart stallion*,
↑
very-violet-sweet!—

8. { These things,
{ these things were here
{ and but the beholder [was] Wanting;

which two when they once meet,
9. The heart { rears wings bold and bolder
{ And { hurls for him, } earth for him
{ O half hurls }
↑
off under his feet.

And the azurous hung hills are his world-wielding shoulder
  Majestic—as a stallion stalwart, very-violet-sweet!—
These things, these things were here and but the beholder
  Wanting; which two when they once meet,
The heart rears wings bold and bolder
  And hurls for him, O half hurls earth for him off under his feet.

9. *azurous:* azure.

10. *stallion:* a virile male horse.

10. *stalwart:* strong, robust.

10. *violet-sweet:* sweet as violets.

11. *but:* only.

12. *Wanting:* lacking in the requisite sensitivity; or, not present.

12. *which two:* (1) these things, (2) the beholder.

13. *heart:* see IH.

13. *rears:* to raise up.

14. *for him:* see IH.

Interpretational Hypothesis

The title informs us that the subject of the poem is exultation, presumably over the collection and storage of the products of the summer's growth; but it is to be noted that "hurrahing" is a word ordinarily employed by a group of joyful celebrants. Who or what these celebrants are remains to be seen.

The speaker begins with a dramatic statement that this is the very moment at which summer ends. The repetition itself of "now" reinforces the drama and the momentary quality of the experience being dramatized. Summer ends, and autumn, the time of harvest, begins. Hence the stooks are presented as "arising." There is a choice here of interpretations. Is "arise" used in the sense that in New York the skyscrapers arise around us? Or is it used in the sense of something growing into a pile? It is the difference between the "The stooks are there," and the "The stooks are being built up." The emphasis in the opening upon the speaker's complete absorption in the moment suggests that the latter interpretation is the consistent one. This notion that they are actively arising, going up as the speaker watches, may be further reinforced, though not proved, by "barbarous," which gives them a human energy. But why are the stooks called "barbarous"? The raising of stooks is a very ancient activity, uncivilized, unsophisticated. "Barbarous" is usually felt to be antithetical to "civilized." The characteristic of barbarous beauty as opposed to civilized beauty is forceful energy as opposed to polished workmanship. This certainly would be consistent with the conception of stooks arising, almost growing, rather than being built. Their growth, or arising, then, symbolizes the human and joyful release of energy in the gathering of the harvest, the oneness of man and nature. In the next line, the shift from statement to exclamation emphasizes the drama of the situation in which the speaker finds himself, and indicates an increase in excitement. The speaker, as it were, is now too excited to make complete statements; he can only utter ejaculations. Even his diction changes; he begins to coin words—"wind-walks," "silk-sacks," "wilful-wavier," "meal-drift"—as if conventional words were not adequate to present his feeling.

To begin with "What wind-walks are up above," the simplest explanation is that "walks" is used as it is in "sidewalks," "a place to walk in." The expression means, "What splendid places for the wind to walk in!" And since a wind fills great spaces, the function of the coinage is to indicate the excitement of suddenly becoming aware of the hugeness of the sky. Further, the effect is one of personification. The wind is given a personality, as are the clouds in the use of the word "behaviour," a word ordinarily applied to human beings. The clouds, again, are likened to sacks made out of silk. Several significances appear to be at work. First, the shape of these particular clouds is indicated by "sack." They are, probably, cumulus clouds. Further, sacks are ordinarily made of a rough coarse material; yet here they are made of silk. The characteristic of silk appropriate here is its smooth, shining appearance. Next, "meal-drift" indicates another function for "sack." The drift of meal as it "moulds" and "melts" refers to the appearance and movement of meal or flour as it is poured out of a bag or as it flows from the mill where it has been ground. First it piles up, and then, as the weight of the pile gets too heavy for its structure to be maintained, the pile settles, shifts, and is re-formed, or "melts." The connection between the two ejaculations lies in the fact that the grinding of meal or flour is part of the harvesting process, and that both unground wheat and ground meal are stored in sacks. The speaker, then, is so dominated by his harvest exuberance that he projects typical harvest images upon the scene; he sees the sky in terms derived from the farm activities of autumn. Further, the energetic activity of the land is ascribed to the behavior of the clouds. The piles of white vapor form and spread, or melt—like meal—across the sky. They are wild, untamed, barbarous, and wavy, or undulating, piling up, and collapsing, in a wilful way, that is, undisciplined, uncivilized, unsophisticated. The implied answer to the question which concludes the stanza is "Never!" and this implication re-emphasizes the uniqueness of the moment of observation. To sum up, in the first stanza, or quatrain, of the sonnet the speaker has fused the human activity and the natural appearances of the landscape at the end of summer and the beginning of autumn.

Now, at the beginning of the next stanza, he moves through the landscape (l. 5). The first difficulty is the repetition of "I lift up." Like the repetition in line 1, it dramatizes the excitement of the speaker. Not only is a kind of excited stammering suggested, but also the repetition of subject and verb without object throws into special relief the verbal idea of "lifting up," of emotional exaltation. The speaker is now at an emotional level higher than at the end of line 4. The next problem is the syntactical peculiarity of "I lift up . . . down." The first stage of the solution is to observe that "down" is used in the sense of "I looked down the street." In the first quatrain, the clouds are presented broadside, moving across the speaker's line of vision. Here suddenly a third dimension is introduced, and the immense depth given the heavens corresponds to the speaker's sudden ascent to a new level of emotional excitement. The second stage of the solution is to interpolate "to look." "I lift up my eyes to look down all that glory in the heavens." However, that still leaves the problem of "heart." Does he mean, "I lift up my heart to look down all that glory in the heavens"? The syntax requires it. The meaning, then, is that the experience is taking place on both a physiological level and a psychological level. He raises his eyes to look down the glory and simultaneously becomes more responsive to the beauty he sees. The result is that he gleans our Saviour, or Christ. A gleaner gathers the last scrap of valuable grain and straw from the fields after the reapers have finished. In the first quatrain, with his vision of stooks and meal-sacks, he thought of the landscape as a harvester would. Now, in his new excitement he plays a new role. Now he is the gleaner. As harvester, he gathered the obvious things, the beauty and power and richness of the landscape. As gleaner, he gathers what he had neglected: God, in the person of the Saviour. The consequences of this perception of God are immediate and dramatic. First he addresses his eyes and heart as something separate from himself. He perceives himself as a self, and his eyes and heart as instruments of that self, instead of, as in line 5, as parts of himself. Just as the role of harvester was superseded by that of gleaner, so the role of gleaner now disappears and the real self emerges. This hypothesis appears to be confirmed by the exclamation that follows, which implies that never has he experienced a realer or rounder response to a movement on his part toward another being. This response is a rapturous response. To be enraptured is to be taken out of, or above, one's normal state. It is a response of love. He has gleaned the Saviour, and the Saviour has responded by raising him to a new level of being, of selfhood. Never has any response been more satisfying and complete ("rounder") or more convincing ("realer"). Although this may imply that at least one other experience has been as real and round, the use of this kind of expression ordinarily implies that nothing has ever been so satisfying. This interpretation, that what is actually implied is that no response has ever been so satisfying, complete, and convincing, is consistent with the idea of being enraptured to a new level of being.

In the next stanza the "and" implies the continuance of this emotional state. He perceives the hills blue from distance as if hung on the sky. That is, being almost as blue as the sky and being distant, they are perceived without depth-perception. They are, then, like the line of a shoulder, the shoulder of the Saviour. But what is meant by world-wielding? To wield a sword, we say, or to wield a mighty power, means to have complete control of some tool or instrument which serves as an extension of the individual's will. He sees the hills as the majestic shoulder with which the

Saviour controls the world. The next comparison reinforces and extends the idea. The shoulder-hills are stalwart as a stallion, powerful, able to exert and withstand immense forces. At the same time, because of their beauty, they are very sweet, like violets. The next sentence changes the mode of speaking. Instead of exclamations and rhetorical questions, the speaker uses a reflective and abstract language. Thus the repetition of "these things" is as much meditative as excited. Sure of himself and his vision, he has his emotion under control. "These things" refers both to the beauty of the landscape and the vision of the Saviour which emerged from the perception of that beauty. But from the vision of the Saviour emerged the heightened awareness of selfhood. All these three qualities were present; only the beholder was wanting. "Wanting" may well mean simply "was absent." But frequently the word, when applied to an individual, means to be lacking something, to be inadequate. When the beauty and the power of the harvest landscape plus the vision of the Saviour ("these things") come together with the speaker ("meet"), then his heart rears its wings with boldness and increasing boldness. ("Two" refers to [1] these things, and [2] the beholder.) But how are we to conceive of "heart"? Simply as emotional intoxication? Traditionally, "heart" means the capacity to love, and in line 8 we have seen that love is involved in the response of the Saviour. That greeting was related to the speaker's new awareness of selfhood. "Heart," then, may be used here in the sense of the central power to love Christ the Saviour. Line 14 raises a series of problems. First is the peculiar use of "hurls." "The heart hurls earth off." "Hurls" means "throw violently away from one." To hurl off means here to rise up on wings from the earth so violently that earth is pushed away. The oddity of the expression lies in its unusual use of "hurl," which ordinarily means that a larger active object throws away a smaller passive object. Here a smaller active entity throws away a larger passive object. Further, we may hurl something away for either of two reasons; the object we hurl may be a missile thrown at something, or it may be simply a powerfully undesired object, thrown away in contempt. The second is the more consistent here. The heart raises its wings and hurls earth off. But what is the antecedent of "him"? The most recent possible antecedent is "beholder" as referred to and carried forward in "two." Thus we may interpret "hurls for him" as "hurls for his sake," i.e. "performs for him the service of hurling." Thus the true antecedent is the speaker as beholder, the speaker in his new role of emergent real self. But why the sudden and immediate correction of "half hurls"? Were the action completed, the self would leave this earth entirely, and the speaker would die. The action is thus arrested; it is half finished. The self is held back in its movement from earth toward Christ. In the final phrase, the antecedent of "him" is "his," i.e. the beholder and real self. Since the soul (i.e. the real self) is traditionally presented as a human figure with wings, "heart" is, as hypothesized, to be best interpreted as not mere emotional capacity but as the specific power of the real self (i.e. soul) to love Christ. Ending the poem with the phrase "under his feet" expresses the connection of the self and the earth, and thus reinforces the arrested, incompleted movement of the self toward Christ the Saviour. The final problem of the line, the interpretation of "O," can now be solved. It is a cry as much of anguish as of joy. It can be either; it is probably both. The poem ends with a sense of almost intolerable frustration and conflict.

The drama of the poem is the emotional progression from a purely physical joy in the beauty of an autumn harvest landscape, to a perception of the ultimate value in the landscape, to a vision of the God who created it and supports it, to a consequent emergence of a sense of selfhood and awareness of one's innermost being or soul, to a bold effort to spurn the earth in a flight toward God, that self's proper home, and then to a sudden and frustrating awareness that the self is still bound to earth. It can yearn toward God, but not yet can it go to Him. We can now see the oddity of the use of "hurrahing" in the title. Since hurrahing is usually done in a group, we can now identify the individual as the speaker and the group as "these things," the harvest landscape. Therefore "hurrahing" indicates here the initial submergence of the individual personality or soul in the emotional excitement of the group. Yet, for the reasons we have seen, the poem ends with a personal cry of anguish.

1. My heart aches,
and a drowsy numbness pains My sense,
as though *I {
had drunk of hemlock*,
Or [had] emptied some dull opiate to the drains
↑
One minute past,
and *had sunk Lethe-wards*:
}

2. 'Tis not {
through envy of thy happy lot,
But [through] being {
too happy in thine happiness,—
[too happy] That thou, Singest of summer in full-throated ease.
↕
light-winged Dryad of the trees,
In some melodious plot Of {
beechen green,
and *numberless shadows*,
}
}
}

JOHN KEATS (1795–1821)

Ode to a Nightingale

I

My heart aches, and a drowsy numbness pains
  My sense, as though of hemlock I had drunk,
Or emptied some dull opiate to the drains
  One minute past, and Lethe-wards had sunk:
'Tis not through envy of thy happy lot,
  But being too happy in thine happiness,—
    That thou, light-winged Dryad of the trees,
        In some melodious plot
  Of beechen green, and shadows numberless,
    Singest of summer in full-throated ease.

2. *sense:* consciousness, *not* the senses; see IH.

2. *as though:* as if.

2. *of:* some.

2. *hemlock:* hemlock reduced to a potion has powerful sedative effects, and, in excess, may kill the drinker. Socrates is thought to have died in this way; see IH.

3. *dull:* dulling, affecting the drinker with dullness.

3. *opiate:* any liquid containing opium and having a narcotic effect.

4. *past:* ago.

4. *Lethe-wards:* toward Lethe, the river of forgetfulness in Greek mythology.

5. *'Tis:* see IH.

5. *through:* because of, out of.

5. *thy:* the nightingale's.

5. *lot:* situation, circumstance, fortune.

7. *Dryad:* in Greek mythology, a nymph supposed to inhabit trees.

9. *beechen:* made green by the leaves of beech trees.

3.

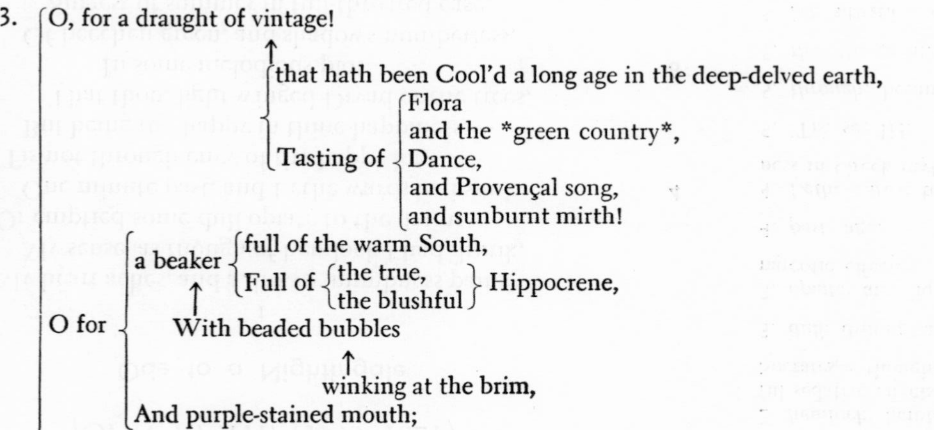
O, for a draught of vintage!
that hath been Cool'd a long age in the deep-delved earth,
Tasting of
Flora
and the *green country*,
Dance,
and Provençal song,
and sunburnt mirth!
O for
a beaker
full of the warm South,
Full of
the true,
the blushful
Hippocrene,
With beaded bubbles
winking at the brim,
And purple-stained mouth;

II

O, for a draught of vintage! that hath been
  Cool'd a long age in the deep-delved earth,
Tasting of Flora and the country green,
  Dance, and Provençal song, and sunburnt mirth!
O for a beaker full of the warm South,
  Full of the true, the blushful Hippocrene,
    With beaded bubbles winking at the brim,
      And purple-stained mouth;

11. *draught:* long drink.

11. *vintage:* wine; see IH.

12. *deep-delved:* deep-dug.

13. *Flora:* in Latin mythology, the goddess of flowers.

14. *Provençal:* Provence is a province of southern France noted for its wines and pleasant living.

15. *beaker:* glass.

16. *blushful:* rosy.

16. *Hippocrene:* Hippocrene is the legendary "fountain of the horse" on Mt. Helicon whose waters are supposed to be a source of poetic inspiration. The legend is that Pegasus, the winged horse of Bellerophon, kicked a stone from which the fountain sprang.

17. *beaded bubbles:* bubbles around the edge of the liquid in a container are round and sparkling like beads.

17. *winking:* twinkling.

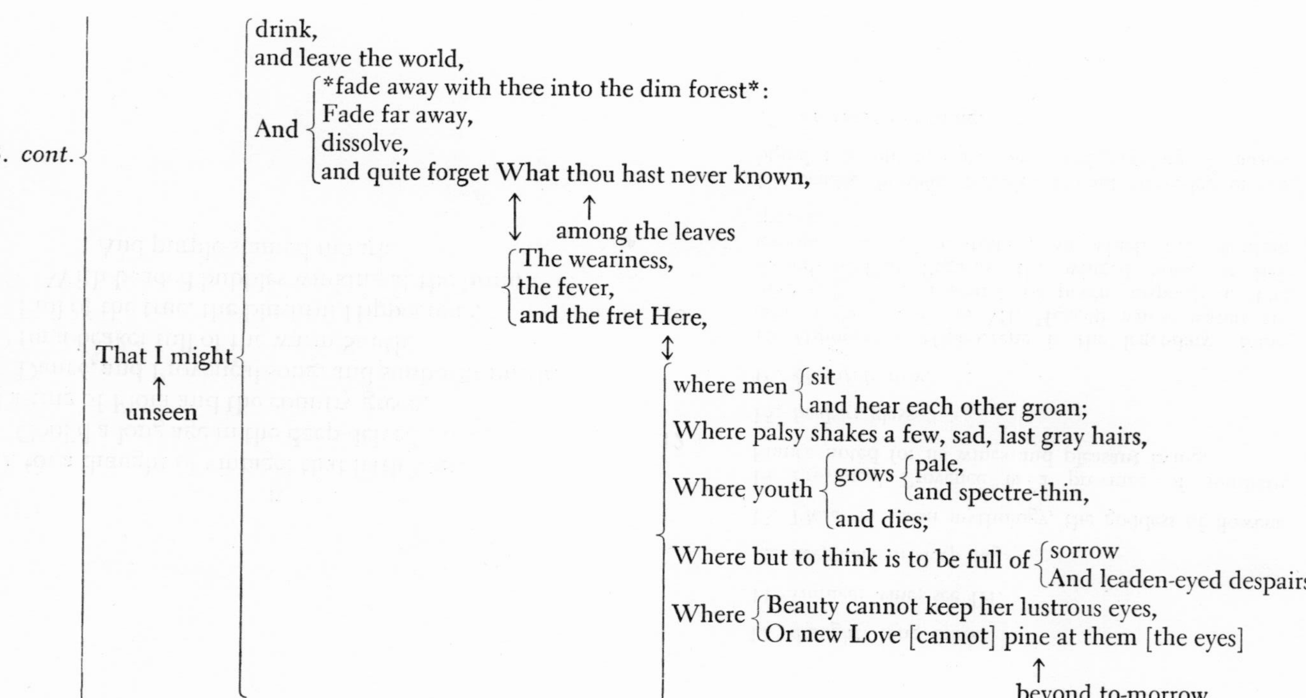
3. cont.
That I might
unseen
drink,
and leave the world,
And
fade away with thee into the dim forest:
Fade far away,
dissolve,
and quite forget What thou hast never known,
among the leaves
The weariness,
the fever,
and the fret Here,
where men
sit
and hear each other groan;
Where palsy shakes a few, sad, last gray hairs,
Where youth
grows
pale,
and spectre-thin,
and dies;
Where but to think is to be full of
sorrow
And leaden-eyed despairs,
Where
Beauty cannot keep her lustrous eyes,
Or new Love [cannot] pine at them [the eyes]
beyond to-morrow.

That I might drink, and leave the world unseen,
  And with thee fade away into the forest dim:

III

Fade far away, dissolve, and quite forget
  What thou among the leaves hast never known,
The weariness, the fever, and the fret
  Here, where men sit and hear each other groan;
Where palsy shakes a few, sad, last gray hairs,
  Where youth grows pale, and spectre-thin, and dies;
    Where but to think is to be full of sorrow
      And leaden-eyed despairs,
  Where Beauty cannot keep her lustrous eyes,
    Or new Love pine at them beyond to-morrow.

19. *That:* so that.

25. *palsy:* a nervous disease of the aged whose chief symptom is involuntary shaking of the muscles.

26. *spectre-thin:* thin as a ghost.

27. *but:* only; merely.

29. *her:* Beauty's.

30. *them:* Beauty's eyes.

4. Away! away! for I will fly to thee,
↑
{Not charioted by Bacchus and his pards,
{But on the viewless wings of Poesy,
Though the dull brain perplexes and retards [me]:

5. [I am] Already with thee!

6. *the night is tender*,
And haply the Queen-Moon is on her throne,
↑
Cluster'd around by all her starry Fays;

7. But here there is no light,
↑
Save what is *blown from heaven with the breezes*
↑
Through {verdurous glooms
{and winding mossy ways.

IV

Away! away! for I will fly to thee,
  Not charioted by Bacchus and his pards,
But on the viewless wings of Poesy,
  Though the dull brain perplexes and retards:
Already with thee! tender is the night,
  And haply the Queen-Moon is on her throne,
    Cluster'd around by all her starry Fays;
        But here there is no light,
  Save what from heaven is with the breezes blown
    Through verdurous glooms and winding mossy ways.

31. *thee:* the nightingale.

32. *Bacchus:* the Latin name for the god of wine.

32. *pards:* leopards, which are reputed to have pulled Bacchus' chariot.

33. *viewless:* invisible.

33. *Poesy:* poetry; poetic creativity.

36. *haply:* by chance; it so happens that.

36. *Queen-Moon:* the Greek goddess of the moon, Artemis, whose train consisted of wood-nymphs, here referred to as "starry Fays."

37. *Fays:* fairies.

38. *here:* see IH.

39. *Save:* except.

39. *what:* that light which.

8. I cannot see
what flowers are at my feet,
Nor what soft incense hangs upon the boughs,

But, [I can] guess each sweet Wherewith the seasonable month endows
The grass,
the thicket,
and the *wild fruit tree*;
in embalmed darkness,
White hawthorn,
and the pastoral eglantine;
Fast fading violets cover'd up in leaves;
And mid-May's eldest child,
The coming musk-rose,
full of dewy wine,
The murmurous haunt of flies on summer eves.

9.
Darkling I listen;
and,
for [because] I have
been half in love with easeful Death,
many a time
Call'd him soft names in many a mused rhyme,
To take *my quiet breath into the air*;
Now more than ever *it seems* rich
to die,
To cease upon the midnight with no pain,
While thou art pouring thy soul abroad
In such an ecstasy!

V

I cannot see what flowers are at my feet,
  Nor what soft incense hangs upon the boughs,
But, in embalmed darkness, guess each sweet
  Wherewith the seasonable month endows
The grass, the thicket, and the fruit-tree wild;
  White hawthorn, and the pastoral eglantine;
    Fast fading violets cover'd up in leaves;
        And mid-May's eldest child,
  The coming musk-rose, full of dewy wine,
    The murmurous haunt of flies on summer eves.

VI

Darkling I listen; and, for many a time
  I have been half in love with easeful Death,
Call'd him soft names in many a mused rhyme,
  To take into the air my quiet breath;
Now more than ever seems it rich to die,
  To cease upon the midnight with no pain,
    While thou art pouring forth thy soul abroad
        In such an ecstasy!

43. *embalmed:* embalming was often done with pleasant-smelling spices and perfumes.

43. *sweet:* sweet-smelling flower.

44. *Wherewith:* with which.

44. *seasonable:* a month whose weather is suitable to the time of year.

46. *hawthorn:* a thorny flowering shrub.

46. *pastoral:* (here) growing in the open country.

46. *eglantine:* the sweetbriar.

49. *coming:* still in the bud.

49. *musk-rose:* a rambling rose with white flowers.

50. *haunt of flies:* place frequented by flies.

51. *Darkling:* in the darkness.

51. *for many a time:* see IH.

52. *easeful:* something that makes one feel easy.

53. *him:* Death.

53. *mused:* pondered or meditated over, contemplated.

57. *abroad:* widely, over a broad surface.

10. *thou wouldst Still sing*,
and I [would] have ears in vain—
↑
[having] *become a sod To thy high requiem*.

11. Thou wast not born for death, <immortal Bird!>

12. No hungry generations tread thee down;

13. The voice was heard In ancient days by emperor and clown:
↑
[that] I hear this passing night

14. Perhaps {
[what I hear is] the self-same song that found a path Through the sad heart of Ruth,
when, She stood in tears amid the alien corn;
↑
sick for home,
[or] The same [song] that oft-times hath Charm'd magic casements,
↑
{opening on the foam Of perilous seas,
{in *forlorn faery lands*.

Still wouldst thou sing, and I have ears in vain—
To thy high requiem become a sod.

VII

Thou wast not born for death, immortal Bird!
No hungry generations tread thee down;
The voice I hear this passing night was heard
In ancient days by emperor and clown:
Perhaps the self-same song that found a path
Through the sad heart of Ruth, when, sick for home,
She stood in tears amid the alien corn;
The same that oft-times hath
Charm'd magic casements, opening on the foam
Of perilous seas, in faery lands forlorn.

59. *Still wouldst thou sing:* you would keep on singing.

59. *I have:* I would have.

60. *high requiem:* noble funeral song.

60. *become:* having become.

60. *sod:* a clod of earth.

61. *for death:* to die.

62. *generations:* the whole bodies of people born at about the same time.

66. *Ruth:* see Ruth, ii. Ruth was a woman of Moab who married into a Jewish family which had emigrated from Bethlehem to Moab at a time of famine. When her father-in-law and her husband died, and when her mother-in-law, Naomi, determined to return to Bethlehem, Ruth courageously and out of love for her mother-in-law accompanied her. They arrived during a barley harvest, and Ruth became a gleaner in the fields of Boaz, whom she ultimately married.

67. *alien:* foreign.

67. *corn:* grainfields.

69. *Charm'd:* put a magical charm on.

69. *casements:* window frames.

70. *faery:* fairy.

70. *forlorn:* far away and utterly lost.

15. Forlorn!
↕
the very word is like a bell To toll me back from thee to my sole self!

16. Adieu! the fancy cannot cheat so well
↑
As she is fam'd to do,
↕
deceiving elf.

17. Adieu!
adieu! { thy plaintive anthem fades { Past the near meadows,
over the still stream,
Up the hill-side;
and now 'tis buried deep In the next valley-glades:

18. Was it { a vision,
or a waking dream?

19. *that music is Fled*:—

20. Do I wake or sleep?

VIII

Forlorn! the very word is like a bell
To toll me back from thee to my sole self!
Adieu! the fancy cannot cheat so well
As she is fam'd to do, deceiving elf.
Adieu! adieu! thy plaintive anthem fades
Past the near meadows, over the still stream,
Up the hill-side; and now 'tis buried deep
In the next valley-glades:
Was it a vision, or a waking dream?
Fled is that music:—Do I wake or sleep?

71. *very word:* the word "forlorn" itself.

73. *fancy:* imagination, particularly of a delusive sort.

74. *she:* the fancy.

75. *plaintive:* mournful.

75. *anthem:* song of praise; here a song praising summer (l. 10).

77. *'tis:* the song is.

78. *valley-glades:* clear, open space.

79. *it:* for referent, see IH.

Interpretational Hypothesis

An ode *to* a god, a spirit, or some other creature is a special kind of prayer. It begs not merely for a favor but that the being addressed should grant to the petitioner its own qualities. (See also Interpretational Hypothesis for Collins for a more detailed discussion; and for Gray and Jonson for discussions of odes *on*.) We may begin our hypothesis for this poem, then, by assuming that the speaker wishes to have for himself some quality of a particular nightingale. (Not all nightingales, or a generic nightingale, be it noted, for then the title would be "Ode to *the* Nightingale.")

The first major statement (ll. 1–4) offers no syntactical difficulties, but a good many of the individual terms require interpretation. An aching heart is so common a metaphor for referring to troubled and unhappy emotions that it seems at first glance probable that it should have that meaning here. However, so many of the terms in the rest of the sentence are physiological that it seems best, at least to begin with, to take "My heart aches" literally as a reference to a sensibly perceived pain in the heart or in the region of the heart. In the next clause it seems reasonable that "sense" means "senses," yet "numbness" refers to the loss of the sense of touch. It is insensitivity to touch; it is a negative sense or a "non-sense." Thus the statement means: one of my senses pains my senses; but this statement is impossible to understand. It seems advisable to take "sense" in some other way—for example, as we use the word in such a phrase as "a sense of duty," i.e. a consciousness of the value of doing one's duty. It seems considerably more satisfactory to read the statement, "A numbness pains my self-awareness," or "An insensitivity to stimuli which affect the sense of touch pains my consciousness." But why "drowsy"? The word means not merely sleepy but having the sensations of going to sleep. But when we go to sleep *all* our senses become increasingly less responsive to stimuli. Hence the function of "drowsy" is to make "numbness" refer to all the senses, not merely to the sense of touch. Thus we have, "A gradual loss of physical sensitivity pains my consciousness." This interpretation appears to be confirmed by the two comparisons which follow. "I feel as if I had drunk hemlock," a poison which kills by attacking the circulatory system over a period of time; the parts of the body farthest from the heart first lose their sensitivity. Socrates, who was administered hemlock, first lost the perception of aliveness in his feet, which turned cold, and so on up. At the same time his brain was still unaffected; he said his farewell to his friends. The psycho-physical state described by the speaker of the poem, then, is a peculiar one. While his sensory apparatus is losing its sensitivity, his mind, or consciousness, remains awake. Hence the pain is one which arises from the disparity between the awareness of the mind and the nonfunctioning of the senses. The mind, as it were, is geared to receive a certain number of messages per second, and its comfort depends upon receiving them. Since it is not receiving them, it feels discomfort. "Opiate," however, has a somewhat different meaning. The function of an opiate is just the opposite of that of hemlock. It affects the nervous system. People take opiates when the mind or consciousness is receiving *more* messages than it can endure or messages which are unendurably painful. Since an opiate alleviates pain, rather than causes it, and sedates the brain before it affects the other parts of the body, it is difficult to see why this comparison is used, until we observe in line 4, "And Lethe-wards had sunk." Lethe is the river of forgetfulness which the souls of the dead cross to reach Hades, the classical afterworld. Merely to emphasize forgetfulness in this phrase, of course, is not to resolve the problem. Forgetfulness, like an opiate, reduces pain; it does not cause it. But if we turn our attention to the notion of the souls of the dead, souls which have been separated from their bodies, we see the relation between the effect of hemlock and the effect of opium. Both separate the consciousness from the sensory apparatus, the mind from the body. Thus the total mind-body unity of the personality is dissolved. Or, to put it a different way, the human organism functions in the real world because the individual thinks of his consciousness and his body as one entity. Aside from moments of philosophical abstraction, it is only in very peculiar psychophysical states that this perceived unity is sundered. The necessary consequence is that the mind feels a loss of reality. The personality feels separated from reality by some incomprehensible barrier. At the same time, deprived of the messages which keep it going, the mind suffers pain, since on the one hand the consciousness continues to function while on the other hand it is being deprived of the stimuli necessary to keep it functioning. The mental pain and the consequent physical ache of the speaker's heart—the sense, perhaps, of oppression that comes of not having enough air—are the result of the hemlock and the opiate, and the conflict between their two opposing effects. The speaker is describing, then, a peculiar mental experience which can be compared to the effects of taking either opium or hemlock; or rather, of being in such a state that he does not know exactly what he feels. It is a dissolution of the normally perceived unity of mind and body, that unity that makes it possible for the individual to operate successfully in the real world. The awareness of that unity is the awareness of the existence and identity of the self. So far, then, we may hypothesize that the speaker is describing a loss of self-identity, or rather, since he still uses "my," a threatened loss of self-identity. It is to be seen if this hypothesis can be maintained.

In the next major statement (ll. 5–10) the first question is, "Is 'it' in ''tis' an expletive or a pronoun?" (An expletive is a word used to fill out a sentence pattern, here, perhaps to fill the place of a subject when the actual subject comes after the verb.) If it is an expletive the sentence must be read: "That thou . . . singest of summer . . . is not through envy of thy happy lot"; i.e. "You do not sing of summer because you envy your own good fortune." But to be envious is to be envious of someone else. "It" cannot, then, be an expletive. If it is a pronoun, what is its antecedent? The only possibility is the total situation described in lines 1–5: the threatened loss of self-identity. The speaker is in this painful state not because he is envious of the good luck of the nightingale, though, it is implied, his luck is not very good, but because he is *too happy* in the nightingale's happiness. To be "too" anything is to be guilty of a fault of excess. The peculiar use of the pronoun "thine" where ordinarily the possessive adjective "thy" would be expected and "correct," puts the emphasis upon the word, draws the idea of possession to our attention. Its opposite is "mine." "My fault of excess is that I am too happy in the nightingale's happiness—and not sufficiently happy in my own happiness." This would seem to indicate that the speaker's threatened loss of self-identity is a consequence of a psychological self-identification with the nightingale. If this is correct, the explanation should be found in the following lines. "Too happy that thou" means "too happy because thou singest . . ." "I have made a mistake by identifying myself with the nightingale, and I identified myself with the nightingale because it sings of summer." But not merely that. It is a dryad, or spirit of the trees. It belongs there. It is light-winged, at ease in its environment. The plot or open space which it is filling with melody takes its color from the green of the beech leaves. There are numberless shadows into which it can blend and hide itself. Thus, perfectly suited to its environment, it sings of summer, it celebrates its world, with an ease that is wholly devoid of any tension that might tighten its throat and reduce the fullness and beauty of its song. But if this sense of the nightingale's being perfectly at home in the world is what has tempted the speaker to identify himself with the nightingale, to commit his error, and thus be threatened with the loss of his own identity, it follows that the speaker is not at home in *his* world, that is, he cannot maintain his identity by operating successfully in his environment. Is the fault his or his environment's? And what is he going to do about it? If the hypothesis so far is on the right track, these subjects should appear. The drama of the poem may be expected to develop along one of three lines of action. His position having been defined, the speaker has only three choices: to maintain the state he is in (but that is painful); to disentangle himself emotionally from the nightingale (but that means returning to an unsatisfactory environment); and to identify himself further and completely with the nightingale, to complete the process begun (but that means a total loss of identity).

His cry at the opening of stanza II tells us immediately that he is going to pursue the third course. He wishes passionately for wine, a long drink of wine ("draught"). But does "vintage" have any particular function? It refers to the process by which grapes are turned into wine and also to a particularly fine wine, "a vintage wine." Thus he wishes for the effects of alcohol, which, because it is a depressant, reduces the sense of anxiety or of being threatened and gives one the feeling of being more at home in the environment; but he also wishes for it with some consciousness of its source and in its most delightful form. Both of these themes are now taken up. He wants wine that has aged and ripened in deep, cool wine cellars, and he wants it to remind him of flowers (which are under the control of the goddess Flora), of the green country, of dancing, of the songs of the south of France, and of the joyous revelry of country folk who have been burned and tanned by the sun, the sun of the grape-growing countries, of France and the Mediterranean. These details share the qualities of the nightingale: its environment, and its relation to its environment; they are natural, spontaneous, easeful. The wine, its age and ripeness, the dancing and singing peasants who make it (i.e. it tastes of them, it reminds him of them), and their surroundings of flowers and green country present a picture of an object and of people perfectly adapted to and fully expressive of the environment. The implication is that if he drinks the wine he will put on the attributes of the environment and of the culture which created it. In line 15 he repeats the wish, with a clear statement that it is the South that he wants, where the environment is less inimical to man than it is in the rainy and cold North, and which has become, to the Northern European, a symbol of perfect adjustment of man to environment. He thinks of the glass of wine as "full of the true, the blushful Hippocrene." As the glossary indicates, Hippocrene was the fountain of poetic inspiration. But what is poetry doing in this setting? We may think of poetic inspiration in two ways, either as the experience of inspiration itself, or as the product of inspiration, poetry. Since the poem so far is about subjectively felt experiences, it would seem that the first meaning is at work here, rather than the second. The typical quality of poetic (or indeed of any kind of aesthetic or intellectual inspiration), thought of psychologically, is that the individual who experiences it feels within himself a more intense sense of vitality and a far richer and more rapid flow of ideas than he is ordinarily accustomed to. He becomes, as poets and other artists and intellectual workers, philosophers and scientists, have so often testified, another person. From this point of view, then, we can see what "Hippocrene" is doing in this stanza. The poet wishes a glass of that drink which will give him the sensation of being another person, and a far better person, because, as we have seen, he will be a person at ease with himself and his environment. He wants (l. 17) an effervescent wine, like champagne (which is notorious for its rapid effects), and he wants his mouth to be stained with the color of the wine. That is, he wishes to be so at ease that he is indifferent to the inhibitions of the ordinary proprieties. He wishes to be perfectly at ease. He desires, then, the attributes of the nightingale. The poem is, then, an "Ode to a Nightingale" because the petitioner wishes for himself the attributes of the being addressed. Had he these attributes, he goes on to say (ll. 19–20), he would leave the world and no one would know it ("unseen") and, identifying himself with the nightingale ("with thee"), he would "fade away." Since he has been talking about the consciousness of himself and of his own identity, to "fade away" means to lose his identity, the third of the possibilities logically implied at the end of the first stanza. Likewise, "into the forest dim" means to become, like the nightingale, so absolutely adjusted to his environment that he becomes in effect continuous with it, unself-conscious, without identity.

Stanza II ends in a colon which seems to indicate that there will follow an explanation of some sort. In stanza III the speaker repeats the "fade away" with a new emphasis on distance and states clearly his desired self-dissolution. He wishes to forget what the nightingale in its perfect continuity with its environment ("amongst the leaves") has never had to be aware of, the quality of human life. As hypothesized above (Is the fault his or his environment's?), he now proceeds to point exactly to those qualities in the human world which make it difficult or impossible for him to operate successfully in his environment. There is the exhaustion consequent upon human effort, the sickness of mind and body, the continuous impatience and sense of frustration which cannot be resolved. In this human world men cannot find satisfaction. They sit, helpless, and listen to those groans of human suffering which are man's principal forms of communication. If a man is old, he shakes from palsy, an inability to control the muscles. If a man is young, instead of enjoying his youth, he becomes ill, thin as a ghost, and dies. (It is worth remembering that in England in the early nineteenth century, life expectancy was considerably shorter than today in either England and America, that a far greater proportion of the population died in youth than today, and that tuberculosis —of the effects of which line 26 is an exact statement—was a kind of endemic and permanent plague.) In such a world one has only to think in order to be depressed by what is going on around him; and he will be full not only of sorrow but of despairs, a hopelessness that deprives one of all vitality (makes one "leaden-eyed"). A beautiful woman does not stay beautiful, nor does love itself last. These final details (ll. 29–30) bring in the factor of time, already implicit in age, and youth. Even if, then, there is something beautiful and even if some emotional gratification can be experienced, it is temporary. Thus in this stanza the speaker explains why he cannot operate successfully in his environment or adjust himself successfully to it; why, therefore, his sense of identity is threatened; and why he is justified in wishing to resolve the suffering caused by that threat by extinguishing his identity entirely and identifying himself with the nightingale.

Consequently in stanza IV he determines not merely to wish to be like the nightingale but to identify himself with the nightingale. "Away! Away!" is addressed to himself. What is the significance of "for"? Is anything added by its inclusion? In the previous stanza he has justified his desire to identify himself with the nightingale. He has converted what he first thought of as fault ("too happy," l. 6) into a virtue. He is right in his desires. He is not "too happy" in the nightingale's happiness but "not happy enough." The effect of the "for," then, is: "I say to myself, Away! for I am compelled to identify myself with the nightingale and I am justified in so doing. I will fly to the nightingale. I will not be dragged there in the leopard-drawn chariot of Bacchus. I will not achieve this state by means of alcohol, but by using my imagination." Here "Poesy" is used, as "Hippocrene" was used in the previous stanza, not to refer to the product of poetic activity but to the inspired activity itself, to the characteristic power of poetic inspiration to take one out of oneself and above oneself. Hence he uses "fly," which means going to higher state of being. This interpretation of "Poesy" is confirmed by "viewless," or invisible. Written poetry, the product of poetic inspiration (or Poesy), would be visible, or at least audible. He wishes an invisible power, as he has already indicated in the "unseen" of line 19. It is a private, a secret activity, for only privacy and secrecy will protect him from being pursued by the groans of men. The dull brain perplexes poetic inspiration and retards it because, as already indicated, to "think is to be full of sorrow." To use the brain, or purely rational faculties, is to be aware of one's environment, but the speaker wishes to rise out of it and above it. And at once the desired effect takes place. The exclamation point indicates that "Already with thee!" is an expression of astonishment. "What, am I already with the nightingale? Is it as easy as that? I had only to surrender to the desire, so reasonable and justified, to flee in imagination from my environment, and the gratification so longed for immediately followed." He now imagines himself in the "plot of beechen green and shadows numberless" from which, in stanza I, he heard emanating the nightingale's voice. It is night, as has been implied but not stated by the fact that the nightingale was singing. The moon is shining. The moon and the stars are compared with a queen surrounded by her maids of honor, as beautiful and gleaming as fairies. Is there a particular reason why the fact that it is night is here introduced for the first time and why the moon is compared with a queen? A queen rules her world; just so the moon rules the night. The difference between the moonlight and the sunlight is that the latter reveals every detail in the environment while the former half conceals them in shadows and bathes them in a flattering light. In the moonlight, reality is less intrusive. Hence it is appropriate that at this point the moon should be introduced, and the time stated, for now the speaker has separated himself from reality. Furthermore, he is so placed within the plot in the forest that even the moonlight scarcely penetrates. Only when the breezes stir the leaves do the repeated reflections of moonlight from one leaf to another travel through the green darkness of leaves and the twisting and turning paths of reflection that wind their way among the moss-covered tree trunks and branches. Only then does a very little light enter into the heart of the woods. (In southern England, because of the dampness and warmth of the climate, trees are often completely covered with bright green moss, especially where the dampness is intensified in the thick woods.)

Stanza V presents few initial difficulties of interpretation. Although the speaker cannot see the flowers on the ground where he is standing, nor the fragrant blossoms on the bushes and trees around him, he can guess each flower from its fragrance. There is white hawthorn, the sweetbriar of the countryside, violets (although, since, as the next line tells us, it is May, their blossoming is almost finished), and the musk rose, which is just beginning to come into flower. It makes him think of the coming summer, when the fragrance of the flowers, intensified by the evening dew, will attract the flies, become the place where they congregate or hang out ("haunt"), and he thinks of the soothing buzz that they will make. Several points, however, require further elucidation. Why is it an "embalmed darkness"? The dead are embalmed with sweet-smelling spices which preserve the corpse. The implication is that this is the darkness of death, but why it should be so is not explained. We may hypothesize, therefore, that this theme will be further developed. Even more important, what is the function of this stanza? Is it merely decorative? When we think of it in terms of what has already taken place in the poem, it is possible to perceive how it develops the emotional drama which the poet is presenting. First, his pleasure in his senses has been restored. Having identified himself with the nightingale, he now has an identity. There is just barely enough light to make the absence of light a distinct pleasure, but above all, his sense of smell is enormously, almost abnormally, improved. Not only can he tell the difference between various kinds of sweet-smelling flowers without the aid of sight, something very difficult to do, but he can even smell fading violets covered with leaves, and the scent that the budding musk rose will have in the summer. We are at once reminded that these are not real pleasures but only imaginary pleasures. Hence the identity that he has now gained is not one that will enable him to operate in the real world. Like the nightingale, he is perfectly, exquisitely, adapted to his environment, but it is not a real environment; hence his adaptation is not real; nor, as already stated, is his consequent self-identity, or, more accurately, his nightingale-identity. This gives us some conception of why it is an "embalmed darkness." The opposite of life, no matter how painful, is death; this, then, is a kind of death. And the theme of death is immediately taken up in the next stanza.

He listens in darkness, and now with his intensely, though imaginatively, sharpened perceptions and his imagined closeness to the bird, the impact of the song may be expected to be more powerful. It must be remembered at this point (it is easily forgotten) that physically, really, the speaker is not inside the wood. He only imagines himself to be there. Thus he can physically hear the real song of the nightingale with all the intensity of his imaginatively sharpened responses. In line 51 the "for" is troublesome. Should we read: "And, I have been in love with Death for many a time, now it seems rich to die"? But there is no connection in this paraphrase between "I . . . . time" and "now . . . die." Thus "I . . . time" becomes a mere parenthetical expression with no syntactical function, although some such function is implied by "and" in line 51. Another possibility is: "and, because I have been in love with death many a time, now it seems rich to die." Actually, such an expression as "many a time" (i.e. "Many times I have done so and so") would be more comprehensible than "For many a time" (i.e. "For many times I have done so and so"), which seems very odd. Further, the second reading provides a connection between the two statements, one of causal dependency. This is virtually confirmed by the comma after "and"; if "for" were read as part of the phrase "for many a time" there would be no reason for that comma. The speaker, then, finds it richer than ever to die now, because in the past he has been half in love with easeful death. We understand why this should be so: the grimness of life as described in stanza III is sufficient explanation.

Only death could give him the ease he desires, the ease which is also characteristic of the nightingale (l. 10). Still, it is not clear what there is about the situation he has imagined that particularly makes him want to die. First, since he has in the past been at least half in love with death, and at least in verse has praised death and asked death to take his breath out of his body, he is already used to wanting to die. It is an attitude which he has experienced often and has confirmed and reinforced by writing down. Second, the "quiet" breath indicates that he has wanted to die not when he is agitated or disturbed, but when he is at ease, as he is now. Thus now it seems rich, intensely and fully gratifying, to die, to die, moreover, without pain, as he has frequently wished to die; and further, to die at the moment when the nightingale is singing in its most rapturous happiness. In the preceding stanza (l. 43) "the embalmed darkness" has already indicated that this is the darkness of death. Now we understand why that detail should have been presented there. The idea of the appropriateness of death under these circumstances had already come to his mind while he was celebrating its beauty and his happiness in it. But there is a still further reason why now, more than ever, it is rich to die. He would die to the song of the nightingale, at ease, and, as we have seen, in perfect identification with the nightingale. It follows that the attempt to solve the problem of the psychological pain of threatened loss of identity by identifying himself with the nightingale necessarily, by a kind of emotional logic, leads him to the desire to destroy all identity. Thus, even though the nightingale might continue singing, its song would have become a requiem (a mass sung for the dead) for the speaker, who would have returned to clay.

Stanza VII presents us with an immediate question. What is the connection between the desire for death and imagined anticipation of death in stanza VI with "Thou wast not born for death"? The line can be interpreted to mean: "After all, I *was born* for death; therefore it is right and proper that I should desire to die. There's nothing wrong in such a wish. It's no fault." And indeed he has already demonstrated man's mortal fate in stanza III. He emphasizes his point by insisting that hungry generations, though they do not kill nightingales as they trample over previous generations in their effort to live, do in fact tread down the speaker. Human beings are always hungry (perfectly true in the early nineteenth century for most of mankind and still true for at least three-quarters of the human race); that is, they are ill adapted to life; nightingales are *not* always hungry and are well adapted to life. The psychological movement between stanza VI and VII, then, is a defensive one. In justifying his desire for death, he implies that he needs justification. In that case, in spite of his protestations, he feels that it is wrong for him to want to die.

The next question is posed by "immortal bird." What is meant by this? For in fact nightingales are not immortal. They die just like human beings. But since the immortality of the bird is the subject of the rest of the stanza, the question is best postponed until we finish the stanza. He goes on, then, to state that the voice that he hears on this night that is passing for him (as a human, he is subject to time) was heard in the distant past by emperors (presumably Roman emperors) and peasants ("clown"). Perhaps even the very same song of this particular ("thou," l. 11) nightingale was heard in the even more remote past of Biblical times. Perhaps Ruth heard it when she stood among the foreign wheat fields and wept for homesickness, and was moved by the song ("found a path into her heart"). But "moved" in what way? Her situation was like the speaker's; she found herself in an unfamiliar and unfriendly world. She, too, then, must have been moved to long for the ease of the nightingale's world, and, by implication, for death. Finally, it was the same voice that by enchantment often controlled windows that opened out on the stormy ("foam") and dangerous seas in lost and forgotten imaginative and mythical countries. The chronological order of the stanza, backward in time from the present to ancient Rome and then back to ancient Palestine, implies that the faery lands are to be thought of as even more remote in time, and hence forgotten. The song of the nightingale disappears into the past, therefore, and the final word "forlorn," which means lost and forgotten, returns the speaker in stanza VIII to a consciousness of his actual living self, not the imagined self in the nightingale's wood but the suffering self with which the poem began.

We are still left, however, with the question of why the nightingale is called immortal. One possible solution is that the song of nightingales has not changed. But that solution is untenable for several reasons. First, human voices have not changed during the centuries either, even though languages have. Second, each generation of nightingales could have been overwhelmed by each succeeding generation without the song having changed. Third, in the second (l. 65) and third (l. 68) appearances of the nightingale's song, it is specifically referred to as the same song of the same nightingale, and in the first (l. 63) there is that possibility. (It is possible to think of "song" as referring to the song common to all nightingales; but it is a little more difficult to interpret "voice," a more individual term, in the same way.) It follows that the speaker is thinking of this individual nightingale as immortal. This interpretation is reinforced by "perhaps" in line 65. If he is thinking of the song common to all nightingales, there would be no more doubt about Ruth's having heard it than about the emperor's and the clown's. But, since it cannot be true that this individual nightingale is really immortal, the statement must be taken as indicative of some attitude on the speaker's part; the feeling that the bird is immortal must be taken as an emotional symbol that stands for and refers to some emotional state. As we have already seen, the nightingale's song has a dual existence, in the real world of the speaker and in his projected world. In stanzas V and VI the real world has ceased to exist. But the thought of his own death, no matter how attractive, brings the speaker's consciousness back to the real world of hungry generations and death. In stanza VII, therefore, the real world and the projected world are not kept separate; both are present in the speaker's mind. And this is consistent with his attempt to justify his desire for death. He begins to feel again the pain he felt at the beginning of the poem. The repeated assertions of the immortality of the bird can now be seen as attempts to maintain the value of the nightingale, in spite of the fact that the self-identification with the nightingale has already failed, and failed at the point where the idea of his own death becomes as imaginatively powerful as the idea of the nightingale. Now, as we have seen (stanza III), the suffering of man, which in the consequence of the inimical conditions under which he lives, is associated in the speaker's mind with time. The nightingale presents the notion of a creature perfectly at home and at ease in its surroundings. For the nightingale, therefore, time does not exist. The requirements for being perfectly at ease and at home in one's world, then, are immortality or timelessness, or freedom from the effects of time. But since nightingales are not in fact immortal, the speaker cannot avoid realizing that it is impossible to give equal validity to the real world of suffering and to the imagined world of happiness into which he has momentarily entered. The imagined song of the nightingale, and everything that it stands for, then, recedes into the past, enters, by way of Rome and ancient Palestine, into a remote, forgotten, and imaginary world, the world of faery. The imagined song of the nightingale loses its validity and only the real song of the nightingale is left, and the speaker is back in the real world. So tenuous has become the imagined nightingale's existence by the end of the stanza that a mere word is sufficient to put it out of existence. But, does not the disappearance of the imagined nightingale and its song also imply the disappearance of the ideal it represented, being perfectly at home and at ease in the world, and thus having a permanently unthreatened and unthreatenable sense of self-identity? If this is correct, we may predict that the nightingale will not reappear in the poem under the aspect it had at the opening, of absolutely easeful happiness.

The word "forlorn" is like a bell because of the exact repetition in the second syllable of the "or" sound in the first. Thus it reminds the speaker of a bell which tolls, each successive sound of the bell coming at a considerable interval. The sound makes him conscious of the difference between himself and the bird. Thus the "fault" of stanza I of being "too happy" is now corrected. He is now alone, but he is alone within himself. He is aware of himself as he was not aware of himself in the first stanza. Why? He wished to identify himself with the nightingale because the suffering and mortality of the human condition made it impossible for him to operate successfully in the real world. But the attempted identification led to a desire for death and thus in fact brought him back to a renewed awareness of the human condition. He is forced to realize that the attempt to solve the problem of threatened identity by identification with another being will not work. The problem is still present, but one proposed solution of it has been revealed as impossible. As was hypothesized at the end of the interpretation of stanza I, to complete the process of identification with the nightingale means a total loss of identity, symbolized through the desire for death. He has also shown by the very drama of the poem that to maintain the sense of threatened identity, as in the opening of the poem, is also impossible. That leaves him with the final alternative: to disentangle himself emotionally from the nightingale, which he has done, and consequently to return to the unsatisfactory environment of reality. That this has happened is indicated in lines 73–74. Simply stated, it means, "Good-by, the imagination cannot serve so well at self-deception as it is supposed to." But observe the downgrading of the imagination that has taken place! In line 33 it was referred to as Poesy, with invisible wings and the power to raise one above and beyond reality. That power is now reduced to the far less imposing "fancy." "Imagination" implies the ability to create an unreal world with the authority and validity of the real one. "Fancy" is simply the mental power to invent something that is not real. Thus instead of a goddess (as the capitalized Poesy indicated) it is merely an elf, a very minor spirit. Instead of creating a new and superior kind of reality, it merely deceives. Again in line 75, he repeats, twice, his farewell to the nightingale, implying an irrevocable emotional disentanglement. And now the real song of the real nightingale also disappears into real space (ll. 76–78) and according to normal time ("now," l. 77) just as the imagined song of the imagined nightingale disappeared into mythical past (the past of the emperor, the clown, Ruth, and the magic casements). Furthermore, no longer is it a song of summer in full-throated ease. It is a plaintive anthem. It too complains of the conditions of life. An anthem is a sung prayer in the Anglican church, a psalm or other part of the service. The nightingale is like the speaker, who prayed to the nightingale to give him its perfect ease and happiness. It too must pray for what it lacks. It goes farther and farther away, beyond the meadow, beyond the stream, up the hillside, and into the woods in the next valley. Once there, it is no longer heard; it is "buried." The implication is that real nightingales are subject like human beings to the ordinary limitations of time, space, and mortality. The perfectly happy nightingale of stanza I never really existed. It was imagined by the speaker.

There is, however, no reconciliation of the speaker with the conditions of human existence, which were the original justification and cause for his attempt to solve the problems of suffering and uncertain self-identity by employing the aid of the imagination. Consequently he is not sure whether it was a vision or a daydream. The difference is that a vision is of something true and valid. A dream is simply a mental illusion. What is the antecedent of "it"? It seems best to identify it as the whole experience of attempted self-identification with the nightingale. Or more precisely, with the idea of being perfectly at home and at ease and happy in one's world, a state which the nightingale symbolized. Does that idea have some kind of validity? Is it important? Should we pay attention to it? Or is it merely an idle daydream of no importance? To that question there is no answer. The bird's music, the stimulus that inspired that idea, is gone. The idea has fled or escaped the speaker's grasp. Consequently, as the punctuation seems to imply, he does not know whether he is now, at the conclusion of the experience, awake or asleep. He does not know if his experience has had any validity, or importance, or "truth," or whether it has been utterly meaningless.

The poem can be summed up, using certain modern terms, as a dramatization of how man comes to perceive the causes and mechanism of psychological escape from a painful reality to which he cannot adequately adjust and which constantly threatens his sense of self-identity. The whole process is, as it were, "seen through." It is understood and in the last stanza it is presented as what it is, an illusory escape. Nevertheless, it did lead to a moment, in stanza V, of perfection, of being exquisitely sensitive to one's environment and completely at home in it, or adapted to it. Consequently, the poem concludes, it is an unresolved question as to whether such moments, although unreal, are in fact invalid, useless to the human being, dangerously self-indulgent. The speaker does not know, but he leaves us with the possibility that such moments do have their validity, their "truth." For example (and this is not in the poem but is presented only to make the point clear): Is it possible that without such moments of perfection, of *feeling* fully adequate (even though such moments are illusions), we could not endure life?

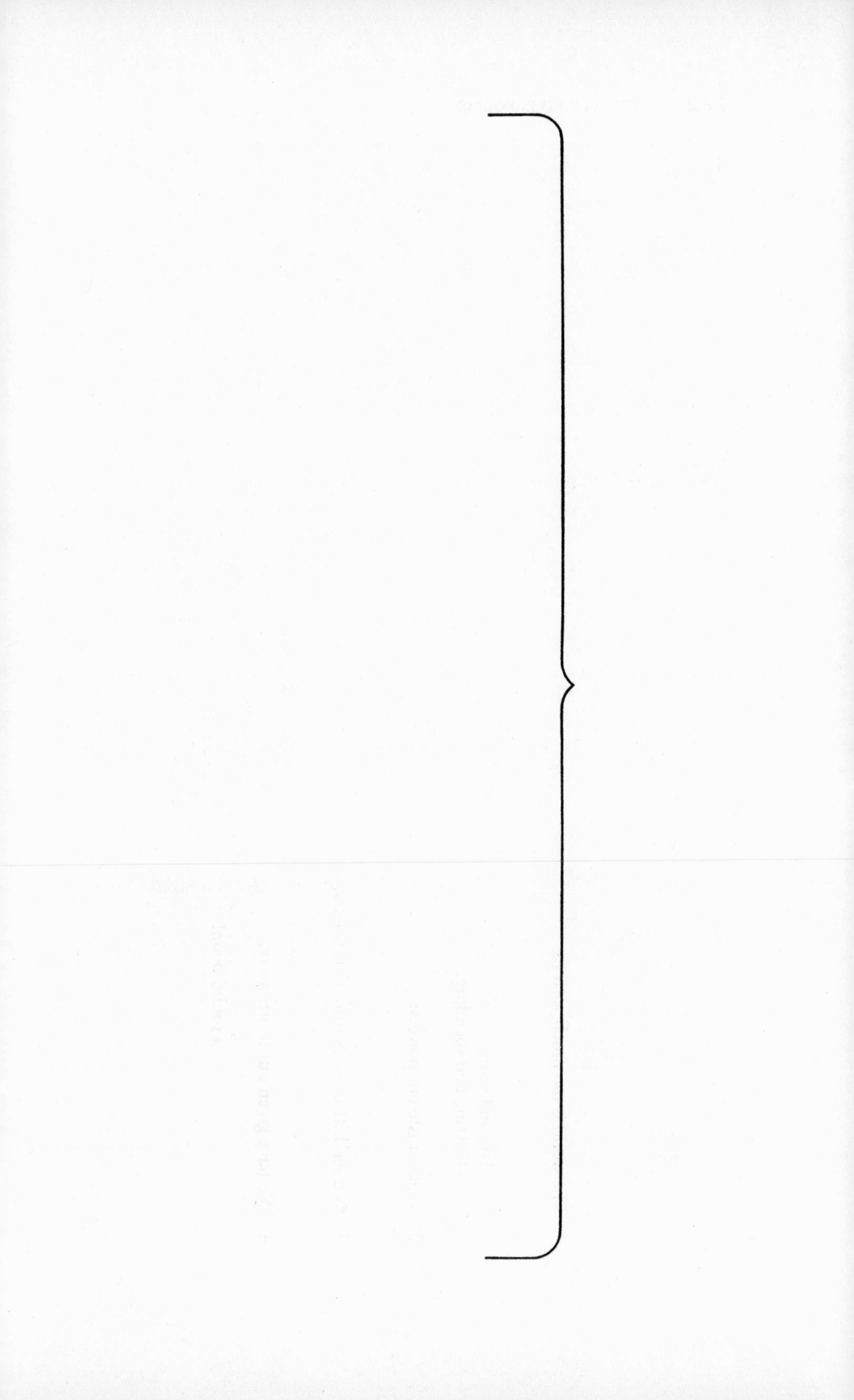

1. The world is too much with us;

{ late and soon,
{ Getting and spending,
↓

2. we lay waste our powers:

3. *we see Little* in Nature that is ours;

4. We have given our hearts away,
↕
a sordid boon!

5.

WILLIAM WORDSWORTH
(1770–1850)

Sonnet 33

From *Miscellaneous Sonnets*

The world is too much with us; late and soon,
Getting and spending, we lay waste our powers:
Little we see in Nature that is ours;
We have given our hearts away, a sordid boon! 4

1. *world:* the class of persons devoted to the affairs, interests, or pursuits of this life; or such activities.

1. *soon:* early.

4. *boon:* a free gift.

5. *we are out of tune;
  For this, ⟷ This Sea that bares her bosom to the moon;
    The winds that will be howling at all hours,
      And are up-gathered now
        ↑ like sleeping flowers;
  for everything*,

6. It moves us not.—

7. Great God! I'd rather be A Pagan suckled in a[n] *outworn creed*;
  ↑ [than what I am]
  So [that] *I might*, Have glimpses that would make me less forlorn;
    Have sight of Proteus rising from the sea;
    Or hear old Triton blow his wreathèd horn.
  ↑ standing on this pleasant lea,

This Sea that bares her bosom to the moon;
The winds that will be howling at all hours,
And are up-gathered now like sleeping flowers;
For this, for everything, we are out of tune;
It moves us not.—Great God! I'd rather be
A Pagan suckled in a creed outworn;
So might I, standing on this pleasant lea,
Have glimpses that would make me less forlorn;
Have sight of Proteus rising from the sea;
Or hear old Triton blow his wreathèd horn.

10. *Pagan:* a heathen.

10. *creed:* a system of religious belief.

10. *outworn:* obsolete, out-of-date.

11. *So might I:* so that I might, if only I could.

11. *lea:* meadow.

13. *Proteus:* sea-god of classical mythology who had the power of assuming different forms.

14. *Triton:* sea-god, son of Poseidon and Amphitrite, depicted as a man with the tail of a fish and carrying a conch-shell horn.

Interpretational Hypothesis

The first question the poem demands that we ask is, "What is meant by 'world' "? The simplest use of the word is to refer to "the world as we know it," that natural world which we experience through our senses. A second use appears in such a phrase as "the world of horse-racing," a segment of the total world of the first meaning. Another use is found in such an expression as "It's a tough world." Here the word refers to the quality of our experience as we make our way through life. A fourth common meaning is found in such expressions as "worldly" and "the world, the flesh, and the devil": "worldly" as opposed to "spiritual." The term, then can be used to designate (1) the totality of which we are aware, (2) any segment of that totality which we wish to abstract, (3) our subjective experience of that totality or some segment of it, or (4) a denial of the goodness, the excellence, the value of whatever is referred to by any of the first three meanings. The question having been raised, it is answered in the next line and a half. It is the world of business, or at least of the economic transactions of life, which require all our time and "lay waste our powers." The second meaning of "world" is being used. "Lay waste" means to destroy utterly; it comes from the practice of destroying completely the agriculture of an area or in completely dismantling a city during war. "To lay waste," then, means to deprive something of its usefulness and value and of one's chance of renewing that usefulness and value, at least without tremendous loss of energy and time. Since "getting and spending," i.e. playing our part in the circulation of money, and in the creation and consumption of goods and services, certainly appears to be a "power" or a capacity to do something, the speaker must also be employing "world" in the meaning it has in the antithesis "world versus spirit," i.e. in the fourth meaning. By identifying "getting and spending" with "world," this negative evaluation of "world" is extended to "getting and spending." These are antithetical in value to "powers," which thus is something good. But to say that economic activity, which is necessary to keep ourselves alive, is totally bad is to utter an absurdity. Nor does the speaker fall into such an attitude. He has said that the world is *too much* with us, not that the world should not be with us at all. Economic activity, then, is bad only when by excessive preoccupation with it we permit our "powers" to be destroyed. Although getting and spending in the world (economic activity in the conduct of the ordinary affairs of life) are not to be utterly denied all value, as we have seen, nevertheless, they are not to be regarded as "powers," which is some other kind of human activity and which we can expect to be defined in the poem without much delay.

The connection between the speaker's first two statements may be thought of as causal. "Because the world is too much with us, we lay waste our powers." Between "powers" and "little," however, there is a colon instead of a semicolon. The relation or connection then will be different from that between the first two clauses. Ordinarily a colon is used to indicate some kind of apposition or equivalence to what has been said, such a connection as "for example" or "that is." The latter seems to be operative here, since an explanation of "powers" is required. Line 3 gives that explanation. "By 'laying waste our powers' I mean that we see little in Nature that is ours." "Seeing something in Nature that is ours," then, is a power.

The connection between the third and fourth statements (l. 4) is again by means of a semicolon. The difference in tense between "see" and "have given" suggests that the two statements are not parallel, though it does not necessarily exclude that possibility. The simplest suggestion is that the causal connection between the first and second statements is here repeated: "We lay waste our powers (that is: we see little in Nature that is ours); consequently, we have given our hearts away." However, the past of "have given" precedes in time the present of the other three statements. It would seem more desirable to assume that the fourth statement refers to the ultimate or original cause of the conditions described in those three statements. "Because we have given our hearts away, the world is too much with us; consequently, we lay waste our powers: that is, we see little in Nature that is ours." Hence the sordid boon of giving our hearts away was the initial act for the chain of consequences. But why is giving our hearts away a *sordid* boon? "Boon" originally meant a prayer or request for something; subsequently it was used to refer to the thing granted to the suppliant. In either sense the transaction was "free," that is, it involved nothing of equivalent value in return. A boon is not an exchange. But "sordid" refers to a low, ignoble, corrupt, or "dirty" act, especially one characterized by mercenary motives or material considerations. "Sordid boon" is a paradox. We have sold for money what we should have given away freely. But this leads to a further difficulty. The transaction involved in giving our hearts away, since it has involved so many bad consequences, was a bad transaction. But to give away is to make a boon, or free gift. But bad boons or false boons are ones that involve an exchange, not a gift. Does the sentence mean that we should have *sold* our hearts? Hardly, since "getting-and-spending" has already been classified as damaging to our powers. It must mean then, first, that we should not have given our hearts away at all; we should have kept them. Further, it was a sordid giving, or boon-making, because instead of giving them away in a free exchange, we traded our hearts for "getting-and-spending." But how can this trading be reconciled with giving? Only by assuming that what we got in return for hearts was something bad, i.e. "getting-and-spending," which was defined above as damaging to our powers. The full conception may be expressed thus: The act that led to our present bad position was one in which we traded our hearts in return for a mercenary life: it was a bad act because we got nothing of real value; on the contrary, we suffered instead a loss of our powers and a sense of alienation from Nature.

A further question now arises. What is meant by "hearts"? "Heart" ordinarily stands for "love," whether purely erotic or otherwise. But something more seems to be involved here, since the poet suggests not only that the emotional capacity referred to by "heart" is valuable but also that when we exercise that capacity toward Nature we get something in return. This further significance comes from "ours" in line 3 and its repetition in line 4. It is just the opposite of a "sordid boon"; it is a "noble exchange." To have or keep our hearts (i.e. *not* to give them away) means that we can respond to Nature and receive from Nature something of importance and value. Yet all of this is more implied than stated, and we may predict, therefore, if our hypothesis is on the right track, that further information will be forthcoming about this "noble exchange."

By contrast the next four lines are a single sentence instead of four separate sentences. This suggests a shift in the emotional drift of the poem. Turning to the main clause of the sentence, we may begin by reading, "We are out of tune for the sea, for the winds, for everything." Returning to the first line, we find that "This" raises a problem. The first four lines have been stated nondramatically. Although the ideas are highly condensed, the tone is what one might encounter in an essay, or a sermon, or from anyone who is making a general statement with no reference to the circumstances in which he makes it. "This sea that bares her bosom to the moon," however, indicates that the speaker is in a place, and that his general statements are, in part at least, a consequence of his being in that place. What appeared to be "general truths" now begin to look like dramatic statements. Nevertheless, it is still not a personal statement, as the "we" of line 8 indicates; it continues the "we," "us," "our", and "ours" of the first four lines. (The first person plural normally refers to mankind in general.) The next thing to notice about line 5 is that the sea is personalized, or anthropomorphized. The reference is to the moonlight on the water, but it is presented in terms that make the sea respond to the moon as would a woman. The same thing is true of the winds in the next two lines. Like human beings they have personal will. They like to howl, always, and now they are gathered up like sleeping flowers. They too have responded to some influence. The notion in "gathered-up" is not "plucked and gathered" but folded up upon themselves, as flowers close at night. They have ceased to exercise their being as winds.

In line 8, "this"—now a pronoun rather than a noun-modifier—creates a problem. What is its antecedent? It can scarcely be just the sea, for the rest of the sentence implies that we are out of tune for the winds as well. Its antecedent is an implication, rather than a word. From the preceding lines may be derived several implications about the natural world, which unites sea and winds. First, each aspect of nature has its own will; the various aspects of nature respond to each other. But we do not respond to them. To the life in nature, then, we are out of tune. Furthermore, the "everything" implies we are indeed out of tune for everything in the natural world whose own powers are genuinely active —at least with everything with which it is possible to have a noble exchange. To be out of tune is a metaphor taken from music. If two musical instruments are in tune they will harmonize together, instead of making a harmonically meaningless noise. Again, if a string is sounded on one instrument, the corresponding string on another instrument, if it is undamped, will also vibrate and produce sound. By using "for" instead of "with," the poet implies that nature offers a stimulus to which we ought to be able to respond sympathetically, but that in fact we cannot. Could we do so, it would be a noble exchange, but we have laid waste our powers. This is confirmed by the first half of line 9. It is the emotional response to nature which is lacking. We remain unmoved by the "spiritual" in nature, even when we are in its very presence.

The tone of the poem now suddenly and dramatically shifts. There is a cry of bitterness and frustration. The tone of this cry has already been established by the previous presentation of a sense of loss and of having been cheated. This is immediately followed by the full personalization of the poem in the use of "I." "Suckle" refers to the act of giving an infant milk at the breast of its mother. A "creed" is a statement of religious faith and has been extended to mean the belief in that faith. An outworn creed is one that no one any longer believes in. The comparative of "rather" implies that a "than" is on the way. But it does not arrive; it is only implied. Its full form is: "I'd rather be a pagan than be what I am." "What I am" has been explained as being one whose powers are inoperative, as being "out of tune" for everything in nature. But the antithesis of pagan is Christian, a creed that is, or is supposed, not to be outworn. But why these references to religion? The implication is that the speaker would rather believe in a creed which is no longer accepted than believe in a creed, the Christianity of his day, which no longer does what he most desires, i.e. provides a satisfactory emotional life. Had he been brought up in such an outworn creed, he might have brief visions as he stands here on this pleasant meadow overlooking the sea, at night, in the moonlight. He might catch a glimpse of Proteus, the god of the changeableness of the sea, rising up out of it; he might hear Triton, a lesser sea-deity, with fishtails instead of legs, blowing on his conch-shell hung with seaweed. Why these particular deities? Had he been a pagan, he would have responded to the life in nature; he would have visualized and symbolized that life in mythology. As a modern, he cannot do so. In lines 5–8 he has presented a seascape for which he was out of tune. Were he a pagan, confronting that same seascape, the divinities of the sea would have made the noble exchange possible. Thus the conclusion, left to be drawn by the reader but firmly implied in the incompleted "rather . . . than" construction, is that our emotional life is dead not merely because we get and spend, but because we have given our hearts away (surrendered our natural emotional inheritance) as a consequence of the failure of our religion. Thus we can see why the poem moves from statements in the form of general truths, through statements related to a particular time and place, to statements that reveal a profound and depressing sense of emotional inadequacy. The psychological pattern or drama of the poem is the gradual realization that our general statements about life arise from attempts to understand the causes of personal and individual emotional and moral dilemmas. Hence the logical pattern is a working back from effect to immediate cause beyond anterior cause until the ultimate cause is uncovered.

PART II

FIFTY POEMS BY THE SAME AUTHORS, WITH LEXICAL GLOSSES, ARRANGED BY DATE OF BIRTH

EDMUND SPENSER (1552?–1599)

Sonnet 89

From *Amoretti*

Like as the Culver on the bared bough,
  sits mourning for the absence of her mate:
  and in her songs sends many a wishful vow,
  for his return that seems to linger late;
So I alone now left disconsolate,
  mourn to myself the absence of my love:
  and wand'ring here and there all desolate,
  seek with my plaints to match that mournful Dove:
Ne joy of ought that under heaven doth hove,
  can comfort me, but her own joyous sight:
  whose sweet aspect both God and man can move,
  in her unspotted pleasance to delight.
Dark is my day, whiles her fair light I miss,
  and dead my life that wants such lively bliss.

Lexical Gloss

1. *Like as:* just as, in the same way as.
1. *Culver:* dove.
4. *that:* refers to the dove, i.e. "who."
4. *linger late:* to be too long delayed.
5. *disconsolate:* uncomforted.
6. *love:* sweetheart, mistress.
7. *desolate:* deprived of companionship, alone.
8. *plaints:* formal expressions of misery.
8. *to match:* to be equal to.
9. *Ne:* nor.
9. *of ought:* at, or derived from, anything.
9. *hove:* short for "hover."
10. *but:* except.
10. *her own joyous sight:* the joyous sight of her, herself.
11. *aspect:* appearance.
11. *move:* to stir emotions.

12. *pleasance:* ability to give pleasure.
13. *whiles:* whilst, while.
13. *fair:* beautiful.
14. *wants:* lacks.
14. *lively:* vital, life-giving.

Prothalamion
or
A Spousal Verse

1

Calm was the day, and through the trembling air,
Sweet breathing *Zephyrus* did softly play
A gentle spirit, that lightly did delay
Hot *Titan's* beams, which then did glister fair:
When I whom sullen care,
Through discontent of my long fruitless stay
In Prince's Court, and expectation vain
Of idle hopes, which still do fly away,
Like empty shadows, did afflict my brain,
Walked forth to ease my pain
Along the shore of silver streaming *Thames,*
Whose rutty Bank, the which his River hems,
Was painted all with variable flowers,
And all the meads adorned with dainty gems,
Fit to deck maidens' bowers,
And crown their Paramours,
Against the Bridal day, which is not long:
Sweet *Thames* run softly, till I end my song.

2

There, in a Meadow, by the River's side,
A Flock of *Nymphs* I chanced to espy,
All lovely Daughters of the Flood thereby,
With goodly greenish locks all loose untied,
As each had been a Bride,
And each one had a little wicker basket,
Made of fine twigs entrailed curiously,
In which they gathered flowers to fill their flasket:
And with fine Fingers, cropp'd full featously

The tender stalks on high.
Of every sort, which in that Meadow grew,
They gathered some; the Violet pallid blue,
The little Daisy, that at evening closes,
The virgin Lily, and the Primrose true,
With store of vermeil Roses,
To deck their Bridegrooms' posies,
Against the Bridal day, which was not long:
Sweet *Thames* run softly, till I end my Song.

3

With that I saw two Swans of goodly hue,
Come softly swimming down along the Lea;
Two fairer Birds I yet did never see:
The snow which doth the top of *Pindus* strew,
Did never whiter shew,
Nor *Jove* himself when he a Swan would be
For love of *Leda*, whiter did appear:
Yet *Leda* was (they say) as white as he,
Yet not so white as these, nor nothing near;
So purely white they were,
That even the gentle stream, the which them bare,
Seem'd foul to them, and bade his billows spare
To wet their silken feathers, lest they might
Soil their fair plumes with water not so fair,
And mar their beauties bright,
That shone as heaven's light,
Against their Bridal day, which was not long:
Sweet *Thames* run softly, till I end my Song.

4

Eftsoons the *Nymphs*, which now had Flowers their fill,
Ran all in haste, to see that silver brood,
As they came floating on the Crystal Flood,
Whom when they saw, they stood amazed still,
Their wond'ring eyes to fill.
Them seem'd they never saw a sight so fair,
Of Fowls so lovely, that they sure did deem
Them heavenly born, or to be that same pair
Which through the Sky draw *Venus*' silver Team,
For sure they did not seem
To be begot of any earthly Seed,

But rather Angels or of Angels' breed:
Yet were they bred of *Summer's-heat* they say,
In sweetest Season, when each Flower and weed
The earth did fresh array,
So fresh they seem'd as day,
Even as their Bridal day, which was not long:
  Sweet *Thames* run softly, till I end my Song.

5

Then forth they all out of their baskets drew
Great store of Flowers, the honour of the field,
That to the sense did fragrant odours yield,
All which upon those goodly Birds they threw,
And all the Waves did strew,
That like old *Peneus*' Waters they did seem,
When down along by pleasant *Tempe's* shore
Scatt'red with Flowers, through *Thessaly* they stream,
That they appear through Lilies' plenteous store,
Like a Bride's Chamber floor:
Two of those *Nymphs*, meanwhile, two Garlands bound,
Of freshest Flowers, which in that Mead they found,
The which presenting all in trim Array,
Their snowy Foreheads therewithal they crown'd,
Whil'st one did sing this Lay,
Prepar'd against that Day,
Against their Bridal day, which was not long:
  Sweet *Thames* run softly, till I end my Song.

6

Ye gentle Birds, the world's fair ornament,
And heaven's glory, whom this happy hour
Doth lead unto your lovers' blissful bower,
Joy may you have, and gentle hearts' content
Of your loves' couplement:
And let fair *Venus*, that is Queen of love,
With her heart-quelling Son upon you smile,
Whose smile they say, hath virtue to remove
All Love's dislike, and friendship's faulty guile
For ever to assoil.
Let endless Peace your steadfast hearts accord,
And blessed Plenty wait upon your board,

And let your bed with pleasures chaste abound,
That fruitful issue may to you afford,
Which may your foes confound,
And make your joys redound,
Upon your Bridal day, which is not long:
  Sweet *Thames* run softly, till I end my Song.

7

So ended she; and all the rest around
To her redoubled that her undersong,
Which said, their bridal day should not be long.
And gentle Echo from the neighbour ground,
Their accents did resound.
So forth those joyous Birds did pass along,
Adown the Lea, that to them murmured low,
As he would speak, but that he lack'd a tongue,
Yet did by signs his glad affection show,
Making his stream run slow.
And all the fowl which in his flood did dwell
Gan flock about these twain, that did excel
The rest, so far, as *Cynthia* doth shend
The lesser stars. So they enranged well,
Did on those two attend,
And their best service lend,
Against their wedding day, which was not long:
  Sweet *Thames* run softly, till I end my Song.

8

At length they all to merry *London* came,
To merry London, my most kindly Nurse,
That to me gave this Life's first native source:
Though from another place I take my name,
An house of ancient fame.
There when they came, whereas those bricky towers,
The which on *Thames*' broad aged back do ride,
Where now the studious Lawyers have their bowers,
There whilom wont the Templar Knights to bide,
Till they decay'd through pride:
Next whereunto there stands a stately place,
Where oft I gained gifts and goodly grace
Of that great Lord, which therein wont to dwell,

Whose want too well, now feels my friendless case:
But Ah! here fits not well
Old woes, but joys to tell
Against the Bridal day, which is not long:
  Sweet *Thames* run softly, till I end my Song.

9

Yet therein now doth lodge a noble Peer,
Great *England's* glory and the World's wide wonder,
Whose dreadful name, late through all *Spain* did thunder,
And *Hercules'* two pillars standing near,
Did make to quake and fear:
Fair branch of Honor, flower of Chivalry,
That fillest *England* with thy triumph's fame,
Joy have thou of thy noble victory,
And endless happiness of thine own name
That promiseth the same:
That through thy prowess and victorious arms,
Thy country may be freed from foreign harms:
And great *Elisa's* glorious name may ring
Through all the world, fill'd with thy wide Alarms,
Which some brave muse may sing
To ages following,
Upon the Bridal day, which is not long:
  Sweet *Thames* run softly, till I end my Song.

10

From those high Towers, this noble Lord issuing,
Like Radiant *Hesper*, when his golden hair
In th' *Ocean* billows he hath Bathed fair,
Descended to the River's open viewing,
With a great train ensuing.
Above the rest were goodly to be seen
Two gentle Knights of lovely face and feature
Beseeming well the bower of any Queen,
With gifts of wit, and ornaments of nature,
Fit for so goodly stature:
That like the twins of *Jove* they seem'd in sight,
Which deck the Baldric of the Heavens bright.
They two forth pacing to the River's side,
Received those two fair Brides, their Loves' delight,
Which at th'appointed tide,

Each one did make his Bride,
Against their Bridal day, which is not long:
  Sweet *Thames* run softly, till I end my Song.

Lexical Gloss

Title. Prothalamion: a marriage song. This poem was written to celebrate the double wedding of Elizabeth and Katherine Somerset to Henry Gilford and William Peter.

2. *Zephyrus*: the mild west wind.
2. *play*: send forth a stream, spout.
3. *spirit*: breeze.
3. *delay*: to mitigate, to lessen the effect of, to temper or lessen.
4. *Titan's*: the sun's.
4. *then*: on that day.
4. *glister*: to sparkle.
4. *fair*: beautifully.
5. *sullen*: gloomy.
6. *of*: at.
6. *fruitless*: profitless.
6. *stay*: "attendance at," in the sense of "seeking patronage at."
7. *vain*: illusory.
8. *idle*: pointless, profitless.
8. *still do fly away*: always fly away.
11. *Thames*: a river in southern England which flows past London. Notice that it rhymes with "hems"; *th* is pronounced *t*.
12. *rutty*: filled with ruts.
13. *painted*: decorated.
13. *variable*: various.
14. *mead*: meadow.
14. *dainty*: precious, rare.
15. *Fit*: worthy.
15. *deck*: to array, adorn.
15. *bowers*: inner private apartments as opposed to general or public halls.
16. *Paramours*: sweethearts, lovers.
17. *Against*: in anticipation of.
17. *long*: far off.
20. *Nymphs*: semi-divine maidens inhabiting beautiful places in nature in classical mythology. These are river nymphs; others lived in the woods, the sea, fountains, and hills.
20. *espy*: catch sight of.
21. *Flood*: the River Thames.
21. *thereby*: near which they played.
22. *goodly*: handsome, attractive.
23. *As*: as if.

24. *wicker:* woven of pliant twigs.
25. *entrailed:* entwined.
25. *curiously:* elaborately, exquisitely, ingeniously, or carefully (all of which may be implied here).
26. *flasket:* a long shallow basket.
27. *fine:* delicate.
27. *cropp'd:* plucked.
27. *featously:* dexterously, deftly.
30. *pallid:* pale.
33. *vermeil:* bright red.
34. *deck:* fit out, adorn.
34. *posies:* bouquets.
37. *With that:* as that happened.
37. *hue:* appearance.
38. *Lea:* a stream that runs into the Thames east of London.
40. *Pindus:* mountain in Greece.
40. *strew:* cover, be spread over.
41. *shew:* show; appear.
42–43. *Jove . . . Leda:* the Greek god Jove, desiring the love of the mortal maiden Leda, appeared to her in the form of a swan.
42. *would be:* wanted to be.
47. *the which:* which.
47. *bare:* bore, carried.
48. *to them:* in comparison to them.
48. *bade:* ordered, instructed.
48. *billows:* waves.
48–49. *spare To:* desist from.
55. *Eftsoons:* at once.
55. *fill:* desired amount.
56. *brood:* swarm, crew, crowd.
57. *Flood:* the River Lea.
59. *to:* in order to.
60. *Them seem'd:* it seemed to them.
63. *Venus' silver Team:* perhaps a reference to a possible source for this poem, W. Vallans' *A Tale of Two Swans* (1590), in which two swans are brought from Greece to England and are yoked to Venus' ivory chariot.
65. *of:* by or from.
65. *Seed:* source or origin.
67. *Summer's-heat:* spelled "Somers-heat" in the original, this is a pun on Somerset, which is the last name of both brides.
74. *honour:* pride, glory, most excellent part.
76. *All which:* all of which.
78. *Peneus:* river in Greece which flows from Mt. Pindus (l. 40).
79. *Tempe:* the valley through which Peneus runs.

80. *Thessaly:* the province of Greece in which are found Pindus, Peneus and Tempe.
81. *plenteous:* abundant, copious.
83. *Garlands:* flower-wreaths.
85. *trim:* well-ordered.
85. *Array:* arrangement.
86. *therewithal:* with all that.
87. *Lay:* song.
95. *couplement:* joining.
96. *that:* who.
97. *quelling:* vanquishing, subduing.
97. *Son:* Cupid.
98. *virtue:* power.
99. *guile:* deception.
100. *assoil:* absolve.
101. *accord:* bring together in friendship.
102. *wait upon:* act as a servant toward.
102. *board:* dining-table.
104. *That:* so that.
104. *fruitful:* a great number of.
104. *issue:* progeny, offspring.
104. *afford:* present, give.
106. *redound:* be overflowing.
109. *she:* the nymph who was singing the "lay" in ll. 87–108.
110. *redoubled . . . undersong:* repeated the refrain.
112. *Echo:* Echo is a nymph of the woods and hills.
112. *ground:* estate, property.
113. *accents:* words.
113. *resound:* re-echo.
115. *Adown:* down.
116. *As:* as if.
120. *Gan:* began.
121. *so far, as:* as much as.
121. *Cynthia:* the moon goddess.
121. *shend:* disgrace, put to shame.
122. *lesser:* smaller (to the eye).
122. *enranged:* arranged, placed around.
123–124. *Did . . . lend:* bestowed.
128. *my . . . Nurse:* Spenser was born in London.
131. *house:* family.
131. *fame:* reputation.
132. *whereas:* where.
132–136. *bricky towers . . . pride:* the Temple was originally the meeting-place of the Templar Knights, a religious and military order founded in 1118 chiefly for the protection of the Holy Sepulcher and Christian pil-

grims visiting the Holy Land. They were suppressed in 1312 and the building was turned over later to law students; hence the later name of the temple, "Inns of Court."

135. *whilom:* formerly.

135. *wont:* were accustomed, used to.

135. *bide:* abide, reside.

137. *whereunto:* next to which.

137. *stately place:* the home of Robert Devereaux, second Earl of Essex (1566–1601).

139. *that great Lord:* Robert Dudley, the Earl of Leicester (c. 1532–1588) was the former owner of the "stately place" which Essex later took over. Leicester was Spenser's patron for some years, helping, for example, to get him an appointment as private secretary to Lord Grey de Wilton, Lord Deputy of Ireland, in 1580.

140. *Whose want:* the lack of whom.

140. *case:* plight.

141. *fits not well:* it is not appropriate.

145. *Peer:* Earl of Essex (l. 137).

146–149. *Great . . . fear:* Essex had recently won a great victory against the Spanish by capturing the city of Cadiz.

148. *Hercules' two pillars:* the ancient name for the Straits of Gibraltar.

150. *Chivalry:* aristocracy.

155. *prowess:* strength.

157. *Elisa's:* Queen Elizabeth's.

158. *wide:* wide-flung, widely dispersed.

158. *Alarms:* sudden calls to arms.

159. *brave:* splendid.

159. *muse:* poet.

163. *issuing:* proceeding forth, when he comes out.

164. *Hesper:* the Evening Star.

166. *viewing:* view.

167. *train ensuing:* followed by a large group of his courtiers.

169. *gentle:* noble, of high rank.

169. *Knights:* Henry Gifford and William Peter.

169. *lovely:* possibly "loving" as well as "lovable" or "handsome."

170. *Beseeming:* well suited for.

171. *ornaments:* adornments.

173. *twins of Jove:* Castor and Pollux, the constellation Gemini. See gloss to Jonson's "Ode to the Immortal Memory and Friendship of that Noble Pair, Sir Lucius Clay and Sir H. Morison," ll. 92–94.

174. *Baldric:* a belt worn over one shoulder and across the chest; here, figuratively, the zodiac.

177. *tide:* time.

WILLIAM SHAKESPEARE (1564–1616)

Sonnet 73

That time of year thou may'st in me behold,
When yellow leaves, or none, or few do hang
Upon those boughs which shake against the cold,
Bare ruin'd choirs, where late the sweet birds sang.
In me thou seest the twilight of such day,
As after Sunset fadeth in the West,
Which by and by black night doth take away,
Death's second self that seals up all in rest.
In me thou seest the glowing of such fire,
That on the ashes of his youth doth lie,
As the death bed, whereon it must expire,
Consum'd with that which it was nourish'd by.
  This thou perceiv'st, which makes thy love more strong,
  To love that well, which thou must leave ere long.

Lexical Gloss

2. *none:* no leaves.
4. *choir:* the part of a church where the church choir sits.
4. *late:* lately.
7. *Which:* the day.
10. *his:* its.
11. *expire:* die.
12. *with:* by.

From Hamlet

Second Quarto: 1604

To be, or not to be, that is the question,
Whether 'tis nobler in the mind to suffer
The slings and arrows of outrageous fortune,
Or to take Arms against a sea of troubles,

And by opposing, end them, to die to sleep
No more, and by a sleep, to say we end
The heart-ache, and the thousand natural shocks
That flesh is heir to: 'tis a consummation
Devoutly to be wished to die to sleep.
To sleep, perchance to dream, Aye there's the rub,
For in that sleep of death what dreams may come
When we have shuffled off this mortal coil
Must give us pause, there's the respect
That makes calamity of so long life:
For who would bear the whips and scorns of time,
Th' oppressor's wrong, the proud man's contumely,
The pangs of despis'd love, the law's delay,
The insolence of office, and the spurns
That patient merit of th' unworthy takes,
When he himself might his quietus make
With a bare bodkin; who would fardels bear,
To grunt and sweat under a weary life,
But that the dread of something after death,
The undiscover'd country, from whose bourn
No traveller returns, puzzles the will,
And makes us rather bear those ills we have,
Than fly to others that we know not of,
Thus conscience does make cowards,
And thus the native hue of resolution
Is sicklied o'er with the pale cast of thought,
And enterprises of great pitch and moment,
With this regard their currents turn awry,
And lose the name of action.

First Folio: 1623

To be, or not to be, that is the Question:
Whether 'tis Nobler in the mind to suffer
The Slings and Arrows of outrageous Fortune,
Or to take Arms against a Sea of troubles,
And by opposing end them: to die, to sleep
No more; and by a sleep, to say we end
The Heartache, and the thousand Natural shocks
That Flesh is heir to? 'Tis a consummation

Devoutly to be wish'd. To die to sleep,
To sleep, perchance to Dream; Aye, there's the rub,
For in that sleep of death, what dreams may come,
When we have shuffl'd off this mortal coil,
Must give us pause. There's the respect
That makes Calamity of so long life:
For who would bear the Whips and Scorns of time,
The Oppressor's wrong, the poor man's Contumely,
The pangs of dispriz'd Love, the Law's delay,
The insolence of Office, and the Spurns
That patient merit of the unworthy takes
When he himself might his *Quietus* make
With a bare Bodkin: Who would these Fardels bear
To grunt and sweat under a weary life,
But that the dread of something after death,
The undiscovered Country, from whose Bourn
No Traveller returns, Puzzles the will,
And makes us rather bear those ills we have,
Than fly to others that we know not of.
Thus Conscience does make Cowards of us all,
And thus the Native hue of Resolution
Is sicklied o'er, with the pale cast of Thought,
And enterprizes of great pith and moment,
With this regard their Currents turn away,
And lose the name of Action.

Lexical Gloss

1. *To be:* to live.
3. *slings:* a weapon for hurling stones with great force.
3. *fortune:* luck, fate.
6. *by:* by means of.
8. *consummation:* ending, winding-up of affairs.
10. *perchance:* perhaps.
10. *rub:* drawback.
12. *shuffled off this mortal coil:* cast off the turmoil of the flesh. Some editors think that a pun is intended, since "coil" may also mean "a ring of rope" and this could stand for the flesh which encircles the soul.
13. *give us pause:* make us stop and wonder.
13. *respect:* consideration, matter for concern.
16. *contumely:* haughty and contemptuous rudeness.
17. *dispriz'd:* (First Folio) not prized, disparaged.
17. *law's delay:* the excessive time it takes to secure justice.

18. *office:* men in high governmental or official position.
19. *takes . . . of:* receives . . . from.
20. *quietus:* full discharge or release from life, death.
21. *bodkin:* dagger.
21. *fardels:* burdens.
23. *But that:* if it were not for the fact that.
24. *bourn:* domain.
28. *conscience:* introspection, self-consciousness.
29. *native hue:* natural coloring, i.e. the natural ruddiness of healthy active persons.
30. *cast:* shade or tinge of color.
31. *pitch:* (Second Quarto) highest point of a falcon's flight.
31. *pith:* (First Folio) strength, vigor.
31. *moment:* importance.
32. *With this regard:* because of this consideration.
32. *current:* course of motion.

BEN JONSON (1572–1637)

A Celebration of Charis

4: Her Triumph

See the Chariot at hand here of Love,
  Wherein my Lady rideth!
Each that draws, is a Swan, or a Dove
  And well the Car Love guideth:
As she goes, all hearts do duty
        Unto her beauty;
And enamour'd, do wish, so they might
        But enjoy such a sight,
That they still were, to run by her side,
Through Swords, through Seas, whither she would ride.

Do but look on her eyes, they do light
  All that Love's world compriseth!
Do but look on her Hair, it is bright
  As Love's star when it riseth!
Do but mark her forehead's smoother
        Than words that soothe her!
And from her arched brows, such a grace

Sheds itself through the face,
As alone there triumphs to the life
All the Gain, all the Good, of the Elements' strife.

Have you seen but a bright Lily grow,
Before rude hands have touch'd it?
Ha' you mark'd but the fall o'the Snow
Before the soil hath smutch'd it?
Ha' you felt the wool o'the Beaver?
Or Swans' Down ever?
Or have smelt o'the bud o'the Brier?
Or the Nard in the fire?
Or have tasted the bag o'the Bee?
O so white! O so soft! O so sweet is she!

Lexical Gloss

Title. A Celebration of Charis: a series of ten lyrics addressed to the beautiful Charis, the object of the poet's love. "Celebration" is used in the sense of "a public proclamation" or "extolling of the fame or beauty of . . ."
Title. Triumph: ceremonial parade and celebration.
1. *Love:* Cupid or Venus.
2. *Wherein:* in which.
3. *Swan:* see Spenser's "Prothalamion," l. 63.
4. *Car:* chariot.
7. *so:* if.
8. *But:* only.
9. *still were, to run:* would keep on running.
10. *whither:* wherever.
17. *brows:* eyebrows.
18. *the face:* her face.
19. *As:* that.
19. *alone there:* only there, there alone.
19. *triumphs:* wins out.
20. *Elements:* earth, air, fire, water.
20. *strife:* the struggle among the elements which in the medieval physiology is seen as the basis of all Nature and therefore of the personality. It was felt that the moral object of all action was to reconcile and harmonize the elements.
21. *but:* only, at least.
24. *smutch'd it:* made it dirty.
28. *Nard:* spikenard, an aromatic plant.

An Ode: To Himself

Where dost thou careless lie
Buried in ease and sloth?
Knowledge, that sleeps, doth die;
And this Security,
It is the common Moth,
That eats on wits, and Arts, and destroys them both.

Are all th'*Aonian* springs
Dried up? lies *Thespia* waste?
Doth *Clarius*' Harp want strings,
That not a Nymph now sings?
Or droop they as disgrac'd,
To see their Seats and Bowers by chatt'ring Pies defac'd?

If hence thy silence be,
As 'tis too just a cause;
Let this thought quicken thee,
Minds that are great and free,
Should not on fortune pause,
'Tis crown enough to virtue still, her own applause.

What though the greedy Fry
Be taken with false Baits
Of worded Balladry,
And think it Poësy?
They die with their conceits,
And only piteous scorn, upon their folly waits.

Then take in hand thy Lyre,
Strike in thy proper strain,
With *Japhet's* line, aspire
Sol's Chariot for new fire,
To give the world again:
Who aided him, will thee, the issue of *Jove's* brain.

And since our Dainty age,
Cannot indure reproof,

Make not thy self a Page,
To that strumpet the Stage,
But sing high and aloof,
Safe from the wolve's black jaw, and the dull Ass's hoof.

Lexical Gloss

5. *common:* ubiquitous, everywhere present.
6. *wits:* inborn talents.
6. *Arts:* learned skills.
7. *Aonian springs:* the well of Aganippe, the nymph, at the foot of Mt. Helicon in Greece, which was thought to be sacred to the Muses and the source of poetic inspiration.
8. *Thespia:* a town on Mt. Helicon, sacred to the Muses.
9. *Clarius:* the clear or bright one, i.e. Apollo. Apollo was the Greek god of music and poetry.
9. *want:* lack.
10. *That:* so that.
12. *Seats:* homes.
12. *Bowers:* secluded private places.
12. *Pies:* magpies, chattering birds.
13. *hence:* from this state of affairs.
15. *quicken:* encourage and enliven.
18. *still:* always.
19. *Fry:* fish, here representing the common run of readers.
21. *Balladry:* popular uncultivated poetry.
22. *Poësy:* poetry.
23. *conceits:* ideas, notions.
24. *waits . . . upon:* accompanies.
25. *Lyre:* harp.
26. *proper strain:* own characteristic melody.
27. *Japhet's:* Titan Japetus, or Japhet, was the father of Prometheus, the mythical giver of fire to mortals. Prometheus stole the fire from the sun.

27–28. *aspire Sol's Chariot:* go up to the sun and fetch fire (as Prometheus did).

30. *issue:* product, offspring.
31. *Dainty:* fastidious, squeamish.
32. *reproof:* blame.
33. *Page:* menial servant, errand boy.
34. *strumpet:* prostitute.
36. *wolve's black jaw . . . Ass's hoof:* vicious and dull critics.

JOHN DONNE (1573–1631)

Sonnet 14

From *Holy Sonnets*

Batter my heart, three person'd God; for, you
As yet but knock, breathe, shine, and seek to mend;
That I may rise, and stand, o'erthrow me,'and bend
Your force, to break, blow, burn and make me new.
I, like an usurp'd town, to'another due,
Labour to'admit you, but Oh, to no end,
Reason your viceroy in me, me should defend,
But is captiv'd, and proves weak or untrue,
Yet dearly'I love you,'and would be lov'd fain,
But am betroth'd unto your enemy,
Divorce me,'untie, or break that knot again,
Take me to you, imprison me, for I
Except you'enthrall me, never shall be free,
Nor ever chaste, except you ravish me.

Lexical Gloss

1. *three person'd:* in Christian theology God consists of three persons: the Father, the Son, and the Holy Ghost.
1. *for:* because.
2. *but:* only.
3. *That:* so that.
3. *bend:* direct, turn.
5. *usurp'd:* conquered.
5. *due:* owed.
7. *viceroy:* person who rules as a deputy to the sovereign.
9. *would:* want to.
9. *fain:* gladly.
10. *enemy:* the devil.
13. *Except:* unless.
13. *enthrall me:* make me a slave.
14. *ravish:* sexually overcome.

The Will

Before I sigh my last gasp, let me breathe,
Great love, some Legacies; Here I bequeathe
Mine eyes to *Argus*, if mine eyes can see,
If they be blind, then Love, I give them thee;
My tongue to Fame; to'Embassadours mine ears;
To women or the sea, my tears;
Thou, Love, hast taught me heretofore
By making me serve her who'had twenty more,
That I should give to none, but such, as had too much before.

My constancy I to the planets give,
My truth to them, who at the Court do live;
Mine ingenuity and openness,
To Jesuits; to Buffoons my pensiveness;
My silence to'any, who abroad hath been;
My money to a Capuchin.
Thou Love taught'st me, by appointing me
To love there, where no love receiv'd can be,
Only to give to such as have an incapacity.

My faith I give to Roman Catholics;
All my good works unto the Schismatics
Of Amsterdam; my best civility
And Courtship, to an University;
My modesty I give to soldiers bare;
My patience let gamesters share.
Thou Love taughtst me, by making me
Love her that holds my love disparity,
Only to give to those that count my gifts indignity.

I give my reputation to those
Which were my friends; Mine industry to foes;
To Schoolmen I bequeathe my doubtfulness;
My sickness to Physicians, or excess;
To Nature, all that I in Rhyme have writ;
And to my company my wit;
Thou Love, by making me adore

Her, who begot this love in me before,
Taught'st me to make, as though I gave, when I did but restore.

To him for whom the passing bell next tolls,
I give my physic books; my written rolls
Of Moral counsels, I to Bedlam give;
My brazen medals, unto them which live
In want of bread; To them which pass among
All foreigners, mine English tongue.
Thou, Love, by making me love one
Who thinks her friendship a fit portion
For younger lovers, dost my gifts thus disproportion.

Therefore I'll give no more; But I'll undo
The world by dying; because love dies too.
Then all your beauties will be no more worth
Than gold in Mines, where none doth draw it forth;
And all your graces no more use shall have
Than a Sundial in a grave.
Thou Love taught'st me, by making me
Love her, who doth neglect both me and thee,
To'invent, and practise this one way, to'annihilate all three.

Lexical Gloss

Title. Will: last testament.
2. *Great love:* Cupid.
3. *Argus:* in Greek mythology, Argus had a hundred eyes. Argus guarded Io, who had been metamorphosed into a cow, but his head was cut off by Hermes. Hera transplanted Argus' eyes in the tail of the peacock.
4. *If . . . thee:* Love, of course, is blind.
5. *Fame:* the spirit of rumor.
7. *heretofore:* up till now.
9. *such, as:* those who.
12. *ingenuity:* ingenuousness, innocence, naïveté.
13. *Jesuits:* a religious order of the Catholic Church known for its sophistication and shrewdness.
13. *Buffoons:* foolish and comical people.
15. *Capuchin:* a monk of one of the Franciscan orders.
20–21. *Schismatics of Amsterdam:* those who had broken with the Church of England and had gone to Holland.
21. *civility:* polite manners.

22. *Courtship:* ability to make oneself agreeable at court.
24. *gamesters:* gamblers.
26. *disparity:* of unequal worth.
29. *industry:* diligence or assiduity in tasks.
30. *Schoolmen:* experts in formal logic and divinity; "scholastics" in the medieval sense of the word.
31. *excess:* intemperance.
33. *company:* companions.
36. *make:* pretend.
37. *passing bell:* funeral bell.
38. *physic books:* medical books.
39. *counsels:* precepts.
39. *Bedlam:* the English hospital of St. Mary of Bethlehem used after 1547 as an asylum for the insane.
40. *brazen:* bronze.
40. *them which:* those who.
41. *In want of:* lacking.
44. *fit:* suitable.
45. *disproportion:* make unequal.
48. *worth:* valuable.
50. *graces:* attractive qualities.
54. *invent:* feign, pretend.

ROBERT HERRICK (1591–1674)

The Hock-Cart, or Harvest Home

Come Sons of Summer, by whose toil,
We are the Lords of Wine and Oil:
By whose tough labours, and rough hands,
We rip up first, then reap our lands.
Crown'd with the ears of corn, now come,
And, to the Pipe, sing Harvest home.
Come forth, my Lord, and see the Cart
Dress'd up with all the Country Art.
See, here a *Maukin*, there a sheet,
As spotless pure, as it is sweet:
The Horses, Mares, and frisking Fillies,
(Clad, all, in Linen, white as Lilies.)
The Harvest Swains, and Wenches bound

For joy, to see the *Hock-cart* crown'd.
About the Cart, hear, how the Rout
Of Rural Younglings raise the shout;
Pressing before, some coming after,
Those with a shout, and these with laughter.
Some bless the Cart; some kiss the sheaves;
Some prank them up with Oaken leaves
Some cross the Fill-horse; some with great
Devotion, stroke the home-borne wheat:
While other Rustics, less attent
To Prayers, then to Merriment,
Run after with their breeches rent.
Well, on, brave boys, to your Lord's Hearth,
Glitt'ring with fire; where, for your mirth,
Ye shall see first the large and chief
Foundation of your Feast, Fat Beef:
With Upper Stories, Mutton, Veal
And Bacon, (which makes full the meal)
With sev'ral dishes standing by,
As here a Custard, there a Pie,
And here all tempting Frumenty.
And for to make the merry cheer,
If smirking Wine be wanting here,
There's that, which drowns all care, stout Beer;
Which freely drink to your Lord's health,
Then to the Plough, (the Common-wealth)
Next to your Flails, your Fans, your Fats;
Then to the Maids with Wheaten Hats:
To the rough Sickle, and crook'd Scythe,
Drink frolic boys, till all be blithe.
Feed, and grow fat; and as ye eat,
Be mindful, that the lab'ring Neat
(As you) may have their fill of meat.
And know, besides, ye must revoke
The patient Ox unto the Yoke,
And all go back unto the Plough
And Harrow, (though they're hang'd up now.)
And, you must know, your Lord's word's true,
Feed him ye must, whose food fills you.
And that this pleasure is like rain,
Not sent ye for to drown your pain,
But for to make it spring again.

Lexical Gloss

Title. The Hock-Cart: the cart which carried home the last load of the harvest.
Title. Harvest Home: the fact, occasion or time of the bringing home of the last harvest.
6. *Pipe:* musical wind instrument.
9. *Maukin:* or "malkin," a coarse colored cloth, a mop.
13. *Swains:* boys.
13. *Wenches:* girls.
15. *Rout:* assemblage, group.
19. *sheaves:* bundles of stalks.
20. *prank them up:* dress up.
21. *cross:* make the sign of the cross.
21. *Fill-horse:* the horse that draws the cart.
23. *attent:* attentive.
25. *rent:* torn.
34. *Frumenty:* a dish made of hulled wheat boiled in milk and seasoned with cinnamon, sugar, etc.
35. *cheer:* meal, fare; and also, entertainment in a more general sense.
36. *wanting:* lacking.
40. *Flail:* one piece of wood tied to another for threshing the chaff from the wheat.
40. *Fans:* winnowing fans, fans for blowing the chaff away from the grain.
40. *Fats:* casks, barrels.
41. *Wheaten:* made of wheat stalks.
42. *Sickle, Scythe:* reaping instruments with short and long handles.
45. *Neat:* cattle, livestock.
46. *meat:* food in general.
47. *revoke:* call back.
50. *Harrow:* a farm implement used to break up clods, pulverize and stir the soil, cover the seed, etc.

Corinna's Going a Maying

Get up, get up for shame, the Blooming Morn
Upon her wings presents the god unshorn.
See how *Aurora* throws her fair
Fresh-quilted colours through the air:
Get up, sweet-Slug-a-bed, and see
The Dew-bespangling Herb and Tree.
Each Flower has wept, and bow'd toward the East,

Above an hour since; yet you not dress'd,
Nay! not so much as out of bed?
When all the Birds have Matins said,
And sung their thankful Hymns: 'tis sin,
Nay, profanation to keep in,
When as a thousand Virgins on this day,
Spring, sooner then the Lark, to fetch in May.

Rise; and put on your Foliage, and be seen
To come forth, like the Spring-time, fresh and green;
And sweet as *Flora*. Take no care
For Jewels for your Gown, or Hair:
Fear not; the leaves will strew
Gems in abundance upon you:
Besides, the childhood of the Day has kept,
Against you come, some *Orient Pearls* unwept:
Come, and receive them while the light
Hangs on the Dew-locks of the night:
And *Titan* on the Eastern hill
Retires himself, or else stands still
Till you come forth. Wash, dress, be brief in praying:
Few Beads are best, when once we go a Maying.

Come, my *Corinna*, come; and coming, mark
How each field turns a street; each street a Park
Made green, and trimm'd with trees: see how
Devotion gives each House a Bough,
Or Branch: Each Porch, each door, ere this,
An Ark a Tabernacle is
Made up of white-thorn neatly interwove;
As if here were those cooler shades of love.
Can such delights be in the street,
And open fields, and we not see't?
Come, we'll abroad; and let's obey
The Proclamation made for May:
And sin no more, as we have done, by staying;
But my *Corinna*, come, let's go a Maying.

There's not a budding Boy, or Girl, this day,
But is got up, and gone to bring in May.
A deal of Youth, ere this, is come
Back, and with *White-thorn* laden home.

Some have dispatch'd their Cakes and Cream,
Before that we have left to dream:
And some have wept, and woo'd, and plighted Troth,
And chose their Priest, ere we can cast off sloth:
Many a green-gown has been given;
Many a kiss, both odd and even:
Many a glance too has been sent
From out the eye, Love's Firmament:
Many a jest told of the Keys' betraying
This night, and Locks pick'd, yet we're not a Maying.

Come, let us go, while we are in our prime;
And take the harmless folly of the time.
We shall grow old apace, and die
Before we know our liberty.
Our life is short; and our days run
As fast away as does the Sun:
And as a vapour, or a drop of rain
Once lost, can ne'er be found again:
So when or you or I are made
A fable, song, or fleeting shade;
All love, all liking, all delight
Lies drown'd with us in endless night.
Then while time serves, and we are but decaying;
Come, my *Corinna*, come, let's go a Maying.

Lexical Gloss

2. *god:* Apollo, the Greek god of the sun.
3. *Aurora:* the Roman goddess of the dawn.
4. *quilted:* the colors are thrown into a variegated design like a patchwork quilt.
5. *Slug-a-bed:* one who lies long in bed through laziness.
6. *bespangling:* brightly decorating.
8. *Above:* more than.
8. *since:* ago.
10. *Matins:* morning prayers.
12. *profanation:* making profane or unholy.
12. *keep in:* stay in.
13. *When as:* read simply "when."
14. *fetch in May:* bring in flowers on May Day, a folk custom with pagan overtones.
15. *Foliage:* garlands, wreaths.
17. *Flora:* goddess of flowers.

17–18. *Take no care For:* do not worry about, pay no attention to.
22. *Against:* for the time when.
22. *Orient:* brilliant, shining, precious.
22. *Pearls unwept:* dewdrops still on the grass.
24. *Dew-locks:* night, personified, has dew on its locks.
25. *Titan:* the sun. (This refers to an earlier Greek sun-god, Helios, who was replaced by Apollo).
28. *Beads:* prayer beads of the rosary, hence few prayers.
28. *go a Maying:* see note on "fetch in May."
29. *mark:* observe.
32. *Devotion:* observance of May.
34. *Ark, Tabernacle:* places of worship, which keep holy objects.
35. *white-thorn:* the white hawthorn was the traditional flower of May day.
39. *abroad:* go out.
45. *deal:* number, group.
47. *dispatch'd:* consumed, eaten.
48. *left to dream:* left off dreaming.
49. *plighted Troth:* got engaged.
51. *green-gown:* gown stained green by the grass.
52. *odd and even:* boys have kissed girls and vice versa.
54. *Firmament:* sky, heaven.
58. *take:* enjoy.
58. *folly:* foolishness, silliness.
59. *apace:* soon enough.
65. *or . . . or:* either . . . or.
66. *fable:* a myth or legend.
66. *shade:* shadow or ghost.
69. *but:* no more than.

GEORGE HERBERT (1593–1633)

The Collar

I struck the board, and cried, No more;
I will abroad.
What? shall I ever sigh and pine?
My lines and life are free; free as the road,
Loose as the wind, as large as store.
Shall I be still in suit?
Have I no harvest but a thorn
To let me blood, and not restore
What I have lost with cordial fruit?

Sure there was wine
Before my sighs did dry it: there was corn
Before my tears did drown it.
Is the year only lost to me?
Have I no bays to crown it?
No flowers, no garlands gay? all blasted?
All wasted?
Not so, my heart: but there is fruit,
And thou hast hands.
Recover all thy sigh-blown age
On double pleasures: leave thy cold dispute
Of what is fit, and not: forsake thy cage,
Thy rope of sands,
Which petty thoughts have made, and made to thee
Good cable, to enforce and draw,
And be thy law,
While thou didst wink and wouldst not see.
Away; take heed.
I will abroad.
Call in thy death's head there: tie up thy fears.
He that forbears
To suit and serve his need,
Deserves his load.
But as I rav'd and grew more fierce and wild
At every word,
Me thoughts I heard one calling, *Child:*
And I reply'd, *My Lord.*

Lexical Gloss

1. *board:* table.
2. *abroad:* get out of here, go where I please.
3. *ever:* always.
3. *pine:* long eagerly.
4. *lines:* lot, situation.
5. *store:* supply or quantity itself.
6. *still:* always.
6. *in suit:* serving some master and making constant requests of him for favor or reward.
8. *let me blood:* bleed me for medical purposes.
9. *cordial:* medicinal.
14. *bays:* wreaths of honor.
15. *blasted:* withered.

19. *sigh-blown:* blasted or wasted by sighs.
19. *age:* life.
20. *On:* by means of.
26. *wink:* keep one's eyes closed, put blinders on.
29. *death's head:* human skull, used as an emblem of man's mortality and hence of the need to resist temptations.
30. *forbears:* abstains from, desists from.
31. *suit and serve:* do personal service to one's lord, in this case one's own "need."
35. *Me thoughts:* it seemed to me.

Mortification

How soon doth man decay!
When clothes are taken from a chest of sweets
To swaddle infants, whose young breath
Scarce knows the way;
Those clouts are little winding sheets,
Which do consign and send them unto death.

When boys go first to bed,
They step into their voluntary graves,
Sleep binds them fast; only their breath
Makes them not dead:
Successive nights, like rolling waves,
Convey them quickly, who are bound for death.

When youth is frank and free,
And calls for music, while his veins do swell,
All day exchanging mirth and breath
In company;
That music summons to the knell,
Which shall befriend him at the hour of death.

When man grows staid and wise,
Getting a house and home, where he may move
Within the circle of his breath,
Schooling his eyes;
That dumb inclosure maketh love
Unto the coffin, that attends his death.

When age grows low and weak,
Marking his grave, and thawing ev'ry year,
Till all do melt, and drown his breath
When he would speak;
A chair or litter shows the bier,
Which shall convey him to the house of death.

Man, ere he is aware,
Hath put together a solemnity,
And dress'd his hearse, while he has breath
As yet to spare.
Yet Lord, instruct us so to die,
That all these dyings may be life in death.

Lexical Gloss

3. *swaddle:* clothe, patricularly clothe a child.
5. *clouts:* clothes.
5. *winding sheets:* burial cloths, shrouds.
6. *consign:* sign them over to.
13. *frank:* unreserved, bounteous.
16. *company:* a group of companions.
17. *knell:* tolling of funeral bells.
22. *Schooling:* disciplining.
24. *attends:* waits upon, accompanies.
26. *Marking:* pointing to.
28. *would:* would like to.
29. *chair:* sedan chair, carried on shoulders of servants.
29. *litter:* a vehicle containing a couch shut in by curtains and carried on men's shoulders or by animals.
29. *shows:* symbolizes; represents.
29. *bier:* coffin.
32. *solemnity:* a serious ceremony.
33. *dress'd:* prepared.
35. *so:* in such a way.

JOHN MILTON (1608–1674)

Sonnet 7

How soon hath time the subtle thief of youth,
Stol'n on his wing my three and twentieth year!

My hasting days fly on with full career,
But my late spring no bud or blossom shew'th.
Perhaps my semblance might deceive the truth,
That I to manhood am arriv'd so near,
And inward ripeness doth much less appear,
That some more timely-happy spirits indu'th.
Yet be it less or more, or soon or slow,
It shall be still in strictest measure ev'n,
To that same lot, however mean or high,
Toward which Time leads me, and the will of Heav'n;
All is, if I have grace to use it so,
As ever in my great task Master's eye.

Lexical Gloss

1. *subtle:* crafty, cunning, sly, wily.
3. *hasting:* hastening.
3. *career:* speed, impetus, (at full) tilt.
4. *shew'th:* showeth
5. *semblance:* appearance.
8. *timely-happy:* happy in that their development is in accordance with their time of life.
8. *spirits:* people, young men.
8. *indu'th:* indues, pervades, fills.
10. *still:* always.
10. *in strictest measure:* according to the most exacting rule.
10. *ev'n:* regular.
11. *lot:* life-situation.
11. *mean:* low.
14. *As ever:* the same.

From Arcades

As they come forward, the Genius of the Wood appears, and turning toward them, speaks.

Gen. Stay gentle Swains, for though in this disguise,
I see bright honour sparkle through your eyes,
Of famous *Arcady* ye are, and sprung
Of that renowned flood, so often sung,
Divine *Alpheus,* who by secret sluice,
Stole under Seas to meet his *Arethuse;*
And ye the breathing Roses of the Wood,

Fair silver-buskin'd Nymphs as great and good,
I know this quest of yours, and free intent
Was all in honour and devotion meant
To the great Mistress of yon princely shrine,
Whom with low reverence I adore as mine,
And with all helpful service will comply
To further this night's glad solemnity;
And lead ye where ye may more near behold
What shallow-searching *Fame* hath left untold;
Which I full oft amidst these shades alone
Have sat to wonder at, and gaze upon:
For know by lot from *Jove* I am the pow'r
Of this fair Wood, and live in Oak'n bow'r,
To nurse the Saplings tall, and curl the grove
With Ringlets quaint; and wanton windings wove.
And all my Plants I save from nightly ill,
Of noisome winds, and blasting vapours chill.
And from the Boughs brush off the evil dew,
And heal the harms of thwarting thunder blue,
Or what the cross dire-looking Planet smites,
Or hurtful Worm with canker'd venom bites.
When Ev'ning gray doth rise, I fetch my round
Over the mount, and all this hallow'd ground,
And early ere the odorous breath of morn
Awakes the slumb'ring leaves, or tassel'd horn
Shakes the high thicket, haste I all about,
Number my ranks, and visit every sprout
With puissant words, and murmurs made to bless,
But else in deep of night when drowsiness
Hath lock'd up mortal sense, then listen I
To the celestial *Sirens'* harmony,
That sit upon the nine enfolded Spheres,
And sing to those that hold the vital shears,
And turn the Adamantine spindle round,
On which the fate of gods and men is wound.
Such sweet compulsion doth in music lie,
To lull the daughters of *Necessity*,
And keep unsteady Nature to her law,
And the low world in measur'd motion draw
After the heavenly tune, which none can hear
Of human mould with gross unpurged ear;
And yet such music worthiest were to blaze

The peerless height of her immortal praise,
Whose lustre leads us, and for her most fit,
If my inferior hand or voice could hit
Inimitable sounds, yet as we go,
Whate'er the skill of lesser gods can show,
I will assay, her worth to celebrate,
And so attend ye toward her glittering state;
Where ye may all that are of noble stem
Approach, and kiss her sacred vestures' hem.

Lexical Gloss

Title. Arcades: Arcadia, although a real district in Greece, became a symbol for a fabled land of rural peace and simplicity. "Arcades" means men from Arcadia. This selection is taken from a *masque*, a form of entertainment popular in the 17th century, which combined the dancing of masked figures, music, and poetic drama. The literary portion consisted of speeches by the participants, among whom might include the members of the court for whom the masque was written. Previous to the appearance of the Genius of the Wood, some noble friends of the Countess Dowager of Derby (to whom this masque was presented) "appear on the scene in pastoral habit [dress], moving toward the seat of state" with a song that praises her "blaze of majesty," which not even Fame has successfully rumored. It is to these "persons" that the Genius of the Wood, the local demigod who protects the inhabitants of his forest, speaks.

Epigraph. Genius: local attending spirit or deity.

1. *gentle Swains:* country lads, that is, here, the young men for whom the masque was written.
2. *honour:* honorable or noble birth.
4. *flood:* river.

5–6. *Alpheus . . . Arethuse:* Alpheus was a river in Arcadia. In legend Alpheus was a young hunter who loved the nymph Arethusa. When she fled to the isle of Ortygia, upon which Syracuse in Sicily is built, he was turned into a river and pursued her by a secret channel ("sluice") under the sea, rising again in Ortygia. There Alpheus and Arethusa joined together into a well which was called, after her, Arethusa.

7. *breathing:* redolent, (sweet-)smelling.
8. *silver-buskin'd Nymphs:* the ladies in the performance wore "buskins" or high, thick-soled, laced boots customarily worn by actors in ancient tragedy.
9. *quest:* see note to title.
9. *free:* noble, of good breeding, generous.
11. *Mistress:* Countess Dowager of Derby.
12. *mine:* my Mistress, i.e. the lady who rules me as well.
13. *comply:* agree, cooperate.

16. *shallow-searching:* not investigating thoroughly.
16. *Fame:* the goddess of rumor.
19. *by lot:* by destiny, by fortune.
19. *Jove:* Jupiter, king of the gods.
19. *pow'r:* ruling deity.
21. *curl:* make curly.
22. *wanton:* sportive, fanciful, unrestrained.
22. *wove:* woven.
24. *noisome:* offensive, harmful.
26. *thwarting:* zigzagging.
27. *what:* the plants which.
27. *cross dire-looking Planet:* the adverse, sinister-appearing planet was probably Saturn, which according to one of Milton's editors "had a *leaden* or dispiriting influence," making its victims "causelessly melancholy."
28. *canker'd:* causing to decay or rot.
29. *fetch my round:* make my rounds or tour of duty.
30. *hallow'd:* sacred.
32. *tassel'd horn:* the horn of the huntsman had tassels attached to it.
34. *Number:* count.
34. *ranks:* those under his control (as an officer's "ranks").
35. *puissant:* powerful.
36. *else:* otherwise, at other times.
38–48. *Sirens' . . . ear:* this passage is based on the Ptolemaic view of the universe. In that view, it was thought that there were nine spheres encircling the earth, which was the center: the Moon, Mercury, Venus, Sun, Mars, Jupiter, and Saturn; outside of Saturn, the seventh sphere, was the eighth, the "crystalline sphere," thought to be liquid, and outside that, the ninth sphere, the *primum mobile,* which was solid. All moved from west to east except the *primum mobile,* which moved from east to west. As a "poetical sub-notion" of this system, Milton presented the ancient belief that the whole Universe turned according to the laws of music. On each of the first nine spheres sat a Siren or Muse whose singing blended in harmony. The relation of the sirens to the Fates of line 40 is described thus in Plato's *Republic* (X, 14): "there is another band, three in number, each sitting upon her throne: these are the Fates, daughters of Necessity, who are clothed in white robes and have chaplets upon their heads, Lachesis and Clotho and Atropos, who accompany with their voices the harmony of the sirens—Lachesis singing of the past, Clotho of the present, Atropos of the future; Clotho from time to time assisting with a touch of her right hand the revolution of the outer circle of the whorl or spindle, and Atropos with her left hand touching and guiding the inner ones, and Lachesis laying hold of either in turn, first with one hand and then with the other."
40. *those that hold the vital shears:* the Fates.
40. *vital:* having life in its control.
41. *Adamantine:* made of a very hard substance. Plato describes the spindle

as follows: "The shaft and hook of this spindle are made of steel, and the whorl is made partly of steel and also partly of other materials."

43. *compulsion:* enforcement, power.
44. *Necessity:* the fundamental rule by which events occur in the universe.
48. *mould:* shape.
48. *gross:* crude, insensitive.
48. *unpurged:* unpurified.
49. *were:* would be.
49. *blaze:* declare, proclaim.
50. *peerless:* without equal.
52. *inferior:* inferior to the sirens.
53. *Inimitable:* not to be imitated.
54. *lesser:* minor.
55. *assay:* try, attempt.
56. *attend toward:* wait upon, accompany and do service to.
56. *state:* chair of state.
57. *stem:* origin, lineage.
58. *vesture:* dress, garment.

JOHN DRYDEN (1631–1700)

Prologue to the University of Oxford

Tho' Actors cannot much of Learning boast,
Of all who want it, we admire it most.
We love the Praises of a Learned Pit,
As we remotely are alli'd to Wit.
We speak our Poet's Wit, and Trade in Ore,
Like those who touch upon the Golden Shore:
Betwixt our Judges can distinction make,
Discern how much, and why, our Poems take.
Mark if the Fools, or Men of Sense, rejoice,
Whether th' Applause be only Sound or Voice.
When our Fop Gallants, or our City Folly
Clap over-loud, it makes us melancholy:
We doubt that Scene which does their wonder raise,
And, for their ignorance contemn their Praise.
Judge then, if We who Act, and They who Write,
Should not be proud of giving You delight.
London likes grossly, but this nicer Pit
Examines, Fathoms all the depths of Wit:

The ready Finger lays on every Blot,
Knows what should justly please, and what should not.
Nature herself lies open to your view,
You judge by Her what draught of Her is true,
Where outlines false, and Colours seem too faint,
Where Bunglers daub, and where True Poets Paint.
But by the Sacred Genius of this Place,
By every Muse, by each Domestic Grace,
Be kind to Wit, which but endeavours well,
And, where you judge, presumes not to excel.
Our Poets hither for Adoption come,
As Nations su'd to be made Free of *Rome*.
Not in the suffragating Tribes to stand,
But in your utmost, last, Provincial Band.
If His Ambition may those Hopes pursue,
Who with Religion loves Your Arts and You,
Oxford to Him a dearer Name shall be,
Than His own Mother University.
Thebes did His Green, unknowing Youth engage,
He chooses *Athens* in His Riper Age.

Lexical Gloss

Title. Prologue: a speech made by a member of the cast of a play to an audience before the play begins.
1. *of:* in the way of.
2. *want:* lack.
3. *Pit:* the audience in the part of a theater which is on the ground floor: what we call the "orchestra."
4. *As:* since.
4. *alli'd:* related.
4. *Wit:* knowledge, learning.
5. *Trade:* i.e. deal in it, but do not create it.
5. *Ore:* precious metals.
6. *Golden Shore:* any place where gold is mined.
8. *take:* to gain public favor, to be popular.
9. *Mark:* observe.
9. *if:* whether.
11. *Fop Gallants:* ultra-fashionable aristocrats.
11. *City Folly:* foolish middle-class men of London.
13. *doubt:* feel distrustful of.
14. *for:* because of.
14. *contemn:* view with contempt.

17. *grossly:* crudely, without discrimination.
17. *nicer:* more exacting in taste.
18. *Fathoms:* reaches and understands to the bottom.
19. *Blot:* artistic failure.
20. *justly please:* please according to correct critical standards.
22. *draught:* sketch, artistic representation.
25. *Genius:* local protecting spirit or deity.
26. *Domestic Grace:* elegant accomplishment.
27. *but:* only.
29–32. *Our . . . Band:* poets felt that to become honorary ("adopted") Oxonians was a great achievement, analogous to being admitted to full rights as Romans even though not of Roman birth. (Thus "free of Rome" does not mean "free from Rome's influence," but rather "free citizens of Rome.") The "suffragating Tribes" were tribes in the Roman Empire who were allowed to vote, but who had not yet achieved the full measure of Roman citizenship.
32. *utmost, last:* most recently "liberated" (in the sense of "free" above).
32. *Provincial:* of the provinces; i.e. the authors would be outlanders, at a far distance from "Rome" (Oxford), who were admitted to Oxonian culture, despite their rusticity.
36. *Mother University:* Dryden had been a student at Cambridge.
37–38. *Thebes . . . Athens:* the culture of the ancient Greek city of Thebes was assumed to be inferior to that of Athens.

The Secular Masque

Enter Janus

Janus. *Chronos, Chronos,* mend thy Pace,
An hundred times the rolling Sun
Around the Radiant Belt has run
In his revolving Race.
Behold, behold, the Goal in sight,
Spread thy Fans, and wing thy flight.

Enter Chronos, *with a Scythe in his hand, and a great Globe on his Back, which he sets down at his entrance*

Chronos. Weary, weary of my weight,
Let me, let me drop my Freight,
And leave the World behind.
I could not bear

Another Year
The Load of Human-kind.

Enter Momus *Laughing*

Momus. Ha! ha! ha! Ha! ha! ha! well hast thou done,
To lay down thy Pack,
And lighten thy Back,
The World was a Fool, e'er since it begun,
And since neither *Janus,* nor *Chronos,* nor I,
Can hinder the Crimes,
Or mend the Bad Times,
'Tis better to Laugh than to Cry.

Cho. of all 3. *'Tis better to Laugh than to Cry.*

Janus. Since *Momus* comes to laugh below,
Old Time begin the Show,
That he may see, in every Scene,
What Changes in this Age have been,
Chronos. Then Goddess of the Silver Bow begin.

Horns, or Hunting-Music within

Enter Diana

Diana. With Horns and with Hounds I waken the Day.
And hie to my Woodland walks away;
I tuck up my Robe, and am buskin'd soon,
And tie to my Forehead a waxing Moon.
I course the fleet Stag, unkennel the Fox,
And chase the wild Goats o'er summits of Rocks,
With shouting and hooting we pierce thro' the Sky:
And Echo turns Hunter, and doubles the Cry.

Cho. of all. *With shouting and hooting, we pierce through the Sky,*
And Echo turns Hunter, and doubles the Cry.

Janus. Then our Age was in its Prime,
Chronos. Free from Rage.
Diana. And free from Crime.

Momus. A very Merry, Dancing, Drinking,
Laughing, Quaffing, and unthinking Time.

Cho. of all. *Then our Age was in its Prime*
Free from Rage, and free from Crime,
A very Merry, Dancing, Drinking,
Laughing, Quaffing, and unthinking Time.

Dance of Diana's *Attendants*

Enter Mars

Mars. Inspire the Vocal Brass, Inspire;
The World is past its Infant Age:
Arms and Honour,
Arms and Honour,
Set the Martial Mind on Fire,
And kindle Manly Rage.
Mars has look'd the Sky to Red;
And Peace, the Lazy Good, is fled.
Plenty, Peace, and Pleasure fly;
The Sprightly Green
In *Woodland*-Walks, no more is seen;
The Sprightly Green, has drunk the *Tyrian* Dye.

Cho. of all. *Plenty, Peace,* &c.

Mars. Sound the Trumpet, Beat the Drum,
Through all the World around;
Sound a Reveille, Sound, Sound,
The Warrior God is come.

Cho. of all. *Sound the Trumpet,* &c.

Momus. Thy Sword within the Scabbard keep,
And let Mankind agree;
Better the World were fast asleep,
Than kept awake by Thee.
The Fools are only thinner,
With all our Cost and Care;
But neither side a winner,
For Things are as they were.

Cho. of all. *The Fools are only,* &c.

Enter Venus

Venus. Calms appear, when Storms are past;
Love will have his Hour at last:
Nature is my kindly Care;
Mars destroys, and I repair;
Take me, take me, while you may,
Venus comes not ev'ry Day.

Cho. of all. *Take her, take her,* &c.

Chronos. The World was then so light,
I scarcely felt the Weight;
Joy rul'd the Day, and Love the Night.
But since the Queen of Pleasure left the Ground,
I faint, I lag,
And feebly drag
The pond'rous Orb around.
Momus. All, all, of a piece throughout;
Pointing to *Diana.* Thy Chase had a Beast in View;
to *Mars.* Thy Wars brought nothing about;
to *Venus.* Thy Lovers were all untrue.
Janus. 'Tis well an Old Age is out,
Chro. And time to begin a New.

Cho. of all. *All, all, of a piece throughout;*
Thy Chase had a Beast in View;
Thy Wars brought nothing about;
Thy Lovers were all untrue.
'Tis well an Old Age is out,
And time to begin a New.

Dance of Huntsmen, Nymphs, Warriors *and* Lovers

Lexical Gloss

Title. Secular: a special Latinic meaning, derived from Latin *saeculum,* "century"; thus this masque is the celebration of the beginning of the new century and also an allegory of the seventeenth century.

Title. Masque: a kind of court festivity chiefly characterized by a procession of figures wearing masks. In the 16th and 17th centuries, poets began to write verse so that the various figures would have lines to speak; the poetry, added to the beauty of the costumes and the lovely music, made the masque a magnificent spectacle. By the time of Dryden, masques could also appear on the stage, and indeed "The Secular Masque" shared the bill on opening night April 29, 1700, with an adaptation of a play by Fletcher called *The Pilgrim.*

Stage direction. Janus: a pre-classical Roman god with two faces looking different ways. He is the god of beginnings (January is named after him) and of gates and doors (which, of course, look both ways).

1. *Chronos:* the personification of Time; in the second stage direction he is depicted in his familiar role as an old man with a scythe in his hand and a globe on his back.

1. *mend thy Pace:* hurry up!

2. *An hundred times:* each rotation of the sun corresponds to one year, according to the Ptolemaic system, in which the sun revolves around the earth.

3. *the Radiant Belt:* the signs of the Zodiac, a belt of stars which, from earth's point of view, girdles the heavens and against which move sun and planets.

4. *Race:* trip, path, onward movement.

6. *Fans:* wings.

8. *Freight:* heavy load.

12–13. *Momus:* the god of mockery and censure, the son of Night.

19. *mend:* improve.

24. *That:* so that.

26. *Goddess of the Silver Bow:* Diana was the goddess of hunting as well as of the moon. She is depicted as dressed in a *chlamys* (a short mantle usually worn by men in ancient Greece) with her legs bare, carrying a bow, quiver, and arrows and accompanied by hunting dogs. The allegorical reference is to the reign of James I (1603–1625), who was extremely fond of hunting.

28. *hie to:* speed off to.

29. *buskin'd:* shod with "buskins," high thick-soled lace boots.

30. *waxing:* growing full. The moon is Diana's emblem.

31. *course:* hunt.

31. *unkennel:* dislodge a fox from its hole.

34. *Echo:* a nymph who was changed into an echo by Hera, wife of Zeus, chief of the Greek gods, for keeping Hera occupied while Zeus sported with other nymphs.

34. *doubles:* repeats.

38. *Rage:* madness, insanity; violent passions.

39–40. A . . . *Time:* reference to "the nightly revels of [James's] court [which] were frequently prolonged to a general turbulence and intoxication" (Montague Summers).

40. *Quaffing:* drinking.

44–45. *Mars:* the god of war represents the period of the English Civil Wars (1642–1653).
45. *Vocal Brass:* resounding trumpets.
46. *Infant Age:* the time of James I.
49. *Martial:* warlike.
52. *Good:* excellence, good thing.
56. *Tyrian Dye:* Tyrian dye was a bright crimson color derived from mollusks by the inhabitants of Tyre.
61. *Scabbard:* sword-case.
63. *Better . . . were:* it would be better if the world . . .
69–70. *Venus:* the goddess of love stands for ' the gallantries and intrigues of the court of Charles II" (Summers).
69. *Calms:* periods of calm.
71. *Nature:* promptings of the natural man or what man and the natural world have in common.
71. *kindly:* natural, fitting; reproductive.
71. *Care:* charge or object of care; "patient," whose nurse is Venus.
75. *then:* during Charles II's reign.
78. *Queen of Pleasure:* a reference to Venus and generally to all the mistresses of Charles II and his courtiers.
81. *pond'rous Orb:* heavy globe.
83. *Chase:* hunt.

ALEXANDER POPE (1688–1744)

An Essay on Criticism

From *Part I*

Still green with bays each ancient altar stands,
Above the reach of sacrilegious hands;
Secure from flames, from envy's fiercer rage,
Destructive war, and all-devouring age.
See from each clime the learn'd their incense bring:
Hear in all tongues consenting *Pæans* ring!
In praise so just let ev'ry voice be join'd,
And fill the gen'ral Chorus of mankind!
Hail, Bards triumphant! born in happier days;
Immortal heirs of universal praise!
Whose honours with increase of ages grow,
As streams roll down, enlarging as they flow!
Nations unborn your mighty names shall sound,

And worlds applaud that must not yet be found!
Oh may some spark of your celestial fire,
The last, the meanest of your sons inspire,
(That on weak wings, from far, pursues your flights;
Glows while he reads, but trembles as he writes)
To teach vain Wits a science little known,
T'admire superior sense, and doubt their own!

Lexical Gloss

1. *bays:* wreaths of praise and glory.
1. *ancient altar:* the altars symbolize the almost religious reverence which is due each ancient writer.
2. *sacrilegious:* disrespectful to sacred things.
5. *clime:* region.
5. *incense:* as offerings.
6. *tongues:* languages.
6. *Pæans:* hymns of thanksgiving to the gods.
8. *gen'ral:* common, universal.
13. *sound:* utter.
14. *must not:* have probably not been.
16. *meanest:* most lowly.
16. *sons:* modern poets. Pope here is referring modestly to himself.
19. *science:* general field of knowledge (not "science" in the modern sense): here, specifically, criticism.

Elegy to the Memory of an Unfortunate Lady

What beck'ning ghost, along the moonlight shade
Invites my steps, and points to yonder glade?
'Tis she!—but why that bleeding bosom gor'd,
Why dimly gleams the visionary sword?
Oh ever beauteous, ever friendly! tell,
Is it, in heav'n, a crime to love too well?
To bear, too tender, or too firm a heart,
To act a Lover's or a *Roman's* part?
Is there no bright reversion in the sky,
For those who greatly think, or bravely die?
Why bade ye else, ye Pow'rs! her soul aspire

Above the vulgar flight of low desire?
Ambition first sprung from your blest abodes;
The glorious fault of Angels and of Gods:
Thence to their Images on earth it flows,
And in the breasts of Kings and Heroes glows!
Most souls, 'tis true, but peep out once an age,
Dull sullen pris'ners in the body's cage:
Dim lights of life that burn a length of years,
Useless, unseen, as lamps in sepulchres;
Like Eastern kings a lazy state they keep,
And close confin'd in their own palace sleep.
  From these perhaps (ere nature bade her die)
Fate snatch'd her early to the pitying sky.
As into air the purer spirits flow,
And sep'rate from their kindred dregs below;
So flew the soul to its congenial place,
Nor left one virtue to redeem her Race.
  But thou, false guardian of a charge too good,
Thou, mean deserter of thy brother's blood!
See on these ruby lips the trembling breath,
These cheeks, now fading at the blast of death:
Cold is that breast which warm'd the world before,
And those love-darting eyes must roll no more.
Thus, if eternal justice rules the ball,
Thus shall your wives, and thus your children fall:
On all the line a sudden vengeance waits,
And frequent hearses shall besiege your gates.
There passengers shall stand, and pointing say,
(While the long fun'rals blacken all the way)
Lo, these were they, whose souls the Furies steel'd,
And curs'd with hearts unknowing how to yield.
Thus unlamented pass the proud away,
The gaze of fools, and pageant of a day!
So perish all, whose breast ne'er learn'd to glow
For others' good, or melt at others' woe.
  What can atone (oh ever-injur'd shade!)
Thy fate unpiti'd, and thy rites unpaid?
No friend's complaint, no kind domestic tear
Pleas'd thy pale ghost, or grac'd thy mournful bier;
By foreign hands thy dying eyes were clos'd,
By foreign hands thy decent limbs compos'd,
By foreign hands thy humble grave adorn'd,

By strangers honour'd, and by strangers mourn'd!
What, tho' no friends in sable weeds appear,
Grieve for an hour, perhaps, then mourn a year,
And bear about the mockery of woe
To midnight dances, and the public show?
What, tho' no weeping Loves thy ashes grace,
Nor polish'd marble emulate thy face?
What, tho' no sacred earth allow thee room,
Nor hallow'd dirge be mutter'd o'er thy tomb?
Yet shall thy grave with rising flowers be dress'd,
And the green turf lie lightly on thy breast:
There shall the morn her earliest tears bestow,
There the first roses of the year shall blow;
While Angels with their silver wings o'ershade
The ground, now sacred by thy relics made.
  So peaceful rests, without a stone, a name,
What once had beauty, titles, wealth, and fame.
How loved, how honour'd once, avails thee not,
To whom related, or by whom begot;
A heap of dust alone remains of thee,
'Tis all thou art, and all the proud shall be!
  Poets themselves must fall, like those they sung,
Deaf the prais'd ear, and mute the tuneful tongue.
Ev'n he, whose soul now melts in mournful lays,
Shall shortly want the gen'rous tear he pays;
Then from his closing eyes thy form shall part,
And the last pang shall tear thee from his heart,
Life's idle business at one gasp be o'er,
The Muse forgot, and thou belov'd no more!

Lexical Gloss

2. *glade:* an open space in a wood.
4. *visionary:* ghostlike.
8. *Roman's part:* a reference to the practice common among the Romans of committing suicide when faced with defeat or disgrace. Such deaths were considered honorable and brave (see l. 10).
9. *reversion:* a returning to her former glory.
10. *greatly:* in a great and noble manner.
11. *else:* otherwise.
11. *Pow'rs:* gods.
11. *aspire:* to rise.

13. *sprung:* sprang.
15. *Thence:* from there.
15. *their Images:* the images of gods and angels are human beings.
20. *sepulchres:* tombs.
21. *Eastern kings:* the courts of kings of the Orient were reputed to have been notoriously luxurious.
21. *state:* court ceremony.
25. *purer spirits:* purer parts of physical constitution.
26. *kindred dregs:* related material which form the residue after the more refined part—the spirits—have flowed upward.
27. *congenial place:* place where it feels most at home.
28. *Race:* her family.
29. *charge:* responsibility, object of care.
35. *ball:* the globe, the earth.
36. *Thus:* in the same way as the unfortunate lady.
37. *line:* lineage, family tree.
41. *Furies:* fearful, winged daughters of Earth or night with serpents twined in their hair and blood dripping from their eyes, who dwelt in the depths of Tartarus. They punished men and gods in both this world and the next. Pope here has them as the source of hardness of heart.
44. *gaze of fools:* object which fools gaze upon.
44. *pageant:* spectacle.
47. *atone:* make up for.
47. *shade:* ghost of the unfortunate lady.
48. *rites unpaid:* unperformed respects due the dead.
49. *complaint:* mourning.
50. *mournful:* causing sorrow.
50. *bier:* coffin.
51. *foreign:* not connected by friendship or blood.
52. *decent:* chaste.
55. *sable:* black.
55. *weeds:* clothes.
57. *bear:* wear, carry.
58. *show:* display, appearance.
59. *What, tho':* what difference does it make if.
59. *Loves:* carved Cupids.
60. *emulate:* try to equal or excel.
61. *sacred earth:* suicides were forbidden burial in holy ground.
62. *hallow'd dirge:* sacred funeral song.
63. *rising:* growing.
66. *blow:* bloom.
68. *relics:* remains, body.
69. *stone:* tombstone.
71. *avails thee not:* does you no good.
75. *sung:* sang about.
77. *lays:* songs, poems.

78. *want:* need (because he'll be dead himself).
80. *last pang:* death pains.
82. *Muse:* spirit of poetic inspiration.
82. *forgot:* forgotten.

THOMAS GRAY (1716–1771)

Ode on the Death of a Favorite Cat, Drowned in a Tub of Gold Fishes

'Twas on a lofty vase's side,
Where China's gayest art had dy'd
  The azure flowers, that blow;
Demurest of the tabby kind,
The pensive Selima reclin'd,
  Gazed on the lake below.

Her conscious tail her joy declar'd;
The fair round face, the snowy beard,
  The velvet of her paws,
Her coat, that with the tortoise vies,
Her ears of jet, and emerald eyes,
  She saw; and purr'd applause.

Still had she gaz'd; but 'midst the tide
Two angel forms were seen to glide,
  The Genii of the stream:
Their scaly armour's Tyrian hue
Thro' richest purple to the view
  Betray'd a golden gleam.

The hapless Nymph with wonder saw:
A whisker first and then a claw,
  With many an ardent wish,
She stretch'd in vain to reach the prize.
What female heart can gold despise?
  What Cat's averse to fish?

Presumptuous Maid! with looks intent
Again she stretch'd, again she bent,

Nor knew the gulf between.
(Malignant Fate sat by, and smil'd)
The slipp'ry verge her feet beguil'd,
She tumbled headlong in.

Eight times emerging from the flood
She mew'd to ev'ry wat'ry God,
Some speedy aid to send.
No Dolphin came, no Nereid stirr'd:
Nor cruel *Tom,* nor *Susan* heard.
A Fav'rite has no friend!

From hence, ye Beauties, undeceiv'd,
Know, one false step is ne'er retriev'd,
And be with caution bold.
Not all that tempts your wand'ring eyes
And heedless hearts, is lawful prize;
Nor all, that glisters, gold.

Lexical Gloss

2. *China's gayest art:* pottery-glazing.
3. *blow:* bloom.
4. *Demurest:* most affectedly grave or decorous.
4. *tabby kind:* striped cats.
7. *conscious:* aware of its own motion, studied.
13. *Still:* yet.
13. *had:* would have.
13. *tide:* exaggerated description of the water in the fishbowl.
15. *Genii:* local deities or spirits.
16. *Tyrian hue:* the bluish-red dye produced by the inhabitants of ancient Tyre was made from certain mollusks.
19. *hapless:* unfortunate.
19. *Nymph:* any charming young female (not supernatural).
29. *verge:* edge.
29. *beguil'd:* tricked.
34. *Dolphin:* the porpoise, a water mammal known for its gregariousness and friendliness to man. Porpoises were of value because their appearance presaged a storm and enabled sailors to steer for safe havens. Classical water gods are sometimes depicted as riding on the backs of dolphins.
34. *Nereid:* sea-nymphs (specifically of the Mediterranean) were believed to be propitious to sailors.
35. *Tom, Susan:* the children of the household.
37. *hence:* this event.
42. *glisters:* glitters.

Ode on a Distant Prospect of Eton College

Ye distant spires, ye antique towers,
That crown the wat'ry glade,
Where grateful Science still adores
Her HENRY's holy Shade;
And ye, that from the stately brow
Of WINDSOR's heights th'expanse below
Of grove, of lawn, of mead survey,
Whose turf, whose shade, whose flowers among
Wanders the hoary Thames along
His silver-winding way.

Ah happy hills, ah pleasing shade,
Ah fields belov'd in vain,
Where once my careless childhood stray'd,
A stranger yet to pain!
I feel the gales, that from ye blow,
A momentary bliss bestow,
As waving fresh their gladsome wing,
My weary soul they seem to soothe,
And redolent of joy and youth,
To breathe a second spring.

Say, Father THAMES, for thou hast seen
Full many a sprightly race
Disporting on thy margent green
The paths of pleasure trace,
Who foremost now delight to cleave
With pliant arm thy glassy wave?
The captive linnet which enthrall?
What idle progeny succeed
To chase the rolling circle's speed,
Or urge the flying ball?

While some on earnest business bent
Their murm'ring labours ply
'Gainst graver hours, that bring constraint
To sweeten liberty:

Some bold adventurers disdain
The limits of their little reign,
And unknown regions dare descry:
Still as they run they look behind,
They hear a voice in every wind,
And snatch a fearful joy.

Gay hope is theirs by fancy fed,
Less pleasing when possess'd;
The tear forgot as soon as shed,
The sunshine of the breast:
Theirs buxom health of rosy hue,
Wild wit, invention ever-new,
And lively cheer of vigour born;
The thoughtless day, the easy night,
The spirits pure, the slumbers light,
That fly th'approach of morn.

Alas, regardless of their doom,
The little victims play!
No sense have they of ills to come,
Nor care beyond to-day:
Yet see how all around 'em wait
The Ministers of human fate,
And black Misfortune's baleful train!
Ah, show them where in ambush stand
To seize their prey the murth'rous band!
Ah, tell them, they are men!

These shall the fury Passions tear,
The vultures of the mind,
Disdainful Anger, pallid Fear,
And Shame that skulks behind;
Or pining Love shall waste their youth,
Or Jealousy with rankling tooth,
That inly gnaws the secret heart,
And Envy wan, and faded Care,
Grim-visag'd comfortless Despair,
And Sorrow's piercing dart.

Ambition this shall tempt to rise,
Then whirl the wretch from high,

To bitter Scorn a sacrifice,
And grinning Infamy.
The stings of Falsehood those shall try,
And hard Unkindness' alter'd eye,
That mocks the tear it forc'd to flow;
And keen Remorse with blood defil'd,
And moody Madness laughing wild
Amid severest woe.

Lo, in the vale of years beneath
A grisly troop are seen,
The painful family of Death,
More hideous than their Queen:
This racks the joints, this fires the veins,
That every labouring sinew strains,
Those in the deeper vitals rage:
Lo, Poverty, to fill the band,
That numbs the soul with icy hand,
And slow-consuming Age.

To each his suff'rings: all are men,
Condemn'd alike to groan,
The tender for another's pain;
Th' unfeeling for his own.
Yet ah! why should they know their fate?
Since sorrow never comes too late,
And happiness too swiftly flies.
Thought would destroy their paradise.
No more; where ignorance is bliss,
'Tis folly to be wise.

Lexical Gloss

Title. Prospect: view.

Title. Eton College: a famous school on the banks of the Thames across from Windsor Castle.

1. *spires:* Gothic pinnacles on Eton College buildings.

1. *antique:* ancient and venerated.

2. *glade:* clearing in a forest.

3. *Science:* all learning, not just what today goes under the name of science.

4. *Henry's holy Shade:* the spirit of Henry VI, who founded the college in 1440.

5. *brow:* projecting edge of a hill.
7. *grove:* thicket, wooded area.
7. *mead:* meadow.
7. *survey:* look out over.
9. *hoary:* old.
9. *Thames:* the most famous of English rivers.
12. *in vain:* because they had to be left.
13. *careless:* carefree.
15. *gales:* gentle breezes.
19. *redolent of:* full of the odor of, smelling from.
20. *second spring:* another period of youth.
22. *sprightly race:* lively group or generation of schoolboys.
23. *Disporting:* frolicking, amusing themselves.
23. *margent:* the space immediately adjacent to a river.
24. *trace:* tread, make one's way over.
25. *cleave:* split, divide.
27. *linnet:* a small bird.
27. *enthrall:* trap.
28. *progeny:* offspring, group of children; but here the spiritual descendants of earlier Etonians.
28. *succeed:* follow Gray's generation or class.
29. *rolling circle's:* hoop's.
32. *murm'ring labours:* studying aloud.
32. *ply:* engage in earnestly.
33. *'Gainst:* in anticipation of.
33. *graver hours:* the more serious periods when they must recite what they have learned.
33. *constraint:* confinement for study.
35. *disdain:* are impatient with, scorn.
36. *reign:* realm, kingdom.
37. *descry:* look for, catch sight of.
38. *Still:* always.
41. *fancy:* imagination.
45. *buxom:* jolly.
46. *wit:* quickness of mind and liveliness of imagination.
46. *invention:* making up new things to do.
47. *cheer:* disposition, mood.
48. *thoughtless:* untroubled by thought.
50. *fly:* flee.
51. *their doom:* their judgment, the fortunes which will befall them (either for good or bad).
56. *Ministers:* agents, instruments, those who put the decisions of fate into effect.
57. *baleful:* full of evil, injurious.
57. *train:* retinue, following band.
59. *murth'rous:* murderous.

61. *These:* one group of the boys.
61. *fury Passions:* the emotions seen as malignant spirits; the Greek Furies were symbolizations of torturing conscience.
63. *pallid:* pale.
65–66. *Or . . . Or:* either . . . or.
66. *rankling:* vexing, causing festering.
67. *inly:* inwardly.
69. *visag'd:* faced.
74. *Infamy:* disgrace, scandal.
75. *try:* tax, put to the test.
78. *Remorse:* anguished guilt and regret for what one has done.
78. *defil'd:* polluted.
82. *grisly:* grim, terrible.
83. *painful:* causing pain.
86. *sinew:* tendon.
87. *vitals:* vital organs of the body.
88. *fill:* fill out, complete.
93. *tender:* one who is sensitive or responsive to.

WILLIAM COLLINS (1721–1759)

Dirge in Cymbeline

SUNG BY GUIDERIUS AND ARVIRAGUS OVER FIDELE,
SUPPOS'D TO BE DEAD.

To fair Fidele's grassy Tomb,
  Soft Maids and Village Hinds shall bring
Each op'ning Sweet, of earliest Bloom,
  And rifle all the breathing Spring.

No wailing Ghost shall dare appear
  To vex with Shrieks this quiet Grove;
But Shepherd Lads assemble here,
  And melting Virgins own their Love.

No wither'd Witch shall here be seen,
  No Goblins lead their nightly Crew:
The Female Fays shall haunt the Green,
  And dress thy Grave with pearly Dew!

The Redbreast oft at Ev'ning Hours
  Shall kindly lend his little Aid:
With hoary Moss, and gather'd Flow'rs,
  To deck the Ground where thou art laid.

When howling Winds, and beating Rain,
  In Tempests shake the sylvan Cell:
Or midst the Chase on ev'ry Plain
  The tender Thought on thee shall dwell.

Each lonely Scene shall thee restore,
  For thee the Tear be duly shed:
Belov'd till Life could charm no more;
  And mourn'd till Pity's self be dead.

Lexical Gloss

Subtitle: in Act IV, Scene 2, of Shakespeare's *Cymbeline*, the brothers Guiderius and Arviragus sing a dirge over Fidele, who is really their own half-sister Imogen in disguise. Fidele is not really dead: she has taken a restorative pill which puts her into a sleep so deep that it seems to be death. The first stanza of their song goes:

Fear no more the heat o' the sun,
  Nor the furious winter's rages;
Thou thy worldly task hast done,
  Home art gone, and ta'en thy wages.
Golden lads and girls all must,
As chimney-sweepers, come to dust.

Thus, Collins' song is a dirge which the reader really knows is not a dirge since its object is not dead.

2. *Hinds:* young men, swains.
4. *rifle:* go through and take the best of.
4. *breathing:* odorous, sweet-scented, fragrant.
8. *own:* confess, admit to.
11. *Fays:* fairies.
12. *dress:* adorn.
15. *hoary:* whitish.
18. *sylvan:* pastoral, woody.
18. *Cell:* hut, small enclosed building.
19. *Chase:* hunt.
23. *charm:* fascinate, powerfully attract.

Ode Occasion'd by the Death of Mr. Thomson

The Scene of the following Stanzas
is suppos'd to lie on the *Thames* near *Richmond.*

In yonder Grave a Druid lies
  Where slowly winds the stealing Wave!
The *Year's* best Sweets shall duteous rise
  To deck *its* Poet's sylvan Grave!

In yon deep Bed of whisp'ring Reeds
  His airy Harp shall now be laid,
That He, whose Heart in Sorrow bleeds,
  May love thro' Life the soothing Shade.

Then Maids and Youths shall linger here,
  And while its Sounds at distance swell,
Shall sadly seem in Pity's Ear
  To hear the Woodland Pilgrim's Knell.

Remembrance oft shall haunt the Shore
  When Thames in Summer-wreaths is dress'd,
And oft suspend the dashing Oar
  To bid his gentle Spirit rest!

And oft as Ease and Health retire
  To breezy Lawn, or Forest deep,
The Friend shall view yon whit'ning Spire,
  And 'mid the varied Landscape weep.

But Thou, who own'st that Earthy Bed,
  Ah! what will ev'ry Dirge avail?
Or Tears, which Love and Pity shed
  That mourn beneath the gliding Sail!

Yet lives there one, whose heedless Eye
  Shall scorn thy pale Shrine glimm'ring near?
With Him, Sweet Bard, may Fancy die,
  And Joy desert the blooming Year.

But thou, lorn Stream, whose sullen Tide
  No sedge-crown'd Sisters now attend,
Now waft me from the green Hill's Side
  Whose cold Turf hides the buried Friend!

And see, the Fairy Valleys fade,
  Dun *Night* has veil'd the solemn View!
—Yet once again, Dear parted Shade
  Meek Nature's Child again adieu!

The genial Meads assign'd to bless
  Thy Life, shall mourn thy early Doom;
Their Hinds, and Shepherd-Girls shall dress
  With simple Hands thy rural Tomb.

Long, long, thy Stone and pointed Clay
  Shall melt the musing Briton's Eyes,
O! Vales, and Wild Woods, shall He say,
  In yonder Grave Your Druid lies!

Lexical Gloss

1. *Druid:* a priest in the Celtic religion of druidism; the etymology "oak-wise" suggests the important role of trees in this religion. The druid priest was a combination prophet, judge, and poet. Collins was thinking of Thomson as a druid because Thomson, the author of *The Seasons,* was a nature poet.
2. *stealing:* the wave is so quiet that it steals along.
3. *Sweets:* flowers.
4. *its:* the Year's: a reference to the fact that Thomson's major poem was called *The Seasons*. It was divided into four parts, each of which depicted the character of one of the four seasons (see Part III).
4. *sylvan:* woody, of the forest.
12. *Pilgrim:* one who visits the shrine of a deity: here, the deity is the God of Nature, to be best found in the woodland.
12. *Knell:* tolling of funeral bell.
17. *retire:* go off to, take a rest in.
22. *Dirge:* a funeral song.
22. *avail:* be of use or value.
25. *heedless:* uncaring, not mourning.
26. *Shrine:* a place endowed with sacredness because of its association with a holy person; here, Thomson's grave.
27. *may:* I hope that.

27. *Fancy:* imagination.
29. *lorn:* forsaken, desolate.
29. *sullen:* moving sluggishly as if melancholy.
30. *sedge-crown'd Sisters:* river nymphs were thought to wear sedge, a kind of water-grass, on their heads.
31. *waft me from:* float me away from.
34. *Dun:* dark and gloomy.
37. *genial:* sympathetically cheerful.
37. *Meads:* meadows.
39. *Hinds:* country lads.
41. *pointed:* the mound over the grave comes to a point.

WILLIAM WORDSWORTH (1770–1850)

"A slumber did my spirit seal"

A slumber did my spirit seal;
  I had no human fears:
She seemed a thing that could not feel
  The touch of earthly years.

No motion has she now, no force;
  She neither hears nor sees;
Rolled round in earth's diurnal course,
  With rocks, and stones, and trees.

Lexical Gloss

5. *force:* vigor, vitality.
7. *diurnal:* daily.
7. *course:* directed movement, path.

Lines
Composed a Few Miles above Tintern Abbey, on Revisiting the Banks of the Wye During a Tour. July 13, 1798

Five years have past; five summers, with the length
Of five long winters! and again I hear

These waters, rolling from their mountain-springs
With a soft inland murmur.—Once again
Do I behold these steep and lofty cliffs,
That on a wild secluded scene impress
Thoughts of more deep seclusion; and connect
The landscape with the quiet of the sky.
The day is come when I again repose
Here, under this dark sycamore, and view
These plots of cottage-ground, these orchard-tufts,
Which at this season, with their unripe fruits,
Are clad in one green hue, and lose themselves
'Mid groves and copses. Once again I see
These hedge-rows, hardly hedge-rows, little lines
Of sportive wood run wild: these pastoral farms,
Green to the very door; and wreaths of smoke
Sent up, in silence, from among the trees!
With some uncertain notice, as might seem
Of vagrant dwellers in the houseless woods,
Or of some Hermit's cave, where by his fire
The Hermit sits alone.
These beauteous forms,
Through a long absence, have not been to me
As is a landscape to a blind man's eye:
But oft, in lonely rooms, and 'mid the din
Of towns and cities, I have owed to them
In hours of weariness, sensations sweet,
Felt in the blood, and felt along the heart;
And passing even into my purer mind,
With tranquil restoration:—feelings too
Of unremembered pleasure: such, perhaps,
As have no slight or trivial influence
On that best portion of a good man's life,
His little, nameless, unremembered, acts
Of kindness and of love. Nor less, I trust,
To them I may have owed another gift,
Of aspect more sublime; that blessed mood
In which the burthen of the mystery,
In which the heavy and the weary weight
Of all this unintelligible world,
Is lightened:—that serene and blessed mood,
In which the affections gently lead us on,—
Until, the breath of this corporeal frame

And even the motion of our human blood
Almost suspended, we are laid asleep
In body, and become a living soul:
While with an eye made quiet by the power
Of harmony, and the deep power of joy,
We see into the life of things.
                                                  If this
Be but a vain belief, yet, oh! how oft—
In darkness and amid the many shapes
Of joyless daylight; when the fretful stir
Unprofitable, and the fever of the world,
Have hung upon the beatings of my heart—
How oft, in spirit, have I turned to thee,
O sylvan Wye! thou wanderer thro' the woods,
How often has my spirit turned to thee!

And now, with gleams of half-extinguished thought,
With many recognitions dim and faint,
And somewhat of a sad perplexity,
The picture of the mind revives again:
While here I stand, not only with the sense
Of present pleasure, but with pleasing thoughts
That in this moment there is life and food
For future years. And so I dare to hope,
Though changed, no doubt, from what I was when first
I came among these hills; when like a roe
I bounded o'er the mountains, by the sides
Of the deep rivers, and the lonely streams,
Wherever nature led: more like a man
Flying from something that he dreads than one
Who sought the thing he loved. For nature then
(The coarser pleasures of my boyish days,
And their glad animal movements all gone by)
To me was all in all.—I cannot paint
What then I was. The sounding cataract
Haunted me like a passion: the tall rock,
The mountain, and the deep and gloomy wood,
Their colours and their forms, were then to me
An appetite; a feeling and a love,
That had no need of a remoter charm,
By thought supplied, nor any interest
Unborrowed from the eye.—That time is past,

And all its aching joys are now no more,
And all its dizzy raptures. Not for this
Faint I, nor mourn nor murmur; other gifts
Have followed; for such loss, I would believe,
Abundant recompense. For I have learned
To look on nature, not as in the hour
Of thoughtless youth; but hearing oftentimes
The still, sad music of humanity,
Nor harsh nor grating, though of ample power
To chasten and subdue. And I have felt
A presence that disturbs me with the joy
Of elevated thoughts; a sense sublime
Of something far more deeply interfused,
Whose dwelling is the light of setting suns,
And the round ocean and the living air,
And the blue sky, and in the mind of man:
A motion and a spirit, that impels
All thinking things, all objects of all thought,
And rolls through all things. Therefore am I still
A lover of the meadows and the woods,
And mountains; and of all that we behold
From this green earth; of all the mighty world
Of eye, and ear,—both what they half create,
And what perceive; well pleased to recognise
In nature and the language of the sense
The anchor of my purest thoughts, the nurse,
The guide, the guardian of my heart, and soul
Of all my moral being.
                                        Nor perchance,
If I were not thus taught, should I the more
Suffer my genial spirits to decay:
For thou art with me here upon the banks
Of this fair river; thou my dearest Friend,
My dear, dear Friend; and in thy voice I catch
The language of my former heart, and read
My former pleasures in the shooting lights
Of thy wild eyes. Oh! yet a little while
May I behold in thee what I was once,
My dear, dear Sister! and this prayer I make,
Knowing that Nature never did betray
The heart that loved her; 'tis her privilege,
Through all the years of this our life, to lead

From joy to joy: for she can so inform
The mind that is within us, so impress
With quietness and beauty, and so feed
With lofty thoughts, that neither evil tongues,
Rash judgments, nor the sneers of selfish men,
Nor greetings where no kindness is, nor all
The dreary intercourse of daily life,
Shall e'er prevail against us, or disturb
Our cheerful faith, that all which we behold
Is full of blessings. Therefore let the moon
Shine on thee in thy solitary walk;
And let the misty mountain-winds be free
To blow against thee: and, in after years,
When these wild ecstasies shall be matured
Into a sober pleasure; when thy mind
Shall be a mansion for all lovely forms,
Thy memory be as a dwelling-place
For all sweet sounds and harmonies; oh! then,
If solitude, or fear, or pain, or grief,
Should be thy portion, with what healing thoughts
Of tender joy wilt thou remember me,
And these my exhortations! Nor, perchance—
If I should be where I no more can hear
Thy voice, nor catch from thy wild eyes these gleams
Of past existence—wilt thou then forget
That on the banks of this delightful stream
We stood together; and that I, so long
A worshipper of Nature, hither came
Unwearied in that service: rather say
With warmer love—oh! with far deeper zeal
Of holier love. Nor wilt thou then forget,
That after many wanderings, many years
Of absence, these steep woods and lofty cliffs,
And this green pastoral landscape, were to me
More dear, both for themselves and for thy sake!

Lexical Gloss

Title. Tintern Abbey: a famous ruin on the River Wye in Monmouthshire in the west of England. The church dates from the 13th century.

4. *inland murmur:* Wordsworth notes: "The river is not affected by the tides a few miles above Tintern."

6. *impress:* imprint in the poet's mind.
11. *orchard-tufts:* clumps of fruit trees.
14. *copses:* thickets.
16. *sportive:* playful, lively.
16. *pastoral:* simple and rustic.
19. *uncertain:* unclear or ambiguous.
19. *notice:* sign.
20. *vagrant:* vagabond, gypsy.
21. *Hermit's:* a solitary dweller's.
22. *beauteous:* beautiful.
28. *along:* within, from one end to another.
29. *purer:* in the old physiology, the mind was thought to be of lighter and purer substance than the other organs.
30. *restoration:* restoring of equanimity and peace.
37. *aspect:* character or sort.
38. *burthen:* burden, heavy weight.
42. *affections:* emotions, feelings.
43. *corporeal frame:* the body.
50. *vain:* idle, fruitless.
56. *sylvan:* woody, of the forest.
67. *roe:* female deer.
73. *coarser:* less fine-grained, less discriminating.
74. *animal:* characterized by healthy vivacity, as in "animal spirits."
76. *cataract:* waterfall.
81. *charm:* power to attract.
85. *raptures:* feelings of ecstatic elation, of being taken out of oneself.
88. *recompense:* payment in return.
93. *chasten:* to correct or discipline.
94. *presence:* divine, spiritual or incorporeal being or influence felt or conceived as present.
96. *interfused:* permeated or penetrated and blended with nature.
106. *they:* eye and ear.
108. *sense:* senses, as vision, hearing, smell, etc.
113. *Suffer:* allow, permit.
113. *genial:* pertaining to one's natural disposition or "genius" (characteristic bent).
125. *inform:* impress, imbue, inspire, in the sense of "give a formative principle to."
131. *intercourse:* business, ordinary dealings between people.
146. *exhortations:* urgings.
152. *hither:* to this place.
153. *service:* act of serving in a religious ritual.

PERCY BYSSHE SHELLEY (1792–1822)

The Two Spirits: An Allegory

FIRST SPIRIT

O thou, who plumed with strong desire
  Wouldst float around the earth, beware!
A Shadow tracks thy flight of fire—
    Night is coming!
Bright are the regions of the air,
  And among the warmth and beams
It was delight to wander there—
    Night is coming!

SECOND SPIRIT

The deathless stars are bright above;
  If I should cross the shade at night,
Within my heart is the lamp of love,
    And that is day!
And the moon will smile with gentle light
  On my golden plumes where'er they move;
The meteors will linger around my flight,
    And make night day.

FIRST SPIRIT

But if the whirlwind of darkness waken
  Hail and lightning and stormy rain;
See the bounds of the air are shaken—
    Night is coming!
The red swift clouds of the hurricane
  Yon declining sun have overtaken,
The clash of the hail sweeps over the plain—
    Night is coming!

SECOND SPIRIT

I see the light, and I hear the sound;
  I'll sail on the flood of the tempest dark
With the calm within and the light around
    Which makes night day:

And thou, when the gloom is deep and stark,
  Look from thy dull earth, slumber-bound,
My moon-like flight thou then may'st mark
      On high, far away.

. . . . .

Some say, there is a precipice
  Where one vast pine is frozen to ruin
O'er piles of snow and chasms of ice
      'Mid Alpine mountains;
And that the languid storm pursuing
  That winged shape for ever flies
Around those hoar branches, aye renewing
      Its aëry fountains.

Some say, when nights are dry and clear,
  And the death dews sleep on the morass,
Sweet whispers are heard by the traveller,
      Which make night day:
And a silver shape like his early love doth pass
  Upborne by her wild and glittering hair,
And when he awakes on the fragrant grass,
      He finds night day.

Lexical Gloss

Title. Allegory: a form of literature in which abstract ideas are personified as the main characters, as Beauty, Evil, Mankind, etc.
1. *plumed:* adorned with feathers.
10. *shade:* shadow.
31. *mark:* observe.
39. *hoar:* frozen.
39. *aye:* forever.
40. *aëry:* of the air, ethereal.
42. *morass:* marsh, boggy land.
46. *Upborne:* carried aloft.

Ode to the West Wind

I

O, wild West Wind, thou breath of Autumn's being,
Thou, from whose unseen presence the leaves dead
Are driven, like ghosts from an enchanter fleeing,

Yellow, and black, and pale, and hectic red,
Pestilence-stricken multitudes: O, thou,
Who chariotest to their dark wintry bed

The winged seeds, where they lie cold and low,
Each like a corpse within its grave, until
Thine azure sister of the spring shall blow

Her clarion o'er the dreaming earth, and fill
(Driving sweet buds like flocks to feed in air)
With living hues and odours plain and hill:

Wild Spirit, which art moving everywhere;
Destroyer and preserver; hear, O, hear!

II

Thou on whose stream, 'mid the steep sky's commotion,
Loose clouds like earth's decaying leaves are shed,
Shook from the tangled boughs of Heaven and Ocean,

Angels of rain and lightning: there are spread
On the blue surface of thine airy surge,
Like the bright hair uplifted from the head

Of some fierce Mænad, even from the dim verge
Of the horizon to the zenith's height
The locks of the approaching storm. Thou dirge

Of the dying year, to which this closing night
Will be the dome of a vast sepulchre,
Vaulted with all thy congregated might

Of vapours, from whose solid atmosphere
Black rain, and fire, and hail will burst: O, hear!

III

Thou who didst waken from his summer dreams
The blue Mediterranean, where he lay,
Lulled by the coil of his crystalline streams,

Beside a pumice isle in Baiæ's bay,
And saw in sleep dim palaces and towers
Quivering within the wave's intenser day,

All overgrown with azure moss and flowers
So sweet, the sense faints picturing them! Thou
For whose path the Atlantic's level powers

Cleave themselves into chasms, while far below
The sea-blooms and the oozy woods which wear
The sapless foliage of the ocean, know

Thy voice, and suddenly grow grey with fear,
And tremble and despoil themselves: O, hear!

IV

If I were a dead leaf thou mightest bear;
If I were a swift cloud to fly with thee;
A wave to pant beneath thy power, and share

The impulse of thy strength, only less free
Than thou, O, uncontrollable! If even
I were as in my boyhood, and could be

The comrade of thy wanderings over heaven,
As then, when to outstrip thy skiey speed
Scarce seemed a vision; I would ne'er have striven

As thus with thee in prayer in my sore need.
Oh! lift me as a wave, a leaf, a cloud!
I fall upon the thorns of life! I bleed!

A heavy weight of hours has chained and bowed
One too like thee: tameless, and swift, and proud.

V

Make me thy lyre, even as the forest is:
What if my leaves are falling like its own!
The tumult of thy mighty harmonies

Will take from both a deep, autumnal tone,
Sweet though in sadness. Be thou, spirit fierce,
My spirit! Be thou me, impetuous one!

Drive my dead thoughts over the universe
Like withered leaves to quicken a new birth!
And, by the incantation of this verse,

Scatter, as from an unextinguished hearth
Ashes and sparks, my words among mankind!
Be through my lips to unawakened earth

The trumpet of a prophecy! O, wind,
If Winter comes, can Spring be far behind?

Lexical Gloss

3. *enchanter:* a wizard; one able to raise the dead.
4. *hectic:* feverish.
9. *azure:* dark blue.
10. *clarion:* a horn used by heralds to announce the presence of a nobleman or king.
21. *Maenad:* a frenzied nymph participating in Bacchus' (the Greek god of wine's) orgies.
21. *verge:* edge.
22. *zenith:* point of the sky directly overhead.
23. *dirge:* funeral song.
25. *sepulchre:* funeral chamber.
26. *Vaulted:* thrown over with a vault or dome, arched.
26. *congregated:* assembled.
27. *atmosphere:* a gaseous envelope.
31. *coil:* noise, roar.
31. *crystalline:* absolutely transparent.
32. *pumice:* lava.
32. *Baiæ's bay:* a bay west of Naples, Italy.
36. *sense:* senses, imagination.
37. *powers:* the waves seen as celestial or spiritual beings.
38. *Cleave:* split.

38. *chasms:* canyons, deep valleys.
38–42. *while . . . themselves:* Shelley writes that the vegetation at the ocean bottom "sympathizes with that of the land in the change of seasons, and is consequently influenced by the winds which announce it."
57. *lyre:* a harplike instrument.
60. *both:* both me and the forest.
64. *quicken:* give life.
65. *incantation:* the chanting of magic words to evoke a spirit.

JOHN KEATS (1795–1821)

Sonnet to Sleep

O soft embalmer of the still midnight,
  Shutting, with careful fingers and benign,
Our gloom-pleas'd eyes, embower'd from the light,
  Enshaded in forgetfulness divine;
O soothest Sleep! if so it please thee, close,
  In midst of this thine hymn, my willing eyes,
Or wait the amen, ere thy poppy throws
  Around my bed its lulling charities;
Then save me, or the passed day will shine
Upon my pillow, breeding many woes;
  Save me from curious conscience, that still lords
Its strength for darkness, burrowing like a mole;
  Turn the key deftly in the oiled wards,
And seal the hushed casket of my soul.

Lexical Gloss

1. *embalmer:* perhaps a pun: (1) one who makes balm, anything healing or soothing, and (2) one who preserves a dead body with spices.
2. *benign:* kindly, gracious.
3. *embower'd:* shaded off, closed off, as in a bower or place of privacy and retirement.
5. *soothest:* most soothing.
7. *wait:* await.
7. *ere:* before.
7. *poppy:* the poppy is an opiate.
11. *curious:* anxious, solicitous, hard to satisfy as well as prying.
11. *conscience:* until 1745 "conscience" meant simply "consciousness," and

this may be an archaism, but more probably the modern sense is meant: moral faculty which pronounces on one's behavior.

11. *lords:* some editors emend this word, which seems to be somewhat peculiar, to "hoards."
12. *for:* in anticipation of.
13. *wards:* the ridges in a lock which prevent the turning of any key whose ridges do not correspond.

To Autumn

I

Season of mists and mellow fruitfulness,
  Close bosom-friend of the maturing sun;
Conspiring with him how to load and bless
  With fruit the vines that round the thatch-eaves run;
To bend with apples the moss'd cottage-trees,
  And fill all fruit with ripeness to the core;
    To swell the gourd, and plump the hazel shells
  With a sweet kernel; to set budding more,
And still more, later flowers for the bees,
Until they think warm days will never cease,
    For Summer has o'er-brimm'd their clammy cells.

II

Who hath not seen thee oft amid thy store?
  Sometimes whoever seeks abroad may find
Thee sitting careless on a granary floor,
  Thy hair soft-lifted by the winnowing wind;
Or on a half-reap'd furrow sound asleep,
  Drows'd with the fume of poppies, while thy hook
    Spares the next swath and all its twined flowers:
And sometimes like a gleaner thou dost keep
  Steady thy laden head across a brook;
  Or by a cider-press, with patient look,
    Thou watchest the last oozings hours by hours.

III

Where are the songs of Spring? Ay, where are they?
  Think not of them, thou hast thy music too,—
While barred clouds bloom the soft-dying day,

And touch the stubble-plains with rosy hue;
Then in a wailful choir the small gnats mourn
Among the river sallows, borne aloft
Or sinking as the light wind lives or dies;
And full-grown lambs loud bleat from hilly bourn;
Hedge-crickets sing; and now with treble soft
The red-breast whistles from a garden-croft;
And gathering swallows twitter in the skies.

Lexical Gloss

2. *maturing:* causing to ripen.
4. *thatch-eaves:* the overhanging edges of a thatched roof.
5. *cottage-trees:* trees around a modest farm worker's house.
7. *plump:* make plump.
11. *o'er-brimm'd:* filled to overflowing.
11. *clammy:* soft and sticky.
12. *store:* supply, abundance.
13. *abroad:* around the countryside, out of doors.
14. *careless:* free from care or apprehension.
14. *granary:* place where the grain is stored after it is threshed, that is, after the grain or seeds are separated from the husks or chaff by beating or flailing.
15. *winnowing:* blowing the chaff away from the grain.
16. *half-reap'd furrow:* the usual meaning of "furrow" is "trenches, made by a plow," but here it is loosely used for plowed land in general.
17. *Drows'd:* made drowsy.
17. *fume:* heavy odor, almost smokelike in its density.
17. *poppies:* the poppy is an opiate.
17. *hook:* reaping hook.
18. *swath:* patch of growing crop, as much as a scythe or sickle can cut in a single stroke.
19. *gleaner:* the one who goes around after the reaper and picks up the grain left over.
20. *laden:* weighted down.
21. *look:* gaze.
25. *barred clouds:* clouds in bars.
26. *stubble-plains:* fields covered with stubble, the stumps of wheat left in the ground after the reaping.
28. *sallows:* willows.
30. *bourn:* boundary between fields.
31. *treble:* high-pitched voices.
32. *garden-croft:* garden plot.

ROBERT BROWNING (1812–1889)

My Last Duchess

FERRARA

That's my last Duchess painted on the wall,
Looking as if she were alive. I call
That piece a wonder, now: Frà Pandolf's hands
Worked busily a day, and there she stands.
Will 't please you sit and look at her? I said
"Frà Pandolf" by design, for never read
Strangers like you that pictured countenance,
The depth and passion of its earnest glance,
But to myself they turned (since none puts by
The curtain I have drawn for you, but I)
And seemed as they would ask me, if they durst,
How such a glance came there; so, not the first
Are you to turn and ask thus. Sir, 't was not
Her husband's presence only, called that spot
Of joy into the Duchess' cheek: perhaps
Frà Pandolf chanced to say "Her mantle laps
Over my lady's wrist too much," or "Paint
Must never hope to reproduce the faint
Half-flush that dies along her throat:" such stuff
Was courtesy, she thought, and cause enough
For calling up that spot of joy. She had
A heart—how shall I say?—too soon made glad,
Too easily impressed; she liked whate'er
She looked on, and her looks went everywhere.
Sir, 't was all one! My favor at her breast,
The dropping of the daylight in the West,
The bough of cherries some officious fool
Broke in the orchard for her, the white mule
She rode with round the terrace—all and each
Would draw from her alike the approving speech,
Or blush, at least. She thanked men,—good! but thanked
Somehow—I know not how—as if she ranked
My gift of a nine-hundred-years-old name
With anybody's gift. Who'd stoop to blame

This sort of trifling? Even had you skill
In speech—(which I have not)—to make your will
Quite clear to such an one, and say, "Just this
Or that in you disgusts me; here you miss,
Or there exceed the mark"—and if she let
Herself be lessoned so, nor plainly set
Her wits to yours, forsooth, and made excuse,
—E'en then would be some stooping; and I choose
Never to stoop. Oh sir, she smiled, no doubt,
Whene'er I passed her; but who passed without
Much the same smile? This grew; I gave commands;
Then all smiles stopped together. There she stands
As if alive. Will 't please you rise? We'll meet
The company below, then. I repeat,
The Count your master's known munificence
Is ample warrant that no just pretence
Of mine for dowry will be disallowed;
Though his fair daughter's self, as I avowed
At starting, is my object. Nay, we'll go
Together down, sir. Notice Neptune, though,
Taming a sea-horse, thought a rarity,
Which Claus of Innsbruck cast in bronze for me!

Lexical Gloss

Title. Ferrara: a city in the Po Valley of Italy, ruled for many centuries by one of the oldest families in Europe, the Estes, who in the sixteenth century were also dukes of nearby Modena. The Estes were expelled from Ferrara in the last decade of the sixteenth century by the Pope.

1. *last:* most recent.
3. *Frà Pandolf:* an imaginary Italian painter. "Frà" is Italian for friar or monk.
6. *by design:* intentionally.
7. *countenance:* face.
9. *But . . . they turned:* without turning.
9. *puts by:* draws aside.
11. *durst:* dared.
16. *mantle:* cloak.
16. *laps:* enfolds, extends.
18. *Must:* has no right to.
25. *favor:* present to be worn by a beloved to identify to whom she is pledged; modern examples are fraternity pins or engagement rings.
27. *officious:* meddlesome.

35. *had you:* if one had.
40. *nor:* and did not.
41. *to:* against.
41. *forsooth:* indeed.
42. *would be:* there would be.
48. *company:* group of people.
49. *munificence:* generosity.
50. *ample warrant:* sufficient guarantee.
50. *pretence:* claim.
51. *dowry:* the sum of money a bride's father gives to the groom as a marriage settlement.
51. *disallowed:* refused.
54. *Neptune:* a statue of the sea-god in the Duke's collection.
56. *Claus of Innsbruck:* an imaginary sculptor. Innsbruck is a city in Austria, in the sixteenth century the home of a famous school of artists in bronze.

Development

My Father was a scholar and knew Greek.
When I was five years old, I asked him once
"What do you read about?"
"The siege of Troy."
"What is a siege, and what is Troy?"
Whereat
He piled up chairs and tables for a town,
Set me a-top for Priam, called our cat
—Helen, enticed away from home (he said)
By wicked Paris, who couched somewhere close
Under the footstool, being cowardly,
But whom—since she was worth the pains, poor puss—
Towzer and Tray,—our dogs, the Atreidai,—sought
By taking Troy to get possession of
—Always when great Achilles ceased to sulk,
(My pony in the stable)—forth would prance
And put to flight Hector—our page-boy's self.
This taught me who was who and what was what:
So far I rightly understood the case
At five years old: a huge delight it proved
And still proves—thanks to that instructor sage
My Father, who knew better than turn straight
Learning's full flare on weak-eyed ignorance,

Or, worse yet, leave weak eyes to grow sand-blind,
Content with darkness and vacuity.

It happened, two or three years afterward,
That—I and playmates playing at Troy's Siege—
My Father came upon our make-believe.
"How would you like to read yourself the tale
Properly told, of which I gave you first
Merely such notion as a boy could bear?
Pope, now, would give you the precise account
Of what, some day, by dint of scholarship,
You'll hear—who knows?—from Homer's very mouth.
Learn Greek by all means, read the 'Blind Old Man,
Sweetest of Singers'—*tuphlos* which means 'blind,'
Hedistos which means 'sweetest.' Time enough!
Try, anyhow, to master him some day;
Until when, take what serves for substitute,
Read Pope, by all means!"
                                        So I ran through Pope,
Enjoyed the tale—what history so true?
Also attacked my Primer, duly drudged,
Grew fitter thus for what was promised next—
The very thing itself, the actual words,
When I could turn—say, Buttmann to account.

Time passed, I ripened somewhat: one fine day,
"Quite ready for the Iliad, nothing less?
There's Heine, where the big books block the shelf:
Don't skip a word, thumb well the Lexicon!"

I thumbed well and skipped nowise till I learned
Who was who, what was what, from Homer's tongue,
And there an end of learning. Had you asked
The all-accomplished scholar, twelve years old,
"Who was it wrote the Iliad?"—what a laugh!
"Why, Homer, all the world knows: of his life
Doubtless some facts exist: it's everywhere:
We have not settled, though, his place of birth:
He begged, for certain, and was blind beside:
Seven cities claimed him—Scio, with best right,
Thinks Byron. What he wrote? Those Hymns we have.
Then there's the 'Battle of the Frogs and Mice,'

That's all—unless they dig 'Margites' up
(I'd like that) nothing more remains to know."

Thus did youth spend a comfortable time;
Until—"What's this the Germans say is fact
That Wolf found out first? It's unpleasant work
Their chop and change, unsettling one's belief:
All the same, where we live, we learn, that's sure."
So, I bent brow o'er *Prolegomena.*

And, after Wolf, a dozen of his like
Proved there was never any Troy at all,
Neither Besiegers nor Besieged,—nay, worse,—
No actual Homer, no authentic text,
No warrant for the fiction I, as fact,
Had treasured in my heart and soul so long—
Ay, mark you! and as fact held still, still hold,
Spite of new knowledge, in my heart of hearts
And soul of souls, fact's essence freed and fixed
From accidental fancy's guardian sheath.
Assuredly thenceforward—thank my stars!—
However it got there, deprive who could—
Wring from the shrine my precious tenantry,
Helen, Ulysses, Hector and his Spouse,
Achilles and his Friend?—though Wolf—ah, Wolf!
Why must he needs come doubting, spoil a dream?

But then, "No dream 's worth waking"—Browning says:
And here 's the reason why I tell thus much.
I, now mature man, you anticipate,
May blame my Father justifiably
For letting me dream out my nonage thus,
And only by such slow and sure degrees
Permitting me to sift the grain from chaff,
Get truth and falsehood known and named as such.
Why did he ever let me dream at all,
Not bid me taste the story in its strength?
Suppose my childhood was scarce qualified
To rightly understand mythology,
Silence at least was in his power to keep:
I might have—somehow—correspondingly—

Well, who knows by what method, gained my gains,
Been taught, by forthrights not meanderings,
My aim should be to loathe, like Peleus' son,
A lie as Hell's Gate, love my wedded wife,
Like Hector, and so on with all the rest.
Could not I have excogitated this
Without believing such men really were?
That is—he might have put into my hand
The "Ethics"? In translation, if you please,
Exact, no pretty lying that improves,
To suit the modern taste: no more, no less—
The "Ethics": 't is a treatise I find hard
To read aright now that my hair is gray,
And I can manage the original.
At five years old—how ill had fared its leaves!
Now, growing double o'er the Stagirite,
At least I soil no page with bread and milk,
Nor crumple, dogsear and deface—boys' way.

Lexical Gloss

4. *Whereat:* in response to which question.
5. *for:* in imitation of.
6. *Priam:* the king of Troy in the *Iliad.*
7. *Helen:* wife of Menelaus, king of Sparta, whose kidnapping by Paris provoked the Greeks to rally around Menelaus and attack Troy.
8. *Paris:* Paris was the second son of Priam and his wife Hecuba. He was very handsome and graceful but a poor fighter.
11. *Atreidai:* sons of Atreus, namely Agamemnon, the leader of the combined Greek armies, and Menelaus.
13. *Achilles:* the great Greek hero, the greatest fighter on the Greek side.
15. *Hector:* Achilles' counterpart, bravest of the Trojans and eldest son of Priam and Hecuba.
19. *sage:* wise.
20. *than turn:* than to turn.
20. *straight:* immediately.
22. *sand-blind:* half-blind, dim-sighted.
23. *vacuity:* vacuum, empty space.
30. *Pope:* Alexander Pope did a translation of the *Iliad* into English (1715–20).
31. *by dint of:* by force of.
32. *Homer's very mouth:* by reading the original in Greek.
33. *Blind old man:* Homer.

37. *for:* as a.
40. *Primer:* beginner's textbook in Greek.
43. *Buttmann:* Philipp Buttmann (1764–1829) wrote a Greek grammar.
46. *Heine:* Christian Heine (1729–1812) edited an edition of the *Iliad* which was standard during the period.
47. *Lexicon:* dictionary of Greek.
57. *Seven cities:* Athens, Rhodes, Argos, Salamis, Smyrna, Colophon, and Scio (Chios).
58. *Byron:* George Gordon, Lord Byron (1788–1824); famous English poet, much traveled in Greece.
58. *Hymns:* poems which are now ascribed by scholars to the rhapsodists or minstrels of early Greece.
59. *'Battle of the Frogs and Mice':* the *Batrachomyomachia,* a comic parody of the *Iliad,* is still extant; modern scholars attribute it to the post-Homeric period.
60. *'Margites':* a lost poem ridiculing a man who knew a lot of things, but knew them badly; this also was written after Homer's death.
64. *Wolf:* F. A. Wolf (1759–1824), in his *Prolegomena in Homerum,* maintained that the *Iliad* and *Odyssey* were not unified poems by Homer but consisted of small epic poems celebrating the separate adventures of heroes and brought together first by Pisistratus, tyrant of Athens (died 527 B.C.). This theory has since been discredited.
65. *chop:* abrupt veering or re-direction.
72. *warrant for:* proof of, justification for believing.
74. *mark you!:* notice! observe!
75. *Spite of:* in spite of.
76. *essence:* that which constitutes the intrinsic and central being of something.
77. *sheath:* sword-case or covering for protecting a sword.
80. *shrine:* a sacred receptacle for holy objects.
80. *tenantry:* inhabitants.
81. *Ulysses:* one of the Greek heroes, whose later adventures were the subject of Homer's *Odyssey.*
81. *his Spouse:* Hector's wife was Andromache.
82. *his Friend:* Patroclus, whose death alone prompted Achilles to return to the war.
88. *nonage:* immaturity, early youth.
90. *chaff:* empty husks of wheat.
93. *strength:* tone, full quality.
99. *forthrights:* direct statements.
99. *meanderings:* roundabout statements, fiction from which one draws a moral.
100. *Peleus' son:* Achilles.
101. *as:* as much as.
103. *excogitated:* thought out.
106. *"Ethics":* treatise on morality by Aristotle.

110. *aright:* correctly.
113. *Stagirite:* Aristotle.
115. *dogsear:* turns down corners of pages as markers.

MATTHEW ARNOLD (1822–1888)

Dover Beach

The sea is calm to-night.
The tide is full, the moon lies fair
Upon the straits;—on the French coast the light
Gleams and is gone; the cliffs of England stand,
Glimmering and vast, out in the tranquil bay.
Come to the window, sweet is the night-air!
Only, from the long line of spray
Where the sea meets the moon-blanch'd land,
Listen! you hear the grating roar
Of pebbles which the waves draw back, and fling,
At their return, up the high strand,
Begin, and cease, and then again begin,
With tremulous cadence slow, and bring
The eternal note of sadness in.

Sophocles long ago
Heard it on the Ægæan, and it brought
Into his mind the turbid ebb and flow
Of human misery; we
Find also in the sound a thought,
Hearing it by this distant northern sea.

The Sea of Faith
Was once, too, at the full, and round earth's shore
Lay like the folds of a bright girdle furl'd.
But now I only hear
Its melancholy, long, withdrawing roar,
Retreating, to the breath
Of the night-wind, down the vast edges drear
And naked shingles of the world.

Ah, love, let us be true
To one another! for the world, which seems

To lie before us like a land of dreams,
So various, so beautiful, so new,
Hath really neither joy, nor love, nor light,
Nor certitude, nor peace, nor help for pain;
And we are here as on a darkling plain
Swept with confused alarms of struggle and flight,
Where ignorant armies clash by night.

Lexical Gloss

3. *straits:* narrow channels.
5. *Glimmering:* giving off faint, flickering light.
8. *-blanch'd:* -whitened.
11. *strand:* beach.
13. *tremulous:* trembling, quivering.
13. *cadence:* measured, regular pace.
15. *Sophocles:* Greek tragedian, 496?–405 B.C.
16. *Ægæan:* sea to the east of Greece.
17. *turbid:* muddy, confused.
21. *Faith:* religious belief.
22. *at the full:* at high tide.
23. *girdle:* belt or sash around the waist.
23. *furl'd:* rolled up tightly, secured.
26. *to:* to the accompaniment of, accompanied by.
27. *drear:* dreary.
28. *shingles:* pebbled or graveled beaches.
34. *certitude:* certainty, assurance.
35. *darkling:* getting darker, dim.
36. *alarms:* sudden trumpet calls to arms.

Lines Written in Kensington Gardens

In this lone, open glade I lie,
Screen'd by deep boughs on either hand;
And at its end, to stay the eye,
Those black-crown'd, red-boled pine-trees stand!

Birds here make song, each bird has his,
Across the girdling city's hum.
How green under the boughs it is!
How thick the tremulous sheep-cries come!

Sometimes a child will cross the glade
To take his nurse his broken toy;
Sometimes a thrush flit overhead
Deep in her unknown day's employ.

Here at my feet what wonders pass,
What endless, active life is here!
What blowing daisies, fragrant grass!
An air-stirr'd forest, fresh and clear.

Scarce fresher is the mountain-sod
Where the tired angler lies, stretch'd out,
And, eased of basket and of rod,
Counts his day's spoil, the spotted trout.

In the huge world, which roars hard by,
Be others happy if they can!
But in my helpless cradle I
Was breathed on by the rural Pan.

I, on men's impious uproar hurl'd,
Think often, as I hear them rave,
That peace has left the upper world
And now keeps only in the grave.

Yet here is peace for ever new!
When I who watch them am away,
Still all things in this glade go through
The changes of their quiet day.

Then to their happy rest they pass!
The flowers upclose, the birds are fed,
The night comes down upon the grass,
The child sleeps warmly in his bed.

Calm soul of all things! make it mine
To feel, amid the city's jar,
That there abides a peace of thine,
Man did not make, and cannot mar.

The will to neither strive nor cry,
The power to feel with others give!

Calm, calm me more! nor let me die
Before I have begun to live.

Lexical Gloss

1. *glade:* open space in woods.
3. *stay:* attract and keep.
4. *red-boled:* with red trunks.
6. *girdling:* surrounding.
8. *tremulous:* trembling, wavering.
12. *employ:* business.
15. *blowing:* blooming.
18. *angler:* fisherman.
20. *spoil:* booty.
21. *hard by:* near by.
24. *Pan:* Greek god of the woodland, patron of shepherds and flocks.
25. *impious:* irreligious.
28. *keeps:* abides.
34. *upclose:* close up, fold together.
38. *jar:* upset.

EMILY DICKINSON (1830–1886)

Poem 341

After great pain, a formal feeling comes—
The Nerves sit ceremonious, like Tombs—
The stiff Heart questions was it He, that bore,
And Yesterday, or Centuries before?

The Feet, mechanical, go round—
Of Ground, or Air, or Ought—
A Wooden way
Regardless grown,
A Quartz contentment, like a stone—

This is the Hour of Lead—
Remembered, if outlived,
As Freezing persons, recollect the Snow—
First—Chill—then Stupor—then the letting go—

Lexical Gloss

2. *ceremonious:* characterized by ceremony and formality.
3. *bore:* had the strength to endure or suffer.
8. *Regardless:* heedless, not caring.
9. *Quartz:* a brilliant hard crystalline mineral.

Poem 986

A narrow Fellow in the Grass
Occasionally rides—
You may have met Him—did you not
His notice sudden is—

The grass divides as with a Comb—
A spotted shaft is seen—
And then it closes at your feet
And opens further on—

He likes a Boggy Acre
A Floor too cool for Corn—
Yet when a Boy, and Barefoot—
I more than once at Noon
Have passed, I thought, a Whip lash
Unbraiding in the Sun
When stooping to secure it
It wrinkled, and was gone—

Several of Nature's People
I know, and they know me—
I feel for them a transport
Of cordiality—

But never met this Fellow
Attended, or alone
Without a tighter breathing
And Zero at the Bone—

Lexical Gloss

4. *notice:* sign of presence.
9. *Boggy:* like a swamp.
14. *Unbraiding:* untwisting, straightening out.
19. *transport:* rapture, a being carried away (by emotion).
20. *cordiality:* warm fellow-feeling.
22. *Attended:* in someone else's company.

ALGERNON CHARLES SWINBURNE
(1837–1909)

Satia Te Sanguine

If you loved me ever so little,
  I could bear the bonds that gall,
I could dream the bonds were brittle;
  You do not love me at all.

O beautiful lips, O bosom
  More white than the moon's and warm,
A sterile, a ruinous blossom
  Is blown your way in a storm.

As the lost white feverish limbs
  Of the Lesbian Sappho, adrift
In foam where the sea-weed swims,
  Swam loose for the streams to lift,

My heart swims blind in a sea
  That stuns me; swims to and fro,
And gathers to windward and lee
  Lamentation, and mourning, and woe.

A broken, an emptied boat,
  Sea saps it, winds blow apart,

Sick and adrift and afloat,
  The barren waif of a heart.

Where, when the gods would be cruel,
  Do they go for a torture? where
Plant thorns, set pain like a jewel?
  Ah, not in the flesh, not there!

The racks of earth and the rods
  Are weak as foam on the sands;
In the heart is the prey for gods,
  Who crucify hearts, not hands.

Mere pangs corrode and consume,
  Dead when life dies in the brain;
In the infinite spirit is room
  For the pulse of an infinite pain.

I wish you were dead, my dear;
  I would give you, had I to give,
Some death too bitter to fear;
  It is better to die than live.

I wish you were stricken of thunder
  And burnt with a bright flame through,
Consumed and cloven in sunder,
  I dead at your feet like you.

If I could but know after all,
  I might cease to hunger and ache,
Though your heart were ever so small,
  If it were not a stone or a snake.

You are crueller, you that we love,
  Than hatred, hunger, or death;
You have eyes and breasts like a dove,
  And you kill men's hearts with a breath.

As plague in a poisonous city
  Insults and exults on her dead,
So you, when pallid for pity
  Comes love, and fawns to be fed.

As a tame beast writhes and wheedles,
  He fawns to be fed with wiles;
You carve him a cross of needles,
  And whet them sharp as your smiles.

He is patient of thorn and whip,
  He is dumb under axe or dart;
You suck with a sleepy red lip
  The wet red wounds in his heart.

You thrill as his pulses dwindle,
  You brighten and warm as he bleeds,
With insatiable eyes that kindle
  And insatiable mouth that feeds.

Your hands nailed love to the tree,
  You stript him, scourged him with rods,
And drowned him deep in the sea
  That hides the dead and their gods.

And for all this, die will he not;
  There is no man sees him but I;
You came and went and forgot;
  I hope he will some day die.

Lexical Gloss

Title. Satia Te Sanguine: satiate yourself with blood.
2. *gall:* vex, irritate, make sore.
10. *Lesbian Sappho:* Sappho of Lesbos (hence Lesbian), fl. 600 B.C., first Greek woman lyric poet. She died for love of Phaon by jumping off a cliff.
15. *windward:* the direction from which the wind blows.
15. *lee:* the direction to which the wind blows.
18. *saps:* drains the vitality from.
20. *waif:* small homeless child.
25. *racks:* instruments of torture.
25. *rods:* clubs or sticks for beating.
29. *corrode:* eat or wear away.
37. *of:* by.
39. *cloven:* split.
39. *in sunder:* in two.
50. *exults:* shouts victoriously.
51. *pallid:* pale.

53. *wheedles:* insinuates one's way into favor, persuades by flattery.
54. *wiles:* sly tricks, winning ways.
56. *whet:* sharpen, as on a grindstone.
61. *thrill:* feel emotional excitement.
63. *insatiable:* not to be satisfied.
63. *kindle:* ignite.
66. *scourge:* whip.

The Garden of Proserpine

Here, where the world is quiet,
  Here, where all trouble seems
Dead winds' and spent waves' riot
  In doubtful dreams of dreams;
I watch the green field growing
For reaping folk and sowing,
For harvest-time and mowing,
  A sleepy world of streams.

I am tired of tears and laughter,
  And men that laugh and weep;
Of what may come hereafter
  For men that sow to reap:
I am weary of days and hours,
Blown buds of barren flowers,
Desires and dreams and powers
  And everything but sleep.

Here life has death for neighbour,
  And far from eye or ear
Wan waves and wet winds labour,
  Weak ships and spirits steer;
They drive adrift, and whither
They wot not who make thither;
But no such winds blow hither,
  And no such things grow here.

No growth of moor or coppice,
  No heather-flower or vine,
But bloomless buds of poppies,

Green grapes of Proserpine,
Pale beds of blowing rushes
Where no leaf blooms or blushes
Save this whereout she crushes
For dead men deadly wine.

Pale, without name or number,
In fruitless fields of corn,
They bow themselves and slumber
All night till light is born;
And like a soul belated,
In hell and heaven unmated,
By cloud and mist abated
Comes out of darkness morn.

Though one were strong as seven,
He too with death shall dwell,
Nor wake with wings in heaven,
Nor weep for pains in hell;
Though one were fair as roses,
His beauty clouds and closes;
And well though love reposes,
In the end it is not well.

Pale, beyond porch and portal,
Crowned with calm leaves, she stands
Who gathers all things mortal
With cold immortal hands;
Her languid lips are sweeter
Than love's who fears to greet her
To men that mix and meet her
From many times and lands.

She waits for each and other,
She waits for all men born;
Forgets the earth her mother,
The life of fruits and corn;
And spring and seed and swallow
Take wing for her and follow
Where summer song rings hollow
And flowers are put to scorn.

There go the loves that wither,
The old loves with wearier wings;
And all dead years draw thither,
And all disastrous things;
Dead dreams of days forsaken,
Blind buds that snows have shaken,
Wild leaves that winds have taken,
Red strays of ruined springs.

We are not sure of sorrow,
And joy was never sure;
To-day will die to-morrow;
Time stoops to no man's lure;
And love, grown faint and fretful,
With lips but half regretful
Sighs, and with eyes forgetful
Weeps that no loves endure.

From too much love of living,
From hope and fear set free,
We thank with brief thanksgiving
Whatever gods may be
That no life lives for ever;
That dead men rise up never;
That even the weariest river
Winds somewhere safe to sea.

Then star nor sun shall waken,
Nor any change of light:
Nor sound of waters shaken,
Nor any sound or sight:
Nor wintry leaves nor vernal,
Nor days nor things diurnal;
Only the sleep eternal
In an eternal night.

Lexical Gloss

Title. Proserpine: also called Persephone, daughter of Demeter and wife of Hades, the god of the underworld.

3. *riot:* violent disorder and disturbance.

6. *reaping:* cutting a crop down.
6. *sowing:* planting seeds.
14. *Blown:* bloomed.
21. *adrift:* floating without direction.
21. *whither:* to which place.
22. *wot:* know.
22. *thither:* to that place.
23. *hither:* to this place.
25. *moor:* open wasteland.
25. *coppice:* thicket of trees.
26. *heather:* a flowering shrub which grows on moors.
27. *poppies:* the poppy is well known for its narcotic effects.
29. *blowing:* blooming; or, waving in wind.
31. *whereout:* out of which.
37. *belated:* late in arriving.
39. *abated:* lessened, made weak.
47. *reposes:* rests, relaxes.
49. *portal:* doorway, entrance.
53. *languid:* drooping, weak, without vitality, languishing.
59. *earth her mother:* Demeter, the goddess of agriculture and the fruit of the earth.
69. *forsaken:* desolate, forlorn.
76. *stoops:* pounces or swoops down on (as a bird of prey).
76. *lure:* bait.
78. *but:* only.
93. *vernal:* springlike, hence fresh and young.
94. *diurnal:* daily.

THOMAS HARDY (1840–1928)

A Commonplace Day

The day is turning ghost,
And scuttles from the kalendar in fits and furtively,
To join the anonymous host
Of those that throng oblivion; ceding his place, maybe
To one of like degree.

I part the fire-gnawed logs,
Rake forth the embers, spoil the busy flames, and lay the ends
Upon the shining dogs;
Further and further from the nooks the twilight's stride extends,
And beamless black impends.

Nothing of tiniest worth
Have I wrought, pondered, planned; no one thing asking blame
or praise,
Since the pale corpse-like birth
Of this diurnal unit, bearing blanks in all its rays—
Dullest of dull-hued Days!

Wanly upon the panes
The rain slides, as have slid since morn my colourless thoughts; and yet
Here, while Day's presence wanes,
And over him the sepulchre-lid is slowly lowered and set,
He wakens my regret.

Regret—though nothing dear
That I wot of, was toward in the wide world at his prime,
Or bloomed elsewhere than here,
To die with his decease, and leave a memory sweet, sublime,
Or mark him out in Time. . . .

—Yet, maybe, in some soul,
In some spot undiscerned on sea or land, some impulse rose,
Or some intent upstole
Of that enkindling ardency from whose maturer glows
The world's amendment flows;

But which, benumbed at birth
By momentary chance or wile, has missed its hope to be
Embodied on the earth;
And undervoicings of this loss to man's futurity
May wake regret in me.

Lexical Gloss

2. *scuttles:* withdraws or runs off from.
2. *kalendar:* calendar.
2. *furtively:* secretly, stealthily, as if guilty.
3. *host:* number, company.
4. *throng:* crowd into.
4. *oblivion:* that which is forgotten.
4. *ceding:* giving up.
5. *degree:* step in social position or rank.
7. *spoil:* destroy, bring an end to.

8. *dogs:* firedogs, andirons, racks upon which logs are burned.
10. *impends:* hangs over, is imminent.
12. *wrought:* achieved.
12. *pondered:* thought about.
14. *diurnal:* daily.
16. *Wanly:* palely.
19. *sepulchre:* a vault for burial.
21. *dear:* precious.
22. *wot:* know.
22. *toward:* promising, favorable.
22. *prime:* best paint.
24. *sublime:* exalted, lofty.
25. *mark . . . out:* distinguish.
27. *undiscerned:* undistinguished, not discovered.
28. *upstole:* stole out of.
29. *enkindling:* igniting, fire-setting.
29. *ardency:* heat, glowing passion.
29. *maturer:* more developed.
30. *amendment:* betterment, improvement.
31. *benumbed:* made numb.
32. *wile:* trick, piece of deceit.
33. *Embodied:* become substantial.
34. *undervoicings:* half-heard hints, expressions uttered by voice not heard clearly because they are drowned out by something else.
34. *futurity:* the future, what shall exist in the future.

A Night of Questionings

On the eve of All-Souls' Day
I heard the dead men say
Who lie by the tottering tower,
To the dark and doubling wind
At the midnight's turning hour,
When other speech had thinned:
    "What of the world now?"
The wind whiffed back: "Men still
Who are born, do good, do ill
Here, just as in your time:
Till their years the locust hath eaten,
Leaving them bare, downbeaten;
Somewhiles in springtide rime,
Somewhiles in summer glow,

Somewhiles in winter snow:—
No more I know."

The same eve I caught cry
To the selfsame wind, those dry
As dust beneath the aisles
Of old cathedral piles,
Walled up in vaulted biers
Through many Christian years:
"What of the world now?"
Sighed back the circuiteer:
"Men since your time, shrined here
By deserved ordinance,
Their own craft, or by chance,
Which follows men from birth
Even until under earth,
But little difference show
When ranged in sculptured row,
Different as dyes although:—
No more I know."

On the selfsame eve, too, said
Those swayed in the sunk sea-bed
To the selfsame wind as it played
With the tide in the starless shade
From Comorin to Horn,
And round by Wrath forlorn:
"What of the world now?"
And the wind for a second ceased,
Then whirred: "Men west and east,
As each sun soars and dips,
Go down to the sea in ships
As you went—hither and thither;
See the wonders of the deep,
As you did, ere they sleep;
But few at home care whither
They wander to and fro;
Themselves care little also!—
No more I know."

Said, too, on the selfsame eve
The troubled skulls that heave

And fust in the flats of France,
To the wind wayfaring over
Listlessly as in trance
From the Ardennes to Dover,
"What of the world now?"
And the farer moaned: "As when
You mauled these fields, do men
Set them with dark-drawn breaths
To knave their neighbours' deaths
In periodic spasms!
Yea, fooled by foul phantasms,
In a strange cyclic throe
Backward to type they go:—
No more I know."

That night, too, men whose crimes
Had cut them off betimes,
Who lay within the pales
Of town and county jails
With the rope-groove on them yet,
Said to the same wind's fret
"What of the world now?"
And the blast in its brooding tone
Returned: "Men have not shown,
Since you were stretched that morning,
A white cap your adorning,
More lovely deeds or true
Through thus neck-knotting you;
Or that they purer grow,
Or ever will, I trow!—
No more I know."

Lexical Gloss

1. *All-Souls' Day:* the day after All Saints' Day, i.e. November 2, a day devoted to the memory of all the dead.
4. *doubling:* changing or reversing direction.
8. *whiffed:* made a sound with a slight blast.
11. *locust:* a voracious insect somewhat like a grasshopper.
13. *Somewhiles:* sometimes.
13. *rime:* frost on ground.
20. *piles:* buildings.

21. *vaulted:* closed up, covered with arched roof.
21. *biers:* places for depositing coffins.
24. *circuiteer:* the wind, which is seen as making a circuit of the earth.
25. *shrined:* put in a holy place.
26. *ordinance:* authoritative directive, order, or decree.
27. *craft:* cunning ability.
38. *Comorin:* Cape Comorin, at the bottom-most tip of India.
38. *Horn:* Cape Horn, at the tip of South America.
39. *Wrath:* Cape Wrath, at the northern tip of Scotland.
42. *whirred:* made a vibrating noise.
45. *hither:* in this direction.
45. *thither:* in that direction.
48. *whither:* to which place.
54. *fust:* to become moldy.
54. *flats:* plains.
56. *Listlessly:* languidly, droopingly, without spirits.
57. *Ardennes:* a forest in northeastern France, site of a great campaign in World War I.
57. *Dover:* the English seaport which is the nearest point in England to France.
59. *farer:* traveler (i.e. the wind).
60. *mauled:* tore up, disfigured.
61. *them:* themselves.
62. *knave:* to accomplish by base devices.
63. *spasms:* convulsions.
64. *phantasms:* ghosts, spirits.
65. *cyclic:* ever-returning.
65. *throe:* pang, upheaval, convulsion.
66. *to type:* characteristic model, biological original.
69. *betimes:* early in life.
70. *pales:* precincts, confines.
72. *rope-groove:* the groove that the hangman's noose made on their necks.
78. *your:* of or on you.
80. *neck-knotting:* hanging.
82. *trow:* trust.

GERARD MANLEY HOPKINS (1844–1889)

Pied Beauty

Glory be to God for dappled things—
  For skies of couple-colour as a brinded cow;
    For rose-moles all in stipple upon trout that swim;

Fresh-firecoal chestnut-falls; finches' wings;
Landscape plotted and pieced—fold, fallow, and plough;
And áll trádes, their gear and tackle and trim.

All things counter, original, spare, strange;
Whatever is fickle, freckled (who knows how?)
With swift, slow; sweet, sour; adazzle, dim;
He fathers-forth whose beauty is past change:
Praise him.

Lexical Gloss

Title. Pied: parti-colored, having different colors in parts, variegated in coloring.
1. *dappled:* pied, parti-colored.
2. *couple-colour:* parti-colored.
2. *brinded:* brindled, streaked.
3. *rose-moles:* red spots.
3. *all in stipple:* as if painted in spots.
4. *chestnut-falls:* chestnuts fallen down out of their husks.
4. *finches:* the family of small birds which includes cardinals, sparrows, canaries, and goldfinches.
5. *pieced:* cut up into (parti-colored) pieces.
5. *fold:* enclosure for domestic animals.
5. *fallow:* plowed ground which is left unsown for a year.
6. *gear and tackle and trim:* equipment.
7. *counter:* contrary.
7. *spare:* rare.
8. *fickle:* changing, various.

The Windhover:

To Christ Our Lord

I caught this morning morning's minion, king-
dom of daylight's dauphin, dapple-dawn-drawn Falcon, in
his riding
Of the rolling level underneath him steady air, and striding
High there, how he rung upon the rein of a wimpling wing
In his ecstasy! then off, off forth on swing,
As a skate's heel sweeps smooth on a bow-bend: the hurl
and gliding

Rebuffed the big wind. My heart in hiding
Stirred for a bird,—the achieve of, the mastery of the thing!

Brute beauty and valour and act, oh, air, pride, plume, here
Buckle! AND the fire that breaks from thee then, a billion
Times told lovelier, more dangerous, O my chevalier!

No wonder of it: shéer plód makes plough down sillion
Shine, and blue-bleak embers, ah my dear,
Fall, gall themselves, and gash gold-vermilion.

Lexical Gloss

Title. The Windhover: a small falcon, noted for its ability to hover against the wind.

1. *caught:* seized with the senses, saw.
1. *minion:* favorite, one preferred above others.
2. *dauphin:* prince, particularly in France.
2. *dapple:* dappled, spotted, parti-colored.
2. *dapple-dawn-drawn:* either pulled along by the variegated dawn or else sketched or outlined by or against it.
4. *rung upon the rein:* like a horse at the end of a long rein.
4. *wimpling:* rippling, twisting and turning.
5. *ecstasy:* exalted joy, rapture, transport.
6. *bow-bend:* wide turn.
6. *hurl:* violent impetuous movement.
7. *Rebuffed:* drove back, checked.
8. *achieve:* achievement.
9. *air:* demeanor, manner and appearance.
10. *Buckle:* collapse, fall apart (or join together?).
11. *told:* counted.
11. *chevalier:* knight.
12. *plod:* plodding, moving laboriously.
12. *down:* from one end to another.
12. *sillion:* furrow, rut dug in ground into which seeds are sown.
14. *gall:* injure by rubbing against something.
14. *gash:* tear open so that the inside of something is exposed.

WILLIAM BUTLER YEATS (1865–1939)

When You Are Old

When you are old and grey and full of sleep,
And nodding by the fire, take down this book,
And slowly read, and dream of the soft look
Your eyes had once, and of their shadows deep;

How many loved your moments of glad grace,
And loved your beauty with love false or true,
But one man loved the pilgrim soul in you,
And loved the sorrows of your changing face;

And bending down beside the glowing bars,
Murmur, a little sadly, how Love fled
And paced upon the mountains overhead
And hid his face amid a crowd of stars.

Lexical Gloss

7. *pilgrim:* one who makes a trip to a religious shrine.
9. *bars:* bars of iron across the front of the fire-basket, an iron basket in which the fire burns.

Vacillation

I

Between extremities
Man runs his course;
A brand, or flaming breath,
Comes to destroy
All those antinomies
Of day and night;
The body calls it death,
The heart remorse.

But if these be right
What is joy?

II

A tree there is that from its topmost bough
Is half all glittering flame and half all green
Abounding foliage moistened with the dew;
And half is half and yet is all the scene;
And half and half consume what they renew,
And he that Attis' image hangs between
That staring fury and the blind lush leaf
May know not what he knows, but knows not grief.

III

Get all the gold and silver that you can,
Satisfy ambition, animate
The trivial days and ram them with the sun,
And yet upon these maxims meditate:
All women dote upon an idle man
Although their children need a rich estate;
No man has ever lived that had enough
Of children's gratitude or women's love.

No longer in Lethean foliage caught
Begin the preparation for your death
And from the fortieth winter by that thought
Test every work of intellect or faith,
And everything that your own hands have wrought,
That are not suited for such men as come
Proud, open-eyed and laughing to the tomb.

IV

My fiftieth year had come and gone,
I sat, a solitary man,
In a crowded London shop,
An open book and empty cup
On the marble table-top.

While on the shop and street I gazed
My body of a sudden blazed;
And twenty minutes more or less
It seemed, so great my happiness,
That I was blessèd and could bless.

V

Although the summer sunlight gild
Cloudy leafage of the sky,
Or wintry moonlight sink the field
In storm-scattered intricacy,
I cannot look thereon,
Responsibility so weighs me down.

Things said or done long years ago,
Or things I did not do or say
But thought that I might say or do,
Weigh me down, and not a day
But something is recalled,
My conscience or my vanity appalled.

VI

A rivery field spread out below,
An odour of the new-mown hay
In his nostrils, the great lord of Chou
Cried, casting off the mountain snow,
'Let all things pass away.'

Wheels by milk-white asses drawn
Where Babylon or Nineveh
Rose; some conqueror drew rein
And cried to battle-weary men,
'Let all things pass away.'

From man's blood-sodden heart are sprung
Those branches of the night and day
Where the gaudy moon is hung.
What's the meaning of all song?
'Let all things pass away.'

VII

The Soul. Seek out reality, leave things that seem.

The Heart. What, be a singer born and lack a theme?

The Soul. Isaiah's coal, what more can man desire?

The Heart. Struck dumb in the simplicity of fire!

The Soul. Look on that fire, salvation walks within.

The Heart. What theme had Homer but original sin?

VIII

Must we part, Von Hügel, though much alike, for we
Accept the miracles of the saints and honour sanctity?
The body of Saint Teresa lies undecayed in tomb,
Bathed in miraculous oil, sweet odours from it come,
Healing from its lettered slab. Those self-same hands perchance
Eternalised the body of a modern saint that once
Had scooped out Pharaoh's mummy. I—though heart might find
relief
Did I become a Christian man and choose for my belief
What seems most welcome in the tomb—play a predestined part.
Homer is my example and his unchristened heart.
The lion and the honeycomb, what has Scripture said?
So get you gone, Von Hügel, though with blessings on your head.

Lexical Gloss

Title. Vacillation: not making up one's mind, hesitating between alternatives.
3. *brand:* torch.
5. *antinomies:* two contradictory principles which are equally logical, reasonable, and necessary.
13. *Abounding:* flourishing in, offering in abundance.
16. *Attis:* the Phyrgian Attis (or Atys), rejected paramour of the great Earth-mother Cybele. Attis castrated himself in despair. It was customary for the priest of Attis to hang the god's image from a tree and for the devotees of Attis to castrate themselves at the time of the yearly festival in March.
20. *animate:* make lively.
22. *maxims:* general truths or moral instructions.
24. *estate:* heritage, inheritance.
27. *Lethean:* pertaining to Lethe, the river of forgetfulness on the edge of Hades, which dead souls must drink from and cross in order to forget their past lives.
44. *gild:* make golden.
48. *thereon:* on that.
55. *appalled:* horrified.
58. *Chou:* Chóu-kung, Duke of Chóu, prime minister of Wu-Wang, first of the Chóu dynasty (12th century B.C.), a great political reformer.
62. *Babylon, Nineveh:* ancient cities in Mesopotamia, capitals of empires.
66. *sodden:* soaked.
73. *Isaiah's coal:* Isaiah, 6:6–7. In a vision, Isaiah sees a seraph fly from God's shoulder, take a live coal from off an altar, and touch Isaiah's mouth with it, whereby his sin and iniquity are purged.
76. *theme:* subject matter of a discourse.
76. *original sin:* Adam's fall from the grace of God by eating the forbidden fruit.

77. *Von Hügel:* Baron Friedrich von Hügel (1852–1925), Catholic scholar, who had maintained in *The Mystical Element of Religion* that the artistic vision was Christian.
78. *miracles:* marvelous events exceeding nature's limits in which God intervenes in behalf of some favored person.
78. *sanctity:* holiness.
79. *Saint Teresa:* St. Teresa was born in Avila, Spain, in 1515 and died in 1582. She was canonized in 1622. An odor of violets and fragrant oil was said to emanate from her tomb, and when the tomb was opened nine months after her death the flesh was found uncorrupted.
81. *slab:* gravestone.
81. *perchance:* perhaps, maybe.
83. *Pharaoh's mummy:* the practice of preserving the bodies of kings of Egypt is well known.
85. *predestined:* decided in advance.
86. *unchristened:* unbaptized.
87. *the lion and the honeycomb:* Judges 14:5–18. Samson kills a young lion with his bare hands and discovers later that bees have built a honeycomb in the carcass of the animal. He makes this event into a kind of riddle, the gist of which is "What has both strength and sweetness?" After he poses the riddle to thirty Philistines, they wheedle the answer from his wife and, in a rage, he slays them.

ROBERT FROST (1875–   )

Birches

When I see birches bend to left and right
Across the lines of straighter darker trees,
I like to think some boy's been swinging them.
But swinging doesn't bend them down to stay
As ice-storms do. Often you must have seen them
Loaded with ice a sunny winter morning
After a rain. They click upon themselves
As the breeze rises, and turn many-colored
As the stir cracks and crazes their enamel.
Soon the sun's warmth makes them shed crystal shells
Shattering and avalanching on the snow-crust—
Such heaps of broken glass to sweep away
You'd think the inner dome of heaven had fallen.
They are dragged to the withered bracken by the load,
And they seem not to break; though once they are bowed

So low for long, they never right themselves:
You may see their trunks arching in the woods
Years afterwards, trailing their leaves on the ground
Like girls on hands and knees that throw their hair
Before them over their heads to dry in the sun.
But I was going to say when Truth broke in
With all her matter-of-fact about the ice-storm
I should prefer to have some boy bend them
As he went out and in to fetch the cows—
Some boy too far from town to learn baseball,
Whose only play was what he found himself,
Summer or winter, and could play alone.
One by one he subdued his father's trees
By riding them down over and over again
Until he took the stiffness out of them,
And not one but hung limp, not one was left
For him to conquer. He learned all there was
To learn about not launching out too soon
And so not carrying the tree away
Clear to the ground. He always kept his poise
To the top branches, climbing carefully
With the same pains you use to fill a cup
Up to the brim, and even above the brim.
Then he flung outward, feet first, with a swish,
Kicking his way down through the air to the ground.
So was I once myself a swinger of birches.
And so I dream of going back to be.
It's when I'm weary of considerations,
And life is too much like a pathless wood
Where your face burns and tickles with the cobwebs
Broken across it, and one eye is weeping
From a twig's having lashed across it open.
I'd like to get away from earth awhile
And then come back to it and begin over.
May no fate willfully misunderstand me
And half grant what I wish and snatch me away
Not to return. Earth's the right place for love:—
I don't know where it's likely to go better.
I'd like to go by climbing a birch tree,
And climb black branches up a snow-white trunk
Toward heaven, till the tree could bear no more,—
But dipped its top and set me down again.

That would be good both going and coming back.
One could do worse than be a swinger of birches.

Lexical Gloss

9. *crazes:* makes a smooth, hard surface, as the glaze on pottery, finely cracked.
9. *enamel:* hard covering.
14. *bracken:* a growth of large, coarse ferns.
16. *right:* straighten up.
35. *poise:* balance.
43. *considerations:* concern with many problems that require close examination.

A Lone Striker

The swinging mill bell changed its rate
To tolling like the count of fate,
And though at that the tardy ran,
One failed to make the closing gate.
There was a law of God or man
That on the one who came too late
The gate for half an hour be locked,
His time be lost, his pittance docked.
He stood rebuked and unemployed.
The straining mill began to shake.
The mill, though many, many eyed,
Had eyes inscrutably opaque;
So that he couldn't look inside
To see if some forlorn machine
Was standing idle for his sake.
(He couldn't hope its heart would break.)

And yet he thought he saw the scene:
The air was full of dust of wool.
A thousand yarns were under pull,
But pull so slow, with such a twist,
All day from spool to lesser spool,
It seldom overtaxed their strength;
They safely grew in slender length.
And if one broke by any chance,

The spinner saw it at a glance.
The spinner still was there to spin.
That's where the human still came in.
Her deft hand showed with finger rings
Among the harp-like spread of strings.
She caught the pieces end to end
And, with a touch that never missed,
Not so much tied as made them blend.
Man's ingenuity was good.
He saw it plainly where he stood,
Yet found it easy to resist.

He knew another place, a wood,
And in it, tall as trees, were cliffs;
And if he stood on one of these,
'Twould be among the tops of trees,
Their upper branches round him wreathing,
Their breathing mingled with his breathing.
If—if he stood! Enough of ifs!
He knew a path that wanted walking;
He knew a spring that wanted drinking;
A thought that wanted further thinking;
A love that wanted re-renewing.
Nor was this just a way of talking
To save him the expense of doing.
With him it boded action, deed.

The factory was very fine;
He wished it all the modern speed.
Yet, after all, 'twas not divine,
That is to say, 'twas not a church.
He never would assume that he'd
Be any institution's need.
But he said then and still would say
If there should ever come a day
When industry seemed like to die
Because he left it in the lurch,
Or even merely seemed to pine
For want of his approval, why
Come get him—they knew where to search.

Lexical Gloss

1. *mill:* factory.
1. *bell:* some old factories use bells rather than whistles to announce opening, lunch, and closing.
2. *tolling:* ringing slowly.
3. *tardy:* those who were late.
8. *pittance:* small allowance of money, low wages.
8. *docked:* to have a small amount deducted from wages by way of penalty.
12. *inscrutably:* obscurely, incomprehensibly, enigmatically.
19. *yarns:* threads spun from raw wool.
19. *pull:* tension.
25. *spinner:* a mill-hand in charge of overseeing the spinning machines.
28. *deft:* quick and skilled.
28. *finger rings:* rings for guiding the threads (or for protecting the fingers?).
33. *ingenuity:* cleverness, originality.
43. *wanted walking:* needed to be walked.
49. *boded:* was an omen of, looked forward to.
51. *speed:* a pun: (1) good fortune, as in "Godspeed"; (2) rapidity, swiftness.
60. *pine:* languish, dwindle, waste away.
61. *want:* lack.

WALLACE STEVENS (1879–1955)

Anecdote of the Jar

I placed a jar in Tennessee,
And round it was, upon a hill.
It made the slovenly wilderness
Surround that hill.

The wilderness rose up to it,
And sprawled around, no longer wild.
The jar was round upon the ground
And tall and of a port in air.

It took dominion everywhere.
The jar was gray and bare.
It did not give of bird or bush,
Like nothing else in Tennessee.

Lexical Gloss

3. *slovenly:* sloppy, messy.
8. *port:* manner in which one carries oneself, demeanor.
9. *dominion:* control.

Peter Quince at the Clavier

I

Just as my fingers on these keys
Make music, so the selfsame sounds
On my spirit make a music, too.

Music is feeling, then, not sound;
And thus it is that what I feel,
Here in this room, desiring you,

Thinking of your blue-shadowed silk,
Is music. It is like the strain
Waked in the elders by Susanna.

Of a green evening, clear and warm,
She bathed in her still garden, while
The red-eyed elders watching, felt

The basses of their beings throb
In witching chords, and their thin blood
Pulse pizzicati of Hosanna.

II

In the green water, clear and warm,
Susanna lay.
She searched
The touch of springs,
And found
Concealed imaginings.
She sighed,
For so much melody.

Upon the bank, she stood
In the cool
Of spent emotions.
She felt, among the leaves,
The dew
Of old devotions.

She walked upon the grass,
Still quavering.
The winds were like her maids,
On timid feet,
Fetching her woven scarves,
Yet wavering.

A breath upon her hand
Muted the night.
She turned—
A cymbal crashed,
And roaring horns.

III

Soon, with a noise like tambourines,
Came her attendant Byzantines.

They wondered why Susanna cried
Against the elders by her side;

And as they whispered, the refrain
Was like a willow swept by rain.

Anon, their lamps' uplifted flame
Revealed Susanna and her shame.

And then, the simpering Byzantines
Fled, with a noise like tambourines.

IV

Beauty is momentary in the mind—
The fitful tracing of a portal;
But in the flesh it is immortal.
The body dies; the body's beauty lives.
So evenings die, in their green going,

A wave, interminably flowing.
So gardens die, their meek breath scenting
The cowl of winter, done repenting.
So maidens die, to the auroral
Celebration of a maiden's choral.
Susanna's music touched the bawdy strings
Of those white elders; but, escaping,
Left only Death's ironic scraping.
Now, in its immortality, it plays
On the clear viol of her memory,
And makes a constant sacrament of praise.

Lexical Gloss

Title. Peter Quince: a carpenter, the leader of the group of commoners who present a play about Pyramus and Thisbe before the Duke of Athens at the latter's wedding in Shakespeare's *A Midsummer-Night's Dream.*

Title. Clavier: an older form of the piano; any keyboard instrument.

8. *strain:* short piece of music, tune, musical theme.
9. *the elders, Susanna:* Daniel, 13 ff. Susanna was the lovely wife of Joachim, a Jew of Babylon. When she refused to lie with two Jewish elders who saw her naked while bathing, they accused her of adultery with an imaginary youth, and she was condemned to death. But Daniel proved the elders were perjurers and Susanna was saved.
13. *basses:* low notes.
14. *witching:* bewitching, causing to be enchanted.
15. *pizzicati:* plural of *pizzicato,* notes plucked instead of bowed on a stringed instrument.
15. *Hosanna:* an exclamation or shout of praise to God.
23. *For:* because there was, or in the presence of.
29. *devotions:* acts of worship.
31. *quavering:* shaking (in music, trilling).
37. *Muted:* muffled or with sound deadened.
42. *Byzantines:* people from Byzantium, ancient city in Turkey, once Eastern capital of Roman Empire, now named Istanbul.

43–44. *cried Against:* accused.

45. *refrain:* tune; or the repeated part of a poem or tune, as a chorus or song.
47. *Anon:* soon.
49. *simpering:* smiling or smirking in a silly way.
52. *fitful:* spasmodically momentary, restless and impulsive.
52. *tracing:* exact imitation by mechanical means of copying.
52. *portal:* gateway or doorway.
58. *cowl:* hood.
59. *auroral:* occurring at dawn, or like the dawn.

60. *choral:* a simple hymn.
61. *bawdy:* indecent, obscene.
63. *ironic:* that which is the opposite of what was expected or considered appropriate.
63. *scraping:* drawing a bow carelessly and raucously across violin strings.
65. *viol:* any instrument of the violin family.
66. *sacrament:* the making sacred of something, for example, sanctifying the human body through rites like baptism; more generally, to spiritualize matter.

THOMAS STEARNS ELIOT (1888–)

Animula

"Issues from the hand of God, the simple soul"
To a flat world of changing lights and noise,
To light, dark, dry or damp, chilly or warm;
Moving between the legs of tables and of chairs,
Rising or falling, grasping at kisses and toys,
Advancing boldly, sudden to take alarm,
Retreating to the corner of arm and knee,
Eager to be reassured, taking pleasure
In the fragrant brilliance of the Christmas tree,
Pleasure in the wind, the sunlight and the sea;
Studies the sunlit pattern on the floor
And running stags around a silver tray;
Confounds the actual and the fanciful,
Content with playing-cards and kings and queens,
What the fairies do and what the servants say.
The heavy burden of the growing soul
Perplexes and offends more, day by day;
Week by week, offends and perplexes more
With the imperatives of 'is and seems'
And may and may not, desire and control.
The pain of living and the drug of dreams
Curl up the small soul in the window seat
Behind the *Encyclopædia Britannica.*
Issues from the hand of time the simple soul
Irresolute and selfish, misshapen, lame,

Unable to fare forward or retreat,
Fearing the warm reality, the offered good,
Denying the importunity of the blood,
Shadow of its own shadows, spectre in its own gloom,
Leaving disordered papers in a dusty room;
Living first in the silence after the viaticum.

Pray for Guiterriez, avid of speed and power,
For Boudin, blown to pieces,
For this one who made a great fortune,
And that one who went his own way.
Pray for Floret, by the boarhound slain between the yew trees,
Pray for us now and at the hour of our birth.

Lexical Gloss

Title. Animula: a bit of life, a little soul.

1. *"Issues . . . soul":* the quotation is from Dante's *Purgatorio,* Canto XVI, lines 85–93. In the translation of Laurence Binyon, the lines read:

> From the hands of him who wistly loves her, ere
> She is, forth comes, like a child frolicking
> That now weeps and now laughs without a care,
> The little, the innocent soul that knows nothing
> Saving that, sprung from a Creator's joy,
> She goes to her own joy and there loves to cling.

1. *Issues:* goes forth.
2. *flat:* without depth or perspective.
7. *corner:* a secluded, protected place.
12. *running stags:* carved deer as a pattern.
13. *Confounds:* confuses.
19. *imperatives:* commands.
22. *window seat:* houses in the earlier part of this century often had seats built onto window sills, large enough for small children to sit in.
25. *Irresolute:* wavering in decision or purpose.
28. *importunity:* urging.
29. *Shadow:* vague apparition.
29. *spectre:* ghost.
31. *viaticum:* the Eucharist given to a person shortly before death.
32, 33, 36. *Guiterriez, Boudin, Floret:* names used to specify imaginary but particular human beings who experience different fates.
36. *boarhound:* the great Dane, or any large dog used for hunting boars.

Gerontion

Thou hast nor youth nor age
But as it were an after dinner sleep
Dreaming of both.

Here I am, an old man in a dry month,
Being read to by a boy, waiting for rain.
I was neither at the hot gates
Nor fought in the warm rain
Nor knee deep in the salt marsh, heaving a cutlass,
Bitten by flies, fought.
My house is a decayed house,
And the jew squats on the window sill, the owner,
Spawned in some estaminet of Antwerp,
Blistered in Brussels, patched and peeled in London.
The goat coughs at night in the field overhead;
Rocks, moss, stonecrop, iron, merds.
The woman keeps the kitchen, makes tea,
Sneezes at evening, poking the peevish gutter.
I an old man,
A dull head among windy spaces.

Signs are taken for wonders. "We would see a sign!"
The word within a word, unable to speak a word,
Swaddled with darkness. In the juvescence of the year
Came Christ the tiger
In depraved May, dogwood and chestnut, flowering judas,
To be eaten, to be divided, to be drunk
Among whispers; by Mr. Silvero
With caressing hands, at Limoges
Who walked all night in the next room;

By Hakagawa, bowing among the Titians;
By Madame de Tornquist, in the dark room
Shifting the candles; Fräulein von Kulp
Who turned in the hall, one hand on the door.
Vacant shuttles
Weave the wind. I have no ghosts,

An old man in a draughty house
Under a windy knob.

After such knowledge, what forgiveness? Think now
History has many cunning passages, contrived corridors
And issues, deceives with whispering ambitions,
Guides us by vanities. Think now
She gives when our attention is distracted
And what she gives, gives with such supple confusions
That the giving famishes the craving. Gives too late
What's not believed in, or if still believed,
In memory only, reconsidered passion. Gives too soon
Into weak hands, what's thought can be dispensed with
Till the refusal propagates a fear. Think
Neither fear nor courage saves us. Unnatural vices
Are fathered by our heroism. Virtues
Are forced upon us by our impudent crimes.
These tears are shaken from the wrath-bearing tree.

The tiger springs in the new year. Us he devours.
    Think at last
We have not reached conclusion, when I
Stiffen in a rented house. Think at last
I have not made this show purposelessly
And it is not by any concitation
Of the backward devils
I would meet you upon this honestly.
I that was near your heart was removed therefrom
To lose beauty in terror, terror in inquisition.
I have lost my passion: why should I need to keep it
Since what is kept must be adulterated?
I have lost my sight, smell, hearing, taste and touch:
How should I use them for your closer contact?
These with a thousand small deliberations
Protract the profit of their chilled delirium,
Excite the membrane, when the sense has cooled,
With pungent sauces, multiply variety
In a wilderness of mirrors. What will the spider do,
Suspend its operations, will the weevil
Delay? De Bailhache, Fresca, Mrs. Cammel, whirled
Beyond the circuit of the shuddering Bear

In fractured atoms. Gull against the wind, in the windy straits
Of Belle Isle, or running on the Horn,
White feathers in the snow, the Gulf claims,
And an old man driven by the Trades
To a sleepy corner.

Tenants of the house,
Thoughts of a dry brain in a dry season.

Lexical Gloss

Title. Gerontion: Greek for "little old man."

Epigraph: this is taken from Shakespeare's *Measure for Measure,* Act III, Scene 1, lines 32–34. These lines are spoken by the Duke Vincentio, who, disguised as a priest, tries to convince Claudio that life is not worth living:

> Reason thus with life:
> If I do lose thee, I do lose a thing
> That none but fools would keep:

5. *cutlass:* curved sword.
9. *Spawned:* bred, like a fish, as part of a great brood.
9. *estaminet:* a café where smoking is allowed; the connotation is "a dive."
12. *stonecrop:* an herb with yellow flowers that grows in ruined walls, etc.
12. *merds:* dung, excrement.
17. "*We . . . sign*": a quotation from a Nativity sermon by Lancelot Andrews, English theologian (1555–1626).
17. *would:* want to.
19. *Swaddled:* wrapped tightly, as an infant.
19. *juvescence:* the state of becoming youthful.
21. *depraved:* morally corrupt because excessively sensual.
21. *flowering judas:* the elder tree, common in Europe, which bears purple flowers in the Spring before the leaves appear.
23, 26, 27, 28. *Silvero, Hakagawa, de Tornquist, von Kulp:* names used to specify imaginary but particular human beings, whose character and interests are specified in the poem.
24. *Limoges:* city in France famous for its fine porcelain.
26. *Titians:* paintings by the Italian master Tiziano Vecellio (1477–1576).
30. *shuttles:* devices used in sewing or weaving which move thread to and fro.
32. *draughty:* drafty.
33. *knob:* a small hill (on top of which the goat coughs, l. 11).
35. *contrived:* schemed, devised.
36. *issues:* exits; or matters for consideration and debate.
37. *vanities:* foolish, meaningless behavior or objects which are ridiculously overvalued.
38. *distracted:* not focused, diverted, drawn away.

39. *supple:* flexible, lithe, limber.
44. *propagates:* reproduces, continues the existence of.
53. *show:* appearance.
54. *concitation:* a stirring up.
55. *backward:* perverse or obsolete.
57. *therefrom:* from that thing.
58. *inquisition:* search for and questioning, sometimes by torture, to determine whether one is or is not a believer.
60. *adulterated:* polluted; made impure or not genuine by the addition of foreign matter.
63. *deliberations:* consideration and debate.
64. *Protract:* lengthen, extend the time of.
64. *delirium:* a temporary state of hallucinations, being "out of one's head."
65. *membrane:* thin, soft pliable sheet or layer of animal tissue functioning as a covering or a lining.
66. *pungent:* having strong, sharp taste or odor.
68. *weevil:* a beetle which feeds destructively on crops.
69. *De Bailhache, Fresca, Mrs. Cammel:* names used in the same way as those in lines 23, 26, 27, and 28, above, and lines 32, 33, and 36 of "Animula."
70. *circuit:* orbit.
70. *Bear:* Ursa Major, a constellation of 53 stars off the North Pole.
71. *straits:* narrow passage of water between two bodies of land.
72. *Belle Isle:* the straits of Belle Isle separate Newfoundland from the coast of Labrador.
72. *running* on: passing, navigating around.
72. *Horn:* Cape Horn, southernmost tip of South America.
73. *Gulf:* the Gulf Stream, a warm ocean current flowing from the Gulf of Mexico out into the Atlantic.
74. *Trades:* trade winds; winds that blow from the northeast and the southeast, across the Atlantic Ocean and toward the equator.

WYSTAN HUGH AUDEN (1907–   )

Petition

Sir, no man's enemy, forgiving all
But will its negative inversion, be prodigal:
Send to us power and light, a sovereign touch
Curing the intolerable neural itch,
The exhaustion of weaning, the liar's quinsy,
And the distortions of ingrown virginity.
Prohibit sharply the rehearsed response

And gradually correct the coward's stance;
Cover in time with beams those in retreat
That, spotted, they turn though the reverse were great;
Publish each healer that in city lives
Or country houses at the end of drives;
Harrow the house of the dead; look shining at
New styles of architecture, a change of heart.

Lexical Gloss

Title. Petition: formal request for a favor.
2. *But:* except.
2. *negative:* opposite in value of positive.
2. *inversion:* a turning upside down.
2. *prodigal:* extremely generous.
3. *sovereign:* royal. The kings of England were once believed to have the power to cure certain skin disease (called "the King's Evil") by touching the sufferer.
4. *intolerable:* not to be put up with.
4. *neural:* of the nerves.
5. *weaning:* gradually ceasing to suckle an infant.
5. *quinsy:* a tonsil inflammation.
7. *rehearsed:* recited aloud, usually in preparation for some kind of performance.
8. *stance:* physical posture.
9. *beams:* rays of light, searchlight beams.
10. *reverse:* check, defeat, misfortune.
11. *Publish:* announce or proclaim the existence of.
13. *Harrow:* break up, lacerate (the ground) for seeding.

"May with its light behaving"

May with its light behaving
Stirs vessel, eye, and limb;
The singular and sad
Are willing to recover,
And to the swan-delighting river
The careless picnics come,
The living white and red.

The dead remote and hooded
In their enclosures rest; but we
From the vague woods have broken,
Forests where children meet
And the white angel-vampires flit;
We stand with shaded eye,
The dangerous apple taken.

The real world lies before us,
Animal motions of the young,
The common wish for death,
The pleasured and the haunted;
The dying master sinks tormented
In the admirers' ring;
The unjust walk the earth.

And love that makes impatient
The tortoise and the roe, and lays
The blonde beside the dark,
Urges upon our blood,
Before the evil and the good
How insufficient is
The endearment and the look.

Lexical Gloss

1. *light:* frivolous, capricious.
1. *behaving:* behavior.
3. *singular:* unusual, queer people.
4. *recover:* recuperate from their distress.
6. *careless:* carefree.
9. *enclosures:* closed-in places.
10. *From . . . broken:* escape.
12. *vampires:* imaginary men who never die and subsist on human blood which they suck from their victims.
20. *ring:* people standing in a circle.
23. *roe:* female deer.
26. *Before:* in the presence of.
27. *insufficient:* inadequate.
28. *endearment:* expression of affection.

PART III

ONE HUNDRED POEMS BY FURTHER POETS: ARRANGED AS A HISTORICAL ANTHOLOGY OF POETIC STYLES IN THE ENGLISH LANGUAGE

SIR THOMAS WYATT (1503–1542)

The Lover Complaineth Himself Forsaken

Where shall I have at mine own will
Tears to complain? Where shall I fet
Such sighs? that I may sigh my fill:
And then again my plaints repeat.

For though my plaint shall have none end:
My tears cannot suffice my woe.
To moan my harm, have I no friend.
For fortune's friend is mishap's foe.

Comfort (God wot) else have I none:
But in the wind to waste my words,
Nought moveth you my deadly moan:
But all you turn it into bordes.

I speak not, now, to move your heart,
That you should rue upon my pain:
The sentence given may not revert:
I know, such labor were but vain.

But since that I for you (my dear)
Have lost that thing, that was my best:
A right small loss it must appear,
To lese these words and, all the rest.

But, though they sparkle in the wind:
Yet shall they show your falsed faith:
Which is returned unto his kind:
For like to like: the proverb saith.

Fortune, and you did me advance.
Me thought, I swam, and could not drown:

Happiest of all, but my mischance
  Did lift me up, to throw me down.

And you, with her, of cruelness,
  Did set your foot upon my neck,
Me and my welfare to oppress:
  Without offence, your heart to wreck,

Where are your pleasant words? alas:
  Where is your faith? your steadfastness?
There is no more: but all doth pass:
  And I am left all comfortless.

But since so much it doth you grieve,
  And also me my wretched life:
Have here my troth; Naught shall relieve,
  But death alone my weary strife.

Therefor, farewell my life, my death,
  My gain, my loss: my salve, my sore:
Farewell also, with you my breath:
  For, I am gone forevermore.

HENRY HOWARD, EARL OF SURREY
(1517?–1547)

Prisoned in Windsor, He Recounteth His Pleasure There Passed

So cruel prison how could betide, alas,
As proud Windsor? where I in lust and joy,
With a king's son, my childish years did pass,
In greater feast than Priam's sons of Troy:
Where each sweet place returns a taste full sour,
The large green courts, where we were wont to hove,
With eyes cast up into the maiden's tower.
And easy sighs, such as folk draw in love:
The stately seats, the ladies bright of hue:
The dances short, long tales of great delight:

With words and looks, that tigers could but rue,
Where each of us did plead the other's right:
The palm play, where, dispoiled for the game,
With dazed eyes oft we by gleams of love,
Have missed the ball, and got sight of our dame,
To bait her eyes, which kept the leads above:
The gravel ground, with sleeves tied on the helm:
On foaming horse, with swords and friendly hearts:
With cheer, as though one should another whelm:
Where we have fought, and chased oft with darts,
With silver drops the mead yet spread for ruth,
In active games of nimbleness, and strength,
Where we did strain, trained with swarms of youth
Our tender limbs, that yet shot up in length:
The secret groves, which oft we made resound
Of pleasant plaint, and of our ladies' praise,
Recording oft what grace each one had found,
What hope of speed, what dread of long delays:
The wild forest, the clothed holts with green:
With reins availed, and swift ybreathed horse,
With cry of hounds, and merry blasts between,
Where we did chase the fearful hart of force,
The wide vales eke, that harbor'd us each night,
Wherewith (alas) reviveth in my breast
The sweet accord: such sleeps as yet delight,
The pleasant dreams, the quiet bed of rest:
The secret thoughts imparted with such trust:
The wanton talk, the diverse change of play:
The friendship sworn, each promise kept so just:
Wherewith we passed the winter night away.
And, with this thought, the blood forsakes the face,
The tears berain my cheeks of deady hue:
The which as soon as sobbing sighs (alas)
Upsupped have, that I my plaint renew:
O place of bliss, renewer of my woes,
Give me accompt, where is my noble fere:
Whom in thy walls thou dost each night enclose,
To others lief, but unto me most dear.
Echo (alas) that doth my sorrow rue,
Returns thereto a hollow sound of plaint.
Thus I alone, where all my freedom grew,
In prison pine, with bondage and restraint,

And with remembrance of the greater grief
To banish the less, I find my chief relief.

GEORGE GASCOIGNE (1542–1577)

Gascoigne's Good Morrow

You that have spent the silent night
In sleep and quiet rest,
And joy to see the cheerful light
That riseth in the East:
Now clear your voice, now cheer your heart,
Come help me now to sing:
Each willing wight come bear a part,
To praise the heavenly King.

And you whom care in prison keeps,
Or sickness doth suppress,
Or secret sorrow breaks your sleeps,
Or dolours do distress:
Yet bear a part in doleful wise,
Yea think it good accord,
And acceptable sacrifice,
Each sprite to praise the Lord.

The dreadful night with darksome storms
Had overspread the light,
And sluggish sleep with drowsiness,
Had overpress't our might:
A glass wherein we may behold
Each storm that stops our breath,
Our bed the grave, our clothes like mold,
And sleep like dreadful death.

Yet as this deadly night did last,
But for a little space,
And heavenly day now night is passed,
Doth show his pleasant face:
So must we hope to see God's face,

At last in heaven on high,
When we have chang'd this mortal place,
For Immortality.

And of such haps and heavenly joys,
As then we hope to hold,
All earthly sights, all worldly toys,
Are tokens to behold:
The day is like the day of doom,
The sun, the Son of man,
The skies the heavens, the earth the tomb
Wherein we rest till than.

The rainbow bending in the sky,
Bedecked with sundry hues,
Is like the seat of God on high,
And seems to tell these news:
That as thereby he promised
To drown the world no more,
So by the blood which Christ hath shed,
He will our health restore.

The misty clouds that fall sometime,
And overcast the skies,
Are like to troubles of our time,
Which do but dim our eyes:
But as such dews are dried up quite,
When *Phoebus* shows his face,
So are such fancies put to flight,
Where God doth guide by grace.

The carrion Crow, that loathesome beast,
Which cries against the rain,
Both for her hue for the rest,
The Devil resembleth plain:
And as with guns we kill the Crow,
For spoiling our relief,
The Devil so must we overthrow,
With gunshot of belief.

The little Birds which sing so sweet,
Are like the angels' voice,

Which render God his praises meet,
And teach us to rejoice:
And as they more esteem that mirth,
Than dread the night's annoy,
So must we deem our days on earth,
But hell to heavenly joy.

Unto which Joys for to attain,
God grant us all his grace,
And send us after worldly pain,
In heaven to have a place.
Where we may still enjoy that light,
Which never shall decay:
Lord for thy mercy lend us might
To see that joyful day.

Haud ictus sapio.

EDMUND SPENSER (1552?–1599)

SIR PHILIP SIDNEY (1554–1586)

Song *from* Arcadia

Let mother earth now deck her self in flowers,
To see her offspring seek a good increase,
Where justest love doth vanquish *Cupid's* powers,
And war of thoughts is swallow'd up in peace,
Which never may decrease,
But like the turtles fair,
Live one in two, a well united pair;
Which that no chance may stain,
O *Hymen* long their coupled joys maintain.

O heav'n awake, show forth thy stately face,
Let not these slumb'ring clouds thy beauties hide,
But with thy cheerful presence help to grace
The honest Bridegroom, and the bashful Bride,
  Whose loves may ever bide,
  Like to the Elm and Vine,
  With mutual embracements them to twine:
  In which delightful pain,
  O *Hymen* long their coupled joys maintain.

Ye Muses all which chaste affects allow,
And have to *Thyrsis* show'd your secret skill,
To this chaste love your sacred favours bow,
And so to him and her your gifts distill,
  That they all vice may kill:
  And like to lilies pure,
  May please all eyes, and spotless may endure.
  Where that all bliss may reign,
  O *Hymen* long their coupled joys maintain.

Ye Nymphs which in the waters empire have,
Since *Thyrsis'* music oft doth yield you praise,
Grant to the thing which we for *Thyrsis* crave.
Let one time (but long first) close up their days,
  One grave their bodies seize:
  And like two rivers sweet,
  When they, though diverse, do together meet:
  One stream both streams contain:
  O *Hymen* long their coupled joys maintain.

Pan, father *Pan*, the god of silly sheep,
Whose care is cause that they in number grow,
Have much more care of them that them do keep,
Since from these good the others' good doth flow,
  And make their issue show
  In number like the herd
  Of younglings, which thy self with love hast rear'd;
  Or like the drops of rain.
  O *Hymen* long their coupled joys maintain.

Virtue (if not a God) yet God's chief part,
Be thou the knot of this their open vow,

That still he be her head, she be his heart,
He lean to her, she unto him do bow:
  Each other still allow:
  Like Oak and Mistletoe.
  Her strength from him, his praise from her do grow;
  In which most lovely train,
  O *Hymen* long their coupled joys maintain.

But thou foul *Cupid* sire to lawless lust,
Be thou far hence with thy impoison'd dart,
Which though of glitt'ring gold, shall here take rust,
Where simple love, which chasteness doth impart,
  Avoids thy hurtful art,
  Not needing charming skill,
  Such minds with sweet affections for to fill,
  Which being pure and plain,
  O *Hymen* long their coupled joys maintain.

All churlish words, shrewd answers, crabbed looks,
All privateness, self-seeking, inward spite,
All waywardness, which nothing kindly brooks,
All strife for toys, and claiming master's right:
  Be hence aye put to flight:
  All stirring husband's hate
  Gainst neighbors good for womanish debate,
  Be fled as things most vain:
  O *Hymen* long their coupled joys maintain.

All peacock pride, and fruits of peacock's pride,
Longing to be with loss of substance gay,
With retchlessness what may thy house betide,
So that you may on higher slippers stay,
  For ever hence away:
  Yet let not sluttery,
  The sink of filth, be counted houswifery:
  But keeping whole your mean,
  O *Hymen* long their coupled joys maintain.

But above all, away vile jealousy,
The evil of evils, just cause to be unjust,
(How can he love suspecting treachery?
How can she love where love cannot win trust?)

Go snake, hide thee in dust,
Ne dare once show thy face,
Where open hearts do hold so constant place,
That they thy sting restrain,
O *Hymen* long their coupled joys maintain.

The earth is deck'd with flowers, the heav'ns display'd,
Muses grant gifts, Nymphs long and joined life,
Pan store of babes, virtue their thoughts well stayed,
Cupid's lust gone, and gone is bitter strife,
Happy man, happy wife.
No pride shall them oppress,
Nor yet shall yield to loathsome sluttishness,
And jealousy is slain:
For *Hymen* will their coupled joys maintain.

SAMUEL DANIEL (1562–1619)

Epistle to Henry Wriothesley, Earl of Southampton

Non fert ullum ictum illaesa foelicitas.

He who hath never warr'd with misery,
Nor ever tugg'd with Fortune and Distress,
Hath had n'occasion nor no field to try
The strength and forces of his worthiness:
Those parts of judgement which felicity
Keeps as conceal'd, affliction must express;
And only men shew their abilities,
And what they are, in their extremities.

The world had never taken so full note
Of what thou art, hadst thou not been undone,
And only thy affliction hath begot
More fame, then thy best fortunes could have done;
For ever, by adversity are wrought
The greatest works of admiration.
And all the fair examples of renown
Out of distress and misery are grown.

Mutius the fire, the tortures *Regulus*,
Did make the miracles of Faith and Zeal;
Exile renown'd, and grac'd *Rutilius*;
Imprisonment and Poison did reveal
The worth of *Socrates*; *Fabricius*
Poverty did grace that Common-weal
More then all *Sulla's* riches got with strife;
And *Cato's* death did vie with *Caesar's* life.

Not to b'unhappy is unhappiness;
And misery not t'have known misery:
For the best way unto discretion, is
The way that leads us by adversity
And men are better show'd what is amiss,
By th'expert finger of Calamity,
Then they can be with all that Fortune brings,
Who never shows them the true face of things.

How could we know that thou could'st have endur'd
With a reposed cheer, wrong and disgrace;
And with a heart and countenance assur'd
Have look'd stern Death, and Horror in the face!
How should we know thy soul had been secur'd
In honest counsels and in ways unbase!
Hadst thou not stood to show us what thou wert,
By thy affliction, that descried thy heart.

It is not but the Tempest that doth show
The Seaman's cunning; but the field that tries
The Captain's courage: and we come to know
Best what men are, in their worst jeopardies:
For lo, how many have we seen to grow
To high renown from lowest miseries,
Out of the hands of death, and many a one
T'have been undone, had they not been undone.

He that endures for what his conscience knows
Not to be ill, doth from a patience high
Look only on the cause whereto he owes
Those sufferings, not on his misery:
The more h'endures, the more his glory grows,

Which never grows from imbecility:
Only the best compos'd and worthiest hearts,
God sets to act the hard'st and constant'st parts.

WILLIAM SHAKESPEARE (1564–1616)

THOMAS CAMPION (1567?–1619)

Song

Sleep, angry Beauty, sleep, and fear not me.
  For who a sleeping lion dares provoke?
It shall suffice me here to sit and see
  Those lips shut up that never kindly spoke.
What sight can more content a lover's mind
Than beauty seeming harmless, if not kind?

My words have charmed her, for secure she sleeps,
  Though guilty much of wrong done to my love.
And in her slumber, see, she close-eyed weeps.
  Dreams often more than waking passions move.
Plead, Sleep, my cause, and make her soft like thee,
That she in peace may wake, and pity me.

BEN JONSON (1572–1637)

JOHN DONNE (1573–1631)

RICHARD BARNFIELD (1574–1627)

From The Affectionate Shepherd

And when th'art weary of thy keeping Sheep
Upon a lovely Down, (to please thy mind,)
I'll give thee fine ruff-footed Doves to keep,
And pretty Pigeons of another kind:
  A Robin-red-breast shall thy Minstrel be,
  Chirping thee sweet, and pleasant Melody.

Or if thou wilt go shoot at little Birds
With bow and bolt (the Thrustle-cock and Sparrow)
Such as our Country hedges can afford's;
I have a fine bow, and ivory arrow;
  And if thou miss, yet meat thou shalt not lack,
  I'll hang a bag and bottle at thy back.

Wilt thou set springes in a frosty Night,
To catch the long-billed Woodcock and the Snipe?
(By the bright glimmering of the Starry light)
The Partridge, Pheasant, or the greedy Gryp?
  I'll lend thee lime-twigs, and fine sparrow calls,
  Wherewith the Fowler silly Birds enthralls.

Or in a misty morning if thou wilt
Make pit-falls for the Lark and Pheldifare;
Thy prop and sweake shall be both over-gilt;

With *Cyparissus*' self thou shalt compare
  For gins and wiles, the Ouzels to beguile;
  Whilst thou under a bush shalt sit and smile.

Or with Hare-pipes (set in a muset hole)
Wilt thou deceive the deep-earth-delving Cony?
Or wilt thou in a yellow Boxen bowl,
Taste with a wooden splint the sweet lithe honey?
  Clusters of crimson Grapes I'll pull thee down;
  And with Vine-leaves make thee a lovely Crown.

Or wilt thou drink a cup of new-made Wine
Frothing at top, mixt with a dish of Cream;
And Strawberries, or Bilberries in their prime,
Bath'd in a melting Sugar-Candy stream:
  Bunnell and Perry I have for thee (alone)
  When Vines are dead, and all the Grapes are gone.

JOHN FLETCHER (1579–1625)

From The Faithful Shepherdess

Enter Clorin, a Shepherdess, having buried her love in an Arbour

  Hail, holy earth, whose cold arms do embrace
The truest man that ever fed his flocks
By the fat plains of fruitful *Thessaly*,
Thus I salute thy grave, thus do I pay
My early vows, and tribute of mine eyes
To thy still loved ashes; thus I free
Myself from all ensuing heats and fires
Of love: all sports, delights, and jolly games
That Shepherds hold full dear, thus put I off.
Now no more shall these smooth brows be girt
With youthful coronals, and lead the dance,
No more the company of fresh fair maids
And wanton shepherds be to me delightful,
Nor the shrill pleasing sound of merry pipes
Under some shady dell, when the cool wind

Plays on the leaves; all be far away,
Since thou art far away, by whose dear side
How often have I sat crown'd with fresh flowers
For summer's queen, whilst every shepherd's boy
Puts on his lusty green, with gaudy hook,
And hanging scrip of finest cordovan.
But thou art gone, and these are gone with thee,
And all are dead but thy dear memory,
That shall outlive thee, and shall ever spring,
Whilst there are pipes, or jolly shepherds sing.
And here will I in honour of thy love,
Dwell by thy grave, forgetting all those joys,
That former times made precious to mine eyes,
Only remembering what my youth did gain
In the dark hidden virtuous use of herbs:
That will I practise, and as freely give
All my endeavours, as I gain'd them free.
Of all green wounds I know the remedies,
In men or cattle, be they stung with snakes,
Or charm'd with powerful words of wicked art,
Or be they love-sick, or through too much heat
Grown wild or lunatic, their eyes or ears
Thicken'd with misty film of dulling rheum;
These I can cure, such secret virtue lies
In herbs appliѐd by a virgin's hand:
My meat shall be what these wild woods afford,
Berries, and Chesnuts, Plantains, on whose cheeks
The Sun sits smiling, and the lofty fruit
Pull'd from the fair head of the straight-grown pine;
On these I'll feed with free content and rest,
When night shall blind the world, by thy side blest.

EDWARD HERBERT (1583–1648)

Elegy over a Tomb

Must I then see, alas! eternal night
Sitting upon those fairest eyes,
And closing all those beams, which once did rise
So radiant and bright,

That light and heat in them to us did prove
Knowledge and Love?

Oh, if you did delight no more to stay
Upon this low and earthly stage,
But rather chose an endless heritage,
Tell us at least, we pray,
Where all the beauties that those ashes ow'd
Are now bestow'd.

Doth the Sun now his light with yours renew?
Have Waves the curling of your hair?
Did you restore unto the Sky and Air
The red, and white, and blue?
Have you vouchsafed to flow'rs since your death
That sweetest breath?

Had not Heav'n's Lights else in their houses slept,
Or to some private life retir'd?
Must not the Sky and Air have else conspir'd
And in their Regions wept?
Must not each flower else the earth could breed
Have been a weed?

But thus enrich'd may we not yield some cause
Why they themselves lament no more?
That must have changed the course they held before,
And broke their proper Laws,
Had not your beauties giv'n this second birth
To Heaven and Earth?

Tell us for Oracles must still ascend,
For those that crave them at your tomb:
Tell us, where are those beauties now become,
And what they now intend:
Tell us, alas, that cannot tell our grief,
Or hope relief.

WILLIAM DRUMMOND (1585–1649)

From Urania

Triumphing, Chariots, Statues, Crowns of Bays,
Sky-threat'ning Arches, *the rewards of worth,*
Books heavenly-wise in sweet harmonious lays,
Which men divine unto the World set forth:
States which Ambitious Minds, in blood, do raise,
From frozen *Tanais* unto sun-burnt *Gange,*
Gigantal Frames held wonders rarely strange,
Like Spiders' webs are made the sport of Days.
Nothing is constant but in constant change,
What's done still is undone, and when undone
Into some other Fashion doth it range;
Thus goes the floating World beneath the Moon:
Wherefore my Mind above Time, Motion, Place,
Rise up, and steps unknown to *Nature* trace.

ROBERT HERRICK (1591–1674)

HENRY KING (1592–1669)

Silence: A Sonnet

Peace my heart's blab, be ever dumb,
Sorrows speak loud without a tongue:
And my perplexed thoughts forbear
To breathe yourselves in any ear:

'Tis scarce a true or manly grief
Which gads abroad to find relief.

Was ever stomach that lacked meat
Nourished by what another eat?
Can I bestow it, or will woe
Forsake me when I bid it go?
Then I'll believe a wounded breast
May heal by shrift, and purchase rest.

But if imparting it I do
Not ease my self, but trouble two,
'Tis better I alone possess
My treasure of unhappiness:
Engrossing that which is my own
No longer then it is unknown.

If silence be a kind of death,
He kindles grief who gives it breath;
But let it raked in embers lie,
On thine own hearth 'twill quickly die;
And spite of fate, that very womb
Which carries it, shall prove its tomb.

GEORGE HERBERT *(1593–1633)*

THOMAS CAREW *(1594/95–1639)*

A Song

Ask me no more where *Jove* bestows,
When *June* is past, the fading rose:

For in your beauty's orient deep,
These flowers as in their causes, sleep.

Ask me no more whither doth stray,
The golden Atoms of the day:
For in pure love heaven did prepare,
Those powders to enrich your hair.

Ask me no more whither doth haste,
The Nightingale when May is past:
For in your sweet dividing throat,
She winters and keeps warm her note.

Ask me no more where those stars light,
That downwards fall in dead of night:
For in your eyes they sit, and there,
Fixed become as in their sphere.

Ask me no more if East or West,
The Phoenix builds her spicy nest:
For unto you at last she flies,
And in your fragrant bosom dies.

EDMUND WALLER (1606–1687)

From The Battle of the Summer Islands

Bermudas wall'd with rocks, who does not know
That happy Island where huge Lemons grow,
And Orange Trees which golden fruit do bear,
Th' Hesperian garden boasts of none so fair?
Where shining Pearl, Coral, and many a pound
On the rich shore, of Ambergris is found:
The lofty Cedar which to Heaven aspires,
The Prince of Trees, is fuel for their fires:
The smoke by which their loaded spits do turn,
For incense might, on sacred Altars burn;
Their private roofs on od'rous timber borne,
Such as might Palaces for Kings adorn:

The sweet *Palmettos* a new *Bacchus* yield
With leaves as ample as the broadest shield:
Under the shadow of whose friendly boughs
They sit carousing, where their liquor grows:
Figs there unplanted through the fields do grow,
Such as fierce *Cato* did the Romans show,
With the rare fruit inviting them to spoil
Carthage the mistress of so rich a soil:
The naked rocks are not unfruitful there,
But, at some constant seasons every year,
Their barren tops with luscious food abound,
And with the eggs of various fowls are crown'd:
Tobacco is the worst of things which they
To English Landlords as their tribute pay:
Such is the mould, that the blest Tenant feeds
On precious fruits, and pays his rent in weeds:
With candied Plantains, and the juicy Pine,
On choicest Melons and sweet Grapes they dine,
And with Potatoes fat their wanton Swine.
Nature these Cates with such a lavish hand
Pours out among them, that our coarse Land
Tastes of that bounty, and does Cloth return,
Which not for Warmth, but Ornament is worn;
For the kind Spring which but salutes us here
Inhabits there, and courts them all the year:
Ripe fruits and blossoms on the same Trees live,
At once they promise what at once they give:
So sweet the air, so moderate the clime,
None sickly lives, or dies before his time.
Heaven sure has kept this spot of earth uncurst
To show how all things were created first.
The tardy plants in our cold Orchards plac'd,
Reserve their fruit, for the next age's taste:
There a small grain in some few months will be
A firm, a lofty, and a spacious Tree.
The *Palma Christi*, and the fair Papà,
Now but a seed (preventing Nature's law)
In half the circle of the hasty year
Project a shade, and lovely fruits do wear.

JOHN MILTON (1608–1674)

SIR JOHN SUCKLING (1609–1642)

Song

1

'Tis now, since I sat down before
  That foolish Fort, a heart;
(Time strangely spent) a year and more,
  And still I did my part:

2

Made my approaches, from her hand
  Unto her lip did rise,
And did already understand
  The language of her eyes.

3

Proceeded on with no less Art,
  My Tongue was Engineer;
I thought to undermine the heart
  By whispering in the ear.

4

When this did nothing, I brought down
  Great Cannon-oaths, and shot
A thousand thousand to the Town,
  And still it yielded not.

5

I then resolv'd to starve the place
  By cutting off all kisses,

Praising and gazing on her face
  And all such little blisses.

6

To draw her out, and from her strength,
  I drew all batteries in:
And brought myself to lie at length
  As if no siege had been.

7

When I had done what man could do,
  And thought the place mine own,
The Enemy lay quiet too,
  And smil'd at all was done.

8

I sent to know from whence and where,
  These hopes, and this relief?
A Spy inform'd, Honour was there,
  And did command in chief.

9

March, march (quoth I) the word straight give,
  Let's lose no time but leave her;
That Giant upon air will live,
  And hold it out for ever.

10

To such a place our Camp remove
  As will no siege abide;
I hate a fool that starves her Love
  Only to feed her pride.

RICHARD CRASHAW (1612/13–1649)

A Letter from Mr. Crashaw to the Countess of Denbigh, Against Irresolution and Delay in Matters of Religion

What Heav'n-besieged Heart is this
Stands Trembling at the Gate of Bliss:
Holds fast the Door, yet dares not venture
Fairly to open and to enter?
Whose Definition is, A Doubt
'Twixt Life and Death, 'twixt In and Out.
Ah! linger not, lov'd Soul: A slow
And late Consent was a long No.
Who grants at last, a great while tri'd,
And did his best to have Deni'd.
What Magic-Bolts, what mystic Bars
Maintain the Will in these strange Wars?
What Fatal, yet fantastic, Bands
Keep the free Heart from his own Hands?
Say, ling'ring Fair, why comes the Birth
Of your brave Soul so slowly forth?
Plead your Pretences, (O you strong
In weakness) why you choose so long
In Labour of your self to lie,
Not daring quite to Live nor Die.
So when the Year takes cold we see
Poor Waters their own Prisoners be:
Fetter'd and lock'd up fast they lie
In a cold self-captivity.
Th'astonish'd Nymphs their Flood's strange Fate deplore,
To find themselves their own severer Shore.
Love, that lends haste to heaviest things,
In you alone hath lost his wings.
Look round and read the World's wide face,
The field of Nature or of Grace;
Where can you fix, to find Excuse
Or Pattern for the Pace you use?

Mark with what Faith Fruits answer Flowers,
And know the Call of Heav'n's kind showers:
Each mindful Plant hastes to make good
The hope and promise of his Bud.
Seed-time's not all; there should be Harvest too.
Alas! and has the Year no Spring for you?
Both Winds and Waters urge their way,
And murmur if they meet a stay.
Mark how the curl'd Waves work and wind,
All hating to be left behind.
Each big with business thrusts the other,
And seems to say, Make haste, my Brother.
The airy nation of neat Doves,
That draw the Chariot of chaste Loves,
Chide your delay: yea those dull things,
Whose ways have least to do with wings,
Make wings at least of their own Weight,
And by their Love control their Fate.
So lumpish Steel, untaught to move,
Learn'd first his Lightness by his Love.
What e're Love's matter be, he moves
By th'even wings of his own Doves,
Lives by his own Laws, and does hold
In grossest Metals his own Gold.
All things swear friends to Fair and Good,
Yea Suitors; Man alone is woo'd,
Tediously woo'd, and hardly won:
Only not slow to be undone.
As if the Bargain had been driven
So hardly betwixt Earth and Heaven;
Our God would thrive too fast, and be
Too much a gainer by't, should we
Our purchas'd selves too soon bestow
On him, who has not lov'd us so.
When love of Us call'd Him to see
If we'd vouchsafe his company,
He left his Father's Court, and came
Lightly as a Lambent Flame,
Leaping upon the Hills, to be
The Humble King of You and Me.
Nor can the cares of his whole Crown
(When one poor Sigh sends for him down)

Detain him, but he leaves behind
The late wings of the lazy Wind,
Spurns the tame Laws of Time and Place,
And breaks through all ten Heav'ns to our embrace.
Yield to his Siege, wise Soul, and see
Your Triumph in his Victory.
Disband dull Fears, give Faith the day:
To save your Life, kill your Delay.
'Tis Cowardice that keeps this Field;
And want of Courage not to Yield.
Yield then, O yield, that Love may win
The Fort at last, and let Life in.
Yield quickly, lest perhaps you prove
Death's Prey, before the Prize of Love.
This Fort of your Fair Self if't be not won,
He is repuls'd indeed, but You're undone.

RICHARD LOVELACE (1618–1687)

The Grasshopper

To my Noble Friend,
Mr. Charles Cotton
Ode

I

Oh thou that swing'st upon the waving hair
Of some well-filled Oaten Beard,
Drunk ev'ry night with a Delicious tear
Dropt thee from Heav'n, where now th' art rear'd.

II

The Joys of Earth and Air are thine entire,
That with thy feet and wings dost hop and fly;
And when thy Poppy works thou dost retire
To thy Carv'd Acorn-bed to lie.

III

Up with the Day, the Sun thou welcom'st then,
Sport'st in the gilt-plates of his Beams,

And all these merry days mak'st merry men,
Thy self, and Melancholy streams.

IV

But ah the Sickle! Golden Ears are Cropt;
Ceres and *Bacchus* bid good night;
Sharp frosty fingers all your Flow'rs have topt
And what scythes spar'd, Winds shave off quite.

V

Poor verdant fool! and now green Ice, thy Joys
Large and as lasting, as thy Perch of Grass,
Bid us lay in 'gainst Winter, Rain, and poise
Their floods, with an o'erflowing glass.

VI

Thou best of *Men* and *Friends!* we will create
A Genuine Summer in each other's breast;
And spite of this cold Time and frozen Fate
Thaw us a warm seat to our rest.

VII

Our sacred hearths shall burn eternally
As Vestal Flames, the North-wind he
Shall strike his frost-stretch'd Wings, dissolve and fly
This *Aetna* in Epitome.

VIII

Dropping *December* shall come weeping in,
Bewail th' usurping of his Reign;
But when in show'rs of old Greek we begin,
Shall cry, he hath his Crown again!

IX

Night as clear *Hesper* shall our Tapers whip
From the light Casements where we play,
And the dark Hag from her black mantle strip,
And stick there everlasting Day.

X

Thus richer than untempted Kings are we,
That asking nothing, nothing need:

Though Lord of all what Seas embrace; yet he
  That wants himself, is poor indeed.

ANDREW MARVELL (1621–1678)

The Garden

I

How vainly men themselves amaze
To win the Palm, the Oak, or Bays;
And their uncessant Labours see
Crown'd from some single Herb or Tree,
Whose short and narrow verged Shade
Does prudently their Toils upbraid;
While all Flow'rs and all Trees do close
To weave the Garlands of repose.

II

Fair quiet, have I found thee here,
And Innocence thy Sister dear!
Mistaken long, I sought you then
In busy Companies of Men.
Your sacred Plants, if here below,
Only among the Plants will grow.
Society is all but rude,
To this delicious Solitude.

III

No white nor red was ever seen
So am'rous as this lovely green.
Fond Lovers, cruel as their Flame,
Cut in these Trees their Mistress' name.
Little, Alas, they know, or heed,
How far these Beauties Hers exceed!
Fair Trees! wheres'er your barks I wound,
No Name shall but your own be found.

IV

When we have run our Passions' heat,
Love hither makes his best retreat.

The *Gods*, that mortal Beauty chase,
Still in a Tree did end their race.
Apollo hunted *Daphne* so,
Only that She might Laurel grow.
And *Pan* did after *Syrinx* speed,
Not as a Nymph, but for a Reed.

V

What wond'rous Life in this I lead!
Ripe Apples drop about my head;
The Luscious Clusters of the Vine
Upon my Mouth do crush their Wine;
The Nectarine, and curious Peach,
Into my hands themselves do reach;
Stumbling on Melons, as I pass,
Ensnar'd with Flow'rs, I fall on Grass.

VI

Meanwhile the Mind, from pleasure less,
Withdraws into its happiness:
The Mind, that Ocean where each kind
Does straight its own resemblance find;
Yet it creates, transcending these,
Far other Worlds, and other Seas;
Annihilating all that 's made
To a green Thought in a green Shade.

VII

Here at the Fountain's sliding foot,
Or at some Fruit-tree's mossy root,
Casting the Body's Vest aside,
My Soul into the boughs does glide:
There like a Bird it sits, and sings,
Then whets, and combs its silver Wings;
And, till prepar'd for longer flight,
Waves in its Plumes the various Light.

VIII

Such was that happy Garden-state,
While Man there walk'd without a Mate:
After a Place so pure, and sweet,
What other Help could yet be meet!
But 'twas beyond a Mortal's share

To wander solitary there:
Two Paradises 'twere in one
To live in Paradise alone.

IX

How well the skilful Gard'ner drew
Of flow'rs and herbs this Dial new;
Where from above the milder Sun
Does through a fragrant Zodiac run;
And, as it works, th' industrious Bee
Computes its time as well as we.
How could such sweet and wholesome Hours
Be reckon'd but with herbs and flow'rs!

HENRY VAUGHAN (1621/22–1695)

Corruption

Sure, It was so. Man in those early days
Was not all stone, and Earth,
He shin'd a little, and by those weak Rays
Had some glimpse of his birth.
He saw Heaven o'er his head, and knew from whence
He came (condemned,) hither,
And, as first Love draws strongest, so from hence
His mind sure progress'd thither.
Things here were strange unto him: Sweet, and till
All was a thorn, or weed,
Nor did those last, but (like himself,) died still
As soon as they did *Seed,*
They seem'd to quarrel with him; for that Act
That fell him, soil'd them all,
He drew the Curse upon the world, and Crack'd
The whole frame with his fall.
This made him long for *home,* as loath to stay
With murmurers, and foes;
He sigh'd for *Eden,* and would often say
Ah! what bright days were those?
Nor was Heav'n cold unto him; for each day

The valley, or the Mountain
Afforded visits, and still *Paradise* lay
In some green shade, or fountain.
Angels lay *Lieger* here; Each Bush, and Cell,
Each Oak, and highway knew them,
Walk but the fields, or sit down at some *well*,
And he was sure to view them.
Almighty *Love!* where art thou now? mad man
Sits down, and freezeth on,
He raves, and swears to stir nor fire, nor fan,
But bids the thread be spun.
I see, thy Curtains are Close-drawn; Thy bow
Looks dim too in the Cloud,
Sin triumphs still, and man is sunk below
The Center, and his shrowd;
All's in deep sleep, and night; Thick darkness lies
And hatcheth o'er thy people;
But hark! what trumpet's that? what Angel cries
Arise! Thrust in thy sickle.

JOHN DRYDEN (1631–1700)

THOMAS TRAHERNE (1637?–1674)

The Vision

1

Flight is but the Preparative: The Sight
Is Deep and Infinite;
Ah me! 'tis all the Glory, Love, Light, Space,
Joy Beauty and Variety
That doth adorn the Godhead's Dwelling Place
'Tis all that Eye can see.

Even Trades themselves seen in Celestial Light,
And Cares and Sins and Woes are Bright.

2

Order the Beauty even of Beauty is,
It is the Rule of Bliss,
The very Life and Form and Cause of Pleasure;
Which if we do not understand,
Ten thousand Heaps of vain confused Treasure
Will but oppress the Land.
In Blessedness itself we that shall miss
Being Blind which is the Cause of Bliss.

3

For then behold the World as thine, and well
Upon the Object Dwell.
See all the Beauty of the Spacious Case,
Lift up thy pleas'd and ravish'd Eyes,
Admire the Glory of the Heav'nly place,
And all its Blessings prize.
That Sight well seen thy Spirit shall prepare,
The first makes all the other Rare.

4

Men's Woes shall be but foils unto thy Bliss,
Thou once Enjoying this:
Trades shall adorn and Beautify the Earth,
Their Ignorance shall make thee Bright,
Were not their Griefs Democritus his Mirth?
Their Faults shall keep thee right.
All shall be thine, because they all Conspire,
To feed and make thy Glory higher.

5

To see a Glorious Fountain and an End
To see all Creatures tend
To thy Advancement, and so sweetly close
In thy Repose: To see them shine
In Use in Worth in Service, and even Foes
Among the rest made thine.
To see all these unite at once in Thee
Is to behold Felicity.

6

To see the *Fountain* is a Blessed Thing.
It is to see the King
Of Glory face to face: But yet the End,
The Glorious Wondrous End is more;
And yet the fountain there we Comprehend,
The Spring we there adore.
For in the End the Fountain best is Shown,
As by Effects the Cause is Known.

7

From One, to One, in one to see *All Things*
To see the King of Kings
At once in two; to see his Endless Treasures
Made all mine own, my self the End
Of all his Labors! 'Tis the Life of Pleasures!
To see my self His friend!
Who all things finds conjoin'd in Him alone,
Sees and Enjoys the Holy one.

SIR CHARLES SEDLEY (1639?–1701)

A Dialogue Between Amintas and Celia

Celia: Amintas, I am come alone,
A silly harmless Maid,
But whither is thy Honour flown?
I fear I am betray'd;
Thy Looks are chang'd and in the Place
Of innocent Desires,
Methinks I see thy Eyes and Face
Glow with unusual Fires.

Amintas: Sees not my *Celia*, Nature wear
One Countenance in the Spring,
And yet another Shape prepare,
To bring the Harvest in?
Look on the Eagle, how unlike
He to the Egg is found,

When he prepares his Pounce to strike
His Prey against the Ground;
Fears might my Infant-love become,
'Twere want of Vigor now
Should Modesty those Hopes benumb,
The Place and You allow.

Celia: Amintas, hold; What could you worse
To worst of Women do?
Ah! how could you a Passion nurse,
So much my Honour's Foe?

Amintas: Make not an Idol of a Toy,
Which every Breath can shake,
Which all must have, or none enjoy,
What Course soe'er we take.
Whilst Women hate, or Men are vain,
You cannot be secure;
What makes my *Celia* then a Pain
So needless to endure?

Celia: Could I the World neglect for thee,
Thy Love, though dear it cost,
In some unkind Conceit of me,
Would be untimely lost:
Thou would'st thy own Example fear,
And every heedless Word,
I chance let fall beyond thy Ear
Would some new Doubt afford.

Amintas: If I am jealous, 'tis because
I know not where you love;
With me obey Love's gentle Laws
And all my Fears remove.

Celia: Women, like Things at Second-hand
Do half their Value lose,
But whil'st all Courtship they withstand,
May at their Pleasure choose.

Amintas: This were a fine Discourse, my Dear,
If we were not alone;

But now Love whispers in my Ear,
  There's somewhat to be done.

She said she never would forgive;
  He kissing, swore she should;
And told her, she was mad to strive
  Against their mutual Good.
What farther pass'd, I cannot tell
  But sure not much amiss;
He vow'd he lov'd her dearly well,
  She answered with a Kiss.

JOHN WILMOT, EARL OF ROCHESTER
(1648–1680)

The Maim'd Debauchee

1

As some brave *Admiral*, in former War
  Depriv'd of Force, but prest with Courage still,
Two Rival Fleets appearing from afar,
  Crawls to the top of an adjacent Hill;

2

From whence (with thoughts full of concern) he views
  The wise, and daring, Conduct of the Fight:
And each bold Action to his Mind renews,
  His present Glory, and his past Delight.

3

From his fierce Eyes Flashes of Rage he throws,
  As from black Clouds when Lightning breaks away,
Transported thinks himself amidst his Foes,
  And absent yet enjoys the bloody Day.

4

So when my Days of Impotence approach,
  And I'm by Love and Wine's unlucky chance,
Driv'n from the pleasing Billows of Debauch,
  On the dull Shore of lazy Temperance

5

My Pains at last some respite shall afford,
  While I behold the Battles you maintain:
When Fleets of Glasses sail around the Board,
  From whose Broad-sides Volleys of Wit shall rain.

6

Nor shall the sight of honourable Scars,
  Which my too forward Valour did procure,
Frighten new-listed Soldiers from the Wars,
  Past Joys have more than paid what I endure.

7

Should some brave Youth (worth being drunk) prove nice,
  And from his fair Inviter meanly shrink,
'Twould please the Ghost of my departed Vice,
  If, at my Counsel, he repent and drink.

8

Or should some cold-complexion'd Sot forbid,
  With his dull Morals, our Night's brisk Alarms;
I'll fire his Blood by telling what I did,
  When I was strong, and able to bear Arms.

9

I'll tell of Whores attack'd their Lords at home,
  Bawds' Quarters beaten up, and Fortress won;
Windows demolish'd, Watches overcome,
  And handsome Ills by my Contrivance done.

10

With Tales like these I will such Heat inspire,
  As to important Mischief shall incline;
I'll make him long some ancient Church to fire,
  And fear no Lewdness they're call'd to by Wine.

11

Thus Statesman-like I'll saucily impose,
  And, safe from danger, valiantly advise;
Shelter'd in Impotence urge you to Blows,
  And, being good for nothing else, be wise.

JOHN SHEFFIELD, DUKE OF BUCKINGHAM AND NORMANBY (1648–1721)

Stanzas

Whene'er my foolish Bent to Public Good,
  Or fonder Zeal for some misguided Prince,
Shall make my dang'rous Humour understood,
  For changing Ministers for Men of Sense:

When vainly proud to show my public Care,
  And ev'n asham'd to see three Nations fool'd,
I shall no longer bear a wretched Share
  In ruling ill, or being over-rul'd:

Then, as old Lechers in a Winter's Night
  To yawning Hearers all their Pranks disclose;
And what Decay deprives them of Delight,
  Supply with vain Endeavours to impose.

Just so shall I as idly entertain
  Some stripling Patriots, fond of seeming wise;
Tell, how I still could great Employments gain,
  Without concealing Truths, or whisp'ring Lies;

Boast of succeeding in my Country's Cause
  Ev'n against some almost too high to blame;
Whom, when advanc'd beyond the Reach of Laws,
  I oft have ridicul'd to Sense and Shame:

Say, I resisted the most potent Fraud;
  But friendless Merit openly approv'd;
And that I was above the being aw'd
  Not only by my Prince, but those he lov'd:

Who knows but my Example then may please
  Such noble, hopeful Spirits as appear

Willing to slight their Pleasures, and their Ease,
For Fame and Honour? Till at last they hear,

After much Trouble borne, and Danger run,
The Crown assisted, and my Country serv'd;
Without good Fortune I had been undone,
Without a good Estate I might have starv'd.

JOHN OLDHAM (1653–1683)

From A Satire Addressed to a Friend, That is About to Leave the University, and Come Abroad in the World

If you're so out of Love with Happiness
To quit a College-Life, and learned Ease;
Convince me first, and some good Reasons give
What Methods, and Designs, you'll take to live:
For such Resolves are needful in the Case,
Before you tread the World's mysterious Maze:
Without the Premises, in vain you'll try
To live by Systems of Philosophy:
Your *Aristotle, 'Cartes,* and *Le Grand,*
And *Euclid* too, in little stead will stand.
How many Men of choice, and noted Parts,
Well fraught with Learning, Languages, and Arts,
Designing high Preferment, in their Mind,
And little doubting good Success to find,
With vast, and tow'ring Thoughts, have flock'd to Town,
But, to their Cost, soon found themselves undone,
Now to repent, and starve at Leisure, left,
Of Misery's last Comfort, Hope, bereft?
These fail'd for Want of good Advice, you cry,
Because, at first, they fix'd on no Employ:
Well then, let's draw the Prospect, end the Scene
To all Advantage possibly we can:
The World lies not before you, let me hear,
What Course your Judgment counsels you to steer:
Always consider, that your whole Estate,

And all your Fortune, lies beneath your Hat:
Were you the Son of some rich Usurer,
That starv'd, and damn'd himself to make his Heir,
Left nought to do, but to inter the Sot,
And spend, with Ease, what he, with Pains, had got;
'Twere easy to advise how you might live,
Nor would there need Instruction then to give:
But you, that boast of no Inheritance,
Save that small Stock, which lies within your Brains,
Learning must be your Trade, and therefore weigh,
With Heed, how you your Game the best may play;
Bethink yourself a while, and then propose
What Way of Life is fitt'st for you to choose,

If you for Orders, and a Gown design,
Consider only this, dear Friend of mine,
The Church is grown so overstock'd of late,
That if you walk abroad, you'll hardly meet
More Porters now, than Parsons, in the Street.
At ev'ry Corner they are forc'd to ply
For Jobs of hawkering Divinity:
And halt the Number of the Sacred Herd
Are fain to stroll, and wander unpreferr'd:

If this, or Thoughts of such a weighty Charge
Make you resolve to keep yourself at large:
For Want of better Opportunity,
A School must your next Sanctuary be:
Go, wed some Grammar-Bridewell, and a Wife
And there beat *Greek*, and *Latin*, for your Life:
With Birchen Scepter, there command at Will,
Greater than *Buby*'s self, or Doctor *Gill:*
But who would be to the vile Drudg'ry bound
Where there so small Encouragement is found?
Where you, for Recompense of all your Pains,
Shall hardly reach a common Fidler's Gains?
For when you've toil'd, and labour'd all you can,
To dung, and cultivate a barren Brain:
A Dancing-Master shall be better paid,
Tho' he instructs the Heels, and you the Head:
To such Indulgence, are kind Parents grown,
That nought costs less in breeding, than a Son:
Nor is it hard to find a Father now,
Shall more, upon a Setting-Dog, allow:

And, with a freer Hand, reward the Care
Of training up his Spaniel, than his Heir.
  Some think themselves exalted to the Sky.
If they light in some noble Family:
Diet, an Horse, and thirty Pounds a Year,
Besides th'Advantage of his Lordship's Ear,
The Credit of the Business, and the State,
Are Things, that, in a Youngster's Sense, found Great.
Little the unexperienc'd Wretch does know,
What Slavery he oft must undergo:
Who tho' in silken Scarf, and Cassock drest,
Wears but a gayer Livery at best;
When Dinner calls, the Implement must wait,
With Holy-Words, to consecrate the Meat:
But hold it for a Favour seldom known,
If he be deign'd the Honour, to sit down.
Soon as the Tarts appear, Sir *Crape*, withdraw!
Those Dainties are not for a Spiritual Maw:
Observe your Distance, and be sure to stand
Hard by the Cistern, with your Cap in Hand:
There, for Diversion, you may pick your Teeth,
Till the kind Voider, comes for your Relief:
For mere Board-wages, such their Freedom sell,
Slaves to an Hour, and Vassals to a Bell:
And if th'Enjoyment of one Day be stole,
They are but Pris'ners, out upon Parole:
Always the Marks of Slavery remain,
And they, tho' loose, still drag about their Chain.
  And where's the mighty Prospect, after all,
A Chaplainship serv'd up, and seven Years Thrall?
The menial Thing, perhaps, for a Reward
Is to some slender Benefice preferr'd,
With this Proviso bound, that he must wed
My Lady's Antiquated-Waiting-Maid,
In Dressing only skill'd and Marmalade.
  Let others, who such Meannesses can brook,
Strike Countenance to ev'ry Great Man's Look:
Let those that have a Mind, turn Slaves to eat
And live contented by another's Plate:
I rate my Freedom higher, nor will I
For Food, and Raiment, truck my Liberty.
But, if I must to my last Shifts be put,

To fill a Bladder, and twelve Yards of Gut;
Rather, with counterfeited wooden Leg;
And my right Arm ti'd up, I'll choose to beg:
I'll rather choose to starve at large, than be
The gawdiest Vassal to Dependency.

THOMAS D'URFEY (1653–1723)

The Fisherman's Song

From *Massaniello*

Of all the World's Enjoyments,
  That ever valu'd were;
There's none of our Employments,
  With Fishing can Compare:
    Some Preach, some Write,
    Some Swear, some Fight,
All Golden Lucre courting,
  But Fishing still bears off the Bell;
For Profit or for Sporting.
  Then who a Jolly Fisherman, a Fisherman will be?
    His Throat must wet,
    Just like his Net,
  To keep out Cold at Sea.

The Country Squire loves Running,
  A Pack of well-mouth'd Hounds;
Another fancies Gunning
  For Wild Ducks in his Grounds:
    This Hunts, that Fowls,
    This Hawks, *Dick* Bowls,
No greater Pleasure wishing,
  But *Tom* that tells what Sport excells,
Gives all the Praise to Fishing,
  Then who, &c.

A good *Westphalia Gammon,*
  Is counted dainty Fare;

But what is't to a *Salmon*,
  Just taken from the Ware:
    Wheat Ears and *Quails*,
    Cocks, Snipes, and *Rails*;
Are priz'd while Season's lasting,
  But all must stoop to Crawfish Soup,
Or I've no skill in tasting.
  Then who, &c.

Keen Hunters always take too
  Their prey with too much pains;
Nay often break a Neck too,
  A Penance for no Brains:
    They Run, they Leap,
    Now high, now deep,
Whilst he that Fishing chooses;
  With ease may do't, nay more to boot,
May entertain the Muses.
  Then who, &c.

And tho' some envious wranglers,
  To jeer us will make bold;
And Laugh at Patient Anglers,
  Who stand so long i' th' Cold:
    They wait on Miss,
    We wait on this,
And think it easier Labour;
  And if you'd know, Fish profits too,
Consult our *Holland* Neighbour.
  Then who, &c.

MATTHEW PRIOR (1664–1721)

From Alma, or the Progress of the Mind

I say, whatever You maintain
Of ALMA in the Heart, or Brain;
The plainest Man alive may tell Ye,
Her Seat of Empire is the Belly:

From hence She sends out those Supplies,
Which make Us either stout or wise:
The Strength of ev'ry other Member,
Is founded on your Belly-Timber:
The Qualms or Raptures of your Blood
Rise in Proportion to your Food:
And if you would improve your Thought;
You must be fed, as well as taught.
Your Stomach makes your Fabric roll;
Just as the Bias rules the Bowl.
That great ACHILLES might employ
The Strength, design'd to ruin TROY;
He Din'd on Lion's Marrow, spread
On Toasts of Ammunition-Bread:
But by His Mother sent away,
Amongst the THRACIAN Girls to play,
Effeminate He sat, and quiet:
Strange Product of a Cheese-cake Diet!
Now give my Argument fair Play;
And take the Thing the t'other Way:
The Youngster, who at Nine and Three
Drinks with his Sisters Milk and Tea,
From Breakfast reads, 'till twelve o'Clock,
BURNET and HEYLYN, HOBBES and LOCKE:
He pays due Visits after Noon
To Cousin ALICE, and Uncle JOHN:
At Ten from Coffee-House or Play
Returning, finishes the Day.
But give him Port, and potent Sack;
From *Milk-sop* He starts up *Mohack:*
Holds that the Happy know no Hours;
So thro' the Street at Midnight scours:
Breaks Watchmen's Heads, and Chairmen's Glasses;
And thence proceeds to nicking Sashes:
Till by some tougher Hand o'ercome,
And first knock'd down, and then led Home;
He damns the Footman, strikes the Maid,
And decently reels up to bed.

Observe the various Operations
Of Food, and Drink in several Nations.
Was ever TARTAR fierce or cruel,

Upon the Strength of Water-Gruel?
But who shall stand His Rage and Force;
If first he rides, then eats his Horse?
Salads, and Eggs, and lighter Fare
Tune the ITALIAN Spark's Guitar.
And, if I take *Dan* CONGREVE right;
Pudding and Beef make BRITONS fight.
TOKAY and COFFEE cause this Work,
Between the GERMAN and the TURK:
And Both, as They Provisions want,
Chicane, avoid, retire, and faint.

Hunger and Thirst, or Guns and Swords,
Give the same Death in diff'rent Words.
To push this Argument no further;
To starve a Man, in Law, is Murther.

As in a WATCH's fine Machine,
Tho' many artful Springs are seen;
The added Movements, which declare,
How full the Moon, how old the Year,
Derive their secondary Pow'r
From that, which simply points the Hour.
For, tho' these Gim-cracks were away;
(QUARE would not swear; but QUARE would say)
However more reduc'd and plain,
The Watch would still a Watch remain:
But if the *Horal* Orbit ceases;
The whole stands still, or breaks to pieces;
Is now no longer what it was;
And You may e'en go sell the Case:
So if unprejudic'd you scan
The Goings of this Clock-work, Man;
You find a hundred Movements made
By fine Devices in his Head:
But 'tis the Stomach's solid Stroke,
That tells his Being, what's o'Clock.
If You take off his *Rhet'ric*-Trigger;
He talks no more in Mode and Figure:
Or clog his *Mathematic*-Wheel;
His Buildings fall; his Ship stands still.
Or lastly, break his *Politic*-Weight;

His Voice no longer rules the State.
Yet if these finer Whims were gone;
Your Clock, tho' plain, would still go on:
But spoil the Engine of Digestion;
And you entirely change the Question.
ALMA's Affairs no Pow'r can mend;
The Jest, alas! is at an End:
Soon ceases all this worldly Bustle;
And you consign the Corpse to RUSSEL.

JONATHAN SWIFT (1667–1742)

Phyllis: Or, The Progress of Love

Desponding *Phyllis* was endu'd
With ev'ry Talent of a Prude:
She trembled when a Man drew near;
Salute her, and she turn'd her Ear:
If o'er against her you were plac'd,
She durst not look above your Waist:
She'd rather take you to her Bed,
Than let you see her dress her Head:
In Church you heard her, through the Crowd,
Repeat the *Absolution* loud;
In Church, secure behind her Fan,
She durst behold that Monster, *Man:*
There practic'd how to place her Head,
And bit her Lips, to make them red;
Or, on the Mat devoutly kneeling,
Would lift her Eyes up to the Ceiling,
And heave her Bosom, unaware,
For neighb'ring Beaux to see it bare.
At length, a lucky Lover came,
And found Admittance to the Dame.
Suppose all Parties now agreed,
The Writings drawn, the Lawyer fee'd
The Vicar and the Ring bespoke:
Guess, how could such a Match be broke?
See then, what Mortals place their Bliss in!

Next Morn, betimes, the Bride was missing.
The Mother scream'd, the Father chid,
Where can this idle Wench be hid?
No news of *Phyl!* The Bridegroom came,
And thought his Bride had skulk'd for shame;
Because her Father us'd to say,
The Girl *had such a bashful way.*
Now, *John*, the Butler, must be sent,
To learn the Road that *Phyllis* went.
The Groom was *wish'd* to saddle *Crop*,
For, *John* must neither light, nor stop,
But find her whereso'er she fled,
And bring her back, alive or dead.
See here again, the Dev'l to do!
For, truly, *John* was missing too.
The Horse and Pillion both were gone!
Phyllis, it seems, was fled with *John.*
Old Madam, who went up to find
What Papers *Phyl* had left behind,
A Letter on the Toilet sees,
To my much honour'd Father. These—
('Tis always done, Romances tell us,
When Daughters run away with Fellows)
Fill'd with the choicest Commonplaces,
By others us'd in the like Cases;
"That, long ago a *Fortune-teller*
Exactly said what now befell her;
And in a *Glass* had made her see
A *serving-Man of low Degree.*
It was her *Fate*, must be forgiven,
For *Marriages were made in Heaven:*
His Pardon begg'd but, to be plain,
She'd *do't* if *'twere to do again.*
Thank God, 'twas *neither Shame, nor Sin;*
For *John* was come of *honest Kin.*
Love never thinks of Rich and Poor,
She'd beg with John *from Door to Door.*
Forgive her, if it be a Crime,
She'll never do't *another Time.*
She ne'r before in all her Life
Once disobey'd him, *Maid nor Wife.*
One Argument she summ'd up all in,
The Thing was done, and past recalling;

And therefore hop'd she should recover
His Favour, when his *Passion's over!*
She valued not what others thought her,
And was—his *most obedient Daughter*."
  Fair Maidens all, attend the Muse,
Who now the wand'ring Pair pursues.
Away they rode in homely Sort,
Their Journey long, their Money short;
The loving Couple well bemir'd
The Horse and both the Riders tir'd:
Their Victuals bad, their Lodging worse;
Phyl cried, and *John* began to curse;
Phyl wish'd, that she had strained a Limb,
When first she ventur'd out with him:
John wish'd, that he had broke a Leg,
When first for her he quitted *Peg*.
  But what Adventures more befell 'em
The Muse has now no time to tell 'em.
How *Johnny* wheedled, threatened, fawn'd,
Till *Phyllis* all her Trinkets pawn'd:
How oft she broke her Marriage Vows,
In Kindness, to maintain her Spouse,
Till Swains unwholesome spoiled the Trade;
For now the Surgeon must be paid,
To whom those Perquisites are gone,
In Christian Justice due to *John*.
  When Food and Raiment now grew scarce,
Fate put a Period to the Farce,
And with exact Poetic Justice,
For John is *Landlord, Phyllis* Hostess;
They keep, at *Stains*, the *old blue Boar*,
Are Cat and Dog, and Rogue and Whore.

WILLIAM SOMERVILE (1675–1742)

From The Chase

  Huntsman! her Gait observe, if in wide Rings
She wheel her mazy Way, in the same Round
Persisting still, she'll foil the beaten Track.

But if she fly, and with the fav'ring Wind
Urge her bold Course; less intricate thy Task:
Push on thy Pack. Like some poor exil'd Wretch
The frighted Chase leaves her late dear Abodes,
O'er Plains remote she stretches far away,
Ah! never to return! For greedy Death
Hov'ring exults, secure to seize his Prey.

Hark! from yon Covert, where those tow'ring Oaks
Above the humble Copse aspiring rise,
What glorious Triumphs burst in ev'ry Gale
Upon our ravish'd Ears! The Hunters shout,
The clanging Horns swell their sweet-winding Notes,
The Pack wide-op'ning load the trembling Air
With various Melody; from Tree to Tree
The propagated Cry, redoubling bounds,
And winged Zephyrs waft the floating Joy
Thro' all the Regions near: Afflictive Birch
No more the School-boy dreads, his Prison broke,
Scamp'ring he flies, nor heeds his Master's Call;
The weary Traveller forgets his Road,
And climbs th'adjacent Hill; the Ploughman leaves
Th'unfinish'd Furrow; nor his bleating Flocks
Are now the Shepherd's Joy; Men, Boys, and Girls
Desert th'unpeopled Village; and wild Crowds
Spread o'er the Plain, by the sweet Frenzy seiz'd.
Look, how she pants! and o'er yon op'ning Glade
Slips glancing by; while, at the further End,
The puzzling Pack unravel Wile by Wile
Maze within Maze. The Covert's utmost Bound
Slily she skirts; behind them cautious creeps,
And in that very Track, so lately stain'd
By all the steaming Crowd, seems to pursue
The Foe she flies. Let Cavillers deny
That Brutes have Reason; sure 'tis something more,
'Tis Heav'n directs, and Stratagems inspires,
Beyond the short Extent of human Thought.
But hold—I see her from the Covert break;
Sad on yon little Eminence she sits;
Intent she listens with one Ear erect,
Pond'ring, and doubtful what new Course to take,
And how t'escape the fierce blood-thirsty Crew,

That still urge on, and still in Volleys loud,
Insult her Woes, and mock her sore Distress.
As now in louder Peals, the loaded Winds
Bring on the gath'ring Storm, her Fears prevail;
And o'er the Plain, and o'er the Mountain's Ridge,
Away she flies; nor Ships with Wind and Tide,
And all their Canvas Wings scud half so fast.
Once more, ye jovial Train, your Courage try,
And each clean Courser's Speed. We scour along,
In pleasing Hurry and Confusion toss'd;
Oblivion to be wish'd. The patient Pack
Hang on the Scent unweary'd, up they climb,
And ardent we pursue; our lab'ring Steeds
We press, we gore; till once the Summit gain'd,
Painfully panting, there we breathe awhile;
Then like a foaming Torrent, pouring down
Precipitant, we smoke along the Vale.
Happy the Man, who with unrival'd Speed
Can pass his Fellows, and with Pleasure view
The struggling Pack; how in the rapid Course
Alternate they preside, and justling push
To guide the dubious Scent; how giddy Youth
Oft babbling errs, by wiser Age reprov'd;
How niggard of his Strength, the wise old Hound
Hangs in the Rear, 'till some important Point
Rouse all his Diligence, or 'till the Chase
Sinking he finds; then to the Head he springs
With Thirst of Glory fir'd, and wins the Prize.
Huntsman, take heed; they stop in full career.
Yon crowding Flocks, that at a Distance gaze,
Have haply foil'd the Turf. See! that old Hound,
How busily he works, but dares not trust
His doubtful Sense; draw yet a wider Ring.
Hark! now again the Chorus fills. As Bells
Sally'd a while at once their Peal renew,
And high in Air the tuneful Thunder rolls.
See, how they toss, with animated Rage
Recov'ring all they lost!—That eager Haste
Some doubling Wile foreshows.—Ah! yet once more
They're check'd,—hold back with Speed—on either hand
They flourish round—ev'n yet persist— 'Tis right,
Away they spring; the rustling Stubbles bend

Beneath the driving Storm. Now the poor Chase
Begins to flag, to her last Shifts reduc'd.
From Brake to Brake she flies, and visits all
Her well-known Haunts, where once she rang'd secure,
With Love and Plenty blest. See! there she goes,
She reels along, and by her Gate betrays
Her inward Weakness. See, how black she looks!
The Sweat that clogs th'obstructed Pores, scarce leaves
A languid Scent. And now in open View
See, see, she flies! each eager Hound exerts
His utmost Speed, and stretches ev'ry Nerve.
How quick she turns! their gaping Jaws eludes,
And yet a Moment lives; 'till round enclos'd
By all the greedy Pack, with infant Screams
She yields her Breath, and there reluctant dies.
So when the furious *Bacchanals* assail'd
Thracian Orpheus, poor ill-fated Bard!
Loud was the Cry, Hills, Woods, and *Hebrus*' Banks,
Return'd their clam'rous Rage; distress'd he flies,
Shifting from Place to Place, but flies in vain;
For eager they pursue, 'till panting, faint,
By noisy Multitudes o'erpower'd, he sinks,
To the relentless Crowd a bleeding Prey.

THOMAS PARNELL (1679–1718)

Health: An Eclogue

Now early Shepherds o'er the Meadow pass,
And print long Footsteps in the glittering Grass;
The Cows neglectful of their Pasture stand,
By turns obsequious to the Milker's Hand.

When *Damon* softly trod the shaven Lawn,
Damon, a Youth from City Cares withdrawn;
Long was the pleasing Walk he wander'd thro',
A cover'd Arbour clos'd the distant view;
There rests the *Youth*, and, while the feather'd Throng
Raise their wild Music, thus contrives a Song.

Here, wafted o'er by mild *Etesian* Air,
Thou Country *Goddess*, beauteous *Health!* repair;
Here let my Breast thro' quivering Trees inhale
Thy rosy Blessings with the Morning Gale.
What are the Fields, or Flow'rs, or all I see?
Ah! tasteless all, if not enjoy'd with thee.

Joy to my soul! I feel the *Goddess* nigh,
The Face of Nature cheers as well as I;
O'er the flat Green refreshing Breezes run,
The smiling Daisies blow beneath the Sun,
The Brooks run purling down with silver Waves,
The planted Lanes rejoice with dancing Leaves,
The chirping Birds from all the Compass rove
To tempt the tuneful Echoes of the Grove:
High sunny Summits, deeply shaded Dales,
Thick Mossy Banks, and flow'ry winding Vales,
With various Prospect gratify the Sight,
And scatter fix'd Attention in Delight.

Come, Country *Goddess*, come: nor thou suffice,
But bring thy Mountain-sister, *Exercise*.
Call'd by thy lively Voice, she turns her Pace,
Her winding Horn proclaims the finish'd Chase;
She mounts the Rocks, she skims the level Plain,
Dogs, Hawks, and Horses, crowd her early Train;
Her hardy Face repels the tanning Wind,
And Lines and Meshes loosely float behind.
All these as Means of Toil the Feeble see,
But these are helps to Pleasure join'd with thee.
Let *Sloth* lie softening till high Noon in Down,
Or lolling fan her in the sultry Town,
Unnerv'd with Rest; and turn her own Disease,
Or foster others in luxurious Ease:
I mount the Courser, call the deep-mouth'd Hounds
The Fox unkennell'd flies to covert Grounds;
I lead where Stags through tangled Thickets tread,
And shake the Saplings with their branching Head;
I make the Falcons wing their airy Way;
And soar to seize, or stooping strike their Prey;
To snare the Fish I fix the luring Bait;
To wound the Fowl I load the Gun with Fate.

'Tis thus through change of Exercise I range,
And Strength and Pleasure rise from every Change.
  Here beauteous *Health* for all the year remain,
  When the next comes, I'll charm thee thus again.

O come, thou *Goddess* of my rural song,
And bring thy Daughter, calm Content, along,
Dame of the ruddy Cheek and laughing Eye,
From whose bright Presence Clouds of Sorrow fly:
For her I mow my Walks, I plait my Bowers,
Clip my low Hedges, and support my Flowers;
To welcome her, this Summer Seat I drest,
And here I court her when she comes to Rest;
When she from Exercise to learned Ease
Shall change again, and teach the Change to please.

Now Friends conversing my soft Hours refine,
And *Tully's Tusculum* revives in mine:
Now to grave Books I bid the Mind retreat,
And such as make me rather Good than Great;
Or o'er the Works of easy *Fancy* rove,
Where Flutes and Innocence amuse the Grove;
The native *Bard* that on *Sicilian* plains
First sung the lowly Manners of the Swains,
Or *Maro's* Muse, that in the fairest Light
Paints rural Prospects and the Charms of Sight:
These soft *Amusements* bring *Content* along,
And *Fancy*, void of Sorrow, turns to *Song*.
  Here beauteous *Health* for all the year remain,
  When the next comes, I'll charm thee thus again.

EDWARD YOUNG (1683–1765)

The Complaint: Or, Night-Thoughts

From *Night IX: The Consolation*

  Then, farewell NIGHT! Of darkness, now, no more:
Joy breaks; shines; triumphs; 'tis eternal day.
Shall that which rises out of *nought* complain

Of a few evils, paid with endless joys?
My soul! henceforth, in sweetest union join
The two supports of human happiness,
Which some, erroneous, think can never meet;
True *taste of life*, and constant *thought of death!*
The *thought* of death, sole victor of its dread!
Hope, be thy *joy*; and *probity* thy *skill*;
Thy *patron He*, whose diadem has dropp'd
Yon gems of heav'n; eternity, thy *prize:*
And leave the racers of the *world* their own,
Their feather, and their froth, for endless toils:
They part with all for that *which is not bread;*
They mortify, they starve, on wealth, fame, power;
And laugh to scorn the *fools* that aim at more.
How must a spirit, late escap'd from earth,
Suppose Philander's, Lucia's, or Narcissa's,
The *truth of things* new-blazing in its eye,
Look back, astonish'd on the ways of men,
Whose lives' whole drift is to forget their graves!
And when our *present privilege* is past,
To scourge us with due sense of its *abuse*,
The *same* astonishment will seize us all.
What *then* must pain us, would preserve us *now*.
Lorenzo! 'tis not yet too late: Lorenzo!
Seize wisdom, ere 'tis torment to be wise;
That is, seize *wisdom*, ere she seizes *thee*.
For, what, my small philosopher! is *hell?*
'Tis nothing, but full knowledge of *the truth*,
When *truth*, resisted long, is sworn our foe;
And calls Eternity to do her right.
  Thus, *darkness* aiding intellectual light,
And sacred *silence* whisp'ring truths divine,
And *truth divine* converting pain to peace,
My song the midnight raven has outwing'd,
And shot, ambitious of unbounded scenes,
Beyond the flaming limits of the world,
Her gloomy flight. But what avails the flight
Of *fancy*, when our *hearts* remain below?
Virtue abounds in flatterers, and foes:
'Tis pride, to praise her; penance, to perform.
To more than words, to more than worth of tongue,
Lorenzo! rise, at this auspicious hour;

An hour, when Heaven's most intimate with man;
When, like a falling star, the ray divine
Glides swift into the bosom of the *just*;
And just are all, *determin'd* to reclaim;
Which sets that title high, within thy reach.
Awake, then: thy PHILANDER calls: awake!
Thou, who shalt wake, when the creation sleeps;
When, like a taper, all these suns expire;
When TIME, like him of *Gaza* in his wrath,
Plucking the pillars that support the world,
In NATURE's ample ruins lies intomb'd;
And MIDNIGHT, *Universal* Midnight! reigns.

JOHN GAY (1685–1732)

The Birth of the Squire: An Eclogue

Ye sylvan Muses, loftier strains recite,
Not all in shades, and humble cots delight.
Hark! the bells ring; along the distant grounds
The driving gales convey the swelling sounds;
Th' attentive swain, forgetful of his work,
With gaping wonder, leans upon his fork.
What sudden news alarms the waking morn?
To the glad Squire a hopeful heir is born.
Mourn, mourn, ye stags, and all ye beasts of chase,
This hour destruction brings on all your race:
See the pleas'd tenants duteous off'rings bear,
Turkeys and geese and grocer's sweetest ware;
With the new health the pond'rous tankard flows,
And old *October* reddens ev'ry nose.
Beagles and spaniels round his cradle stand,
Kiss his moist lip and gently lick his hand;
He joys to hear the shrill horn's echoing sounds,
And learns to lisp the names of all the hounds.
With frothy ale to make his cup o'er-flow,
Barley shall in paternal acres grow;
The bee shall sip the fragrant dew from flow'rs,
To give metheglin for his morning hours;

For him the clust'ring hop shall climb the poles,
And his own orchard sparkle in his bowls.

His Sire's exploits he now with wonder hears,
The monstrous tales indulge his greedy ears;
How when youth strung his nerves and warm'd his veins,
He rode the mighty *Nimrod* of the plains:
He leads the staring infant through the hall,
Points out the horny spoils that grace the wall;
Tells, how this stag thro' three whole Counties fled,
What rivers swam, where bay'd, and where he bled.
Now he the wonders of the fox repeats,
Describes the desp'rate chase, and all his cheats;
How in one day beneath his furious speed,
He tir'd seven coursers of the fleetest breed;
How high the pale he leapt, how wide the ditch,
When the hound tore the haunches of the witch!
These stories which descend from son to son,
The forward boy shall one day make his own.

Ah, too fond mother, think the time draws nigh,
That calls the darling from thy tender eye;
How shall his spirit brook the rigid rules,
And the long tyranny of grammar schools?
Let younger brothers o'er dull authors plod,
Lash'd into *Latin* by the tingling rod;
No, let him never feel that smart disgrace:
Why should he wiser prove than all his race?

When rip'ning youth with down o'ershades his chin,
And ev'ry female eye incites to sin;
The milk-maid (thoughtless of her future shame)
With smacking lip shall raise his guilty flame;
The dairy, barn, the hay-loft and the grove
Shall oft' be conscious of their stolen love.
But think, *Priscilla,* on that dreadful time,
When pangs and wat'ry qualms shall own thy crime;
How wilt thou tremble when thy nipple's prest,
To see the white drops bathe thy swelling breast!
Nine moons shall publicly divulge thy shame,
And the young Squire forestall a father's name.

When twice twelve times the reaper's sweeping hand
With levell'd harvests has bestrown the land,
On fam'd *St. Hubert*'s feast, his winding horn
Shall cheer the joyful hound and wake the morn!
This memorable day his eager speed
Shall urge with bloody heel the rising steed.
O check the foamy bit, nor tempt thy fate,
Think on the murders of a five-bar gate!
Yet prodigal of life, the leap he tries,
Low in the dust his groveling honour lies,
Headlong he falls, and on the rugged stone
Distorts his neck, and cracks the collar bone;
O ventr'ous youth, thy thirst of game allay,
Mayst thou survive the perils of this day!
He shall survive; and in late years be sent
To snore away Debates in *Parliament*.

The time shall come, when his more solid sense
With nod important shall the laws dispense;
A Justice with grave Justices shall sit,
He praise their wisdom, they admire his wit.
No greyhound shall attend the tenant's pace,
No rusty gun the farmer's chimney grace;
Salmons shall leave their covers void of fear,
Nor dread the thievish net or triple spear;
Poachers shall tremble at his awful name,
Whom vengeance now o'ertakes for murder'd game.

Assist me, *Bacchus*, and ye drunken Pow'rs,
To sing his friendships and his midnight hours!

Why dost thou glory in thy strength of beer,
Firm-cork'd, and mellow'd till the twentieth year;
Brew'd or when *Phœbus* warms the fleecy sign,
Or when his languid rays in *Scorpio* shine.
Think on the mischiefs which from hence have sprung!
It arms with curses dire the wrathful tongue;
Foul scandal to the lying lip affords,
And prompts the mem'ry with injurious words.
O where is wisdom, when by this o'erpower'd?
The State is censur'd, and the maid deflower'd!

And wilt thou still, O Squire, brew ale so strong?
Hear then the dictates of prophetic song.

Methinks I see him in his hall appear,
Where the long table floats in clammy beer,
'Midst mugs and glasses shatter'd o'er the floor,
Dead-drunk his servile crew supinely snore;
Triumphant, o'er the prostrate brutes he stands,
The mighty bumper trembles in his hands;
Boldly he drinks, and like his glorious Sires,
In copious gulps of potent ale expires.

ALEXANDER POPE (1688–1744)

ROBERT BLAIR (1690–1746)

From The Grave

Whilst some affect the Sun, and some the Shade,
Some flee the City, some the Hermitage;
Their Aims as various, as the Roads they take
In Journeying through Life;—the Task be mine
To paint the gloomy Horrors of the *Tomb;*
Th' appointed Place of Rendezvous, where all
These Travellers meet.—Thy Succours I implore,
Eternal King! whose potent Arm sustains
The Keys of Hell and Death.—The GRAVE, dread Thing!
Men shiver, when thou'rt nam'd: Nature appall'd
Shakes off her wonted Firmness.—Ah! how dark
Thy long-extended Realms, and rueful Wastes!
Where nought but Silence reigns, and Night, dark Night,

Dark as was *Chaos*, ere the Infant Sun
Was roll'd together, or had tried his Beams
Athwart the Gloom profound!—The sickly Taper,
By glimm'ring through thy low-brow'd misty Vaults,
(Furr'd round with mouldy Damps and ropy Slime,)
Lets fall a supernumerary Horror,
And only serves to make thy Night more irksome.
Well do I know thee by thy trusty *Yew*,
Cheerless unsocial Plant! that loves to dwell
'Midst Skulls and Coffins, Epitaphs and Worms:
Where light-heel'd Ghosts and visionary Shades,
Beneath the wan cold Moon (as Fame reports)
Embodi'd, thick, perform their mystic Rounds.
No other Merriment, Dull Tree, is thine.

See yonder Hallow'd Fane! The pious Work
Of Names once fam'd, now dubious or forgot,
And buried 'midst the Wreck of Things which were:
There lie interr'd the more illustrious Dead.
The Wind is up: Hark! how it howls! Methinks
Till now, I never heard a sound so dreary:
Doors creak, and Windows clap, and Night's foul Bird,
Rook'd in the Spire, screams loud: The gloomy Aisles
Black plaster'd, and hung round With shreds of 'Scutcheons
And tatter'd Coats of Arms, send back the Sound
Laden with heavier Airs, from the low Vaults,
The Mansions of the Dead. Rous'd from their Slumbers,
In grim Array the grisly Spectres rise,
Grin horrible, and obstinately sullen,
Pass and repass, hush'd as the Foot of Night:
Again! the screech owl shrieks: Ungracious Sound!
I'll hear no more; it makes one's Blood run chill.

Quite round the Pile, a row of Reverend Elms,
Coeval near with that, all ragged shew,
Long lash'd by the rude winds: some rift half down
Their branchless Trunks: Others so thin a-Top,
That scarce Two Crows could lodge in the same Tree.
Strange Things, the Neighbours say, have happen'd here:
Wild shrieks have issued from the hollow Tombs,
Dead men have come again, and walk'd about,
And the Great Bell has toll'd, unrung, untouch'd.

(Such Tales their Cheer at Wake or Gossiping,
When it draws near to Witching-Time of Night.)

MATHEW GREEN (1696–1737)

From The Spleen

When fancy tries her limning skill
To draw and colour at her will,
And raise and round the figures well,
And shew her talent to excel,
I guard my heart, lest it should woo
Unreal beauties, fancy drew,
And disappointed feel despair
At loss of things, that never were.

When I lean politicians mark
Grazing on aether in the park,
Who e'er on wing with open throats
Fly at debates, expresses, votes,
Just in the manner swallows use,
Catching their airy food of news,
Whose latrant stomachs oft molest
The deep-laid plans, their dreams suggest;
Or see some poet pensive sit,
Fondly mistaking spleen for wit,
Who, tho' short-winded, still will aim
To sound the epic trump of fame,
Who still on Phœbus' smiles will dote,
Nor learn conviction from his coat;
I bless my stars, I never knew
Whimseys, which close pursu'd, undo,
And have from old experience been
Both parent, and the child of spleen.
These subjects of Apollo's state,
Who from false fire derive their fate,
With airy purchases undone
Of lands, which none lend money on,
Born dull, had follow'd thriving ways,

Nor lost one hour to gather bays.
Their fancies first delirious grew,
And scenes ideal took for true.
Fine to the sight Parnassus lies,
And with false prospects cheats their eyes;
The fabl'd goods, the poets sing,
A season of perpetual spring,
Brooks, flow'ry fields, and groves of trees
Affording sweets, and similes,
Gay dreams inspir'd in myrtle bow'rs,
And wreaths of undecaying flow'rs,
Apollo's harp with airs divine,
The sacred music of the Nine,
Views of the temple rais'd to fame,
And for a vacant niche proud aim
Ravish their souls, and plainly shew,
What fancy's sketching power can do:
They will attempt the mountain steep,
Where on the top, like dreams in sleep,
The muses revelations shew,
That find men crack'd, or make them so.

You, friend, like me, the trade of rhyme
Avoid, elab'rate waste of time,
Nor are content to be undone,
And pass for Phœbus' crazy son.
Poems, the hop-grounds of the brain,
Afford the most uncertain gain;
And lott'ries never tempt the wise,
With blanks so many to a prize.
I only transient visits pay,
Meeting the Muses in my way,
Scarce known to the fastidious dames,
Nor skill'd to call them by their names.
Nor can their passports in these days
Your profit warrant, or your praise.
On poems by their dictates writ
Critics, as sworn appraisers, sit,
And, mere upholster'rs, in a trice
On gems and paintings set a price.
These tail'ring artists for our lays
Invent cramp'd rules, and with strait stays

Striving free nature's shape to hit,
Emaciate sense, before they fit.

JAMES THOMSON (1700–1748)

The Seasons

From *Summer*

Among the crooked Lanes, on every Hedge,
The glow-worm lights his *Gem;* and, thro' the Dark,
A moving Radiance twinkles. *Evening* yields
The World to *Night;* not in her Winter-Robe
Of massy Stygian Woof, but loose array'd
In Mantle dun. A faint erroneous Ray,
Glanc'd from th' imperfect Surfaces of Things,
Flings half an Image on the straining Eye;
While wavering Woods, and Villages, and Streams,
And Rocks, and Mountain-tops, that long retain'd
Th' ascending gleam, are all one swimming Scene,
Uncertain if beheld. Sudden to Heaven
Thence weary Vision turns; where, leading soft
The silent Hours of Love, with purest Ray
Sweet *Venus* shines; and from her genial Rise,
When Day-Light sickens till it springs afresh,
Unrival'd reigns, the fairest Lamp of Night.
As thus th' Effulgence tremulous I drink,
With cherish'd Gaze, the lambent Lightnings shoot
Across the Sky or horizontal dart
In wondrous shapes: by fearful murmuring Crowds
Portentous deem'd. Amid the radiant Orbs
That more than deck, that animate the Sky,
The Life-infusing Suns of other Worlds,
Lo! from the dread Immensity of Space
Returning, with accelerated Course,
The rushing comet to the sun descends;
And as he sinks below the shading Earth
With awful Train projected o'er the Heavens,
The guilty Nations tremble. But, above
Those superstitious Horrors that enslave

The fond sequacious Herd, to mystic Faith
And blind Amazement prone, th' enlighten'd Few,
Whose Godlike Minds Philosophy exalts,
The glorious Stranger hail. They feel a Joy
Divinely great; they in their Powers exult,
That wondrous Force of Thought, which mounting spurns
This dusky Spot, and measures all the Sky;
While, from his far Excursions thro' the Wilds
Of barren Ether, faithful to his Time,
They see the blazing Wonder rise anew,
In seeming Terror clad, but kindly bent
To work the Will of all-sustaining *Love:*
From his huge vapoury Train perhaps to shake
Reviving Moisture on the numerous Orbs,
Thro' which his long Ellipsis winds; perhaps
To lend new Fuel to declining Suns,
To light up Worlds, and feed th' eternal fire.

With Thee, serene Philosophy, with Thee,
And thy bright Garland, let me crown my Song!
Effusive Source of Evidence and Truth!
A Lustre shedding o'er the ennobled Mind,
Stronger than Summer-Noon; and pure as That,
Whose mild Vibrations soothe the parted Soul,
New to the Dawning of celestial Day.
Hence thro' her nourish'd powers, enlarg'd by thee,
She springs aloft, with elevated Pride,
Above the tangling Mass of low Desires,
That bind the fluttering Crowd; and Angel-wing'd,
The heights of Science and of Virtue gains,
Where all is calm and clear; with Nature round,
Or in the starry Regions, or th' Abyss,
To Reason's and to Fancy's Eye display'd:
The *First* up-tracing, from the dreary Void,
The Chain of Causes and Effects to Him
The world-producing Essence, who alone
Possesses Being; while the *Last* receives
The whole magnificence of Heaven and Earth,
And every Beauty, delicate or bold,
Obvious or more remote, with livelier Sense,
Diffusive painted on the rapid Mind.

TUTOR'D by thee, hence POETRY exalts
Her Voice to Ages; and informs the Page
With Music, Image, Sentiment, and Thought,
Never to die! the treasure of mankind!
Their highest Honour, and their truest Joy!

SAMUEL JOHNSON (1709–1784)

The Winter's Walk

Behold my fair, where'er we rove,
  What dreary prospects round us rise,
The naked hills, the leafless grove,
  The hoary ground, the frowning skies.

Nor only through the wasted plain,
  Stern winter, is thy force confest,
Still wider spreads thy horrid reign,
  I feel thy pow'r usurp my breast.

Enliv'ning hope, and fond desire,
  Resign the heart to spleen and care,
Scarce frighted love maintains his fire,
  And rapture saddens to despair.

In groundless hope, and causeless fear,
  Unhappy man! behold thy doom,
Still changing with the changeful year,
  The slave of sunshine and of gloom.

Tir'd with vain joys, and false alarms,
  With mental and corporeal strife,
Snatch me, my *Stella,* to thy arms,
  And screen me from the ills of life.

WILLIAM SHENSTONE (1714–1763)

Ophelia's Urn

Thro' the dim veil of ev'ning's dusky shade,
  Near some lone fane, or yew's funereal green,
What dreary forms has magic fear survey'd!
  What shrouded spectres superstition seen!

But you secure shall pour your sad complaint,
  Nor dread the meagre phantom's wan array;
What none but fear's officious hand can paint,
  What none, but superstition's eye, survey.

The glimm'ring twilight and the doubtful dawn
  Shall see your step to these sad scenes return:
Constant, as crystal dews impearl the lawn,
  Shall Strephon's tear bedew Ophelia's urn.

Sure nought unhallow'd shall presume to stray
  Where sleep the relics of that virtuous maid:
Nor aught unlovely bend its devious way,
  Where soft Ophelia's dear remains are laid.

Haply thy muse, as with unceasing sighs
  She keeps late vigils on her urn reclin'd,
May see light groups of pleasing visions rise;
  And phantoms glide, but of celestial kind.

Then fame, her clarion pendent at her side,
  Shall seek forgiveness of Ophelia's shade;
"Why has such worth, without distinction, died?
  Why, like the desert's lily, bloom'd to fade?"

Then young simplicity, averse to feign,
  Shall unmolested breathe her softest sigh:
And candour with unwonted warmth complain,
  And innocence indulge a wailful cry.

Then elegance, with coy judicious hand,
  Shall cull fresh flow'rets for Ophelia's tomb;
And beauty chide the fates' severe command,
  That show'd the frailty of so fair a bloom!

And fancy then with wild ungovern'd woe,
  Shall her loved pupil's native taste explain;
For mournful sable all her hues forego,
  And ask sweet solace of the muse in vain!

Ah gentle forms expect no fond relief;
  Too much the sacred Nine their loss deplore:
Well may ye grieve, nor find an end of grief—
  Your best, your brightest fav'rite is no more.

JOHN BROWN (1715–1766)

Fragment of a Rhapsody, Written at the Lakes in Westmoreland

Now sunk the sun, now twilight sunk, and night
Rode in her zenith; nor a passing breeze
Sigh'd to the groves, which in the midnight air
Stood motionless; and in the peaceful floods
Inverted hung; for now the billow slept
Along the shore, nor heav'd the deep, but spread
A shining mirror to the moon's pale orb,
Which, dim and waning, o'er the shadowy cliffs,
The solemn woods and spiry mountain-tops
Her glimmering faintness threw. Now every eye
Oppress'd with toil, was drown'd in deep repose,
Save that the unseen shepherd in his watch,
Propt on his crook, stood listening by the fold,
And gaz'd the starry vault and pendant moon.
Nor voice nor sound broke on the deep serene,
But the soft murmur of swift gushing rills,
Forth issuing from the mountain's distant steep
(Unheard till now, and now scarce heard) proclaim'd
All things at rest, and imag'd the still voice
Of quiet whispering to the ear of night.

THOMAS GRAY (1716–1771)

WILLIAM COLLINS (1721–1759)

CHRISTOPHER SMART (1722–1771)

Hymn 14: The Ascension of Our Lord Jesus Christ

"And other wond'rous works were done
No mem'ry can recall;
Which were they number'd every one,
Not all the space beneath the sun
Cou'd hold the fair detail of all."

The text is full, and strong to do
The glorious subject right;
But on the working mind's review
The letter's like the spirit true,
And clear and evident as light.

For not a particle of space
Where'er his glory beam'd,
With all the modes of site and place,
But were the better for his grace,
And up to higher lot redeem'd.

For all the motley tribe that pair,
And to their cover skim,
Became his more immediate care,
The raven urgent in his pray'r,
And those that make the woodland hymn.

For every creature left at will
The howling WASTE to roam,
Which live upon the blood they spill,
From his own hands receive their fill,
What time the desert was his home.

They knew him well, and could not err,
To him they all appeal'd;
The beast of sleek or shaggy fur,
And found their natures to recur
To what they were in Eden's field.

For all that dwell in depth or wave,
And ocean—every drop—
Confess'd his mighty pow'r to save,
When to the floods his peace he gave,
And bade careering whirlwinds stop.

And all things meaner, from the worm
Probationer to fly;
To him that creeps his little term,
And countless rising from the sperm
Shed by sea-reptiles, where they ply.

These all were bless'd beneath his feet,
Approaching them so near;
Vast flocks that have no mouths to bleat,
With yet a spirit to intreat,
And in their rank divinely dear.

For on some special good intent,
Advancement or relief,
Or some great evil to prevent,
Or some perfection to augment,
He held his life of tears and grief.

'Twas his the pow'rs of hell to curb,
And men possess'd to free;
And all the blasting fiends disturb
From seed of bread, from flow'r and herb,
From fragrant shrub and stately tree.

The song can never be pursu'd
When Infinite's the theme—
For all to crown, and to conclude,
He bore and bless'd ingratitude,
And insult in its worst extreme.

And having then such deeds achiev'd
As never man before,
From scorn and cruelty repriev'd,
In highest heav'n he was receiv'd,
To reign with God for evermore.

THOMAS WARTON, THE YOUNGER
(1728–1790)

The Hamlet

Written in Whichwood Forest

The hinds how blest, who ne'er beguil'd
To quit their hamlet's hawthorn wild;
Nor haunt the crowd, nor tempt the main,
For splendid care, and guilty gain!

When morning's twilight-tinctur'd beam
Strikes their low thatch with slanting gleam,
They rove abroad in ether blue,
To dip the scythe in fragrant dew:
The sheaf to bind, the beech to fell,
That nodding shades a craggy dell.

Midst gloomy glades, in warbles clear,
Wild nature's sweetest notes they hear:
On green untrodden banks they view

The hyacinth's neglected hue:
In their lone haunts, and woodland rounds,
They spy the squirrel's airy bounds:
And startle from her ashen spray,
Across the glen, the screaming jay:
Each native charm their steps explore
Of Solitude's sequester'd store.

For them the moon with cloudless ray
Mounts, to illume their homeward way:
Their weary spirits to relieve,
The meadows incense breathe at eve.
No riot mars the simple fare
That o'er a glimmering hearth they share:
But when the curfew's measured roar
Duly, the darkening valleys o'er,
Has echoed from the distant town,
They wish no beds of cygnet-down,
No trophied canopies, to close
Their drooping eyes in quick repose.

Their little sons, who spread the bloom
Of health around the clay-built room,
Or through the primrosed coppice stray,
Or gambol in the new-mown hay;
Or quaintly braid the cowslip-twine,
Or drive afield the tardy kine;
Or hasten from the sultry hill
To loiter at the shady rill;
Or climb the tall pine's gloomy crest
To rob the raven's ancient nest.

Their humble porch with honey'd flow'rs
The curling woodbine's shade embow'rs:
From the small garden's thymy mound
Their bees in busy swarms resound:
Nor fell Disease, before his time,
Hastes to consume life's golden prime:
But when their temples long have wore
The silver crown of tresses hoar;
As studious still calm peace to keep,
Beneath a flowery turf they sleep.

OLIVER GOLDSMITH (1730–1774)

Elegy on the Death of a Mad Dog

Good people all, of every sort,
 Give ear unto my song;
And if you find it wondrous short,
 It cannot hold you long.

In Islingtown there was a man,
 Of whom the world might say,
That still a godly race he ran,
 Whene'er he went to pray.

A kind and gentle heart he had,
 To comfort friends and foes;
The naked every day he clad,
 When he put on his clothes.

And in that town a dog was found,
 As many dogs there be,
Both mongrel, puppy, whelp, and hound,
 And curs of low degree.

This dog and man at first were friends;
 But when a pique began,
The dog, to gain some private ends,
 Went mad and bit the man.

Around from all the neighbouring streets,
 The wondering neighbours ran,
And swore the dog had lost his wits,
 To bite so good a man.

The wound it seem'd both sore and sad,
 To every christian eye;
And while they swore the dog was mad,
 They swore the man would die.

But soon a wonder came to light,
  That show'd the rogues they lied,
The man recover'd of the bite,
  The dog it was that died.

WILLIAM COWPER (1731–1800)

The Negro's Complaint

Forc'd from home and all its pleasures,
  Afric's coast I left forlorn,
To increase a stranger's treasures,
  O'er the raging billows borne.
Men from England bought and sold me,
  Paid my price in paltry gold;
But, though slave they have enroll'd me,
  Minds are never to be sold.

Still in thought as free as ever,
  What are England's rights, I ask,
Me from my delights to sever,
  Me to torture, me to task?
Fleecy locks, and black complexion
  Cannot forfeit nature's claim;
Skins may differ, but affection
  Dwells in white and black the same.

Why did all-creating Nature
  Make the plant for which we toil?
Sighs must fan it, tears must water,
  Sweat of ours must dress the soil.
Think, ye masters, iron-hearted,
  Lolling at your jovial boards,
Think how many backs have smarted
  For the sweets your cane affords.

Is there, as ye sometimes tell us,
  Is there One who reigns on high?
Has He bid you buy and sell us,

  Speaking from his throne, the sky?
Ask Him, if your knotted scourges,
  Matches, blood-extorting screws,
Are the means which duty urges
  Agents of his will to use?

Hark! He answers!—Wild tornadoes,
  Strewing yonder sea with wrecks,
Wasting towns, plantations, meadows,
  Are the voice with which he speaks.
He, foreseeing what vexations
  Afric's sons should undergo,
Fix'd their tyrants' habitations
  Where his whirlwinds answer—No.

By our blood in Afric wasted,
  Ere our necks receiv'd the chain;
By the miseries that we tasted,
  Crossing in your barks the main;
By our suff'rings, since ye brought us
  To the man-degrading mart,
All sustain'd by patience, taught us
  Only by a broken heart:

Deem our nation brutes no longer,
  Till some reason ye shall find
Worthier of regard and stronger
  Than the colour of our kind.
Slaves of gold, whose sordid dealings
  Tarnish all your boasted powers,
Prove that you have human feelings
  Ere you proudly question ours!

JAMES BEATTIE (1735–1803)

The Minstrel, or the Progress of Genius

From *Book I*

Oft when the winter-storm had ceas'd to rave,
He roam'd the snowy waste at even, to view,
The cloud stupendous, from th' Atlantic wave
High-towering, sail along th' horizon blue:
Where midst the changeful scenery ever new
Fancy a thousand wondrous forms descries
More wildly great than ever pencil drew,
Rocks, torrents, gulfs, and shapes of giant size,
And glittering cliffs on cliffs, and fiery ramparts rise.

Thence musing onward to the sounding shore,
The lone enthusiast oft would take his way,
Listening with pleasing dread to the deep roar
Of the wide-weltering waves. In black array
When sulphurous clouds roll'd on the vernal day,
Even then he hasten'd from the haunt of man,
Along the darkening wilderness to stray,
What time the lightning's fierce career began,
And o'er heaven's rending arch the rattling thunder ran.

Responsive to the sprightly pipe when all
In sprightly dance the village-youth were join'd,
Edwin, of melody aye held in thrall,
From the rude gambol far remote reclined,
Sooth'd with the soft notes warbling in the wind.
Ah then, all jollity seem'd noise and folly.
To the pure soul by Fancy's fire refined
Ah what is mirth, but turbulence unholy,
When with the charm compared of heavenly melancholy!

Is there a heart that music cannot melt?
Ah me! how is that rugged heart forlorn!

Is there, who ne'er those mystic transports felt
Of solitude and melancholy born?
He needs not woo the Muse; he is her scorn.
The sophist's rope of cobweb he shall twine;
Mope o'er the schoolman's peevish page; or mourn,
And delve for life, in Mammon's dirty mine;
Sneak with the scoundrel fox, or grunt with glutton swine.

For Edwin Fate a nobler doom had plann'd;
Song was his favourite and first pursuit.
The wild harp rang to his adventurous hand,
And languish'd to his breath the plaintive flute.
His infant muse, though artless, was not mute:
Of elegance as yet he took no care;
For this of time and culture is the fruit;
And Edwin gain'd at last this fruit so rare:
As in some future verse I purpose to declare.

Meanwhile, whate'er of beautiful, or new,
Sublime, or dreadful, in earth, sea, or sky,
By chance, or search, was offer'd to his view,
He scann'd with curious and romantic eye.
Whate'er of lore tradition could supply
From Gothic tale, or song, or fable old,
Rous'd him, still keen to listen and to pry.
At last, though long by penury controll'd,
And solitude, his soul her graces 'gan unfold.

Thus on the chill Lapponian's dreary land,
For many a long month lost in snow profound,
When Sol from Cancer sends the season bland,
And in their northern cave the storms hath bound;
From silent mountains, straight, with startling sound,
Torrents are hurl'd; green hills emerge; and lo,
The trees with foliage, cliffs with flowers are crown'd;
Pure rills through vales of verdure warbling go;
And wonder, love, and joy, the peasant's heart o'erflow.

ANNA BARBAULD (1743–1825)

To Mr. S. T. Coleridge

1797

Midway the hill of science, after steep
And rugged paths that tire the' unpractised feet,
A grove extends; in tangled mazes wrought,
And filled with strange enchantment:—dubious shapes
Flit through dim glades, and lure the eager foot
Of youthful ardour to eternal chase.
Dreams hang on every leaf: unearthly forms
Glide through the gloom; and mystic visions swim
Before the cheated sense. Athwart the mists,
Far into vacant space, huge shadows stretch,
And seem realities; while things of life,
Obvious to sight and touch, all glowing round,
Fade to the hue of shadows—Scruples here,
With filmy net, most like the autumnal webs
Of floating gossamer, arrest the foot
Of generous enterprise; and palsy hope
And fair ambition with the chilling touch
Of sickly hesitation and blank fear.
Nor seldom Indolence these lawns among
Fixes her turf-built seat; and wears the garb
Of deep philosophy, and museful sits,
In dreamy twilight of the vacant mind,
Soothed by the whispering shade; for soothing soft
The shades; and vistas lengthening into air,
With moonbeam rainbows tinted.—Here each mind
Of finer mould, acute and delicate,
In its high progress to eternal truth
Rests for a space, in fairy bowers entranced;
And loves the softened light and tender gloom;
And, pampered with most unsubstantial food,
Looks down indignant on the grosser world,
And matter's cumbrous shapings. Youth beloved
Of Science—of the Muse beloved,—not here,

Not in the maze of metaphysic lore,
Build thou thy place of resting! lightly tread
The dangerous ground, on noble aims intent;
And be this Circe of the studious cell
Enjoyed, but still subservient. Active scenes
Shall soon with healthful spirit brace thy mind;
And fair exertion, for bright fame sustained,
For friends, for country, chase each spleen-fed fog
That blots the wide creation.—
Now Heaven conduct thee with a parent's love!

GEORGE CRABBE (1754–1832)

The Village

From *Book I*

Ye gentle souls, who dream of rural ease,
Whom the smooth stream and smoother sonnet please;
Go! if the peaceful cot your praises share,
Go look within, and ask if peace be there:
If peace be his—that drooping weary sire,
Or theirs, that offspring round their feeble fire;
Or hers, that matron pale, whose trembling hand
Turns on the wretched hearth th' expiring brand!
Nor yet can Time itself obtain for these
Life's latest comforts, due respect and ease;
For yonder see that hoary swain, whose age
Can with no cares except his own engage;
Who, propp'd on that rude staff, looks up to see
The bare arms broken from the withering tree,
On which, a boy, he climb'd the loftiest bough,
Then his first joy, but his sad emblem now.
He once was chief in all the rustic trade;
His steady hand the straightest furrow made;
Full many a prize he won, and still is proud
To find the triumphs of his youth allow'd;
A transient pleasure sparkles in his eyes,
He hears and smiles, then thinks again and sighs:

For now he journeys to his grave in pain;
The rich disdain him; nay, the poor disdain:
Alternate masters now their slave command,
Urge the weak efforts of his feeble hand,
And, when his age attempts its task in vain,
With ruthless taunts, of lazy poor complain.
  Oft may you see him, when he tends the sheep,
His winter-charge, beneath the hillock weep;
Oft hear him murmur to the winds that blow
O'er his white locks and bury them in snow,
When, roused by rage and muttering in the morn,
He mends the broken hedge with icy thorn:—
  "Why do I live, when I desire to be
At once from life and life's long labour free?
Like leaves in spring, the young are blown away,
Without the sorrows of a slow decay;
I, like yon wither'd leaf, remain behind,
Nipp'd by the frost, and shivering in the wind;
There it abides till younger buds come on,
As I, now all my fellow-swains are gone;
Then, from the rising generation thrust,
It falls, like me, unnoticed to the dust.
  "These fruitful fields, these numerous flocks I see,
Are others' gain, but killing cares to me:
To me the children of my youth are lords,
Cool in their looks, but hasty in their words:
Wants of their own demand their care; and who
Feels his own want and succours others too?
A lonely, wretched man, in pain I go,
None need my help, and none relieve my woe;
Then let my bones beneath the turf be laid,
And men forget the wretch they would not aid!"
  Thus groan the old, till, by disease oppress'd,
They taste a final woe, and then they rest.
  Theirs is yon house that holds the parish poor,
Whose walls of mud scarce bear the broken door;
There, where the putrid vapours, flagging, play,
And the dull wheel hums doleful through the day;
There children dwell, who know no parents' care;
Parents, who know no children's love, dwell there!
Heart-broken matrons on their joyless bed,
Forsaken wives, and mothers never wed;

Dejected widows with unheeded tears,
And crippled age with more than childhood fears;
The lame, the blind, and, far the happiest they!
The moping idiot and the madman gay.
Here too the sick their final doom receive,
Here brought, amid the scenes of grief, to grieve,
Where the loud groans from some sad chamber flow,
Mix'd with the clamours of the crowd below;
Here, sorrowing, they each kindred sorrow scan,
And the cold charities of man to man:
Whose laws indeed for ruin'd age provide,
And strong compulsion plucks the scrap from pride;
But still that scrap is bought with many a sigh,
And pride embitters what it can't deny.

WILLIAM BLAKE (1757–1827)

London

Text as engraved by Blake

I wander thro' each charter'd street,
Near where the charter'd Thames does flow
And mark in every face I meet
Marks of weakness, marks of woe,

In every cry of every Man,
In every Infant's cry of fear,
In every voice: in every ban,
The mind-forg'd manacles I hear

How the Chimney-sweeper's cry
Every black'ning Church appalls,
And the hapless Soldier's sigh
Runs in blood down Palace walls

But most thro' midnight streets I hear
How the youthful Harlot's curse
Blasts the new born Infant's tear
And blights with plagues the Marriage hearse

Edited text

I wander thro' each charter'd street,
Near where the charter'd Thames does flow
And mark in every face I meet
Marks of weakness, marks of woe;

In every cry of every Man,
In every Infant's cry of fear,
In every voice, in every ban,
The mind-forg'd manacles I hear,

How the Chimney-sweeper's cry
Ev'ry black'ning Church appalls
And the hapless Soldier's sigh
Runs in blood down Palace walls;

But most thro' midnight streets I hear
How the youthful Harlot's curse
Blasts the new-born Infant's tear
And blights with plagues the Marriage hearse.

WILLIAM LISLE BOWLES (1762–1850)

Sonnet 24

May, 1793

How shall I meet thee, Summer, wont to fill
  My heart with gladness, when thy pleasant tide
  First came, and on the coomb's romantic side
Was heard the distant cockoo's hollow bill!
Fresh flowers shall fringe the margin of the stream,
  As with the songs of joyance and of hope
  The hedge-rows shall ring loud, and on the slope
The poplars sparkle in the transient beam;
The shrubs and laurels that I lov'd to tend,
  Thinking their May-tide fragrance might delight,

With many a peaceful charm, thee, my best friend,
  Shall put forth their green shoots, and cheer the sight!
But I shall mark their hues with sick'ning eyes,
And weep the more for her who in the cold ground lies!

SAMUEL ROGERS (1763–1855)

The Alps

From *Italy*

Who first beholds those everlasting clouds,
Seed-time and harvest, morning noon and night,
Still where they were, steadfast, immovable;
Those mighty hills, so shadowy, so sublime,
As rather to belong to Heaven than Earth—
But instantly receives into his soul
A sense, a feeling that he loses not,
A something that informs him 'tis an hour,
Whence he may date henceforward and for ever?
  To me they seemed the barriers of a World,
Saying, Thus far, no farther! and as o'er
The level plain I travelled silently,
Nearing them more and more, day after day,
My wandering thoughts my only company,
And they before me still—oft as I looked,
A strange delight was mine, mingled with fear,
A wonder as at things I had not heard of!
And still and still I felt as if I gazed
For the first time!—Great was the tumult there,
Deafening the din, when in barbaric pomp
The Carthaginian on his march to Rome
Entered their fastnesses. Trampling the snows,
The war-horse reared; and the towered elephant
Upturned his trunk into the murky sky,
Then tumbled headlong, swallowed up and lost,
He and his rider.—Now the scene is changed;
And o'er the Simplon, o'er the Splugen winds
A path of pleasure. Like a silver zone
Flung about carelessly, it shines afar,

Catching the eye in many a broken link,
In many a turn and traverse as it glides;
And oft above and oft below appears,
Seen o'er the wall by him who journeys up,
As if it were another, thro' the wild
Leading along he knows not whence or whither.
Yet thro' its fairy-course, go where it will,
The torrent stops it not, the rugged rock
Opens and lets it in; and on it runs,
Winning its easy way from clime to clime
Thro' glens locked up before.—Not such *my* path!
The very path for them that dare defy
Danger, nor shrink, wear he what shape he will;
That o'er his caldron, when the flood boils up,
Hang as in air, gazing and shuddering on
Till fascination comes and the brain turns!
The very path for them, that list, to choose
Where best to plant a monumental cross,
And live in story like EMPEDOCLES;
A track for Heroes, such as He who came,
Ere long, to win, to wear the Iron Crown;
And (if aright I judge from what I felt
Over the DRANCE, just where the Abbot fell,
Rolled downward in an after-dinner's sleep)
The same as HANNIBAL'S. But now 'tis passed,
That turbulent Chaos; and the promised land
Lies at my feet in all its loveliness!
To him who starts up from a terrible dream,
And lo, the sun is shining, and the lark
Singing aloud for joy, to him is not
Such sudden ravishment as now I feel
At the first glimpses of fair ITALY.

WILLIAM WORDSWORTH *(1770–1850)*

SAMUEL TAYLOR COLERIDGE (1772–1834)

Kubla Khan

In Xanadu did Kubla Khan
A stately pleasure-dome decree:
Where Alph, the sacred river, ran
Through caverns measureless to man
Down to a sunless sea.
So twice five miles of fertile ground
With walls and towers were girdled round:
And there were gardens bright with sinuous rills,
Where blossomed many an incense-bearing tree;
And here were forests ancient as the hills,
Enfolding sunny spots of greenery.

But oh! that deep romantic chasm which slanted
Down the green hill athwart a cedarn cover!
A savage place! as holy and enchanted
As e'er beneath a waning moon was haunted
By woman wailing for her demon-lover!
And from this chasm, with ceaseless turmoil seething,
As if this earth in fast thick pants were breathing,
A mighty fountain momently was forced:
Amid whose swift half-intermitted burst
Huge fragments vaulted like rebounding hail,
Or chaffy grain beneath the thresher's flail:
And mid these dancing rocks at once and ever
It flung up momently the sacred river.
Five miles meandering with a mazy motion
Through wood and dale the sacred river ran,
Then reached the caverns measureless to man,
And sank in tumult to a lifeless ocean:
And 'mid this tumult Kubla heard from far
Ancestral voices prophesying war!

The shadow of the dome of pleasure
Floated midway on the waves;

Where was heard the mingled measure
From the fountain and the caves.
It was a miracle of rare device,
A sunny pleasure-dome with caves of ice!

A damsel with a dulcimer
In a vision once I saw:
It was an Abyssinian maid,
And on her dulcimer she played,
Singing of Mount Abora.
Could I revive within me
Her symphony and song,
To such a deep delight 'twould win me,
That with music loud and long,
I would build that dome in air,
That sunny dome! those caves of ice!
And all who heard should see them there,
And all should cry, Beware! Beware!
His flashing eyes, his floating hair!
Weave a circle round him thrice,
And close your eyes with holy dread,
For he on honey-dew hath fed,
And drunk the milk of Paradise.

WALTER SAVAGE LANDOR (1775–1864)

A Friend to Theocritos in Egypt

Dost thou not often gasp with longdrawn sighs,
Theocritos, recalling Sicily?
Glorious is Nile, but rather give me back
Our little rills which fain would run away
And hide themselves from persecuting suns
In summer, under oleander boughs,
And catch its roses as they flaunt above.
Here are no birds that sing, no sweeter flower
Than tiny fragile weak-eyed resida,
Which faints upon the bosom it would cool.
Altho' the royal lotos sits aloof

On his rich carpet, spread from wave to wave,
I throw myself more gladly where the pine
Protects me, loftier than the palace-roof,
Or where the linden and acacia meet
Across my path, in fragrance to contend.
Bring back the hour, Theocritos, when we
Shall sit together on a thymy knoll,
With few about us, and with none too nigh,
And when the song of shepherds and their glee
We may repeat, perchance and gaily mock,
Until one bolder than the rest springs up
And slaps us on the shoulder for our pains.
Take thou meanwhile these two papyrus-leaves,
Recording, one the loves and one the woes
Of Pan and Pitys, heretofore unsung.
Aside our rivers and within our groves
The pastoral pipe hath dropt its mellow lay,
And shepherds in their contests only try
Who best can puzzle.
Come, Theocritos,
Come, let us lend a shoulder to the wheel
And help to lift it from this depth of sand.

LEIGH HUNT (1784–1859)

The Fish, the Man, and the Spirit

TO FISH

You strange, astonish'd-looking, angle-faced,
Dreary-mouth'd, gaping wretches of the sea,
Gulping salt-water everlastingly,
Cold-blooded, though with red your blood be graced,
And mute, though dwellers in the roaring waste;
And you, all shapes beside, that fishy be,—
Some round, some flat, some long, all devilry,
Legless, unloving, infamously chaste:—

O scaly, slippery, wet, swift, staring wights,
What is't ye do? what life lead? eh, dull goggles?

How do ye vary your vile days and nights?
How pass your Sundays? Are ye still but joggles
In ceaseless wash? Still naught but gapes, and bites,
And drinks, and stares, diversified with boggles?

A FISH ANSWERS

Amazing monster! that, for aught I know,
With the first sight of thee didst make our race
Forever stare! O flat and shocking face,
Grimly divided from the breast below!
Thou that on dry land horribly dost go
With a split body and most ridiculous pace,
Prong after prong, disgracer of all grace,
Long-useless-finn'd, hair'd, upright, unwet, slow!

O breather of unbreathable, sword-sharp air,
How canst exist? How bear thyself, thou dry
And dreary sloth! What particle canst share
Of the only blessed life, the watery?
I sometimes see of ye an actual *pair*
Go by! link'd fin by fin! most odiously.

THE FISH TURNS INTO A MAN, AND THEN INTO A SPIRIT, AND AGAIN SPEAKS

Indulge thy smiling scorn, if smiling still,
O man! and loathe, but with a sort of love:
For difference must its use by difference prove,
And, in sweet clang, the spheres with music fill.
One of the spirits am I, that at his will
Live in whate'er has life—fish, eagle, dove—
No hate, no pride, beneath nought, nor above,
A visitor of the rounds of God's sweet skill.

Man's life is warm, glad, sad, 'twixt loves and graves,
Boundless in hope, honour'd with pangs austere,
Heaven-gazing; and his angel-wings he craves:—
The fish is swift, small-needing, vague yet clear,
A cold, sweet, silver life, wrapp'd in round waves,
Quicken'd with touches of transporting fear.

GEORGE GORDON BYRON, LORD BYRON
(1788–1824)

"River that rollest by the ancient walls"

River that rollest by the ancient walls
Where dwells the Lady of my love, when she
Walks by thy brink, and there perchance recalls
A faint and fleeting memory of me:

What if thy deep and ample stream should be
A mirror of my heart, where she may read
The thousand thoughts I now betray to thee,
Wild as thy wave, and headlong as thy speed?

What do I say—a mirror of my heart?
Are not thy waters sweeping, dark and strong?
Such as my feelings were and are, thou art;
And such as thou art, were my passions long.

Time may have somewhat tamed them, not for ever;
Thou overflow'st thy banks, and not for aye;
Thy bosom overboils, congenial river!
Thy floods subside, and mine have sunk away—

But left long wrecks behind, and again
Borne in our old unchanged career, we move;
Thou tendest wildly onwards to the main,
And I to loving *one* I should not love.

The current I behold will sweep beneath
Her native walls, and murmur at her feet;
Her eyes will look on thee, when she shall breathe
The twilight air, unharm'd by summer's heat.

She will look on thee; I have looked on thee,
Full of that thought, and, from that moment ne'er
Thy waters could I dream of, name, or see,
Without the inseparable sigh for her.

Her bright eyes will be imaged in thy stream;
Yes, they will meet the wave I gaze on now:
Mine cannot witness, even in a dream,
That happy wave repass me in its flow!

The wave that bears my tears returns no more:
Will she return by whom that wave shall sweep?
Both tread thy banks, both wander on thy shore;
I by thy source, she by the dark-blue deep.

But that which keepeth us apart is not
Distance, nor depth of wave, nor space of earth,
But the distraction of a various lot,
As various as the climates of our birth.

A stranger loves the lady of the land,
Born far beyond the mountains, but his blood
Is all meridian, as if never fanned
By the black wind that chills the polar flood.

My blood is all meridian; were it not,
I had not left my clime;—I shall not be
In spite of tortures, ne'er to be forgot,
A slave again of love, at least of thee.

'Tis vain to struggle—let me perish young—
Live as I lived, and love as I have loved:
To dust if I return, from dust I sprung,
And then at least my heart can ne'er be moved.

PERCY BYSSHE SHELLEY (1792–1822)

JOHN CLARE (1793–1864)

Secret Love

I hid my love when young till I
Couldn't bear the buzzing of a fly;
I hid my love to my despite
Till I could not bear to look at light:
I dare not gaze upon her face
But left her memory in each place;
Where e'er I saw a wild flower lie
I kissed and bade my love good bye.

I met her in the greenest dells
Where dewdrops pearl the wood blue bells
The lost breeze kissed her bright blue eye,
The bee kissed and went singing by,
A sunbeam found a passage there,
A gold chain round her neck so fair;
As secret as the wild bee's song
She lay there all the summer long.

I hid my love in field and town
Till e'en the breeze would knock me down,
The bees seemed singing ballads o'er,
The fly's bass turned a lion's roar;
And even silence found a tongue,
To haunt me all the summer long;
The riddle nature could not prove
Was nothing else but secret love.

WILLIAM CULLEN BRYANT (1794–1878)

Inscription for the Entrance to a Wood

Stranger, if thou hast learned a truth which needs
No school of long experience, that the world

Is full of guilt and misery, and hast seen
Enough of all its sorrows, crimes, and cares,
To tire thee of it, enter this wild wood
And view the haunts of Nature. The calm shade
Shall bring a kindred calm, and the sweet breeze
That makes the green leaves dance, shall waft a balm
To thy sick heart. Thou wilt find nothing here
Of all that pained thee in the haunts of men,
And made thee loathe thy life. The primal curse
Fell, it is true, upon the unsinning earth,
But not in vengeance. God hath yoked to guilt
Her pale tormentor, misery. Hence these shades
Are still the abodes of gladness; the thick roof
Of green and stirring branches is alive
And musical with birds, that sing and sport
In wantonness of spirit; while below
The squirrel, with raised paws and form erect,
Chirps merrily. Throngs of insects in the shade
Try their thin wings and dance in the warm beam
That waked them into life. Even the green trees
Partake the deep contentment; as they bend
To the soft winds, the sun from the blue sky
Looks in and sheds a blessing on the scene.
Scarce less the cleft-born wild-flower seems to enjoy
Existence, than the wingèd plunderer
That sucks its sweets. The mossy rocks themselves,
And the old and ponderous trunks of prostrate trees
That lead from knoll to knoll a causey rude,
Or bridge the sunken brook, and their dark roots,
With all their earth upon them, twisting high,
Breathe fixed tranquillity. The rivulet
Sends forth glad sounds, and tripping o'er its bed
Of pebbly sands, or leaping down the rocks,
Seems, with continuous laughter, to rejoice
In its own being. Softly tread the marge,
Lest from her midway perch thou scare the wren
That dips her bill in water. The cool wind,
That stirs the stream in play, shall come to thee,
Like one that loves thee nor will let thee pass
Ungreeted, and shall give its light embrace.

JOHN KEATS (1795–1821)

THOMAS HOOD (1799–1845)

The Bridge of Sighs

"Drowned! drowned!"—HAMLET

One more Unfortunate,
Weary of breath,
Rashly importunate,
Gone to her death!

Take her up tenderly,
Lift her with care;
Fashion'd so slenderly,
Young, and so fair!

Look at her garments
Clinging like cerements;
Whilst the wave constantly
Drips from her clothing
Take her up instantly,
Loving, not loathing.—

Touch her not scornfully,
Think of her mournfully,
Gently and humanly;
Not of the stains of her,
All that remains of her
Now is pure womanly.

Make no deep scrutiny
Into her mutiny
Rash and undutiful:
Past all dishonor,
Death has left on her
Only the beautiful.

Still, for all slips of hers,
One of Eve's family—
Wipe those poor lips of hers
Oozing so clammily.

Loop up her tresses
Escaped from the comb,
Her fair auburn tresses;
Whilst wonderment guesses
Where was her home?

Who was her father?
Who was her mother?
Had she a sister?
Had she a brother?
Or was there a dearer one
Still, and a nearer one
Yet, than all other?

Alas! for the rarity
Of Christian charity
Under the sun!
Oh! it was pitiful!
Near a whole city full,
Home she had none.

Sisterly, brotherly,
Fatherly, motherly
Feelings had changed:
Love, by harsh evidence,
Thrown from its eminence;
Even God's providence
Seeming estranged.

Where the lamps quiver
So far in the river,
With many a light
From window and casement,
From garret to basement,
She stood, with amazement,
Houseless by night.

The bleak wind of March
Made her tremble and shiver;
But not the dark arch,
Or the black flowing river:
Mad from life's history,
Glad to death's mystery,
Swift to be hurl'd—
Anywhere, anywhere,
Out of the world!

In she plunged boldly,
No matter how coldly
The rough river ran,—
Over the brink of it,
Picture it—think of it,
Dissolute Man!
Lave in it, drink of it,
Then, if you can!

Take her up tenderly,
Lift her with care;
Fashion'd so slenderly,
Young, and so fair!

Ere her limbs frigidly
Stiffen too rigidly,
Decently,—kindly,—
Smoothe and compose them:
And her eyes, close them,
Staring so blindly!

Dreadfully staring
Through muddy impurity,
As when with the daring

Last look of despairing
Fixed on futurity.

Perishing gloomily,
Spurred by contumely,
Cold inhumanity,
Burning insanity,
Into her rest.—
Cross her hands humbly,
As if praying dumbly,
Over her breast!

Owning her weakness,
Her evil behavior,
And leaving, with meekness,
Her sins to her Saviour!

THOMAS LOVELL BEDDOES (1803–1849)

Song of the Stygian Naiades

I

Proserpine may pull her flowers,
Wet with dew or wet with tears,
Red with anger, pale with fears,
Is it any fault of ours,
If Pluto be an amorous king,
And come home nightly, laden,
Underneath his broad bat-wing,
With a gentle earthly maiden?
Is it so, Wind, is it so?
All that I and you do know
Is that we saw fly and fix
'Mongst the flowers and reeds of Styx,
Yesterday,
Where the Furies made their hay
For a bed of tiger cubs,
A great fly of Beelzebub's,

The bee of hearts, which mortals name
Cupid, Love, and Fie for shame.

II

Proserpine may weep in rage,
    But, ere I and you have done
    Kissing, bathing in the sun,
What I have in yonder cage,
Bird or serpent, wild or tame
    She shall guess and ask in vain;
    But, if Pluto does 't again,
It shall sing out loud his shame.
    What hast caught then? What hast caught?
Nothing but a poet's thought,
    Which so light did fall and fix
    'Mongst the flowers and reeds of Styx,
            Yesterday,
Where the Furies made their hay
For a bed of tiger cubs,—
A great fly of Beelzebub's,
The bee of hearts, which mortals name
Cupid, Love, and Fie for shame.

RALPH WALDO EMERSON (1803–1882)

Bacchus

Bring me wine, but wine which never grew
In the belly of the grape,
Or grew on vine whose tap-roots, reaching through
Under the Andes to the Cape,
Suffer no savor of the earth to scape.

Let its grapes the morn salute
From a nocturnal root,
Which feels the acrid juice
Of Styx and Erebus;
And turns the woe of Night,
By its own craft, to a more rich delight.

We buy ashes for bread;
We buy diluted wine;
Give me of the true,—
Whose ample leaves and tendrils curled
Among the silver hills of heaven
Draw everlasting dew;
Wine of wine,
Blood of the world,
Form of forms, and mould of statures,
That I intoxicated,
And by the draught assimilated,
May float at pleasure through all natures;
The bird-language rightly spell,
And that which roses say so well.

Wine that is shed
Like the torrents of the sun
Up the horizon walls,
Or like the Atlantic streams, which run
When the South Sea calls.

Water and bread,
Food which needs no transmuting,
Rainbow-flowering, wisdom-fruiting,
Wine which is already man,
Food which teach and reason can.

Wine which Music is,—
Music and wine are one,—
That I, drinking this,
Shall hear far Chaos talk with me;
Kings unborn shall walk with me;
And the poor grass shall plot and plan
What it will do when it is man.
Quickened so, will I unlock
Every crypt of every rock.

I thank the joyful juice
For all I know;—
Winds of remembering
Of the ancient being blow,
And seeming-solid walls of use
Open and flow.

Pour, Bacchus! the remembering wine;
Retrieve the loss of me and mine!
Vine for vine be antidote,
And the grape requite the lote!
Haste to cure the old despair,—
Reason in Nature's lotus drenched,
The memory of ages quenched;
Give them again to shine;
Let wine repair what this undid;
And where the infection slid,
A dazzling memory revive;
Refresh the faded tints,
Recut the aged prints,
And write my old adventures with the pen
Which on the first day drew,
Upon the tablets blue,
The dancing Pleiads and eternal men.

ALFRED, LORD TENNYSON (1809–1892)

The Hesperides

Hesperus and his daughters three,
That sing about the golden tree.
COMUS

The Northwind fall'n, in the newstarrèd night
Zidonian Hanno, voyaging beyond
The hoary promontory of Soloë
Past Thymiaterion, in calmèd bays,
Between the southern and the western Horn,
Heard neither warbling of the nightingale,
Nor melody o' the Libyan lotusflute
Blown seaward from the shore; but from a slope
That ran bloombright into the Atlantic blue,
Beneath a highland leaning down a weight
Of cliffs, and zoned below with cedarshade,
Came voices, like the voices in a dream,
Continuous, till he reached the outer sea.

Song

I

The golden apple, the golden apple, the hallowed fruit,
Guard it well, guard it warily,
Singing airily
Standing about the charmèd root.
Round about all is mute,
As the snowfield on the mountain-peaks,
As the sandfield at the mountain-foot.
Crocodiles in briny creeks
Sleep and stir not: all is mute.
If ye sing not, if ye make false measure,
We shall lose eternal pleasure,
Worth eternal want of rest.
Laugh not loudly: watch the treasure
Of the wisdom of the west.
In a corner wisdom whispers. Five and three
(Let it not be preached abroad) make an awful mystery.
For the blossom unto threefold music bloweth;
Evermore it is born anew;
And the sap to threefold music floweth,
From the root
Drawn in the dark,
Up to the fruit,
Creeping under the fragrant bark,
Liquid gold, honeysweet, thro' and thro'.
Keen-eyed Sisters, singing airily,
Looking warily
Every way,
Guard the apple night and day,
Lest one from the East come and take it away.

II

Father Hesper, Father Hesper, watch, watch, ever and aye,
Looking under silver hair with a silver eye.
Father, twinkle not thy steadfast sight;
Kingdoms lapse, and climates change, and races die;
Honor comes with mystery;
Hoarded wisdom brings delight.

Number, tell them over and number
How many the mystic fruittree holds,
Lest the redcombed dragon slumber
Rolled together in purple folds.
Look to him, father, lest he wink, and the golden apple be stol'n away,
For his ancient heart is drunk with over-watchings night and day,
Round about the hallowed fruittree curled—
Sing away, sing aloud evermore in the wind, without stop,
Lest his scalèd eyelid drop,
For he is older than the world.
If he waken, we waken,
Rapidly levelling eager eyes.
If he sleep, we sleep,
Dropping the eyelid over the eyes.
If the golden apple be taken,
The world will be overwise.
Five links, a golden chain, are we,
Hesper, the dragon, and sisters three,
Bound about the golden tree.

III

Father Hesper, Father Hesper, watch, watch, night and day,
Lest the old wound of the world be healèd,
The glory unsealèd,
The golden apple stol'n away,
And the ancient secret revealèd.
Look from west to east along:
Father, old Himala weakens, Caucasus is bold and strong.
Wandering waters unto wandering waters call;
Let them clash together, foam and fall.
Out of watchings, out of wiles,
Comes the bliss of secret smiles.
All things are not told to all.
Half-round the mantling night is drawn,
Purplefringèd with even and dawn.
Hesper hateth Phosphor, evening hateth morn.

IV

Every flower and every fruit the redolent breath
Of this warm seawind ripeneth,
Arching the billow in his sleep;
But the landwind wandereth,

Broken by the highland-steep,
Two streams upon the violet deep:
For the western sun and the western star,
And the low west wind, breathing afar,
The end of day and beginning of night
Make the apple holy and bright;
Holy and bright, round and full, bright and blest,
Mellowed in a land of rest;
Watch it warily day and night;
All good things are in the west.
Till midnoon the cool east light
Is shut out by the tall hillbrow;
But when the fullfaced sunset yellowly
Stays on the flowering arch of the bough,
The luscious fruitage clustereth mellowly,
Goldenkernelled, goldencored,
Sunset-ripened above on the tree.
The world is wasted with fire and sword,
But the apple of gold hangs over the sea.
Five links, a golden chain, are we,
Hesper, the dragon, and sisters three,
        Daughters three,
        Bound about
        All round about
The gnarlèd bole of the charmèd tree.
The golden apple, the golden apple, the hallowed fruit,
Guard it well, guard it warily,
        Watch it warily,
        Singing airily,
Standing about the charmèd root.

ROBERT BROWNING (1812–1889)

EMILY BRONTË (1818–1848)

The Philosopher

"Enough of thought, philosopher;
Too long hast thou been dreaming
Unenlightened, in this chamber drear,
While summer's sun is beaming!
Space-sweeping soul, what sad refrain
Concludes thy musings once again?"

"Oh, for the time when I shall sleep
Without identity,
And never care how rain may steep,
Or snow may cover me!
No promised heaven, these wild desires,
Could all our half fulfil;
No threatened hell, with quenchless fires,
Subdue this quenchless will!"

"So said I, and still say the same;
Still, to my death, will say—
Three gods, within this little frame,
Are warring night and day;
Heaven could not hold them all, and yet
They all are held in me;
And must be mine till I forget
My present entity.
Oh, for the time, when in my breast
Their struggles will be o'er!
Oh, for the day, when I shall rest,
And never suffer more!"

"I saw a spirit, standing, man,
Where thou dost stand—an hour ago,
And round his feet three rivers ran,
Of equal depth and equal flow—
A golden stream and one like blood;

And one like sapphire seemed to be;
But, where they joined their triple flood
It tumbled in an inky sea.
The Spirit bent his dazzling gaze
Down through that ocean's gloomy night
Then, kindling all, with sudden blaze,
The glad deep sparkled wide and bright—
White as the sun, far, far more fair
Than its divided sources were!"

"And even for that spirit, seer,
I've watched and sought my lifetime long;
Sought him in heaven, hell, earth and air—
And endless search, and always wrong!
Had I but seen his glorious eye
Once light the clouds that 'wilder me,
I ne'er had raised this coward cry
To cease to think, and cease to be;
I ne'er had called oblivion blest,
Nor, stretching eager hands to death,
Implored to change for lifeless rest
This sentient soul, this living breath—
Oh, let me die—that power and will
Their cruel strife may close;
And conquered good, and conquering ill
Be lost in one repose."

ARTHUR HUGH CLOUGH (1819–1861)

Italy

O land of Empire, art and love!
What is it that you show me?
A sky for Gods to tread above,
A soil for pigs below me!
O in all place and shape and kind
Beyond all thought and thinking,
The graceful with the gross combined,
The stately with the stinking!

Whilst words of mighty love to trace,
Which thy great walls I see on,
Thy porch I pace or take my place
Within thee, great Pantheon,
What sights untold of contrast bold
My ranging eyes must be on!
What though uprolled by young and old
In slumbrous convolution
Neath pillared shade must lie displayed
Bare limbs that scorn ablution,
Should husks that swine would never pick
Bestrew that patterned paving,
And sores to make a surgeon sick
For charity come craving?
Though oft the meditative cur
Account it small intrusion
Through that great gate to quit the stir
Of market-place confusion,
True brother of the bipeds there,
If Nature's need requireth,
Lifts up his leg with tranquil air
And tranquilly retireth:
Though priest think fit to stop and spit
Beside the altar solemn,
Yet, boy, that nuisance why commit
On this Corinthian column?—
O richly soiled and richly sunned,
Exuberant, fervid, and fecund!
Are these the fixed condition
On which may Northern pilgrim come
To imbibe thine ether-air, and sum
Thy store of old tradition?
Must we be chill, if clean, and stand
Foot-deep in dirt in classic land?

So is it: in all ages so,
And in all places man can know,
From homely roots unseen below
In forest-shade in woodland bower
The stem that bears the ethereal flower
Derives that emanative power;
From mixtures fetid foul and sour

Draws juices that those petals fill.
Ah Nature, if indeed thy will
Thou own'st it, it shall not be ill!
And truly here, in this quick clime
Where, scarcely bound by space or time,
The elements in half a day
Toss off with exquisitest play
What our cold seasons toil and grieve,
And never quite at last achieve;
Where processes, with pain and fear
Disgust and horror wrought, appear
The quick mutations of a dance,
Wherein retiring but to advance,
Life, in brief interpause of death,
One moment sitting, taking breath,
Forth comes again as glad as e'er
In some new figure full as fair,
Where what has scarcely ceased to be,
Instinct with newer birth we see—
What dies already, look you, lives;
In such a clime, who thinks, forgives;
Who sees, will understand; who knows,
In calm of knowledge find repose,
And thoughtful as of glory gone,
So too of more to come anon,
Of permanent existence sure,
Brief intermediate breaks endure.
  O Nature, if indeed thy will,
Thou ownest it, it is not ill!
And e'en as oft on heathy hill,
On moorland black, and ferny fells,
Beside thy brooks and in thy dells,
Was welcomed erst the kindly stain
Of thy true earth, e'en so again
With resignation fair and meet
The dirt and refuse of thy street
My philosophic foot shall greet,
So leave but perfect to my eye
Thy columns set against thy sky!

WALT WHITMAN (1819–1902)

As I Ebb'd with the Ocean of Life

1

As I ebb'd with the ocean of life,
As I wended the shores I know,
As I walk'd where the ripples continually wash you Paumanok,
Where they rustle up hoarse and sibilant,
Where the fierce old mother endlessly cries for her castaways,
I musing late in the autumn day, gazing off southward,
Held by this electric self out of the pride of which I utter poems,
Was seiz'd by the spirit that trails in the lines underfoot,
The rim, the sediment that stands for all the water and all the land of the globe.

Fascinated, my eyes reverting from the south, dropt, to follow those slender windrows,
Chaff, straw, splinters of wood, weeds, and the sea-gluten,
Scum, scales from shining rocks, leaves of salt-lettuce, left by the tide,
Miles walking, the sound of breaking waves the other side of me,
Paumanok there and then as I thought the old thought of likenesses,
These you presented to me you fish-shaped island,
As I wended the shores I know,
As I walk'd with that electric self seeking types.

2

As I wend to the shores I know not,
As I list to the dirge, the voices of men and women wreck'd,
As I inhale the impalpable breezes that set in upon me,
As the ocean so mysterious rolls toward me closer and closer,
I too but signify at the utmost a little wash'd-up drift,
A few sands and dead leaves to gather,
Gather, and merge myself as part of the sands and drift.

O baffled, balk'd, bent to the very earth,
Oppress'd with myself that I have dared to open my mouth,
Aware now that amid all that blab whose echoes recoil upon me I have not once had the least idea who or what I am,

But that before all my arrogant poems the real Me stands yet untouch'd,
untold, altogether unreach'd,
Withdrawn far, mocking me with mock-congratulatory signs and bows,
With peals of distant ironical laughter at every word I have written,
Pointing in silence to these songs, and then to the sand beneath.
I perceive I have not really understood any thing, not a single object, and
that no man ever can,
Nature here in sight of the sea taking advantage of me to dart upon me
and sting me,
Because I have dared to open my mouth to sing at all.

3

You oceans both, I close with you,
We murmur alike reproachfully rolling sands and drift, knowing not why,
These little shreds indeed standing for you and me and all.

You friable shore with trails of debris,
You fish-shaped island, I take what is underfoot,
What is yours is mine my father.

I too Paumanok,
I too have bubbled up, floated the measureless float, and been wash'd on
your shores,
I too am but a trail of drift and debris,
I too leave little wrecks upon you, you fish-shaped island.

I throw myself upon your breast my father,
I cling to you so that you cannot unloose me,
I hold you so firm till you answer me something.

Kiss me my father,
Touch me with your lips as I touch those I love,
Breathe to me while I hold you close the secret of the murmuring I envy.

4

Ebb, ocean of life, (the flow will return,)
Cease not your moaning you fierce old mother,
Endlessly cry for your castaways, but fear not, deny not me,
Rustle not up so hoarse and angry against my feet as I touch you or gather
from you.
I mean tenderly by you and all,

I gather for myself and for this phantom looking down where we lead, and
following me and mine.

Me and mine, loose windrows, little corpses,
Froth, snowy white, and bubbles,
(See, from my dead lips the ooze exuding at last,
See, the prismatic colors glistening and rolling,)
Tufts of straw, sands, fragments,
Buoy'd hither from many moods, one contradicting another,
From the storm, the long calm, the darkness, the swell,
Musing, pondering, a breath, a briny tear, a dab of liquid or soil,
Up just as much out of fathomless workings fermented and thrown,
A limp blossom or two, torn, just as much over waves floating, drifted at
random,
Just as much for us that sobbing dirge of Nature,
Just as much whence we come that blare of the cloud-trumpets,
We, capricious, brought hither we know not whence, spread out before you,
You up there walking or sitting,
Whoever you are, we too lie in drifts at your feet.

MATTHEW ARNOLD (1822–1888)

BAYARD TAYLOR (1825–1878)

The Mystic Summer

'T is not the dropping of the flower,
The blush of fruit upon the tree,
Though summer ripens, hour by hour,
The garden's sweet maternity:

'T is not that birds have ceased to build,
And wait their brood with tender care;

That corn is golden in the field,
  And clover balm is in the air;—

Not these the season's splendor bring,
  And crowd with life the happy year,
Nor yet, where yonder fountains sing,
  The blaze of sunshine, hot and clear.

In thy full womb, O Summer! lies
  A secret hope, a joy unsung,
Held in the hush of these calm skies,
  And trembling on the forest's tongue.

The lands of harvest throb anew
  In shining pulses, far away;
The Night distils a dearer dew,
  And sweeter eyelids has the Day.

And not in vain the peony burns
  In bursting globes, her crimson fire,
Her incense-dropping ivory urns
  The lily lifts in many a spire:

And not in vain the tulips clash
  In revelry the cups they hold
Of fiery wine, until they dash
  With ruby streaks the splendid gold!

Send down your roots the mystic charm
  That warms and flushes all your flowers,
And with the summer's touch disarm
  The thraldom of the under powers,

Until, in caverns, buried deep,
  Strange fragrance reach the diamond's home,
And murmurs of the garden sweep
  The houses of the frighted gnome!

For, piercing through their black repose,
  And shooting up beyond the sun,
I see that Tree of Life, which rose
  Before the eyes of Solomon:

Its boughs, that, in the light of God,
  Their bright, innumerous leaves display,—
Whose hum of life is borne abroad
  By winds that shake the dead away

And, trembling on a branch afar,
  The topmost nursling of the skies,
I see my bud, the fairest star
  The ever dawned for watching eyes.

Unnoticed on the boundless tree,
  Its fragrant promise fills the air;
Its little bell expands, for me,
  A tent of silver, lily-fair.

All life to that one centre tends;
  All joy and beauty thence outflow;
Her sweetest gifts the summer spends,
  To teach that sweeter bud to blow.

So compassed by the vision's gleam,
  In trembling hope, from day to day,
As in some bright, bewildering dream,
  The mystic summer wanes away.

DANTE GABRIEL ROSSETTI (1828–1882)

The Monochord

(Written during Music)

Is it this sky's vast vault, or ocean's sound
  That is Life's self and draws my life from me,
  And by instinct ineffable decree
Holds my breath quailing on the bitter bound?
Nay, is it Life or Death, thus thunder-crown'd,
  That 'mid the tide of all emergency
  Now notes my separate wave, and to what sea
Its difficult eddies labour in the ground?

Oh! what is this that knows the road I came,
The flame turned cloud, the cloud returned to flame
  The lifted shifted steeps and all the way?—
That draws round me at last this wind-warm space,
And in regenerate rapture turns my face
  Upon the devious coverts of dismay?

GEORGE MEREDITH (1828–1909)

Hymn to Colour

I

With Life and Death I walked when Love appeared,
And made them on each side a shadow seem.
Through wooded vales the land of dawn we neared,
Where down smooth rapids whirls the helmless dream
To fall on daylight; and night puts away
    Her darker veil for grey.

II

In that grey veil green grassblades brushed we by;
We came where woods breathed sharp, and overhead
Rocks raised clear horns on a transforming sky:
Around, save for those shapes, with him who led
And linked them, desert varied by no sign
    Of other life than mine.

III

By this the dark-winged planet, raying wide,
From the mild pearl-glow to the rose upborne,
Drew in his fires, less faint than far descried,
Pure-fronted on a stronger wave of morn:
And those two shapes the splendour interweaved,
    Hung web-like, sank and heaved.

IV

Love took my hand when hidden stood the sun
To fling his robe on shoulder-heights of snow.
Then said: There lie they, Life and Death in one.

Whichever is, the other is: but know,
It is thy craving self that thou dost see,
Not in them seeing me.

V

Shall man into the mystery of breath,
From his quick beating pulse a pathway spy?
Or learn the secret of the shrouded death,
By lifting up the lid of a white eye?
Cleave thou thy way with fathering desire
Of fire to reach to fire.

VI

Look now where Colour, the soul's bridegroom, makes
The house of heaven splendid for the bride.
To him as leaps a fountain she awakes,
In knotting arms, yet boundless: him beside,
She holds the flower to heaven, and by his power
Brings heaven to the flower.

VII

He gives her homeliness in desert air,
And sovereignty in spaciousness; he leads
Through widening chambers of surprise to where
Throbs rapture near an end that aye recedes,
Because his touch is infinite and lends
A yonder to all ends.

VIII

Death begs of Life his blush; Life Death persuades
To keep long day with his caresses graced.
He is the heart of light, the wing of shades,
The crown of beauty: never soul embraced
Of him can harbour unfaith; soul of him
Possessed walks never dim.

IX

Love eyed his rosy memories: he sang:
O bloom of dawn, breathed up from the gold sheaf
Held springing beneath Orient! that dost hang
The space of dewdrops running over leaf;
Thy fleetingness is bigger in the ghost
Than Time with all his host!

X

Of thee to say behold, has said adieu.
But love remembers how the sky was green,
And how the grasses glimmered lightest blue;
How saint-like grey took fervour: how the screen
Of cloud grew violet; how thy moment came
        Between a blush and flame.

XI

Love saw the emissary eglantine
Break wave round thy white feet above the gloom;
Lay finger on thy star; thy raiment line
With cherub wing and limb; wed thy soft bloom,
Gold-quivering like sunrays in thistle-down,
        Earth under rolling brown.

XII

They do not look through love to look on thee,
Grave heavenliness! nor know they joy of sight,
Who deem the wave of rapt desire must be
Its wrecking and last issue of delight.
Dead seasons quicken in one petal-spot
        Of colour unforgot.

XIII

This way have men come out of brutishness
To spell the letters of the sky and read
A reflex upon earth else meaningless.
With thee, O fount of the Untimed! to lead;
Drink they of thee, thee eyeing, they unaged
        Shall on through brave wars waged.

XIV

More gardens will they win than any lost;
The vile plucked out of them, the unlovely slain.
Not forfeiting the beast with which they are crossed,
To stature of the Gods will they attain.
They shall uplift their Earth to meet her Lord,
        Themselves the attuning chord!

XV

The song had ceased; my vision with the song.
Then of those Shadows, which one made descent

Beside me I knew not: but Life ere long
Came on me in the public ways and bent
Eyes deeper than of old: Death met I too,
And saw the dawn glow through.

EMILY DICKINSON (1830–1886)

Poem 512: "The Soul has Bandaged moments" 303
Poem 341: "After great pain, a formal feeling comes" 462
Poem 986: "A narrow Fellow in the Grass" 463

CHRISTINA ROSSETTI (1830–1894)

Song

When I am dead, my dearest,
  Sing no sad songs for me;
Plant thou no roses at my head,
  Nor shady cypress tree:
Be the green grass above me
  With showers and dewdrops wet:
And if thou wilt, remember,
  And if thou wilt, forget.

I shall not see the shadows,
  I shall not feel the rain;
I shall not hear the nightingale
  Sing on, as if in pain:
And dreaming through the twilight
  That doth not rise nor set,
Haply I may remember,
  And haply may forget.

WILLIAM MORRIS (1834–1896)

Error and Loss

Upon an eve I sat me down and wept,
Because the world to me seemed nowise good;
Still autumn was it, and the meadows slept,
The misty hills dreamed, and the silent wood
Seemed listening to the sorrow of my mood:
I knew not if the earth with me did grieve,
Or if it mocked my grief that bitter eve.

Then 'twixt my tears a maiden did I see,
Who drew anigh me on the leaf-strewn grass,
Then stood and gazed upon me pitifully
With grief-worn eyes, until my woe did pass
From me to her, and tearless now I was,
And she mid tears was asking me of one
She long had sought unaided and alone.

I knew not of him, and she turned away
Into the dark wood, and my own great pain
Still held me there, till dark had slain the day,
And perished at the grey dawn's hand again;
Then from the wood a voice cried: "Ah, in vain,
In vain I seek thee, O thou bitter-sweet!
In what lone land are set thy longed-for feet?"

Then I looked up, and lo, a man there came
From midst the trees, and stood regarding me
Until my tears were dried for very shame;
Then he cried out: "O mourner, where is she
Whom I have sought o'er every land and sea?
I love her and she loveth me, and still
We meet no more than green hill meeteth hill."

With that he passed on sadly, and I knew
That these had met, and missed, in the dark night,

Blinded by blindness of the world untrue,
That hideth love, and maketh wrong of right.
Then midst my pity for their lost delight,
Yet more with barren longing I grew weak,
Yet more I mourned that I had none to seek.

THOMAS BAILEY ALDRICH (1836–1907)

Accomplices

The soft new grass is creeping o'er the graves
  By the Potomac; and the crisp ground-flower
  Lifts its blue cup to catch the passing shower;
The pine-cone ripens, and the long moss waves
Its tangled gonfalons above our braves.
  Hark, what a burst of music from yon bower!—
  The Southern nightingale that hour by hour
In its melodious summer madness raves.
Ah, with what delicate touches of her hand,
  With what sweet voices, Nature seeks to screen
The awful Crime of this distracted land,—
  Sets her birds singing, while she spreads her green
Mantle of velvet where the Murdered lie,
As if to hide the horror from God's eye.

ALGERNON CHARLES SWINBURNE (1837–1909)

THOMAS HARDY (1837–1909)

SIDNEY LANIER (1842–1881)

Sunrise

In my sleep I was fain of their fellowship, fain
Of the live-oak, the marsh, and the main.
The little green leaves would not let me alone in my sleep;
Up-breathed from the marshes, a message of range and of sweep,
Interwoven with wafture of wild sea-liberties, drifting,
Came through the lapped leaves sifting, sifting,
Came to the gates of sleep.
Then my thoughts, in the dark of the dungeon-keep
Of the Castle of Captives hid in the City of Sleep,
Upstarted, by twos and by threes assembling:
The gates of sleep fell a-trembling
Like as the lips of a lady that forth falter *yes*,
Shaken with happiness:
The gates of sleep stood wide.

I have waked, I have come, my beloved! I might not abide:
I have come ere the dawn, O beloved, my live-oaks, to hide
In your gospelling glooms,—to be
As a lover in heaven, the marsh my marsh and the sea my sea.

Tell me, sweet burly-bark'd, man-bodied Tree
That mine arms in the dark are embracing, dost know
From what fount are these tears at thy feet which flow?
They rise not from reason, but deeper inconsequent deeps.
Reason's not one that weeps.
What logic of greeting lies
Betwixt dear over-beautiful trees and the rain of the eyes?

O cunning green leaves, little masters! like as ye gloss
All the dull-tissued dark with your luminous darks that emboss
The vague blackness of night into pattern and plan,
So,
(But would I could know, but would I could know,)
With your question embroid'ring the dark of the question of man,—

So, with your silences purfling this silence of man
While his cry to the dead for some knowledge is under the ban,
Under the ban,—
So, ye have wrought me
Designs on the night of our knowledge,—yea, ye have taught me,
So,
That haply we know somewhat more than we know.

Ye lispers, whisperers, singers in storms,
Ye consciences murmuring faiths under forms,
Ye ministers meet for each passion that grieves,
Friendly, sisterly, sweetheart leaves,
Oh, rain me down from your darks that contain me
Wisdoms ye winnow from winds that pain me,—
Sift down tremors of sweet-within-sweet
That advise me of more than they bring,—repeat
Me the woods-smell that swiftly but now brought breath
From the heaven-side bank of the river of death,—
Teach me the terms of silence,—preach me
The passion of patience,—sift me,—impeach me,—
And there, oh there
As ye hang with your myriad palms upturned in the air,
Pray me a myriad prayer.

My gossip, the owl,—is it thou
That out of the leaves of the low-hanging bough,
As I pass to the beach, art stirred?
Dumb woods, have ye uttered a bird?

. . . . .

Reverend Marsh, low-couched along the sea,
Old chemist, rapt in alchemy,
Distilling silence,—lo,
That which our father-age had died to know—
The menstruum that dissolves all matter—thou
Hast found it: for this silence, filling now
The globèd clarity of receiving space,
This solves us all: man, matter, doubt, disgrace,
Death, love, sin, sanity,
Must in yon silence's clear solution lie.
Too clear! That crystal nothing who'll peruse?
The blackest night could bring us brighter news.
Yet precious qualities of silence haunt

Round these vast margins, ministrant.
Oh, if thy soul's at latter gasp for space,
With trying to breathe no bigger than thy race
Just to be fellow'd, when that thou hast found
No man with room, or grace, enough of bound
To entertain that New thou tell'st, thou art,—
'Tis here, 'tis here, thou canst unhand thy heart
And breathe it free, and breathe it free,
By rangy marsh, in lone sea-liberty.

The tide's at full: the marsh with flooded streams
Glimmers, a limpid labyrinth of dreams.
Each winding creek in grave entrancement lies,
A rhapsody of morning-stars. The skies
Shine scant with one forked galaxy,—
The marsh brags ten: looped on his breast they lie.

Oh, what if a sound should be made!
Oh, what if a bound should be laid
To this bow-and-string tension of beauty and silence a-spring,—
To the bend of beauty the bow, or the hold of silence the string!
I fear me, I fear me yon dome of diaphanous gleam
Will break as a bubble o'er-blown in a dream,—
Yon dome of too-tenuous tissues of space and of night,
Over-weighted with stars, over-freighted with light,
Over-sated with beauty and silence, will seem
  But a bubble that broke in a dream,
If a bound of degree to this grace be laid,
    Or a sound or a motion made.

But no: it is made: list! somewhere,—mystery, where?
        In the leaves? in the air?
In my heart? is a motion made:
'Tis a motion of dawn, like a flicker of shade on shade.
In the leaves 'tis palpable: low multitudinous stirring
Upwinds through the woods; the little ones, softly conferring,
Have settled my lord's to be looked for; so; they are still;
But the air and my heart and the earth are a-thrill,—
And look where the wild duck sails round the bend of the river,—
  And look where a passionate shiver
  Expectant is bending the blades
Of the marsh-grass in serial shimmers and shades,—

And invisible wings, fast fleeting, fast fleeting,
Are beating
The dark overhead as my heart beats,—and steady and free
Is the ebb-tide flowing from marsh to sea
(Run home, little streams,
With your lapfulls of stars and dreams),—
And a sailor unseen is hoisting a-peak,
For list, down the inshore curve of the creek
How merrily flutters the sail,—
And lo, in the east! Will the East unveil?
The East is unveiled, the East hath confessed
A flush: 'tis dead; 'tis alive: 'tis dead, ere the West
Was aware of it: nay, 'tis abiding, 'tis unwithdrawn:
Have a care, sweet Heaven! 'Tis Dawn.

Now a dream of a flame through that dream of a flush is uprolled:
To the zenith ascending, a dome of undazzling gold
Is builded, in shape as a bee-hive, from out of the sea:
The hive is of gold undazzling, but oh, the Bee,
The star-fed Bee, the build-fire Bee,
Of dazzling gold is the great Sun-Bee
That shall flash from the hive-hole over the sea.

Yet now the dew-drop, now the morning gray,
Shall live their little lucid sober day
Ere with the sun their souls exhale away.
Now in each pettiest personal sphere of dew
The summ'd morn shines complete as in the blue
Big dew-drop of all heaven: with these lit shrines
O'er-silvered to the farthest sea-confines,
The sacramental marsh one pious plain
Of worship lies. Peace to the ante-reign
Of Mary Morning, blissful mother mild,
Minded of nought but peace, and of a child.

Not slower than Majesty moves, for a mean and a measure
Of motion,—not faster than dateless Olympian leisure
Might pace with unblown ample garments from pleasure to
pleasure,—
The wave-serrate sea-rim sinks, unjarring, unreeling,
Forever revealing, revealing, revealing,
Edgewise, bladewise, halfwise, wholewise,—'tis done!

Good-morrow, lord Sun!
With several voice, with ascription one,
The woods and the marsh and the sea and my soul
Unto thee, whence the glittering stream of all morrows doth roll,
Cry good and past-good and most heavenly morrow, lord Sun.

O Artisan born in the purple,—Workman Heat,—
Parter of passionate atoms that travail to meet
And be mixed in the death-cold oneness,—innermost Guest
At the marriage of elements,—fellow of publicans,—blest
King in the blouse of flame, that loiterest o'er
The idle skies yet laborest fast evermore—
Thou, in the fine forge-thunder, thou, in the beat
Of the heart of a man, thou Motive,—Laborer Heat:
Yea, Artist, thou, of whose art yon sea's all news,
With his inshore greens and manifold mid-sea blues,
Pearl-glint, shell-tint, ancientest perfectest hues
Ever shaming the maidens,—lily and rose
Confess thee, and each mild flame that glows
In the clarified virginal bosoms of stones that shine,
It is thine, it is thine:

Thou chemist of storms, whether driving the winds a-swirl
Or a-flicker the subtiler essences polar that whirl
In the magnet earth,—yea, thou with a storm for a heart,
Rent with debate, many-spotted with question, part
From part oft sundered, yet ever a globèd light,
Yet ever the artist, ever more large and bright
Than the eye of a man may avail of:—manifold One,
I must pass from thy face, I must pass from the face of the Sun:
Old Want is awake and agog, every wrinkle a-frown;
The worker must pass to his work in the terrible town:
But I fear not, nay, and I fear not the thing to be done;
I am strong with the strength of my lord the Sun:
How dark, how dark soever the race that must needs be run,
I am lit with the Sun.

Oh, never the mast-high run of the seas
Of traffic shall hide thee,
Never the hell-colored smoke of the factories
Hide thee,
Never the reek of the time's fen-polities

Hide thee,
And ever my heart through the night shall with knowledge abide thee,
And ever by day shall my spirit, as one that hath tried thee,
Labor, at leisure, in art,—till yonder beside thee
My soul shall float, friend Sun,
The day being done.

GERARD MANLEY HOPKINS (1844–1889)

ROBERT BRIDGES (1844–1930)

"The sea keeps not the Sabbath day"

The sea keeps not the Sabbath day,
His waves come rolling evermore;
His noisy toil grindeth the shore,
And all the cliff is drencht with spray.

Here as we sit, my love and I,
Under the pine upon the hill,
The sadness of the clouded sky,
The bitter wind, the gloomy roar,
The seamew's melancholy cry
With loving fancy suit but ill.

We talk of moons and cooling suns,
Of geologic time and tide,
The eternal sluggards that abide
While our fair love so swiftly runs,

Of nature that doth half consent
That man should guess her dreary scheme

Lest he should live too well content
In his fair house of mirth and dream:

Whose labour irks his ageing heart,
His heart that wearies of desire,
Being so fugitive a part
Of what so slowly must expire.

She in her agelong toil and care
Persistent, wearies not nor stays,
Mocking alike hope and despair.

—Ah, but she too can mock our praise,
Enchanted on her brighter days,

Days, that the thought of grief refuse,
Days that are one with human art,
Worthy of the Virgilian muse,
Fit for the gaiety of Mozart.

WILLIAM ERNEST HENLEY (1849–1903)

London Voluntaries

4

Largo e mesto

Out of the poisonous East,
Over a continent of blight,
Like a maleficent Influence released
From the most squalid cellarage of hell,
The Wind-Fiend, the abominable—
The Hangman Wind that tortures temper and light—
Comes slouching, sullen and obscene,
Hard on the skirts of the embittered night;
And in a cloud unclean
Of excremental humours, roused to strife
By the operation of some ruinous change,
Wherever his evil mandate run and range,

Into a dire intensity of life,
A craftsman at his bench, he settles down
To the grim job of throttling London Town.

So, by a jealous lightlessness beset
That might have oppressed the dragons of old time
Crunching and groping in the abysmal slime,
A cave of cut-throat thoughts and villainous dreams,
Hag-rid and crying with cold and dirt and wet,
The afflicted City, prone from mark to mark
In shameful occultation, seems
A nightmare labyrinthine, dim and drifting,
With wavering gulfs and antic heights, and shifting,
Rent in the stuff of a material dark,
Wherein the lamplight, scattered and sick and pale,
Shows like the leper's living blotch of bale:
Uncoiling monstrous into street on street
Paven with perils, teeming with mischance,
Where man and beast go blindfold and in dread,
Working with oaths and threats and faltering feet
Somewhither in the hideousness ahead;
Working through wicked airs and deadly dews
That make the laden robber grin askance
At the good places in his black romance,
And the poor, loitering harlot rather choose
Go pinched and pined to bed
Than lurk and shiver and curse her wretched way
From arch to arch, scouting some threepenny prey.
Forgot his dawns and far-flushed afterglows,
His green garlands and windy eyots forgot,
The old Father-River flows,
His watchfires cores of menace in the gloom,
As he came oozing from the Pit, and bore,
Sunk in his filthily transfigured sides,
Shoals of dishonoured dead to tumble and rot
In the squalor of the universal shore:
His voices sounding through the gruesome air
As from the Ferry where the Boat of Doom
With her blaspheming cargo reels and rides:
The while his children, the brave ships,
No more adventurous and fair,
Nor tripping it light of heel as home-bound brides,

But infamously enchanted,
Huddle together in the foul eclipse,
Or feel their course by inches desperately,
As through a tangle of alleys murder-haunted,
From sinister reach to reach out—out—to sea.

And Death the while—
Death with his well-worn, lean, professional smile,
Death in his threadbare working trim—
Comes to your bedside, unannounced and bland,
And with expert, inevitable hand
Feels at your windpipe, fingers you in the lung,
Or flicks the clot well into the labouring heart:
Thus signifying unto old and young,
However hard of mouth or wild of whim,
'Tis time—'tis time by his ancient watch—to part
From books and women and talk and drink and art.
And you go humbly after him
To a mean suburban lodging: on the way
To what or where
Not Death, who is old and very wise, can say:
And you—how should you care
So long as, unreclaimed of hell,
The Wind-Fiend, the insufferable,
Thus vicious and thus patient, sits him down
To the black job of burking London Town?

LIZETTE WOODWORTH REESE (1856–1935)

Wild Geese

The sun blown out;
The dusk about:
Fence, roof, tree—here or there,
Wedged fast in the drab air;
A pool vacant with sky,
That stares up like an eye.

Nothing can happen. All is done—
The quest to fare,

The race to run—
The house sodden with years,
And bare
Even of tears.

A cry!
From out the hostelries of sky,
And down the gray wind blown;
Rude, innocent, alone.

Now, in the west, long sere,
An orange thread, the length of spear;
It glows;
It grows;
The flagons of the air
Drip color everywhere:
The village—fence, roof, tree—
From the lapsed dusk pulls free,
And shows
A rich, still, unforgotten place;
Each window square,
Yellow for yellow renders back;
The pool puts off its foolish face;
The wagon track
Crooks past lank garden-plot,
To Rome, to Camelot.

A cry!

FRANCIS THOMPSON (1859–1927)

The Poppy

To Monica

Summer set lip to earth's bosom bare,
And left the flushed print in a poppy there:
Like a yawn of fire from the grass it came,
And the fanning wind puffed it to flapping flame.

With burnt mouth red like a lion's it drank
The blood of the sun as he slaughtered sank,
And dipped its cup in the purpurate shine
When the Eastern conduits ran with wine.

Till it grew lethargied with fierce bliss,
And hot as a swinkèd gipsy is,
And drowsed in sleepy savageries,
With mouth wide a-pout for a sultry kiss.

A child and man paced side by side,
Treading the skirts of eventide;
But between the clasp of his hand and hers
Lay, felt not, twenty withered years.

She turned, with the rout of her dusk South hair,
And saw the sleeping gipsy there;
And snatched and snapped it in swift child's whim,
With—"Keep it, long as you live!"—to him.

And his smile, as nymphs from their laving meres,
Trembled up from a bath of tears;
And joy, like a mew sea-rocked apart,
Tossed on the waves of his troubled heart.

For *he* saw what she did not see,
That—as kindled by its own fervency—
The verge shrivelled inward smoulderingly:

And suddenly 'twixt his hand and hers
He knew the twenty withered years—
No flower, but twenty shrivelled years.

"Was never such thing until this hour,"
Low to his heart he said; "the flower
Of sleep brings wakening to me,
And of oblivion memory."

"Was never this thing to me," he said,
"Though with bruisèd poppies my feet are red!"
And again to his own heart very low:
"O child! I love, for I love and know;

"But you, who love nor know at all
The diverse chambers in Love's guest-hall,
Where some rise early, few sit long:
In how differing accents hear the throng
His great Pentecostal tongue;

"Who know not love from amity,
Nor my reported self from me;
A fair fit gift is this, meseems,
You give—this withering flower of dreams.

"O frankly fickle, and fickly true,
Do you know what the days will do to you?
To your love and you what the days will do,
O frankly fickle, and fickly true?

"You have loved me, Fair, three lives—or days:
'Twill pass with the passing of my face.
But where *I* go, your face goes too,
To watch lest I play false to you.

"I am but, my sweet, your foster-lover,
Knowing well when certain years are over
You vanish from me to another;
Yet I know, and love, like the foster-mother.

"So, frankly fickle, and fickly true!
For my brief life-while I take from you
This token, fair and fit, meseems,
For me—this withering flower of dreams."

. . . . .

The sleep-flower sways in the wheat its head,
Heavy with dreams, as that with bread:
The goodly grain and the sun-flushed sleeper
The reaper reaps, and Time the reaper.

I hang 'mid men my needless head,
And my fruit is dreams, as theirs is bread:
The goodly men and the sun-hazed sleeper
Time shall reap, but after the reaper
The world shall glean of me, me the sleeper.

Love, love! your flower of withered dream
In leavèd rhyme lies safe, I deem,
Sheltered and shut in a nook of rhyme,
From the reaper man, and his reaper Time.

Love! *I* fall into the claws of Time:
But lasts within a leavèd rhyme
All that the world of me esteems—
My withered dreams, my withered dreams.

ALFRED EDWARD HOUSMAN (1859–1936)

A Shropshire Lad

32

From far, from eve and morning
  And yon twelve-winded sky,
The stuff of life to knit me
  Blew hither: here am I.

Now—for a breath I tarry
  Nor yet disperse apart—
Take my hand quick and tell me,
  What have you in your heart.

Speak now, and I will answer;
  How shall I help you, say;
Ere to the wind's twelve quarters
  I take my endless way.

RUDYARD KIPLING (1865–1936)

An American

The American Spirit speaks:

"If the Led Striker call it a strike,
  Or the papers call it a war,
They know not much what I am like,
  Nor what he is, my Avatar."

Through many roads, by me possessed,
  He shambles forth in cosmic guise;
He is the Jester and the Jest,
  And he the Text himself applies.

The Celt is in his heart and hand,
  The Gaul is in his brain and nerve;
Where, cosmopolitanly planned,
  He guards the Redskin's dry reserve.

His easy unswept hearth he lends
  From Labrador to Guadeloupe;
Till, elbowed out by sloven friends,
  He camps, at sufferance, on the stoop.

Calm-eyed he scoffs at sword and crown,
  Or panic-blinded stabs and slays:
Blatant he bids the world bow down,
  Or cringing begs a crust of praise;

Or, sombre-drunk, at mine and mart,
  He dubs his dreary brethren Kings.
His hands are black with blood—his heart
  Leaps, as a babe's, at little things.

But, through the shift of mood and mood,
  Mine ancient humour saves him whole—

The cynic devil in his blood
  That bids him mock his hurrying soul;

That bids him flout the Law he makes,
  That bids him make the Law he flouts,
Till, dazed by many doubts, he wakes
  The drumming guns that—have no doubts;

That checks him foolish-hot and fond,
  That chuckles through his deepest ire,
That gilds the slough of his despond
  But dims the goal of his desire;

Inopportune, shrill-accented,
  The acrid Asiatic mirth
That leaves him, careless 'mid his dead,
  The scandal of the elder earth.

How shall he clear himself, how reach
  Your bar or weighed defence prefer?
A brother hedged with alien speech
  And lacking all interpreter.

Which knowledge vexes him a space;
  But while Reproof around him rings,
He turns a keen untroubled face
  Home, to the instant need of things.

Enslaved, illogical, elate,
  He greets th' embarrassed Gods, nor fears
To shake the iron hand of Fate
  Or match with Destiny for beers.

Lo, imperturbable he rules,
  Unkempt, disreputable, vast—
And, in the teeth of all the schools,
  I—I shall save him at the last!

WILLIAM BUTLER YEATS (1865–1939)

LIONEL JOHNSON (1867–1902)

Upon Reading Certain Poems

I come, a lost wind from the shores
Of wondering dull misery:
With muttered echoes, heartsick plaints,
And sullen sorrows, filling me.
But all this flowery world abhors
Me, wretched wind and heavy cloud:
Beneath me, as beneath a shroud,
　　The spirit of summer faints.

The golden angel of delight
Gleams past me, and I shrink away:
A dimness on the dawn am I,
A mist upon the merry day.
Here should be none but Muses bright,
Whose airs go delicately sweet:
With swallow wings, and faery feet,
　　Eager to dance or fly.

I will drift back to Wearyland,
To wondering dull misery:
No champaign rich, nor rosy lawn,
Shall wither by the fault of me.
Where no one takes loved hand in hand,
But with his shadow crawls alone:
They miss the comfort of my moan,
　　My melancholy long-drawn.

EDWIN ARLINGTON ROBINSON (1869–1935)

Old Trails

(Washington Square)

I met him, as one meets a ghost or two,
Between the gray Arch and the old Hotel.
"King Solomon was right, there's nothing new,"
Said he. "Behold a ruin who meant well."

He led me down familiar steps again,
Appealingly, and set me in a chair.
"My dreams have all come true to other men,"
Said he; "God lives, however, and why care?

"An hour among the ghosts will do no harm."
He laughed, and something glad within me sank.
I may have eyed him with a faint alarm,
For now his laugh was lost in what he drank.

"They chill things here with ice from hell," he said;
"I might have known it." And he made a face
That showed again how much of him was dead,
And how much was alive and out of place,

And out of reach. He knew as well as I
That all the words of wise men who are skilled
In using them are not much to defy
What comes when memory meets the unfulfilled.

What evil and infirm perversity
Had been at work with him to bring him back?
Never among the ghosts, assuredly,
Would he originate a new attack;

Never among the ghosts, or anywhere,
Till what was dead of him was put away,

Would he attain to his offended share
Of honor among others of his day.

"You ponder like an owl," he said at last;
"You always did, and here you have a cause.
For I'm a confirmation of the past,
A vengeance, and a flowering of what was.

"Sorry? Of course you are, though you compress,
With even your most impenetrable fears,
A placid and a proper consciousness
Of anxious angels over my arrears.

"I see them there against me in a book
As large as hope, in ink that shines by night
Surely I see; but now I'd rather look
At you, and you are not a pleasant sight.

"Forbear, forgive. Ten years are on my soul,
And on my conscience. I've an incubus:
My one distinction, and a parlous toll
To glory; but hope lives on clamorous.

" 'Twas hope, though heaven I grant you knows of what—
The kind that blinks and rises when it falls,
Whether it sees a reason why or not—
That heard Broadway's hard-throated siren-calls;

" 'Twas hope that brought me through December storms,
To shores again where I'll not have to be
A lonely man with only foreign worms
To cheer him in his last obscurity.

"But what it was that hurried me down here
To be among the ghosts, I leave to you.
My thanks are yours, no less, for one thing clear:
Though you are silent, what you say is true.

"There may have been the devil in my feet,
For down I blundered, like a fugitive,
To find the old room in Eleventh Street.
God save us!—I came here again to live."

We rose at that, and all the ghosts rose then,
And followed us unseen to his old room.
No longer a good place for living men
We found it, and we shivered in the gloom.

The goods he took away from there were few,
And soon we found ourselves outside once more,
Where now the lamps along the Avenue
Bloomed white for miles above an iron floor.

"Now lead me to the newest of hotels,"
He said, "and let your spleen be undeceived:
This ruin is not myself, but some one else;
I haven't failed; I've merely not achieved."

Whether he knew or not, he laughed and dined
With more of an immune regardlessness
Of pits before him and of sands behind
Than many a child at forty would confess;

And after, when the bells in *Boris* rang
Their tumult at the Metropolitan,
He rocked himself, and I believe he sang.
"God lives," he crooned aloud, "and I'm the man!"

He was. And even though the creature spoiled
All prophecies, I cherish his acclaim.
Three weeks he fattened; and five years he toiled
In Yonkers,—and then sauntered into fame.

And he may go now to what streets he will—
Eleventh, or the last, and little care;
But he would find the old room very still
Of evenings, and the ghosts would all be there.

I doubt if he goes after them; I doubt
If many of them ever come to him.
His memories are like lamps, and they go out;
Or if they burn, they flicker and are dim.

A light of other gleams he has to-day
And adulations of applauding hosts;

A famous danger, but a safer way
Than growing old alone among the ghosts.

But we may still be glad that we were wrong:
He fooled us, and we'd shrivel to deny it;
Though sometimes when old echoes ring too long,
I wish the bells in *Boris* would be quiet.

WALTER DE LA MARE (1873–1956)

Forests

Turn, now, tired mind unto your rest,
Within your secret chamber lie,
Doors shut, and windows curtained, lest
Footfall or moonbeam, stealing by,
Wake you, or night-wind sigh.

Now, Self, we are at peace—we twain;
The house is silent, except that—hark!—
Against its walls wells out again
That rapture in the empty dark;
Where, softly beaming, spark by spark,

The glow-worms stud the leaves with light;
And unseen flowers, refreshed with dew—
Jasmine, convolvulus, glimmering white,
The air with their still life endue,
And sweeten night for me and you.

Be mute all speech; and not of love
Talk we, nor call on hope, but be—
Calm as the constant stars above—
The friends of fragile memory,
Shared only now by you and me.

Thus hidden, thus silent, while the hours
From gloom to gloom their wings beat on,
Shall not a moment's peace by ours,

Till, faint with day, the east is wan,
And terrors of the dark are gone?

Nay—in the forests of the mind
Lurk beasts as fierce as those that tread
Earth's rock-strown wilds, to night resigned,
There stars of heaven no radiance shed—
Bleak-eyed Remorse, Despair becowled in lead.

With dawn these ravening shapes will go
Though One at watch will still remain:
Till knell the sunset hours, and lo!
The listening soul once more will know
Death and his pack are hot afield again.

ROBERT FROST (1875–   )

JOHN MASEFIELD (1878–   )

Sonnet

Here in the self is all that man can know
Of Beauty, all the wonder, all the power,
All the unearthly color, all the glow,
Here in the self which withers like a flower;
Here in the self which fades as hours pass,
And droops and dies and rots and is forgotten,
Sooner, by ages, than the mirroring glass
In which it sees its glory still unrotten.
Here in the flesh, within the flesh, behind,
Swift in the blood and throbbing on the bone,
Beauty herself, the universal mind,
Eternal April wandering alone.

The god, the holy ghost, the atoning lord,
Here in the flesh, the never yet explored.

CARL SANDBURG (1878–   )

Interior

In the cool of the night time
The clocks pick off the points
And the mainsprings loosen.
They will need winding.
One of these days . . .
                    they will need winding.

Rabelais in red boards,
Walt Whitman in green,
Hugo in ten-cent paper covers,
Here they stand on shelves
In the cool of the night time
And there is nothing . . .
To be said against them . . .
Or for them . . .
In the cool of the night time
And the clocks.

A man in pigeon-gray pajamas.
The open window begins at his feet
And goes taller than his head.
Eight feet high is the pattern.

Moon and mist make an oblong layout.
Silver at the man's bare feet.
He swings one foot in a moon silver.
And it costs nothing.

One more day of bread and work.
One more day . . . so much rags . . .
The man barefoot in moon silver
Mutters "You" and "You"

To things hidden
In the cool of the night time,
In Rabelais, Whitman, Hugo,
In an oblong of moon mist.

Out from the window . . . prairielands.
Moon mist whitens a golf ground.
Whiter yet is a limestone quarry.
The crickets keep on chirring.

Switch engines of the Great Western
Sidetrack box cars, make up trains
For Weehawken, Oskaloosa, Saskatchewan;
The cattle, the coal, the corn, must go
In the night . . . on the prairielands.

Chuff-chuff go the pulses.
They beat in the cool of the night time.
Chuff-chuff and chuff-chuff . . .
These heartbeats travel the night a mile
And touch the moon silver at the window
And the bones of the man.
It costs nothing.

Rabelais in red boards,
Walt Whitman in green,
Hugo in ten-cent paper covers,
Here they stand on shelves
In the cool of the night time
And the clocks.

WALLACE STEVENS *(1879–1955)*

DAVID HERBERT LAWRENCE (1885–1930)

Dolour of Autumn

The acrid scents of autumn,
Reminiscent of slinking beasts, make me fear
Everything, tear-trembling stars of autumn
And the snore of the night in my ear.

For suddenly, flush-fallen,
All my life, in a rush
Of shedding away, has left me
Naked exposed on the bush.

I on the bush of the globe
Like a newly-naked berry shrink
Disclosed; but 'tis I who am prowling
As well in the scents that slink

Abroad: I in this naked berry
Of flesh that stands dismayed on the bush!
And I in the stealthy, brindled odours
Prowling about the lush

And acrid night of autumn!
My soul, along with the rout
Rank and treacherous, prowling
Disseminated out.

For the night, with a great breath taken
Has drawn my spirit outside
Me, till I reel with disseminated consciousness
Like a man who has died.

At the same time stand exposed
Here on the bush of the globe,
A newly-naked berry of flesh
For the stars to probe.

EZRA POUND (1885–)

From The Cantos

17

So that the vines burst from my fingers
And the bees weighted with pollen
Move heavily in the vine-shoots:
chirr—chirr—chir-rikk—a purring sound,
And the birds sleepily in the branches.
ZAGREUS! IO ZAGREUS!
With the first pale-clear of the heaven
And the cities set in their hills,
And the goddess of the fair knees
Moving there, with the oak-wood behind her,
The green slope, with white hounds
leaping about her;
And thence down to the creek's mouth, until evening,
Flat water before me,
and the trees growing in water,
Marble trunks out of stillness,
On past the palazzi,
in the stillness,
The light now, not of the sun.
Chrysophrase,
And the water green clear, and blue clear;
On, to the great cliffs of amber.
Between them,
Cave of Nerea,
she like a great shell curved,
And the boat drawn without sound,
Without odour of ship-work,
Nor bird-cry, nor any noise of wave moving,
Nor splash of porpoise, nor any noise of wave moving,
Within her cave, Nerea,
she like a great shell curved
In the suavity of the rock,
cliff green-gray in the far,

In the near, the gate-cliffs of amber,
And the wave
green clear, and blue clear,
And the cave salt-white, and glare-purple,
cool, porphyry smooth,
the rock sea-worn.
No gull-cry, no sound of porpoise,
Sand as of malachite, and no cold there,
the light not of the sun.
Zagreus, feeding his panthers,
the turf clear as on hills under light.
And under the almond-trees, gods,
with them, *choros nympharum.* Gods,
Hermes and Athene,
As shaft of compass,
Between them, trembled—
To the left is the place of fauns,
sylva nympharum;
The low wood, moor-scrub,
the doe, the young spotted deer,
leap up through the broom-plants,
as dry leaf amid yellow.
And by one cut of the hills,
the great alley of Memnons.
Beyond, sea, crests seen over dune
Night sea churning shingle,
To the left, the alley of cypress.
A boat came,
One man holding her sail,
Guiding her with oar caught over gunwale, saying:
"There, in the forest of marble,
"the stone trees—out of water—
"the arbours of stone—
"marble leaf, over leaf,
"silver, steel over steel,
"silver beaks rising and crossing,
"prow set against prow,
"stone, ply over ply,
"the gilt beams flare of an evening"
Borso, Carmagnola, the men of craft, *i vitrei,*
Thither, at one time, time after time,

And the waters richer than glass,
Bronze gold, the blaze over the silver,
Dye-pots in the torch-light,
The flash of wave under prows,
And the silver beaks rising and crossing.
Stone trees, white and rose-white in the darkness,
Cypress there by the towers,
Drift under hulls in the night.

"In the gloom the gold
Gathers the light about it." . . .

Now supine in burrow, half over-arched bramble,
One eye for the sea, through that peek-hole,
Gray light, with Athene.
Zothar and her elephants, the gold loin-cloth,
The sistrum, shaken, shaken,
the cohort of her dancers.
And Aletha, by bend of the shore,
with her eyes seaward,
and in her hands sea-wrack
Salt-bright with the foam.
Koré through the bright meadow,
with green-gray dust in the grass:
"For this hour, brother of Circe."
Arm laid over my shoulder,
Saw the sun for three days, the sun fulvid,
As a lion lift over sand-plain;
and that day,
And for three days, and none after,
Splendour, as the splendour of Hermes,
And shipped thence
to the stone place,
Pale white, over water,
known water,
And the white forest of marble, bent bough over bough,
The pleached arbour of stone,
Thither Borso, when they shot the barbed arrow at him,
And Carmagnola, between the two columns,
Sigismundo, after that wreck in Dalmatia.
Sunset like the grasshopper flying.

EDITH SITWELL (1887–   )

The Higher Sensualism

Queen Circe, the farmer's wife at the Fair,
Met three sailor-men stumping there,

Who came from the parrot-plumed sea, Yo-Ho!
And each his own trumpet began to blow.

"We come," said they, "from the Indian seas,
All bright as a parrot's feathers, and these

Break on gold sands of the perfumed isles,
Where the fruit is soft as a siren's smiles,

And the sun is as black as a Nubian.
We singed the beard of the King of Spain. . . .

Then we wandered once more on the South Sea strand
Where the icebergs seem Heavenly Mansions fanned

By the softest wind from the groves of spice,
And the angels like birds of paradise

Flit there: and we caught this queer-plumaged boy
(An angel, he calls himself) for a toy."

. . . . .

The Angel sighed: "Please, ma'am, if you'll spare
Me a trumpet, the angels will come to the Fair;

For even an angel must have his fling,
And ride on the roundabout, in the swing!"

She gave him a trumpet, but never a blare
Reached the angels from Midsummer Fair,

Though he played, "Will you hear a Spanish lady?"
And "Jack the Sailor," "Sweet Nelly," "Trees shady"—

For only the gay hosannas of flowers
Sound, loud as brass bands, in those heavenly bowers.

Queen Circe said, "Young man, I will buy
Your plumaged coat for my pig to try—

Then with angels he'll go a-dancing hence
From sensuality into sense!"

The Fair's tunes like cherries and apricots
Ripened; the angels danced from their green grots;

Their hair was curled like the fruit on the trees . . .
Rigaudon, sarabande, danced they these.

And the pig points his toe and he curves his wings,
The music starts, and away he flings—

Dancing with angels all in a round,
Hornpipe and rigaudon on the Fair's ground.

THOMAS STEARNS ELIOT (1888–)

ARCHIBALD MACLEISH (1892–)

Immortal Autumn

I speak this poem now with grave and level voice
In praise of autumn, of the far-horn-winding fall.

I praise the flower-barren fields, the clouds, the tall
Unanswering branches where the wind makes sullen noise.

I praise the fall: it is the human season.
                                                            Now
No more the foreign sun does meddle at our earth,
Enforce the green and bring the fallow land to birth,
Nor winter yet weigh all with silence the pine bough,

But now in autumn with the black and outcast crows
Share we the spacious world: the whispering year is gone:
There is more room to live now: the once secret dawn
Comes late by daylight and the dark unguarded goes.

Between the mutinous brave burning of the leaves
And winter's covering of our hearts with his deep snow
We are alone: there are no evening birds: we know
The naked moon: the tame stars circle at our eaves.

It is the human season. On this sterile air
Do words outcarry breath: the sound goes on and on.
I hear a dead man's cry from autumn long since gone.

I cry to you beyond upon this bitter air.

WILFRED OWEN (1893–1918)

Dulce et Decorum Est

Bent double, like old beggars under sacks,
Knock-kneed, coughing like hags, we cursed through sludge,
Till on the haunting flares we turned our backs,
And towards our distant rest began to trudge.
Men marched asleep. Many had lost their boots,
But limped on, blood-shod. All went lame, all blind;
Drunk with fatigue; deaf even to the hoots
Of gas-shells dropping softly behind.

Gas! GAS! Quick, boys!—An ecstasy of fumbling
Fitting the clumsy helmets just in time,
But someone still was yelling out and stumbling
And flound'ring like a man in fire or lime.—

Dim through the misty panes and thick green light,
As under a green sea, I saw him drowning.

In all my dreams before my helpless sight
He plunges at me, guttering, choking, drowning.

If in some smothering dreams, you too could pace
Behind the wagon that we flung him in,
And watch the white eyes writhing in his face,
His hanging face, like a devil's sick of sin,
If you could hear, at every jolt, the blood
Come gargling from the froth-corrupted lungs
Bitten as the cud
Of vile, incurable sores on innocent tongues,—
My friend, you would not tell with such high zest
To children ardent for some desperate glory,
The old Lie: *Dulce et decorum est*
Pro patria mori.

EDWARD ESTLIN CUMMINGS (1894–)

"anyone lived in a pretty how town"

anyone lived in a pretty how town
(with up so floating many bells down)
spring summer autumn winter
he sang his didn't he danced his did.

Women and men (both little and small)
cared for anyone not at all
they sowed their isn't they reaped their same
sun moon stars rain

children guessed (but only a few
and down they forgot as up they grew
autumn winter spring summer)
that noone loved him more by more

when by now and tree by leaf
she laughed his joy she cried his grief

bird by snow and stir by still
anyone's any was all to her

someones married their everyones
laughed their cryings and did their dance
(sleep wake hope and then) they
said their nevers they slept their dream

stars rain sun moon
(and only the snow can begin to explain
how children are apt to forget to remember
with up so floating many bells down)

one day anyone died i guess
(and noone stooped to kiss his face)
busy folk buried them side by side
little by little and was by was

all by all and deep by deep
and more by more they dream their sleep
noone and anyone earth by april
wish by spirit and if by yes.

Women and men (both dong and ding)
summer autumn winter spring
reaped their sowing and went their came
sun moon stars rain

ROBERT GRAVES (1895–   )

The Cool Web

Children are dumb to say how hot the day is,
How hot the scent is of the summer rose,
How dreadful the black wastes of evening sky,
How dreadful the tall soldiers drumming by.

But we have speech, that cools the hottest sun,
And speech that dulls the hottest rose's scent.

We spell away the overhanging night,
We spell away the soldiers and the fright.

There's a cool web of language winds us in,
Retreat from too much gladness, too much fear:
We grow sea-green at last and coldly die
In brininess and volubility.

But if we let our tongues lose self-possession,
Throwing off language and its wateriness
Before our death, instead of when death comes,
Facing the brightness of the children's day,
Facing the rose, the dark sky and the drums,
We shall go mad no doubt and die that way.

HART CRANE (1899–1932)

To Brooklyn Bridge

From *The Bridge*

How many dawns, chill from his rippling rest
The seagull's wings shall dip and pivot him,
Shedding white rings of tumult, building high
Over the chained bay waters Liberty—

Then, with inviolate curve, forsake our eyes
As apparitional as sails that cross
Some page of figures to be filed away;
—Till elevators drop us from our day . . .

I think of cinemas, panoramic sleights
With multitudes bent toward some flashing scene
Never disclosed, but hastened to again,
Foretold to other eyes on the same screen;

And Thee, across the harbor, silver-paced
As though the sun took step of thee, yet left
Some motion ever unspent in thy stride,—
Implicitly thy freedom staying thee!

Out of some subway scuttle, cell or loft
A bedlamite speeds to thy parapets,
Tilting there momently, shrill shirt ballooning,
A jest falls from the speechless caravan.

Down Wall, from girder into street noon leaks,
A rip-tooth of the sky's acetylene;
All afternoon the cloud-flown derricks turn . . .
Thy cables breathe the North Atlantic still.

And obscure as that heaven of the Jews,
Thy guerdon . . . Accolade thou dost bestow
Of anonymity time cannot raise:
Vibrant reprieve and pardon thou dost show.

O harp and altar, of the fury fused,
(How could mere toil align thy choiring strings!)
Terrific threshold of the prophet's pledge,
Prayer of pariah, and the lover's cry,—

Again the traffic lights that skim thy swift
Unfractioned idiom, immaculate sigh of stars,
Beading thy path—condense eternity:
And we have seen night lifted in thine arms.

Under thy shadow by the piers I waited;
Only in darkness is thy shadow clear.
The City's fiery parcels all undone,
Already snow submerges an iron year . . .

O Sleepless as the river under thee,
Vaulting the sea, the prairies' dreaming sod,
Unto us lowliest sometime sweep, descend
And of the curveship lend a myth to God.

KENNETH FEARING (1902–)

Art Review

Recently displayed at the Times Square Station, a new Vandyke on the face-cream girl.
(Artist unknown. Has promise, but lacks the brilliance shown by the great masters of the Elevated age)
The latest wood carving in a Whelan telephone booth, titled "O Mortal Fools WA 9-5090," shows two winged hearts above an ace of spades.
(His meaning is not entirely clear, but this man will go far)
A charcoal nude in the rear of Flatbush Ahearn's Bar & Grill, "Forward to the Brotherhood of Man," has been boldly conceived in the great tradition.
(We need more, much more of this)
Then there is the chalk portrait, on the walls of a waterfront warehouse, of a gentleman wearing a derby hat: "Bleecker Street Mike is a double-crossing rat."
(Morbid, but powerful. Don't miss)

Know then by these presents, know all men by these signs and omens, by these simple thumbprints on the throat of time,
Know that Pete, the people's artist, is ever watchful,
That Tuxedo Jim has passed among us, and was much displeased, as always,
That George the Ghost (no man has ever seen him) and Billy the Bicep boy will neither bend nor break,
That Mr. Harkness of Sunnyside still hopes for the best, and has not lost his human touch,
That Phantom Phil, the master of them all, has come and gone, but will return, and all is well.

RICHARD EBERHART (1904–)

If I Could Only Live at the Pitch That Is Near Madness

If I could only live at the pitch that is near madness
When everything is as it was in my childhood

Violent, vivid, and of infinite possibility:
That the sun and the moon broke over my head.

Then I cast time out of the trees and fields,
Then I stood immaculate in the Ego;
Then I eyed the world with all delight,
Reality was the perfection of my sight.

And time has big handles on the hands,
Fields and trees a way of being themselves.
I saw battalions of the race of mankind
Standing stolid, demanding a moral answer.

I gave the moral answer and I died
And into a realm of complexity came
Where nothing is possible but necessity
And the truth wailing there like a red babe.

ROBERT PENN WARREN (1905–   )

Crime

Envy the mad killer who lies in the ditch and grieves,
Hearing the horns on the highway, and the tires scream:
He tries to remember, and tries, but he cannot seem
To remember what it was he buried under the leaves.

By the steamed lagoon, near the carnivorous orchid,
Pirates hide treasure and mark the place with a skull,
Then lose the map, and roar in pubs with a skinful,
In Devon or Barbados; but remember what they hid.

But what was it? But he is too tired to ask it.
An old woman mumbling her gums like incertitude?
The proud stranger who asked the match by the park wood,
Or the child who crossed the park every day with the lunch-basket?

He cannot say, nor formulate the delicious
And smooth convolution of terror, like whipped cream,

Nor the mouth, rounded and white for the lyric scream
Which he never heard, though he still tries, nodding and serious.

His treasure: for years down streets of contempt and trouble,
Hugged under his coat, among sharp elbows and rows
Of eyes hieratic like foetuses in jars;
Or he nursed it unwitting, like a child asleep with a bauble.

Happiness: what the heart wants. That is its fond
Definition, and wants only the peace in God's eye.
Our flame bends in that draft; and that is why
He clutched at the object bright on the bottom of the murky pond.

Peace, all he asked: past despair and past the uncouth
Violation, he snatched at the fleeting hem, though in error;
Nor gestured before the mind's sycophant mirror,
Nor made the refusal and spat from the secret side of his mouth.

Though a tree for you is a tree, and in the long
Dark, no sibilant tumor inside your enormous
Head, though no walls confer in the silent house,
Nor the eyes of pictures protrude, like a snail's, each on its prong,

Yet envy him, for what he buried is buried
By the culvert there, till the boy with the air-gun
In spring, at the violet, comes; nor is ever known
To go on any vacations with him, lend money, break bread.

And envy him, for though the seasons stammer
Past pulse in the yellow throat of the field-lark,
Still memory drips, a pipe in the cellar-dark,
And in its hutch and hole, as when the earth gets warmer,

The cold heart heaves like a toad, and lifts its brow
With that bright jewel you have no use for now;
While puzzled yet, despised with the attic junk, the letter
Names over your name, and mourns under the dry rafter.

WYSTAN HUGH AUDEN (1907–   )

LOUIS MACNEICE (1907–   )

Picture Galleries

Strolling, guidebook in hand, along the varnished parquet
We meet the calm of opium in the long galleries,
    An under-water dream, a closed
World whose people live in frames, the flames of their self-centred
Affections frozen, the bread and fruit on their tables fossil,
    A curfew—once for all—imposed
Upon their might-be wanderings; their might-be applications
    For resurrection in advance refused.

Yet were violent monsters, whom the retiring ocean
Left embedded in sandstone: Michelangelo's tortured
    Urge to God, Greco's fugue of fire,
Goya's sleight-of-hand that fooled his patrons, Blake's ingenuous
Usurpation of reality, Daumier watching the bubbles rising
    From mouths of the drowned; panic, desire,
Fantasy, joy of the earth—the rhythm lurks in the canvas, sometimes
    If we look long, is more than we can bear.

Or viewed as history they remind us of what we always
Would rather forget—that what we are or prefer is conditioned
    By circumstances, that evil and good
Are relative to ourselves who are creatures of period; seeing
That what, for instance, Zurbaran found in his Carthusians
    Serene in white, with rope girdle and hood,
Lautrec discovered in brothel and circus; the answers were even
    Even though we today may find them odd.

A curator rings a bell: tourists, connoisseurs and loafers,
School-children with their teachers, hustle for the door, many
Of their faces tired or showing relief
At leaving a silence which was a crowd of voices, the language
Like that of a paralytic hard to follow; they descend the staircase
Into the open air, a sheaf
Of inklings fluttering in their minds, and now even the open
Air is half-articulate and unsafe.

STEPHEN SPENDER (1909–)

Polar Exploration

Our single purpose was to walk through snow
With faces swung to their prodigious North
Like compass iron. As clerks in whited banks
With bird-claw pens column virgin paper,
To snow we added foot-prints.
Extensive whiteness drowned
All sense of space. We tramped through
Static, glaring days, Time's suspended blank.
That was in Spring and Autumn. Summer struck
Water over rocks, and half the world
Became a ship with a deep keel, the booming floes
And icebergs with their little birds:
Twittering Snow Bunting, Greenland Wheatear,
Red-throated Divers; imagine butterflies
Sulphurous cloudy yellow; glory of bees
That suck from saxifrage; crowberry,
Bilberry, cranberry, *Pyrola Uniflora*.
There followed Winter in a frozen hut
Warm enough at the kernel, but dare to sleep
With head against the wall—ice gummed my hair!
Hate Culver's loud breathing, despise Freeman's
Fidget for washing: love only the dogs
That whine for scraps, and scratch. Notice
How they run better (on short journeys) with a bitch.
In that, different from us.
Return, return, you warn. We do. There is

A network of railways, money, words, words, words.
Meals, papers, exchanges, debates,
Cinema, wireless: the worst, is Marriage.
We cannot sleep. At night we watch
A speaking clearness through cloudy paranoia.
These questions are white rifts:—Was
Ice our anger transformed? The raw, the motionless
Skies, were these the Spirit's hunger?
The continual and hypnotized march through snow,
The dropping nights of precious extinction, were these
Only the wide inventions of the will,
The frozen will's evasion? If this exists
In us as madness here, as coldness
In these summer, civilized sheets: Is the North,
Over there, a tangible, real madness,
A glittering simpleton, one without towns,
Only with bears and fish, a staring eye,
A new and singular sex?

HENRY TREECE (1912–)

Poem

In the dark caverns of the night,
Loveless and alone,
Friendless as wind that wails across the plains,
I sit, the last man left on earth,
Putting my fear on paper,
Praying that love will flow from my dry pen
And watching the tears make havoc on my page.

And I remember then,
Under the night's still mask,
The gallant geese
Making their way through storms,
The fieldmouse scuttering to my door
Away from the black cloud,
And the gay snail
Garnishing the twig before leaves came.

The old ones told me,
"When you grow grey you think on little things;"
Now these dreams kiss the bruises from my mind
Under the night's still mask,
As loveless and alone
I sit, till dawn the last man left
Who knows the sound of rain on summer leaves,
The graceful swan breasting the blood-red stream,
And heart's incompetence.

DELMORE SCHWARTZ (1913–   )

The Repetitive Heart

7

I am to my own heart merely a serf
And follow humbly as it glides with autos
And come attentive when it is too sick,
In the bad cold of sorrow much too weak,
To drink some coffee, light a cigarette
And think of summer beaches, blue and gay.
I climb the sides of buildings just to get
Merely a gob of gum, all that is left
Of its infatuation of last year.
Being the servant of incredible assumption,
Being to my own heart merely a serf.

I have been sick of its cruel rule, as sick
As one is sick of chewing gum all day;
Only inside of sleep did all my anger
Spend itself, restore me to my rôle,
Comfort me, bring me to the morning
Willing and smiling, ready to be of service,
To box its shadows, lead its brutish dogs,
Knowing its vanity the vanity of waves.

But when sleep too is crowded, when sleep too
Is full of chores impossible and heavy,

The looking for white doors whose numbers are
Different and equal, that is, infinite,
The carriage of my father on my back,
Last summer, 1910, and my own people,
The government of love's great polity,
The choice of taxes, the production
Of clocks, of lights and horses, the location
Of monuments, of hotels and of rhyme,
Then, then, in final anger, I wake up!
Merely wake up once more,
                                        once more to resume
The unfed hope, the unfed animal,
Being the servant of incredible assumption,
Being to my own heart merely a serf.

KARL SHAPIRO (1913–   )

Elegy for a Dead Soldier

I

A white sheet on the tail-gate of a truck
Becomes an altar; two small candlesticks
Sputter at each side of the crucifix
Laid round with flowers brighter than the blood,
Red as the red of our apocalypse,
Hibiscus that a marching man will pluck
To stick into his rifle or his hat,
And great blue morning-glories pale as lips
That shall no longer taste or kiss or swear.
The wind begins a low magnificat,
The chaplain chats, the palmtrees swirl their hair,
The columns come together through the mud.

II

We too are ashes as we watch and hear
The psalm, the sorrow, and the simple praise
Of one whose promised thoughts of other days
Were such as ours, but now wholly destroyed,
The service record of his youth wiped out,

His dream dispersed by shot, must disappear.
What can we feel but wonder at a loss
That seems to point at nothing but the doubt
Which flirts our sense of luck into the ditch?
Reader of Paul who prays beside this fosse,
Shall we believe our eyes or legends rich
With glory and rebirth beyond the void?

III

For this comrade is dead, dead in the war,
A young man out of millions yet to live,
One cut away from all that war can give,
Freedom of self and peace to wander free.
Who mourns in all this sober multitude
Who did not feel the bite of it before
The bullet found its aim? This worthy flesh,
This boy laid in a coffin and reviewed—
Who has not wrapped himself in this same flag,
Heard the light fall of dirt, his wound still fresh,
Felt his eyes closed, and heard the distant brag
Of the last volley of humanity?

IV

By chance I saw him die, stretched on the ground,
A tattooed arm lifted to take the blood
Of someone else sealed in a tin. I stood
During the last delirium that stays
The intelligence a tiny moment more,
And then the strangulation, the last sound.
The end was sudden, like a foolish play,
A stupid fool slamming a foolish door,
The absurd catastrophe, half-prearranged,
And all the decisive things still left to say.
So we disbanded, angrier and unchanged,
Sick with the utter silence of dispraise.

V

We ask for no statistics of the killed,
For nothing political impinges on
This single casualty, or all those gone,
Missing or healing, sinking or dispersed,
Hundreds of thousands counted, millions lost.

More than an accident and less than willed
Is every fall, and this one like the rest.
However others calculate the cost,
To us the final aggregate is *one*,
One with a name, one transferred to the blest;
And though another stoops and takes the gun,
We cannot add the second to the first.

VI

I would not speak for him who could not speak
Unless my fear were true: he was not wronged,
He knew to which decision he belonged
But let it choose itself. Ripe in instinct,
Neither the victim nor the volunteer,
He followed, and the leaders could not seek
Beyond the followers. Much of this he knew;
The journey was a detour that would steer
Into the Lincoln Highway of a land
Remorselessly improved, excited, new,
And that was what he wanted. He had planned
To earn and drive. He and the world had winked.

VII

No history deceived him, for he knew
Little of times and armies not his own;
He never felt that peace was but a loan,
Had never questioned the idea of gain.
Beyond the headlines once or twice he saw
The gathering of a power by the few
But could not tell their names; he cast his vote,
Distrusting all the elected but not law.
He laughed at socialism; *on mourrait*
Pour les industriels? He shed his coat
And not for brotherhood, but for his pay.
To him the red flag marked the sewer main.

VIII

Above all else he loathed the homily,
The slogan and the ad. He paid his bill
But not for Congressmen at Bunker Hill.
Ideals were few and those there were not made
For conversation. He belonged to church

But never spoke of God. The Christmas tree,
The Easter egg, baptism, he observed,
Never denied the preacher on his perch,
And would not sign Resolved That or Whereas.
Softness he had and hours and nights reserved
For thinking, dressing, dancing to the jazz.
His laugh was real, his manners were home made.

IX

Of all men poverty pursued him least;
He was ashamed of all the down and out,
Spurned the panhandler like an uneasy doubt,
And saw the unemployed as a vague mass
Incapable of hunger or revolt.
He hated other races, south or east,
And shoved them to the margin of his mind.
He could recall the justice of the Colt,
Take interest in a gang-war like a game.
His ancestry was somewhere far behind
And left him only his peculiar name.
Doors opened, and he recognized no class.

X

His children would have known a heritage,
Just or unjust, the richest in the world,
The quantum of all art and science curled
In the horn of plenty, bursting from the horn,
A people bathed in honey, Paris come,
Vienna transferred with the highest wage,
A World's Fair spread to Phoenix, Jacksonville,
Earth's capitol, the new Byzantium,
Kingdom of man—who knows? Hollow or firm,
No man can ever prophesy until
Out of our death some undiscovered germ,
Whole toleration or pure peace is born.

XI

The time to mourn is short that best becomes
The military dead. We lift and fold the flag,
Lay bare the coffin with its written tag,
And march away. Behind, four others wait
To lift the box, the heaviest of loads.

The anesthetic afternoon benumbs,
Sickens our senses, forces back our talk.
We know that others on tomorrow's roads
Will fall, ourselves perhaps, the man beside,
Over the world the threatened, all who walk:
And could we mark the grave of him who died
We would write this beneath his name and date:

EPITAPH

Underneath this wooden cross there lies
A Christian killed in battle. You who read,
Remember that this stranger died in pain;
And passing here, if you can lift your eyes
Upon a peace kept by a human creed,
Know that one soldier has not died in vain.

DYLAN THOMAS (1914–1953)

Do Not Go Gentle into That Good Night

Do not go gentle into that good night,
Old age should burn and rave at close of day;
Rage, rage against the dying of the light.

Though wise men at their end know dark is right,
Because their words had forked no lightning they
Do not go gentle into that good night.

Good men, the last wave by, crying how bright
Their frail deeds might have danced in a green bay,
Rage, rage against the dying of the light.

Wild men who caught and sang the sun in flight,
And learn, too late, they grieved it on its way,
Do not go gentle into that good night.

Grave men, near death, who see with blinding sight
Blind eyes could blaze like meteors and be gay,
Rage, rage against the dying of the light.

And you, my father, there on the sad height,
Curse, bless, me now with your fierce tears, I pray.
Do not go gentle into that good night.
Rage, rage against the dying of the light.

ROBERT LOWELL (1917–)

Mr. Edwards and the Spider

I saw the spiders marching through the air,
Swimming from tree to tree that mildewed day
In latter August when the hay
Came creaking to the barn. But where
The wind is westerly,
Where gnarled November makes the spiders fly
Into the apparitions of the sky,
They purpose nothing but their ease and die
Urgently beating east to sunrise and the sea;

What are we in the hands of the great God?
It was in vain you set up thorn and briar
In battle array against the fire
And treason crackling in your blood;
For the wild thorns grow tame
And will do nothing to oppose the flame;
Your lacerations tell the losing game
You play against a sickness past your cure.
How will the hands be strong? How will the heart endure?

A very little thing, a little worm,
Or hourglass-blazoned spider, it is said,
Can kill a tiger. Will the dead
Hold up his mirror and affirm
To the four winds the smell
And flash of his authority? It's well
If God who holds you to the pit of hell,
Much as one holds a spider, will destroy,
Baffle and dissipate your soul. As a small boy

On Windsor Marsh, I saw the spider die
When thrown into the bowels of fierce fire:
There's no long struggle, no desire
To get up on its feet and fly—
It stretches out its feet
And dies. This is the sinner's last retreat;
Yes, and no strength exerted on the heat
Then sinews the abolished will, when sick
And full of burning, it will whistle on a brick.

But who can plumb the sinking of that soul?
Josiah Hawley, picture yourself cast
Into a brick-kiln where the blast
Fans your quick vitals to a coal—
If measured by a glass,
How long would it seem burning! Let there pass
A minute, ten, ten trillion; but the blaze
Is infinite, eternal: this is death.
To die and know it. This is the Black Widow, death.

ALEC COMFORT (1920–)

A Rider Turned to Stone

A rider turned to stone
caught in mid-leap by time
even the hoof-sparks frozen to glittering dust

or a stone footprint where
scales and enormous claws
frighten the quarrymen even so long after

something blown from Northward
or between us and the sun
makes words fall frozen as we spit them out

all those dark glaciers
come down from history
the songs themselves tinkle like icicles

perhaps more durable
transparent as the cage
which holds a mammoth, lifelike but not living

somehow preserved, we are
waiting the thaw, the axes,
to bring us out again, no hair destroyed

but in another time
when glaciers go back
and only leave round boulders on the fields

cold, cold; come closer, closer.

RICHARD WILBUR (1921–   )

Love Calls Us to the Things of This World

The eyes open to a cry of pulleys,
And spirited from sleep, the astounded soul
Hangs for a moment bodiless and simple
As false dawn.
Outside the open window
The morning air is all awash with angels.

Some are in bed-sheets, some are in blouses,
Some are in smocks: but truly there they are.
Now they are rising together in calm swells
Of halcyon feeling, filling whatever they wear
With the deep joy of their impersonal breathing;

Now they are flying in place, conveying
The terrible speed of their omnipresence, moving
And staying like white water; and now of a sudden
They swoon down into so rapt a quiet
That nobody seems to be there.
The soul shrinks

From all that it is about to remember,
From the punctual rape of every blessèd day,

And cries,
"Oh, let there be nothing on earth but laundry,
Nothing but rosy hands in the rising steam
And clear dances done in the sight of heaven."

Yet, as the sun acknowledges
With a warm look the world's hunks and colors,
The soul descends once more in bitter love
To accept the waking body, saying now
In a changed voice as the man yawns and rises,

"Bring them down from their ruddy gallows;
Let there be clean linen for the backs of thieves;
Let lovers go fresh and sweet to be undone,
And the heaviest nuns walk in a pure floating
Of dark habits,
keeping their difficult balance."

SIDNEY KEYES (1922–1944)

The Promised Landscape

For R.-J.

How shall I sing for you—
Sharing only
The scared dream of a soldier:
A young man's unbearable
Dream of possession?
How shall I sing for you
With the foul tongue of a soldier?

We march through new mountains
Where crows inhabit
The pitiful cairns.
At morning, the rock-pools
Are matted with ice.
But you are the mountains
And you the journey.

We lie in a ruined farm
Where rats perform
Marvels of balance
Among the rafters.

And rain kisses my lips
Because you are the sky
That bends always over me.

How shall I sing for you
Knowing only
The explorer's sorrow,
The soldier's weariness?
New ranges and rivers
Are never quite revealing
Your promised figure.

How dare I sing for you
I the least worthy
Of lovers you've had:
You the most lovely
Of possible landscapes?

DONALD HALL (1928–)

The Body Politic

I shot my friend to save my country's life,
And when the happy bullet struck him dead,
I was saluted by the drum and fife
Corps of a high school, while the traitor bled.

I never thought until I pulled the trigger
But that I did the difficult and good.
I thought republics stood for something bigger,
For the mind of man, as Plato said they stood.

So when I heard the duty they assigned,
Shooting my friend seemed only sanity;

To keep disorder from the state of mind
Was mental rectitude, it seemed to me.

The audience dispersed. I felt depressed.
I went to where my orders issued from,
But the right number on the street was just
A rickety old house, vacant and dumb.

I tried to find the true address, but where?
Nobody told me what I really wanted;
Just secretaries sent me here and there
To other secretaries. I was daunted.

Poor Fred. His presence will be greatly missed
By children and by cronies by the score.
The State (I learn too late) does not exist;
Man lives by love, and not by metaphor.

ROBERT PACK (1929–)

The Way We Wonder

What has become of our astonishment
For simple things: colors, sounds, the hour of day?
We wonder, now our early gift is spent,

About imagined reasons to repent
For joy, and words we've heard our parents say.
What has become of our astonishment

For night and stars and things we can't invent?
(While crickets tick the perfect night away.)
We wonder, now our early gift is spent,

Whether some miraculous event
Will soon reveal (we're told old men are gay)
What has become of our astonishment.

The questioning of ultimate intent
Is still continued in the abstract way
We wonder, now our early gift is spent.

O who among us would have ever dreamt 16
The very best of our ideas betray?

What has become of our astonishment
We wonder, now our early gift is spent.

APPENDICES

I: Prosodic Patterns for the Poems in Part I

In this appendix are to be found the basic prosodic or formal patterns of each of the poems in Part I. We assume that though few lines are exactly regular in rhythm, there is an underlying or implied rhythm for most poetry, at least until the second decade of this century. This rhythm depends upon stressing some syllables more strongly than others, just as in ordinary speech, or to use another term, accenting one syllable and not accenting another. Thus:

x equals an unaccented syllable
/ equals an accented syllable.

Example from Herrick's *His Farewell to Sack,* line 2:

x   / x   /   x   /   x   /   x   /
To me as blood to life and spir it: Near

A superscription, or number or series of numbers directly after and slightly above the stress pattern, indicates which lines in a stanza have that particular pattern.

After each stress pattern is indicated whether or not the line regularly has a caesura or pause within the line. Thus:

C equals a caesura normally present.

Example from the same poem, line 15:

Comets we see by night; (pause) whose shagg'd portents

After each C, if it is present, or otherwise after each stress pattern, is the rhyme scheme, the repetition of an identical sound at the ends of successive lines. This identity is schematized by using letters for identical sounds. "aabb . . ." means that the pattern continues throughout the poem. Number superscriptions indicate which stanzas use that particular rhyme scheme: a single superscription indicates the number of stanzas that use the same rhyme scheme. "x" indicates that the line does not rhyme.

It must be emphasized that the reader will find here the *underlying* or *implied* pattern for rhythm and for rhyme and stanza. Thus the stress patterns for only the opening lines of the Auden, Stevens, and Hopkins poems are given. The sign ". . ." indicates that this same kind of irregularity persists throughout the poem and that there is no identifiable regular stress pattern. In the Swinburne poem the rhythm is not so irregular as in these three, but an underlying pattern like those of the remainder of the poems cannot be found. Similar irregularities are to be found in the rhyme patterns. Thus the Dryden excerpt begins with an exception from the couplet pattern: it begins, that is, with a triplet. The sign ". . ." after the rhyme scheme for the first two patterns of Herbert's poem indicates that each subsequent stanza uses three rhymes but in a continually differing order, with the exception of one stanza. Other irregularities will be observed. Stanza 6 in Jonson's "Ode" differs in its first four lines from the normal rhyme scheme of the other three "Stands." In Donne the "a" rhyme is identical in each stanza. Dickinson's poem has, in terms of rhythm, six stanzas, in terms of rhyme, five, since five plus six have the same rhyme scheme as four; at the same time stanza four departs so strongly from the rhyme scheme of one and three as to call in question the existence of a rhyme scheme at all. Is it xaxa, axax, abab, or xxxx? That is, do "Rose" and "Paradise" rhyme? Do "borne" and "more" rhyme? Or is there no rhyme at all?

Herrick: *His Farewell to Sack*
x / x / x / x / x /: C: aabb . . .

Pope: *Timon's Villa*
x / x / x / x / x /: C: aabb . . .

Arnold: *To Marguerite*
x / x / x / x /: C: ababcc^{4}

Spenser: A *Hymn to Venus*
x / x / x / x / x /$^{1-8}$ x / x / x / x / x / x /^{9}: C: ababbcbcc^{4}

Hardy: *He Abjures Love*
x / x / x /^{1,3,5,7} x / x /^{2,6} x / x / x^{4,8}: abcdabcd$^{1,3-6}$: xaabxccb^{2}

Jonson: *To the Immortal Memory . . .*
x / x / x / x /^{1,2,7,8}: C: x / x / x / x / x /^{3,4,9,10}: C: x / x / x /^{5,6}: aabbccddee^{1,2,4,5,7,8,10,11}

x / x / x / x / x /^{1,3,7,11,12}: C: x / x /^{2,4} x / x / x /^{5,6,8,9}: x / x / x / x /^{10}: C: ababccdeedff^{3,6,9,12}

Donne: *The Canonization*
x / x / x / x / x /: C: ^{1,3,4,7} x / x / x / x /: C: ^{2,5,6,8}: C: x / x / x /^{10}: abbacccaa, addaeeeaa . . .^{5}

Milton: *From* Paradise Lost
x / x / x / x / x /: C

Shelley: *Ode to Heaven*
/ x / x / x /: aabcbcddd^{6}

Dryden: *From* Absalom and Achitophel
x / x / x / x / x /: C: aabb . . .

Browning: *Two in the Campagna*
x / x / x / x /$^{1-4}$ x / x / x /^{5}: ababa^{12}

Herbert: *Man*
x / x / x /^{1,6} x / x / x / x / x /: C: ^{2,5} x / x / x / x /^{3,4}: abccba^{1}: abcabc^{2} . . .$^{3-9}$

Gray: *Ode on the Spring*
x / x / x / x /$^{1,3,5–9}$ x / x / x /^{2,4,10}: ababccdeed^{5}

Collins: *Ode to Evening*
x / x / x / x / x /^{1,2,5,6,9,10} . . .: C: x / x / x /^{3,4,7,8,11,12} . . .

Frost: *In Time of Cloudburst*
/ x / x / x /, x / x x / x /, x / x x / x /, x / x / x x / . . .: abab^{7}

Swinburne: *A Ballad of Dreamland*
x / x / x x / x / x, / x x / / / x x /, x x / x / x x / / / /, / x x / x x / x /, / x x / / / x x /, x / x x / x x / / /, / / / / x x / x /, / x x / x x / x / . . .: C: ababbcbc,^{3} bcbc^{4}

Yeats: *Sailing to Byzantium*
x / x / x / x / x /: C: abababcc^{4}

Auden: *Casino*
/ x x / x / x x x / x / x, x / x / / / x x / / x x /, x x / x / x x / x x / x, x / x x / x x / . . .: C: ^{6}

Shakespeare: *Sonnet 116*
x / x / x / x / x /: C: ababcdcdefefgg

Dickinson: *Poem 512*
x / x / x / x^{1,3,5}, x / x / x /^{2,4,6}: xaxa^{1,3,4}, xaxaxa$^{2,5+6}$

Stevens: *Not Ideas about the Thing but the Thing Itself*
x x / x x / x x / x, x / x / x / x / /, / x x / x x /, x / x x / x, x / / x / / x x /, x x / x / / . . .: xxa, xxa, xxb, xxb, xxx xxx

Eliot: *A Cooking Egg*
x / x / x / x /: xaxa$^{1–7}$ a baxx

Hopkins: *Hurrahing in Harvest*
/ x / / / / x x x / x x / x, x / / x / / / / / / x x / x, x / / / x / x / x / x x, / / / x / x x / x x / / . . .: C: abbaabbacdcdcd

Keats: *Ode to a Nightingale*
x / x / x / x / x /$^{1–7,9,10}$: C: x / x / x /^{8}: ababcdecde^{8}

Wordsworth: *Sonnet*
x / x / x / x / x /: C: abbaabbacdcdcd

II: Bibliography

Aldrich, Thomas Bailey, "Accomplices" (c. 1861–5?); text from *Early Poems,* New York, 1908.

Arnold, Matthew, "Switzerland: 5. To Marguerite—Continued," "Lines Written in Kensington Gardens," *Empedocles on Etna, and Other Poems,* London, 1852; "Dover Beach," *New Poems,* London, 1867; texts from *The Works,* London, 1903.

Auden, Wystan Hugh, "Sir, no man's enemy, forgiving all," *Poems,* London, 1930; "May with its light behaving," "Casino," *Look, Stranger!,* London, 1936; texts from *The Collected Poetry,* New York, 1945.

Barbauld, Anna L., "To Mr. S. T. Coleridge: 1797," *Works,* ed. Lucy Aikin, London, 1825.

Barnfield, Richard, *The Affectionate Shepherd,* London, 1594; text from *The Complete Poems,* ed. A. B. Grosart, London, 1876.

Beattie, James, *The Minstrel,* London, 1771; text from 4th ed., 1774.

Beddoes, Thomas L., "Song of the Stygian Naiades," *Poems Posthumous and Collected,* ed. T. F. Kelsall, London, 1850; text from 1851 ed.

Blair, Robert, *The Grave,* London, 1743.

Blake, William, "London," *Songs of Innocence, Songs of Experience,* London, 1794.

Bowles, William Lisle, "Sonnet 24: May, 1793," *Fourteen Sonnets,* Bath, 1789; text from *Sonnets and Other Poems,* 4th ed., London, 1796.

Bridges, Robert, "The sea keeps not the Sabbath day," *New Poems,* London, 1899; text from *The Poetical Works,* London, 1914.

Brontë, Emily, "The Philosopher," *Poems by Currer, Ellis and Acton Bell,* London, 1846.

Brown, John, "Fragment of a Rhapsody" (before 1766?), *Anderson's British Poets,* London, 1795.

Browning, Robert, "My Last Duchess," *Dramatic Lyrics,* London, 1842; "Two in the Campagna," *Men and Women,* London, 1855; "Development," *Asolando,* London, 1889; texts from *Poetical Works,* London, 1889.

Bryant, William Cullen, "Inscription for the Entrance to a Wood," *Poems,* New York, 1821; text from *Poems,* ed. Bryant, New York, 1856.

Byron, George Gordon, Lord Byron, "River that rollest by the ancient walls," Thomas Medwin, *Conversations of Lord Byron,* London, 1824.

Campion, Thomas, "Sleep, angry Beauty, sleep, and fear not me," *The Third and Fourth Book of Ayres,* London, c. 1617; text from *English Madrigal Verse,* ed. E. H. Fellowes, London, 1920.

Carew, Thomas, "Ask me no more where *Jove* bestows," *Poems,* London, 1640; text from 2nd ed., 1642.

Clare, John, "Secret Love," *Poems Chiefly from Manuscript*, ed. E. Blunden and A. Porter, 1920.

Clough, Arthur Hugh, "O land of Empire, art and love," ll. 35–88, *Poems and Prose Remains*, London, 1869; text from *Poems*, ed. H. F. Lowry, A. L. P. Norrington, and F. L. Mulhausen, Oxford, 1951.

Coleridge, Samuel Taylor, "Kubla Khan," *Kubla Khan, Christabel, etc.*, London, 1816; text from *The Poems*, London, 1844.

Collins, William, "Ode to Evening," *Odes on Several Descriptive and Allegorical Subjects*, London, 1746. *Ode Occasion'd by the Death of Mr. Thomson*, London, 1749. "*Dirge in Cymbeline*," *An Epistle: Addresst to Sir Thomas Hanmer*, etc., London, 1744; text from *The Poems*, ed. E. Blunden, London, 1765.

Comfort, Alec, "A Rider Turned to Stone," *And All but He Departed*, London, 1951.

Cowper, William, "The Negro's Complaint," *Poems*, 11th ed., London, 1800; text from *The Works*, ed. R. Southey, London, 1837.

Crabbe, George, *The Village*, London, 1783; text from *The Works*, London, 1823.

Crane, Hart, "To Brooklyn Bridge," *The Bridge*, New York and Paris, 1930; text from *Collected Poems*, ed. Waldo Frank, N.Y., 1933.

Crashaw, Richard, "A Letter from Mr. Crashaw to the Countess of Denbigh," etc., London, 1653?; text from *The Poems*, ed. L. C. Martin, Oxford, 1957.

Cummings, E. E., "anyone lived in a pretty how town," *Collected Poems*, New York, 1938; text from *Collected Poems 1923–1954*, New York, 1954.

Daniel, Samuel, "Epistle to Henry Wriothesley, Earl of Southampton," *A Panegyrike Congratulatorie to the Kings Majestie. Also Certain Epistles*, London, 1603.

De la Mare, Walter, "Forests," *The Fleeting*, New York, 1933.

Dickinson, Emily, "After great pain, a formal feeling comes," *Further Poems*, ed. M. D. Bianchi and A. L. Hampson, Boston, 1929; "The Soul has Bandaged moments," *Bolts of Melody*, ed. M. L. Todd and M. T. Bingham, New York, 1945; "A narrow Fellow in the Grass," *Poems, Second Series*, Boston 1891; texts from *The Poems*, ed. T. H. Johnson, Cambridge, Mass., 1955.

Donne, John, "The Canonization," "The Will," "Batter my heart, three person'd God," *Poems*, London, 1633.

Drummond, William, "Urania," *Poems*, Edinburgh, 1616; text from *Poems*, London, 1656.

Dryden, John, "A Character of Og," *The Second Part of Absalom and Achitophel*, London, 1682; "Prologue to the University of Oxford," *Miscellany Poems*, London, 1684; "The Secular Masque," *The Pilgrim*, London, 1700.

D'Urfey, Thomas, "The Fisherman's Song," *Wit and Mirth*, London, 1700; text from 1719 ed.

Eberhart, Richard, "If I could only live at the pitch that is near madness," *Song and Idea*, New York, 1942; text from *Poems New and Selected*, 1944.

Eliot, Thomas Stearns, "Gerontion," "A Cooking Egg," *Poems*, London, 1920; "Animula," *Ariel Poems*, London, 1929; texts from *The Complete Poems and Plays*, New York, 1952.

Emerson, Ralph Waldo, "Bacchus," *Poems*, Boston, 1846; text from 1872 ed.

Fearing, Kenneth, "Art Review," *Afternoon of a Pawnbroker*, New York, 1943; text from *New and Selected Poems*, Bloomington, Ind., 1956.

Fletcher, John, *The Faithful Shepherdess*, London, 1609?; text from 3rd ed., 1634.

Frost, Robert, "Birches," *North of Boston*, New York, 1914; text from *Complete Poems*, New York, 1949. "In Time of Cloudburst," "A Lone Striker," *A Further Range*, New York, 1936.

Gascoigne, George, "Gascoigne's Good-morrow," *A Hundreth Sundrie Flowers*, London, 1573.

Gay, John, "The Birth of the Squire: An Eclogue," *Poems on Several Occasions*, London, 1720; text from 3rd ed., 1737.

Goldsmith, Oliver, "Elegy on the Death of a Mad Dog," *The Vicar of Wakefield*, London, 1766.

Graves, Robert, "The Cool Web," *Poems (1914–26)*, London, 1927; text from *Collected Poems, 1955*, New York, 1955.

Gray, Thomas, "Ode on a Distant Prospect of Eton College," London, 1747; "Ode on the Spring," "Ode on the Death of a Favourite Cat," *Designs by Mr. R. Bentley for Six Poems by Mr. T. Gray*, London, 1753; texts from *Poems*, London, 1768.

Green, Matthew, *The Spleen*, London, 1737; text from 2nd ed., 1737.

Hall, Donald, "The Body Politic," *New Poets of England and America*, New York, 1957.

Hardy, Thomas, "A Commonplace Day," *Poems of the Past and Present*, London, 1901; "He Abjures Love," *Time's Laughingstocks*, London, 1909; "A Night of Questionings," *Human Shows—Far Phantasies*, London, 1925; texts from *Collected Poems*, New York, 1926.

Henley, William Ernest, "London Voluntaries: 4," *London Voluntaries and Other Verses*, London, 1893; text from *Poems*, New York, 1898.

Herbert, Edward, "Elegy over a Tomb," *Occasional Verses*, London, 1665.

Herbert, George, "The Collar," "Man," "Mortification," *The Temple*, Cambridge, 1633; text from 2nd ed., Cambridge, 1633.

Herrick, Robert, "His Farewell to Sack," "Corinna's Going a-Maying," "The Hock-Cart," *Hesperides*, London, 1648.

Hood, Thomas, "The Bridge of Sighs," *Hood's Magazine*, 1844; text from *The Works*, ed. by his son and daughter, London, 1870.

Hopkins, Gerard Manley, "The Windhover," "Pied Beauty," "Hurrahing in Harvest," *The Poems*, ed. R. Bridges, London, 1918; texts from ed. of Bridges and Gardner, New York, 1948.

Housman, A. E., "From far, from eve and morning," *A Shropshire Lad*, London, 1895; text from *The Collected Poems*, London, 1940.

Howard, Henry, Earl of Surrey, "Prisoned in Windsor," *Tottel's Miscellany,* London, 1557; text from ed. of A. Arber, Birmingham, 1870.

Hunt, Leigh, "The Fish, the Man, and the Spirit," *Poetical Works,* London, 1844.

Johnson, Lionel, "Upon Reading Certain Poems," *Ireland, with Other Poems,* London, 1897.

Johnson, Samuel, "The Winter's Walk," *The Gentleman's Magazine,* May, 1747.

Jonson, Ben, "A Celebration of Charis," "To the Immortal Memory . . . ," "An Ode: To Himself," *The Works,* London, 1640.

Keats, John, "Ode to a Nightingale," "Autumn," *Lamia, Isabella, The Eve of St. Agnes, and Other Poems,* London, 1820; "To Sleep," *Life, Letters, and Literary Remains,* ed. R. M. Milnes, London, 1848.

Keyes, Sidney, "The Promised Landscape," *The Cruel Solstice,* London, 1944.

King, Henry, "Silence: A Sonnet," *Poems, Elegies, Paradoxes, and Sonnets,* London, 1657.

Kipling, Rudyard, "An American," *Verses 1889–96,* London, 1896; text from *Works,* Vol. 10, New York, 1920.

Landor, Walter Savage, "A Friend to Theocritos in Egypt," *Heroic Idylls,* London, 1863; text from *Works,* ed. J. Forster, London, 1876.

Lanier, Sidney, "Sunrise," *Poems,* New York, 1884.

Lawrence, David Herbert, "Dolour of Autumn," text from *The Collected Poems,* London, 1928.

Lovelace, Richard, "The Grasshopper," *Lucasta,* London, 1649.

Lowell, Robert, "Mr. Edwards and the Spider," *Lord Weary's Castle,* New York, 1944.

MacLeish, Archibald, "Immortal Autumn," *New Found Land,* Boston, 1930; text from *Collected Poems, 1917–1952,* Boston, 1952.

MacNeice, Louis, "Picture Galleries," *Poems, 1925–1940,* New York, 1940.

Marvell, Andrew, "The Garden," *Miscellaneous Poems,* London, 1681.

Masefield, John, "Here in the self is all that man can know," *Good Friday and Other Poems,* London, 1916; text from *The Poems,* New York, 1935.

Meredith, George, "Hymn to Colour," *A Reading of Earth,* London, 1888; text from *Poetical Works,* London, 1896.

Milton, John, "How soon hath time the subtle thief of youth," *Arcades, Poems, etc.,* 1645; texts from *Poems on Several Occasions,* 1673; *Paradise Lost,* 1667; text from 2nd ed., 1674.

Morris, William, "Error and Loss," *Poems by the Way,* London, 1891.

Oldham, John, "A Satire Addressed to a Friend," *Poems and Translations,* London, 1683; text from *Works,* London, 1722.

Owen, Wilfred, "Dulce et Decorum Est," *Poems,* New York, 1921.

Pack, Robert, "The Way We Wonder," *Poets of To-Day, II,* New York, 1955.

Parnell, Thomas, "Health," *Poems on Several Occasions,* ed. A. Pope, London, 1747.

Pope, Alexander, "An Essay on Criticism," London, 1711; text from *The Works,* London, 1717; "Elegy to the Memory of an Unfortunate Lady,"

The Works, 1717; *An Epistle to the Right Honourable Richard Earl of Burlington*, London, 1730; text based on 3rd ed., 1731.

Pound, Ezra, "Canto XVII," *A Draft of Cantos XVII to XXVII*, London, 1927; text from *Selected Poems*, Norfolk, Conn., 1957.

Prior, Matthew, "Alma," *Poems on Several Occasions*, London, 1718.

Reese, Lizette Woodworth, "Wild Geese," *The Selected Poems*, New York, 1926.

Robinson, Edward Arlington, "Old Trails," *The Man Against the Sky*, New York, 1916; text from *Collected Poems*, New York, 1927.

Rogers, Samuel, *Italy*, London, 1822; text from ill. ed., London, 1836.

Rossetti, Christina G., "When I am dead," *Goblin Market, and Other Poems*, London, 1862; text from 2nd ed., 1865.

Rossetti, Dante Gabriel, "The Monochord," *Poems*, 1870; text from *The Collected Works*, ed. W. M. Rossetti, London, 1887.

Sandburg, Carl, "Interior," *Cornhuskers*, New York, 1918; text from *Complete Poems*, New York, 1950.

Schwartz, Delmore, "I am to my own heart," *In Dreams Begin Responsibilities*, Norfolk, Conn., 1938.

Sedley, Sir Charles, "A Dialogue between Amintas and Celia," *A Collection of Poems, Written upon Several Occasions. By Several Persons*, London, 1672; text from *The Miscellaneous Works*, London, 1702.

Shakespeare, William, "Sonnets 73 and 116," *Shakespeares Sonnets*, London, 1609. *Hamlet*, London, 1603; texts from Second Quarto, London, 1604, and First Folio, London, 1623.

Shapiro, Karl, "Elegy for a Dead Soldier," *V-Letter and Other Poems*, New York, 1944; text from *Poems 1940–1953*, New York, 1953.

Sheffield, John, Duke of Buckingham, "Stanzas," *Works*, 1723; text from *Works*, ed. A. Pope, London, 1740.

Shelley, Percy Bysshe, "Ode to Heaven," "Ode to the West Wind," *Prometheus Unbound*, London, 1820; "The Two Spirits," *Posthumous Poems*, London, 1824.

Shenstone, William, "Ophelia's Urn," *The Works in Verse and Prose*, London, 1765.

Sidney, Sir Philip, "Let mother earth now deck herself in flowers," *Arcadia*, London, 1593.

Sitwell, Edith, "The Higher Sensualism," *Bucolic Comedies*, London, 1923; text from *Façade and Other Poems*, London, 1950.

Smart, Christopher, "Hymn 14," *A Translation of the Psalms of David*, London, 1765.

Somerville, William, *The Chase*, London, 1735, text from 3rd ed., 1735.

Spender, Stephen, "Polar Exploration," *The Still Centre*, London, 1934.

Spenser, Edmund, *The Faerie Queene, Books I to VI*, London, 1596; *Amoretti and Epithalamium*, London, 1595; *Prothalamion*, London, 1596; texts based on *The Faerie Queene*, London, 1611.

Stevens, Wallace, "Peter Quince at the Clavier," "Anecdote of the Jar," *Harmonium*, New York, 1923; "Not Ideas about the Thing but the

Thing Itself," *The Collected Poems,* New York, 1955; texts from the same.

Suckling, Sir John, "'Tis now, since I sat down before," *Fragmenta Aurea,* London, 1658.

Swift, Jonathan, "Phyllis," *Poems on Several Occasions,* Dublin, 1735.

Swinburne, Algernon, "The Garden of Proserpine," "Satia Te Sanguine," *Poems and Ballads,* London, 1866; texts from new ed., 1897. "A Ballad of Dreamland," *Poems and Ballads, Second Series,* London, 1878; text from 3rd ed., 1882.

Taylor, Bayard, "The Mystic Summer," *The Poet's Journal,* Boston?, 1862; text from *The Poetical Works,* Boston and New York, 1892.

Tennyson, Alfred, Lord, "The Hesperides," *Poems,* London, 1833.

Thomas, Dylan, "Do Not Go Gentle into That Good Night," *The Collected Poems,* New York, 1953.

Thompson, Francis, "The Poppy," *Poems,* 1893.

Thomson, James, *Summer: A Poem,* London, 1727; text from *The Works,* London, 1750.

Traherne, Thomas, "The Vision," *Poetical Works,* ed. B. Dobell, London, 1903; text from *Centuries, Poems and Thanksgivings,* ed. H. M. Margoliouth, London, 1958.

Treece, Henry, "In the dark caverns of the night," *The Haunted Garden,* London, 1947.

Vaughan, Henry, "Corruption," *Silex Scintillans,* London, 1650; text from *The Works,* ed. L. C. Martin, Oxford, 1914.

Waller, Edmund, "The Battle of the Summer Islands," *Poems,* London, 1645.

Warren, Robert Penn, "Crime," *Eleven Poems on the Same Theme,* Norfolk, Conn., 1942.

Warton, Thomas, the Younger, "The Hamlet," *Poems,* London, 1777; text from *Poems on Various Subjects,* London, 1791.

Whitman, Walt, "As I Ebb'd with the Ocean of Life," *Leaves of Grass,* Boston, 1860; text from same, Boston, 1897.

Wilbur, Richard, "Love Calls Us to the Things of This World," *Things of This World,* New York, 1956.

Wilmot, John, Earl of Rochester, "The Maim'd Debauchee," *Poems, etc., on Several Occasions,* London, 1691; text from 1696 ed.

Wordsworth, William, "Lines Composed a Few Miles above Tintern Abbey," *Lyrical Ballads,* London, 1798; "A slumber did my spirit seal," *Lyrical Ballads,* London, 1800; "The world is too much with us," *Poems in Two Volumes,* London, 1807; texts from *The Poetical Works,* London, 1849.

Wyatt, Sir Thomas, "The Lover Complaineth Himself Forsaken," *Tottel's Miscellany,* London, 1557; text from ed. of E. Arber, Birmingham, 1870.

Yeats, William Butler, "When You Are Old," *Countess Kathleen and Various Legends and Lyrics,* London, 1892; "Sailing to Byzantium," *The Tower,* London, 1928; "Vacillation," *The Winding Stair and Other Poems,* London, 1933; texts from *The Collected Poems,* New York, 1950.

Young, Edward, *The Consolation,* London, 1745; text from *The Works,* rev. and corr. by the author, London, 1768.

Index: Authors, Titles, and First Lines

Page numbers for titles and first lines indicate only the page on which text of a poem begins.